TALES OF THE
UNCANNY

TALES
OF THE UNCANNY

Selected by the Editors of
Reader's Digest

The Reader's Digest Association, Inc.
Pleasantville, New York
Cape Town, Hong Kong, London, Montreal, Sydney

READER'S DIGEST CONDENSED BOOKS

Editor: Joseph W. Hotchkiss

Executive Editor: John S. Zinsser, Jr.

Senior Managing Editor: Anthony Wethered

Managing Editor: Barbara J. Morgan

Assistant Managing Editors: Anne H. Atwater, Ann Berryman, Tanis H. Erdmann,
Marjorie Palmer

Senior Staff Editors: Doris E. Dewey, Fredrica S. Friedman

Senior Editors: Barbara Bradshaw, Olive Farmer, Thomas Froncek, Angela C. Gibbs,
Virginia Rice (Rights), Margery D. Thorndike, Angela Weldon

Associate Editors: Jean E. Aptakin, Catherine T. Brown, Linn Carl, Estelle T. Dashman,
Daniel H. Frank, Joseph P. McGrath, James J. Menick, Alice Murtha

Art Editor: William Gregory

Senior Art Editors: Marion Davis, Soren Noring, Thomas Von Der Linn

Associate Art Editor: Angelo Perrone

Art Research: George Calas, Jr., Katherine Kelleher

Senior Copy Editors: Claire A. Bedolis, Jeane Garment

Associate Copy Editors: Rosalind H. Campbell, Dorothy G. Flynn, Jean S. Friedman

Assistant Copy Editors: Jean G. Cornell, Jane F. Neighbors

CB PROJECTS

Executive Editor: Herbert H. Lieberman

Senior Staff Editors: Sherwood Harris, John E. Walsh

Senior Editors: John R. Roberson, Ray Sipherd, Carol D. Tarlow

Associate Editor: Dana Adkins

CB INTERNATIONAL EDITIONS

Executive Editor: Noel Rae

Senior Editor: Sigrid MacRae

Associate Editors: Gary Q. Arpin, Istar H. Dole

CONTENTS

Dr. Holmes's Murder Castle

by
Robert Bloch

ILLUSTRATED BY RICK McCOLLUM

He appeared to be one of Chicago's most respectable citizens. Medical school graduate and successful entrepreneur, Dr. Henry Howard Holmes was also a devoted husband and father. In 1892 he designed an enormous structure containing a pharmacy, sundry shops and, on the second and third floors, lodgings for visitors to the World's Fair. It was called the Holmes Castle. But strangely, Holmes's business partners began to disappear, one by one. So did a whole procession of secretaries hired by him—all attractive young women. And visitors to the Fair who rented rooms in the Castle. What was Holmes: medical man or madman? Or was he a man possessed, the Devil's own?

Robert Bloch, who achieved international acclaim for his novel *Psycho,* wrote an earlier fictional account of Dr. Holmes. What he learned about the monster of the Murder Castle continued to haunt him long after his novel, *American Gothic,* was completed. He decided that to rid himself of the demon he must write the true story. He calls it "a work of exorcism."

THE CASTLE

1

THE CREATURE CAME out of the night.

For a time it simply stood there, small and silent in the shadows. Then, as darkness faded into dawn and dawn gave way to daylight, the creature began to change. Slowly at first, then with startling rapidity, its size doubled, redoubled, grew greater still. And with growth it found its voice, a low growl that soon rose to a roar. Turning restlessly, peering in every direction with a hundred eyes, the creature's appetite and thirst increased.

In all nature there is no animal comparable to that of our own creation—the creature we call a crowd. Nothing can match its appetite for excitement, its thirst for sensation.

And the crowd that formed on a street corner in suburban Chicago this sunny morning of July 20, 1895, had a special hunger all its own—a hunger for blood.

For many months now that hunger had been nourished by headlines and newspaper stories regarding the activities of Dr. Henry Howard Holmes.

The building on the corner of Wallace and Sixty-third Street before which the crowd now gathered had been built by Dr. Holmes in 1892. Officially called the Holmes Block, the three-storied structure was soon popularly identified as the "Holmes Castle" because of its imposing battlements and unusual architecture. Here Holmes had operated a pharmacy, conducted a variety of other businesses, rented out office space and stores, and furnished upstairs lodgings to visitors attending the World's Columbian Exposition of 1893.

Late that year he'd departed from Chicago after a fire damaged the Castle roof. Since then the building's top two floors had been locked and left vacant, but local residents vividly remembered their colorful owner. Many of those assembled here today had known him personally or by reputation as a pillar of the community, but in the year and a half since his departure the newspapers had supplied them with new information.

Holmes's former business partner, Benjamin Pitezel, was found dead in Philadelphia following a mysterious explosion. Holmes turned up to identify the body and helped the widow's lawyer collect on a ten-thousand-dollar insurance policy. Now Dr. Holmes was accused of fraud in the matter.

Further investigation revealed that Holmes had jumped bail on a swindling charge in Saint Louis. He was also wanted for horse stealing in Texas.

It was learned that his real name was Herman W. Mudgett. While visiting his wife in New Hampshire, he had told her a weird tale to account for many years of absence.

Another Mrs. Holmes was found living in Wilmette, just north of Chicago.

And there was a third Mrs. Holmes, with whom he had been traveling across the country.

After his arrest in Boston, Holmes confessed to fraud. He said Ben Pitezel was still alive and had fled the country with three of his children. Two other children were with Pitezel's wife, who was also arrested.

Mrs. Pitezel revealed her part in the scheme and then Holmes began changing his story. Each new version was wilder than the last. After being convicted of fraud, he was pressed to produce the three missing Pitezel children last seen in his company as he transported them throughout the East.

Meanwhile, back in Chicago, an army of creditors came forth, testifying they'd been deceived, cheated and swindled in a variety of ways by H. H. Holmes, operating for years under an assortment of names.

Others told authorities of strange circumstances surrounding the building of the Castle. And there were those who claimed to know what went on inside that Castle after its construction. They repeated rumors regarding Exposition visitors who had rented lodgings there and were never seen again. They spoke of the countless number of "typewriters"—as secretaries were then called—whom Holmes had hired over the years. These girls had worked briefly in the Castle and then they too had disappeared.

Now, as speculation soared into suspicion, a shocking story broke in the news. An insurance company set a Philadelphia police detective on Holmes's trail. He followed it to a house in Toronto which had been rented by Holmes under another name. Buried in the cellar were the bodies of two of Pitezel's little girls.

That discovery had been made five days ago. And now, on this sultry July morning in Chicago, the Holmes Castle itself was to be entered at last. As horse-drawn streetcars clattered past on Sixty-third Street and freight trains rumbled over the tracks paralleling Wallace, the milling mob murmured in anticipation. Newspapers stated that the court-appointed receiver of Holmes's assets had given the police permission to enter the Castle seeking clues, but what were they really looking for?

The eyes of the crowd roved restlessly over the elaborate edifice. Its sheer size—50 x 125 feet—was made still more imposing by battlements and wooden bay windows covered with sheet iron. The doorway of the corner drugstore was quite impressive; other entrances gave access to stores and shops. The two upper stories were studded with a profusion of glittering glass windows hinting at the presence of eighty or ninety rooms. What did those rooms contain? And what might be found in the windowless basement below? The summer sun shone brightly on the Castle's outer walls, but behind them lay dark secrets.

The investigators arrived, uniformed firemen and police officers plus a number of others in street clothes. Some were recognized—dignified Fire Marshal James Kenyon, portly Detective Sergeant Fitzpatrick and thin Detective Sergeant Norton whose slouch hat and drooping mustache gave him a somewhat sinister look. Few identified Dr. C. P. Stringfield, a medical doctor working with the police, or Frank Wind, a special operator from the famous Pinkerton Detective Agency.

But there was no doubt that these men meant business. Some carried kerosene lanterns; others shouldered shovels, crowbars or pickaxes. The police bore clubs and revolvers in preparation for any emergency. Underscoring the importance of the occasion was the presence of a large number of reporters brandishing notebooks and sketch pads. These too were weapons.

Policemen cleared a path through the crowd and forced spectators aside as the search party, together with members of the press, entered the drugstore and disappeared into the darkness beyond.

The excited throng surged forward but police wielded their nightsticks and pressed them back again. Now the crowd could only watch and wait—and wonder.

Horsecars continued to rattle by, crossing the railroad tracks. The trains chugged and clanked, engine smokestacks showering cinders. The noonday sun rose high in the heavens to beat down upon the heads of those who stood staring at the Castle.

Where were the men who had vanished into its depths? What had they found there?

No answer came. Hours passed and still the Castle stood silent, the mob massed before it.

Suddenly the silence was shattered by a blast that shook the cobblestone street and rattled the windows of the structure above. Deep within its walls something had exploded.

The crowd roared an echo, and once again police forced frantic onlookers to stand clear. In the confusion several minutes elapsed before order was restored, but no one yet knew what had taken place inside the Castle. Even the officers peered at the dark entrance in nervous expectation of what might emerge.

As they watched, a disheveled figure reeled forth from the doorway, gasping for breath. Dignified no longer, Fire Marshal Kenyon was scarcely recognizable; his bulging eyes were bloodshot and his face was purple as he stood panting at the entryway.

Several of his men moved out from behind to grasp his arms in support. Babbling incoherently, Kenyon broke free of their grip and started to run past the side of the building. Shouting, the firemen pursued him. After capturing the delirious fire marshal in an alley a block away, they carried him into a nearby store where a doctor was called to attend him.

By this time the crowd's attention was centered elsewhere. Others of the search party burst forth shouting orders; in response some police officers ran into the building. Those remaining managed to hold the crowd back. Cries arose—"What happened?" "Was it an explosion?" "Where are the others?" "Are they dead?"

Reporters rushing out of the doorway heard the questions but didn't answer them. Haggard and shaken, they scattered in search of nearby telephones, clutching notebooks in their trembling hands.

Soon the shouting was drowned out by the clanging bell of an ambulance. A lathered horse pulled up at the corner and white-coated attendants leaped out and hurried into the Castle. In a few minutes they reappeared, bearing grim burdens—the limp forms of four firemen, which they placed, one by one, in the ambulance before it wheeled away again.

Now there was another exodus from the Castle's open doorway: an emanation of smoke and reeking fumes slowly filtered forth. The smell of gas and the fear of fire sent the crowd stumbling back across the street.

It wasn't until the next morning that newspapers revealed what had occurred. In the days and weeks that followed, the local and national press poured out incredible disclosures as the search of the Castle continued. But few accounts agreed as to what had been concealed within its walls, and all were so riddled with rumor, conjecture and hearsay that it was virtually impossible to separate truth from fiction. Not that there was any need of the latter. The facts were more horrifying than any fantasy.

2

IF THE CROWD had been free to follow the search party into the Castle on that July morning, it might at first have met with disappointment. The ornate entrance was complemented by the drugstore's dramatic interior, with its diamond-shaped black-and-white-tiled floor, frescoed stucco walls and winding staircase at the back. But it was a drugstore, nothing more. And the adjoining shops seemed like ordinary places of business.

After conferring with the detectives, Fire Marshal Kenyon faced the group assembled in the pharmacy. "No point in wasting time here," he told them. "I want to take a look upstairs and down."

A reporter from an out-of-town paper spoke up. "What about that fire on the roof two years ago? Didn't you inspect the building then?"

Kenyon shrugged. "Holmes dropped his claim when the insurance people started to investigate, so they called a halt right there. Then he left town. Nobody's been upstairs since except the caretaker. Now let's stop blabbing and get on with what we're here for."

Detective Sergeant Fitzpatrick nodded at the fire marshal. "Where do you want to begin?"

"I'd like to examine the furnace in the basement," Kenyon said.

"Good enough. We'll go upstairs." Fitzpatrick glanced at his partner. "Norton, you take the third floor, I'll cover the second." He looked at Pinkerton investigator Frank Wind. "What about you?"

Wind shrugged. "Dr. Stringfield and I will go downstairs with the fire marshal. Okay, Doctor?"

Stringfield nodded affirmatively. "Do we have enough lanterns?"

"Enough and some to spare." Fitzpatrick turned to the waiting police officers and firemen and quickly divided them into three groups. "Let's get one thing straight," he said to them. "No matter which floor you're assigned to, I want you boys to stick together." He faced the reporters. "That goes double for you—there'll be no nosying around on your own, understand? It could be dangerous."

The journalist from out of town ventured a sniff. "But there's no one here except ourselves. Unless you believe those stories about ghosts—"

"May the Devil take the ghosts, and you as well, if you disobey orders." Fitzpatrick turned and gestured to his men. "Come along now, and be quick about it."

Fitzpatrick's party clambered up the staircase at the back of the store and dispersed on the second floor, while Norton's group found its way to the floor above.

The third story was dark, dusty and deserted. A musty odor left the searchers gasping in the hot air. At the top of the stairs Detective Norton halted, removed his slouch hat, wiped his forehead and glanced upward. Looming overhead was a flimsy roof, obviously constructed in haste to replace the one damaged by the flames. The side walls of the staircase were charred and smoke-smudged.

Norton shook his head. "Kenyon's about to have himself a fit when he sees this firetrap."

A local reporter nodded. "You can bet your boots it's some kind of a trap." He stared down the long hallway extending almost to the front of the building and at the doors lining it on both sides. "A trap or a maze."

His words proved prophetic. As they cautiously moved forward along the hall, light from their lanterns disclosed three side passageways to the right, flanked by more doors on either side. Now, as Norton issued commands, some of these doors were flung open, disclosing empty rooms. Those at the rear were unfurnished and seemed never to have been occupied. Many were windowless. After passing through these rooms, the party entered others that were dead ends; they could not be reached directly from any hall. If the single entrance was locked, these rooms would become sealed chambers.

"Look at this!" An officer lowered his lantern to the bare floor of a small compartment and dim rays disclosed the outline of a trapdoor. He tugged at the latch but the door didn't budge.

"Here's another one." A second officer standing in the doorway had found a similar trapdoor in the corridor just outside. A fireman nodded at Norton. "Want me to pry it up?" He hefted his crowbar, but the detective shook his head.

"Not now. Let's see the rest of this layout first."

The group moved toward the front where the third passageway branched right. Here another door was opened, disclosing a bedroom.

"Holmes slept here?" a reporter murmured.

"If he did, he wasn't sleeping alone." Norton's mouth formed the hint of a smile beneath the straggly mustache. "That vanity table and mirror don't belong in a man's room."

But an inspection of the bare closet and empty vanity drawers disclosed no clues as to the room's occupants. The group moved across the hallway to a more rewarding area—two small offices and a bedroom. In the first office a desk drawer still contained a few scraps of paper. Norton rummaged through them and pulled out a bankbook, which he inspected in the lantern light.

"First National Bank," he said.

The out-of-town reporter peered over Norton's shoulder, then held out his hand. "Can I see it?"

"None of your business. This here's evidence." The detective closed the passbook and slipped it into his pocket.

"Sergeant!"

A police officer was calling from the second office. "Would you step in here, sir? I think we've found something—"

The detective turned and crossed through the connecting doorway to the other room, followed by the rest of the party.

At first glance the adjoining office looked very much like the first. Its only distinguishing feature was a large cast-iron stove standing in one corner. The bulky unit was almost six feet high and unusually wide; it seemed designed to heat an entire house rather than this small third-floor room.

"That's what set me thinking," the officer told his superior. "So I took a look inside the ash pan here and I found this."

He held up a small yellowish object. Norton grasped it and stared down with puzzled eyes.

"What do you make of it?" he said.

"Looks like part of a bone," the uniformed man answered. "Feels like it, too."

"Look and feel don't cut any mustard." Norton shook his head. "Besides, you were warned not to go snooping around on your own."

"Sorry, sir." The officer stooped and picked up something from the floor. "But there was more stuff, too. I got this out of the grate."

Now there was no mistaking it. The other, much larger yellowish object he displayed was definitely a bone.

A collective gasp rose from the group gathered inside the doorway. "It's a rib," someone murmured. "A human rib!"

Norton turned to silence the source of the disturbance, but before he could do so, the zealous police officer reached down again and came up with several items that needed no identification. One of them was a piece of cloth, obviously the remnant of a dress. The other, scorched and covered with ash, was a woman's slipper.

Norton made no effort to still the babble that now broke out. "Put that down," he muttered. "I want Fitzpatrick to see this."

He led the party back into the hall. There, turning a corner into the long corridor, he noticed a small door standing ajar on the right wall. On impulse Norton pushed it open, revealing a closet. Motioning to the others to stand aside, the detective took a lantern and entered the cubicle alone. He surveyed it with a practiced eye.

At first glance there was nothing unusual to be seen. The closet was bare and had apparently never been used for storage purposes.

But there was a trapdoor in the floor.

Norton unfastened the latch and pulled the door up. Holding his lantern over the opening, he stared down into the second-floor room below. After a long moment he lowered the trapdoor again and walked back into the hallway.

One of the police officers approached him. "What's down there?" he asked.

"Nothing. It's just an opening in the ceiling over a bathroom downstairs."

"Bathroom?" The officer shook his head. "Now what would he be after needing a trapdoor for that?"

Norton scowled. "Don't ask foolish questions. You sound like a reporter. . . . Speaking of which, where are they?"

The officer glanced up apologetically. "Back in the offices, I guess."

"We're supposed to stick together!" Norton started down the hall. "Wait until I get my hands on those snooping—"

When he reached the office suite he found the reporters had indeed been snooping. And in the course of satisfying their curiosity they had come across a few discoveries.

In the closet of the bedroom next to the two offices was a series of cutoffs which apparently regulated the flow of gas to lights throughout the Castle. There was also a bell with wiring attached. And on the underside of one office desk was a row of buzzers linked to another wiring system that wasn't operating.

"You savvy?" said the reporter whose queries had first annoyed the detective. "Holmes could control the gaslight all over the building anytime he pleased. When he sat at his desk these buzzers would signal whenever someone moved anywhere in the Murder Castle."

"Murder Castle!" Norton exploded. "Will you stop with that malarkey now?"

"I'm afraid we're only starting," the reporter said softly. "Let me show you what else we ran into."

"Go ahead." Norton spoke just as softly, but there was a hard edge to his voice. "It'd better be good."

"After your man found those bones in the stove along with the cloth and the slipper"—the reporter glanced at his companions—"we got to wondering just who Holmes incinerated there—"

"Incinerated be damned!" Norton muttered. "For all we know, those could be a couple of soup bones and maybe he burned some old clothes, but that doesn't prove he did away with whoever wore them."

"This does."

The reporter turned and took something from the desk top behind him as he spoke. "We lifted off the stovepipe and looked inside the chimney to see if the draft had pulled anything up. Here's what was stuck against the brickwork."

Holding out his hand, he displayed a clump of hair.

"Take a good look," the reporter said. "See how long and thick it is? This came from a woman's head."

"Holy Mother of God!" Norton turned and charged out into the hall. "Wait until Fitzpatrick hears this!"

But Fitzpatrick's own explorations had led to even more disconcerting discoveries.

If the third floor was a maze, the second floor seemed like a labyrinth. Fitzpatrick and his party wandered through the weird world of an architectural nightmare.

There was no open hallway extending the full length of the building; the back corridor branched off into two side halls and ended abruptly in a blind alley dividing the second story into two separate sections. Another hall up front could be reached only by passing through a series of rooms off the dead end.

Not all of the thirty-five separate rooms on this floor were visible from outside. Some could be reached only from adjoining chambers, others were concealed by secret panels in the hallway walls. Many were windowless, several had hidden doors which, when closed, transformed the rooms into airless cells. A few were bedrooms—women's bedrooms, by the look of the furnishings.

But there was no explaining the purpose of certain connecting closets, soundproof cubicles or the strange double-level rooms with low ceilings and trapdoors in the floors where ladders led down into tinier rooms beneath. Nor could anyone account for the room that was entirely filled by a gigantic steel walk-in safe the size of a bank vault. Oddly enough, there was an opening inside that proved to be the outlet for a gas pipe.

Equally puzzling was another bare chamber with sheet-iron walls lined in asbestos. The asbestos was scorch-marked as though something had been burned in the room; again a gas pipe had been set in the wall.

Many rooms had similar pipes, each equipped with a shut-off valve. But the firemen in the party told Fitzpatrick the valves were fakes; the flow of gas could be controlled only from some outside source.

Holmes would know where that control was located. Holmes would be able to prowl through the hidden passageways and climb the closet staircases to enter any room at will.

Holmes would have access to the peepholes in the walls of the bedchambers of his unsuspecting guests. He would also have the keys to the heavy metal locks affixed to the outside of some of the doors.

And Holmes would know about the concealed chute which ran from the third floor all the way into the basement; a dummy elevator shaft into which a large object could be dropped. Its sides appeared to have been greased.

All this Fitzpatrick revealed to Norton and his companions when the two parties joined forces on the second floor.

"But that's not the worst of it," Fitzpatrick said. "We found these in one of the bedrooms." He nodded at a police officer, who held up a bloodstained undershirt and a pair of overalls mottled by reddish streaks.

"And this." Fitzpatrick nodded again and a second officer stepped forward and handed him three more objects to display. "We broke into one of the back rooms and here's what was stuck under the doorsill."

Norton gazed at the findings—a wool shirt, a pair of shoes, and a girl's dress, tattered and threadbare.

"Must have been there a long time," he muttered.

"Is that all you've got to say?" Fitzpatrick frowned. "What did you see upstairs?"

His colleague told him quickly and now Fitzpatrick nodded. "It's beginning to make sense. I'll just go have a look at that office and the stove—"

"Wait." Norton gestured quickly. "There's one thing has me stumped. That closet trapdoor opening into the bathroom ceiling on the second floor. Why would he be having the two rooms connected?"

"Maybe to drop something from up above," Fitzpatrick said. "But it's just a bathroom. Nothing special about it."

"I'd like to see for myself," Norton said.

"Come along then—it's right here off the end of the hall."

The party trooped after them, then halted at the corner doorway. As Fitzpatrick stood guard, Norton entered alone and made a quick inspection.

The medicine cabinet, washbowl, toilet with overhead flush tank and pull chain seemed ordinary enough. The room was carpeted; next to the conventional four-legged tub was a bath mat, nailed to the floor.

It was this feature that aroused Norton's professional interest. Why the nails? He remembered stories about World's Fair visitors and their zeal as souvenir hunters; as the old saying had it, they'd steal anything that wasn't nailed down. But a bath mat—?

He stooped and ran his fingers along the edge.

All at once his hand halted, curling around a piece of metal set in the flooring beneath the mat. Tracing its outline by touch, he recognized the shape of a latch which loosened and gave as he pressed against it.

Suddenly the bath mat rose.

Norton jumped back, startled, then stared down into the blackness below.

The crowd in the hall clustered around the doorway, jostling for a better view. Fitzpatrick motioned them away, calling over his shoulder to his colleague. "What is it?"

"Another trapdoor." Norton eyed the opening. "There's a stairway below." Turning, he gestured with his lantern. "I'm going down."

"Want me to come with you?"

"I can manage." Norton moved to the rear, disappearing from view behind the upraised door. "Wait here."

For a moment those in the hall could hear the muffled footsteps echoing through the flooring below. Gradually they died away into silence.

As the minutes passed, the silence was broken by the murmurs of those who watched from above.

"What's keeping him so long?"

"Think somebody ought to go after him?"

Fitzpatrick scowled. "I'm giving the orders here. Just stay put until he gets back."

"Suppose he doesn't come back?"

"Hold it—I hear something. He must be climbing up now."

"Somebody's climbing, that's for sure. But how do we know it's Norton?"

Fitzpatrick drew his revolver. "Whoever it is, we're ready for him."

"Put that damn thing away before it goes off!" Norton said as he clambered up out of the opening.

"All right." Fitzpatrick holstered his weapon. "Suppose you tell us what you found."

"The stairs come out to a room on the ground level behind the drugstore. But there's another set goes on down to the basement."

Fitzpatrick nodded. "So Holmes could use this secret route and come out below wherever he had a mind to." His eyes narrowed thoughtfully. "But why go to all that trouble? Unless he was carrying something he didn't want anyone to see."

Fitzpatrick turned abruptly. The party followed. There was no need for him to announce a destination. The time had come to follow Holmes's trail to the basement. And it was there, in the dungeonlike darkness, that the ultimate horror lurked.

3

IT WAS HARD to believe that the midday sun was beating down outside the Castle walls. Here beneath the seven-foot ceiling of the huge basement the air was so clammy that Norton and Fitzpatrick stood shivering. But what Kenyon was to tell them proved far more chilling than the atmosphere of the chamber itself.

Dreadful discoveries had been made in an area extending under the entire building and beyond, for a concealed portion was tunneled out below the sidewalk of Sixty-third Street. Now the fire marshal led them on a guided tour of the cellar.

One of the first things that had attracted his attention was a wood-burning stove. It proved larger than the one in Holmes's office upstairs and contained more sinister relics—several pieces of women's jewelry and a half-dozen large bones.

In a nearby ash heap were scraps of bloody linen and a thick lock of hair. Coal had been removed from a small bin in the north corner; underneath, a shirt and a pair of drawers were found.

Digging into the floor, firemen had discovered a barrel bound with heavy metal hoops and filled with some sort of corrosive acid. Continuing their search, they unearthed two brick-lined vaults filled with quicklime. From them Dr. Stringfield's gloved hands lifted eight ribs and part of a human skull.

Loose quicklime was piled in a corner room; in it was a naked footprint.

"A woman's footprint," Kenyon told his companions. "Dr. Stringfield said he'd swear to that."

Norton and Fitzpatrick exchanged glances. Before they could comment, Fire Marshal Kenyon led them into a small storeroom against the wall. From the doorway they saw nothing inside but a bare workbench with a coil of rope below it. But the bench top was spattered with dark red rivulets, and the rope, which had been fashioned into a noose, was crusted with bloodstains.

"Will you look at it now," Fitzpatrick muttered. "A hangman's rope and a bloody butcher's block!"

"There's more." Kenyon moved back across the cellar. At the far end firemen were wielding pickaxes against the brick wall of what appeared to be a large coal bin. Rising above the thudding echoes came the outcries of reporters huddling before several curiously constructed metal machines. As Kenyon and the two detectives approached, the journalists drew back, affording a clearer view.

"What do you make of these?" the fire marshal said.

Norton squinted down, one hand rising to tug at the corner of his mustache. "Beats me. I never saw the like of such contraptions."

"That long one with the pulleys at both ends," Fitzpatrick murmured. "Reminds me of the torture racks used in the olden days for pulling prisoners' bones apart until the poor devils confessed."

"It must be the Elasticity Determinator," one of the reporters told him.

"The *what*?"

"I've heard Dr. Holmes experimented with an invention to test the tension of the muscular system. He had an idea that by gradual treatments he could stretch the human body to twice its normal length and turn people into giants."

Fitzpatrick stared at his informant. "You believe this?"

"I don't know." The reporter shrugged. "But Holmes does seem to have some kind of reputation as an inventor."

Kenyon cleared his throat. "Come along. There's more."

He led Fitzpatrick and Norton to a doorway opening into the south end of the basement. He rounded its corner and ushered them over to a room that had been concealed by a wall. Poised at the entrance, he pointed down.

"Don't try going in," he cautioned. "There's no floor—just dirt and manure. I had the boys dig in to see if they could find anything underneath. They uncovered a woman's shoe." He waved across the opening. "There's a stairway leading into this room from above, but it's blocked off."

"Blocked off?" Fitzpatrick frowned at Norton. "I thought you said you found one that came all the way down here."

"So I did." Norton looked puzzled. "There must be another—"

"There is." Fire Marshal Kenyon nodded.

Grim-faced, he moved back into the central portion of the basement. And it was here that the purpose of the trapdoor and stairwell beneath the bathroom floor above became fully evident.

Behind false paneling was a metal table on which rested a black leather case. The lid had been flung open to reveal its contents—a row of gleaming surgical instruments.

But not all of them gleamed. Some of the knives and scalpels had cutting edges smudged with reddish stains.

"A dissecting table," Kenyon said.

Fitzpatrick frowned. "Not so fast. Let's stick to the facts. All we've got here is a table and a medical bag."

Fire Marshal Kenyon ignored him, addressing Norton instead. "See that box under the table? I suggest you take a look inside."

Norton moved forward and stooped to tug at the heavy wooden

crate Kenyon had indicated. He pulled it toward him, lifted the lid and peered inside.

"Holy Mother!" Norton gestured Fitzpatrick forward. "Skeletons!"

Three bony forms lay in the box, entwined in an obscene embrace. Three fleshless skulls grinned up in the wavering light.

Kenyon turned and removed a loose panel from the base of the wall to reveal a gaping opening. He tapped the wall above and a hollow sound echoed as he spoke.

"There's some kind of chute from up above—"

Fitzpatrick nodded. "We know about that."

"And now we know what it's for," Norton said. "Holmes had his choice, didn't he? Either drop the bodies down the chute from the third floor or carry them down the staircase from the second." He grimaced wryly. "I guess I owe those newspaper fellows an apology. Here I was bawling them out for calling this place a Murder—"

He halted abruptly and for a moment the three men stood in silence, sharing their unspoken thoughts with the shadows looming down upon them in this domain of death.

DEATH. IT WAS A palpable presence now, lurking everywhere. Death dwelt in Dr. Holmes's office on the third floor, hiding away in the grate and chimney pipe of an old-fashioned stove. Death haunted the hallways of the second floor, in airtight rooms locked from outside, in asphyxiation chambers with gas connections, in a metal vault and an asbestos-lined compartment. Death prowled dark corridors to peer through peepholes at sleeping victims, crept along secret passageways, slithered through panels and rose from trapdoors to seize its prey in the midnight maze. Death bore its burden down the hidden staircase to the cellar.

And here, in the basement, Death racked and ripped, cut and chopped, burned and buried, gloated and gloried in its dark delights.

"WHAT IN BLAZES—?"

Kenyon looked up as the thudding, which had been continuously echoing from the far end of the basement, suddenly stopped. He and the detectives hurried toward the area where the firemen had been attacking the brickwork of the supposed coal bin. Now that the bricks had given way beneath their picks and crowbars, an opening into a chamber behind the barrier had been revealed.

Pinkerton man Frank Wind approached it as reporters converged from other parts of the cellar. By the time Kenyon and the two detectives reached the gap, the firemen had enlarged it sufficiently to get a good view of what lay beyond.

Set against the far wall was a cylindrical cedarwood tank from which a tangle of pipes zigzagged in all directions. A sickening stench slowly filtered forth from the dark recess and the reporters fell back, gagging and coughing.

"Smells like a sewer," Norton wheezed.

"More like the stockyards," Fitzpatrick told him. He cleared his throat. "Wait a minute—it's going away." Gradually the smell subsided and the onlookers breathed freely again. Kenyon glanced up as Frank Wind stepped forward to peer through the opening.

"Funny-looking gizmo," Wind murmured.

Kenyon nodded. "Any idea what it is?"

"Beats me," Wind told him. "But I intend to find out." Lantern in hand, he started through the space between the tumbled brickwork, but Kenyon grabbed his shoulder.

"Hold your horses," the fire marshal said. "I wouldn't go in there if I were you."

"Since when are you giving *me* orders?"

"It's just a matter of taking precautions, what with that smell and all." Kenyon squinted into the shadows. "Do you have any idea what those pipes are for?"

"How would I know?" Wind snapped. "I'm not a plumber."

"Exactly," Kenyon said. "That's why I asked one of my men to send for one."

Wind glared at the fire marshal. "This is an official investigation. We can't waste time waiting."

"It'll only be a minute. There's a shop just down the street. I told my man to bring the plumber in through the rear so there'd be no delay."

"You had no business bringing in another—"

Fitzpatrick stepped between the two men. "Now don't go getting hot under the collar," he said. "I think maybe Kenyon is right."

"Oh do you, now?"

The detective nodded. "Look at it this way. Everything we've found here tells us that Holmes is a slippery customer. And if he went to the trouble of hiding this gadget of his behind a brick wall, it must be something pretty special. Chances are it could be dangerous. No sense fooling around with all those pipes until we know what we're up against."

Wind hesitated as murmurs of agreement rose from the group gathered behind him. If he had any intentions of arguing further, his objections were stilled when a fireman cleared a path through the huddle of onlookers and produced the plumber.

The short, stocky man nodded perfunctorily as introductions were exchanged, then moved to the fissure in the wall. He peered at the cylinder beyond, rubbing his fingers across a stubbly chin.

"It's some kind of tank," he said.

"We know that," Wind growled. "But what's it for?"

"Give me a lantern and I'll tell you."

A fireman fulfilled his request and the plumber moved through the gap. Inspecting the container, he muttered to himself, "Ten by six. Flue must run under the alleyway. Got to have a sealer—probably double."

He squatted and ran his thumb along the side of the tank and located a latch. After unfastening it, he glanced at a strip of metal embedded in the wood beneath, then nodded. "Just like I figured." Turning, he called to Kenyon, "This here's a double tank. Tell some of your men to give me a hand and we'll see what's inside."

Kenyon started through the opening, followed by four firemen. The group outside stood watching as the plumber directed the quartet to unscrew pipe attachments and tip the cedar cylinder forward. Two of them unfastened the lid at the top while the other two held the tank steady.

The plumber nodded at the fire marshal. "Look inside here. All that black stuff, it's some kind of oil burned away. The zinc lining— that's to protect the wood. Could take some pretty high temperatures if you ask me."

"What about that little box down at the bottom?" Kenyon asked.

"Don't know. Have to see it close-hand."

Kenyon thrust his arm down into the tank. "Ah, here we go—"

He lifted the box out and turned and unscrewed the lid, revealing a powdery deposit. For a moment he stared down, then recoiled as a swirl of fuming vapor spiraled up to envelop his head and shoulders.

Retching, Kenyon reeled back, eyes widening as he fought for breath. As Frank Wind reached forward to pull him out of the recess, the box dropped from his numbed fingers.

"What happened?" Wind muttered.

But Kenyon couldn't speak. His lips moved soundlessly as he pointed toward the opening. Now a nauseating odor surged forth, clouding the cubicle and obscuring the forms of the firemen holding the tank. They too were gasping. One of them stumbled, knocking over the lantern which the plumber had placed on the floor. Its light flickered out and the figures grouped around the tank were lost in darkness and billowing haze. Blinking and half blinded, the plumber dipped a hand into his pocket and drew out a box of matches.

From outside Fitzpatrick caught the gesture and called quickly, "Hey—don't do that—"

His warning came too late.

There was a single flash of bluish flame that burst like a gigantic bubble, the roar resounding through the cellar and resonating in the building above.

"Gas explosion!" yelled Norton, but his voice was lost amid the cries of reporters scattering back across the basement. As the echo of the blast died away, police officers dragged the firemen from the opening in the wall. The plumber staggered out on his own, dazed but unharmed.

"I was just gonna light the lantern," he whispered.

The noxious vapor poured through the confines of the cellar but there was no further outburst of flame. The reporters halted their flight as Fitzpatrick took over, quelling the confusion. Quickly he directed his officers to remove the injured firemen from the premises. Two of Kenyon's men had stayed clear of the cubicle; now they grasped his arm and led him, stumbling and babbling incoherently, to the stairs.

It took several hours before order was restored. By then the ambulance had come and gone outside and the basement was cleared of fumes. Fire Marshal Kenyon, after receiving medical treatment at the pharmacy down the street, now insisted on returning to the Castle and rejoining the search party.

Throughout the rest of the afternoon and in the days that followed, the investigation continued. More journalists swarmed over the scene, scribbling and sketching. Other officials arrived, including E. F. Laughlin, a city building inspector. His report, issued on July 23, was confined to a description of the structure itself. He outlined the areas where he had found damage and fire hazards. The roof was faulty, interior repairs were inadequate, sanitary conditions "horrible." The stores passed inspection but he recommended that the rest of the Castle be condemned as unsafe.

While a building inspector might be horrified by sanitation defects, the police, press and public were upset by other findings.

More areas had been excavated now, including a subbasement section where a mixture of human and animal bones was unearthed. One source described three graves containing unidentifiable bodies; other accounts were more cautious.

Those not content with bones were given an additional bonus. Microscopic examination revealed bloodstains on the floor and walls of the upstairs sleeping room where the overalls and undershirt had been found. More stains of human blood were discovered in the bathroom and its secret stairway below.

But the biggest sensation was created by the description of a furnace built into one of the basement walls which had two separate grates—one to hold the fire and the other, fitted with rollers, on which a large object could be slid into the flames. From the furnace a flue led to a sealed tank. Apparently Dr. Holmes, not completely satisfied with grave digging, vats of quicklime and ordinary stoves, had also provided himself with a private crematorium.

Clarence Phillips, once swindled by Holmes in a deal involving an all-night restaurant operation, now came forward. He said he'd built the tank as part of Holmes's apparatus used in experiments for the Warner Glass Bending Company. The enterprise was abandoned but an anonymous furnace agent told one newspaper reporter that he had later added a burner which used oil from a tank in the alley, and explained how the furnace could be operated without telltale odors escaping. Whether or not this device was connected to the double tank behind the false brick wall was never made clear.

Nor were other explanations much more enlightening. Pat Quinlan, Holmes's longtime janitor and handyman, gave out revelations of how Holmes had constructed the Castle with many separate groups of workmen.

It was his practice to let each group perform a single task, then halt them before they finished the job. Complaining about the use of poor materials or slipshod methods, he would dismiss them—usually without payment—then hire another crew to complete the task. In this way only Holmes would know the full details of how the Castle was built and exactly what it contained.

A bricklayer, George Bowman, corroborated this when he described his work on the upstairs vault. He too had been removed from the project midway. The huge safe Holmes had ordered went into an unfinished room; another workman then erected the walls around it so that it couldn't be removed.

A builder named Cole told of installing some of the secret passageways upstairs and noted that there often seemed to be gas leaks in the basement.

Several different workmen were employed at separate times to handle construction jobs in the cellar.

And Charles Chopmen, a Chicago mechanic, stated that in 1892 and 1893 he had been hired to perform a delicate task—stripping the flesh from the bodies of a man and two women, which Holmes said he'd procured from the morgue. He was paid thirty-six dollars for each stint, including the articulation of the skeletons so that Holmes could sell them to medical schools. If true, this could possibly explain the presence of the three skeletons found in the box beneath the table in the basement.

Understandably upset by the avalanche of atrocity stories thundering from the press, some skeptical citizens began to protest that too much was being made of purely circumstantial evidence.

Apparently these objectors had forgotten the discovery of the bodies in the Toronto house Holmes had rented under another name for himself and his two "nieces." The naked, decomposing corpses of fifteen-year-old Alice Pitezel and her younger sister, Nellie, were unearthed in the tiny basement. An examination showed that the cause of death was asphyxiation.

A trunk Holmes had in his possession when he was arrested in Boston offered damning evidence as to the likely method. A round hole drilled in the lid was just wide enough to accommodate the insertion of a rubber tube. It was probable that the children had been drugged and then placed in the trunk, whereupon Holmes introduced the tube and attached the other end to a gas jet. When he turned on the gas, the two helpless girls suffocated to death. And there was one other grisly touch, never explained—both of little Nellie's feet were missing.

Still unaccounted for was their younger brother, Howard Pitezel, who had also accompanied H. H. Holmes during his travels. The detective who had unearthed the bodies of his sisters now joined with his chief inspector to continue the search.

On August 27 their investigation led them to a cottage Holmes had rented in Irvington, Indiana, while in the company of a young boy he described as his "nephew."

Once more a cellar yielded up a grisly secret. While dismantling the chimney leading from the basement to the roof, the detectives discovered bits of bone, part of a jaw and human teeth. Also, a pelvis and the charred and baked remains of internal organs were found. In a barn outside they came across a package containing pieces of bone and the skull of a small child. The barn had a coal stove; its top was bloodstained and inside was a residue of mingled blood and grease.

A local youth told of assisting Holmes to install the stove one afternoon, while the "nephew" was present. A man operating a repair shop in nearby Indianapolis offered additional information. Holmes, accompanied by a small boy, had brought him two cases of surgical instruments to be sharpened; he picked them up again five days later.

Those who discounted Dr. Holmes's homicidal deeds could not explain away the facts. Three children had last been seen alive in the company of a man answering to his description. Now little Howard Pitezel and his two sisters were dead.

And a few weeks later, on September 12, 1895, in Philadelphia, Herman W. Mudgett, aka H. H. Holmes, was indicted for the murder of the children's father, Benjamin F. Pitezel.

By then, back in Chicago, the twisted tunnels of the Murder Castle had been completely explored.

Now it is time to explore the twisted mind of the Castle's lord and master—the ogre who called himself H. H. Holmes.

THE OGRE

1

FOLKS IN GILMANTON remembered Herman Mudgett.

Reckon they would, seeing as how Gilmanton wasn't all that big of a place—just a little bitty town plunked down in easterly New Hampshire, south of Laconia. It's a mite more populous today, but back then it weren't hardly big enough to have a post office.

Old Levi Mudgett used to be postmaster there but his main line was farming. Did pretty well at it too; ended up marrying a school-marm name of Theodate Price.

Theodate—now there's a fancy moniker for you! But she was a good woman and a good Methodist, like her husband. Brought up her young 'uns in the faith too.

Funny thing about those kids; some say as how she had five and others swear they was only three. Not that it matters because none of them ever amounted to a hill of beans, outside of Herman.

Born in 1860, on May 16. That makes him a Taurus, according to astrologers. But most folks don't hold with that line of thinking, and if Herman was a bit bullheaded, nobody paid it much heed at the time.

The time being just before the start of the Civil War, so folks had other things to worry about. Old Abe Lincoln run for president and got himself elected. Then come the secession trouble and we had us a real ruckus on our hands. Some of the local boys volunteered to join up and whip the Johnny Rebs, and later on another bunch got drafted, leaving the folks back home with their hands full, what with farming chores and all. So hardly anyone kept an eye on little Herman Webster Mudgett.

Webster—that was for Daniel Webster, of course. Must of been his ma's idea, seeing as how she'd been a teacher. By the time the war was over, Herman was going to school himself and he turned out to be a right smart scholar.

Thing of it is, he was a tad on the puny side. Older boys picked on him, called him a sissy, and that could be what drove him to settle down to book learning. His pa was a God-fearing man; "Children should be seen and not heard" was his motto, along with "Spare the rod and spoil the child." So young Herman toed the line and studied his lessons. People recollect he made high marks when he went on to the Gilmanton Academy.

Some say he was cruel to animals and played the bully with younger boys, but maybe they're just stretching things a bit on account of what he turned into later. By the time he graduated—1876 it was, which makes him sixteen—he looked to be a well brought up young fellow on the serious side. Used to hire out for farm work up north every summer to earn himself some money. Minute he graduated he went into teaching school on his own; got a job schoolmastering in Gilmanton the very first year, then skedaddled off to a better deal in Alton. Even then he was always one to keep a sharp lookout for the main chance.

Kept a sharp lookout for the fair sex too, and first thing you know he up and married a girl name of Clara Lovering on the Fourth of July, 1878. She was a farmer's daughter; they say her father was well off, and maybe that had something to do with Herman eloping so sudden-like. One thing for sure, she did come into an inheritance about this time and that was the last Gilmanton saw of Herman W. Mudgett. Moved his wife clear over to Burlington, Vermont, and started studying at the university there. Said he wanted to be a doctor.

Some years later his wife come traipsing back home with a baby boy she said was Herman's son—but Herman wasn't with her. Close-mouthed woman she was; never told where her husband went or what he'd been up to, only that they'd moved from Vermont to Michigan so's he could finish his schooling there. Now he'd be looking around for a place to start up a doctoring practice, and meantime she aimed to settle down and wait till he sent for her.

Folks being what they are, you could hear a lot of talk—gossip or worse—about how Herman flew the coop and left his lawful wedded wife for another woman. Others figured that maybe he'd gotten into a scrape with the law over in Michigan and was laying low until things cooled down. Never did get a chance to make hide or hair of it, because wife Clara and the child moved about ten miles away, to Tilton.

But she never went for a divorce and gradual-like everybody simmered down and just plumb forgot all about Herman W. Mudgett.

WHEN YOUNG MR. MUDGETT enrolled in the medical school at Ann Arbor, the state of Michigan was flourishing.

The state of medicine, however, was another matter.

During the final decades of the century most physicians were still practicing an art rather than a science. Though Koch and Pasteur had established the germ theory of communicable disease, thousands of their colleagues still carried deadly microorganisms into the sickroom in their bushy beards. President Garfield was shot by an assassin in 1881, but it is now believed he actually met death at the hands of his physicians—the unclean hands groping for the bullet lodged in his body. Twenty years later another American President, William McKinley, was shot, and again it's been alleged that he died only because of medical bungling. Meanwhile millions of less prominent patients suffered, succumbed or sometimes survived in an era when quack treatments and patent nostrums flourished.

Those who mistrusted doctors put their faith in remedies laced with alcohol and laudanum. Opiates could be purchased over the counter at any drugstore, along with "miracle cures" for female disorders, venereal complaints, stammering, epilepsy, cancer and chilblains. Fevers were allayed with oatmeal baths, pneumonia victims wore mustard plasters, and consumptives were advised to sleep with wide-open windows in below-zero weather, then awaken to roll naked in the snow.

But progress was being made. The introduction of anesthesia led to surgical advances, and the study of anatomy became a major concern of the profession.

There is no reliable firsthand account of Herman Mudgett's medical education. On the basis of his previous scholastic record it can be assumed he was a diligent student. No doubt he distinguished himself in his anatomy classes.

Dissecting cadavers is one thing; stealing them is another matter. Though in later years he would admit to murder, he steadfastly denied that he had ever been a ghoul. Everyone has to draw the line somewhere; while Mudgett apparently had no qualms about putting a man in the grave, he balked at taking him out of one.

But stories persist about his body-snatching exploits—often with a reverse twist. Instead of seeking a corpse from the cemetery, he took advantage of a much more convenient source and stole one from the dissecting laboratory itself. One version states that such a theft occurred while he was still a student at Ann Arbor; in collusion with a friend he rigged an insurance fraud.

The first step was to take out a sizable insurance policy on his fellow student's life. When a corpse bearing a general resemblance to his accomplice appeared among the "specimens" at the lab, Mudgett stole it. Meanwhile his partner in crime disappeared, whereupon Mudgett shipped the cadaver out of town in a trunk. After claiming the trunk at its destination, he disfigured the corpse and planted it in a lonely spot amid circumstantial evidence of an accidental death. By the time it was discovered, decomposition had set in and Mudgett conveniently showed up to identify his missing colleague and collect the insurance money.

He himself told a somewhat similar tale in his alleged confessions, but claimed the episode occurred in another city, and after his graduation. In this account the role of the accomplice was merely to provide a properly mutilated corpse from a medical school morgue which Mudgett, under another name, could later identify as himself. The yarn he spun involved a perilous railroad journey with the body concealed in a trunk, a hairbreadth escape from a "secret service man" who somehow got on his trail and the eventual disposition of the stolen cadaver under a fallen tree in a Michigan forest.

If this or similar incidents occurred, it's likely that they took place during the summer months. Summer brought freedom and the opportunity to augment the dwindling resources of wife Clara's small inheritance. He had taken the precaution of ensconcing her in the town of Maple Rapids, some distance away from Ann Arbor; thus his own movements were unimpeded by the presence of his spouse.

One summer vacation was spent in northern Illinois representing a Chicago textbook firm. When September came, he disappeared, together with the money accumulated from his sales efforts.

Broadened by travel, nourished by education, enriched by experience, his life was rapidly evolving into one in which his country bride played little part. It was later alleged that he had a fling with a young lady in Ann Arbor and there were hints of a breach-of-promise suit which he apparently averted.

Nevertheless, Mudgett was still a married man—and the fact was forcibly brought home to him when Clara announced her pregnancy. Almost before he fully realized it he found himself the possessor of a brand-new medical diploma and a brand-new baby boy.

Herman W. Mudgett was no longer a carefree college student; instead he'd become the head of a household, with all the attendant responsibilities and obligations. His diploma looked handsome enough but it was not contributing to his financial support at the moment. Without an established medical practice, the diploma was of no more use to him than one of the baby's diapers.

His first step was to convey the glad tidings of their grandparent-hood to Clara's folks back home and to solicit a loan from them to tide him over until he could start a professional career. But the Lovering family had never forgiven the upstart who had eloped with their daughter and they promptly advised him—in the then current catchphrase—to make a noise like a hoop and roll away.

Instead it was Clara and the baby who rolled away, sent home by a loving husband and father until he could locate the proper spot in which to hang out his shingle and begin medical practice.

The exact chronology of Mudgett's movements during the next few years is difficult to verify, but he managed to establish himself on a temporary footing in a number of locations.

One of them was Minnesota, where he used his medical credentials to obtain a position as a drugstore clerk in Minneapolis. Apparently it was here that he learned the pharmacy business.

Soon he mastered the ins and outs of another operation—the credit swindle. He moved on to Saint Paul and somehow wangled an appointment as receiver for a bankrupt store. After setting up a going-out-of-business sale to liquidate its assets, he augmented the inventory by ordering a huge supply of additional merchandise on account from various wholesalers. The goods were sold at a loss, with Mudgett pocketing the proceeds and skipping town.

He turned up in the state of New York. There he traveled as an agent for a shrubbery and plant nursery, then taught for a time in a district school at Mooers Forks near the Canadian border. The site was convenient because he could hop across the line to Canada whenever it became necessary to do so.

He was also working as a country doctor during a short period; his practice was precarious and brought in little revenue. But he had access to information regarding deaths in the area and access to insurance records.

Whether or not his medical ministrations hastened some of the local deaths is open to conjecture. So is the possibility that he conveyed corpses to Canada for sale at medical schools. In his confessions he admitted contemplating another insurance fraud involving false identification of a body but said the notion was finally abandoned as too dangerous.

However cautious he might have been in dealing with the dead, Mudgett failed to safeguard himself in his affairs with the living.

Affairs of the heart?

Some allege that he was forced to abandon his budding career as a physician because he became too friendly with female patients, the wives and daughters of local farmers. Others cite business affairs, such as unpaid rent, to account for his sudden flight from Mooers Forks. One version combines both—a disappointed landlord and an expectant landlady—as reasons for his abrupt departure.

He surfaced next in Philadelphia for a short stint as an attendant at the Norristown Asylum.

During the 1880s the polite euphemism of "mental hospital" had yet to be invented and an asylum was just that: a "lunatic asylum" or a "madhouse." In one of Philadelphia's hospitals the unfortunate inmates were incarcerated, three or four together, in cells as small as 8 x 10 feet. Starved and straitjacketed, the poor wretches were punished by blows from brutal guards and sometimes given the "water treatment." In winter a patient might be tied to the wall of his cell while cold water was poured over his head and shoulders until it froze to ice. Even worse was the custom of pouring alcohol on epileptics and setting them on fire.

What Mudgett did in such a hellhole and what he learned there will never be known. But certainly the man whose medical training had inured him to the sight of death and dismemberment now received a postgraduate course in the callous infliction of suffering on helpless living victims.

His tenure proved brief, for he soon reverted to his previous role as drugstore clerk, this time in Philadelphia. Then, in July of 1886, he set out for Chicago.

2

CHICAGO HAD RISEN from the ashes of the Great Fire of 1871 to establish itself as an intercontinental railroad center and, thanks to the stockyards, as "Hog Butcher of the World." The combination of rail access and opportunities for manual labor lured vast hordes of foreign immigrants to the city. The large Irish population later celebrated in Finley Peter Dunne's "Mister Dooley" stories soon dominated the political life of the community, but not always to good effect. Lack of education, man-killing hours of work and the manifold temptations of urban existence took a tremendous toll. The first fourteen-storied "skyscrapers" were rising, but so was the number of saloons, gambling joints and brothels. Politicians winked at reform, and crime increased to the point where muggings and robberies were commonplace occurrences. At the time Mudgett arrived there, the homicide rate had quadrupled over a period of a few short years—the annual death toll from murder in Chicago was eight times that of Paris. By 1893, *one out of every eleven persons* was arrested during the course of a year. And the mayor himself, Carter Harrison, was shot dead on his own doorstep.

The city was a place of peril. Carriage collisions, traffic accidents and railroad wrecks added to the carnage. Disease was rampant, and no wonder, with one hundred thousand pounds of manure dumped daily in the streets.

It was in this atmosphere of death that Herman W. Mudgett arrived and flourished. But from this point on he would live as—and others would die at the hands of—Dr. Henry Howard Holmes.

Exactly when he adopted his new name permanently is not known. But over the past half-dozen years he had undergone a transformation far more extensive than that of a mere name change.

The bright student had become a brilliant alumnus of what was then termed the school of hard knocks. He'd learned the arts of unscrupulous survival—lying, cheating, dissembling and fraud.

Travel and sojourns in both small towns and major cities had gained him full knowledge of human nature and its frailties. His experiments at seduction had evolved into expertise. The dissecting room, the morgue, the graveyard and the asylum had completed an education in evil.

Chicago was ripe for the coming of H. H. Holmes, and H. H. Holmes was ready for Chicago.

His new career began quietly enough, in the southern suburb of Englewood. Here, at a safe distance from downtown squalor, the local citizenry rejoiced in an atmosphere of what was popularly known as genteel refinement.

Englewood was a residential community, tree-shaded by day and gaslit by night. But in 1886—the time of Holmes's arrival—it was beginning to bustle with the first signs of mercantile activity.

Holmes strolled along cobblestone streets which echoed with the clop of hooves and the clatter of wheels. Cabs and carriages, sulkies and surreys, proudly outpaced the peddlers' carts, ice wagons and the creaking conveyances of junk men, ragpickers and scissors grinders.

He surveyed the corner groceries, adorned outside with pickle barrels and smelling inside of freshly made sauerkraut. He observed and inhaled the aroma of livery stables, the sooty fumes of blacksmiths' forges, the leather smell of harness shops.

There were dry-goods stores dealing in ribbons and lace, cloth yardage, pearl buttons and sundries. Dressmakers' establishments catered to chattering customers seeking appointments for fittings. Milliners created headgear from a stock of ostrich plumes, peacock feathers, stuffed birds and fancy felt imported "direct from Paris." In front of barber shops were the obligatory red-and-white-striped poles, and every cigar store was guarded by the upraised tomahawk of a wooden Indian. Taxidermists displayed glass-eyed animals mounted and menacing. Butchers festooned their windows with the carcasses of fresh-killed poultry dangling head down; the floor inside the premises was heaped with sawdust to absorb the spattering blood. Fish markets boasted barrels of oysters packed in ice; the reek of their principal wares was its own advertisement. Another distinctive odor emanated from the corner saloons—a commingling of malt and hops. Here, as in every establishment where men gathered, the most important item of furnishing was the ubiquitous spittoon.

Holmes studied the scene with cool calculation. In addition to commercial establishments he noted a number of small offices occupied by realtors, attorneys and physicians. In a booming business area such professionals were bound to thrive.

But the practice of medicine was impractical for Holmes. His degree had been granted to Herman W. Mudgett, and for obvious reasons he felt it wise not to use a name that might attract the attention of his abandoned wife, to say nothing of creditors and victims of other past misdeeds.

The time had come to start with a clean slate upon which would be inscribed the name of Henry Howard Holmes. And while he might call himself a doctor on occasion or speak of his training as a physician, he couldn't risk setting himself up as an M.D. on a full-time basis.

In the course of his surveillance of the community Holmes had made a mental note of a pharmacy on the corner of Wallace and Sixty-third Street. It occupied the ground floor of an apartment building known as the Englewood Flats. The location wasn't fully developed; there were still vacant lots directly across the street. But businesses in the vicinity were prospering and Holmes learned that a streetcar line would be running on Sixty-third within the next few years. That, together with the nearby railroads, made the spot attractive.

And when he discovered the pharmacy was run by a doctor's widow whose husband had bequeathed her the business, he lost no time in applying for a position as a clerk. By catering to customers, he soon transformed the pharmacy from an old-fashioned apothecary's shop into a modern drugstore. Mrs. E. S. Holton gradually entrusted him with all the business dealings and details involved in managing the operation.

But Mrs. Holton and her small daughter were not the only beneficiaries of the new employee's charisma. There was also a young lady named Myrta Z. Belknap whom he'd met while residing in Minneapolis a few years earlier. At that time she was clerking in a music store and apparently their acquaintance had been a casual one. In any case, she didn't know him by his real name.

In the interim her father, a railroad man from a well-to-do family, retired and moved to Chicago. Just how and where Holmes renewed contact with Myrta Belknap was never revealed, but the quiet and demure young woman attracted him. So did the financial status of her parents.

The result was a whirlwind courtship, culminating in marriage on January 28, 1887.

It would seem that Holmes was pleased with his new bride, for after a two-week honeymoon he paid a secret visit to the courthouse downtown. There, in Cook County Superior Court, he used his real name for the last time when filing for divorce against Clara A. Lovering. But he never followed through on the suit and eventually the action was dismissed without anyone—including the defendant—being the wiser.

Meanwhile Holmes had involved himself in a variety of other actions, some, like bigamy, illegal.

Exactly what occurred during the next five years will never be accurately known. It is here that rumor, gossip, conflicting testimony, faulty memory, self-serving and face-saving accounts create confusion clouding the most important period in Holmes's life. For these were the years in which a man turned into a monster.

It wasn't an overnight transformation, and at the outset all seemed normal enough. Apparently Holmes and Myrta began their married life in an apartment above the drugstore. In due time they became the parents of a baby girl. Myrta's family moved to the suburb of Wilmette, north of Chicago, in 1889. Holmes followed soon thereafter and took up residence in a substantial two-storied house which he had had built next door to a church.

That part seems clear enough, but there are certain discrepancies in chronology. For example, when interviewed following Holmes's arrest, Myrta told reporters they had been married "about nine years." Actually they'd been wedded for only seven and had been informally separated for at least the final three.

Myrta described her husband as a prosperous businessman whose affairs took him away from home on frequent and lengthy trips. But, she emphasized, he always kept in close touch with his family and was conscientious about supplying funds for their upkeep. Within the confines of the household he was a kind husband and a devoted father. He loved children and animals, and they responded adoringly to his attentions. She knew nothing about his alleged bigamy or larceny, let alone any other scandalous accusations, and there had never been any trouble between them.

Other reports of Holmes's domestic life are less charitable. Some allege he financed the building of his Wilmette home by borrowing twenty-five hundred dollars from Myrta's great-uncle Jonathan, then forging another note for a similar amount. Some declare Myrta's uncle refused to make the loan and the forgery followed.

Kate Durkee, a longtime friend of Myrta's, visited Wilmette, and Holmes wormed his way into her confidence. In a series of complicated transactions she never completely understood, he deeded his property to her as a means of avoiding bankruptcy, then managed to be appointed as its administrator, whereupon the property was deeded again to a man named Campbell. Miss Durkee never met Hiram S. Campbell, nor could she—for Mr. Campbell didn't exist.

There are those who tell of Holmes's later attempts to poison Myrta's ailing father. The efforts were foiled when the old man became suspicious and took his son-in-law's prescriptions to a doctor who identified one of the ingredients as arsenic. It was this disclosure, they say, that led to Holmes's withdrawal from his Wilmette residence. Prosecution was avoided on the grounds of "What will the neighbors say?" but the breach with Myrta dated from the doctor's discovery.

How much of all this Myrta was aware of is a moot question. Perhaps her uncle and father shielded her from the full truth and perhaps Miss Durkee didn't reveal her curious role in Holmes's financial maneuvers. To Myrta, Holmes may really have seemed a faithful husband and good provider whose business necessitated frequent travel. Young matrons concerned with bringing up a small child and running a household weren't expected to understand such things; business was a man's affair.

And at this point Holmes's business affairs were complicated indeed.

THE LOVING HUSBAND and father in Wilmette was also the trusted manager of Mrs. Holton's pharmacy in Englewood. He ran the store, placed orders for supplies and merchandise, handled the books and gained her trust as well. One day he came to his employer with a brilliant idea. Taking Mrs. Holton by the hand, he led her to the front window overlooking the street and gestured toward the large empty space directly across the way.

"Do you realize what's over there?" he said.

"Of course." Mrs. Holton gave him a puzzled look. "It's a vacant lot."

"A double lot," Holmes corrected her. "That's why the building is so large."

"What building are you talking about? I don't see anything there."

"Then close your eyes." Holmes smiled and nodded. "That's it! Go ahead and close them."

The woman glanced at him hesitantly, then obeyed. Holmes's voice softened, deepened. "Now you can see what I see. Just picture it for yourself in your mind's eye—a big brand-new office building—two, perhaps three stories high. Look at the turrets rising from the walls. No wonder everyone in the neighborhood is enchanted with the place—it's just like a fairy castle! Do you notice all those upstairs windows? Plenty of rooms and offices up there, every one of them bringing in rent, regular as clockwork. And those stores on the ground floor—they're fetching a fancy price month after month, on long-term leases."

"Have you gone crazy? You're imagining things." Mrs. Holton's eyelids fluttered, but Holmes spoke quickly.

"No, keep your eyes closed. Please—just hear me out. I haven't gone crazy. Perhaps I *am* imagining things, but this can all be real if you'll just imagine along with me." Again his voice deepened.

"Now look at those stores again. Do you see the big one right on the corner? That's the new pharmacy, the one everybody's talking about. *Your* pharmacy."

"Mine?"

This time Mrs. Holton's eyes opened and Holmes made no attempt to restrain her.

"That's right. First you close your eyes and dream. Then you open your eyes to what's around you and turn that dream into a reality." His smile vanished and he gazed at her intently. "You can do it. You can build that castle."

"I don't understand. I've already got a store here—why would I want to move across the street?"

"You're renting this property. The landlord can turn you out of the building the moment your lease expires, or double your rent, triple it, charge anything he likes."

"Now how can you say a thing like that? He and I are old friends."

"My dear lady." Holmes shook his head and uttered a mournful sigh. "Ordinarily I would be the last one on earth to question your judgment, but in this instance I perceive you are in error. Experience has taught me that business and friendship don't mix. Mark my words—the day of reckoning is at hand."

"What day?"

"Why, the one we're all waiting for. The day that will mark the opening of the World's Columbian Exposition."

"The World's Fair?" Mrs. Holton smiled. "But that's years away! And we don't even know if Chicago will get the bid." Her smile faded. "Even if it does, I still don't see what it has to do with the drugstore."

"Then allow me to explain." Holmes stroked his mustache as he spoke. "I happen to have access to inside information. My business contacts downtown assure me that Chicago will be chosen, and the site of the Fair will be directly east of us, in Jackson Park."

"But that's nothing but swampland—" Mrs. Holton frowned.

"Exactly." Holmes nodded. "Filling it in would be a boon to South Side real estate interests, and the Fair is a perfect excuse to do so. Millions of visitors are going to come to Chicago from all parts of the country, from all over the world. They'll arrive at the fairgrounds by train on new, specially built spur lines, and on the elevated railway from downtown. And where will these lines end? Why, right here, in Englewood! Englewood is going to be the gateway to the whole Fair.

"Just think of what that's going to mean—all those people passing through this neighborhood, and not just passing—some will be staying for days, even weeks. They'll need food, lodging, all the necessities of life. And you can provide them with everything they require—right here across the street."

"But this building you're talking about would cost a fortune!"

"Not if you act quickly. When other merchants figure out the possibilities, they'll buy up every piece of property in sight. But you can get the jump on everyone now. Once you finish construction the rush will be on and you can rent out the stores immediately. There'll be enough money coming in to meet the mortgage payments and give you the pharmacy at no cost to yourself. Then you'll have rooms upstairs for lodgers. All you have to do is advertise. Once out-of-town visitors learn they can find accommodations virtually within walking distance of the Fair, you'll get more customers than you can handle. Take my word for it, dear lady."

"I don't know." Mrs. Holton's eyes had brightened as Holmes described the prospects but now they clouded with uncertainty. "It takes money to buy up those lots and pay the building costs—"

"Precisely." Holmes spoke swiftly. "You know me well enough by now to realize I'm a man with a good head for business. I've analyzed this proposition thoroughly and in my opinion it just can't lose. And I've got resources of my own, enough to go halves with you on buying those lots and constructing the building."

Mrs. Holton stared at him. "You mean you'd share the expense?"

Holmes smiled. "What I'm proposing is an equal partnership, share and share alike. It's a once-in-a-lifetime opportunity for both of us. Now what do you say?"

Mrs. Holton didn't answer immediately; she needed time to think. Holmes claimed he had inside information, he seemed to know what he was talking about, but what if he was wrong? On the other hand, he'd already proven himself capable in his management of the drugstore, and if he was willing to put up his own money for this new venture, it must be a good thing.

There was also her daughter's welfare to consider. A widowed mother with a small child had no easy burden. But if this project worked out as Holmes promised, she and her little girl might be taken care of for life.

Mrs. Holton agreed to the proposal.

And disappeared.

"Sold me the business," Holmes told customers who noted her absence from the pharmacy. "Traveling in California. Said she intends to settle there with her youngster. It's a healthy climate, you know."

Nobody questioned him further. Later hearsay would allude to Holmes's creative bookkeeping, his embezzlement of store profits, a faking of estimates on costs of the proposed building so that her savings were signed away to meet the inflated expense figures.

Things may or may not have happened that way. But the upshot of it all was that Mrs. Holton and her daughter vanished from Englewood. Even after Holmes was arrested and accorded months of nationwide publicity, the widow and her offspring were never heard from.

Possibly the California climate wasn't as healthy as Holmes had pictured it to be and the mother and child went elsewhere. Or perhaps Holmes evolved a project that did take care of Mrs. Holton and her little girl—not for life, but for death.

3

HOLMES EXPANDED THE drugstore's business to include a sideline of paints and oils and also began selling Linden Grove Mineral Spring Water—a tonic obtained, so he said, from an artesian well. At five cents a glass it was a bargain for ailing customers. It was also a bargain for Holmes who—later on—was discovered to be getting his supply of the miraculous fluid by tapping the city water mains on an adjoining street.

Holmes now branched out into yet another career in downtown Chicago. Frederick C. Nind had purchased a patent on an English invention called a "copier"—a forerunner of the mimeograph machine. After taking a partner named Bryan, he had set up the A.B.C. Copier Company on Dearborn Street. Holmes learned of the enterprise and came to them with an offer to buy out Bryan's interest. He ended up in charge of the Chicago office and sent Nind off to New York to start up a branch agency there.

During Nind's absence Holmes used his new business as a front for various shady transactions, at the same time spreading the word that the A.B.C. Copier was his own invention. As a child he'd dreamed about becoming an inventor and from now on this would be one of his favorite roles.

When Nind returned to Chicago he was told the business was in trouble and the only way to get out of debt was to sell the rights to a Pittsburgh firm in return for twenty-five thousand dollars' worth of finished copiers. Actually the attorney for the purchasers was working for Holmes, who took over the business. Nind found himself squeezed out of the operation with nothing to show for it.

Nind later claimed that Holmes had originally bought an interest in the company with a worthless note signed by his wife's friend, Kate Durkee. As an added tidbit, he spoke of the possible murder of a girl whom Holmes had "put in the family way," as the polite phrase had it. But apparently Nind didn't have sufficient proof to back up either accusation at the time and didn't present charges to the authorities.

Meanwhile Holmes joined forces with another patent holder named Warner and advertised himself as manager of the Warner Glass Bending Company. He had a number of other schemes going under various names, his credentials vouched for by the same attorney who had participated in the A.B.C. Copier swindle.

The busy pharmacist-physician-inventor-businessman could no longer function alone. He gained assistance from several sources. One was in the form of a pipe-smoking handyman and jack-of-all-trades named Pat Quinlan whom Holmes first encountered in Wilmette. He had a wife and child, an eye for the ladies and a fondness for the bottle. It was said that Holmes made his acquaintance after selling him a patent medicine he'd concocted as a cure for alcoholism. As might be expected, the cure didn't work, and neither did Pat until Holmes provided him with various odd jobs around the premises. Looking ahead, he planned to use Quinlan as a bricklayer and construction worker on his building project, then employ him as janitor when it was completed.

While in Wilmette Holmes had also befriended a man from Kansas, one Benjamin Fuller Pitezel. He and his wife, Carrie, had five children and little else. Ben Pitezel was another jack-of-all-trades, including carpentry and contracting. Pitezel liked his liquor, too, but he was several cuts above Pat Quinlan in intelligence. He was also a petty grafter and his willingness to turn a dishonest dollar fitted in with Holmes's needs. After using him as an accomplice in some of his downtown deals, Holmes installed Pitezel and his family in an apartment in Englewood.

Fortune smiled. The two vacant lots across the street from the drugstore were owned by a woman in New York, and Holmes managed to purchase the land for a low price with notes which may have been secured by manipulating Kate Durkee's fictitious ownership of his assets or with his fraudulently acquired rights in the A.B.C. Copier Company. In any case, he secured the property.

Holmes hadn't lied to Mrs. Holton about his faith in the future. Plans for a World's Fair to commemorate the four hundredth anniversary of Columbus' discovery of America were well under way. Just as Holmes had predicted, Chicago won out over the other cities bidding for the site. Then ensued another power struggle among supporters of various locations within the community, but—again as Holmes had anticipated—the final choice was Jackson Park. Though only an uninhabited strip of barren sand and desolate marshland exposed to the encroachment of flooding from Lake Michigan, the area was ideally situated and the necessary improvements could be made.

In 1890 the first ground was broken, and from that moment on, the project went forward without delay. The marsh was drained and converted into waterways connecting with the lake beyond; grading and filling, followed by landscaping and gardening, would transform the waste into a beautiful and picturesque setting. Railroad tracks were laid, along with sewers, viaducts, gas pipes, water mains, power lines and other fixtures. By 1891 an army of engineers, architects, designers, mechanics and laborers descended upon the newly created fairgrounds and began the construction of towering buildings to house the attractions of the Exposition.

Meanwhile excitement grew as representatives of nations from all over the world pledged and planned exhibits. While hundreds of domestic organizations and commercial enterprises clamored for space and concessions, ten thousand workmen toiled in Jackson Park to prepare the site. Even so, it was apparent that though the actual commemorative date of October 12, 1892, could be celebrated by appropriate ceremonies, the Exposition itself would not be ready to open its gates until the spring of 1893. In spite of this setback the city of Chicago seethed with expectation. And exploitation.

Just as Holmes had prophesied, the price of local real estate soared in anticipation of the demands for space and services on the part of the millions of visitors soon to be arriving.

When they came, Holmes would be ready for them. He had designed his Castle.

Nothing in his background would seem to qualify him as an architect, nor had he ever posed as one. But the plan of the two-storied building which was to rise on the vacant frontage at Sixty-third and

Wallace did not spring from the mind of a master builder. It came from the mind of a master murderer.

The unscrupulous nature of the construction operation itself evolved from Holmes's experience as a swindler. In addition to hiring and firing separate groups of workers without paying them, he juggled loans, liens and mortgages. And he revived an old dodge: stocking the premises with furnishings and equipment which could be quickly resold at a profit without payment to the original suppliers.

All of this required precise timing, careful coordination and constant attention to every detail—evidence of Holmes's gift for organization.

What cannot be so easily explained is the planning *behind* the plan. Putting together that monstrous maze of hidden rooms, secret staircases, concealed panels, trapdoors, drops, peepholes and remote-control devices called for consummate cunning. Holmes must have taken many months in preparation—visualizing the layout, scribbling notes and rough sketches, figuring dimensions, estimating the amount of money, material and manpower required to carry out his concept. Without any architectural or construction-engineering experience, working secretly and alone, Holmes created his Castle. One can only marvel at his achievement.

Until one stops to reflect upon his purpose.

The Castle—including the third story, which was added to the structure a year later—was conceived, constructed and completed with full knowledge of what was to come. How else to account for the elaborate labyrinth, the fake gas cutoffs, the vault, the soundproof and windowless and doorless rooms, the oversize stove, the greased chute leading to the cellar's chamber of horrors?

Holmes's creation rose, and not too long thereafter, at the fairgrounds, other structures soared against the sky—palatial pavilions; vast display centers, elaborate edifices designed for education, enlightenment or entertainment; the world's first Ferris wheel; exhibition buildings and areas representing cities, states, the federal government and nations from both civilized and uncivilized portions of the world.

Thousands labored to fashion the Fair. One enterprise alone—the Palace of Manufactures and Liberal Arts—required the services of seven hundred men working day and night, through sultry summer and subzero winter weather, for eighteen months. Towering to a height of 236 feet over an artificial lagoon, the Palace extended 1,687 feet in length and 787 in breadth. Into its massive walls went 16,500,000 feet of lumber, 200 tons of nails and 60 tons of paint; its skylights and 900 windows were supplied with 76 carloads of glass. The central hall alone covered nearly twelve acres. And this was only one among scores of buildings. All of which makes Holmes's enterprise pale by comparison—until once again comes the realization that it was originated by just one man for just one sinister purpose.

ENGLEWOOD WAS NOW expanding in preparation for the coming rush of Fair visitors. Just as Holmes had foretold, the area had become a magnet attracting speculators, business firms and job hunters alike.

One of those seeking employment was a jeweler from Davenport, Iowa, whose name, Icilius L. Conner, seemed too grand for everyday use. Generally he went by the nickname of Ned.

Ned Conner moved his pretty young wife, Julia, and their eight-year-old daughter, Pearl, into the Englewood Flats, across the street from the Castle. Soon Holmes struck up an acquaintance with the family, and shortly after Mrs. Holton had been dispatched on her lengthy trip to California or elsewhere, Conner was offered a position in the drugstore by its new proprietor. He operated the jewelry department that Holmes had installed, and his wife became a clerk. Soon she was promoted to bookkeeper. Meanwhile, elated by prospects of prosperity, Ned Conner summoned his sister Gertie from Muscatine, Iowa, hoping that she too could find a job in Englewood.

She didn't have much difficulty in doing so. One glimpse of the lovely eighteen-year-old-girl and Holmes offered her an opportunity to become his secretary.

By this time the good doctor had other irons in the fire—a mail-order business promoting his "cure" for alcoholism, and a scientific formula to prevent baldness. Gertie handled the correspondence and orders. Holmes himself was often called away from the store to conduct matters involving the Copier company, the Warner Glass Bending enterprise and the tangled transactions involved in financing the construction of the Castle. But it was not all work and no play. When the opportunity arose, he again enlarged the scope of comely Mrs. Conner's duties, promoting her to the role of his mistress.

Apparently not content with stealing Ned Conner's wife, Holmes had designs on his worldly goods as well. Soon, he told Conner, he would be moving across the street into the new Holmes Block, where he'd be involved full time in his other enterprises and thus much too busy to operate the pharmacy. Conner rose to the bait and bought the store; then found to his dismay that he had acquired not only a pharmacy but also its debts for merchandise and fixtures.

Just how Holmes placated Conner is not clear, but he managed to convince him that it was all the result of an innocent mistake. Perhaps he placed the blame on the former owner, now missing. It was she who hadn't paid the bills and concealed the fact from Holmes, so he as well as Conner had been victimized. However the story went, Conner believed it and agreed to let bygones be bygones.

What happened next is equally uncertain. One version has the cuckolded husband discovering his wife's infidelity and promising forgiveness if she'd leave with him, only to have her refuse. In another account Holmes went to Ned Conner and gallantly confessed all. In either case the upshot is a matter of record. Conner departed and took a watchmaking job in downtown Chicago, while Julia remained at the store with her daughter and sister-in-law Gertie.

Holmes next sent Julia off to take a business college course, probably painting pictures of a lifelong partnership in which she would handle the finances and he would handle the management of the Holmes Block's many enterprises.

What he actually handled, during Julia's absence at school, was Gertie, his attractive young secretary. It may have been Gertie whom Holmes referred to when he told his Copier associate, Frederick Nind, about getting a girl in the family way. And it may be that when Julia discovered the affair, Holmes promised to send Gertie back home. While Nind later hinted Holmes had murdered the girl by means of "medicine" he'd procured for purposes of abortion, he also admitted seeing Gertie herself three months later at the Copier office downtown. There she announced plans for returning to Iowa and bid him good-by.

The following week Holmes told Nind he'd received a letter from Gertie's mother, telling him the girl was dead.

"I wheeled right around in my chair," Nind reported, "and said: 'Holmes, you have killed her!' He turned it off in that suave way of his, saying with the utmost *sang froid:* 'Bah. What makes you think that?' We had no further conversation about the matter."

Ned Conner maintained to the end that his little sister was a pure and innocent girl who had never had intimate relations with Holmes. He said Gertie had gone back to Iowa. It's likely that she had; likely, too, that Holmes had provided her with his own special form of medication—a slow-acting poison that brought about her death after she'd arrived home.

In any event, the girl vanished and Julia Conner remained with her lover. The fact that he'd sent Gertie away undoubtedly helped make Julia confident of her hold on his affections. That confidence increased when he took a "business trip" to Texas, leaving her in charge of the pharmacy. By this time the Castle had been completed to the point where Holmes could establish himself in office space there. When he returned from Texas, he moved into the new building and installed Julia and her daughter in an upstairs apartment.

Now he sold the old drugstore across the street to another sucker, pledging that he himself would stay out of that line of business. Of course he immediately opened up a new pharmacy in the Castle, just as he'd planned all along, and the owner of his former property was stuck with the unpaid debts routine.

Holmes leased the other stores on the ground floor of the Holmes Block to various merchants, including a confectioner; an ironware dealer; another jeweler, named Davis; and restaurant operator Phillips, whom he promptly cheated by selling him mortgaged equipment.

To expedite these transactions, Holmes once more employed the services of his attorney, Wharton Plummer, who'd been his accomplice in fleecing Nind. Together Holmes and his lawyer created a fictitious ownership for the new building—the Campbell-Yates Manufacturing Company—with Ben Pitezel posing as Mr. Campbell. The others involved in the corporation were employees at the store, including a porter named Joseph Owens. Mr. Yates was never seen, and Holmes himself claimed he was merely the company's business agent.

All this came in handy when he decided to add a third story to the Castle before the Fair opened. Again Holmes spent time and effort on the new addition; here his permanent offices would be set up, together with such thoughtful touches as the stove, the chute, and trapdoors leading to the laboratory and bathroom on the floor below. Once more he swindled suppliers and workmen on the project.

Meanwhile the pharmacy below was prospering. In addition to selling Linden Grove Mineral Spring Water over the counter, he now set up the Holmes Chemical Water Gas Company. Using one of his basement tanks, which he rigged up with a weird assortment of pipes and valves, Holmes demonstrated its powers to potential investors. After adding a dash of "secret chemicals" to the water in the tank, he would light the gas jet connected to one of the pipes issuing from the vat. There, before the very eyes of the gullible, was proof that Holmes's invention did indeed transform water into illuminating gas.

What the investor did not see was another pipe, hidden amid the coils at the bottom of the tank, which happened to be connected to a city gas main outside the premises. Not content with fleecing those who bought shares in the new invention, Holmes also lighted his property upstairs from the same clandestine source of supply. Just how he escaped charges when the ruse was discovered is not established, but quite probably he bribed his way out of the mess.

It is likely he resorted to bribery on other occasions as well. Paying off venal police officers, city inspectors and petty officials may partially account for Holmes's constant need of additional funds. It would certainly explain how he continued to avoid arrest and prosecution despite his many extralegal activities over the years. It might also be the reason why so few of his activities are a matter of public record, and why no official account exists of the number of his victims (it has been surmised that he did away with a hundred or even two hundred people during the course of his career) or the precise order and manner in which they met their fates.

WE DO KNOW THAT Gertie Conner disappeared. And not too long thereafter Julia Conner and her daughter vanished. Julia's tenure as Holmes's public housekeeper and private mistress apparently ended on Christmas Day in 1891. New tenants of the rooms she had previously occupied with her daughter found their clothing still on the premises, and breakfast dishes had been left untouched on the table.

Holmes explained that the Conners had left abruptly when informed of illness in the family. He repeated much the same story to his porter, Joseph Owens, saying that Julia had gone home to Davenport, Iowa. But Pat Quinlan was informed she'd married a doctor and moved to California, and Ned Conner was told his ex-wife and daughter had departed for Saint Louis. Apparently these explanations were satisfactory and nobody bothered to check one against another. All we can be certain of is that Julia and her child vanished, never to be seen again.

Then there was the blacksmith's daughter, Annie Redmond, who may or may not have been involved in a kidnapping plot. And a wealthy widow named Lee who moved into quarters upstairs and presumably made a sudden departure after Holmes arranged to "invest" her inheritance at a profit—to him. There was a man named Cole, a Castle resident not related to the builder, who joined the ranks of missing persons, allegedly with Holmes's assistance, as did another tenant, a Dr. Russell or Russler. It is not clear whether a certain Mr. Rodgers lived in the Castle or not, but it was said he knew Holmes well enough to accompany him on a fishing trip from which he never returned. Supposedly all of these deaths were engineered for the doctor's financial enrichment, but money wasn't always the motive.

Lizzie was a servant girl whom Holmes facetiously described as his "understudy." He moved her into one of his specially furnished upstairs rooms but her tenure there was so brief that no one ever recalled hearing her last name. One version has it that she became infatuated with Pat Quinlan and Holmes did away with the girl before his right-hand man could run off with her. Another account infers she learned too much about Holmes's affairs. Most likely Lizzie died of suffocation in the sealed vault, and it may be that Holmes, knowing she had no relatives or friends who might ask questions about her disappearance, used her as a guinea pig to test the vault's efficiency. In any case, no one ever bothered about the girl's absence except Quinlan. Holmes told Pat that Lizzie had gone to Omaha.

During the late summer and throughout the following fall of 1892 another Lizzie was very much in evidence—Lizzie Borden. Everyone in the country was anxious to learn if she had indeed taken an ax to give her mother "forty whacks" and then bestowed an additional forty-one on her father. The double murder in Fall River, Massachusetts, received headline publicity in the Chicago press. No doubt Dr.

Holmes read the newspapers as eagerly as his friends and neighbors. It would be enlightening to know if he ever discussed the crimes with them, and what his comments may have been. Enlightening and ironic—for during the time of Lizzie Borden's arrest, incarceration and acquittal, he himself was engaged in a full-scale career of homicide which made the Borden case seem minor by contrast. While an entire nation focused its attention on a dowdy spinster who may or may not have committed two murders in the heat of passion on an August day, not one person seemed to remotely suspect that a dapper Chicago doctor and businessman was establishing himself as a wholesale butcher of human beings.

By this time Holmes had launched his practice of offering employment to a series of "typewriters"—young girls seeking secretarial jobs. And they flocked to the Castle, filling temporary positions that soon became all too permanent.

There was a Miss Mary Haracamp who arrived in the company of her pregnant aunt, Mrs. Cook. Holmes carelessly supplied them with a master key to the upstairs rooms. One night they surprised him while he was disposing of a body, and as he so sensibly stated later in his confession, "It was a time for quick action."

Another secretary, young Kittie Kelly, enjoyed Holmes's favors until she presumably put her signature on an insurance policy naming him as beneficiary. Very shortly thereafter he volunteered the information that she'd left to get married.

Late in 1892 Holmes engaged a voluptuous nineteen-year-old blonde named Emmeline Cigrand. In some memoirs a year was added to her age and an "m" subtracted from her first name, but there is universal agreement as to her charms.

Miss Cigrand had been recommended by Ben Pitezel, who found her working as a stenographer at the Keeley Institute in Dwight, Illinois. Pitezel went there to take a cure for alcoholism and on his return he told his boss about the lovely girl. Holmes immediately wrote to Miss Cigrand offering her a handsome salary and she soon became his employee at the Castle. Apparently, however, she balked at the bedroom door. As a result she was fated to vanish behind the door of the concealed vault.

Castle residents Dr. M. B. Lawrence and his wife later recalled Miss Cigrand's abrupt disappearance. The day after their last conversation with her, Holmes had remained closeted in his office, to which only Pat Quinlan was admitted. In the evening he emerged and asked two male tenants for help in carrying a heavy trunk downstairs. After an express wagon came to pick up the trunk, Holmes left the Castle and didn't return for two days. When he came back, the Lawrences questioned him about Emmeline Cigrand's absence and he explained she'd married a traveling salesman. As proof he produced two cards—one announcing her marriage on December 7 to a "Mr. Robert E. Phelps" and the other a calling card which was inscribed "Mr. and Mrs. Robert E. Phelps." The cards were not engraved, and the plain printing had been done on cheap stationery stock.

Some accounts say that Robert E. Phelps was indeed Emmeline Cigrand's fiancé, an older man of considerable means. One source has him showing up at the Castle for information regarding her whereabouts, after which he too joined the ranks of missing persons. Another has him actually living there for a time while awaiting her return from a "business trip," which Holmes had cited as the reason for her absence. In this version the doctor tortured him on his "Elasticity Determinator" until he signed over his funds, then finished him off. Holmes himself confessed to using Phelps in an "experiment." Further complicating the matter is the fact that Ben Pitezel had used the name Phelps as his alias when he took the Keeley Institute cure.

Emmeline's sister Phyllis and her family were informed that the girl had eloped with Robert Phelps. A letter bearing her typed signature reached the parents, telling them of unfortunate discoveries made after the hasty wedding—her new husband proved to be a gambler, drunkard and womanizer. Presumably unable to bear the consequences of her misplaced trust, she left him and ran off to parts unknown.

To substantiate the fact, Holmes wrote letters in his own name to the Cigrand family, imploring them to locate his missing employee whose signature was needed on important business documents. But she was never found and neither was Phelps. Emmeline's mother and father didn't seek aid in tracing their daughter. Apparently they could only shake their heads and reflect upon the perils of life in the wicked city.

4

THE CALENDAR MARKED the advent of 1893. This, at long last, was the year of the World's Fair—the event for which the city had yearned. During the four months prior to the official opening date of May 1, work on the grounds and buildings redoubled. The costs were heavy, not only in terms of money, but also in terms of human lives. Already no fewer than twenty-three laborers had died in accidents, nine of them perishing after falls from great heights during the construction of the Manufactures building. Over two thousand injuries had required surgery and an additional thousand had needed medical treatment. Now the mishaps increased as the grueling pressure drove the builders toward their deadlines.

Official activity increased. Special guards numbering into the thousands were organized and trained. The Chicago police force was augmented and a camp was erected outside the grounds to house National Guard contingents. All this manpower would be committed to ensure the safety of Fair visitors.

There was a large fire department, a complete hospital, and five full acres of dining and refreshment rooms. Arrangements were made with the railroad companies to offer special fares on excursion trains. A bureau was established to facilitate guest housing in hotels, boarding places and private homes. Millions of Fair tickets were ordered in advance; concessions for refreshment sales went to the highest bidders. Since horses would not be admitted to the grounds, another concession was established to provide twenty-four hundred "roller chairs," each with a husky young attendant.

Buildings and display sites were readied for seventeen foreign nations and all forty-four states. There were thirty-eight additional structures ranging from a Children's Exhibit to the Sewage Cleansing Works. Along the separate strip of land called the Midway Plaisance another forty-three exhibits were completed—an Ice Railway, Panoramas of the Kilauea Volcano and the Bernese Alps, a Japanese Bazaar, the Street of Cairo where Little Egypt would soon dance, a model of Saint Peter's Cathedral, the Hagenbeck Animal Show. Work was finished on villages of every description—East Indian, American Indian, Chinese, Austrian, Dutch, Irish, even one from

Lapland. Fair attendees could dine at a Chinese teahouse or sample the fare of Vienna while gazing skyward at the captive balloon which swayed above the great Ferris wheel.

By the time of the gala downtown parades and the arrival of President Grover Cleveland for the opening ceremonies, all was miraculously in readiness. And on Monday, May 1, over a quarter of a million people gathered on the grounds to watch the Chief Executive press a single button which set the entire machinery of the Fair in motion. Fountains hurled their spray to the skies, flags of the United States and Spain jointly unfurled, the national anthem blared forth, and the crowd roared its welcome to the Columbian Exposition.

No one seems to know whether or not Holmes was among those present on this eventful day. He might well have been, for his own preparations had been finalized. The new third floor had been added to the sinister structure and the entire Castle was in operating order: the trapdoors oiled, the chutes greased, the stoves and furnaces stoked. In the vault and concealed chambers the gas jets hissed. Poisons filled the phials, and resting within Dr. Holmes's medical bag were the dissecting knives, sharp and gleaming.

Notices advertising lodgings to let now appeared in the papers. Rooms had been cleaned and linen changed. Amid the shadows of the cellar squatted the apparatuses of destruction—the racks, the quicklime pits, the crematorium.

Welcome, Fair Visitors. Welcome to the Holmes Castle! Your Host Awaits You!

How many read the ads and applied for accommodations during the next six months is anybody's guess. Attendees arrived for a single night, a weekend or a longer stay, coming and going in such profusion and confusion that their numbers cannot even be estimated. But later, after the police mounted their investigation, they managed to list some of the many missing persons who had disappeared on a trip to the Fair. At least fifty were traced to the point where they took up residence in the Castle. These fifty were never seen alive again.

HOLMES'S CAREER OF CARNAGE hadn't halted during the months preceding the opening of the Fair. His confessions cite the death of his janitor, Robert Latimer, who—he said—had attempted to blackmail him in return for his silence concerning insurance swindles. Latimer was effectively silenced without payment; he was starved to death in a secret room where he vainly attempted to claw his way out through the solid walls. "Finally, needing its use for another purpose," Holmes writes, "I ended his life." The other purpose can all too easily be imagined.

A Wisconsin banker was brought to the Castle by one of Holmes's accomplices, according to the doctor's confession. He too was starved until he signed over his assets, whereupon chloroform terminated his existence and a medical school may have acquired another body.

Mr. Warner, founder of the Warner Glass Bending Company in which Holmes had acquired an interest during his downtown activities, was promoted from partner to victim. Holmes explains in his confession how he had built a large kiln in the basement for glass-bending demonstrations in accordance with Warner's instructions. After tricking the inventor into entering the kiln, he then closed the door and turned on the oil and steam jets. "In a short time," Holmes continues, "not even the bones of my victim remained."

One unnamed victim was a girl from Omaha—that exotic locale to which several of Holmes's previous associates had purportedly traveled. Following a complicated financial arrangement which assigned him the proceeds from the sale of her Chicago property without subjecting himself to investigation, he introduced her to his special accommodations in the vault.

Then there was Anna Betts, who died after Holmes substituted poison for the ingredients of a prescription she brought to his pharmacy. One must remember that in those long-ago times such remedies were not poured out of containers; the pharmacist compounded each concoction literally by hand, grinding the raw materials with the aid of an old-fashioned mortar and pestle. No reason is cited for Holmes's administration of a lethal dose to Miss Betts; perhaps he was experimenting with the preparation to ascertain the length of time it required to take effect. The scientific mind is always searching for answers.

But even scientists must have moments of relaxation. And H. H. Holmes had already shown that he preferred to relax in the company of an attractive woman.

One of them was Emily Van Tassel, which may or may not have been a misnomer for Rosine Van Jassand. The name differs in various accounts but all agree that she was young and fair and fatally fond of her employer. Her residence upstairs was brief; soon she took up permanent quarters downstairs.

During this period two other young women enjoyed life with Holmes and, subsequently, death. These were the Williams sisters, Minnie and Nannie. The girls were born in Mississippi and had been orphaned when very young.

Accounts of the complicated circumstances of their lives and deaths differ widely, but it is generally agreed that Minnie was the first to arrive on the scene. In short order she became involved with Holmes as a partner in both business and bed. One source would have her married to Holmes under the name of Harry Gordon and inviting her sister Nannie to join them in Chicago. Some writers state that Minnie was only engaged to the supposed Harry Gordon. Police say Holmes rented an apartment on Wrightwood Avenue, in North Side Chicago, and that he and Minnie welcomed Nannie there. Some accounts state that Holmes gallantly escorted sister Nannie to the Fair, and that soon she, too, was added to his list of conquests.

Was Minnie actually deceived as to Holmes's identity? It seems unlikely. Witnesses later said they had seen her at the Castle, where in all probability she learned that Harry Gordon was also known as Henry Howard Holmes.

How much more did she learn?

Again, versions differ. One school of thought pictures Minnie as a neurotic, completely duped by Holmes. Others portray her as a shrewd and intelligent woman who must soon have discovered her lover's true nature but—through passion, greed or a combination of both—became his willing partner in crime. Was one of these crimes murder? Later Holmes would say as much.

Whatever actually went on between the two sisters and Holmes, the fact remains that both Minnie and Nannie Williams vanished before the year was out.

How many others appeared and disappeared at the Castle between May and October 1893 is anyone's guess. The hiring and firing of young stenographers went on amid the hectic round of room rental and financial wheeling and dealing. It is impossible to unsort the tangle; during those long summer months Holmes's activities accelerated to an incredible degree. Dividing his attentions among official mistress Minnie, her sister, the girls lured to his lair and the transients trapped in their lodgings, he indulged in an endless series of deceptions.

One pictures him scurrying down into the cellar to dissect and dispose of a corpse, hurrying through a concealed passageway to join his latest inamorata in an upstairs bedroom, then disappearing through a hidden panel for a rendezvous with another potential paramour. The comings and goings, the opening and closing of doors as though on cue, are reminiscent of a French farce.

In reality they were part of a horror show, and when the Fair ended, it was Holmes who rang down the curtain.

After bricking up the Castle's concealed cellar confines and locking the upstairs rooms following his unsuccessful arson attempt on an incomplete fourth floor, Holmes turned the custody of the building over to Pat Quinlan. He himself was ready to open a new act in the drama with a change of scene.

IT BEGAN WITH a wedding.

Fantastic as it may seem, considering Holmes's constant involvement with Castle visitors and employees, he had found time to cultivate yet another young woman—Georgiana Yoke, a charming young blonde from Indiana. Again the data are conflicting; her residence was either Franklin or Richmond, and he was said to have met her several years previously, or in March of 1893 or during the following summer when she visited the Fair. Whenever the meeting occurred, it is agreed that he became engaged to her in November under the alias of Henry Mansfield Howard, and under that name he entered into his third marriage on January 17, 1894.

The ceremony took place in Denver, Colorado, after Holmes's abrupt departure from Chicago. If we are to believe his confessions, he chose that city for reasons that had little to do with sentiment. He had discovered an insurance policy in which Minnie Williams had named her brother Baldwin as beneficiary. Baldwin Williams lived in Leadville, Colorado, and it was there, one story goes, that Holmes shot him. Shortly after, the newly wedded couple left Denver.

Holmes whisked Georgiana off to a honeymoon in Fort Worth, Texas. There he identified himself to her as H. H. Holmes, and explained why it had been necessary to employ an alias. Henry

Mansfield Howard was actually his uncle and he'd adopted the name when the old man had made him heir to his estate of Texas ranchland. Now his uncle was dead and it was time to secure the inheritance, but greedy private interests and corrupt local officials were seeking to thwart him. For this reason he didn't wish to be known either as Howard or Holmes, but registered himself and Georgiana at their hotel as Mr. and Mrs. D. T. Pratt.

His bride swallowed the story and settled down to wait while Holmes pressed his claim to the property. But the actual land he sought wasn't an inheritance from a mythical uncle; it had belonged to the real uncle of the Williams sisters, and it was located right there in urban Fort Worth. Holmes intended to build a store on this prime location.

In short order Ben Pitezel appeared on the scene, using an alias of his own, Benton Lyman. Together with a local insurance man named Harris and a crooked contractor, James C. Allen, Holmes and Pitezel soon set in motion a series of swindles. Since all the members of the group used a variety of phony identities, their activities are almost impossible to follow. But the upshot was the construction of the Fort Worth store which Holmes presumably meant to serve as his new Castle.

Building proceeded with all the tricks he'd learned in Chicago, but somewhere along the line Holmes and his confederates overreached themselves. Passing off worthless notes under assumed names and taking genuine notes from investors led to the threat of discovery. There was nothing for Holmes to do but swallow his losses and get out of town while he was still free to do so. He told Georgiana that his uncle's enemies were now seeking his life; he'd decided to sell the ranchland at once and leave for Saint Louis where the money could be transferred to him in safety.

Actually there were other matters awaiting his attention there. It was in Saint Louis that Ben Pitezel had established his wife and five children. He'd scouted the area and found it a likely place in which he and Holmes could do their kind of business. James Allen, their Texas associate, was already on his way to the city with a carload of stolen horses.

To throw Texas creditors off the scent, Holmes dropped the Pratt alias and took on the Howard name again as he traveled a roundabout route to Saint Louis via Denver. In the meantime, Pitezel went back to Chicago to check on affairs at the Castle.

Holmes arrived in Saint Louis with his bride toward the end of May and waited for his partners to join him there. Pitezel turned up with bad news. Chicago creditors were closing in and the insurance adjusters had become increasingly suspicious about the fire and refused to pay without further investigation.

To make matters worse, Allen didn't show up at all. He'd been arrested in Little Rock, Arkansas, while en route with his cargo of horseflesh and would be extradited to Texas. As a final blow, warrants had been issued naming his partners, "Lyman" and "Pratt," as horse thieves. The devious doctor found himself between a rock and a hard place. H. H. Holmes was in trouble in Chicago; D. T. Pratt was wanted on criminal charges in Fort Worth. But for the moment Henry Mansfield Howard and Ben Pitezel were names that seemed safe enough for use in Saint Louis. The big question was what to use them for.

The immediate need was money. Rather than risk another disaster in this new location by acting too hastily, the two men decided to search for a temporary source of funds elsewhere. They visited Memphis, where they hoped to perpetrate one of their old insurance frauds, but for various reasons the scheme was abandoned. After returning to Saint Louis in June, Holmes came up with an alternative proposal, which he laid out to Ben Pitezel and his wife, Carrie.

SOMETIME BACK, PITEZEL had taken out a ten-thousand-dollar life insurance policy with the Fidelity Mutual Life Insurance Company of Philadelphia, through its Chicago office. This particular policy was legitimate and in Pitezel's actual name, with his wife listed as beneficiary.

"How would you like to collect on that policy right now?" Holmes asked Mrs. Pitezel.

Carrie stared at him. "What on earth are you talking about?"

"Easy money," Holmes said to Ben. "We'll take a little jaunt to Philadelphia and set you up in the patent business. You can call yourself B. F. Perry."

Pitezel scowled. "Not on your life! The name's too close. And I don't know anything about inventions."

"Exactly." Holmes nodded. "The name *has* to be close. And I want you to be involved in inventions you don't understand. That's what will help explain the explosion."

"Explosion!" exclaimed Carrie Pitezel.

"Don't worry." Holmes gave her a reassuring smile. "When it takes place Ben will be far, far away. I'll get hold of a look-alike corpse as a substitute. The explosion is only to explain the manner of death and complicate identification of the victim."

"I don't get it." Pitezel said. "How can you collect on a policy made out to me if the victim is identified as somebody named Perry?"

"That's the kicker." Holmes beamed. "A few days after the body is discovered, the insurance company will get a letter from an attorney stating that the dead man is actually Ben Pitezel, one of their policy-holders who was living under an assumed name. Then Carrie goes to Philadelphia and identifies the corpse—"

"Not me!" Carrie frowned. "I'm not getting mixed up in such a scheme."

"Very well then. I'll come and make the identification myself." Holmes turned to his partner. "This is foolproof. The insurance people will never suspect you of trying to hornswoggle them out of a claim because you were using an alias. When they find out some of the deals you were mixed up in, the reasons for passing yourself off as Perry will be obvious. As for the explosion itself, it's going to look like an unfortunate accident—something that happened when you meddled with an invention without realizing its perils."

"What happens then?" Pitezel asked. "After you've blown me and my reputation to smithereens?"

Holmes shrugged. "You'll be legally dead, so your reputation won't matter. All you'll have to do is to take on a new identity. You'll never have to worry about that Texas warrant again. And when the lawyer collects on the policy and turns the principal sum over to Carrie as beneficiary, you'll be ten thousand dollars richer. That's a lot of cash, Ben. Think about it."

"I am." Pitezel's eyes narrowed as he glanced at Holmes. "You're not one to be handing out money for nothing. What I want to know is where you come in."

"As your partner," Holmes said. "Look, Ben, we've been together a long time now. I've got some great plans for the future, but they require money. If you like, you can take the ten thousand and leave; that's your privilege. But I'm hoping you'll decide to stay and throw in your lot with me. This could be the chance you and I have been waiting for. And this time, if you deal yourself in, you'll do so on a fifty-fifty basis, an equal partner from now on."

Holmes turned to include Carrie in his smile. "It's not just for your sake. Remember, you've got your family to consider." Now he confronted Ben once more. "Well, old friend—how does that strike you?"

Pitezel eyed his wife before replying. "Give me a little time to think about it."

"Take all the time you want," Holmes told him. "Meanwhile there's another little deal cooking that may tide us over for a spell."

The little deal he was referring to involved the pending purchase of a pharmacy from the Merrill Drug Company of Saint Louis. Posing as Henry Mansfield Howard, he engineered the transaction, then sold the mortgage to a man named Brown. Brown may well have been another name used by Pitezel, who then sold the store to a third party. But somewhere along the line the Merrill Drug Company got wind of the paper shuffling and on July 19 Holmes, under the alias of Howard, suddenly found himself jailed for fraud. It was quite a shock to a man who had for so many years successfully avoided arrest and incarceration. But Georgiana listened to his cock-and-bull explanations and promptly bailed him out, not once but twice.

Saint Louis was now much too hot a place for H. H. Holmes. He left it for the East and Georgiana joined him a few days later in Philadelphia. He told her he was setting up a deal to sell a lease on his A.B.C. Copier to the Pennsylvania Railroad.

But while she waited patiently in Adella Alcorn's boardinghouse, Holmes was busily setting up another kind of deal. He telegraphed the semiannual premium on Ben Pitezel's ten-thousand-dollar policy to the Chicago office of the Fidelity Mutual Life Insurance Company on the day before it would have lapsed for nonpayment. His partner had now agreed to carry out the insurance scheme and was on his way to join him. Poor Ben Pitezel would never leave Philadelphia.

Once he arrived, Holmes set him up in a house on Callowhill Street. A window sign lettered on a sheet of muslin said: *B. F. Perry, Patents Bought and Sold.*

It was there, on the morning of September 4, that a carpenter interested in marketing his invention of a saw sharpener arrived to interview the self-styled patents expert. Upon entering the house, he discovered "Perry's" partially decomposed corpse lying on the floor, its face badly burned and disfigured. A corncob pipe, a burnt match and a broken bottle of benzine added up to an obvious conclusion: the dead man had carelessly lighted his pipe and was killed when the volatile fumes ignited and exploded. The city morgue happened to be conveniently located just behind the house, and there an autopsy disclosed "death due to chloroform poisoning."

In the room where the deceased was found were several bottles containing mixtures of ammonia, benzine and chloroform; probably the victim had been inspecting such a compound when the explosion occurred. A coroner's jury decided that B. F. Perry died from "congestion of the lungs, caused by inhalation of flame, or of chloroform, or other poisonous drug."

Obviously both the autopsy and the inquest were quite routine; Perry seemed to be a loner, a stranger in town, and without the intervention of interested parties the proceedings raised no questions and caused no comment. Since no one claimed the body, it was buried in Potter's Field on September 13.

By then Holmes was long gone from the scene. On the evening of September 2 he and Georgiana had caught the train for Indianapolis, where they took up residence in a boardinghouse. A few days later he slipped off to Saint Louis, where he told an anxious Carrie Pitezel that everything was going according to plan; he'd substituted a corpse for identification and Ben had gone into hiding. Now it was time for her to contact the insurance company through Jeptha D. Howe, a Saint Louis attorney whom Holmes had hired.

A letter was duly composed and mailed to the Fidelity Mutual people, informing them that Mrs. Pitezel had read a newspaper account of B. F. Perry's accidental death and had reason to believe that the man was actually her husband.

The insurance company responded, asking her to go to Philadelphia and identify the body. Carrie Pitezel pleaded a nervous breakdown; instead her fifteen-year-old daughter, Alice, made the trip with attorney Howe.

Meanwhile Holmes, in his role as an old friend and former employer of Pitezel, contacted the company and volunteered to view the remains; all he asked was that he be reimbursed for his travel expenses.

The corpse was exhumed on the twenty-second of the month and the gruesome charade proceeded without a hitch. Poor little Alice made the actual identification, though the body and face were mercifully covered so that she saw nothing but the mouth and teeth. This seemed to be enough for purposes of recognition and her statement was accepted without further question.

In short order the money was paid. Holmes went to Saint Louis and told Mrs. Pitezel he'd left Alice with friends in Covington, Kentucky. Now he volunteered to take two other children, Nellie and Howard, and join Alice there. Mrs. Pitezel would go to her parents' home in Galva, Illinois, with her oldest and youngest offspring; after two weeks the whole family would be reunited in Detroit, together with Ben Pitezel. There they could start life under another name.

Somehow this sounded logical to the distraught woman. By breaking up the family and traveling separately under an alias with only two of the children, she'd throw authorities off the scent in case anyone secretly suspected Ben was still alive and about to rejoin her. Keeping the oldest child to help care for the youngest also made sense; meanwhile Holmes would see to it that the other three youngsters never learned their father had participated in a fraud. Soon their troubles would be over.

To sweeten the prospects, Carrie Pitezel received seventy-two hundred dollars of the insurance money; attorney Howe supposedly got the rest as fee and expenses.

Mrs. Pitezel scarcely had time to cash the check before Holmes borrowed sixty-seven hundred dollars on his personal note—later discovered to be worthless. He needed the money, he explained, to "bail out" some extremely valuable Fort Worth property owned in Ben's name. Once free of entailments, it could promptly be sold for an astronomical sum and they'd all be rich.

Money in hand, Holmes departed with Nellie and Howard to rejoin Alice and travel as the children's "uncle," after fond farewells at the railroad station.

Holmes, of course, had no intention of reuniting the Pitezels. Staging a fake explosion after murdering Ben was all in a day's work;

resurrecting him was a shade beyond his power. What he had to do was keep the family separated, stall the promised reunion and kill them off before their suspicions were fully aroused.

At the same time he had Georgiana to consider. She knew nothing whatsoever of all this, and he didn't intend to inform her. Amazingly enough, in view of his previous relationships, Holmes seems to have fallen in love with her. And the fantastic lies he told during their life together were apparently fabricated only to maintain her affection. Most probably he planned to leave Georgiana in Indiana while he went off on a prolonged "business trip," and then to return to her after it—and the Pitezels—had been finished.

But something happened that he had failed to anticipate.

BACK IN SAINT LOUIS the police notified the Fidelity Mutual people of an unexpected development. They had received a letter from a Mr. Marion C. Hedgepeth, a notorious outlaw and train robber now jailed and awaiting sentence in that city. Hedgepeth wrote that he had occupied a cell with Holmes back in July when Holmes—under the name of H. M. Howard—had been arrested for his drug company–mortgaging caper. During that time Holmes offered Hedgepeth five hundred dollars to recommend a trustworthy—i.e., crooked—attorney whose services he required in a scheme to cheat an insurance company. The plan involved procuring a corpse and planting it in a fake explosion, then identifying the body as Ben Pitezel's and collecting on his insurance. It sounded pretty slick, so Hedgepeth put him in touch with his own lawyer—none other than Jeptha D. Howe. Since that time Hedgepeth had learned the swindle had taken place, with Howe's complicity.

Subsequently Hedgepeth repeated his story in a sworn statement, but added another detail. Since writing his letter, he'd spoken with Howe, and now thought Ben Pitezel had been murdered.

Since both the letter and statement contained details not publicly known, such as the expiration date of the insurance policy, it seemed that Hedgepeth was telling the truth. And he had a convincing reason for blowing the whistle on his old cell mate—Holmes had never paid him the five hundred dollars.

Indeed, the only puzzling aspect of the matter is one which has never been resolved. Why did Holmes confide his plans to Hedgepeth in the first place? All he really needed to do was ask him to recommend a crooked lawyer. But like every criminal, Holmes was prey to human failings, including vanity. The mere fact of being arrested must have been a crushing blow to his ego. Even worse was his incarceration with Hedgepeth—a man whose misdeeds made him an aristocrat of crime who probably condescended to Holmes as just another bungling amateur. Perhaps pride prompted him to seek Hedgepeth's respect by outlining the details of his plot against the insurance company. Now it was too late to rectify the error. Fidelity Mutual was taking action. According to press notices, they had called in the Pinkerton Detective Agency to locate the missing Mr. Howard, aka H. H. Holmes.

If he left Georgiana behind in Indiana, the Pinkerton blood-hounds would be bound to sniff her out in short order; the only sensible thing for Holmes to do was to take her along on his journey. At the same time he had the three Pitezel youngsters to consider; somehow their presence must remain unknown to Georgiana, or else their eventual absence would raise doubts in her mind. Simultaneously he must supervise the movements of Mrs. Pitezel and the other two children. And on top of everything else, he had to see to it that all three groups traveled under assumed but acceptable identities. Until, of course, he managed to reduce the three groups to one, consisting merely of Georgiana and himself. This would take considerable doing but he thought he could handle it. After all, he'd be using three different aliases and playing three different roles—a man traveling with his wife, a man traveling with a relative and her two children, and an uncle traveling with a nephew and two nieces.

Over the next seven weeks he embarked on a hectic round of misdirection, crisscrossing from Indiana to Cincinnati to Detroit to New York State to Canada to Vermont. Meanwhile he kept switching identities and changing residences regularly at his various stopping places. Later the Chicago *Journal* would report that "during these travels Holmes carried with him three separate detachments—Mrs. Pitezel, Miss Yoke, and the children—all within four blocks of each other in all the different cities, almost traveling together, under Holmes's leading strings, and yet each detachment ignorant of the presence of the other two."

In addition to keeping the three groups unaware of one another,

Holmes was constantly supplying new stories to account for their movements. To Georgiana, he spun yarns about business trips to explain his frequent absences; to the children in his custody, he promised a speedy family reunion. Alice and Nellie thought their mother was still back in the Midwest and wrote her regularly—until Holmes murdered them in Toronto. Little Howard had already become his victim in Irvington, Indiana.

Holmes's biggest problem was placating Mrs. Pitezel, who—with the remaining two children—was moved from city to city in expectation of rejoining her husband. Holmes repeatedly came up with fresh excuses for Ben's absence, each more intricate than the last; at the same time he sought a spot where it would be safe to kill off the mother and her surviving youngsters too. Eventually he established them in a rented house in Burlington, Vermont, told them once again to be patient and took Georgiana to Boston.

Then, leaving Georgiana in Boston, he went north again. This time to New Hampshire. Here he took on a previous role—none other than that of Herman W. Mudgett!

Under this, his real name, he sought out Clara, his real wife. To her and to his son he recited the most outrageous story of all. He told them he'd been injured in a train wreck back in 1886 and had suffered total amnesia. Unaware of his true identity, he'd elected to call himself H. M. Howard and later married the nurse who had ministered to him in the hospital. Now in the East on business, his memory had finally returned.

Apparently Clara believed him. Together the reunited couple drove over to Gilmanton, where the prodigal son related the same tragic tale to his parents.

What made him do it? The most obvious motive would be to further baffle the authorities. If they ever succeeded in tracing him this far, they'd find a mother, father, wife and child all prepared to swear that he was merely the victim of a blackout, a cruel prank of fate. Even if the law enforcement agencies were able to prove his crimes, he could plead innocent on grounds of mental illness.

Now he was ready to return to Boston, ostensibly to confess his sorry mistake to Georgiana and bid her a contrite farewell. Actually he planned to book passage on a ship bound for foreign soil. Then, just before the scheduled departure, he'd find an excuse to slip back to Burlington where Mrs. Pitezel and the surviving children were still awaiting their promised meeting with Ben. What really awaited them was a hole he'd dug in the yard behind the rented house.

But Holmes never sailed, nor did he make the trip to Burlington.

The Pinkerton operatives had picked up his trail as he ventured East and had been shadowing him ever since. Now, growing fearful their quarry might skip the country, they decided to close in. They arrested him in a Boston hotel lobby on November 17, 1894.

Holmes found himself facing two warrants—one charging insurance fraud in Philadelphia and the other issued for horse stealing in Fort Worth. Fully aware that horse thieves were regarded as major criminals in Texas and knowing his presence there might lead to exposure of further offenses, Holmes opted to confess fraud against the Philadelphia insurance company.

Mrs. Pitezel was also arrested for the insurance fraud, and her account contradicted the statements Holmes made to his captors. First she denied all knowledge of the scheme, then admitted awareness but not complicity. Meanwhile Holmes claimed Pitezel was in Central America. So were Alice, Nellie and Howard, whom he'd secretly turned over to his partner after the insurance claim was paid.

After failing to contact or locate Pitezel by cable or letter, the police pressed Holmes further. Now he revised his story and said Pitezel was actually dead; he'd committed suicide with chloroform during a fit of depression. After discovering the body, Holmes had set the scene to look as though an accident had occurred, because suicide would void payment on the insurance policy. He'd kept the news from Mrs. Pitezel, he said, in order to spare the poor woman's feelings. Fearing the children suspected the truth and might talk, he had entrusted them to his former secretary, Minnie Williams, who took them to London where she was opening a massage parlor. He even gave the police Minnie's London address.

When the address proved nonexistent, he suggested Minnie may have misled him and gone into hiding—she herself, Holmes said, was guilty of murdering her sister Nannie in Chicago. However, he could still reach her by placing an item in the personal column of the New York *Herald* written according to a prearranged code. Minnie would be reading that paper regularly to secure messages from Holmes.

The notice was composed and duly run but there was no response.

Holmes declared she'd double-crossed him; now he was baffled.

So were the authorities, as their prisoner continued to play his cat-and-mouse game while awaiting trial. On May 28, 1895, he finally went to court on the insurance company indictment and shortly thereafter pleaded guilty. It was advantageous to do so; a two-year sentence for fraud would keep him safe in Philadelphia from any possible charges arising elsewhere. At least he was buying time and during imprisonment he'd find a way out of the mess.

But the judge anticipated his reasoning and deferred passing sentence. The charges against Mrs. Pitezel were dropped on June 19 with the understanding that she'd be available to testify.

By now Holmes's continual lying had raised suspicions about the missing children and the Philadelphia police were determined to get at the truth. Their truth seeker was veteran detective Frank P. Geyer.

To aid him in his search, Geyer carried a batch of photos of Holmes and the Pitezel family, plus photos of pieces of luggage used in their travels. Geyer also had some of the letters written by Alice and Nellie, plus letters Mrs. Pitezel had written to the children during the trip. Of course Holmes had volunteered to mail these missives; actually none had ever been sent. But instead of destroying them, he had for some unknown reason preserved the letters in a tin box where they were discovered after his arrest.

Armed with his exhibits, Geyer established Holmes's escape route and followed it from city to city. Not content with searching for entries in hotel registers, he also checked house rentals. By enlisting the aid of realtors and local authorities, he was able to trace Holmes's movements under his many aliases. Within two months he had located the remains of Alice and Nellie in Toronto, then those of little Howard in Irvington. Meanwhile the Chicago Castle had been explored and its grisly contents exposed.

Holmes himself had not been idle. Over the protests of his lawyers he wrote and sold a booklet, which was published in the summer of 1895. In it he proclaimed his innocence of anything except insurance frauds involving falsely identified corpses procured from medical schools. He even included excerpts from his prison diary carefully calculated to tug at the heartstrings of readers.

He also took pains to offer a startling revelation. Now that the bodies of the Pitezel children had been found, he added to his earlier accusations against the missing Minnie Williams. He alleged that she had killed the youngsters with the aid of an accomplice, one Edward Hatch. Hatch was Miss Williams' fiancé, and for a time he had accompanied Holmes during his travels with the children.

The motive for murder, Holmes now stated, was jealousy. Minnie Williams, outraged when she learned of his marriage to Myrta Belknap, had plotted to do away with the Pitezel offspring and pin the crimes on Holmes. After engaging herself to Hatch, an old suitor from her past career in the theater, she had persuaded him to participate in the vile scheme.

Unfortunately the facts didn't jibe with the fiction. Minnie Williams had never been an actress, and Holmes had married Myrta Belknap long before he met Minnie. As for his supposed traveling companion, Edward Hatch, none of the many witnesses in the cities he had visited ever saw the man. There was no proof that he existed at all, except in Holmes's fevered imagination.

Such inconsistencies in testimony, together with the ghastly discoveries in Toronto, Irvington and the Chicago Castle, spurred Philadelphia authorities to mount new proceedings against their prisoner. On September 12 a grand jury indicted Herman W. Mudgett, alias H. H. Holmes, for the murder of Benjamin F. Pitezel.

Pleading not guilty, Holmes and his attorneys now attempted a series of delaying actions. But on October 28 he was brought to trial.

By this time technical findings had refuted the possibility of Pitezel's having committed suicide with chloroform, as Holmes claimed; medical witnesses for the prosecution made it clear that the poison had been administered by another. Holmes was found guilty of first-degree murder. His motion for a new trial was overruled and on November 30 he was sentenced to death by hanging.

His attorneys appealed to the state Supreme Court. The appeal was denied.

In March 1896, having exhausted his options, Holmes contracted to write an exclusive confession for the Hearst newspaper syndicate. He was paid a substantial sum by the standards of that day—variously reported as five thousand, seventy-five hundred, and as much as ten thousand dollars—for a lurid disclosure of his criminal career. The result appeared in the Sunday papers on April 12 and filled nearly three full pages. Penned possibly with the aid of a ghostwriter but full of touches that could only have come from the mind of Holmes himself, it created a sensation.

His admission of twenty-seven murders shocked the nation. Abandoning the air of injured innocence he'd tried to maintain from the moment of arrest until the present, he now compared himself to a man-eating tiger whose appetite for blood sent him on a ceaseless search for fresh victims.

Holmes detailed the death of little Howard Pitezel in Irvington: he gave him a fatal dose of "medicine," then cut his body up and burned the pieces in the stove.

Alice and Nellie Pitezel were locked inside a trunk and asphyxiated by means of a hose connected to a gas jet, just as had been conjectured. After stripping the girls, he buried their bodies in the basement graves he'd dug for them at the Toronto house.

Now he revealed how Ben Pitezel met his death. Holmes forged heartrending letters from Carrie Pitezel, which he knew would goad his partner into remorseful recourse to the bottle. When Ben fell into a drunken stupor, Holmes tied his hands and feet, doused his face and clothing with benzine, and burned him alive.

Following the agonizing death, and satisfied that Ben's features had been sufficiently disfigured to hinder accurate identification, Holmes poured chloroform down the dead man's throat. If Pitezel's demise didn't appear to be due to the fake explosion, the chloroform in his stomach was designed to indicate evidence of suicide.

After the publication of this cold-blooded confession, Holmes made a sudden conversion to Catholicism. Then he promptly petitioned the governor of Pennsylvania for executive clemency. The petition was just as promptly denied.

He next attempted to gain time by asking Carrie Pitezel, of all people, to intercede in his behalf for a stay of execution. He told her he owned a house and lot under a false name; given a month or so, he could prove ownership and arrange to sign the real estate over to her. By selling or renting it, she would be provided with some income by way of amends for his offenses; he felt he owed her that much at least.

Investigation soon disclosed that no such property existed.

But Holmes didn't give up. He now wrote to none other than Frank Geyer, the detective whose brilliant efforts had led to his undoing. Holmes claimed he'd lied in his newspaper confessions regarding the deaths of the three Pitezel children; the actual murders were carried out in his absence by a confederate. If Geyer would use his influence to get him a reprieve, he would furnish information to help identify and locate the accomplice in the interests of justice.

Geyer refused.

The day of execution loomed.

There was nothing left for Holmes now except to confer with his attorneys about funeral arrangements. Several physicians were eager to dissect his body and examine his brain for the sake of science—to say nothing of publicity. But under state law no autopsy could be performed without the subject's permission, and Holmes—who had carved up so many corpses without a qualm—shuddered at the thought of sharing a similar fate.

Nor did this confessed body snatcher want his own remains stolen from their final resting place. He directed that his coffin be encased in cement and buried in a grave ten feet deep, under a two-foot layer of cement poured as a further precaution.

On the morning of May 7, 1896, he was led from his cell to the scaffold. There, on the platform, Holmes made his final statement. Now he reversed himself yet again, denying any guilt for the murders of Ben Pitezel and the children. All he had done, he declared, was to inadvertently take the lives of two women—Julia Conner and Emmeline Cigrand.

After a hasty prayer and a brief farewell he was handcuffed. A black satin bag was drawn down over his head and face. The noose encircled his neck.

Holmes murmured a last good-by.

The noose tightened.

For a moment he stood alone on the gallows and the crowd held its breath.

Then the man who had affixed the noose stepped back and dropped a white handkerchief. It was the signal for a concealed prisoner to activate a lever and release the trap.

The boards beneath Holmes's feet parted and he dropped through the opening.

His death throes were hideous.

But no one shed a single tear.

THE LEGACY

So CONCLUDES THE STRANGE career of Dr. H. H. Holmes, alias Howard, Gordon, Pratt and heaven knows how many other assumed identities—all united in the single shape of Herman W. Mudgett and neatly tied together by a rope knotted around his neck.

Recreating the story today, the inclination is to emulate a film director who—trapped without a proper ending for his picture—freezes the frame as a solution to the problem. Thus one is tempted to leave Dr. Holmes dangling from the scaffold and walk away.

But in a sense Holmes's end is really the beginning of our story, for the most puzzling, weird and uncanny elements remain to be explored. And there are still so many questions.

How, for example, was Holmes able to perpetrate his crimes under the very noses of employees, business associates and intimates? Was it the power of suggestion that made him appear to be all things to all men—and all women? His ability to hoodwink supposedly hard-bitten businessmen on short acquaintance, his almost instant appeal to the opposite sex, the ease with which he dismissed creditors and claimants, can only be explained by a charisma reinforced through some additional element of suggestion.

The popular novel *Trilby*, published in 1894 shortly before Holmes's downfall, presents contemporary misconceptions regarding hypnotic techniques. Its evil genius, Svengali, transfixes the heroine with his evil eye; he teaches her to sing and she becomes a vocalizing puppet animated by the psychic power of his gaze. Eventually the intense concentration required to command her drains Svengali's strength and he dies while conducting Trilby in a concert.

Today we know hypnotic control can be attained without the aid of burning glances, mysterious hand passes or hoked-up histrionics borrowed from the performances of stage magicians. We can safely hazard that Holmes, through trial and error, might easily have learned that a high percentage of his adoring "typewriters," already bedazzled by his magnetic personality, could be controlled and deceived simply because they *wanted* to believe whatever he told them.

As for Holmes's other victims—those wittingly or unwittingly involved in his various shady swindles, and the long list of missing persons who presumably took up all too temporary residence in the Castle—we can only conjecture if hypnosis played a part in their final fate. A man bending over a desk to sign a business contract and a woman asleep in bed don't need to be subjected to mesmeric control; they can be placed in a deep trance by a simple blow on the head with a blunt instrument or the introduction of gas into a sleeping chamber.

But there are still other questions.

What happened to first wife Clara Mudgett and brides Myrta and Georgiana? Clara remained in the East following Holmes's execution, Myrta in Wilmette, Georgiana in Indiana after appearing at the trial. But what *finally* became of them? Did they assume new names to avoid discovery, or perhaps marry again?

And what of the children—Holmes's son by Clara and the little daughter Myrta bore him? Did they reach adulthood under other identities, wed and have children of their own? Is the bloodline and genetic strain of Herman W. Mudgett still carried today by unsuspecting great-great-grandchildren?

We shall never know, any more than we know the antecedents of their infamous ancestor. He himself is our greatest mystery.

What was in his own gene pool that might possibly account for the life he led and the deaths he dealt? What elements in his ordinary middle-class rural background could have shaped a seemingly insignificant little man into a full-fledged fiend? How did he, without any known experience or assistance, create the elaborate architectural maze of his Castle and equip it with a score of devices designed to trap and kill and dispose of victims?

We are coming to the heart of the horror now.

Holmes himself beckons us in his memoirs. Speaking of his early years as a country boy in Gilmanton, he says, "I had daily to pass the office of one village doctor, the door of which was seldom if ever barred. Partly from its being associated in my mind as the source of all the nauseous mixtures that had been my childish terror and partly because of the vague rumors I had heard regarding its contents, this place was one of peculiar abhorrence to me, and this becoming known to two of my older schoolmates, they one day bore me struggling and shrieking beyond its awful portals; nor did they desist until I had been brought face to face with one of its grinning skeletons, which, with arms outstretched, seemed ready in its turn to seize me. It was a wicked and dangerous thing to do to a child of tender years and health, but it proved an heroic method of treatment, destined ultimately to cure me of my fears, and to inculcate in me, first, a strong feeling of curiosity, and, later, a desire to learn, which resulted years afterwards in my adopting medicine as a profession."

Did a part of Holmes remain there in the doctor's office, forever imprisoned in a skeleton's embrace? If so, did Holmes translate this childhood trauma into a grim and gruesome reality?

But there are those who demur. They choose to believe Holmes innocent of all but the Pitezel murders; there is, they insist, no "proof" that he killed those girls in the Castle. The many discrepancies in accounts of his career, they say, add up to one conclusion: sensation-seeking journalists created an imaginary monster.

But the Castle itself, with its secret horrors, stands as Holmes's confession of guilt. And it does not stand alone. What of his own admissions written in prison and published while he was still alive?

"I was born with the devil in me . . . I was born with the evil one standing as my sponsor, beside the bed where I was ushered into the world, and he has been with me since."

Born with the Devil in him? Unbelievers might scoff at such a statement and assert that no man is born evil. If so, let them read further as Holmes assumes the role of medical observer.

"Ten years ago I was thoroughly examined by four men of marked ability and by them pronounced as being both mentally and physically a normal and healthy man. Today I have every attribute of a degenerate—a moral idiot. Is it possible that the crimes, instead of being the result of these abnormal conditions, are in themselves the occasion of the degeneracy?"

He goes on to say, "Even at the time of my arrest in 1894, no defects were noticeable under the searching Bertillon system of measurements to which I was subjected, but later, and more noticeably within the past few months, these defects have increased with startling rapidity, as is made known to me by each succeeding examination until I have become thankful that I am no longer allowed a glass with which to note my rapidly deteriorating condition."

Apparently Holmes reached a point where he couldn't bear to look at himself in the mirror any longer and the opinions of others brought him full circle to belief in demoniac possession.

"I am convinced that since my imprisonment I have changed woefully and gruesomely from what I was formerly in feature and figure. My features are assuming a pronounced Satanical cast; I have become afflicted with that dread disease, rare but terrible, with which physicians are acquainted, but over which they have no control whatsoever. That disease is a malformation or distortion of the osseous parts . . . my head and face are gradually assuming an elongated shape. I believe fully that I am growing to resemble the devil—that similitude is almost completed. In fact, so impressed am I with this belief, that I am convinced I no longer have anything human in me."

The "rare but terrible" disease Holmes refers to is probably acromegaly, a disorder of the pituitary gland which brings about some of the physical changes described—but only gradually—and is not marked by any resemblance to an artist's conception of Satan or accompanied by personality changes.

The skeptic might point out that the authorities did not notice any "degeneration" whatsoever. Holmes lost weight and shaved off his beard while in prison but his head was not elongated. The abnormalities he cited were figments of his imagination. Holmes, the doubters would maintain, was a pathological liar to the end.

Suppose we grant as much. But add to the compulsive fantasizing his excessive sex drive, his insatiable greed, his cunning ability to assume a dozen different personas at will, his apparent mastery of hypnotic techniques and his obsession with death, and what emerges is indeed a monster.

Removing the Devil's horns from his brow and replacing them with a psychiatric label seems much more "scientific" by today's standards. But while it may reassure us, it still doesn't cast out the Devil completely.

And though belief in Satan may appear quaint and old-fashioned, it cannot be confined to the unsophisticated members of a past generation. We need only recall a modern instance—the brutal and horrifying murder of five innocent people in the home of Sharon Tate Polanski. The first words the victims heard were uttered by one of the killers, who announced, "I'm the Devil. I'm here to do the Devil's business."

Does a man who thinks he is the Devil actually exercise diabolic powers? Is it possible that Holmes truly believed, as he asserted, that he was the Evil One incarnate? And that, sane or insane, his belief was in itself a source of supernatural or supernormal powers which governed his own life and extended beyond the grave?

Before we decide, we must consider the curse.

As in so many of the events throughout Holmes's career, there is no general agreement on the details of its conclusion. His gallows speech is not open to question, nor is the impression he gave of being cool and collected. We know that he prayed in his cell before execution, but to whom was he praying? Did he go to his death calmly because he had made his peace with heaven or because he had made a final, secret pact with hell?

At least one chronicler, Walter Gibson, leads us to suspect the latter. He states flat out that sometime before his last few moments Holmes "burst forth with imprecations, hurling curses upon everyone who had played a part in his conviction. People who heard that curse shuddered, so viciously had it been voiced."

True or false? And if Holmes did pronounce such a malediction, is there any reason to believe that the Devil lurking within granted him the power to inflict death or torment on others even after his own life was ended?

Let us rely solely upon facts for a reply to these questions. And while each of us may have his own answer, beyond doubt or dispute these facts remain:

• The first attorney who defended Holmes was suspended from the practice of law.

• Shortly after Holmes's execution his Chicago attorney died.

• The superintendent at Holmes's Philadelphia prison committed suicide.

• The coroner's physician who testified against Holmes at the trial met a gruesome death from blood poisoning.

• The coroner who performed the inquest on Ben Pitezel suffered a near-fatal illness.

• So did the judge who sentenced Holmes to death.

• The office of the supervisor of city agents for the Fidelity Mutual

Life Insurance Company was swept by a fire of unexplained origin. Desk, carpet and papers were destroyed. A frame hanging on the wall behind the desk was burned and its glass cracked in the heat of conflagration. But what it contained—the warrant for Holmes's arrest—was untouched by the blaze.

• One of the priests attending Holmes at the gallows died under most peculiar circumstances. The official verdict was uremia, but why, then, was he found dead in a yard outside the church with no evidence of hemorrhage or injury from what seemed to be just a commonplace fall?

• The foreman of Holmes's jury met an even stranger fate. On the day of Holmes's arrest, a telephone wire made contact with a telegraph wire above the roof of his house, and fire broke out. It was extinguished safely, but after Holmes was hanged, another fire started during a storm. The foreman climbed up on the roof to battle the flames and fell dead, electrocuted.

• The undertaker who buried Holmes went insane. He lingered on to die twenty years later, on the anniversary of the day he put Holmes in the grave.

The exact fate of many others involved in the case—like those of the victims in the Murder Castle—remains unknown.

As for the Castle itself, it too met disaster. At 2:00 a.m. on August 19, 1895, it caught fire and burned. Two men, never identified or apprehended, were reportedly observed running from the scene; later a gasoline can was discovered in the ruins. The structure survived, however, and stores remained open on the ground floor. Finally, in 1938 the Castle was razed to make room for a post office.

And so the mysterious Castle vanished, as did its mysterious owner, the enigmatic man who called himself H. H. Holmes but in the end declared he was the Devil. Presumably his curse, if he indeed pronounced it, is finally laid to rest.

Yet there are those who still believe in devils and those who still perform the Devil's deeds. In a world where mass murder occurs all too frequently, we would do well to consider this. Superstition may be set aside, but not grim reality.

The real curse—Holmes's bloodstained heritage of horror—remains to haunt our dreams.

And our waking lives, today.

CURIOUS ENCOUNTER

Curious
Encounter
by John G. Fuller

ILLUSTRATED BY MITCHELL HOOKS

The sky that night was brilliant with stars and the road through the mountains deserted as Barney and Betty Hill drove south toward their home in Portsmouth, New Hampshire. With Barney at the wheel, Betty sat relaxed, watching the dark outline of the surrounding peaks and the sky above them. Suddenly one star grew brighter and appeared to change course. What the Hills were about to see was to leave them terrified, incredulous and, at times, even doubtful of their sanity. It was an experience that would change their lives forever.

John G. Fuller, author of the best-selling book *The Ghost of Flight 401*, first covered the Hill case in a special two-part series for *Look* magazine. Here he dramatically captures the terror and bewilderment of the Hills as, under hypnosis, they relive an encounter too frightening for the conscious mind to remember, too powerful for the unconscious to forget.

INTRODUCTION

As I SAT ACROSS the desk from Benjamin Simon, M.D., one afternoon back in 1965, I felt as if I were a character in a science fiction story. The office, in a fashionable remodeled town house on Boston's Bay State Road, was perfectly normal and fitting for a professional man of Dr. Simon's stature. His credentials were absolutely impeccable. Lecturer at Yale. Rockefeller Fellow in neurology. Director of psychiatry at one of the largest state hospitals in Massachusetts. Colonel and former chief of neuropsychiatry at the U.S. Army's giant Mason General Hospital during World War II. Recipient of the Legion of Merit Medal. Yet the story we were now talking about was as bizarre as one any science fiction writer could conjure up.

Still, the strange case of Barney and Betty Hill was true and documented in medical records. I was there in Dr. Simon's office to track down that story, a tale that continues to leave me utterly baffled, because by all rational yardsticks it could not be true. As a reporter on assignment for *Look* magazine, a documentary film producer and a columnist for the *Saturday Review* at that time, I felt I had no business poking my nose into a tale as incredible as this one.

It involved flying saucers, of all things, a phrase that smacks of modern mythology, and which I dislike intensely. I even have trouble accepting the sanitized synonym: unidentified flying objects, or UFOs. Until a short time before my visit to Boston I knew little or nothing about UFOs. In fact, I was extremely skeptical about them, a position shared by Dr. Simon.

The facts that emerged from Dr. Simon's tapes and medical records were hard, tough and unassailable. This was either one of the most unusual cases in the history of psychiatry or the first extraterrestrial visit to be documented in detail. Either way, the story was gripping and mind-boggling.

The conscious memory of the Hills could not illuminate the story, except in fragments. The incident involved two hours of lost time for both of them, time that had somehow been eradicated from their conscious minds. This strange trauma of sudden double amnesia came to them when they saw an enormous UFO over their car on a lonely mountain road along the Vermont–New Hampshire border. They woke up two hours later, still in their car, but some forty miles away from where the craft had originally approached them.

For two years the Hills tried to reconstruct what happened in those missing hours. They developed serious anxiety symptoms as a result of the inexplicable twin amnesia. A psychiatrist diagnosed their mutual problem as traumatic anxiety from their experience, and from their amnesia. The only specific treatment for amnesia is skilled regression by sodium amobarbital, sodium pentothal, or regressive hypnosis to break down the threshold that bars the memories from reaching consciousness. The Hills were referred to Dr. Simon, a leading specialist in this form of therapy.

Because of his World War II experience, the Boston physician was well practiced in dealing with amnesia among soldiers whose battle experiences had left them unable to function. Through regressive hypnosis, Simon had enabled them to relive, often painfully, their experiences so that their amnesia was gone, their anxiety lifted and their health restored.

But this case was different. Amnesia from an encounter with a UFO? Unheard of in the annals of psychiatric history. Double simultaneous amnesia? Never before recorded. Unidentified flying objects? Dr. Simon had no interest in them, doubted their existence. But he did have two patients who needed help, and he set about to treat them as he would any of his other patients.

As part of the treatment, Dr. Simon hypnotized Betty and Barney Hill separately, once a week, for six months. Every session was tape-recorded. Two identical stories emerged—yet neither Betty nor Barney knew what the other was saying. They were also instructed to forget all they had said during each session. The result: nearly forty taped hours of a dramatic reliving of a "close encounter of the third kind," of an abduction by humanoid beings to a large UFO, where the Hills were given physical examinations and then returned to their car without a conscious memory of the event.

I had already visited the Hills before I went to see Dr. Simon. They had impressed me with their sincerity, their frankness and their intelligence. They were leaders in the Portsmouth, New Hampshire, community and in the local Unitarian Church. Their IQs were both over 130, high on the scale. They were as puzzled about the whole sequence of events as Dr. Simon and I were.

In Dr. Simon's office I leafed through a transcript of one of the regressive hypnosis tapes. There was a stack of them as thick as a dictionary on his desk. Then I asked, "How can you possibly account for this story?"

"There are many things to consider," Dr. Simon said. "Remember that I was treating them professionally for one specific purpose: to relieve their anxiety symptoms and their amnesia."

"But what about the UFO and the purported abduction?" I asked.

"That is entirely out of my area."

"Do you believe UFOs could exist?" I asked.

"I believe anything exists if I see hard, palpable evidence."

"Do you see that here?"

"I can only say this," the doctor replied. "It is very difficult to lie under carefully administered hypnosis. Especially six months of it. Therefore I'm convinced the Hills were not lying. Second, after careful examination of the tapes I'm convinced they were not hallucinating. Third, there is no evidence of psychosis, or of a rare condition known as *folie à deux*, where two people can create psychosis between themselves."

I was puzzled. "But if they're not lying, not psychotic and not hallucinating—does that mean it actually could have happened?"

"All I can say," said Dr. Simon, "is that I'm a scientist. That's as far as I can go."

I listened to the tapes with Dr. Simon over a period of five weeks, several hours at a time. The impact on hearing them was shocking, startling, frightening. The Hills, under hypnosis, were not merely describing the purported abduction on a lonely New Hampshire road; they were *living* it all over again, experiencing every detail, all the emotions of the event as it had happened. The story that springs out from the tapes is one that I will never forget, and certainly will never be able to explain.

CHAPTER ONE

SEPTEMBER IN THE White Mountains is the cruelest month. The gaunt hotels, vestiges of Victorian tradition, are either shuttered or about to be. Motels and overnight cabins flash their neon vacancy signs for only a few fitful hours before the owners give up and retire for the night. The New Hampshire ski slopes are barren of snow and skiers, the trails appearing as great brownish gashes beside the silent tramways and chair lifts. The Labor Day exodus has swept most of the roads clear of traffic.

A few solitary vacation trailers and roof-laden station wagons straggle toward Boston or the New York thruways. Winter is already here on the chilled and ominous slopes of Mount Washington, where the summit weather station once clocked the highest wind velocity ever recorded on any mountaintop in the world. Bears and red foxes roam occasionally. Soon hunters in scarlet or luminous orange jackets would be on the trails, intent on deer or ruffed grouse or anything legal in sight. The skiers would follow later, their minds on powder snow and hot buttered rum, bringing back with them the gay holiday mood of summer. Once again the White Mountains would take on new life.

It was in the doleful mid-September period of 1961—September 19, to be exact—that thirty-nine-year-old Barney Hill and his wife, Betty, forty-one, began their drive from the Canadian border down U.S. 3, through the White Mountains, on their way home to Portsmouth, New Hampshire. It was to be a night drive, brought on by a sense of urgency. The radio of their 1957 Bel Air hardtop made it clear that Hurricane Esther was coming up the coast and might cut inland, an event that in previous years had uprooted trees and spilled high-tension wires across the roads. On their holiday trip the Hills had driven leisurely to Niagara Falls, then circled up through Montreal and back toward home.

They had cleared U.S.–Canadian customs at about nine that evening, winding along the lonely top of Vermont's Northeast Kingdom. The traffic was sparse. They had seen few other cars before approaching the welcome lights of Colebrook, about fifteen minutes later. An ancient New Hampshire settlement founded in 1770, Colebrook lies in the shadow of Mount Monadnock, just across the river from Vermont. The lights of the village were few. A forlorn glow came from the windows of a single restaurant. Realizing that this might be their last chance for refreshment for the rest of the trip, the Hills decided to turn back even though they had driven past it.

The restaurant was nearly deserted. A few teenagers gathered in a far corner. Only one woman, a waitress, seemed to show any reaction at all to the fact that Betty and Barney's marriage was a mixed one: Barney, a handsome descendant of a proud Ethiopian freeman, whose great-grandmother was born into slavery but raised in the house of the plantation owner because she was his daughter; Betty, whose ancestors bought three tracts of land in York, Maine, in 1637, only to have one family member cut down by the Indians.

Regardless of what attention their mixed marriage drew in public places, they were no longer self-conscious about it themselves. Their first attraction to each other, one that still remained, was of intellect and mutual interests. Together they stumped the state of New Hampshire speaking for the cause of civil rights. Barney, a Boston post office employee and legal redress chairman of the Portsmouth NAACP, was also a member of the state Advisory Board of the United States Civil Rights Commission and the Board of Directors of the Rockingham County Poverty Program. Both he and Betty were proud to display the award he had received from Sargent Shriver for his work. As a child welfare worker for the state of New Hampshire, Betty carried a heavy case load. After hours she was assistant secretary and community coordinator for the NAACP and United Nations envoy for the Unitarian Church.

But what was to happen that night of September 19, 1961, had nothing whatever to do with the Hills' marriage or their dedication to social progress. Nor was there any hint of what was to happen as they sat in the pine-paneled restaurant in Colebrook, Barney unceremoniously eating a hamburger, Betty a piece of chocolate layer cake. They didn't linger too long at the counter, just long enough for a cigarette and a cup of black coffee before continuing down U.S. 3 toward home.

The distance from Colebrook to Portsmouth is a hundred and sixty-five miles, with U.S. 3 remarkably smooth and navigable considering the deep mountain gorges it must negotiate. Farther south, below Plymouth, nearly thirty miles of four-lane highway—more than that now—invited safe speeds of up to seventy miles an hour. For the other roads, Barney Hill liked to drive between fifty and fifty-five, even if this should be a shade above the limit.

The clock over the rest room in the Colebrook restaurant read 10:05 when they left that night. "It looks," said Barney as they got in their car, "like we should be home by two thirty in the morning—or by three at the latest."

Betty agreed. She had confidence in Barney's driving, even though she sometimes chided him for pushing too fast. It was a bright, clear night with an almost full moon. The stars were brilliant, as they always are in the New Hampshire mountains on a cloudless night, when they seem to illuminate the peaks with a strange incandescence.

The car was running smoothly through the night air, the road ahead unwinding effortlessly along the flat ground of the upper Connecticut River valley, ancient Indian and lumbering country rich in history and legend. The thirty miles south to Northumberland passed quickly. Betty, an inveterate sightseer, enjoyed watching the moonlit valley and the mountains in the distance—both in New Hampshire to the east and over the river in Vermont to the west. Delsey, the Hills' scrappy little dachshund, lay peacefully on the floor at Betty's feet.

Through Lancaster—a village with a wide main street and fine old pre-Revolutionary houses, all dark now on this September night— U.S. 3 continues south, as the Connecticut River swings westward to widen New Hampshire's territory and narrow Vermont's. Here the wide valley changes to a more uncertain path through the mountains. The serrated peaks of the Pilot Range have been described lushly by one writer as "a great rolling rampart which plays fantastic tricks with the sunshine and shadow, and towards sunset assumes the tenderest tints of deep amethyst."

There was no sunshine or amethyst now, only the luminous moon, very bright and large, and a two-lane blacktop road that appeared to be totally deserted. To the left of the moon, and slightly below it, was a particularly bright star, perhaps a planet, Betty Hill thought, because of its steady glow. Just south of Lancaster Betty was a little startled to notice that another star or planet, a bigger one, had appeared above the first. It had not been there, she was sure, when she had looked before. Even more curious was the fact that the new celestial visitor clearly appeared to be getting bigger and brighter.

For several moments she watched it, but said nothing to her husband as he negotiated the road through the mountains. Finally, when the strange light persisted, she nudged Barney, who slowed the car somewhat and looked out the right-hand side of the windshield to see it. "When I looked at it first," Barney Hill said later, "it didn't seem anything particularly unusual, except that we were fortunate enough to see a satellite. It had no doubt gone off its course, and it seemed to be going along the curvature of the earth. It was quite a distance out, making it look like a star in motion."

They drove on, frequently glancing at the bright object and finding it difficult to tell if the light itself was moving or if the movement of the car was making it *seem* to move. The object would disappear behind trees, or a mountaintop, then reappear again as the obstruction was passed. Delsey, the dog, was beginning to get restless, and Betty mentioned that perhaps they should let her out and take advantage of the road stop to get a better look. Barney agreed. He was an avid plane watcher who sometimes liked to take his two sons from a former marriage, living now in Philadelphia, to watch Piper Cub seaplanes land and take off on Lake Winnipesaukee. He pulled the car over to the side of the road at a spot where the visibility was reasonably unobstructed.

There were woods nearby. Barney, a worrier at times, mentioned they might keep an eye out for bears, a distinct possibility in this part of the country. Betty laughed off his suggestion, snapped the chain lead on Delsey's collar and walked the dachshund along the side of the road. At this moment she noted that the star, or the light or whatever it was in the September sky was definitely moving. As Barney joined her on the road, she handed Delsey's leash to him and went back to the car. From the front seat she took the 7 x 50 Crescent binoculars they had brought along to better view the scenery. Barney, noting that the light in the sky *was* moving, was now fully convinced that it was a straying satellite.

Betty put the binoculars up to her eyes and focused carefully. What both she and Barney were about to see was to change their lives forever, and generate worldwide controversy that still continues.

THE OBJECT THEY WERE watching in the sky near Lancaster continued its unpredictable movement as they passed through Whitefield and the village of Twin Mountain. They stopped briefly several times, and by now Barney was frankly puzzled. His only alternative to the satellite theory was that the object was a star or planet, an idea he discounted because it was moving and changing its course in an erratic manner. At one of their stops Betty had said, "Barney, if you think that's a satellite or a star, you're being ridiculous."

With his naked eye Barney could now tell that she was right. It was obviously not a celestial object. "We've made a mistake, Betty," he said. "It's a commercial plane, probably on its way to Canada." He got back in the car and they continued driving on.

Betty, in the passenger seat, kept the object in view as they moved down Route 3. It seemed to her that it was getting bigger and brighter, and she grew increasingly puzzled and curious. Barney would note it through the windshield on occasion, but was more worried about a car coming around one of the now-frequent curves of the road. The theory that it was a commercial airliner headed for Canada soothed his annoyance at being confronted with something that might be unexplainable.

The road was completely deserted. There were no welcome lights of villages or farms. They hadn't seen a car or truck in either direction for miles now. Through long-standing custom and superstition, some natives of northern New Hampshire prefer never to drive through these roads after dark. In winter a patrol known as the Blue Angels checks the roads and looks for frozen or disabled cars. It is too easy to freeze to death in these lonely stretches, and the state troopers cannot possibly cover the wide territory frequently enough. Barney, his concern growing, hoped that he would soon see a trooper or at least another car which he could flag down. He would have liked to compare notes with someone else.

Around eleven o'clock they approached the enormous and somber silhouette of Cannon Mountain, looming westward on their right. Barney slowed the car down near a picnic turnout commanding a wide view to the west and looked again at the strange moving light. In amazement, he noted that it swung suddenly from its northerly course, turning to the west. Then, after completing its turn, it headed back directly toward them. Barney braked the car sharply and turned off into the picnic area.

"Whatever you're calling it, Barney," Betty said, "it's still up there, and it's still following us. If anything, it's coming right toward us."

"It's got to be a plane," Barney said. They were standing in the picnic area now, looking up at the light, which was growing bigger still. "A commercial liner."

"With a crazy course like that?" Betty said.

"Well, then it's a Piper Cub. That's what it is. With some hunters who might be lost."

"It's not the hunting season yet," Betty said as Barney took the binoculars from her. "And I don't hear a sound."

Neither did Barney, although he desperately wanted to.

"It might be a helicopter," he said as he looked through the binoculars. He was sure that it wasn't, but was reaching for any kind of explanation that made sense. "The wind might be carrying the sound in the other direction."

"There *is* no wind, Barney. Not tonight."

Through the binoculars, Barney made out a shape, like that of the fuselage of an airplane. But he could see no wings. There also seemed to be a series of blinking lights along the side in an alternating pattern. When Betty took the glasses, the object passed in front of the moon, in silhouette. It appeared to be flashing thin pencils of different-colored lights, rotating around a cigar-shaped object. Just a moment before, it had changed its speed from slow to fast, then slowed down again as it crossed the face of the moon. The lights were flashing persistently red, amber, green and blue. She turned to Barney and asked him to take another look.

"It's *got* to be a plane," Barney said. "Maybe a military plane. A search plane. Maybe it's a plane that is lost."

He was getting irritated at Betty now for refusing to accept a natural explanation. At one time, eight years before in 1953, Betty's sister Janet had described seeing an unidentified flying object in Kingston, New Hampshire, where she lived. Betty, who had confidence in her sister's reliability and capacity for observation, believed the story of the sighting. Barney neither believed nor disbelieved it. He was indifferent to the subject as a whole and, if anything, after hearing the sister's story was more skeptical about flying objects than before. He felt that for the first time in many years Betty was about to bring up the subject.

Beside them, the dachshund was whining and cowering. Betty gave the binoculars to Barney, took Delsey to the car, got in and shut the door. Barney focused the glasses on the object and again wished for the comfort of comparing notes with a passing motorist. Above all, he wanted to hear a sound: the throb of a propeller-driven plane or the roar of a jet. None came. For the first time, he felt they were being observed, that the object was actually coming closer and attempting to circle them. If it's a military craft, he thought, it should not do this. His mind went back to a few years before when a military jet had buzzed close by, shattering the sound barrier and cracking the air with an explosion.

After getting back in the car Barney mentioned to Betty that he thought the craft had seen them and was playing games. He tried not to let Betty know that he was afraid, something he didn't like to admit.

They drove on toward Cannon Mountain at not much more than five miles an hour, catching glimpses of the object as it moved erratically in the sky. From the mountain, the only light they had seen for miles glowed like a beacon, appearing to be on the top of the closed and silent aerial tramway, or perhaps the restaurant there. Wouldn't it be nice, Barney thought, if the restaurant were open. Just the thought of some people around would be comforting, even far up on the mountain. Or a state trooper. The sight of a police cruiser was all he asked for.

They stopped again near the base of the mountain, as the object suddenly swung behind its dark silhouette and disappeared. Just then, the light at the top of the mountain went out, inexplicably.

As the car moved by the darkened outline of the mountain, the object reappeared. It was gliding silently, leisurely, parallel to the car, along the Vermont border to the west. They were going through woods now, making it more difficult to keep the object in sight as it glided behind the trees. But it was there, moving with them. Near the turnoff for the The Flume, a now-deserted tourist attraction, they stopped, and almost got a sharp, clear look at the object, but again the trees intervened.

Just beyond the turnoff for The Flume, they passed a small hotel, the first sign of life they had seen for miles. The tidy hostelry looked comforting, although Barney, his eyes alternately moving between the curves of the road and the object in the sky, barely noticed it. Betty caught sight of the sign, beaming with AAA approval, and the light in a single window. A man was standing in the doorway of one of the cottages, and Betty thought how easy it would be to end the whole situation right then by simply pulling into the motel. She was thinking this—but she didn't say anything to Barney. Her curiosity about the object was now overwhelming, and she was determined to see more of it. Barney, still concerned that another car would come around a blind curve, was trying to keep one eye on the object when suddenly it moved almost directly in front of them.

It was only a few hundred feet off the ground, and it was huge. Farther off, it had seemed to Betty to be spinning. Now the spinning had stopped and the light pattern had changed from blinking multi-colored lights to a steady white glow. In spite of the vibrations of the car, she put the binoculars to her eyes and looked again.

She drew a quick involuntary breath because she could see a double row of windows. Without the binoculars, the windows had appeared only as a streak of light. Now it was clear that this was a structured craft of enormous dimension, just how large she couldn't tell because both distance and altitude were hard to judge exactly. Then, slowly, a red light came out of the left side of the object, followed by a similar one on the right.

"Barney," she said, "I don't know *why* you're trying *not* to look at this. Stop the car and look at it."

"It'll go away by the time I do that," Barney said. He was not at all convinced that it would.

"Barney, you've got to *stop*. You've never seen anything like this in your life."

He looked through the windshield and could see it plainly now, not more than two hundred feet in the air and coming closer. A curve in the road seemed to shift the object to the right of the car, but the distance remained the same.

Also on the right, not far south of Indian Head, where the historic stone face surveys the mountains and valleys, Barney saw two commercial imitation wigwams at an enterprise known as Natureland. Here during the summer months hundreds of youngsters swarm with their parents. At this moment, however, it was silent and tomblike.

Barney stopped the car almost in the center of the road, forgetting in the excitement the possibility of there being any other traffic. "All right, give me the binoculars," he said. It sounded to Betty as if he was trying to humor her.

Barney got out, the motor still running, and leaned his arm on the side of the car. By now the object had swung toward them and hovered silently in the air, two treetops high and not more than a short city block away. Its full shape—that of a large glowing pancake—was apparent for the first time. But the vibration from the car's motor jostled Barney's arm, blurring his vision. He stepped away from the side of the car to get a better look.

"Do you see it? Do you *see* it?" Betty said excitedly.

Barney, he admitted frankly later, was scared, perhaps as much because Betty rarely became emotional as because of the nearness of this strange and utterly silent object.

"It's just a plane or something," he snapped.

"Okay," Betty said. "It's a plane. But did you ever see a plane standing still in the air—with no sound? And with two red lights instead of one red and one green?"

"Well, I didn't get a good look at it," he said. "The car was shaking the binoculars." A few feet away now, he looked again.

As he did so, the huge object swung in a silent arc across the road directly toward him. The enormous disc was now raked on an angle. The two finlike projections on either side were sliding out farther, each with a red light on it. The windows curving around the perimeter of the craft glowed with a brilliant white light. Still there was no sound. Shaken, but experiencing an overpowering urge to move closer, Barney continued walking across the field, coming within fifty feet of the craft as it suddenly dropped down to the height of a tall tree. He did not estimate its size in feet, except that he knew it was as big or bigger than the length of a jet airliner, though circular in shape rather than elongated.

Back in the car, Betty was not at first aware that Barney was walking away from her. She was thinking that the middle of the highway wasn't a very smart place to park the car. The vehicle was neither to the right nor to the left—it was splitting the white dotted line down the middle of the road. She would watch, she thought, to see if headlights appeared, and at least pull out of the way quickly. She busied herself doing this for several moments, and then suddenly became aware that Barney had disappeared into the blackness of the field. Instinctively, she called for him.

"Barney! Barney, come back here." If he didn't reappear in a moment, she resolved to go out after him. "*Barney!* What's wrong with you? Do you hear me?"

There was no answer. She started to slide across the front seat, toward the open door on the driver's side of the car.

Out on the dark field, near a shuttered vegetable stand and a single gnarled apple tree, Barney put the binoculars up to his eyes. Then he froze.

It was clearly not a plane. There were windows, but they were nothing like those of a jet or any other plane. They curved around the edge of the circular craft. Barney tried to regain control of himself. He did not want Betty to see how utterly frozen with fear he was. He shook his head, and said to himself, "My *God*, this can't be. This can't be here. Can't somebody come along the road and tell me this thing is not there?"

He shook off his fear and, on an irresistible impulse, walked closer. It was still there. Dropping the binoculars from his eyes, he let them dangle on the strap. Maybe, he thought, if I start over, it won't be there. But it was. If only he had a weapon of some kind. He ran to the car, yanked the tire wrench out of the trunk and ran back to the field. He did not even hear Betty yelling at him.

After slipping the tire wrench through his belt, he put the binoculars up to his eyes again. Behind the curved windows he could see figures, at least half a dozen living beings. They seemed to be bracing themselves, as the craft tilted down in his direction. They were, as a group, staring directly at him. He became vaguely aware that they were wearing some kind of uniform.

The binoculars felt as if they were glued to his eyes. Then, on some seemingly invisible, inaudible signal, the members of the crew stepped back to a large panel a few feet behind the windows.

Only one, apparently the leader, remained there looking intently at Barney. Through the binoculars Barney could see the appendages of the crew in action at what seemed to be a control board behind the windows. Slowly the craft descended. As the fins bearing the red lights moved out farther on the sides, an extension was lowered from underneath—perhaps a ladder, he could not be sure.

Barney sharpened the focus of the binoculars on the face remaining at the window. For a reason he could not explain, he was certain that he was about to be captured. He tried to pull the glasses away from his eyes, to turn away, but he couldn't. As the focus became sharp, he saw the eyes of the figure at the window. Barney had never seen eyes like that before. They were enormous. And for some crazy reason, they seemed to be telling him: *Stay there—and keep looking. Just keep looking—and stay there. Just keep looking.* The strange part was that he didn't hear any voice. He *knew* what was being told him, yet no lips were moving, and the face was expressionless.

A strange scene from Barney's boyhood went through his head. He had been hunting for rabbits in Virginia. A small one ran into a skimpy bush. His cousin Marge was on one side of the bush, and he was on the other—with a hat. Barney had been amused that the rabbit hid behind a slender stalk for security. Dropping his hat over the animal, Barney had captured it.

Now, with the craft hovering near him, he felt like that rabbit. He knew he had to get the binoculars away from his eyes. Those words were pounding in his head: *Stay there. Just keep looking.* Those large, silent, slanted eyes kept telling him that. But then he thought: I've got to get hold of myself. I have courage. I can drive a car. With all his strength, Barney ripped the binoculars from his eyes, breaking the strap with his neck as he did so. He ran screaming across the field to Betty and the car. "They're going to capture us, Betty!"

He tossed the binoculars and the tire wrench on the seat, barely missing Betty, who had just straightened up after getting ready to slide out of his side of the car.

Barney was near hysteria. He jammed the car into first gear and sped off down the road, shouting again that he was sure they were going to be captured. He ordered Betty to look out the window to see where the craft was. She rolled down the window on the passenger side and looked out. The object was nowhere in sight. Craning her neck, she looked directly above the car. Everything was black. The strange craft did not seem to be there. But neither were the stars. Barney kept yelling that he was sure the object had swung directly above them. Betty checked again, but all she could see was total darkness. She looked out the rear window and saw nothing—except the stars, once again visible through that window.

Then, suddenly, they heard a strange electronic-sounding beeping. The car seemed to vibrate with it. It had an irregular rhythm, beep-beep—beep-beep-beep, and seemed to come from behind the car. Her hand on the metal door, Betty felt a mild electric shock.

Barney said, "What's that noise?"

"I don't know," Betty replied.

They each began to feel an odd tingling drowsiness. Betty was half aware of her memory slowly slipping away as if she were sliding down a well. Barney felt as though he were floating in space. Those terrifyingly large eyes burned in his head as if pressed inside his brain. Betty tried to fight off the irresistible blanket of sleep that came down over her, but found it impossible to do so.

A VEIL OF AMNESIA descended on both of them at exactly the same time, at exactly the same place in the road. It would be two years later, under Dr. Simon's deep probing with regressive hypnosis, that Betty and Barney would recover their memories as they listened with disbelief to the tapes. Then, their own voices would reveal an experience that even they would find impossible to believe.

CHAPTER TWO

THROUGH THE HAZE, as Barney recalled two years later, the eyes remained pressed against his brain. Route 3 was somewhere in his consciousness, but shadowy and disconnected. He was driving the car, but he was not conscious of Betty being beside him; he was barely conscious of the car itself. The road was ahead of him, and then there was no road. Just that feeling of floating in space. Then the road was ahead of him again—but it was not Route 3. It was small and winding. He must have turned off the main road, but he had no idea where.

In between these fragmentary glimpses of the road, there were the eyes again, still inside his head, still burning. Now they were telling him something new: *Don't be afraid.* The eyes had no body connected to them. He tried to rationalize them away. Suddenly, he began to comfort himself with what they could be: a wildcat up a tree. But there was no tree, and there was no wildcat. He even thought of the Cheshire cat from *Alice in Wonderland.* Hadn't it disappeared and left only the smile? Couldn't it do so again and leave only the eyes? Either way, though, it was all absurd.

But then, so was the scene he saw down the winding road—the road he had had no intention of taking. What was it? A huge orange and red light ahead which looked like a glowing moon standing on its edge. But there was the real moon in the sky. Was it an accident? Were there men standing in the road? Was he being robbed? He fought to clear his mind, but then slipped back into that strange floating sensation with the eyes still telling him not to be afraid.

THE FIRST THING Betty thought of when the beeping noise occurred was that she wished she knew Morse code so she could decipher some kind of message. Immediately after that she lost consciousness—at least to the degree that everything became blurred and hazy as she fought to overcome the drowsiness that had engulfed her. As with Barney, only fragments of awareness came through.

She knew they continued down the road, but she had no idea where they were. She knew Barney was at the wheel, but neither of them spoke. She did not feel afraid, but sensed something was going to happen. In her hazy awareness she felt Barney slam on the brakes and swerve to the left. He began driving along a narrow road she had never been on before. Then, fading in and out of consciousness, she saw figures standing in the road. They were backlit by a bright orange glow coming from behind some trees nearby.

She was sure that it was either an accident or a disabled car, but in her dazed state she felt indifferent. She knew only that she wanted to wake herself up. She felt Barney slam on the brakes again and come to a sudden stop. Two groups of silhouetted figures came toward the car. The motor died. As the shadowy forms approached, she began to be afraid for the first time. She heard Barney trying to start the car. The engine turned over and over, but there was no ignition. The figures were coming closer. The engine still did not respond. She was gripped with fear.

Her first thought was to get away, to run and hide in the woods. She reached for the door handle, her hand moving as if in a dream. Finally she got hold of it and started to open the door. But now there were two figures on either side of the car. Before she could escape, one of them opened the door for her.

She was terrified. She could not see or determine what kind of figures they were, but they had arms and legs, and seemed to be dressed in some kind of uniform. One of the figures suddenly put his hand out. There was some kind of instrument in it, about the size of a flashlight. He pointed it toward her eyes. As he did so, another wave of drowsiness seized her.

BARNEY, IN THE DRIVER'S seat, was trying to start the car in vain. He was barely aware of the men coming toward them, but the "eyes" were still with him. He caught glimpses of the approaching forms, and the bright orange glow behind the trees on the side of the road. He thought of grabbing the tire wrench again, then decided against it. Somehow, in his dazed condition he sensed he would be harmed if he tried that.

He felt very weak, and for some reason he did not even question what was happening to him. Instead he recalled a motion picture he had seen years before. One scene showed a man being carried to the electric chair. He pictured himself in the same position, yet he knew he was not. His eyes automatically closed. He knew there were men there, although he was not looking at them. He also knew he was being assisted out of the car.

As he felt both feet dragging along the ground, the toes of his shoes bumping on the rocks, he thought of Betty, but he had no will to resist what was happening to him. Again, he felt as if he were floating, almost as if he were dreaming. "Disassociated" was the only word he could think of later. With his eyes still tightly closed, a series of mental pictures came to him. Was he being half carried up a slight incline? For some reason, he kept telling himself to keep his eyes closed. He was sure he was being supported on each side, yet he couldn't really feel those who were doing it.

For a fraction of a second Barney opened his eyes, then closed them again quickly. In that fraction he saw a ramp of some kind leading up to the doorway of the craft. He could feel the tops of his shoes bump over a sort of bulkhead. As he closed his eyes, he "heard" the same silent voice that had communicated with him on the highway, telling him that no harm would come to him. It was as if the eyes he had seen through the binoculars were sending commands into his mind. He was instructed not to open his eyes. But he did—just long enough to see that he was in a curved corridor leading to an open door. Someone was holding him up on each side. Beyond the door was a small pie-shaped room that looked like an operating room. It contained an examining table.

Now he could hear voices—but they were nothing more than a humming sound: mmm-mmmmm-mm-mmmmmmm-mmm. He was moved toward the table, and sensed without question that he was to lie down on it.

As SHE WAS BEING lifted out of the car in her comatose state, Betty continued to fight to wake up. She struggled intensely to do so, only to slip back into sleep. Suddenly she was able to break through into awareness. She opened her eyes, and realized she was walking on a path through trees. There were men on each side of her, small men, shorter than she was; far shorter than Barney. She turned her head. Barney was behind her, his eyes closed, his shoes dragging on the ground as he was half carried along the path.

Then she began to get mad. "Who the heck are these men," she said to herself, "and what do they think they're doing?" She forced her head around again, and called out, "Barney! Wake up! Barney! Why don't you wake up?"

Barney appeared to pay no attention; his eyes were still closed. Then she felt rather than heard the man beside her say, "Is his name Barney?" At first she wasn't surprised the man had spoken. In any case, she felt it wasn't any of his business. As she was being led along the path, she called back again, "Barney, Barney, wake up!"

And again, she felt she heard the one beside her say, "Is Barney his name?" She refused to answer, but then the man continued, "Don't be afraid. You don't have any reason to be afraid. We're not going to harm you, we just want to do some tests. When the tests are over, we'll take you and Barney back and put you in the car. You'll be on your way in no time."

This seemed reassuring, but she didn't trust what she heard. Was this man really talking to me? she thought. She tried to figure it out. He was and he wasn't. He was not speaking English. He was not really speaking any language, yet he was perfectly understandable. Was it telepathy? There was a sound, an accented sound. The only thing she could compare it to was when she was beginning to learn French. She could listen to it being spoken and get a sense of the meaning, without being able to translate it directly. Yet these thoughts were more articulate than that. She could understand precisely what was being told her—yet it was more a sound than a language. She was sure it was some form of telepathy, but she was in no mood to analyze it. By now her fear had changed to anger and she just wanted to get free.

Betty was led into a clearing. The large craft was on the ground in front of her. It was no longer glowing brightly, neither orange nor white. She could make out a ramp going up to a doorway. Now she balked. They were leading her toward it. Her curiosity was gone. She did not want to go aboard. She looked back toward Barney, but his eyes were still closed. She called to him again, but still he did not respond. There was no way he could help her.

At the foot of the ramp Betty continued to resist. Again the man on her left spoke, or transferred his thoughts or made cryptic sounds that became understandable in English—whatever the process was. But she understood, and knew that her captors meant business.

"Go on," the one on her left said. "The longer you fool around out here, the longer it's going to take. You might as well go on and get it over with, and get back to your car. We haven't got much time, either." Was he speaking such colloquial English, or was she just interpreting it that way? She still had no idea, except that the meaning was clear.

Betty was overcome by a feeling of helplessness. There was not much she could do except to go up the ramp with them. Still being led, she stepped inside the craft. It was illuminated and clean, with a strange smell in the air, like that of marigolds. She was guided left in

the corridor and up to the doorway of a room. She stopped there and waited to see what they were going to do with Barney. She watched them lead him past her, toward another room down the curved corridor. Angry again, she demanded, "What are you doing with Barney? Bring him in where I am."

"No," her escort told her. "We only have equipment enough in one room to do one person at a time. If we took both of you in the same room, it would take too long. Barney will be all right. They're going to take him into the next room. Then, as soon as we get through testing both of you, you will go back to your car. You don't have to be afraid."

There it was again. That strange mode of communication that added up to being understood in colloquial English. This phenomenon disturbed Betty almost as much as the abduction itself. She watched them take Barney into the next room, then turned and compliantly went into hers. Resistance, she now felt, was futile.

Betty permitted herself to open her eyes in brief flashes. The room was pie-shaped, with the point cut off bluntly. There was a stool and an examining table. The room was illuminated by a shadowless fluorescent sort of glow and the walls were metallic-looking. As she was led toward the stool by her two captors, two others entered the room and seemed to take command. She wasn't sure, but they seemed a little taller than those who had brought her to the craft. They were speaking to each other in that strange humming sound, but Betty could not understand what they were saying.

For the first time now, in the illuminated room, Betty could get a clear idea of what they looked like. Her impression was that most were not over five feet tall. Their heads were wide at the top, narrowing down markedly toward the chin. The skin was a bluish gray, perhaps a little whiter than that. The bodies seemed out of proportion, with large broad chests and short spidery legs. For some reason, she didn't notice the clothing—except that it seemed like a tight-fitting uniform. There were no buttons or zippers evident.

Most prominent of all were the eyes. They were extremely large, almost catlike, with clearly defined pupils, and they moved as human eyes do. There was a form of lips: a thin membrane that did not seem to open when the humming sound was made.

Along the walls of the room was what looked like a battery of electronic instruments, but far stranger and more complex ones than the EEGs and EKGs Betty had encountered.

The two leaders—she came to identify them as the leader and the examiner—placed her on the stool without communicating with her. She somehow felt more confident with these two, sensing they were more intelligent than the other crew members, now out in the hallway. Without ceremony, the leader and the examiner pushed up the sleeve of her dress and began intently studying the skin of her arm. They rubbed it briskly, as if it were a strange foreign material, then turned her arm over and examined the other side. As they did, they made sounds to each other, but again Betty could not understand anything they were saying.

In a moment they brought over an instrument that looked like a microscope with an extraordinarily large lens and examined the surface of her skin. Shortly afterward they took something resembling a letter opener and scraped the upper part of her arm. Some particles of skin flaked off, which they placed on a piece of transparent plastic. The examiner then rolled the plastic up and put it in a drawer.

Although Betty was still frightened, she was beginning to calm down under the influence of the leader and examiner. Her mind was hazy, but she was fighting to keep it clear so that she could observe what was happening to her. She felt them place her head in some sort of brace or bracket behind her. It held her head firmly as the examiner peered into her eyes with a light, very much in the style of an ophthalmologist. Then he opened her mouth and carefully inspected her throat and teeth. The examination of her ears followed. A swab of some sort was used to remove a smear from them, which again was rolled up in the plastic material and put in the drawer.

Betty had little idea of how long this was taking; she had lost all sense of time. The two men were working swiftly and efficiently, still without comment to her and with only the obscure humming between themselves. Next came the examination of her hair. The examiner ran his strange clawlike hands through the hair at the back of her neck. He pulled out several strands and handed them to the leader, who wrapped them and placed them in the drawer.

Working with the same methodical precision, the leader probed Betty's neck, chin, shoulders and collarbone, in addition to running an instrument under her fingernails and taking a sample. The light in the room was intensely bright, and Betty opened her eyes at fewer intervals, partly because of the brightness and partly because the appearance of the un-human creatures was hard to bear.

The foot examination was next—part of the process that so closely paralleled a full medical examination. They took off her shoes and began a careful probe of her feet and toes. Then the examiner spoke directly to Betty for the first time. Through the same semitranslation process that ended up as English in Betty's mind, he told her that he was now going to examine her nervous system.

Betty was beginning to get irritated by this invasion of her privacy. At that moment she was instructed to take off her dress.

The dress had a zipper down the back, and before Betty knew it, the examiner had unzipped it and removed the dress. In moments she was moved from the stool and placed on her back on the examining table. Another instrument that looked like a cluster of needles was brought over. Each needle had a wire running from it to a computer screen where various wavy lines were visible.

The examiner moved the needles behind her ears, along her neck and on various parts of her scalp. She felt no pain, and the only noticeable response came from his placing the instrument on her knee, where the usual reflex reaction took place: her leg jumped. After sitting her up and probing down her back, both the leader and the examiner seemed satisfied with their examination and eased her back down on the table.

Betty opened her eyes again at this point and looked up. She was startled to see the examiner coming toward her with a large needle, a needle larger than any she had ever seen. She shuddered with fear and quickly closed her eyes.

A BRIEF GLIMPSE before closing his eyes again had told Barney that the room they were leading him into appeared to have pale blue walls and was spotless. Those catlike eyes seen through the binoculars still burned in his mind. They seemed to keep telling him to stay calm, that he would not be harmed. But even in his daze he was frustrated. How could those eyes communicate with him? He was hearing a voice plainly in English within him, and it was not his voice. Fragmented thoughts filled his mind: the feeling of the tops of his shoes being dragged over an apparent bulkhead; the craft glowing on the ground, looking as big as the moon; the feeling of weakness and total submission overcoming him as the creatures approached the stalled car; the snap of the binocular strap when he wrenched it from his neck; the irresistible power of the eyes pulling him toward the craft as it hovered over the field; the firm instruction to keep his eyes closed, which he sometimes failed to follow; the humming sound as the crew members talked among themselves.

Now he was lying on his back on a table in what seemed to be an operating room. He was afraid to open his eyes because the message not to again came through clearly. He felt weak and somnambulistic. He wanted to ball his hands into fists and strike out, yet he was powerless to do so. He felt relaxed and frightened at the same time.

He was aware that his feet extended over the edge of the table, and he felt his shoes being removed. The humming sound of the voices continued in his ears. They turned him over on his stomach and Barney felt them examining his spinal column, as if counting his vertebrae. They were using their fingers, but strange fingers that felt long and clawlike, making him shudder at every touch. They moved up and down his back, and finally one was pressed at the base of his spine. He wanted to fight back more than ever, but he could not.

In his dazed state Barney wondered where Betty was, but could do nothing about it. He was suddenly turned over on his back again, and he felt two fingers pull his mouth open. He wanted to raise his eyelids, but could not. He felt some sort of instrument scratch the skin of his left arm. He sensed that there were three or more of the crew in the room, but only one seemed to be conducting the examination.

The fragmented images he'd had of the crew went through his head: the large cranium and small chin; the eyes that swept to the sides of the head in oriental fashion, but far wider, so that it appeared the lateral vision was greater than normal. The mouth, too, puzzled him. It seemed to be one horizontal line with a short perpendicular line at each end. He felt he had seen it part slightly at one moment, when the humming sound came out, but it appeared to be a closed membrane rather than an opening. There did not seem to be a nose—just two slits representing the nostrils. He had failed to notice any hair—or headgear. All these details had penetrated Barney's hazy state, yet he had no strength, or even will, to resist what was taking place.

As the examiner probed in Barney's mouth, Barney felt him slide his fingers across the bridge of his two false teeth. They were removed, and Barney sensed confusion in the room. He was not alert enough at the time to know whether or not his false teeth had caused puzzlement among his abductors. He simply waited for what was going to happen next.

He did not have long to wait. He felt them taking down his trousers to expose his groin. Barney shuddered, but could do absolutely nothing. The voice—whatever it was and wherever it was coming from—continued to assure him that he would not be harmed. Then he felt a cold sensation in the area of his genitals. He wasn't sure, but it seemed as if they were putting some kind of metal cup over them and the lower part of his stomach. Now he was telling himself that if he kept very quiet and still, he would not be harmed.

But the sensation of the cup, although it actually did not hurt, was terrifying. He wanted to cry out and tell them not to do it, but he could not speak. What were they doing? Were they drawing out sperm? And if so, why? He thought of God and Jesus, and began to pray. Somehow he had to get through this, he had to get free.

ALL THROUGH THE EARLY part of her examination Betty Hill had the feeling that her captors were working with remarkable efficiency. The ones she had designated as the leader and the examiner seemed more proficient and intelligent than the others, and what little communication she had with them was smoother and more understandable than with those who had led her up into the craft. Both seemed very concerned about her fears and were constantly trying to reassure her that the ordeal would be over very soon.

But when the examiner approached her with what appeared to be a six-inch-long needle, she was again gripped with fear. The previous tests had been bad enough, if only because of the grotesque appearance of the aliens. Now there was a clear and immediate threat as the examiner drew the needle near her navel. Betty tried to fight, to squirm away, but in her hazy state she wasn't able to move. She called out and asked them what they were going to do.

The examiner responded by telling her that it was just a simple test they would be making through the navel, that it would be over quickly, that there was nothing to worry about. Betty broke out crying, screaming that it would hurt and pleading with him not to do it. But without hesitation, the examiner plunged the needle deeply into the navel. Betty cried in anguish, "It's hurting, it's hurting. Please take it out, please!"

The pain was more like that of a knife than of a needle.

Quickly the leader came to the table. He rubbed his hand over her eyes and told her she would be all right, she would not feel the pain at all. Just as quickly, the pain stopped. The moment the leader's hand went across her eyes, Betty felt relaxed. All her fear left her. She began to have confidence in the leader, to trust him.

But her curiosity had not stopped. After the needle was withdrawn, she asked what the test was for. She was told that it was a simple pregnancy test. Betty didn't tell them that she was unable to have children because of an operation, and she almost laughed at his explanation anyway. In her job as a social worker she was aware of many types of medical tests relating to childbearing. To her knowledge, no doctor in his right mind would explore a possible fetus by driving a needle through the abdomen. The idea was absurd, and she said, "I don't know what you expect, but there is no such pregnancy test like this."

Her remark was ignored, but Betty was grateful that the pain was gone, and that the leader had taken immediate steps to stop it. The examiner gave her her shoes, helped her put her dress back on, and then went out into the corridor and turned toward Barney's room on the right. There had been no sexual advances of any kind.

Left alone with the leader, Betty asked if she could go back to the car. She was told that she could as soon as Barney was ready, but that they had not finished examining him yet. Now that she was relaxed and calm, Betty felt she could easily put up with the waiting. Her new respect for the leader after he had saved her from the pain of the needle made it that much easier. Finding she could keep her eyes open now, she glanced around the strange room. There was a complete absence of color in it, and it was illuminated by a bright light, the source of which she could not determine, except for one bluish overhead light that seemed more a supplementary than primary source. The equipment was located in one corner of the room—a strange assortment of instruments that Betty could not fathom, some of which were mounted in the wall.

Her relief at the examination being over helped dissipate the strangeness of both the craft and the creature she was now facing alone in the room. He was not a man, there was no question about that. Although definitely a humanoid, he was physically alien to anything Betty had ever dreamed of. Yet because she sensed his intelligence, his lack of hostility, his kindness in relieving her pain, there was a feeling of normalcy that alleviated her concerns.

Betty's curiosity continued to be overwhelming. Dozens of questions she wanted to ask rushed through her mind. She was now ready to ask them, in spite of the strange form of communication they had been using. She was certain that he had *not* been speaking English, but whatever he was saying to her seemed like English.

As the leader appeared to be adjusting or putting away some of the instruments, Betty remarked that this had been an incredible experience, something she had never in her life been through before. As she spoke, she was a little surprised that she was able to use such a normal conversational tone of voice in such an abnormal situation. She was equally surprised by the informal attitude of this strange creature, who responded as if they were having a chat over a cup of tea.

The leader told her that he knew she and Barney had been badly frightened when they had been brought aboard, and he regretted that. He wanted to do all he could to alleviate their fear. Betty responded by saying that she was now completely recovered and was actually enjoying this chance to talk with him, that there were so many questions she wanted to ask. In a manner she found very pleasant, the leader agreed to try to answer her questions.

But at that moment some of the crew came into Betty's examination room in apparent excitement. They were communicating with the leader in sounds she could not understand. The leader suddenly left her room with the others, and Betty became frightened that something had gone wrong during Barney's examination.

Shortly afterward, however, the leader came back. He opened her mouth and began touching her teeth. One by one, he tried to wiggle them. It even seemed as if he wanted to dislodge them. But he stopped the examination and stated that he was puzzled: some of Barney's teeth were removable, and hers were not. In moments the examiner came in from Barney's room and repeated the process. He was also puzzled. Betty was amused, and explained that Barney had dentures because some of his teeth had been removed, but none of hers had been. Neither the leader nor the examiner seemed able to take this in.

Betty tried to explain that when people got older, they often had to have teeth removed and replaced by dentures. This created more consternation on the part of the leader. He wanted to know what "older" meant. Betty had some difficulty in explaining this to him. She tried to point out that old age meant a progression in years in which the body functions slowed down. She added that a life span could run as long as a hundred or so years, but that most people died earlier from degeneration or disease, or from accidents and illnesses at all ages.

The leader seemed completely puzzled by the idea of a life span and the reference to years. Betty confessed she did not know exactly how it had been figured out, but it had something to do with the number of days, and the days had so many hours, and the hours had so many minutes and the minutes had so many seconds—depending on the rotation of the earth, the positions of the planets around the sun, the seasons and so forth.

She was wearing her watch, and she tried to point out to him the hours from twelve to twelve and the segments in between. He did not appear to understand what she was saying. She tried to explain wrinkles and aging, but without success.

All the time she was talking, she was aware of how ridiculous it was for them to be communicating in English, without him ever speaking. But whatever was happening, they *were* communicating.

The conversation took a turn when the leader asked her what she ate. Betty explained that people ate meat, potatoes and other vegetables, milk, and different foods. This immediately brought forth the question: "What are vegetables?" Betty told him that this was a broad term used to cover a great variety of a certain kind of food, that there were too many to explain them all.

But the leader revealed his curiosity. He wanted to know if there was one special vegetable that Betty liked. She told him that she liked a great many, but that her favorite was squash. The leader wanted to know more about that. Betty told him that it was usually yellow in color. This elicited another question: "What is yellow?"

Betty looked around the room. There was nothing yellow in it, nor was there anything of a rich, bright color that she could use to illustrate it. Nor was she wearing anything yellow or particularly colorful. She tried to explain that it was a bright color, that we considered sunlight yellow.

Her frustration was growing. There was no sense talking more about vegetables because she couldn't explain them without demonstrating, and there was nothing with which to demonstrate. Then the subject shifted to the earth and its place in relation to the other stars or planets. "All these things you ask me—" she said, "I am a very limited person when trying to talk to you. But there are other people in the country who are not like me. They would be happy to talk to you, and could answer all your questions. And if you came back, maybe all your questions could be answered."

Betty was now reassured enough to actually want to meet the leader again if he did come back. She told him so and indicated that she would have to know where she should arrange to be for such an encounter. The leader seemed amused. He assured her that if they did decide to come back, they would be able to find her. Betty felt the rapport between them increasing. Her anxieties had lifted by now, and she was firmly convinced that neither she nor Barney would be harmed or kept captive.

Getting back to the utter unbelievability of her situation, Betty indicated to the leader that no one anywhere in the world knew that such a craft and such a crew existed, and that she would be unable to convince anyone of her experience. She wanted to know if he could supply some kind of proof of this, clear evidence that she could show people when she was released. The leader again seemed amused, and asked her what she had in mind.

Betty looked around. She asked if there was something from the craft that she could take with her. She was told to see what she could find. There wasn't much other than the fixed instruments, but she noticed for the first time that there was a rather large book on a cabinet, almost the size of a dictionary. She asked if she could open it, and was told she could. Inside, it had many pages inscribed with a kind of writing she had never seen before. The hieroglyphic characters were not arranged horizontally; they ran up and down. Yet they were not oriental. There were straight lines, curved lines—some thin, some medium, some very heavy—and dots.

The leader indicated that Betty would be totally unable to read the material, but Betty insisted that she did not want it for the content, but as proof of the experience. She was surprised and pleased when he told her she could have it. It was more than she had hoped for, a completely unearthlike trophy.

Now, wanting to know more than ever where the craft had come from, she asked him. He countered by asking if she knew anything about the stellar systems. She told him what she knew from school: that the sun was the center of the solar system, and that there were nine planets. She also spoke of reading a book by the Harvard astronomer Harlow Shapley and studying photographs in it of the millions of stars and galaxies.

At that, the leader moved to a part of the wall and revealed a wide oblong chart that appeared to be of a star system—one that was unrecognizable to Betty. Some of the dots representing stars were pinpoints; others were as large as a nickel. The chart seemed to be three-dimensional. There were curved lines connecting some of the dots, broken lines connecting others, and one larger circle that had a lot of heavier unbroken lines going out from it.

When Betty asked the leader what these lines were, he told her the heavy lines were trade routes; the thinner but still solid lines were to places they went occasionally; finally, the dotted lines were where expeditions had been sent. Betty asked where his home "port" was, and he indicated to her that if she didn't know where the earth was in relation to the chart, there wouldn't be any point in trying to show her where he was from. He closed the chart from her view and refused to open it again when she requested him to do so. Betty comforted herself by thinking that at least she would be able to take the strange book with her when she left the craft. As she picked it up and held it, she heard sounds coming from the corridor in the direction of Barney's room.

ON HIS EXAMINING table Barney could feel the examiner removing the bowllike instrument from the area of his groin. He still did not dare to open his eyes, but the discomfort and terror of the experience seemed to stop once the instrument was removed. Nonetheless, he was immensely relieved when he felt his shoes being put back on. He was helped as he stepped down from the table, still in a dazed state, his eyes closed. As he was led into the corridor and toward the bulkhead door, he could sense the outside night air rushing at him. There seemed to be a distinct difference between the atmosphere inside and outside the craft. He still had no idea where Betty was, but in his hazy condition he was convinced that she was all right.

FROM THE DOORWAY of her examining room Betty watched as the crew members guided Barney along the corridor. The leader and another one of the crew members led her out into the corridor also, stopping Barney to let her move ahead of him. She saw him there with great relief, but his eyes were still shut and he was in the somnambulistic state he had been in when they were taken aboard the craft. Clutching the book in her arms, Betty was led toward the open bulkhead door. For a moment there was some commotion among the crew members, and Betty was halted in the process. Then the leader came over and said that he had to take the book away.

Betty was furious. To her, a promise had been broken, and she protested vigorously, claiming it was the only proof she had. She was told firmly, but not unkindly, that this was the reason she was being prohibited from taking it. "You are not to remember what has happened here," he said. "You are to forget about it completely."

Betty became more riled. "I *won't* forget about it," she said. "You can take the book, but you can never, never, never make me forget about it. I'll remember this experience if it's the last thing I do!"

The leader seemed amused at her anger. "Maybe you will remember," he told her. "I don't know. But I hope you don't. And it won't do you any good if you do, because Barney won't. Barney probably won't remember a single thing. And if he should remember anything at all, he is going to remember it differently from you. And all you are going to do is to get each other so confused you will not know what to do. If you do remember, it will be better if you decide to forget it anyway."

Betty would not give in. "Why?" she asked. "Are you trying to threaten me? Because you can't scare me, because I won't forget. I will remember it somehow."

Betty was standing beside the doorway to the ramp. During her discussion with the leader the other crew members had taken Barney past her and down the ramp. Then she, too, was escorted down to the path in the woods that they had taken earlier. The walk seemed much shorter than it had on the way up to the craft. Something was bothering Betty and suddenly she realized what it was. At some point during her talk with the leader she had heard the phrase "Wait a minute—" This was inconsistent. How could he have said that if he didn't know what time itself was? It was a nagging question, but she put it out of her mind. There were many other inexplicable things more complicated than that.

Near the car the leader and the rest of the crew stopped. The leader turned to her and said, "I am going to leave you here. Why don't you stand by the side of the car and watch us leave?"

Betty said, "I would like that if we are not in danger from it."

Then the leader apologized and said he was sorry that she had been so frightened in the beginning. Betty indicated that she was not frightened now, that she was relieved and even exhilarated in spite of the loss of the book. She told him it had been an amazing experience, and she hoped that somehow they would meet again. Maybe he would come back. He said he would try. Then the leader and the other crew members turned and started toward the craft.

AHEAD OF BETTY in the corridor, Barney had been too dazed to be aware of much of anything. He had felt his shoes again being dragged over the top of the bulkhead, and himself being taken down the ramp. Then he seemed to be walking on rough ground. On opening his eyes, he was surprised to find himself utterly alone. His mind was a complete blank; there was no memory at all of how he had gotten where he was. He thought: I must have walked into the woods to take a break from driving. That's what must have happened. I'll just go back to the car.

The car was sitting by the side of the road with the lights and motor turned off. This struck Barney as odd. He didn't usually turn off the lights and motor when he took a brief roadside rest stop. He opened the driver's door and got in. As he did so, he found himself sitting on top of the tire wrench. That's funny, he wondered. How did the tire wrench get here on the front seat? He pulled it from under him and placed it in the well between the door and the seat.

Then he heard Delsey whimpering. She was cowering under the front seat. His mind was terribly foggy and he was groping for full consciousness. He could not seem to get it back. The sound of Delsey was also strange. He had assumed that Betty had taken the dog for a walk in the woods. Trying to clear his head, he started the car and turned the headlights on. Then, looking up, he saw Betty coming down the path in the woods. She was alone. Now he reasoned that he had stopped the car by the side of the road at Betty's request. And yet strange, elusive and undefined images faded in and out of his mind.

BETTY SAW BARNEY sitting behind the wheel. She noticed that his eyes were open but he was in a dazed condition. Still, he seemed to be more normal than when she had seen him back in the corridor of the craft. She opened the door on the passenger side and saw Delsey sitting on the seat of the car. The dog was trembling badly. Betty quickly picked her up and cradled her. "Don't be afraid, Delsey," she said. "There's nothing to be afraid of." Then she turned to Barney and said, "Come out and watch it leave."

Barney thought: That's ridiculous. Watch *what* leave? But he decided to humor her. He got out and stood beside her by the car, and both of them looked up the path toward the craft. Once again, sitting on end and glowing a luminous orange, it looked like a large moon. But it was nothing like a normal moon, this enormous disc that was changing to a silvery color and slowly beginning to roll. They watched in amazement as the huge swirling disc lifted off the ground, and then with tremendous speed faded into a pinpoint of silvery light and disappeared. Barney felt both a sense of elation and a sense of fear. Half to himself, he said, "I'm *never* going to tell anybody about this. Never."

Betty said, "Now do you believe in flying saucers, Barney?"

"Don't be ridiculous, Betty," he replied.

In his haziness he put the car into gear and began to drive toward what he hoped was Route 3. Fragmented images of his experience floated like bobbing corks to his consciousness, then disappeared again. But a sense of elation and relief remained with him. "That's the funniest thing, Betty," he said. "I never believed in flying saucers—but I don't know. It's too ridiculous, isn't it? Wonder where they came from? Maybe this will prove the existence of God."

They drove on in silence. The road wound and twisted, and Barney was able to follow it, even able to feel that at one moment he was back on Route 3. Then suddenly both of them heard the strange beeping sound again. Beep-beep—beep-beep-beep. With that sound—the same sound that had buzzed the car at Indian Head—Barney and Betty seemed to return to full consciousness. It surprised both of them. They tried to put things back together, to communicate with each other with clear minds, but it was inordinately difficult. They were not even sure where they were. Their last distinct memory was at Indian Head, beside the road, when the craft had hovered over the field. Even that memory was foggy.

Suddenly Barney saw a sign on the road. It read: CONCORD—17 MILES. Now he knew where they were. But it was a long way from Indian Head—forty miles or so. His head had cleared at the sound of the beeps, but his recall of the abduction part of the encounter had been totally wiped out.

They drove on toward Concord, saying little. They did decide, though, that their now-conscious memory of the beginning of the experience at Indian Head was so strange, so unbelievable, that they would tell no one about it. "No one would believe it anyway," Barney said. "I find it hard to believe myself."

Betty agreed. Near Concord, they looked for a place to have a cup of coffee, but nothing was open. Still groggy and uncommunicative, they plowed on, turning east on Route 4 and moving across the state toward the ocean and Portsmouth.

Just outside Portsmouth they noticed dawn streaking the sky in the east. As they drove through the streets of the slumbering city, no one was stirring. The birds were already chattering, though, and it was nearly full daylight when they pulled up in front of their home at 953 State Street. Barney looked at his watch, but it had stopped running. Shortly afterward Betty looked at hers, which had also stopped. Inside, the kitchen clock read just after five. "It looks," said Barney, "like we've arrived home a little later than expected."

Betty took Delsey out on her leash for a morning airing, while Barney unloaded the car. The birds were in full chorus now, a background for Betty's still haunted thoughts of the night before. Barney, too, was thoughtful. They said little. For a reason she couldn't pinpoint, Betty asked him to put the luggage on the back porch instead of bringing it into the house. Barney complied, and then went out to unload the rest of the car. Picking up the binoculars, he noticed for the first time that the leather strap, which had been around his neck the night before, was freshly and cleanly broken in half. He had no recollection whatever of that happening.

From Concord on down, during the silent drive, both Betty and Barney had looked to the sky at regular intervals, wondering if the strange object would appear again. Even after they went into their house, a red frame structure on a small lot in Portsmouth, they found themselves occasionally going to the windows to look up at the morning sky.

Both had a strange, clammy feeling. They sat down at the kitchen table over a freshly brewed cup of coffee, but not before Barney went into the bathroom to examine his lower abdomen, which, for no reason he could explain or recall, was bothering him. The question as to why he made this examination continued to plague him over the years that followed.

When Barney came out of the bathroom, he and Betty reviewed the events of the night before. The latter part of the trip was extremely vague; they couldn't recall much of anything from Indian Head to the sign to Concord. They had fragmentary recollections of going through Plymouth, north of the second series of beeps. Barney was baffled by the absence of sound from the craft. He was still trying to classify it as a known aircraft in spite of the foreign appearance, the otherworldly feeling it had created in them.

They mulled over the two distinct series of beeps. But the sandwich of missing time in between was tantalizing. Betty, with the aid of a strong cup of coffee, could faintly recall some of the things that had happened right after Indian Head. She remembered seeing a road marker that divided the towns of Lincoln and North Woodstock, but it was a flashing and momentary impression. She recalled passing a store in North Woodstock, and then, later, a large, luminous moon-shape, which seemed to be touching the roadside, sitting on end under some pines. Betty, straining to remember, thought that Barney had made a sharp left turn from Route 3, but could not in any way identify where this had been. She recalled her reaction to Barney's denial that the moon-shaped craft could be an unidentified flying object. She thought: That's the way Barney is. If something frightens him, or he doesn't like it, he just says to himself that it never happened. Barney agreed with her that he sometimes did this.

They collapsed into bed after a light breakfast, and their sleep was undisturbed. They were hoping that the incident would fade quickly from their minds and remain only an interesting anecdote that they might someday tell someone. They were unaware that it would affect their lives profoundly for many years to come.

CHAPTER THREE

SOME TEN DAYS after the sighting Betty began having a series of vivid dreams. They continued for five successive nights. Never in her memory had she recalled dreams of such detail and intensity. They dominated her waking life during that week and the memory of them continued to plague her afterward, even though the dreams themselves stopped abruptly after five days. In a sense, they assumed the proportion of nightmares. They were so awesome and of such magnitude that she hesitated to mention them to Barney, who was working those five nights and therefore not with her when the dreams took place. When she eventually did mention rather casually that she was having a series of nightmares, Barney was sympathetic but not too concerned.

Realizing that Barney was attempting to put the UFO event out of his mind, Betty refrained from discussing the nightmares with him. But she did tell a few close friends, one of whom was a fellow social worker, who urged her to write down her dreams. Feeling that this might relieve her conscious preoccupation with them, she sat down at her typewriter and wrote.

In her dreams Betty encountered a strange roadblock on a lonely New Hampshire road as a group of men approached the car. The men were dressed alike. As soon as they reached the car, she slipped into unconsciousness. She awoke to find herself and Barney being taken aboard a wholly strange craft, where she was given a complete physical examination by intelligent humanoid beings. Barney was taken off down a corridor, curving to the contour of the ship, for apparently the same reason. They were assured, in the dream, that no harm would come to them and that they would be released without any conscious memory of the strange episode.

A few weeks later another puzzling incident occurred that neither

Barney nor Betty could explain. They were driving through the sparsely populated countryside near Portsmouth when they noticed a parked car partially blocking the road ahead. A group of people were standing outside the car, and Barney began to slow down gradually to avoid an accident.

Suddenly Betty was overcome with fear. She could not explain it, even to herself. "Barney," she said. "Barney—keep going. Please don't slow down. Keep going, keep going!" And she found herself starting to open the car door on the passenger side, with an almost uncontrollable impulse to jump out and run.

Barney was startled and tried to find out what was wrong. Betty was nearing a state of panic. Without asking any more questions, he speeded up as fast as was practicable with people partially blocking the road, and Betty recovered her equilibrium. What disturbed her most was that she was not at all inclined to be this emotional; she had never before experienced such a sensation.

The impact of this unexplainable incident stayed with them for many days afterward, along with the lingering effect of the nightmares on Betty.

One day in March of 1962 Betty had lunch with Gail Peabody, a friend of hers who was a state probation officer and in whom Betty had full confidence. During the lunch Betty mentioned the idea of trying hypnosis to recreate the lost time, and Gail responded promptly by recommending a psychiatrist who was medical director of a private sanatorium in Georgetown, Massachusetts, about thirty miles from Portsmouth.

On March 12, 1962, Betty typed a letter to the doctor, Patrick J. Quirke, and Betty and Barney's interview with him took place on March 25, at eleven in the morning.

"At no time did I feel uncomfortable," Barney said. "The doctor sat across from us at his desk, while we sat in comfortable chairs, and I felt relieved to talk to this man about our experience, particularly since he did not look at it as if we were two persons talking about an obvious hallucination—and he was giving his professional attention to it. He acknowledged that we had had an unusual experience, but he felt that we might gradually begin to remember some of the missing things, since we had probably suppressed much of the experience as a protective device. He felt that at this stage it might not be a good idea to explore this block of mine and Betty's disturbing reactions, forcibly at least."

The decision was to postpone any action at the time, but that if problems should persist, then therapy might be indicated.

THE LONG COMMUTING drive from Portsmouth to Boston, a night work schedule, the separation from his sons, who were living in Philadelphia with his former wife, the doubts about the Indian Head experience and a recurring problem with ulcers all began to take their toll on Barney. His condition was further complicated by high blood pressure, which he could not successfully lower without the removal of the other problems. Another disturbing symptom began at this time, more of an annoyance than anything else: A series of warts developed in an almost geometrically perfect semicircle in the area of his groin. While they were a minor problem, they added to his concern.

By the summer of 1962 Barney's exhaustion and general malaise prompted him to seek a psychiatrist for his overall condition. He did not associate his need for therapy with the UFO incident, feeling mainly that the conflict over his relationship with his two sons in Philadelphia was the basis of his problem, the long distance making it impossible for him to be a full-time father.

His physician recommended a distinguished psychiatrist in nearby Exeter, New Hampshire, Dr. Duncan Stephens, and the process of therapy began during the summer of 1962.

At first, the incident at Indian Head was ignored altogether by Barney. But as he examined scenes from his past, his curiosity grew regarding his violent reaction to the craft that had hovered over him in the sky at Indian Head. What confused Barney most about the incident was that he was not inclined to panic, not afraid of facing a traumatic crisis. This attitude was reflected when, carrying his binoculars, he had walked steadily across the road and out onto the field toward the enormous object on the night of September 19, 1961. It was not until he had put the binoculars to his eyes and focused on the craft that he had panicked and run back to the car. The unexplained panic, which he knew to be foreign to his general reactions, plagued him, in addition to the curtain of blankness that had descended with the beeps.

ONE EVENING IN September 1963, over a year after Barney had begun seeing Dr. Stephens, the Hills were invited by their church discussion group to relate their experience with the UFO in the White Mountains. They had mentioned the incident to their minister, who along with others in the church had a growing curiosity about the subject in light of increasing unidentified flying object reports throughout New England, especially in New Hampshire and Vermont. The Hills had mixed feelings about the idea, as usual, although Betty was now becoming convinced that their story should be told. If it should represent a landmark in the history of the phenomenon, did they have a right to confine it to themselves?

At this group meeting was another invited speaker, Captain Ben H. Swett, from the nearby Pease Air Force Base, who was well known in the area for his study of hypnosis, a subject which, together with the story the Hills would tell, might make up an interesting evening.

"After the captain listened to our story—as much as we could tell with the blanking out of memory that took place at that moment at Indian Head—he was interested that the account was cut off as if by a cleaver at that point," Barney recalled. "We mentioned the fact that various people had recommended hypnosis, and as a man well acquainted with it himself, the captain agreed that it might be a good idea, especially if it were conducted by a psychiatrist. Hypnosis is indicated as a course of action to recover lost memory, but as a layman, Captain Swett told us, he wouldn't dream of doing it himself. We, too, were aware of the danger of indiscriminate hypnosis. But it did stimulate our interest in the idea, which had been dormant for a long time."

At his next session with Dr. Stephens, Barney brought up the subject of hypnosis. The doctor found it advisable at this point to have the opinion of the well-known Boston psychiatrist and neurologist Dr. Benjamin Simon.

IN HIS OFFICE on Bay State Road in Boston Dr. Simon received a call from Barney Hill early in December of 1963 and set up an appointment for a consultation at eight a.m. on December 14. Barney and Betty left Portsmouth well before seven o'clock the morning of the fourteenth. They approached the consultation with mingled feelings of curiosity, nervousness and some apprehension, although these feelings were tempered by relief at taking a decisive step in a direction they thought would help.

Dr. Simon was aware that Barney had been undergoing therapy for his anxiety state and that it was increasingly apparent that the experience with the unidentified flying object was an important factor in his condition. He was similarly aware of the nightmares leading to Betty's anxiety. It became quickly apparent that both Barney and Betty needed treatment.

Dr. Simon instructed the Hills that they would not remember anything they revealed under hypnosis unless they were directed to. Until he had the whole story and could assess its emotional effect, he was careful to make sure that the amnesia was reinstated after each session. His war experiences with battle amnesia had clearly shown that the conscious mind is often incapable of withstanding the traumatic shock of repressed events. The reinstatement of amnesia after each session also prevented communication between the Hills on the subject, thus avoiding distortions that might arise from their discussing material revealed under hypnosis.

It was not until after a number of introductory sessions and five sessions of intensive regressive hypnosis, during which the Hills independently told the story of their abduction, that on March 21, 1964, the doctor finally permitted them to recall part of what they had revealed. Then they were directed to remember only those things that didn't trouble them. Barney recalled two years after the therapy that no major part of the repressed material came through at this point. There seemed to be only leaks or flashes of recall.

During their March 28 session, for the purpose of reinforcement, Dr. Simon put both the Hills into a trance and reemphasized that they would continue to remember only aspects of their experiences that were tolerable to them. He also indicated that in the near future, if the Hills were willing, they would be permitted to hear the playback of the recordings, so that the complete experience—not just fragments—would be relived on a conscious level.

To Betty and Barney, the chance to hear recorded experiences marked a milestone in their treatment. They reacted with intense curiosity—and some apprehension.

"When I first began hearing my voice under hypnosis," Barney later described their session of April 4, "I was lifted out of my seat. I couldn't believe it. I knew it was my voice, but it was difficult for me to understand that this was me, saying that this had actually happened. It was as if I had been asleep and had talked in my sleep. I wasn't concerned about the first part of the tapes—coming down through Canada, and the first part of our leg through upper New Hampshire. I had remembered practically all this detail consciously. But as the tapes moved along toward Indian Head, I didn't know what was going to happen. I could feel my stomach churning, my muscles tightening. I just didn't know what to expect. I know I sat on the edge of my chair, shifting my position frequently.

"Every once in a while, I would look over at Betty. And she has a way of looking at me and being reassuring. It's sort of a look that she can give, almost to say, 'I'm in love with you, Barney.' And I felt this reassurance. And it helped.

"I think you can say the best description was that I was numb as I listened. Information was flooding back into my mind, but my emotions were numb. I continued to feel that if it became too distressing, the doctor would be able to control it.

"And then, as the tapes went deeper and deeper into the part I had never remembered, there was the feeling as if heavy chains were lifted off my shoulders. I felt that I need no longer suffer the anxieties of wondering what [had] happened."

CHAPTER FOUR

WHEN I FIRST ARRANGED with the doctor and the Hills to listen to the regressive hypnosis tapes, I was not at all sure I wanted to write the story. On the surface, the events were simply unacceptable. If the sighting and abduction were true, they would have a greater impact on history than almost any recorded event. Therefore it was reasonable to assume that they were not true. If they were not true, then I didn't want to write about the case—except possibly as one of the most unusual in psychiatric history. Either way, I was very wary of putting myself in a position where my credibility as a journalist could be challenged.

And yet I found myself inexorably drawn to the story. So, in fact, were the editors of *Look*. In listening to a portion of the tapes, the intensity of emotion revealed by the Hills as they relived the experience was so vivid and gripping that there seemed to be little doubt that the Hills, at least, believed fully they were experiencing a trauma that was bitingly real.

I finally took the position that I would assess every detail in an attempt to prove that it was *not* true. I would look for those false notes and discrepancies as intensely as the doctor had in his medical probe. I would look for rational alternative explanations. But the main question in my mind was: Could I rule the story out completely? The most important factor going for the story was Dr. Simon's clinical appraisal that the Hills were not lying, not hallucinating and not psychotic. This was both puzzling and provocative.

I began the long series of sessions with Dr. Simon in 1965, four years after the original sighting by the Hills, and two years after the Hills had undergone their treatments with him. The forty hours of tape recordings of the regressive hypnosis were stacked neatly in a rack beside the doctor's tape deck. As Dr. Simon prepared the tape of Barney's first session under hypnosis, my anticipation was high. I had never had any direct experience with hypnosis, and was very curious about it.

"Just how did you go about this technique with Barney and Betty?" I asked.

"There's nothing mysterious about it, really," Dr. Simon said. "Hypnosis is based on suggestion. The patient is carefully brought into a condition that's halfway between sleep and waking. His memory becomes razor-sharp. His unconscious is exposed. He may go into a light trance, or a deep trance as Barney and Betty did. They were exceptionally good subjects. Otherwise, I would have used sodium amobarbital or pentothal. They achieve the same results. But the patient takes a long time to come out of them, and the drugs are much harder to control."

"Those are the truth serums?" I asked.

"So-called," said the doctor. "But absolutely no different in effect than hypnosis on a good subject."

Dr. Simon pushed the start button on his tape recorder, and Barney, already in a trance state, was speaking. What was at first obvious was the flat, dull, somnambulistic tone of his voice. It was almost eerie, not at all like his lively tone when he talked naturally.

His phrasing was precise, unemotional at first, the sound of a robot. He was in the process of reliving the drive down Route 3 the night of the sighting. As he got closer to Indian Head, however, his voice became more animated, more intense.

DR. SIMON: *(On the tape.)* You're in a deep sleep. You are comfortable, relaxed. This is not going to trouble you. Go on. You can remember everything now.

BARNEY: *(His voice is now measurably excited.)* It's over my right! God! What is it? *(His voice begins to tremble.)* And I am trying to maintain control, so Betty cannot tell I am *scared. God,* I'm scared!

DR. SIMON: *(His voice is very calm and firm in the face of Barney's rising emotion.)* It's all right. You can go right on, experience it. It will not hurt you now.

BARNEY: *(He breaks into breathless sobbing, then screams.)* I gotta get a weapon! *(He screams again, as his sobs become uncontrollable.)*

The doctor stopped the recorder and spoke to me. "What happened here," he said, "is that I was faced with a hard decision. Barney literally leaped off his chair at this point, and I had to guide him back into it. I had to decide quickly whether to impose an amnesia on him and bring him out of the trance, or to keep him moving through the experience for what is called an abreaction—a discharge of feeling—which could be cathartic and helpful for his anxiety symptoms."

I was almost reluctant to have the doctor start up the tape recorder again, the scene was so chilling. But of course I asked him to continue. He did so.

DR. SIMON: Go to sleep. You can forget now. You've forgotten. *(He is providing Barney with momentary relief.)* You're calm now. Relaxed. Deeply relaxed. You do not have to make an outcry. But you can remember it now. Keep remembering. You feel you have to get a weapon.

BARNEY: *(Still breathing heavily.)* Yes.

DR. SIMON: This is going to harm you, you felt.

BARNEY: *(Still excited.)* Yes. I open the trunk of my car. I get the tire wrench . . . part of the jack. *(Again his panic seems to be rising.)*

DR. SIMON: All right. Just keep reasonably calm.

BARNEY: *(He speaks with great excitement again.)* And I keep it by me. Then I look through the binoculars. *(Now with quiet terror.)* And it is *there*. And I look. And it is just over the field. And I think, I think—I'm *not* afraid. I'm *not* afraid. I'll fight it off. I'm *not* afraid. And I walk. And I walk out, and I walk across the road. *There it is!* Up there! Ohhhhh, God!

On the tape the doctor's voice remained cool and composed, as Barney's voice was registering unearthly terror. The contrast was striking.

It was the same with Betty's tapes.

> BETTY: We're driving along . . . I don't know where we are . . . I don't even know how we got here . . . Barney and I . . . we were driving. I don't know how long . . . I don't know how long . . . And we haven't been talking . . . I've just been sitting here . . . feeling that something is going to happen. *(Now she cries outright.)* And I'm not really too afraid . . . except right now I am . . . at the time I didn't feel afraid. . . . *(But she bursts out in tears.)*
>
> DR. SIMON: Why are you crying if you're not afraid?
>
> BETTY: I'm afraid now . . . but I wasn't . . . I don't . . . I wasn't afraid . . . I *was* afraid when I saw the men in the road.
>
> DR. SIMON: Men in the road?
>
> BETTY: *(Now she breaks out with an anguished cry.)* I've *never* been so afraid in my life before!

As I listened to the first of forty hours of tapes (about half recorded by Barney and half by Betty), one thing was obvious: No actor in the world could have simulated the terror they were experiencing as they pieced together the story of their abduction in vivid detail, and with no inconsistencies other than those of two different witnesses reliving the same experiences from two different points of view.

All through the tapes the doctor continued the reality testing, asking them the same questions in different forms, quietly challenging them, posing questions that would reveal fantasy or attempts to fabricate. All through the tapes both Barney and Betty held to their stories; nothing would shake them.

I SAT DOWN WITH the Hills in their Portsmouth home shortly after my long sessions with Dr. Simon, which had taken five weeks of listening, on a stop-and-go basis, in a series of two- and three-hour sittings. The experience of listening to the tapes was staggering enough for me. What had it been like for the Hills?

Barney, the realist who opposed any such concept as a flying saucer, had listened with total disbelief. Neither he nor Betty could believe the story coming out in their own voices in such detail.

Slowly, as the tape began to approach Indian Head, Barney knew he was getting to the point where he had only partial memory. "I felt quite secure being with the doctor in his office, and I had complete confidence in him. I knew that if the going got too rough, he could take me out of it. Then I was suddenly startled. When I put the binoculars up to my eyes, I couldn't believe I had reacted that way. And the eyes. I saw the eyes. The eyes that seemed to come toward me. Then I heard myself saying that the eyes seemed to be burning into my senses, like an indelible imprint. Suddenly the lost pieces began to come together. Even while listening to the tapes, I felt this. I realized how I had broken my binocular strap. And I remembered that for days after Indian Head, I had an intense soreness in the back of my neck. Listening to the tapes, this came back to me sharply—the violent thrust of my arms breaking the binocular strap. All of this was unfolding—not just on the tapes, but beginning to unfold in my mind, my conscious mind."

For both Betty and Barney, the experience came back vividly while listening to the tapes, so much so that they ultimately felt the two hours missing from their lives had been restored, and the experience *had* to be real to survive such intensive probing.

Also, the results of the therapy were encouraging. The anxiety symptoms of both Barney and Betty receded. They felt more comfortable and relaxed, to the point where Dr. Simon felt they could stop therapy, even though there was no scientific conclusion that the abduction had or had not taken place.

There was also the question of economics. Although the Hills had a medical policy that would cover part of the therapy, it would not cover all of it, and the financial stress was heavy. Interestingly, the insurance company allowed the claim to be paid—possibly the first time in history that people were compensated for an encounter with a flying saucer.

AT THE END OF the sessions Dr. Simon felt that on the basis of available evidence, and our present knowledge of mental functioning, he could accept the probability that the Hills had experienced an unusual aerial phenomenon, a sighting that had stimulated an intense emotional experience in both of them.

He searched deeply for every possible explanation of the abduction. One theory had to do with the dreams Betty had following the experience. They were repetitive and startling in detail. They matched many of the incidents that came out during the regressive hypnosis sessions, but she had avoided telling these dreams to Barney. Dr. Simon's hypothesis was that Betty had telepathically transferred her dreams to Barney to such an extent that he had absorbed them and they had become part of his reality.

"I'm not absolutely convinced," the doctor said later. "I had to come to my conclusion. If you can call it a conclusion. It never really was one. Therapeutically, we had reached a good place to stop under the practical conditions existing, and the Hills' basic improvement. It was acceptable in my judgment to leave it not fully answered."

When I questioned Barney about his reaction to Dr. Simon's dream theory, he brought up an interesting point. In the period before the amnesia began, a time period that the doctor accepted as being a valid conscious memory, Barney had not only seen the unusual object, but had viewed living persons aboard the craft. Further, Betty had not participated in this incident; it was not a part of her dreams and could not possibly have been transferred. This, and Barney's recall under hypnosis of scenes purportedly aboard the craft that Betty did not participate in, and definitely did not dream about, further strained the dream theory.

Betty had her own thoughts about the doctor's theory. "When Dr. Simon first suggested the idea that maybe it could be possible that I had converted the dreams about the amnesiac period into false reality, I thought: Well, this is wonderful. And I was able to go along with it for about two weeks, I guess, after the therapy was over. Then all of a sudden one morning I woke up with the thought: Who do I think I'm kidding? Zoom—it was back again. And I haven't been successful in telling myself it was a dream ever since."

ALL THROUGH MY interviews with the Hills I was trying to observe them objectively. Their sincerity, articulateness and rationality were impressive. Beyond that, I had the professional appraisal of Dr. Simon as to their integrity and sanity even under conditions of stress.

The first thing that I examined in depth was the minutiae that followed in the wake of the incident. It was important to keep in mind that neither of the Hills had any memory whatever at that time of what had happened between the two series of beeps—some forty miles apart. The beeps served as a barrier that prevented them from having any recall of being taken aboard the craft or being given the purported medical examination. What interested me was the sudden descent of the amnesiac veil at exactly the same time and place, as Barney tried to gun the car to escape what he thought was inevitable capture. They both heard the beeping consciously, and then there was the missing time—a span which Barney and Betty figured as being just about two hours.

This interested the doctor, too. It was strange, eerie and medically unprecedented. Amnesia is caused by injury, shock, senility, severe illness or mental disease. All of these had been carefully screened out by the doctor. Amnesia itself is rare; a case of duplicate amnesia has never been recorded.

Then there was the series of puzzling things that emerged after Barney and Betty returned to their home in Portsmouth. Barney, experiencing a strange clammy feeling, went almost immediately to the bathroom to examine his groin. He had no idea why at the time because none of the experiences aboard the craft had filtered into his conscious mind. Yet he was compelled to do this by some unknown force that he could not understand.

Later, four months later, a semicircle of warts grew on his lower abdomen in an arc so perfectly symmetrical it could have been drawn with a compass. Then, after his therapy with Dr. Simon began, the small circle of warts became inflamed. As the conscious memory of what he had revealed under hypnosis came back to him, he remembered that in the examination on the craft a circular instrument had been placed at exactly the same point where the warts had now appeared. Barney realized the warts might have been a psychosomatic symptom connected with the feelings experienced under hypnosis. And yet, he reasoned, they had initially appeared back in 1962, when he had no conscious memory of the events aboard the craft. And in 1964, during the sessions, they became inflamed.

Neither Dr. Simon, to whom Barney mentioned the warts, nor the skin specialist he visited appeared to be concerned about them and they were easily removed by electrolysis. But Barney had the gnawing thought that this could be evidence—if indeed there was anything to this totally incredible story.

There was also the broken binocular strap. Barney had no recollection about how this could have happened. He did, however, recall the severe soreness on the back of his neck, but for some reason never bothered to put the two facts together. Listening to his own voice tell on tape how he had wrenched the binoculars from his eyes brought the experience back to him sharply, and another puzzlement was removed from his mind.

Perhaps the detail that bothered Barney the most was the tops of his shoes. He was a very careful dresser and had the habit of keeping all his shoes well shined, whether for vacation, business or social wear. When he took off his shoes early that morning after the incident, he noticed the tops were not only scuffed but had gouges in them. But why the *tops?* He recalled their various stops on the way toward Indian Head, but he had not scraped his shoes on anything. Even going out on the field with his binoculars, he was careful where he stepped and had not tripped over anything. But on this morning after, the tops of *both* shoes were almost beyond repair. All through the months after the event until the time he heard himself on the tape, apparently being half carried along the ground with his feet dragging, he had pondered the question of those shoes. Hearing the tapes, he felt that at least a possible explanation was presented—in spite of his strong resistance to accepting a story involving a flying saucer.

In my discussions with Dr. Simon I found one of his greatest objections to the validity of Betty Hill's recollection of her abduction was her description under hypnosis of the long needle that was inserted into her abdomen for a so-called pregnancy test. Betty agreed with the doctor that the idea seemed medically ridiculous. She had reported this incident in 1964 during her hypnotherapy. Several years later, two pregnancy-related procedures involving needle insertion came into prominence. One was amniocentesis, a technique developed to test amniotic fluid. The other involved the use of a laparoscope to permit the introduction of a needle into the lower abdomen that could be used to aspirate the egg from its follicle. This technique has been used for the creation of test-tube babies.

I went back to the tapes again to replay Betty's recall of the insertion of the needle, keeping in mind that all this was recorded before the amniotic and the test-tube baby techniques were general knowledge.

BETTY: So they roll me over on my back. And the examiner has a long needle in his hand. And I see the needle. And it's bigger than any needle that I've ever seen. And I ask him what he's going to do with it. . . . *(She starts to get very upset on the tape.)* It won't hurt, he says. And I ask him what and he said he just wants to put it in my navel, it's just a simple test. *(There is sobbing.)* And I tell him, no, it will hurt, don't do it, don't do it! And I'm crying and I'm telling him, "It's hurting, it's hurting, take it out, take it out!" And the leader comes over and he puts his hand, rubs his hand in front of my eyes, and he says it will be all right. I won't feel it. *(She becomes calmer.)* And all the pain goes away. The pain goes away, but I'm still sore from where they put that needle. I don't know why they put that needle into my navel. Because I told them they shouldn't do it. . . .
DR. SIMON: Did they make any sexual advances to you?
BETTY: No. I asked the leader, I said, "Why did they put that needle in my navel?" And he said it was a pregnancy test. I said, "I don't know what they expected, but that was no pregnancy test." And he didn't say anything more.

I couldn't blame either Betty or the doctor for discounting this explanation back in 1964. But later it raised the very serious question, if true, as to whether these strange humanoids were intent on a specific mission: the creation of a test-tube baby. The implications were staggering.

CHAPTER FIVE

BY THE TIME I had finished the long two-part series for *Look* magazine, my mind was spinning. The story was just too much. Would anyone believe it? Could I believe it? One thing I was certain of was that I had written in the lowest possible key, with no exaggeration or extrapolation. Further, I had stuck to the facts and had avoided drawing any conclusion whatever.

At the table in the *Look* conference room I went over the script carefully, line by line, with editors Bob Meskill and Gerry Zimmermann. They were both tough realists, and I was grateful not to feel so alone with the story. We were all grateful for Dr. Simon's stance: He simply would not accept any easy solutions to the events, and maintained his dispassionate clinical posture toward the subject of flying saucers. He was unwavering in his determination not to accept or reject anything summarily.

The consensus of all of us at *Look* was that the story should not be released without the most rigorous testing we could think of to check it out. What, for instance, if the deepest part of the Hills' unconscious minds now rejected the whole episode? What if now, in 1966, two years after their intensive therapy, they had shifted into disbelieving their own memories? Consciously, they remained convinced of the veracity of the tapes, but theirs was a story that had been dredged from the unconscious, where the truth spills out and the ego censor is not operating to guard it from doing so.

There was only one obvious way to check out the facts as they stood near publication time. Would both the doctor and the Hills volunteer to go through a new hypnosis session in which the *Look* editors and I could ask our own questions—and double-check their belief that the abduction had actually taken place? Only in this way could we confirm that the Hills still believed the story they had told two years earlier.

The Hills and Dr. Simon concurred that it would be a good idea to review the case after the long inactive time span. They agreed that hypnosis was the only real way of probing deep enough to see if the veracity still held up. We asked the doctor to concentrate on Barney, since he had been more resistant to the idea of UFOs. A time and date were set for the session at Dr. Simon's office.

Earlier Barney had told me about his first session with Dr. Simon, before the actual regressive hypnosis had started. At the beginning of the therapy the doctor had spent three weeks in one-hour sessions with each of them to satisfy himself that they would make good subjects and would be able to attain the depth of trance desired without the use of sodium pentothal or amobarbital. The repetition of the hypnosis process over that preliminary three-week period had served to reinforce the induction and to establish specific posthypnotic cue words to replace lengthy future induction procedures.

Now, two years later, *Look* editor Zimmermann and I talked with the doctor before the Hills arrived about the new "verification" session, as we called it. Dr. Simon told us that because of the long reinforcement of the hypnotic technique, all he needed to use were two simple cue words to put either Barney or Betty into a trance state. The words chosen were ones not likely to come up in ordinary conversation and he had conditioned the Hills to respond only to his voice. Nevertheless, he suggested that we never repeat them in voice or in print, on the remote chance that the Hills might see or hear them and go into an unwanted trance state. Unsupervised hypnosis is not something to be treated lightly.

When the session started, Barney sat comfortably in a chair in the doctor's office, facing the three of us—Dr. Simon, Gerry Zimmermann and myself. The atmosphere was light and informal, and after some small chatter the doctor told Barney he was now ready to induce the trance state. Barney nodded in agreement and leaned back against the chair. After a pause the doctor gave him the two cue words.

In a matter of moments Barney sank slightly lower in the chair, his eyes closed quickly and he looked as if he were sleeping comfortably. The doctor began the questioning with a general review of the trip, coming down toward Indian Head. As Barney started talking, I was again struck by the somnambulistic quality of his voice. It was flat, eerie, abnormally sonorous. His face was expressionless; his eyes remained closed. The story he was telling was unchanged. There was no evasion in his answers to the doctor's questions, and because this was not a medical or therapeutic session, the doctor was able to be more firm than ever in his questions. We had asked the doctor to press particularly hard on the abduction part of the event—the most difficult part to accept on any terms.

At one point in the session the doctor leaned forward in his chair and assumed the tone of a lawyer conducting a cross-examination.

"What is your feeling *now?*" Dr. Simon asked. "*Were* you abducted or weren't you?" His tone was harsh and challenging.

Barney, his eyes still closed in trance, spoke in even tones. "I feel I was abducted."

Dr. Simon drove hard again. "*Were* you abducted? Not how do you *feel. Were* you abducted?"

Barney's voice remained calm. "Yes. But I don't want to believe I was abducted."

"But you are convinced that you *were?*"

"I said 'I feel,' " Barney replied in his trance, "because this makes it more comfortable for me to accept something I don't want to accept."

"You mean," Dr. Simon went on, "it would be worse to say, 'I actually *was* abducted'?"

"I'm comfortable the other way," Barney said.

The doctor now took another tack. "What are you uncomfortable about?"

Barney replied with a statement he had made before in my interviews with him. "Because it is such a weird story. If anyone else told me that this had happened to them, I would not believe them."

"Well," Dr. Simon challenged him again, "suppose that you have just absorbed Betty's *dreams?*"

This was a direct question, and a good one. Even though the dream transference theory was almost as strange as an actual abduction by humanoids, it was a possible answer to the puzzle, and one that would help rule out an abduction. But Barney replied without hesitation, "I would like that."

The answer implied that Barney would prefer any alternative to accepting the abduction as real. But it further implied that he couldn't accept the dream premise.

The doctor pressed on. "You would like that?" He paused a moment, then added, "Could that be *true?*"

Barney responded quickly and sharply. "No!"

The doctor shot back the question, "Why not?"

Now Barney suddenly began heavy breathing—deep, emotional, intense. I looked over at Gerry Zimmermann. He was as tense as I was. Barney was no longer in a calm trance. He opened and closed his hands and began writhing about in his chair. His eyes were still closed tightly. Then he screamed out, *"Because—I didn't like them putting that on me!"*

Gerry Zimmermann and I both winced. When he said *"that,"* Barney seemed to be referring to the instrument put on his groin. You could sense the terror in him as he yelled out. I was relieved when Dr. Simon immediately cut in, "That's all right, Barney. You don't have to be upset. Take it easy!"

But Barney didn't seem to hear. He was now crying openly. He continued twisting in his chair. "I didn't like them putting that on me! *I don't like them putting their hands on me!*" he repeated. "I don't like them *touching* me!"

I had to admit I was frightened. I admired Dr. Simon's coolness. "Okay, Barney," he said reassuringly. "They're not touching you now. *They're not touching you now!* You can let that go. . . ."

Barney calmed down almost instantly. Dr. Simon began to take him gradually out of the trance state and eventually closed with the usual command: "You may wake now, Barney."

I looked down at my hands. They were sweating. Gerry Zimmermann took out a pocket Kleenex and wiped his forehead. Then he leaned over to me and said quietly, "Okay. We'll run the story as scheduled."

I DROVE BACK TO Portsmouth from Boston with the Hills to their house to do some factual line checking with them on the galley proofs. All the way back Barney kept begging me to replay the tape of his new session because he was curious to hear consciously what he had said unconsciously. I didn't think the idea was a good one because the emotions were so highly charged. I thought we ought to check with the doctor first.

When we arrived at the Hills' house I finally gave in, and Barney put the tape on his machine. We sat down at the kitchen table over a cup of coffee and prepared to listen. The tape began with the doctor's voice reviewing the purpose of the exercise with Barney. Before any of us thought anything more about it, the two cue words came out clearly from the speaker. I was about to take a sip of coffee when I looked over at Barney. He had suddenly slumped back on his chair, his eyes closed. His breathing turned long and slow, just as it had in the doctor's office a few hours before.

Betty jumped up from her chair and started slapping Barney's face. I immediately shut off the tape recorder. But it was too late. Barney was in a deep trance and none of our efforts could wake him up. Betty went to the phone and called Dr. Simon's office. There was no one there. She also called his home, and got no answer there either. We tried splashing Barney's face with cold water and giving him instructions to wake up, with no effect at all.

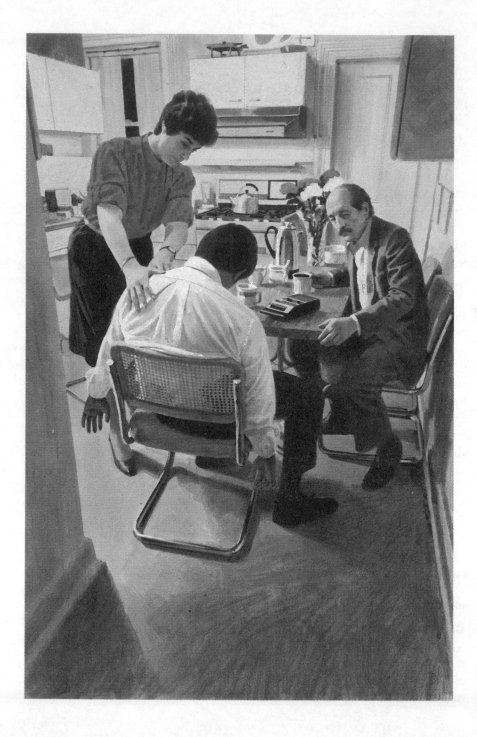

The trance state in hypnosis is not directly dangerous, unless it happens in a place where injury from a fall or other hazards could occur. There was no such danger here. The worst that could happen to Barney was that he would eventually fall into a natural sleep and wake up feeling refreshed in three or four hours.

Suddenly I had an idea that might work. I picked up the tape recorder, put it in fast forward and spun the tape ahead. I stopped it at the point where the doctor began his instructions for Barney to wake up, and I turned up the volume. "When I count to five," the doctor was saying, "you will be completely awake. You will be comfortable and relaxed, no aches, no pains, no anxieties. One-two—three—comfortable and relaxed. No aches, no pains, no anxieties. Four—you're getting wider and wider awake. *Five.* You may wake up now, Barney."

I was watching Barney very closely all through the playing of the tape. At the count of three, his eyelids began to flutter. At the count of five, his eyes snapped open, he shook his head and said, "What in the hell happened?"

We could laugh about it now that it was over, but it dramatized for me the incredible power of hypnosis and its capacity to be effective even on a remote-control basis. I couldn't help speculating whether some kind of remote-control technique could have been used by the abductors.

In fact, Dr. Simon himself had advanced a theory about the strange electronic beeps which had apparently started the amnesiac period for the Hills at Indian Head. His hypothesis bore on the theory of hypnosis by remote control. In electrical shock treatment for severe depression, electrical currents are used to affect the central nervous system, including both the conscious and unconscious states of mind. One related shred of evidence along this line had shown up immediately after the encounter when Betty and Barney both noticed a cluster of highly polished, perfectly round spots on the trunk of their car, each about the size of a half-dollar. Betty had become extremely interested in them. She took a pocket compass and discovered that the needle wavered far off its northerly fix when she placed it on the spots. Barney, wanting to get the whole incident out of his mind, discouraged her from following up, and the spots eventually disappeared without further exploration. There did not at the time seem to be any great incentive to investigate the cause of the spots, since neither Barney nor Betty was then aware that any such thing as an abduction might have taken place.

CHAPTER SIX

THE HILLS' WAS not an isolated case. The Air Force was being swamped with inexplicable reports of UFO sightings from every part of the country. In exploring this matter I found that since the Air Force authorities didn't want to admit that they had no explanations, they were trying to sweep the reports under the rug. There was no evidence of a "government conspiracy," however.

Probably the most important scientist investigating the phenomenon was Dr. J. Allen Hynek, then chairman of the Department of Astronomy at Northwestern University. He also had been the official scientific consultant on UFOs for the United States Air Force. He had started as an avowed skeptic, but his long perusal of the Air Force files and his personal investigation of many UFO sightings had brought him to the conclusion that UFOs represented an unknown but very real phenomenon that demanded the most serious scientific attention.

I met Dr. Hynek shortly after the Hills' story came out in 1966. We met for a strange reason. The late U Thant, then secretary-general of the United Nations, had read the story of Barney and Betty Hill in *Look* and noticed that it showed similarities to stories that had been reported by many member nations of the U.N. Curious to learn more, he arranged for Dr. Hynek and me to meet with him at his U.N. office in New York. As a leading astronomer and former Air Force consultant on UFOs, Dr. Hynek could fill in the secretary-general on the technical aspects. As a journalist, I could perhaps fill him in on the human reaction.

I met Dr. Hynek in the lobby of the United Nations building. While waiting to be called up to U Thant's office on the top floor, Hynek told me that he had been able to knock down over four fifths of the cases reported to the Air Force as inaccurate or illusory sightings. But there was a large residue of hundreds of unexplained and unidentified cases that continued to bother him. He referred to himself as the "resident skeptic" of the Air Force. By the time a large wave of sightings hit the country in 1966, Hynek was becoming more convinced that the sightings by pilots, ground control personnel, police and other responsible, intelligent observers could no longer be ignored.

We were ushered into U Thant's office on a bright June Saturday morning. The secretary-general greeted us cordially, and we were glad to be the only visitors there at the time. Our conversation centered first on the psychological reaction of a populace to the possible visit of aliens from another star system. I told the secretary-general that in my survey and interviews in the New Hampshire area those who had observed the objects at close range (many sightings were reported as low as twenty feet over a car or house) were naturally apprehensive at first, but their curiosity soon overcame their fear. Hynek agreed with this, indicating that the concern of government officials about mass hysteria developing was probably unfounded. In fact, the reluctance of officials to discuss the subject was a major stumbling block in establishing intelligent scientific study.

The conversation then turned to an interesting theoretical aspect of the subject. U Thant had noted that many scientists had disclaimed the possibility of UFOs visiting from another stellar system because of the imponderable distances between stars and galaxies. The nearest star capable of supporting a planetary system, for instance, was Alpha Centauri, and it was 4.28 light-years away.

A big difficulty in speculating about man's capacity to reach interstellar systems is that his life span is relatively short. But Dr. Hynek had a theory. Wasn't it egocentric to assume that the life span of a man applied to the whole universe? In fact, right here on earth there are markedly varying life spans. A fruit fly lives ten days. A man can live for one hundred years, or 3650 times as long as a fruit fly.

If there is this much variance on earth, an even greater variance could exist elsewhere in the universe. Suppose that a species on a theoretical planet of Alpha Centauri had a life span many thousands of times longer than ours? An earth-year to them might be the blink of an eye. Suppose that advanced civilization was able to travel close to the speed of light. At such a speed, the time element is slowed, along with life processes, so that fifty thousand earth-years would seem to be only a handful of years to the traveler.

The secretary-general arranged for Hynek and me to visit informally with the U.N. Outer Space Affairs Division. Our conversation with the staff members we met there was fascinating, and I left with the conviction that something was going on, beyond the incredible story of Barney and Betty Hill.

Afterward Dr. Hynek and I stopped for a cup of coffee in a nearby coffee shop and I had a chance to tell him more about the Hill case. Hynek was interested because he had never encountered a UFO incident that had been so carefully and professionally documented. He asked me if he might question the Hills directly, under hypnosis by Dr. Simon, so that he could learn more details to compare with the hundreds of cases he was examining. I told him that I thought both Barney and Betty were still anxious to learn more about their own case and would probably welcome a responsible scientific inquiry.

I was right. Both the Hills and Dr. Simon agreed. A meeting was set up at Dr. Simon's home in Arlington, just outside of Boston, at which both the Hills would be put into a trance state by the doctor so that Professor Hynek could query them directly on their encounter. This would be the first time that both Barney and Betty would be regressed together in the same room. All the other sessions had been conducted separately.

I met Dr. Hynek at the Boston airport and we drove out to Arlington with considerable anticipation. One thing we were both interested in exploring was how Barney and Betty would interact in a dual state of regression. Even Dr. Simon was not sure about this. I was particularly interested in whether a dialogue would take place between Barney and Betty in their trance state.

Hynek and I agreed that we would not ask the doctor to run through the entire story in sequence. We planned instead to select certain points that might reveal more details concerning the abduction experience, without any particular chronology. Since the trance state of the Hills would allow Dr. Simon to shift the focus at will, and since he could, by a given signal, suspend the consciousness of either one of the Hills at any time, we could explore those portions of the experience likely to throw the most light on the UFO aspect.

As the session began, we arranged the furniture so that Dr. Simon, Professor Hynek and I sat facing the Hills. Barney was in a comfortable chair on Betty's right. The microphone for the tape recorder was placed halfway between the two groups. The trance state came on quickly, and within moments Barney and Betty were settled back in their chairs, eyes closed, completely relaxed.

At the completion of his instructions for the trance Dr. Simon said, "In this session Dr. Hynek may talk to you. And Mr. Fuller may talk to you. And you will both carry out their instructions as if they were mine." Hynek began the questioning first.

DR. HYNEK: Barney, you will remember everything clearly. And I want you to tell me what is happening. You have just heard the beep-beep-beep. I want you to tell me what it sounded like, and then each of you just relive those moments when you first heard the beeping sounds as you were driving down the road. . . . *(At this point Barney begins stirring uneasily in his chair. There are signs of distress. Dr. Simon immediately cuts in.)*

DR. SIMON: You will not be upset, Barney. You will not have any anxiety, or upset feelings. Just tell us what is happening, without having any emotional disturbance.

BETTY: *(Her voice shows some stress, but she remains quiet in her chair.)* I don't see anything! *(She now begins to breathe very heavily.)* I don't see anything! *(She is apparently referring to the time when she looked out the window of the car and the large object was blocking the view of the sky.)*

BARNEY: *(He is also breathing heavily.)* Betty, it's out there.

BETTY: *(Very tense.)* Oh, God!

BARNEY: This is crazy.

BETTY: I don't see it. I don't see it. I don't see anything.

BARNEY: Where am I? *(His voice is very frightened.)* Ohhhhh. Oh, I don't believe it. There are men in the road. I don't want to go over. It can't be there. It's the moon. It's the moon. *(Barney is apparently trying to rationalize the appearance of the object.)*

DR. HYNEK: Go on, Barney. You remember everything clearly. Everything is clear.

BARNEY: I gotta get out.

DR. SIMON: This won't bother you now. But you can tell about it. Same for you, Betty. It won't bother you, but you can tell about it.

BARNEY: I am coming down the road into the woods. There is an orange glow. There's something there. Ohhhhhh—if I only had a gun. What do they want? Those crazy eyes are with me. They're with me. Go up a ramp. I'd love to lash out, but I can't. I'd love to strike out, but I can't! *(Now Barney appeals directly to Dr. Simon.)* Dr. Simon, give me my emotions back! I've got to strike out, I've got to strike out!

DR. SIMON: You have as much emotion as you need. Just keep right on telling us.

BARNEY: I can't, though.

DR. SIMON: *(Calmly.)* You can't do anything, of course. So just go on and tell us about it.

BARNEY: *(Apparently quite surprised.)* There's a difference in the temperature. There's a corridor. I don't know where Betty is.

DR. SIMON: Where are you now?

BARNEY: My feet just bumped. I'm in a corridor. I don't want to go. I don't know where Betty is. The eyes are telling me to be calm. If I'm not harmed, I will not strike out. But I will strike out if I'm harmed in any way! *(Now his tone changes sharply, to one of fear again.)* I'm numb. I'm numb! *(Loud and sharp.)* I don't have any feeling in my fingers!

DR. SIMON: Okay. Okay. It's okay now.

BARNEY: My legs are numb!

DR. SIMON: It's all right now, Barney.

BARNEY: I'm on a table.

DR. SIMON: Stop there. You're on the table, but you're quiet. And you're relaxed. You can just rest now. Until I say, "Listen, Barney," you won't hear anything for a little while. *(Now Dr. Simon addresses Betty.)* Betty, what's going on?

BETTY: We're riding, and Barney's putting on the brakes and they squeal. But he turns to the left very sharply. *(This apparently refers to the turn off Route 3 to a back road.)* And I don't know why he's doing this. We're going to be lost in the woods. The car is stopping. Barney tries to start it. It won't start. There's some men coming up to the car. There's something about the first man.

DR. HYNEK: Where is Barney now, Betty?

BETTY: *(Her voice is low and sleepy.)* Barney is still in the car.

DR. HYNEK: And then what happens?

BETTY: There is one man ahead of the others coming up. And he's got something in his hand. I don't know what it is. I think they're men—but they're *not* men!

DR. SIMON: Have you seen anyone like this? *(Suddenly Barney, who has been leaning back in his chair with closed eyes, begins stirring and squirming.)* Stop, Betty. Stop for a moment. I don't want you to hear anything I say for a moment. *(Now he addresses Barney.)* Barney?

BARNEY: *(Yelling loudly.)* Betty! *(Barney suddenly leaps out of his chair and drops to his knees on the floor.)*

DR. SIMON: *(Commanding.)* Barney! Barney! It's all gone. It's all gone. You can go to sleep now. It's all stopped. It's all stopped. No more until

I tell you to. Do you hear me, Barney? All right. Deep sleep, deep asleep. You're completely relaxed, and it's all stopped for now. *(Turns to Betty, as he helps Barney back in his chair.)* Betty—you can hear me now. Go on. *(Dr. Simon's instructions have the effect of turning Barney and Betty on and off like tape recorders.)*

BETTY: I'm going to open the car door and run out and hide in the woods. They opened the door . . . *(Her voice drifts off as if she is asleep.)*

DR. SIMON: Then what did you do? *(Betty remains silent.)* What did you do, Betty?

BETTY: I went to sleep.

DR. SIMON: Where?

BETTY: In the car. I think.

DR. SIMON: What happened while you were asleep?

BETTY: *(She is alternating between past and present tense, a common response in regression.)* I tried to wake myself up. I don't want to be asleep.

DR. SIMON: Did the man make you go to sleep?

BETTY: Somehow. I don't want to be asleep.

DR. HYNEK: Then what, Betty?

BETTY: I'm trying to wake up.

DR. SIMON: Did you wake up, Betty?

BETTY: Yes. I try to wake up. I keep trying and trying and trying. I walk in a path in the woods. There's a man behind me, and men—I don't know where I am. I am sleepwalking, and there is a man on each side of me to hold me up.

DR. SIMON: Is this after you woke up, or while you were asleep?

BETTY: I was awake. And I keep saying, "Barney, Barney, Barney, wake up!" *(At this point Barney begins stirring from his relaxed position in the chair. In order to give him instructions to relax again, it is necessary for Dr. Simon to suspend Betty's present line of regression.)*

DR. SIMON: Stop a minute, Betty. When I touch your head, you will not hear anything more from anybody until I touch it again. *(The doctor leans over and touches her head. She remains silent, eyes closed, as he turns to Barney.)* Barney—you can hear me now. You are deep asleep. Fully relaxed. You are comfortable now—nothing is troubling you. When I touch your head, you will not hear anybody else until I touch you again. *(He reaches over and touches Barney's head, then does the same to Betty.)* Now, Betty, you can begin again. How far did you walk? How long did it take? Was it a short or long walk?

BETTY: *(Still in a very sleepy tone.)* A fairly long walk, I think. I don't know how long I was walking before I woke up.

DR. HYNEK: Were your eyes quite open when you were walking?

BETTY: When I woke up, my eyes were open.

DR. HYNEK: Where were the men taking you?

BETTY: In a path in the woods. Toward the craft.

DR. HYNEK: Did the craft look anything like a helicopter?

BETTY: No.

DR. HYNEK: Did you ever see anything that resembled it?

BETTY: No.

DR. HYNEK: What color was it?

BETTY: It was—it was a metal. It was shiny.

DR. HYNEK: Was the moon shining down on it?

BETTY: It was quite a moonlit night. I could see that it was on the ground. There was like a rim around the edge.

DR. HYNEK: Was it resting on legs, or was it flat on the ground?

BETTY: The rim was a little bit above the ground. And there was a ramp that came down. If it was on legs, the legs were in a hole.

DR. SIMON: Keep right on, Betty.

BETTY: I don't think that it was on legs. I didn't see any.

DR. HYNEK: What were your thoughts as you drew closer to it?

BETTY: *(After a brief pause.)* To get the "H" out of there if I could.

DR. SIMON: And why couldn't you?

BETTY: The man beside me—I kept saying, "Barney, Barney, wake up . . ." And the man asked me if his name was Barney. I didn't answer because I didn't think it was any of his business. And when I saw this craft thing, I knew they were going to want us to go on it. I kept telling him I don't want to go—I won't go. They said they just wanted to do a simple test, and as soon as it was over, I could go back to the car.

DR. SIMON: What about when you were in the room with the leader or with the examiner? What kind of sounds did he make?

BETTY: He didn't make a mumbling sound, like the crew.

DR. SIMON: What kind of sounds did he make?

BETTY: It was more like words. Like sounds of words.

DR. SIMON: English words?

BETTY: No.

DR. SIMON: But you understood them?

BETTY: Yes.

Later Professor Hynek presses down on this point.

DR. HYNEK: *How* did they tell you what to do? Did they talk to you?

BETTY: The man I call the leader said, "Is his name Barney?"

DR. HYNEK: Did he actually say this in English? Clearly now, you can recall all these details. Did you hear him say this with your ears?

BETTY: I heard sounds.

DR. SIMON: You hear them now. Whatever they are, they are clear and sharp.

BETTY: He makes a sound, and I understand it in English.

DR. SIMON: Did you hear sounds coming out of their throats, their mouths?

BETTY: Yes.

DR. HYNEK: Tell me how they sounded to you.

BETTY: The crew made different sounds. Like a—like a humming sound. It went up and down, but it was a humming.

DR. SIMON: (He rises, crosses to Betty's chair.) All right, Betty. When I touch your head, you'll be rested and relaxed. I don't want you to hear anything until I touch your head again. (He touches her head, and she remains quiet. Then he turns to Barney and touches his head.) Barney, you can hear me now. You are comfortable and relaxed. You told me that you had gone into this vehicle. Is that right? They have taken you and put you on a table. And they talked to you. Is that right? Tell us how they talked. Answer Dr. Hynek on that . . .

DR. HYNEK: Did you see them, Barney, open their mouths? And if so, how wide did they open them?

BARNEY: (He is completely calm now.) They were not talking to me. There were these eyes that burned into my head. They stayed in my head, and I knew whatever I was supposed to do, and they kept me calm. Whenever they wanted me to do something, this bright light was always in my head.

DR. HYNEK: Is there any animal, Barney, that you can think of that made the sound that they were making?

BARNEY: No. It was no animal.

DR. HYNEK: Any human?

BARNEY: It was no human.

DR. HYNEK: They were not human? (Barney begins to show signs of distress again, moving uncomfortably in his chair.)

DR. SIMON: Easy, Barney!

BARNEY: They came down the road. They had spindly legs. They carried me out of the car. But the men inside did not have spindly legs. They moved. Their mouths moved. I could see them.

DR. HYNEK: And when their mouths moved, was there a sound coming from them?

BARNEY: Yes.

DR. HYNEK: Try to tell me what the sounds were. Do they represent anything you know?

BARNEY: No. *(Then Barney suddenly makes an eerie humming sound that is partly a gargle as well as a hum.)* Eergglhmmmmmmm . . . hmmmmm . . .

DR. HYNEK: Did you understand what they were saying?

BARNEY: No I did not.

DR. SIMON: *(After consultation with Dr. Hynek.)* All right, Barney. I want to move ahead to the point after the abduction. You have just left the craft. You have been taken back to the car. . . . I want you both to tell exactly what happened. *(Dr. Simon touches Betty's head to bring her back into the session.)*

BARNEY: *(He is apparently addressing their dachshund who had been left in the car.)* Delsey!

BETTY: *(Her voice in the trance is now measurably relieved.)* Delsey is scared to death!

BARNEY: Delsey! Delsey! Where's Delsey, Betty? *(He sounds confused.)*

BETTY: *(She is laughing in relief.)* Barney, are you awake?

BARNEY: Yes, Betty.

BETTY: You have your eyes open now.

BARNEY: *(He is apparently referring to Betty's acceptance that they are actually dealing with a UFO.)* Come on, Betty. Don't be ridiculous. . . . Let's go.

BETTY: I want to see it leave, Barney.

BARNEY: *(Suddenly his voice begins quivering in awe.)* There's an orange glow! Hey—look at that! Isn't that something? *(He talks as if he is watching the object begin to glow from a nearby location.)*

BETTY: Delsey, Delsey—look at that! *(She is very excited.)*

BARNEY: *(Not at all convincing.)* It's the moon. I know. That's what it is. The moon!

BETTY: It's not the moon, Barney.

BARNEY: I'm not going to talk to you, Betty. I don't care. I'm getting in the car.

BETTY: Delsey's still excited.

BARNEY: *(Sharply.)* Come on, Betty! Get in. You'd better, because I'm going to leave. *(He gets angrier.)* I'm not going to hang around here. Come get in the car, dammit. Geeez, I'm tired of this foolishness. Get in the car, Betty!

BETTY: Okay. But look at Delsey. She's the only dog in the world who has seen something like this.

BARNEY: *(The awe and wonder return to his voice.)* It looks like a satellite! Look at it go! *(He pauses, then resolutely:)* Oh, boy—I'll *never* tell anybody about this!

BETTY: I wonder where it's going . . .

DR. SIMON: *(Driving hard for facts.)* Okay, now. Tell me now. What does it look like? How big is it? What is its color? What kind of movement does it show? Describe it in detail. Both of you. Just before it gets far from you. While it's still close.

BETTY: *(Analytically.)* It has a swirling orange glow.

BARNEY: It's getting brighter and brighter. And it's turning silvery in color. And it's moving very fast. And it's gone up in the sky.

DR. SIMON: *(Firmly.)* Which direction? Straight up? Angle?

BARNEY: *(Indicating with his hands. His eyes, of course, remain closed in trance.)* It goes from this way—to this way. It never hit the trees. . . .

At one point in the session an unusual thing happened. In the room Barney was sitting on Betty's right. Yet in the flow of regression Barney was supposed to be in the driver's seat of the car. Regression in a trance state is so real to the subject that he actually believes he is back at the scene. In this case, it seemed to Barney that Betty was on the driver's side of the car, when he should be there. It suddenly disturbed him greatly.

BARNEY: Wait a minute. This is ridiculous. Betty's over here—when she should be there! . . . *I'm* driving the car.

DR. SIMON: Easy, easy. It's all right. Go on, Betty.

BETTY: Barney is still somewhat in a daze, after we see the object leave and get back in the car. And Barney is driving, and I say to him, "Do you believe in flying saucers?" And he says, "Don't be ridiculous." And then we hear the beeping sounds again, and Delsey jumps up on the back seat and looks out the window.

DR. HYNEK: Was it at this time that you saw the craft cross between you and the moon?

BETTY: That was much earlier. But the moon is there.

DR. HYNEK: Was it above or below the moon, Betty?

BETTY: It was on the left-hand side of the moon, about the middle of the moon, or a little bit lower. *(At this point Barney becomes more disturbed about the "driver's seat" problem.)*

BARNEY: *I'm* driving this car . . .

DR. SIMON: Just a minute . . . *(Dr. Simon rises and helps Barney and Betty change seats with each other, each of them still remaining in the trance state, eyes closed. Barney becomes considerably more comfortable after the change.)* Okay, Barney. Are you still confused? *(Barney shakes his head. Dr. Simon instructs them to go back to the point where they first saw the object in the sky, before the abduction took place.)*

BETTY: We're driving along . . . and Barney stops to look at it. I'm standing out there looking at it, and it goes across the moon . . .

DR. SIMON: You tell it to Barney. You're both in the car now.

BARNEY: *(The puzzlement is in his voice again. It is as if they are driving in the car on Route 3.)* It turned, Betty.

BETTY: What do you mean, it turned?

BARNEY: Look out the window. You can see it's a plane. Geez.

BETTY: Where are the binoculars?

BARNEY: *(There is stress in his voice.)* Stop it, Delsey! Get down.

BETTY: *(Chuckling.)* You see a plane coming towards us, and you're acting as if you're in the Twilight Zone.

BARNEY: Just make the dog keep quiet. Delsey's agitated, and you're making me agitated. You're aggravating me.

DR. SIMON: *(Interrupting.)* Now—we'll skip a little time . . . until it comes real close. It's coming real close, is it?

BETTY: I think. Barney, start the car. Barney, have you ever seen anything like this before?

BARNEY: *(More awe and wonder in his voice.)* I can see it! *(Again Barney becomes disturbed in his chair. He leans forward tensely.)*

DR. SIMON: That's all now, Barney! It's all gone now. Sit back in your chair!

BARNEY: *(Shouting.)* Look at that!

DR. SIMON: Okay, Barney. You can do it from the chair.

DR. HYNEK: Describe it now.

BARNEY: *(His voice trembling.)* Ohhhhhhh—it's *huge!* Ohhhhh, my goodness.

DR. SIMON: What do you see through your binoculars?

BARNEY: I can see it! It's there!

DR. SIMON: Yes?

BARNEY: And . . . and . . . there's lights. I don't believe this! *(Breathless.)* I don't *believe* this.

DR. SIMON: Okay, okay. It's all right. Okay. Now tell us what you see.

BARNEY: *(He is at the critical point of the encounter now, where his reaction has always been strong.)* Ohhhhhhhhhh! A huge, huge, big thing! There are people and they are looking down. *(He begins to sob.)* God, help me get these binoculars down! God, help me get these binoculars down!

DR. SIMON: Calm, Barney. Calm. Tell us what you see . . . describe the craft . . . What's the shape, Barney?

BARNEY: Like a pancake. *(Stressing.)* I'm not going to say it! I don't believe it, flying saucers. I'm not going to say it. I don't ever want to say that word again.

DR. HYNEK: How do you know what flying saucers look like?
BARNEY: *(Calm again.)* I was looking in a magazine. I think it was *The Saturday Evening Post* magazine . . .
DR. HYNEK: It looked like what you saw in the *Post* magazine, is that it?
BARNEY: Yes.
DR. SIMON: Yes, all right. Betty, what were you doing?
BETTY: I was in the car.
DR. SIMON: What was Delsey doing?
BETTY: I was sitting on the seat waiting for Barney, and I think Delsey was in the back seat. I'm waiting for Barney to come back, and I'm getting worried why he isn't coming back . . . and then he comes running to the car. He throws the binoculars in on the seat, and I don't know if he's laughing or crying, but he said, "They're going to capture us!" *(Betty continues with the story of their experience as the first beeping sound is heard, to bring the session back full circle.)*

WHEN DR. SIMON CLOSED the session and took the Hills out of the trance state, I felt a strong sense of relief. The consistency of their recall was indisputable. They obviously had nothing to hide or hold back, or they would never have volunteered for a grueling interrogation that had lasted over two hours. The variations in their new session were so minor that they served only to buttress the validity of their recall. As before, their responses to the hard-driving questions were immediate and uncontrived. Their emotional response to the reliving of the scenes was convincing.

Dr. Hynek and I drove toward Logan Airport mostly in silence. I was reflecting on the scenes recreated this time in contrast to those in the original tapes, and the session for *Look* magazine. The lack of false notes among the three segments of recall made it impossible for me to accept any theory other than that the abduction had actually taken place. I finally broke the silence and spoke to Dr. Hynek.

"Well," I said, "after sweating through these last two hours, what do you think? Do you believe it?"

There was a long pause before Hynek finally spoke. "I don't know what else to say," he finally said, "except that I don't know how you can disbelieve it. If this were just a plain and simple court case with all this testimony and evidence laid before a jury, you would have to say that the evidence was overwhelmingly positive, and the jury would have to vote 'yes.' But it's not a trial, and there's no jury, and we're still left hanging. There's one thing for sure, however, and that is that a lot of people have won or lost court cases on a lot less testimony and evidence than this."

Later Dr. Hynek made an important discovery. In checking Air Force records of UFO activity at the exact time and date of the Hills' encounter with the vehicle, he and a former associate discovered a previously overlooked Air Force report that showed radar contact with an unidentified flying object in the vicinity where the Hills had had their experience.

CHAPTER SEVEN

IN THE LATE 1960s and early 1970s UFO reports continued to increase across the country and the world. The Hill case no longer had to be examined in a vacuum. Yet the field was so large, the reports so vast in number and the sources so scattered that I couldn't possibly personally investigate all of them, and the Hill story had taught me that personal investigation was the only way to appraise a case intelligently. I did, however, go over the testimony by six leading scientists, including Dr. Hynek, who appeared before the House Committee on Science and Astronautics in July 1968.

In his testimony Dr. Hynek said, "The cumulative weight of continued reports from groups of people around the world whose competence and sanity I have no reason to doubt, reports involving close encounters with unexplainable craft, with physical effects on animals, motor vehicles, and on the ground, has led me reluctantly to the conclusion that there is a scientifically valuable subset of reports in the UFO phenomena."

Dr. James E. McDonald, then senior physicist in atmospheric physics at the University of Arizona and a member of the National Academy of Sciences, told the hearing that he had studied the UFO situation for about two years on an intensive basis, and that he was astonished by what he had found. He pointed out that meteorites were once scoffed at as unreal. He quoted General Samford, former director of Air Force Intelligence, who said, "Credible observers are observing relatively incredible objects." McDonald concluded by saying, "My position is that UFOs are entirely real and we do not know what they are because we have laughed them out of court. The possibility that these are extraterrestrial devices, that we are dealing with surveillance from some advanced technology, is a possibility I take very seriously."

Among others, noted educator and astronomer Dr. Carl Sagan indicated that "moderate support of investigations of UFOs might very well have some scientific paydirt in it," while social psychologist Robert L. Hall, then head of the Department of Sociology at the University of Illinois, concluded that the whole UFO matter "badly needs to be treated as something deserving serious study."

In a book published by Prentice-Hall entitled *The Andreasson Affair*, an experienced and reliable UFO investigator named Raymond Fowler documented the story of Betty Andreasson, who was involved in a strange UFO abduction case in a small Massachusetts town. Fowler spent a year investigating the case, utilizing the help of a skilled hypnotist from the New England Institute of Hypnosis.

On January 25, 1967, Mrs. Andreasson found her home plunged into darkness as a pulsating glow showed up outside her window, in her backyard. Several members of her family were stunned and unable to move when a number of humanoid figures entered her kitchen, took her out to a strange craft and, as in the case of the Hills, subjected her to a physical examination.

The investigation revealed many marked similarities to the Hill case. First, Betty Andreasson's daughter explained under hypnosis what one of the aliens looked like:

Sideways, he didn't have a mouth. When he turned, he did. It was like a *wrinkle* in clay—not a line, but like a line. . . . I can't see any nose. . . . The only thing I can see really good was the big . . . eyes. . . . I can't do anything—can't move. I'm not afraid of him because there's a feeling that he's not going to hurt me. . . .

In her trance Mrs. Andreasson described an oval craft very much like the one the Hills described, containing an examination room and complicated instruments. Her sketches of the aliens show them with huge slanted eyes, holes for the nose and a small slit for the mouth. They knew her name.

. . . he called me Betty. It seemed like an oral sound, but . . . I think it was a transformation of thought. . . .

Describing her physical examination under hypnosis, Betty Andreasson went into further detail:

> There's a big block . . . they had me on . . . lights coming from the walls . . . wires, *needle* wires . . . they inserted . . . a long silver thing through my belly button—my navel . . . they said there were some parts missing . . . because I had a hysterectomy, I guess. . . .

On December 3, 1967, a patrolman named Herbert Schirmer, of Ashland, Nebraska, was in his police cruiser on a road near Highway 63 shortly before three in the morning. He saw ahead of him what he thought was a truck that had broken down. Within moments the vehicle took off abruptly in the air, with lights flashing around its perimeter. He entered the incident on the police blotter, but it was only later, when a writer named Eric Norman arranged for Schirmer to undergo hypnosis, that the detailed story emerged.

Amnesia had set in the moment Schirmer saw the craft. With his memory sharpened, he recalled seeing the object settling on the ground as it extended a sort of telescopic landing gear.

One detail after another paralleled the Hill case. The crewmen appeared to be about five feet tall. One pair of eyes burned into Schirmer's consciousness. A ladder descended from the ship. The mouth was a slit that did not move. There were large oriental-type eyes. And the purported spaceman seemed to communicate by "making a sound and speaking through the mind."

Shreds of parallel evidence continued to pile up. Perhaps the most startling was the incident in October 1973 that stunned and threw into amnesia two shipyard workers in the town of Pascagoula, Mississippi. They were fishing from a dock when they saw an odd-looking airborne craft hovering behind them. It moved closer, emitting a strange blue haze. Both the men, Charles Hickson and Calvin Parker, were frozen with fear as three humanoid beings emerged from the craft and seemed to float through the air toward them. The men reported that they suddenly became numb, and then began to feel themselves being lifted and taken toward the craft.

Parker lost consciousness, but Hickson remembers feeling as if he were being floated toward the craft, airborne by its creatures. He recalled being given a scanning examination by a machine, and described the purported humanoids as pale and about five feet tall.

Within forty-eight hours Dr. Hynek had arrived in Mississippi with a writer named Ralph Blum, sent by NBC-TV, and an investigation was begun. Dr. James Harder, a professor of engineering at the University of California at Berkeley, came in from California. He is a consultant to the Aerial Phenomena Research Organization and a cautious researcher in the UFO field.

What attracted this group was the assurance of the sheriff's department that the men were genuinely upset by the experience and were not perpetrating a hoax. Later both Hickson and Parker volunteered for lie detector tests, which they passed with flying colors.

Statements by Charles Hickson bore striking similarities to the Hills' account:

—One of [the men] made a little buzzing noise . . . and two of them never made no noise. . . .
—[It was] a little buzzing sound   nnnnnnnn, nnnnnn.
—No force. They didn't hurt me. I didn't feel nothing. . . .
—Some kind of instrument, I don't know what it was. . . .
—I couldn't move. Just my eyes could move. . . .
—[The mouth was] like a slit—and I never saw that opening move. . . .

At a press conference Dr. Hynek said, "There's simply no question in my mind that these men have had what was to them a very real, frightening experience, the physical nature of which I am not certain about—and I don't think we have any answers to that. These men are absolutely honest. They have had a fantastic experience, and I also believe it should be taken in context with experiences that others have had elsewhere in the country and the world."

IN 1983, TWENTY-TWO years after the Hill encounter, nineteen years after hypnosis revealed the apparent abduction, and seventeen years after I first wrote the story, the event still lingers in my mind. In the intervening years three sad events took place. On February 25, 1969, Barney Hill suffered a stroke and died almost immediately. By tragic coincidence, Gerry Zimmermann, the *Look* editor who had worked with me on the story, died at almost the same time on the same day. Both were in their forties. In 1981 Dr. Simon finally succumbed to a long illness.

The voices of the doctor and Barney remain on the tapes as loud and clear as when they were alive. Each of them had probed and searched in a clinical attempt to solve the mystery, without evasion or self-deception. What still grips me is that, in spite of a devil's advocate position on the part of the doctor, Gerry Zimmermann and myself, the story clearly *cannot be ruled out*. And if it can't, then what? The implications are enormous.

I still remain wary of overacceptance of the UFO phenomenon, but I am equally wary of those who dismiss it without full and open-minded examination. Intelligent appraisal of the evidence is hindered by two types of people. On one side is the nondiscriminating enthusiast who is gullible enough to buy everything that comes down the pike. On the other side is the closed-minded skeptic who refuses even to examine the data, or if he does, seizes on irrelevancies to dismiss the entire subject. Unfortunately some scientists, in an attempt to discredit *all* UFOs simply because *some* reports concerning them are unfounded, resort to unscientific means to do so.

Many years after writing the story I was directing and producing a documentary film for ABC-TV about the future of space travel in the NASA space program. I interviewed at length Chris Kraft, a top NASA official, on the subject of possible contact with extraterrestrial civilizations. He stated without equivocation, "There is no question in my mind that in the future we will visit other civilizations, and they will visit us."

The question still remains in the light of the Hill case: Have we already been visited? Only further, deeper, unprejudiced investigation into the hundreds of UFO sightings that continue to be reported daily will give us the answer.

THE POSSESSION
OF SISTER JEANNE

The Possession
of Sister Jeanne

by
Norah Lofts

ILLUSTRATED BY ROBERT QUACKENBUSH

The year is 1626.

The place is Loudun, France, a small city about one hundred eighty-six miles southwest of Paris. Old stone houses and small shops spread upward along the slope of a hill, dominated by the spires of Saint Peter's church and the tall Gothic tower of the fortified castle.

It is a rainy, dull day when the nuns arrive, making their way along narrow streets to the crumbling, broken-down house where they are to live and begin a school for girls. No one could have guessed at that time anything of the strange, inexplicable phenomena that would soon overtake them there.

Here is a truly terrifying story of possession, exorcism and ultimate redemption told by the best-selling author Norah Lofts. Her many novels include *How Far to Bethlehem?*, a warm, compassionate recreation of the gospel story of the birth of Christ, and *The King's Pleasure*, a vibrant portrayal of Henry VIII's first wife, Katharine of Aragon.

CHAPTER ONE

WE CAME INTO LOUDUN in the rain. Gray rain falling from a gray sky; and there was the little gray town, and brooding over it the huge gray castle.

It could have been depressing, but we, weary and soaked as we were, were jubilant. We had arrived and we were about to begin the work for which we had been chosen.

We were Ursulines, commonly called black-and-white nuns, a teaching order. Eight of us had been sent to Loudun to establish a religious house and to start a school.

We were all weary, but I was the nearest to exhaustion, for I am a dwarf, barely four feet in height. I am also a hunchback with one shoulder higher than the other, and as a consequence, unless I make an effort to correct it, my head slightly awry. I found it very difficult to keep up with those who took normal strides; every now and then I had to put in some extra steps, like a child.

We knew our destination. Reverend Mother at Poitiers, who had chosen and dispatched us, had spoken with satisfaction and some merriment about the house she had secured for us. "We have obtained it so very cheaply," she had said, "because the foolish towns-folk believe it to be haunted." She had laughed, and dutifully we had also laughed, but I had felt an inward shudder. Still, the middle-aged sister now suddenly promoted to be prioress of the Loudun house had not taken any notice of the word but had asked in a brisk and practical manner, "Of what size, Reverend Mother?" Reverend Mother had laughed again. "Oh, vast," she had said, "vast! There will be room for more pupils than the eight of you can manage."

Pupils! I had felt another little shudder. Nobody could know how I dreaded the idea of standing with my crooked back and short legs before a class of girls, all well grown and straight.

But I was a nun. I had taken the vow of obedience. Of self-abnegation. Of resignation to God's will.

WE REACHED THE HOUSE. It was, as Reverend Mother had said, vast, and at two hundred and fifty livres a year, ridiculously cheap. But it was also completely unfurnished. That night, and several successive nights, we slept on the bare floor. Nuns do not expect comfort. The flesh must be mortified but even the strictest regime allows straw-stuffed mattresses. And here again, perhaps this deprivation affected me more than the others. It was impossible for me to arrange myself in any position that did not cause actual pain.

The house had ample larders, all completely empty, and on the first night we supped scantily on the remains of the food we had been given for the journey. The prioress distributed the morsels—about two mouthfuls each—with painstaking fairness. "A little extra fasting will hurt nobody," she said, "but this is a case when we must take thought for the morrow. To starve would make us weak and useless. Our confessor must help us. I rather wonder that he . . ." She cut short that remark. One does not criticize one's confessor.

When we saw Father Moussaut we understood. He was a sick man whom the slightest exertion rendered breathless. But that day he did exert himself on our behalf and before nightfall several of the leading Catholic families in the town had sent food. I emphasize Catholic because Loudun had a large Huguenot section, heretics who followed the teaching of that arch-heretic Martin Luther. There had been a time when the Huguenots had been persecuted and forced into exile; then somebody in a high place had realized that France was losing—to England and the Netherlands—a number of skilled people of thrifty habit. So now Huguenots were protected and *just* tolerated; but they had been dispersed. Loudun had been a reception area. Of the Huguenots, of course, nothing could be expected; they regarded religious houses with distrust.

And even to Catholics Father Moussaut had explained our situation badly, or been misunderstood. Somebody sent us, I remember, a prime joint of beef. But *raw*, and we had no kitchen utensils and no fuel for hearth or oven. And we had no money; absolutely none, not so much as a sou. Reverend Mother at Poitiers had performed an act of faith by sending us into the world with nothing but our clothes. For a day or two we could not even clean our new house; we had no broom, no scrubbing brush.

However, this situation soon righted itself. When people understood, gifts poured in. Most things were already well used, some of them shabby. I was born, I think, with the gift of a vivid imagination and I had kept it well exercised, so it was easy for me to visualize the mistress of a prosperous household saying, "Oh, those poor nuns in the rue Paquin! What can we spare for them?" And looking around, selecting the thing most easily to be spared: the cracked dish, the battered saucepan, the candlestick which lurched. But one must be grateful, not critical.

A Monsieur Caron was perspicacious enough to send us a carpenter with a bag of good tools and orders to do whatever the prioress told him. Her first request was that he should make the parlor *suitable*, as she called it. We are an enclosed order and not supposed—except in certain circumstances—to mingle freely with other people. Therefore we needed, across the room chosen as a reception place, a wall with a grille in it.

I heard the man ask, "At what level, Reverend Mother?"

"So that those who are behind it *stand*. That should discourage lingering and idle chatter."

She was a tall woman and she went and stood by the newly boarded wall, and the carpenter used his chalk. The grille, when made and barred, was well above my head level. I mention this seemingly irrelevant trifle because of the part which the parlor and the grille were to play in my life.

I did my share of cleaning, once we had the implements for it. Only two of us had ever before done manual labor. We developed blisters on our palms, we grazed our knuckles, we wore our knees so raw that we had to wad up our habits as pads to make further kneeling possible. The house had been unoccupied for so many years that the brushing and scrubbing seemed endless.

As with the walking, I strained myself to keep up with the others. In my compulsion to equal, or excel, and to be noticed, not pityingly, but with approbation, I drove myself to extremes, always trying to think of Our Lord, toiling under the weight of the Cross up the slope of Calvary, his back newly scourged. What were my paltry sufferings compared to His Agony?

Mine ended ignominiously. One afternoon a black cloud rolled in and engulfed me; I fell forward, my head in the bucket of dirty water. Sister Seraphima claimed afterward that only prompt action on her part saved me from drowning.

After that the prioress decreed that I was unfit for scrubbing. She said it with a justifiable degree of impatience. I could almost read her thought: Sent here to deal with a difficult situation, why could I not at least have had able-bodied women?

Her decision distressed me. I said meekly, "May I speak?"

"You have permission."

I said, "Mother, what happened this afternoon was but a passing weakness. Hitherto I have done my share. I have kept up with the others—"

She said, quite curtly, "I have other work for you. Well within your scope."

My heart rebounded. I thought: In the infirmary!

For that work I was especially suited because nothing repulsed me. In the Poitiers infirmary I had dealt matter-of-factly with terrible sores and shocking wounds. Once a woman had brought in her son whom a dog had bitten. His nose was, literally, hanging by a thread. I clapped it back into place, applied a liberal dressing of healing ointment and then a plaster to hold it firmly. Ten days later when I flaked off the plaster, there was his nose as good as new. I had most sedulously studied many herbals; I could prepare my own unguents and healing tonics. But of course in an established house like Poitiers I could not hope to be more than an acolyte. Could I, should I, be in a position of authority here?

"I am placing you in charge of the parlor," the prioress said.

I thought, but did not say: Oh, but my head reaches only to the lower edge of the grille! However, she had taken that into consideration and there was a tall stool. Seated upon it, I appeared, from the parlor, to be of normal size.

So, by sheer accident, I was given what I craved—contact with ordinary people, a finger on the pulse of the outer world, which may sound a strange thing for an Ursuline to crave. But the truth was—a truth which I admitted to myself, and was humiliated by—I had taken the veil in what I can only call a fit of pique.

But before judgment is issued on such a grave matter, let my childhood and early youth be considered. I was the seventh, and completely unwanted, child of my parents, both of them noble by birth. I had four sisters and two brothers, not one to be relied upon. There were rare flashes of kindness, but far more prevalent was a mood of teasing and derisory comment. At age ten I was shuttled off to a convent at Saintes. My aunt was mother superior there. In me she detected no aptitude and she sent me home, where again I was thoroughly miserable because so unwanted. Husbands must be found and dowries provided for the four properly shaped, fairly pretty girls. What hope for the misshapen one? Though my face was, and is, quite beautiful.

To my second convent I was not sent, I went of my own volition. That was the Ursuline house at Poitiers, and while I was there, my novitiate completed, my final vows not yet taken, a most singular thing happened. All my sisters and brothers died within a year; not in an epidemic, just accident, illness, illness, accident. Then, of course, my parents wanted me home—their sole heir.

But I thought of the twenty-one years of neglect, of the lack of love or care for my well-being. I ignored their pleas, took my final vows and the veil. Revenge is, I know, an unworthy thing. But oh! How sweet!

I paid for it, of course, and the price was high. A lifetime of boredom! I minded that more than anything else, being by nature gregarious, yearning for excitement, eager always for an audience. Admittedly, in the eyes of the outer world I was a cripple, but I had compensating gifts: a sharp but witty tongue, a keen sense of the ridiculous, the ability to mimic—all wasted in an Ursuline nun, living, speaking, even thinking according to rule. There must have been thousands of times when I regretted my choice and thought how much happier I should have been at home in my father's castle at Cozes, an heiress whom some man might marry for her money.

At Poitiers, once I was in the infirmary, the tedium was relieved and the regrets eased; for there I came into contact with ordinary people, people who did not speak and think to rule, people whom I could impress. My name in religion was Sister Jeanne of the Angels, and many a grateful patient had said how apt it was.

Would the parlor at Loudun offer me as much?

PEOPLE CAME TO THE convent for a variety of reasons. First and foremost, perhaps, curiosity. Ordinary women displayed an almost morbid interest in nuns and their way of life. Nobody, naturally, walked into that parlor and said: I have come to look at you who have shut the world away. And what they saw was just a rather sparsely furnished parlor, a rickety table, some oddly assorted chairs and my face behind the grille.

Many women said they had called to ask about the school. Was it true that a school was opening here? Yes, I said. Yes. And when would it open? I said when there were sufficient paying pupils to make it practical. I smiled; I was very civil; I was charming. Soon they were coming for other reasons. Would somebody write a letter? Did anybody know of a cure for a persistent cough? Or for ringworm? So my other skills were brought into play, and thanks to the Blessed Virgin and to Saint Teresa of Avila, to whom I felt a special devotion, four out of five of my cures worked. When the school opened there was no question of my standing before a group of contemptuous girls. "You are altogether too valuable here," the prioress said. She did not praise readily and maybe on this occasion she was influenced by the fact that I had begun to charge for my medicines! I adjusted my price to the dress or demeanor of my customer. I always apologized for marketing a gift that came from God. "But," I would say, "we are a poor house and some of the ingredients I use are very costly." Nobody objected to paying; some even added a little gift as well. Soon my purges and fever remedies, my cough potions and ointments, were providing a small but reasonably steady income at a time when we had no other.

Then people, mainly mothers, but a few fathers, began making application for places in the school for their daughters. And here again I was of great help to the prioress. I used to take a fresh sheet of paper and write down all relevant particulars—father's name and occupation; the girl's name and age and educational record, if any.

And all the while I was observing and assessing. Given permission to make free comment, I would say, "I think it would be unwise to take Mademoiselle X. When I mentioned the payment of fees in advance, her father did not protest, but I noticed that his hand tightened on his cane." The prioress gave me a sharp look, but she said, "I will trust your judgment." And it was as well that she did, for within a few months that man was bankrupt. I warned the prioress against another girl, sixteen years old, who had been in four separate educational establishments. "And why," I said to the prioress, "seek further schooling for a girl of marriageable age?" The answer to that was provided shortly afterward when the young woman eloped with her mother's coachman.

Finally, a sufficient number of girls having been enrolled, the school opened, and it prospered. The old house was full of lively young things, aged from about ten to fifteen, a few awkward—they would grow out of that; a few suffering from acne—and for that I had a sovereign remedy.

The parlor became even busier. There were loving parents, anxious parents, parents wishful to ascertain that they were getting value for their money.

I enjoyed it most when two or three females met in the parlor. Because I was behind the grille, they would talk together in low voices. But I had only to slide off the stool to become invisible. Then they would speak in more natural voices, laugh or exclaim in horror.

The chief subject of their gossip was a Father Grandier, the priest in charge of Saint Peter's.

Urbain Grandier.

I had never seen the man, but Grandier, I gathered, was very handsome, more like a gentleman of fashion than a parish priest. He was tall and of muscular build; his hair and eyes were black, the hair curly. He was invariably well dressed. He preferred the company of the well-to-do, and himself lived like a lord, for he added to his stipend by accepting various offices which, in a small town, are offered to a man of education.

Such a man need not be sexually attractive, but I heard, with my own ears, one lady confide in another that even with the curtain of the confessional box between them, the mere sound of his voice so thrilled her that she almost swooned with ecstasy. "And I have been twice married," she said. They laughed together in a suggestive manner, sharing something completely outside my experience.

And had I been as pure of heart as I wished to be, as I prayed to be made, I should not have recognized the suggestiveness, nor been affected by it. As I was. To the peril of my immortal soul, I was.

It began insidiously. Just a quickening of interest whenever I heard his name. I would slide off my stool and stand, almost holding my breath, willing the speaker to speak more loudly, to say more, to be more explicit. There was never—or almost never—anything to Grandier's credit in what I overheard. His behavior, if half of what I heard and pieced together was true, would have been intolerable even in a layman; and this was a priest, vowed to celibacy. But—and here was the contradiction which was so fascinating—he was superbly brave; he thought the celibacy of the secular clergyman a mistake and he was not afraid to say so.

Handsome, sexually irresistible, brave and arrogant. What better—or more dangerous—mixture could be devised?

Women might whisper and flutter and hint. Men were more outspoken, and their voices carried better.

Men sometimes came to the parlor; some were fond fathers, unlike mine. Often they were somewhat sheepish, saying that since they found themselves on our street, or since they happened to be in town, they would just like to know how little Marie or Madeleine was settling down. Some men came on business: men who had worked on the tumbledown house or, once we were established, had contracts to supply us with essentials. Such things as contracts and bills the prioress now left entirely to me.

One quite regular caller was Monsieur Adam, the apothecary, whose business was always with me, for even the most skillful herbalist needs some substances that she cannot grow or gather—bitter aloes and opium, to name only two. Adam was a most virulent enemy of Grandier's and one evening he said to another man, "Cocky swine—he'll come to no good, mark my words. He has an enemy in Cardinal Richelieu."

"But the cardinal is in Paris."

"He is *now*. But years ago . . . Surely you know the story. No? Well, years ago, Richelieu paid a visit to Saint Peter's. Even then he outranked Grandier, and in the procession should have preceded him.

But that arrogant swine took Richelieu by the arm and pulled him back. 'In *my* church,' he said, '*I* go first.' "

"The cardinal has probably forgotten."

"If His Eminence has—*he could be reminded!*"

I felt, absurdly, as though I were threatened. Contrary to my custom when Grandier was under discussion, I clambered up upon my stool and hit the little bell with which I had been provided. I said, "Gentlemen, I am ready to give you some attention."

I found myself looking at the apothecary with disfavor. For I was now committed. In my mind I had already been seduced by Urbain Grandier.

It began with dreams, so vivid, so real-seeming, that I would go about all day feeling his arms about me, his mouth on mine.

There I was, crookbacked little Sister Jeanne of the Angels, fulfilling her pleasurable but mundane duties. In my dreams I was transfigured; all the rest of me as beautiful as my face; and happy. So happy.

I fought this obsession; let nobody believe otherwise. I went into retreat for seven days: complete solitude, and one small slice of coarse stale bread, one cup of water, a day. It availed me nothing. He still came to me in my dreams; and in those dreams we drank rare wines and ate exotic fruit together. I scourged myself mercilessly, lay down scarcely able to bear the touch of the rough blanket upon my torn flesh; I fell asleep and there he was, waiting to embrace me. And at his touch I was healed.

He invaded my days, too. And looking back, I think how ironic, considering all that happened, how ironic it is that in all my waking thoughts he should be associated with something beautiful: the scent of a flower, a tree coming into leaf, a sunset or a sunrise, even a pleasant color in a gown worn by another woman. All, everything, led me directly back to Urbain.

The prioress, who was observant in a detached way, stopped me one evening and said, "Sister Jeanne, are you well? You have grown very thin."

I said the first thing that came into my head.

"Reverend Mother, a delicate frame runs in the family."

She said, "Have a care to yourself. We can none of us afford to fall ill these days."

That was all too true; now that the school was in being, everybody was overworked. Sister Seraphima, a woman of the people, did all the cooking, helped by one raw young maid. Sister Marie, also a peasant, was bravely tackling the overgrown garden. I was in the parlor, so that left only five nuns to teach almost fifty girls of varying age and ability. The prioress herself had little learning as such, but she was musical and had a good head for figures. Her accounts were most meticulously kept.

CHAPTER TWO

IT WAS AT ABOUT this time that the haunting began. Six of the senior girls occupied a large bedroom, with Sister Marie-Céleste in a curtained cubicle near the door. One night they all rushed out in their nightclothes, screaming that their wing of the house was falling down. It was possible; we had been able to afford only the very minimum in the way of restoration.

The prioress said, "I must investigate," and moved along the passage. I followed without drawing attention to myself.

The room stood foursquare; there were the beds, hastily vacated but otherwise ordinary. No timber had collapsed, no brick or bit of plaster had fallen. There was a perceptible chill, but the month was November.

The prioress was very angry. She scolded Marie-Céleste for losing her head, asked her how she would behave in a real emergency, such as a fire, reduced her to tears and set her a moderate penance. Then she sent her to me for a sedative, not a sleeping draft, because work must go on as usual. So I had a firsthand account.

"The noise was terrible," Marie-Céleste said. "I veritably believed that the wall was falling. And the wind blew in, that I swear. My curtains swayed."

Three mornings later a woman rustled into the parlor and came straight to the grille. A woman of substance, very well dressed. By craning my neck to the window I could see a good coach, good horses. The woman's manner, however, was anything but assured; rather, a mixture of deference, aggressiveness and embarrassment.

"Good morning, Sister. I am Madame Laval. I have come—come

to take my daughter, Anne, away. I cannot allow—her father will not allow her to remain in a haunted house."

"Madame, I myself went into the room within five minutes. And there was nothing of which anyone need be frightened."

"So it may seem. But there is more to it. My husband knows. Some forty years ago friends of his parents rented this house. It suited them, they needed space: six children, *their* parents, on both sides, and some aunts. They stayed, my husband says, a bare six months. They found it intolerable. The haunting was so bad that nobody could sleep."

That inward shudder shook me again, but I said, "Madame Laval, why, knowing this, and evidently believing it as you do, did you send your daughter here in the first place?"

"Ah! It was not done without consideration. My husband and I talked many times with Father Moussaut. He said that the place being occupied by holy women, and the chapel being consecrated by the bishop, any evil, if evil there was, would have been exorcised. Now it seems to be otherwise. I have two sons, but Anne is my only daughter. I cannot risk her being driven mad!"

"Has anyone ever been driven mad?"

"Oh," she said. "In the past, several. I paid no heed to such old tales until the school opened." Her voice became wistful. "I did so wish—and my husband also wished—that Anne should have a little schooling. And not too far away."

I knew that the prioress would grieve over the loss of a pupil, not because Anne Laval could not be easily replaced, but because the school would gain a bad name. So I tried again.

"Madame Laval, I can assure you there is nothing to fear. I think a gust of wind in the chimney wakened one girl, who screamed and started a little panic."

"That is how it begins. When Anne's letter came, my husband remembered. A sound as though heavy furniture were being moved. But that is only the beginning."

"What follows?" I asked in a light voice as though asking advice about a recipe for making a cake.

"Worse things. The sound of a child wailing pitiably—where no child is. Spectral figures. And things thrown about in the kitchen. . . . Then madness."

I was to spend a great deal of time—after Anne Laval had been removed—brooding over the things that her mother had mentioned: in particular, *holy women.*

I was presumably one of them. But what of my dreams, and the memories of dreams that brimmed over into my waking day? Urbain Grandier and I under flowering trees that shed perfume; in warm, firelit, tapestried rooms.

THE HAUNTING CONTINUED and it took the form that Madame Laval had described. It was oddly selective. One evening as we returned from chapel, the prioress, who was walking ahead, stopped and stiffened.

"Oh!" she said. "So they've begun *that* now! Well, I must make it abundantly clear that we cannot start an orphanage here. We have not the facilities." She strode to the main entrance, unbolted the bolts, which were shut at sunset, and looked out into the quiet street. She seemed surprised, confused.

"I am sure I heard a baby wailing."

"So did I."

"Yes, assuredly."

"I heard it, too."

"It was unmistakable."

Four, like the prioress, had heard the cry; three had not, and I was one of the unhearing.

Sister Seraphima, with good peasant sense, said, "It was a cat, Reverend Mother. Cats at times make human noises."

That was accepted, a trifle too easily.

And a few days later a possible explanation was forthcoming.

Sister Marie was intent upon making an asparagus bed. The vegetable is not only delicious, but has blood-purifying qualities, just at the time of year when they are most needed, especially by the young.

An asparagus bed requires special preparation: deep digging, a thick layer of broken crockery or broken bricks to ensure good drainage. So Sister Marie dug deep. She dug like a man, but on that day she came back into the house tremulous and pale as a young girl.

She had unearthed the skeleton of a child!

We did our best to rectify matters—a proper coffin for the poor little bones and a requiem mass for the child's soul.

Naturally we kept the truth from the students, and Sister Marie chose another site for her asparagus bed.

There it should have ended; but it did not. The wailing recurred, in this dormitory or that, in a passageway or on the stairs. And always there were those who heard and those who did not.

Then, equally mystifying, and more disruptive, pandemonium broke loose in the kitchen. Sister Seraphima remained staunchly skeptical. When a saucepan fell from a shelf she blamed herself or the young maid. "It was not placed securely," she said. When a thing disappeared, often to reappear in some unlikely place, "I must have done it myself," she said. "Absentmindedness grows with age and I am almost seventy."

But the young maid, who had been so grateful for the job, said she could stand no more and left abruptly. And although it was in many ways an enviable job, if only because in the convent no young girl was in danger of seduction from the master or sons of the household, and although there was in Loudun, as elsewhere, a plentitude of poor girls, members of large families glad to have one less mouth at the table, no one came forward. Since Sister Seraphima could not possibly manage unaided, we all took turns helping.

I assumed responsibility for the preparation of vegetables. I could shell peas, skin onions, peel potatoes, and also keep an eye on the parlor. I used the kitchen as a pharmacy, so I was often there in the evening, when the parlor had closed. I never heard or saw or sensed anything uncanny in the kitchen, yet it was as a result of my work there that I suffered my first supernatural experience.

Because I was now virtually doing three jobs—in the parlor, in the infirmary, and in the kitchen—the prioress, who noticed more than she ever seemed to, excused me from all attendance at chapel after sunset. It was within her power to do so; a nun in disgrace could be banned from chapel altogether, the deprivation being part of her punishment. But I was not in disgrace; in fact, for the first time, the prioress regarded me and spoke to me with something approaching approval. She said that she had observed my exertions, realized that I missed the usual recreation hour and thought I needed fresh air. "Go walk a little, and then sit in the garden," she said. "Take advantage of the fine weather. You can tell your beads."

By this time Sister Marie's labors in the garden were having visible effect. Several tough bushes, freed of entanglements, had revived amazingly, and in cleared patches she was growing flowers, always white ones, for the altar. On that particular evening—it was June, the eve of Saint Peter's and Saint Paul's Day—a patch of those lilies known by the Madonna's name was in full flower. There was honeysuckle, too.

It was a sultry evening and after walking conscientiously for about five minutes I sat down on a stone bench.

Scents can be very sensual. My rosary hung at my waist, untouched. I relinquished myself to thoughts of Grandier, of Urbain, the lover of my dreams.

For the first time my two worlds—the waking one so bleak, so virginal, so busy, and the dream one so utterly otherwise—seemed to come together. The warmth, the fragrance, and the sound of sweet singing from the little chapel combined to form an atmosphere not unlike that of fantasy.

I let myself go and was brought to with a jolt.

It was a voice. Male, but not Urbain's. I had never in real life heard him speak but I had heard a great deal about his voice: so low and soothing and seductive, yet capable of resonance, when required. Adam, the apothecary, had once said, in my hearing, "He could talk himself out of an iron trap."

This was not such a voice. It was harsh, grating, a trifle shrill. No, it is impossible to describe it, for we poor humans have only human words, worn smooth with use.

"We have been watching," the voice said. "We have been listening. We disapprove. You will all be punished."

The voice was very distinct. A saw, penetrating the mind. Yet I was alone. Completely alone in the scented garden, and whereas I had been warm, basking in the lingering heat of the day, I was suddenly cold as though a barrelful of iced water had been emptied over my head.

The shock of it rendered me breathless, but I just managed to gasp out, "Who . . . what are you?"

"I am Asmodeus. One day you will know me well." There was laughter, mocking and jeering. Then nothing.

When I could move, though still all ashudder, I got up and went in search of the prioress. As I walked, I thought again of my conversation with Madame Laval.

I found the prioress in her own small private parlor. She was not a woman to panic easily but at the sight of me she rose up in alarm.

"Sister Jeanne! What is the matter? Are you ill?"

I shook my head, struggling for speech. "Not ill. I have . . . just received . . . a bad shock."

"Well, we know the cure for that, don't we?" She eased me into a chair. She recovered her composure; she even ventured a mild joke. "You have so often prescribed for others, now *I* will prescribe for *you*." She unlocked the cupboard in which our small, precious supply of cognac was kept. Whenever I needed a little to add to my potions, I had to apply to her, and I had seen her unlock that cupboard in precisely the same unhurried way countless times.

"Drink that," she said, handing me a full measure. It was excellent brandy, probably produced at my father's own small distillery. It ran through my veins, warming and steadying.

"Now," the prioress said, "tell me."

I told her, word for word. She was not a well-read woman and the dread name Asmodeus meant nothing to her.

"And who is he, pray?"

"A demon. One of Satan's angels. The demon of envy and possessiveness."

She gave me one of her sharp looks. "And how did you come by such knowledge?"

"When I was dismissed from Saintes I could read. My grandfather had accumulated a library of sorts. I read many books—some very old."

"Books no nun would read?"

"I was not a nun then."

"And now you are! I must ask you to remember your vows when you took the veil. You renounced the world, did you not? And all this unseemly pagan nonsense should have gone with it. I can tell you exactly what happened to you in the garden. You fell into a doze and dreamed. This *taint*, the result of unwise reading, took charge of your sleeping mind. Are you a habitual dreamer?"

"Yes, Mother. I dream."

"There you are, then." She was prepared to dismiss the whole thing.

I said, "You are my superior. I must not argue. But may I venture an opinion? Thank you. I fear there is more to it. Madame Laval told me exactly." I recounted what the woman had said. "Until this evening I have been immune. I have heard nothing—"

"There was nothing to hear."

"Reverend Mother, forgive me, *but you yourself heard a child crying.*"

She looked at me with a serene, untroubled stare. "Oh, that! It was a cat. There is *always* some logical explanation. There must be."

I used Madame Laval's word and said, "Then you do not think that the house should be exorcised?"

She jumped as though a hornet had stung her. "I do *not!* What a suggestion! The idea is benighted. Only certain priests, specially trained, are allowed to attempt it—and that by special permission from a bishop. And even so, the results are often calamitous."

"Why? If, as you hold, there is nothing to be exorcised, nothing not subject to logical explanation?"

There was quite a long silence. Then she said, "You should not argue with me. I think the very notion of exorcism is bad, and the men who do it, even with the permission of a bishop, are encroaching; taking to themselves powers which belong to God alone. Do you follow me? I know I lack your handiness with words. I can only say plainly that I know firsthand of two attempted exorcisms. Both exorcists went mad. One killed himself."

I stayed silent and she said, "You have been overworking. You are not robust. You were overtired, you sat in the garden. I always find the scent of lilies conducive to slumber. You slept. You dreamed of an evil but, I assure you, nonexistent thing. Now, would you wish to be relieved of some of your hours in the parlor? Perhaps Sister Mathilde, or I myself—"

I was so alarmed that I interrupted her. "Reverend Mother, no. Please do not even consider it. I *was* overtired. I fell asleep, as you say. I am sorry that I troubled you."

She looked faintly pleased. "I have always regarded you as a sensible woman. Go to bed now. The brandy should bring you sound sleep."

It brought me the strangest dream yet. In my dream I relived exactly what had happened in the garden, and hurried in to find the prioress. But it was not the prioress who awaited me in the private parlor; it was Urbain. He took me, cold and shivering, into his warm embrace. He said: I will save you. Only believe in me. Only believe . . .

Two days later, in the parlor, I heard voices, regretful or gloating, talking about what had happened to Father Grandier.

IT BEGAN WITH a certain section of Grandier's parishioners appealing to the bishop at Poitiers for permission to take the sacrament from "hands less impure" than his. The bishop asked in what way were his hands impure, and he was told.

I can hold no brief for Urbain. During his many years in Loudun more than one girl had been obliged to marry hastily and pretend that her baby was slightly premature. The latest of these was Philippe Trincant. Her father was a man of wealth and position—and Urbain's sworn enemy.

Against these sins of the flesh his virtues were set out for the bishop's consideration. Grandier was very charitable. He preached such wonderful sermons that his church of Saint Peter in the Market was always crowded and its offertory boxes crammed.

I heard all this in bits and pieces. It was like making a patchwork quilt, but frankly there was so much evidence against him, the word *impure* was so fully justified, that the bishop had no choice. He deprived Urbain of his living.

And then, with an effrontery and arrogance that the unregenerate part of me could only admire, Urbain went to the archbishop and with his golden voice and gifted tongue persuaded him to overrule the bishop.

It was what I had prayed for, day and night, night and day—when I should have been praying for the safety of my soul, and for strength to deal with my duties, which were formidable.

ONE EVENING AFTER SUPPER the prioress sent for me.

"Sit down," she said. "I have something of importance to tell you. I have been recalled."

I thought: Why tell *me?* I said, "I am sorry. We shall miss you, Mother." It was true; she had represented something—an effortless authority, practical good sense. Rather stern but always just.

"Our feelings are of no importance," she reminded me. "In this case there is an undesirable element of haste. I leave tomorrow. But the very haste brings me a certain advantage. I am empowered to choose my successor."

I thought: She has chosen Sister Mathilde and is informing me first because she knows that Mathilde and I do not get on well together. She outranked me, her father being a marquis, and she never failed to remind me. But then, I often reminded others of my own high origin, so I could not well resent Mathilde's attitude. However, apart from that, we were personally antagonistic.

"I have chosen you, Sister Jeanne of the Angels."

I reeled as from a heavy physical blow. I opened my mouth to protest, to ask *why,* but my mouth had dried up. She wanted no words from me; she wasted no time in compliments, or in telling me why she had reached her decision. She said briskly, "Well now, what remains is for me to hand over." And there were her accounts, so well kept, clear and explicit, and in a hand which resembled that of a six-year-old child. I found it all very touching. Touching, too, the fact that she did not know her own destination. Merely that it was a disorderly house needing a firm hand. "I shall be told more when I reach Poitiers," she said with simple trust.

As we pored over the books the magnitude of the task she had set me seemed to grow, to become overwhelming; I shrank from it. When she closed the last book and inquired, "Is there anything you wish to ask?" I said, "Yes, Reverend Mother. . . . Why not Sister Mathilde?"

"The letter bringing me my orders arrived yesterday evening. Do you not think I have pondered and prayed for guidance? Why do *you* suggest Mathilde?"

"She is older. She has dignity. She is not . . . malformed."

"Also she has no talent for getting on with people. She offends—often unwittingly. We are an enclosed order but the head of a school is forced into contact with parents and others. I have watched you in the parlor, you have tact. People like you. Of dignity you have sufficient. I would advise you to forget your lack of inches, your uneven shoulders."

She stood up, dismissing me. She had decided, and there was no appeal.

Then at the last minute something of her iron composure fell away. She said in a low voice but with great intensity, "I made this place from nothing. I have watched it grow. I took pride in my own achievement. God observed, and in His great mercy has seen fit to remove me from further temptation in that regard."

I thought: That is the correct attitude. I also thought: How can I measure up to such a standard, not of behavior only, but of thought?

She said, composed again, "I will not say that I hand it to you as a sacred trust. No earthly thing warrants such words. I leave you a piece of unfinished work, trusting that you will add a little, and when the time comes, hand over as confidently as I do. Sister Jeanne of the Angels, I shall pray for you. I request your prayers."

"Constantly," I said, near to tears, "constantly."

WHAT I NOTICED first was the fact that nobody, not even Sister Mathilde, seemed to resent my sudden promotion. It was as though my misshapenness, and my duties in the parlor, had always set me a little apart, and that that was why I had been chosen. And accepted by all.

The second thing I noticed was how easily the mantle of authority slipped over me. I had dreaded the responsibility of the post, but I soon saw that it consisted in making day-to-day decisions and I found that I could do it easily, with no hesitation and no self-distrust.

One of my first decisions was to relax the rules. I let it be known that I was accessible at any hour. I dealt drastically with the question of beds. When we first came to Loudun we had slept on the bare floor; then we had straw-stuffed pallets between our bones and the boards, and then a few charitable people had sent us beds. There was not one for each of us and the prioress had made that the excuse to send them all back. Sister Mathilde had ventured to suggest that we use the beds in rotation, but the answer to that was that one night in a soft bed would make the pallet seem harder.

When the school opened, every student had a bed. Some brought their own; others were made by the carpenter: simple structures, each an oblong of sailcloth stretched over a wooden frame, supported by four legs. We sisters had rather hoped that while these were in the making some might be made for us. But my predecessor had been adamant.

Now I ordered a bed for everybody. Also, I introduced a little wine on Sundays and feast days. Most nuns suffer from thin blood and the best cure is a sound diet. I arranged for more meat to be delivered and for fresh fish, whenever possible, to be served on Fridays instead of the everlasting stockfish.

I did not think that I was overindulgent, merely a trifle less Spartan. And I was not extravagant, for the school was now a paying concern. During that first scare two other girls had been removed, but one had actually come back and there had been no further withdrawals. For no harm had ever come to any girl, and in Loudun snobbery was rife. What did the occasional scare count against the advantage of being taught the use of the globes by the daughter of a marquis?

AMID ALL THIS BUSYNESS my dreams and some of my waking thoughts continued to be obsessed by Urbain Grandier. I had retained for myself the parlor duties, so I was well, if patchily, informed. After almost a year's absence Grandier was back in triumph. His enemies were furious, his supporters gloating. He gave a great feast for his friends and supporters, his friends gave feasts for him. By this time the Ursulines were established, largely approved and often the subject of casual charities. One of Urbain's friends sent us a haunch of venison from his overloaded table and I wondered if Urbain had himself suggested it. Did I figure in his mind as he did in mine? I soon knew the answer to that!

In June 1631 Father Moussaut, our confessor and spiritual director, died and I had to choose someone to replace him. I knew I was playing with fire but I seemed to have no choice in the matter. The idea of hearing that wonderful voice, of actually having some physical proximity, was too much for me. I even indulged in sophistry— perhaps on closer acquaintance I should like him less. I might even be delivered from an infatuation which stood between me and God.

I wrote Urbain Grandier a brief, dignified letter inviting him to become our confessor.

After two days of racking anxiety I received his answer. It was civil, brief and definite. He had so many subsidiary offices, he wrote, that he could not undertake any more. He was sorry . . .

I knew a moment of utter desolation, the old feeling of being rejected which, once suffered, is so easily renewed, swamping me. And then a searing anger came to my aid.

I have always had a hot temper; since my taking the veil, reined, disciplined, I would have said extinct. Now it flared up. It literally scorched me. I was flushed and shaking as though in a high fever. Then, as a fever bout does, it passed into a healing sweat. Great drops, like tears, rolled down my face and fell upon that detestable letter.

This seems incredible, even to me, but when I was calm again and the sweat had dried, I hated Urbain Grandier as much as I had once loved him, despised him as much as I had once secretly admired him. Mentally I aligned myself with his enemies, and could I have thought of a way to injure him, I would have taken it promptly and joyfully. But a cloistered nun was unlikely to find a way of working harm against a man who plainly stood high in the favor of the archbishop.

Nevertheless, I was to do Urbain Grandier irreparable harm. But not in any ordinary way. Not, ironically, of my own spiteful will.

CHAPTER THREE

JUNE IS THE MONTH of roses, and thanks to Sister Marie, a few of ours, freed from choking growths, had flowered. But they had produced blooms much akin to wild ones, pale and fragile. That morning, as I opened the door upon the street, I became aware of an overpowering scent of roses, sweeter than any in our garden, and there on the top step lay a little bunch of six superb dark red ones. They were at the best stage, buds half open. I picked them up, held them to my nose; they were most heavily perfumed. I then tucked them into my waistband.

This was the kind of indulgence which the former prioress would never have permitted, but I was not strict about such things. I had even allowed Sister Seraphima to adopt a stray cat. The pretense was that it would deal with any mice, but in reality it was a pet upon which poor old Seraphima could lavish much affection.

Now and then during the day I wondered who had placed the roses there. Occasionally people, too shy to make a close approach, did leave little offerings on the steps, but usually of a practical nature. And the bunch had not been dropped by accident from a flower seller's basket. It had been deliberately placed.

That day two of the sisters remarked upon my nosegay. Sister Mathilde stooped her tall proud head and smelled the flowers. Later in the day Sister Marie said, "Mother, what fine roses! But they are flagging. May I take them, and revive them?" She said something about crushing their stems and plunging them up to their necks in water. "They'll be as good as new in the morning; even better, more open."

She sniffed them as she carried them away.

Since Grandier's refusal and my cleansing anger about it, I had enjoyed, until that day, great peace of soul and felt nearer to God than I had ever been.

At that season of the year the light lingered so that the only candles needed were on the altar. The evening, like dark blue velvet, pressed against the windows. The day's work completed, the world shut away. Total peace. Even the scent of the lilies, prolific again this year, did not remind me of that similar evening.

Inside my head all went silent. Then Asmodeus' rasping voice said, "Jeanne of the Angels, you remember me, I am Asmodeus. I claimed you first." A deeper, more masculine voice said, "I am new to you. My name is Isacaaron. You would do better with me. I am the demon of impurity. Choose!"

"I cannot! I cannot! I want neither of you. Go away, leave me. Oh, God the Father, God the Son, God the—"

"Stop that! We will decide." And they proceeded to tear me between them.

Those who think that demoniac possession is a thing of the imagination, or something to be made a show of or something to mock at should think again and believe me. It is more painful than any torture man has yet devised. I had never been supple, but I ended on the floor, seated with my legs spread out at right angles. The pain was excruciating. I screamed, "Help me! Help me!"

Only old Sister Seraphima came forward, and she came gingerly. As she helped me toward the door I saw the bodies of two nuns lying prone. I pulled myself together and remembered that under God I was in charge of this house, responsible for all that happened within it. To the other nuns, huddled together, all pale as paper and some of them crying, I spoke with authority: "Help your sisters. Don't stand there like silly sheep!" Even that much exertion exhausted me and I was obliged to lean heavily on Seraphima. Almost in a whisper I asked, "Which? And what happened to them?"

"Sister Mathilde and Sister Marie. They suffered smaller seizures. And less real. Never mind them. It is a matter of imitation. I've seen it often enough. One faints with good cause and others drop down for none."

It sounded reasonable, especially when said in that grudging, grumbling country voice. But I thought: Mathilde and Marie—they also smelled those roses!

Sister Seraphima helped me to bed and brought me a glass of milk, well laced with brandy. "It will help you to sleep."

"What form did my seizure take?"

"It was awful, Reverend Mother. You screamed, as though in great agony; you threw yourself about; you called strange words. And called upon God." She stopped a moment, then continued rather timidly, "If I may say so, it was like the madness that comes upon dogs in hot weather. Except for the words."

"Asmodeus? Isacaaron?"

"Yes! Yes! Are they saints? Two I have never heard of?"

Unfair to unload upon this good, simple soul the burden of my loathsome knowledge, so I quickly changed the direction of the conversation.

"And the others?"

"The same in form, but much less severe; they did not cry out. Sleep now. And may I offer one word of advice? If you can, sleep through." She meant not to rise at midnight to pray in the chapel. I had no wish to do so, though I slept little, churning things over in my mind.

I decided that the one person in whom I could and must confide was our new confessor, Father Mignon. I had chosen him deliberately, for he was one of Grandier's enemies. For one thing, he envied him those many offices; for another, he was related to the Trincant family, cousin to the Philippe Trincant whom Grandier had made pregnant.

Father Mignon was not worldly or flamboyant, as Grandier was, nor old and almost passive, as Father Moussaut had become. He was of a mystical, rather nervous disposition; nerves twitched in his face, his hands were rarely still.

When I rose next morning I was surprised—and yet not surprised—to find myself absolutely covered with bruises. Possession by devils is supposed to affect the soul and the mind, but I bore visible signs. Not so very different from the stigmata that exceptionally holy women can show. But of how different an origin!

I sent a servant—we had some now, mostly old and rather crack-brained—to ask Father Mignon to meet me in the chapel. I felt that it would be slightly less embarrassing to be frank with the curtain between us.

I told him everything. My long obsession with Urbain Grandier. . . I heard Father Mignon draw a sharp, hissing breath at the mention of that name. I told him of my experience in the garden and of last evening's events.

He listened most patiently. At the end he asked only one question. "You are *sure* of this? It is not the product of an overheated imagination?"

"Father, I am sure."

"Then," he said, like a doctor prescribing a remedy, "what we need is an exorcist."

I remembered what my predecessor had said of exorcism. I said, falteringly, "Is that necessary, Father? I mean . . . I had rather hoped that you . . . I have now confessed all. Could you not absolve . . . and liberate me?"

"I have no such power. I will apply to the Carmelites."

I said, "At the beginning . . . the then Reverend Mother told me that exorcism could be dangerous. I think the word she used was *calamitous*."

"That is correct. In the wrong hands. But the Carmelites will send an experienced exorcist."

IN FACT THEY SENT three. All grave but self-assured men.

Oh, I can still hear the sonorous phrases: "I exorcise thee, most unclean spirit, every onslaught of the Adversary, every specter, every legion, in the name of Our Lord Jesus Christ, be thou uprooted and put to flight from this creature of God."

Such exhortations were worse than useless. The devils became more violent and soon we were all possessed, except Seraphima, whose staunch disbelief in the demons seemed to protect her, and Marie, who had been one of the first to be affected, but who claimed she had cured herself by eating garlic, an old remedy against witchcraft.

So we all ate garlic and went about stinking, but gained no relief.

When I say *all* I mean a larger community than the eight of us who had originally trudged to Loudun. As the school expanded, we had, of necessity, expanded too, and there were now seventeen of us, fifteen possessed in varying degrees, two apparently immune.

And despite what was said afterward, no pupil was ever affected. The devils moved against only those who had taken the veil.

It was a time of great confusion, of terror and of pain, but we tried to keep it private, and there must be few places on earth more suited for privacy than a convent. Even the grille in the parlor had its shutter. We managed somehow to see that the pupils' routine was not disrupted, and so far the exorcisms had been performed behind locked doors in the chapel.

I, the most possessed, the most accursed of all, was the one who first broke through this carefully preserved facade.

ONE MORNING, BEING HAPPILY free of the devils, I was behind the parlor grille when a woman entered. She was young, pretty, and elegantly dressed. As she moved toward me I could smell her sweet perfume.

She had come, she said, to ask leave to take one of our boarders— her niece—out for the day to celebrate the girl's birthday. (More latitude in such things had been one of my innovations. I could see no logical reason for treating pupils as though they were nuns.)

I said, "Certainly. If I may just have your name."

"I am Mademoiselle de Brou."

Grandier's latest mistress!

Except for the fact that any love affair indulged in by a priest is scandalous, this liaison had been relatively innocuous; no cuckolded husband or heartbroken father had been involved. Mademoiselle de Brou was of full age and had independent means.

I looked at her and realized that she had known in fact those embraces of which I had merely dreamed. And as I stared, Asmodeus, demon of envy and possessiveness, took possession of me. He pushed me so that I leaned closer to the grille, and he used my voice.

"Whore!" I shrieked. "Strumpet! Debaucher of priests! Committer of the ultimate sacrilege!" Then I spat at her.

She put her hands over her ears and ran, stumbling, to the door while Asmodeus took me by the nape of the neck and banged my head, with great violence, three times against the grille. Then he snatched the stool from under me so that I lay, crumpled and crooked and in great pain, on the floor.

If my words—Asmodeus' words—shamed Madeleine de Brou, she recovered quickly, and was able to tell of her experience. By nightfall the story was all over the town, with a most curious result. In the parlor I had always been treated with the respect due me; now there was a kind of awed admiration combined with a certain familiarity. Adam, the apothecary, coming to deliver to me some items I had requested, said, "Reverend Mother, there are things which should be said openly. And you have said them."

PRESENTLY IT WAS DISMALLY apparent that our first exorcists had failed, and Father Mignon decided to call in Father Barré, who lived in Chinon and who had a great reputation as an exorcist. Father Barré came, all agog, very confident of his power to deal with any manifestation of evil. At our first meeting he told me that it was essential that exorcisms be held in public; that previous failure to drive out the devils was due to the secrecy.

Those who say that I rushed headlong to seek publicity do me wrong. I hesitated. I protested. I said, "Father, a public exorcism would make plain what we have tried to conceal. I must think first of our school. We have all taken great pains to keep our pupils in ignorance."

"So! You place a mercenary consideration before the glory of God? There is your error. The power of God must not be displayed in a corner; it must be seen and recognized by as many people as possible. To put it bluntly, madame, I exorcise in public—or not at all."

What choice had I?

How CAN I DESCRIBE the horror of those public exorcisms with a gaping crowd crammed into our small chapel? The devils throve on the attention and made us do even more outrageous things.

Possession itself is inconceivable to those who have not suffered it. For one thing, it is far from consistent. There were times when we were so completely possessed as to be like people in a trance, unaware of our actions and words. The other times were far worse, for then we were half conscious of the use the demons were making of our voices and our bodies; we shared the mob's horror at what we said and did, yet we were helpless.

The people who watched were entertained, but not amused. The devils had no sense of humor; they specialized in lewdness and obscenity; they made us defile the altar, insult the very Host. And once Isacaaron, using my voice, screamed out that Urbain Grandier had bewitched us.

I had told Father Mignon the whole story—but under the seal of the confessional. Among those who now heard me were both friends and enemies of Grandier; the friends rushed to warn him, and I learned later that he had laughed and shrugged, and said, "Why heed mad women with so many sane ones around?"

The most immediate result of this publicity was the withdrawal of pupils from the school. Some parents demanded a return of fees that had been paid in advance. It was impossible for me not to think—in my lucid intervals—of my predecessor, Mother Bernard, and that one wistful moment when, leaving her work unfinished, she had handed it over to me. With confidence. Oh, how misplaced! I also remembered how she had once said that the result of exorcism could be calamitous.

With the school practically disbanded, Father Barré made the horrifying suggestion that at each public exorcism the collecting bag should be passed around.

I resisted that too. "Rather let us be poor," I said. "When we came here we had nothing. We slept on the bare floor and depended upon charity for our bread. We could do it again."

"Except that charity would not be forthcoming."

"Then we must support ourselves. We have skills. Sister Agnes paints pretty pictures; Sister Gabrielle does beautiful embroidery. Everyone can do plain sewing. I make simple medicines. Our garden is productive and our bees do well."

Father Barré waited and then said, "And who would buy so much as a jar of honey *now?*"

He was right, of course. People came to watch our antics, to listen to our blasphemies. Otherwise we were avoided by all, except . . .

I cannot explain how it came about that our prim parlor should have become a meeting place for *men.* All enemies of Grandier.

Perhaps, since I had made the accusation against him, they felt an affinity which I, in my right mind, never acknowledged.

Perhaps I should now be thankful that they chose the convent parlor as a place to talk; otherwise I should never have gathered so much information.

God have pity on me!

EARLY IN DECEMBER Grandier was arrested. Fully robed, he had been on his way to church when a contingent of archers had surrounded him and thrust him into a waiting coach. He was driven to Angers and put into a cell.

His arrest was ordered and his trial arranged by a Monsieur de Laubardemont who had first come to Loudun on very different business—to oversee the demolition of the great castle. Cardinal Richelieu was aware that a strongly fortified place could be used by rebels against total rule from Paris. All over France castles were being destroyed or made indefensible. The castle at Loudun was an exceptionally strong one, doubly walled, doubly moated. Its previous occupant, the town governor, had wished the castle to be preserved, at least in part, so he had been removed and Laubardemont, a Cardinalist to his fingertips, had taken his place.

These political references may seem irrelevant to my story, but Grandier had been a friend of the previous governor's and had spoken against the demolition. He had thus shown himself to be anti-Cardinalist, and in the unlikely event of Richelieu having forgotten that old insult about precedence, he now had new reason for hating Grandier.

THE TRIAL WAS UNFAIR.

I whom he had bewitched, I whom he had caused to suffer so much, say that his trial was unfair.

I was not present, of course; I heard only bits and pieces from the men who had made our parlor into a kind of headquarters. They hated Grandier, and spoke with shameless gloating about the way in which people were bribed or terrorized into bearing false witness; about the way in which one open-minded man among the judges was silenced; about the prejudice and trickery employed.

After his arrest Grandier's house was searched, with particular attention paid to his library.

He was about to be tried for practicing witchcraft, and if one book on Black Magic, one shred of writing dealing with the subject, had been found, it would have been valid evidence against him. The complete absence of such things was not mentioned in his favor. Instead, other and utterly irrelevant things were dragged in. He had kept letters which spoke disrespectfully of Cardinal Richelieu; therefore, it was argued, he had written letters similar in tone. He had among his papers a copy of a scurrilous pamphlet which had been published anonymously—this was taken as positive proof that he was the author of it.

But he was not standing trial on his attitude toward Richelieu, or his authorship.

Nor did the searchers bother to deal properly with his papers. They found one recording his dismissal on the charge of immorality and one referring to his reinstatement. The former was preserved, the latter conveniently "lost."

His accusers were anxious to prove that he had not only practiced witchcraft but had been a member of a coven of witches, a regular attendant at the Sabbats. At first there was no evidence of this, but then—too apt and timely to be completely credible—a simple country woman came forward to say that Father Grandier had promised to take her to a Sabbat and give her high rank at the court of the Prince of Darkness.

To me the whole thing rang false.

The third open injustice that Laubardemont inflicted upon Grandier was in the matter of the test for witch-marks. I know more about that than any other aspect of the trial, for I had heard firsthand when Monsieur Mannoury, the surgeon, boasted, laughing, to his cronies.

Grandier had been brought back to Loudun and had been lodged in a high room in Father Mignon's house. The castle had had dungeons, but as walls were demolished, the dungeons had been used as repositories for stones and rubble. So, as a prison Father Mignon had offered a room in his own house, its window bricked up, its door reinforced, some straw on the floor for a bed.

Grandier was fed at intervals—his enemies wanted him alive for a time—but this proud, fastidious man lay in his own filth.

What his enemies wanted was a confession.

Grandier was anything but a fool and he must have known that confession would mean death by hanging, infinitely preferable to a session of torture and then death at the stake. However, he would not confess to witchcraft; he would only say, "I have been a great sinner, but never a magician."

Therefore he was subjected to the pricking test. This was based upon a belief that the Devil could give his followers certain areas completely insensitive to pain. Anybody can—under supervision—apply this test, but in Grandier's case it was made by the surgeon, Mannoury, one of Grandier's bitter enemies. Here is Mannoury's own account:

"Well, first of all they shaved him completely. Not a hair left anywhere! Remember those black curls? That mustache in the latest fashion? All gone. He did look comic! I'd rather hoped he might have some witch-mark on him—a third teat or a mole—but his skin was clear. So I took a well-sharpened probe and gave a jab or two. I thought to myself: That's for the time you said I was a man of little education! Ah, I had several grudges to work off. Most times I pierced to the bone and he yelled. Every now and then I just touched him lightly with the handle of the probe. You follow me? It was warm from my hand. Of course he felt nothing. The Capuchins in charge told their clerk to note down the spots that had no feeling—four of them. I could have found more, but Father Tranquille said four were enough to condemn him."

The surgeon's hearers laughed.

I did not. After all there is a thing called justice, and such a story made mock of it. I think that it was then, overhearing Mannoury, that I felt my first pang of compunction. Yet, was I to blame? I had spoken privately of the bewitchment; Isacaaron had shouted the public accusation.

"So, what now?" Adam, the apothecary, asked Marmoury.

"Oh, they're set on confession. Makes everything so simple. They'll wring it out of him, somehow. Most likely the Boot."

The Boot it was.

It works this way: The one to be tortured is placed on his back and between his legs are laid two stout planks, unfixed. On the outer side of each leg—and fixed—are set similar stout planks. The torturer takes a wedge, a small one to start with, and hammers it between the inner planks. There is some pain, but no great injury. And they say, "Confess!"

Grandier would not. Bigger wedges were driven in. Under the increasing pressure the bones of his legs cracked; in places they pierced the skin. At each new agony he cried out, but confess he would not. When his legs were mere bloody pulp, they released him and revived him with wine.

His courage under torture gained him many adherents. There had always been some: people who remembered his charity, and almost everybody who had worked for him in whatever capacity. In fact, public opinion now swung around so much to his favor that Laubardemont was obliged to issue an order. It was strictly forbidden to say a word of sympathy for Grandier, or to express a doubt about his guilt.

I tried to pray that he would die. I say *tried* because since I was first possessed I had not prayed easily. The devils did not wish the possessed to pray and they came between us and God. Still, I tried. I prayed, fasting: Oh God, let him die. Please, dear God, let him die.

Not an unreasonable request, considering his injuries. I had heard of men who had become fevered and died with a hundredth part of his hurt.

But Grandier lived to hear his sentence, which was death by burning, though even that was not to happen until he had done penance. He was to kneel, holding a taper weighing two pounds, at the door of his church, which he was said to have betrayed, and at the door of our convent, which he had bewitched.

I LAY SLEEPLESS and watched, toward the foot of my bed, a radiance grow. A light not of this world. No sun, no moon, had ever shed such light. And then, in the center of it, a figure which I took to be an angel: golden-haired, white robed, and so beautiful that looking at him I realized that what we, on earth, think of as beauty in human beings is but a poor, pallid reflection of Beauty's self. I thought that, but I could not speak. Propped on my elbows, I could only stare.

He said, "Not so far wrong, Sister Jeanne of the Angels. I am the Fallen Angel. I am Lucifer."

In other words, Satan's self, and always associated with darkness. With blackness. With physical deformity—artists and sculptors portrayed the Devil with horns, with hooves like a goat's, and often with a tail.

"You love Urbain Grandier?" Unlike his minions, who had on the whole unpleasant voices, he spoke melodiously.

I fought for speech, which finally came, sounding as though I were being strangled. I said, "No. . . . But I pity him now."

"Why?"

"His trial was unfair."

"Then you are willing to help him?"

"I have already tried."

He laughed. "I know. You were naïve enough to tell Laubarde-mont that perhaps you were mistaken. *Not* what he wished to hear, so he ignored it. No, you must understand that no *human* agency can possibly help Urbain Grandier now. Only I can do that. If you will play your part."

It was true that, thinking Grandier had suffered sufficiently, I had approached Laubardemont with the suggestion that I could have been mistaken. A futile effort! Now, thinking of the long imprison-ment, the unfair trial, the trickery of the witch test, I said, "I would do anything."

"Then kneel down and worship me."

Exactly the temptation that had been offered to Our Lord during His sojourn in the wilderness. I could see what a triumph that would have been for Satan. There would have been no Christianity, no Church. And the luring away of Son from Father would have been the perfect revenge for the expulsion from heaven. But of what possible value could I be? An obscure nun in a provincial house—and already the prey of devils.

I said, "Why me?"

"You have spiritual promise. You are not—you never have been—snugly and smugly wrapped up in your human flesh. You do not fall into hoggish slumber when you sleep—you dream. You have a lively mind, a passionate nature. All misdirected and wasted. Everything could be remedied for you, and Urbain Grandier freed and healed, by one simple act of submission."

"Which I cannot make."

"Then he will suffer. But briefly. Your ordeal will be longer: physical pain and pangs of remorse."

With that, the radiance faded. Lucifer had gone, but Isacaaron and Asmodeus fell upon me and this time they did me permanent damage.

Hitherto my spine, though crooked and unsightly, had served me well. It would ache now and then from overexertion or uncomfort-able posture—like sleeping on the floor. But that night, Grandier's last on earth, the devils gave me such a twist that I have not since been free of pain. Not acute, just a dull, nagging ache, resistant to opium. I have since suffered other ills and been cured, by medicines, by miracle, but nothing shifts Lucifer's legacy to me.

OF THE NEXT DAY I write of what I saw myself and what I heard recounted. This I saw, looking down from an upper window:

A procession worthy of a better cause. A cart drawn by six mules, riding in it the condemned man—his legs dangling like a puppet's. Present also were the executioner who was to light the fire; two rough-handed guards; a company of archers; two priests—Father Tranquille, a Capuchin, and Father Lactance, a Franciscan; and Monsieur de Laubardemont and the magistrates who had connived. The mules halted; the guards dragged Grandier down and literally threw him at our doorway.

So I saw him with my own eyes for the first time. Completely hairless, waxy pale, a grotesque, nightmare figure. He had been ordered to kneel—but he had no knees. He fell forward and lay on his face. And yet, in his extremity, when the lighted taper was thrust into his hand, he held it steady and said in a loud, ringing voice, "I have been ordered to ask pardon of the Ursuline Sisters; but I have never done them any harm. I pray God to forgive them."

Resolute to the end, but not what his enemies wanted.

And not all in the crowd were his enemies. Most of them had come to see a witch burned, much as they would have gone to see a bearbaiting; but there were others, women weeping, men with sorrowful faces.

The guards hauled him up and flung him back into the cart. At a word—no whip needed—the mules began to trot toward the Place Sainte-Croix where the stake and the fire waited. One of the Capuchins who waited with the crowd shouted that Grandier was a condemned magician and that to pray for him, even to pity him, would be a very serious sin.

So much I saw. The rest is hearsay, but reliable hearsay because from varying angles all the tales coincided.

The Place Sainte-Croix is, I understand, small, and a quarter of the space was devoted to the site of the execution, yet about six thousand spectators had squeezed in; many watched from rented windows or from precarious perches on roofs. The stake was fifteen feet high, and since Grandier could not stand, an iron seat was attached to it. He was lifted onto this and the rope, already noosed about his neck, was secured. He sat with his back to the Church of Sainte-Croix, and his face toward the house of Monsieur Trincant whose daughter, Philippe, he had seduced. Trincant, with Father Mignon and other friends, sat at a window and watched and drank wine.

The captain of the archers, who must give the word for the fire to be lighted, went toward Grandier and formally asked pardon for what he was about to do. Those of the crowd near enough to hear afterward swore that the captain also made two promises—that the condemned man should be allowed to make a last speech, and that he would be mercifully strangled before the fire was well alight. But the captain was reckoning without the Capuchin fathers, who were determined to grant no favor and show no mercy until they had extracted a full confession. Pacing around the piles of combustible materials, they shouted, "Confess! Confess!" and sprinkled holy water everywhere.

Grandier's resolution never wavered, nor did his dignity fail. He said, "I am about to meet the God who is my witness that I have spoken the truth."

Father Lactance, the Franciscan, shouted, "Confess! You have only a moment to live."

"Only a moment," Grandier replied. "Then I go to that just and fearful judgment to which you, too, Reverend Father, must soon be called."

Those words were to be remembered.

After that Grandier was not allowed to speak; every time he attempted to do so one of the Capuchins silenced him by throwing holy water in his face or striking him on the mouth with an iron crucifix. To shrink away from such a blow was called repudiation of the Lord.

Two other men, both priests, showed courage, pushing their way to the stake. One embraced Grandier and promised to say masses for his soul. The other begged his forgiveness. He had been one of those who had borne witness against Grandier during his trial.

By this time even the Capuchins saw that no confession would be forthcoming and made ready to kindle the fire. The executioner went forward with a noosed cord with which he intended to strangle Grandier. But somebody had tied a knot so that the noose would not slip, and before the bewildered man could perform his act of mercy, the Capuchins had started the fire.

It blazed fast and fiercely. Grandier screamed once, and Father Lactance yelled that that was the Devil being driven out. Then from the church roof came a great flock of pigeons, wheeling so low over the pyre that some of their feathers were singed. Grandier's enemies claimed that these were the sorcerer's attendants come to escort his soul to hell. His friends remembered the dove—a very similar bird—which appeared at Our Lord's baptism in the Jordan.

In the end the fire was merciful to him; a great flame leaped and burned through the bonds which held him to the stake. Falling forward, he cried, "Forgive them. Forgive my enemies." Then he was consumed.

With a long-handled shovel the executioner performed the last rite of scattering the remains to the four winds. And before they were cool enough to handle, the crowd was upon them, seeking teeth, and the bits of bone most resistant to fire. They were to become cherished relics, significantly enough, regarded as effective love charms or as a guard against the malice of enemies.

CHAPTER FOUR

I WAS SO COMPLETELY possessed on the day Urbain Grandier died that I could hardly have been said to be in this world at all. It was as though the devils were intent upon showing me how wrong I had been in my accusation. With Grandier dying, with Grandier dead, I was still under a spell.

I suffered pain, as Lucifer had threatened, for the devils bent me backward until my head touched my heels. They threw me about until I was bruised all over. Of the other sisters, only Agnes was afflicted, and she much more lightly. Then, toward evening—and it was August, with the days shortening—the devils left me and the remorse set in.

Useless to tell myself that it was Isacaaron, not I, who had made the public denunciation of Grandier; useless to tell myself that I had believed those roses to be a means of enchantment. The stark truth was that my infatuation, then my revulsion, had acted as a lever.

Seized upon by Grandier's enemies. But between a human being and the most painful experience, days and nights build a barrier. Urbain Grandier gradually became part of the past. I salved my remorse by remembering what Seraphima had once told me. "If he hadn't been such an evil-living man," she had said, "and made so many enemies, nobody would have taken much notice." Innocent as she was of the truth, she had been right, for if he had lived as a priest should live, I should never have heard of him, never become obsessed and opened the way for the devils. Sometimes it was just possible for me to see him as the guilty one and myself as the innocent victim.

And soon I had something else to worry about.

A missed month—then two—then three. My figure changed. I knew I was pregnant. Yet it was not possible, for despite the lascivious postures and lewd words, the ultimate surrender had never been made—or even demanded.

I agonized over the scandal this would bring upon our already discredited house. I prayed, oh, how I prayed. I wore a hair shirt and a heavy belt studded with nails, points inward. I did everything that was calculated to make prayer effective. I ate no meat, made frequent fasts of twenty-four hours' duration, but my prayers were not answered. God seemed to have abandoned me and even the devils had for a time withdrawn. I was alone with my burden, steadily growing.

MY ONLY DIVERSION came from parlor gossip—and dramatic things were happening in the outer world. Grandier had said that Father Lactance would soon face God. On the night of the burning, the Franciscan priest had said, not surprisingly, that he felt tired and he had gone to his bed without waiting for supper. Next day he was fevered and showed every sign of being possessed. He writhed about, frothed at the mouth, and shouted obscenities and blasphemies, just as we had. He was dead within days. Had Grandier's words been a witch's threat or the prophecy of a saintly man?

Monsieur Mannoury was next. One evening he was called out to bleed a patient who lived a short distance from the town. He took with him a manservant to carry his bag and to light the way with a lantern. On the way home Mannoury stopped suddenly, trembled violently and began to talk to somebody who, as the servant expressed it, wasn't there. He seemed to be begging forgiveness and finally flung himself down on the ground. Not without difficulty his man hauled him up and took him home to bed. There he talked about having seen Grandier just as he had been at the witch test, naked and shaven. In a week Mannoury was dead.

And Father Tranquille had begun his more prolonged ordeal. He went mad: neighing like a horse, barking like a dog and displaying a revolting physical symptom. Whatever he ate, however wholesome, he vomited up. Still, he must have derived some nourishment from what he swallowed, for he lived, in dire misery, for almost two years.

I would listen and be momentarily diverted; then I would remember my own condition. At some time, without my knowledge, let alone my consent, I had been impregnated by one of the devils, and unless freed by some miracle or some magic, would bring to birth, probably in May, that most beautiful month, some horrible hybrid thing.

Better be dead. Oh, far better dead. I faced the fact that I was contemplating the most mortal of sins and was condemning my soul to hell, but even that thought, hideous as it was, seemed preferable to the alternative.

I went into the kitchen and took Seraphima's favorite strong knife, then proceeded to the chapel and fetched half a cupful of holy water. I intended to cut the embryo out of my body, and baptize it. I said, "God forgive me." Then I took the knife in a steady hand.

And dropped to the floor.

THERE ARE NO WORDS with which to describe heaven. It is futile even to try. To speak of color having sound, or of music having flavor. All the limitations of our poor human senses were abolished. Even size and space ceased to exist. A wide sunset could be held in the palm of a hand; one could lie down in the heart of a rose.

Yet I had a body. I felt my shoulders, and they were level; I looked at my legs, they were long and slim. Red-gold hair rippled down to my waist. I was naked and unashamed. I was Eve in the Garden of Eden.

I was surprised to find myself in heaven. I was surprised to find myself alone. Unconsciously one thinks of heaven as being occupied by angels and archangels, and saints. And somewhere, probably bathed in such ineffable light that it would blind one to look, God on His throne, with Christ at His right hand. And somewhere near, Mary the Mother, serene and gentle in blue.

But there was nothing celestial about the place in which I found myself. Except for the blending and expansion of the senses, it was an earthly paradise. Lacking only one thing. Somebody with whom to share it.

And then he came, as once in my dreams he had come. Urbain Grandier. Not the pitiable figure that he had been on the only occasion when I had seen him in the flesh. No—he was upright, handsome, superbly confident. And in love with me!

He took my hands, drew me toward him, held me tenderly yet closely. I said, "Now is heaven complete."

He laughed. Then he said, "Beloved, this is hell."

He seemed to loose me, and I lost my hold on him. I began to fall . . .

Down and down and down, through the dark abyss of time, through the cold reaches of eternity.

I landed with a jolt, on my own bed.

It was night. A candle burned on a table and I could see dear old Seraphima, her placid face furrowed, her eyes red-rimmed.

To speak was like carrying a load of stones up a steep slope, but I managed it. I said, "Seraphima."

"Ah, thanks be to God! You have come to yourself."

She was delighted. She bustled about, raising me on my pillows, holding a cup of wine to my lips, urging me to take a mouthful of sponge cake. "You have not eaten for six days. The doctor despaired; but I did not. As a token of faith I have had everything ready for this moment—fresh wine and fresh cake every day."

How could she sound so jubilant? She must know what I was coming back to. She brought a damp cloth and wiped my face and hands, promising to wash me all over as soon as the doctor gave permission. She sounded so innocent that I began to wonder how much she knew. She even remarked, in a tone of grievance, that her best knife had vanished.

I managed to speak again. "Did I rave?"

"Oh, no. There was no fever or delirium. You just lay—as though you were dead. Now I will call Dr. du Chêne."

"Who?"

"Monsieur de Laubardemont sent for him. He is from Le Mans. He is said to be very clever." It was plain from her tone that she did not share this opinion.

The doctor came in, carrying a thick candle in a heavy brass stand which he set down on the table where my rosary lay. Then, with a bow, he introduced himself. He was of middle age, a spare man with a narrow, rather ratlike face, a long probing nose, small, alert dark eyes. He seemed to be laboring under some embarrassment, and I understood why. I was prioress, he should address me as Reverend Mother, or at least as madame, but I was also a nun whose very condition was proof of evil, unchaste behavior.

I called upon my reserves of breeding and upbringing. I said, "Please be seated." He dragged up the stool upon which poor Seraphima had kept her long vigil and said, "You must have struck your head when you fainted, and suffered a concussion."

"So it would seem."

"But you must have known that you were pregnant."

"I knew. I still know that I *appear* to be so. But I also know that it is impossible. I am a virgin!"

He looked at me with disbelief, with distaste.

"As you say, *impossible*. It is my duty to inform you that a claim to virginity is susceptible to proof. A panel of matrons—"

"I am willing to submit to any test you care to propose. Your panel of matrons will find me *virgo intacta*. But first, would you answer one question? Does Sister Seraphima know? Or anyone else in this house?"

"No. Your method of concealment, though dangerous to both you and the child, was most effectual. That nailed belt—few women, however desperate, could have sustained the pressure, and the pain . . ." He was at odds with himself, giving a word of praise to one of whom he thoroughly disapproved. "Your self-appointed nurse had her own explanation for your distended abdomen—a general swelling resulting from the sores. I did not contradict her."

"Thank you. That was kind."

He made a deprecating gesture and asked, "Is there a side entrance to this place?"

"Two."

"Good. The women I have in mind are discreet. But this you must understand. Whatever their verdict, you *are* pregnant. At least five months. More scandal to add to that which is already so grievous to every good Catholic."

"Nobody can be more aware of that than I. But we did not ask to be possessed by devils. I did not ask to be made pregnant in this most mystifying way."

He gave a little barking laugh, cut it off and said, nastily, "Just *how* mystifying remains to be seen."

THE THREE WOMEN CAME by night. I lay on the bed, my face and the upper part of my body covered by a light scarf. They smelled of garlic, onions, pigs, goats. They had rustic voices. What they did to me was humiliating, but not painful.

They came and they went, and after quite a short time Dr. du Chêne visited me again. He seemed a changed man. His neat, orderly world had been shattered; he even stammered a little. "Reverend M-Mother. You were c-correct. The verdict—and it was unanimous—was *virgo intacta.*"

"As I said."

"As you said. But it is physically impossible."

"So is the idea of me, with my crooked back, turning somersaults, or walking on my hands. Yet I have done both."

"Yes, so I heard. I attributed much to hysteria, and some to exaggeration. But, madame, this is fact. We must look to the future. Is there anywhere you could go and bear your child? In secrecy?"

"I can think of nowhere."

"Your parents?"

"The last people on earth." I explained, as briefly as possible.

"There are other Ursuline houses. One, I think, in Marseilles."

"But I cannot move without a direct order from Poitiers. And what house would accept me *now?*"

"It is very difficult," he admitted. He nibbled at a fingernail, looked at the result with disfavor and said, "The child will be born in four months' time. Possibly less."

"I know." Hopelessness and lethargy swept over me. I had even considered suicide as a way to avoid scandal; and hell itself had rejected me! I said, "Leave me now."

He went away and I was alone. Possibly the loneliest person on the face of the earth. Even the demons had deserted me, at a time when I would have welcomed the blankness of mind and the physical pain of an attack.

I was wrong. Isacaaron came; not to wrench and twist me, not to use my voice to yell obscenities. He spoke to me from outside my head. Like a friend dropped in for a gossip.

"I understand that you have paid a visit to our homeland," he said. "Was it not delightful? Now you can understand—as no other human being can—how much we resent being sent on errands such as this. However, I am to be recalled. I have only two things more to do."

The hateful, jeering quality had left his voice and he sounded like a boarding pupil with just two exercises to complete before going home for a vacation.

"And they are?" I asked, fearing the answer.

"I must help you."

"How could anybody help me now? Even you?"

"What I implanted, I can destroy. You shall void it by vomit. Do not be alarmed. And then I have to make sure of Father Surin."

The name was new to me, but Isacaaron was well informed. The jeering tone back, he said, "Jean-Joseph Surin is a Jesuit; strict, pious, ascetic, but of unstable mind. In fact, his superiors did not wish him to have anything to do with Loudun, thinking him too vulnerable. However, he insisted, having a great opinion of his spiritual power. Rather ignorant—you will hear him address me as Leviathan! But he will learn."

Isacaaron went away and almost immediately I felt sick. Within a few minutes I literally emptied myself. My body returned to its normal size and shape and I was ready for Father Surin when he arrived.

HE WAS FAIRLY TALL, emaciated and so frail that he looked old. His voice was a constant surprise, seeming much too deep and powerful for a man of his size. His eyes were extraordinary, deep set, a pale gray in color, and for most of the time expressionless and chill as though he looked inward. But there were times when they could assume a piercing look. At these times Father Surin seemed to see to the very soul.

He was ruthless. He said that my great fault was pride.

"You have never yet accepted fully the infirmity with which you were born."

"I have tried to ignore it. To overcome it. Was that so wrong?"

"Yes. You fought against it. Always anxious to prove that you were equal to, or better than, people with no physical infirmity."

"And is that a sin?"

"Certainly. All the time you were trying to impress people, to draw attention to yourself. A form of spiritual pride. A thing most abhorrent to God. You must be humble. I suggest that you—head of this convent—go to work in the kitchen."

I said, "I have worked there before. First because everybody had to, and again, later, when I went voluntarily. As a penance."

"Set by yourself? Was that not arrogance?"

"If you say so."

"I do. This time you will do menial work in the right spirit. Not thinking: Look how humble I am, look how adept, despite my affliction. This time go humbly, remembering that the only approval worth having is that of God."

Meanwhile Cardinal Richelieu had provided us with some much needed financial help, and Monsieur de Laubardemont had given us a pleasant surprise by moving us from the moldering old house to a relatively new one which he had confiscated from the Huguenots. I never learned what offense these Protestants had committed that their properties should be taken away from them. There was probably some trumped-up excuse. Laubardemont hated all Protestants and must surely have enjoyed seeing one of their places of learning turned into a house for nuns. It had been built as a residential college, capable of accommodating sixty young men in small open-fronted sleeping chambers forming large dormitories. There was a huge hall, formerly used as a lecture room.

I was still so weak. I had actually suffered a kind of miscarriage, and I had had to be carried from the old house to the new. There I improved rapidly and was soon to obey Father Surin's order to work in the kitchen.

Seraphima strongly disapproved and did her not inconsiderable best to mitigate this penance. No matter what time I presented myself for kitchen duty, the really onerous or disagreeable tasks had just that minute been performed. Once, anxious to show that I was not unobservant, I expostulated, and she responded in a most curious way. "God forgive me for criticizing a priest," she said, "but I sometimes think Father Surin is a bit deranged." She touched her forehead significantly.

"What makes you say that?"

"The look in his eyes. And he knows how ill you have been, Reverend Mother, yet he sets you a penance which would exhaust the strongest. Also, he is disappointed because the—attacks have died down."

It was true. Only two of the younger sisters had shown any sign of being possessed since we had come to the new house, and both attacks had ended before Father Surin could attempt to exorcise the demons. As for me, I had not been aware of Isacaaron since the night when he promised to liberate me; and had kept his word!

Then one morning Isacaaron took possession of me again. Father Surin was talking to me about the value of mental prayer, which should be practiced at all times since it deflects the mind from earthly things. Isacaaron gave his loud, jeering laugh and made me stick out my tongue. Using my voice, he said, "Who would have suspected an old man in petticoats to cherish carnal desires? If you want her, why not take her?"

It was terrible to hear such things being spoken not *by* me, but *through* me. But I was helpless. Father Surin was not. He had been sitting down; now he stood up, trembling but resolute. In his firm, authoritative voice he spoke the now familiar words of the exorcism ritual. *"Exorciso te, immundissime spiritus . . ."*

Isacaaron said, quite seriously, "You order me away. But where to? Answer that and perhaps I may go."

In leaving me this time he gave me such a cruel wrench that I screamed. Cold sweat broke out on my forehead and rolled, like tears, down my face. And I was ashamed, after what had been said in my voice, to look Father Surin in the eye. But he was unperturbed. He said, "I pity you. You have indeed suffered. But I know now what to do. Invite the demons to leave you and to infest me."

"No! Father, that is one thing you must not do. It is what the devils—particularly Isacaaron—want. He said to me that he had to make sure of Father Surin. And that you would learn. He spoke threateningly."

"But truly. I shall indubitably learn."

"And suffer. Not merely physical pain, but shame and humiliation as well."

"I am prepared for that."

I spoke even more urgently. "Father, if *I* die possessed and am lost to God, it will be no great loss. I have not been a good nun. I have been selfish, worldly, weak-minded. By thinking impure thoughts I opened the door to the demons. I have given way to despair; planned to commit suicide. Perhaps I am already lost. But you are almost saintly. For Isacaaron to get possession of you would be a great loss to God. I implore you, I beg you, take no such risk."

But he remained unconvinced. "It may be a demon speaking through you now," he said, "and he naturally wishes to avoid the confrontation that I plan. If I can get him out of you and into me it will be a singular triumph—not for me, for God."

Although I admired him and appreciated his saintly quality, he had not yet endeared himself to me in any way. Still I tried to deal justly with him, and when I heard that he planned a special exorcism for the following Friday I said, "But, Father, I may not be possessed on that day. What happens then?"

"We must leave that to God."

What he was apparently not willing to leave to God was the setting of the scene, which was as carefully prepared as though a masque were about to take place.

The big hall in which Protestants had held meetings and heard lectures had a large platform along its inner wall. This platform had been covered with red carpet, probably provided by Laubardemont, and an altar had been set up. Easter was past, but the altar cloth was white and gold, the Easter colors. There was the little light burning before the reserved Host; there were the silver candlesticks; the silver bowl of holy water; the censer. And there upon the plain whitewashed wall hung a large crucifix.

The hall was crowded and many of the people there were Huguenots; some, I suppose, come to see what their Protestant college had been turned into, but most of them anxious to see me, possessed by devils, and Father Surin's attempt to exorcise the devils.

I knew that the well-staged scene would fail, for I had no demon in me that day, and remembering what Isacaaron had said about Father Surin being taught a lesson, I was worried. What could be more ridiculous than a priest in full canonicals trying to exorcise an evil spirit which was not there?

I voiced a last-minute protest. I said, "I am not possessed today. Devils do not make appointments. By their very absence, Father, they will mock you. Please, postpone this exorcism."

Father Surin then said the only worldly thing I ever heard him utter. He said, "It cannot be postponed. The King's brother, Prince Gaston of Orléans, is here. Not an evil man, but frivolous. Much addicted to swearing. And to love affairs. A truly spiritual experience could redeem him."

This regard for rank in a man who had supposedly renounced the world angered me a little. I thought: Very well then, I will put on a performance for the prince.

But I was not forced to such a measure, for as I entered the crowded hall Isacaaron gave my hunched shoulder a cruel tweak, so that I cried out with pain. When I had mounted the platform he propelled me forward; I almost knocked Father Surin over and I did collide heavily against the altar, which, being only a temporary structure, shifted under the impact.

Then Isacaaron entered my body, and using my tongue, but his own voice, cried, "What an undignified entrance! With a prince of the blood royal present! And how strange that the prince should have no lover with him."

Though possessed, *I* was still there. I saw the prince's color deepen. I heard the sounds of disapproval from the audience. Somebody shouted from the back of the hall, "Get on with the exorcism."

Father Surin stood in a waiting attitude. I had no doubt that he was indulging in mental prayer.

Isacaaron cried, "A few tricks first! The mob must be entertained." He set me to walking on my hands and turning somersaults. But now I was weakened by illness, and even devils cannot use what is not there. When I finally collapsed, Isacaaron lifted me by the nape of my neck so that I appeared to levitate across the platform. Then he dropped me into a chair that stood ready.

"And now, you man of God, what can we do for you?" Isacaaron asked, imitating the servility of a shopkeeper.

Father Surin sprinkled holy water and recited the whole order of exorcism. Nothing happened. Then he abandoned Latin and said, "In the name of the Father and of the Son, I command you. Come out of her! Come to me!" He spread his arms in a welcoming gesture. "Leviathan, I offer you sanctuary."

I felt Isacaaron leave me, but there was a moment in which we all held our breath. Then Father Surin fell to the floor, screamed, writhed, foamed at the mouth. He rolled toward the altar, seized the cloth in both hands and pulled. All the things, so lovingly assembled, came crashing down while Father Surin cried, "Away with all false gods!"

In the hall there was pandemonium. Women screamed and fainted. Men shouted and groaned. Prince Gaston had attendants and servants, and the effortless authority of his rank. He stood up and said, "Clear this room!"

Two DAYS LATER Father Surin came to see me. He looked very ill, he had a heavy bruise on one cheek and two fingers of his left hand were swollen, probably broken when he rolled on the platform. But he was jubilant about the success of what he called his experiment.

"It is something which has not been tried before. And it worked, did it not?"

"It seemed to," I said cautiously.

"You are freed, are you not?"

"All has been well with me for two days. But I have had peaceful interludes before. Isacaaron may be mocking us both."

"Even so, I now *know* what it means to be possessed." He gave me one of his rare, exceptionally sweet smiles. "Who would trust a doctor who had never felt a twinge of pain?" Then, grave again, he said, "I

shall now most certainly be recalled and rebuked for overenthusiasm and for making a public spectacle of myself. I am somewhat concerned for *you*. Now that I have sampled the power of these demons, I think that spiritually you are very strong, not to have been destroyed. But strength, unless channeled, can in itself be a danger. I think you need a personal, intervening saint. Have you a particular preference?"

"I have always had an interest in, and admiration for, Saint Teresa of Avila."

He considered that and said, "No! Too proud to be of service to you. A humbler saint would serve you better."

I said, "Saint Joseph was humble."

"The very model of self-abnegation! Yes, pray to him. Meditate upon his saintly life. Make him your ideal."

FATHER SURIN HAD BEEN right when he said that he would be recalled. He left promptly, taking, he said, all the devils with him. The other, less successful exorcists also left, and the quiet, conventional life of the convent finally resumed.

CHAPTER FIVE

THE DEVILS, OF COURSE, had always mishandled us; I was quite accustomed to suffering minor injuries at their hands, bruises and scratches which soon healed. Father Surin had been gone a week before I realized that Isacaaron, in pushing me against the altar, had done me more lasting damage. I now had, in addition to the dull, nagging ache in my back, a sharp pain in my right side. There was nothing, not even a bruise, to be seen, and when I probed, very gingerly, with my fingers, I could find no broken rib. Perhaps, I thought, a cracked one, or a bruise gone inward.

I mentioned it to no one, nor did I let it interfere with my work in the kitchen. Saint Joseph had been a carpenter, and had worked with his hands. In an attempt to establish an affinity with him, I worked with mine, despite Seraphima's protests and tricks to forestall me.

So little is really known of Saint Joseph. In the gospels he is hardly mentioned after the Holy Family's return from Egypt. We only know that he was called upon by God to face an impossible, incredible situation and that he did it with dignity and kindliness. God communicated with him through dreams and he was implicitly obedient. He took the Mother and Child safely to Egypt when danger threatened, and brought them back when the danger was over. He may for a time have supervised the youth of Jesus, watching Him play, then letting Him help in the carpenter's shop. Beyond these few facts—and speculation—there is nothing but myth and legend.

Seraphima continued her attempt to outwit me, and one day I felt that I must have it out with her. I prepared to scrub the kitchen floor and she said, "Reverend Mother, it has already been done. See, it is still damp."

"Then I must do it again, since that is my self-appointed task for today."

She muttered something under her breath as she turned away, and I put the empty bucket under the pump and filled it. When I tried to lift it down, the pain lanced through my side, a nauseating pang. Seraphima pretended to be busy at the stove, but I felt that she was watching me from the back of her head and would in a second or two come to my aid with a what-did-I-tell-you air of triumph. So, without thinking, I prayed, "Saint Joseph, help me!"

The bucket lifted, light as a feather. It was exactly as though a strong hand were on the handle alongside my feeble one. On my knees, scrubbing brush in hand, I thanked him. I glowed with the sense of having achieved personal contact. How could I show my gratitude? The answer came as I scrubbed.

At Saintes, as a child, I had shown some skill at drawing and had once received a rare word of praise from my aunt, the abbess. At Poitiers, I had not pursued the art, mainly because there was always some sister more gifted than I. Here at Loudun, the more gifted one was Sister Agnes, who during the early days of our possession had drawn some most horrifying pictures of the demons as she imagined they looked. Father Barré had solemnly burned them.

When I went to select the materials I needed, Sister Agnes meekly offered to draw or paint anything I wanted. Remembering to be humble, I said, "I have no doubt you would make a much better job of it, but I am under an obligation to do this myself."

I can say without undue pride that nobody could have made a

better job of it, for I worked under direct guidance and produced a masterpiece of simplicity, no fussiness, no decoration, not a stroke of the brush wasted. I drew a big muscular man standing by a workbench planing a plank of wood. Behind him on a whitewashed wall hung a saw and hammers of various sizes, a water bottle, one of the reed baskets in which carpenters carry their tools, and a bag which I thought of as containing nails. That was all, but the man's stance, his expression of concentration and the look of movement in the arm that worked the plane were all perfect.

Of course, it is possible that at some time I had watched a carpenter at work, but I had no memory of it and preferred to think that Saint Joseph himself had guided my hand. The very speed and surety with which I worked make it seem probable that he in some way had helped me.

Before it was time for vespers, my picture, the paint on it still not quite dry, hung in the chapel, where until that moment Saint Joseph had had no memorial at all. I had it hung just to the right of the only good statue of Mary and the Child we owned. And holding to the theme of wood, I had placed below it a plain wooden bench and two wooden candlesticks.

IT HAD BEEN A full, busy, satisfactory day and I should have slept well but for the pain in my side. I could arrange my spine comfortably on a reasonably soft mattress such as we all had now. But the cracked rib would not cease its stabbing. From sheer exhaustion, I would fall asleep, only to be wakened again by a particularly vicious pang.

So I cannot say with any certainty whether I saw Saint Joseph in a sleeping dream or a waking one. But I saw him. Just as I had limned him that afternoon.

He said, "You need help, poor child."

He sounded so utterly fatherly; and I had never had any paternal love. Under the comfort and the promise of help in that deep, steady voice, I almost melted into childish tears.

"I do," I said. "I do. I have had such terrible experiences. . . . And now suffer such pain."

"Where?"

"In my side." I heard myself telling him how I had come by this hurt, and it was like talking to an old, trusted friend.

"On earth," he said slowly, "in Nazareth, I could sometimes help with certain injuries—those to bones; those within a mere carpenter's range. Show me where."

I pointed to the site of the pain.

I was wearing a simple garment called a shift or a chemise—the latter the more refined term. With us it was a plain linen garment, worn day and night and changed once a week. In the days when I had been punishing myself I had worn the hair shirt and the nailed belt under my chemise. I think Seraphima had done away with them while I lay unconscious.

Now Saint Joseph reached out his left hand. I observed that even for a big man it was a large hand, broadened by labor, but it touched me lightly.

And the pain ceased.

I was able, for the first time since I had been thrown against the altar, to draw a deep, painless breath. I used it to thank him.

He withdrew his hand. "Sleep now," he said.

And I did. I slept well, and woke to the sweet, unmistakable scent of balsam, which seemed to increase as I pushed back the bedclothes. It was emanating from my chemise.

I looked down, and just where Saint Joseph had touched me were five marks: four fairly close together, the fifth slightly apart. His fingerprints.

The marks were of no particular color, just a shade darker than the unbleached linen of the shift, as though the fingers had been damp. Perhaps with oil.

There are plenty of skeptical people about, and I have been accused of fabricating this tale and of having made the marks myself. They forget that I lived in close proximity to Sister Seraphima, a resolute skeptic who had not believed in the ghosts in the old house, had not been possessed by the devils herself, and was still convinced that possession was a sickness of the mind, an extreme form of hysteria. In her stolid peasant fashion she had managed to ignore what she could not credit.

I called her and she came. I began gently. I asked could she smell anything. She sniffed, thought about it, sniffed again and said, "Yes, flowers."

I showed her the marks, told her what they were, and saw fear as well as disbelief in her eyes. Once again she took refuge in practicalities. She said, "I'll fetch you a clean shift and give that one a good wash."

And a good wash it would certainly be!

The marks remained after a scrubbing, a soaking overnight, another scrubbing and a day's bleaching in full sun. They were still there, and still fragrant. Seraphima said, almost angrily, "It is a mystery."

IF SERAPHIMA MIGHT be called my first—though unwilling—convert, I soon had another; no less a person than Madame de Laubardemont. Through parlor gossip I heard that she was having a very difficult and prolonged labor, trying to bear a child which would not be born.

My feelings toward Monsieur de Laubardemont were ambivalent; as a person, I could not like him, and I felt that he had been unjust to Grandier. On the other hand, he had always been a friend to us and he had brought Dr. du Chêne to me. So I determined to go and see if the chemise could help the poor woman at all.

I found a disrupted household. Madame de Laubardemont was in the last stage of exhaustion. Laubardemont was distraught, and the parish priest who had succeeded Grandier stood by, ready to administer extreme unction. Dr. Fanton was there. He was said to be clever, but he was a Huguenot; Laubardemont must have been desperate to call him in. And there was the surgeon, ready to perform the crude operation that might at least save the mother's life should the child be dead.

With more confidence than I actually felt, I said to Madame, "Here is Saint Joseph come to help you." I spread the chemise across her. And I prayed.

Almost immediately a little child came into the world. It was stillborn. Yet the mother lived.

I did not claim that the chemise had worked a miracle. It was the other people about the bed who did that. I said, as I was to say many times in the future, "It was Saint Joseph's kind, helping hand."

And what of my own? I noticed on my left hand a red smear which puzzled me. Neither in spreading the chemise nor in taking it up again had I been aware of touching either the dead child or the afterbirth. But there it was, and as soon as I was back in the convent I went to wash my hands. The red smear defied soap and water. Slowly, under my disbelieving eyes, the smear took shape, and there, on the back of my left hand, between the wrist bone and the knuckle of my little finger, was the word *Joseph*, printed plain in large vermilion letters.

Those who decry me, calling me cheat and poseur, have put forward the suggestion that I myself wrote this—and the names which were to follow. But with what? Red dye, they say, or colored starch. But such substances could not withstand a resolute scrubbing with soap and water. Skeptics say that the letters vanish and are renewed by me, and it is true that they *seem* to vanish, but only because my sensitive skin goes crimson under friction and the lighter color is engulfed. As the crimson fades, the letters emerge again.

Anyone who believes that I wrote them myself is reckoning without Seraphima, who was not only difficult to convince but at heart frightened. If there had been the slightest trickery, how eagerly she would have pounced on it! And with what relief!

To please her, I agreed not to say anything about my hand for a week and I allowed her to fix a bandage. She not only tied it in a most complicated knot but sealed it. I was spared having to give an untruthful or evasive answer to any question about the bandage by the fact that, despite everything, I was still prioress and it would have been incorrect for any sister to comment.

At the end of a week Seraphima took her scissors and cut away the bandage, not breaking the seals. And in clear scarlet were four names: *Joseph, Jesus, Mary* and *Francis de Sales*. We both stared, and Seraphima threw down the scissors and the bandage and broke into loud sobs. "So it is true, then. God pity us! What will happen now?"

I comforted her as well as I could, but I was puzzled and confused. For I knew nothing whatever about Francis de Sales except that I could say positively that he was not a saint. At least not one mentioned in any book I had read.

The only person in our house likely to know was Sister Mathilde, also a great reader. I sent for her and she came. Keeping the back of my hand pressed against my lap, I asked her if she knew anything about Francis de Sales.

"He was bishop of Geneva. A noted preacher and quite famous for his success in converting Huguenots. He died about fifteen years ago."

"I must confess I have never read anything about him. How do you know so much?"

She gave me her cool, unfriendly look. "I am a Savoyard. Sales, where Francis was born, adjoins my father's estate. And so does Annecy, where he is buried."

I thought: I cannot go on hiding this hand forever. Sister Mathilde will be one of the incredulous. A good test. I lifted my hand and held it so that she could see easily. She turned very pale, lost her well-bred composure and asked, "What does it mean?"

"I don't know. The first name appeared a week ago. The others developed inside the bandage."

"We did wonder about your hand. We thought perhaps it was some kind of penance. Reverend Mother, may I ask a blunt question? Is this *also* to be exploited?"

"Why do you say *also*? What else has been exploited?"

"The whole matter of the possession by demons." She spoke as though she blamed me for everything.

"You were possessed yourself," I reminded her. "Explain to me what you mean by exploited."

"It was publicized. Made much of. *You*, Reverend Mother, admitted the first exorcist. *You* consented to public exorcisms."

"And in my place you would have done differently?"

"Yes. And let the whole dreadful thing take its course, die down of its own accord."

I said, almost with meekness, "That may have been the wiser course. But I was acting upon the advice of our confessor."

"Yes. And with what result? Our mother house at Poitiers has disowned us. Our name is blackened beyond all hope. I sometimes think that a hundred years from now we shall still be infamous."

I realized that she was speaking much as my predecessor would have. *She* would have ignored even her own demon, closed the convent door firmly and left the demons to grow weary.

I said, "Perhaps even now the situation may be redeemed. Will you go to the cell I now occupy and bring the linen bag which is under my pillow?"

She brought it; and after opening it, I pulled out the chemise, told her the story, pointed out the marks, asked her to smell the balsam, described how Seraphima had tried to wash the marks away and how Madame de Laubardemont had been helped. Mathilde looked and listened.

I said, "It is a curious thing, but when Mother Bernard first told me that I was to be prioress in her place, I suggested you, Sister Mathilde, as a better choice. So tell me, quite frankly, what would *you* do if you were in my place now? With this." I stuck out my left hand. "And this." I touched the chemise.

She thought before she answered and then said, "For the time being, nothing. Nothing that would attract attention. Because—who knows?—it might be another device of the Devil. He is infinitely cunning."

"I suppose all things are *possible*," I said, "but I pray God that this is not deception. However, I will be cautious."

But it was already too late for caution.

MADAME DE LAUBARDEMONT talked; so did her husband and the surgeon—all acclaiming a miracle. Even Dr. Fanton talked, denying that anything miraculous had happened. People began to flood in, begging, beseeching that some small miracle should be performed on their behalf.

And how could I deny them?

The father carrying a child with a withered leg.

The mother leading a blind child.

The numerous sufferers from scrofula, with their swollen, suppurating glands.

And why should Saint Joseph not be asked to help? And thanked if he helped even a little? I looked upon myself as a channel, a go-between, always careful to name him: "May Saint Joseph relieve you."

Faith in itself is a wonderful healer and the amount of faith, as well as the strength of it, was astonishing. There were people who were content to touch the chemise with a piece of paper, a rosary, a rag, and to go away convinced that they were taking Saint Joseph's healing balsam with them.

Not since I had worked in the infirmary at Poitiers had I been in such close touch with the really poor and simple, and it was a heartening experience. Those who were cured—and many were—were so grateful, and they came back to thank me. I always refused to take any credit. Even some of those for whom no miracle had been performed said that though not cured, they *felt* better knowing that Saint Joseph was interceding for them.

Many people brought little gifts, which I always directed should be placed below the picture of the saint in the chapel. Often at the end of the day the plain wooden table which had replaced the bench beneath the picture was piled with flowers, eggs, homemade candles, fruit and vegetables.

At first I kept my hand concealed, but after consultation with our new confessor, a very pious, unworldly man, I displayed it. Father Ressès said, "In times like these anything which encourages faith should be used to the glory of God." He seemed to think that even the possession by devils had been ordered by God, perhaps as a test of our faith, or in order to focus attention upon us, preparing the way, as it were, for this demonstration of Saint Joseph's power.

If possible, the miraculous writing on my hand evoked more interest, more wonder, than the chemise. Many people, at the sight of the names, fell to their knees.

One evening, just as the crowd was thinning, Monsieur de Laubardemont arrived, tired and dusty from travel, but with a kind of excitement about him.

"I have ridden as fast as possible from Paris, Reverend Mother. My Lord Cardinal, His Majesty and the Queen are all most anxious to see you. How soon can you leave?"

Some of his excitement communicated itself to me; but I reminded myself that worldly things must be put away.

"It is unlikely that I shall be able to leave at all. I should require permission from Poitiers, which will not be forthcoming. The abbess wrote me one most vituperative letter when our—trouble began. Since then, I have written several letters. They have not even been acknowledged."

He gave me a sly little smile. "When Cardinal Richelieu expresses a wish, it would be very unwise, even for an abbess, to stand in his way. Actually I called in at Poitiers on my way here. The abbess was most—reasonable."

"You mean she consented?"

"With conditions." That smile showed again. "You are to be accompanied by one of your sisters, preferably a senior one. You are to have a suitable escort—that I will arrange. Also she thought it advisable for you to take a priest with you. Whom would you like?"

I felt almost dizzy. It had all happened so quickly. I, from the cloister, being wafted to Paris! But there was just something about Laubardemont's manner which warned me. What of, I couldn't say, except that I felt I was being manipulated. And that made me feel that I needed a spiritually *strong* priest.

I said, on impulse, "Father Surin."

The animation left Laubardemont's face. He said, speaking slowly, "I am afraid that would not be possible, Reverend Mother. His state of health would forbid it."

"I did not know that he was ill. I wrote and he answered. He made no mention . . ."

"No. I understand that he can *write*. Have you a second choice?"

"I must think, monsieur."

"Certainly. But not too long. Her Majesty the Queen is pregnant. She is not young and she suffers. She is anxious to see if the garment which did my wife such service would benefit her in any way."

"I see. . . . Well, if you can arrange an escort, and a priest, I can be ready to leave tomorrow."

He stared.

I said, "A nun has no possessions and can travel light."

And I thought of the time when the eight of us, owning nothing, had walked into Loudun in the rain.

I CHOSE SERAPHIMA to accompany me. She made only a feeble protest: "But who will cook here when I am in Paris?"

"Who cooked when you watched beside me for six days and nights?"

"The young girls under instruction."

"Then they can do it again."

I next spoke with Sister Mathilde, the obvious one to leave in charge during my absence. She accepted the duty willingly, but her tongue betrayed her. She said, "I will do my best so that if . . . *when* you return, you will find everything in order."

"Why did you say *if*, Sister?"

"Did I? How stupid of me! It was merely that I was thinking some promotion might come to you, Reverend Mother."

In all honesty I could not rebuke her, for my own thoughts were running along the same line. I was going to Paris, to the court, to the very fountainhead of all favor, patronage, privilege. Who could tell what the result might be?

From that nonsensical thought I was swiftly cast down.

What with one thing and another I was late to bed that night and had hardly put my head on the pillow when Saint Joseph was there.

He said, "Last time I came to help. This time to warn. I am regarded as a simple man; my surroundings were a workshop and a small village. But I spent some time in the most sophisticated society in the world. Cities are dangerous places."

"I shall be well guarded."

"In body—yes. I am concerned for your soul. There will be adulation and flattery, attacks upon your integrity. You must not allow your head to be turned. I will lend what support I can, but if at any time you seek to exploit, for profit or for honor, the small gift I made you, it will lose all virtue. Will you remember that?"

"In every situation. At all times."

"Some cunning may be required of you. I judge that you can supply it. Much physical exertion too. But above all, regard yourself, as I did, as God's caretaker. Then all will be well."

"Why was I chosen? I have often wondered."

He smiled. "Why are any of us chosen? You have had a unique experience. You also have a gift for language. Perhaps it was meant that you should write a book."

The idea was new to me, but agreeable.

"Could I? Should I?"

"Surely, an honest account would be valuable. But remember, you are only the tool."

THE GRANDEUR—AGAINST which I must perpetually be on guard—began next day. Seraphima and I had walked into Loudun; we left in a fine light carriage drawn by two spirited horses. On the seat beside the coachman sat the secular priest, Father Paul, whom Monsieur de Laubardemont had produced at such short notice. Alongside the carriage rode our escort, Monsieur de Montglat, and behind came two sturdy serving men, also well mounted.

But except for the sweet-scented chemise all that Seraphima and I brought away with us was one change of linen apiece.

It should have been a swift journey. But Monsieur de Laubardemont's genius for organization had defeated itself. He had sent a rider ahead to secure fresh horses and comfortable accommodations, and word had been let slip, so that everywhere crowds had assembled.

At Tours, for example, I was delayed for twenty-four hours. I first received the archbishop, who was eighty and plainly in his dotage, yet

inclined to be skeptical. He brought with him a number of physicians, less interested in the chemise than in my hand. Every test they applied failed in its purpose: long immersion in almost scalding water, violent scrubbing. The names seemed to fade, and then emerged, as clearly as ever. The archbishop was convinced and sent for Prince Gaston of Orléans, who was staying in the neighborhood. The prince, at least, required no further proof; he said that the exorcism he had attended at Loudun had changed his life.

Then it was the turn of the ordinary people. I sat far into the night with my hand lying on the sill of an open window. Seraphima sat beside me holding the chemise. A serving man bearing a torch stood on either side of the window; others ran about the courtyard, urging the crowd to keep on the move. Finally, well after midnight, Seraphima said, "That is all for tonight!" and would have slammed down the window but for the fact that my arm seemed to have turned into wood. She had to move it for me, and she scolded all the time we were making ready for bed. "If people think I'm going to let you kill yourself," she said, "they're wrong!" She grumbled on. I was too exhausted even to speak.

In the morning the crowd was thicker than ever. I sat all day at the window, with only the briefest intervals, my posture slightly relieved by a cushion which Seraphima had placed on the sill. An estimated thirty thousand people filed past.

It was the same at Amboise, and at Orléans. Then finally we arrived in Paris.

My mother had spent her girlhood there. My father had paid one visit in connection with some small property left him by an aged relative, met my mother, married her and carried her off to Cozes. My mother always said that Paris was the center of the world; my father said it was a cesspit. Now I could judge for myself.

And they were both right!

Most of the streets were narrow, dark and filthy, crowded with people who looked very poor, undersized and underfed. And most of them were pale. There were poor people everywhere, of course, but in the country, or in country towns, which were all I had hitherto known, food, grown nearby, is reasonably cheap, and fresh air is free.

In the dirty, crowded streets the servants of Monsieur de Montglat, our escort, rode ahead of us, clearing the way, overroughly, I thought. Then a sudden turn would bring the carriage into a wider street, or an open square where, behind tall iron gates, were the houses of the wealthy, spacious in themselves and surrounded by gardens, or even miniature parks.

Monsieur de Laubardemont's house was such a one, a veritable palace. Here, in rooms specially assigned to us, Seraphima and I were to spend our time while we were in Paris.

Our host was there to greet us. And Madame de Laubardemont came forward and welcomed me as though I were her dearest friend. She personally conducted us to our apartments, which were very grand, with carpets on the floors and silk curtains at the windows and about the beds. The washbowl and ewer and chamber pot were of silver.

I was not overawed by the magnificence around us. After all, I had been born in a castle. But splendor made Seraphima uncomfortable, and her discomfort took the form of intense disapproval. Such waste! Such extravagance! And the food, though lavish, was not well cooked. Given the ingredients, she could have done far better. She developed a Puritan streak, and with hot water to be had by the ringing of a bell, would wash only in cold; of a seven-course meal, would eat only one dish, and that very sparingly. She spoke often of Loudun, wondering how things were going in the kitchen now that she was not there to supervise. A dish of green peas could spur her nostalgia: "Sister Marie's will be another two weeks before they are ready, but they are sweeter."

WE SPENT TWO DAYS in virtual isolation until I was informed that His Eminence was ready to receive us. I had not been told that the cardinal was not in good health, but as soon as I entered the room I knew.

A window stood wide, admitting the scent of limes and early roses. In a far corner of the enormous room a brazier glowed, emitting the odors of incense, which I recognized, and other substances unknown to me. But nothing, nothing could override the terrible stench of putrefaction that emanated from the bed. I had encountered it once before, in the infirmary at Poitiers; a man had suffered an injury to his foot and stupidly refused all treatment until it had begun to rot.

Cardinal Richelieu half sat, half reclined against satin pillows, rose-colored. He wore on his head the scarlet cap of his rank, and over as much of his torso as showed above the satin coverlet, a loose robe of silk. He had been a handsome man, and now, in his middle fifties and ill, he was far from ordinary in appearance. Color fades, flesh sags, bones remain. And eyes. Out of a face the color of parchment, and furrowed by pain and the strain of responsibilities, his eyes positively shone, a bright crystalline gray, cold, hard, observant.

We approached him and curtsied. With his left hand the cardinal removed his scarlet cap, a gesture of supreme courtesy to two nuns from an obscure provincial convent. He was far from bald, but his hair had a dull, lifeless look, like frayed rope.

There were two chairs, padded and cushioned in velvet. "Please sit," he said. And it did not surprise me that his voice should be compelling. "I have been very anxious to meet you," he said. "And no reports did you justice. They exaggerated your slight—*very* slight—affliction, and omitted to tell me that you were beautiful."

I remembered what Saint Joseph had said about flattery. But flattery is invariably used to some purpose. Here I could see none. What could he possibly want of me?

I made what I hoped was the correct answer. "My Lord Cardinal," I said, "a nun, when she renounces the world, must shed all vanity."

"Well said." He smiled a thin-lipped smile. "And ambition?"

"That too."

"Ah! Now, if I may see the famous hand . . ."

I placed it on the coverlet and he took my wrist in a firm clasp, using his left hand. Then he moved his right arm. The sleeve fell back and I saw that his arm was bandaged from just below the elbow to as near the shoulder as was visible. On the table to the right of the bed was a small silver bowl from which he took a damp sponge. "I have your permission?" I nodded, but Seraphima cried, "No acid! I forbid it! Somebody tried acid once and raised blisters."

I think it must have been a very long time since anyone had used the word *forbid* to Cardinal Richelieu, but he laughed and said, "Sit down, Sister Tigress. It is a harmless bleach. A mere test."

"But *why?* If Reverend Mother says a thing is true, so it is."

"What touching confidence!" he said. A drop of the liquid fell onto the rose-pink of the coverlet, made a dark spot which rapidly faded to near white. A bleach indeed, and a powerful one.

He dabbed at my hand. There was a stinging sensation, but no burning, and because the sponge was soft and used gently, none of the reddening which resulted in a temporary eclipse. The cardinal stared and stared, relinquished my hand, looked up at me and said, "I am convinced." Then he dropped back against his pillows and gave a little sigh.

And all at once, aware of his discomfort, I was not the nun who had been possessed and delivered and then made into a walking relic; I was back in the infirmary at Poitiers, young, eager to learn, anxious to help. I turned to Seraphima and said, "May I have the chemise?"

She opened the linen bag in which we carried it and handed it to me. I breathed a silent prayer to Saint Joseph and spread the chemise in such a way that its lower edge covered the cardinal's right arm and the rest of it lay across his body. To do this, I had to approach even nearer to the bed, lean across it. The evil odor was overpowering.

Then, very slowly, some of the pain lines eased from his face.

"Better," he said, half in wonder, half in disbelief.

I said, "Thanks to Saint Joseph," and took the chemise and handed it back to Seraphima, who folded it and would have replaced it in the bag, but a word from the bed stopped her.

"Wait!" This great man then showed himself as much a believer in transferred miracles as the poorest peasant who had tried to rub a scrap of rag against the balsam marks. He wore on his finger his cardinal's ring, a ruby of great size and beauty. He called to Seraphima to hold out the chemise, and then he rubbed the ring against the balsam marks.

Then his mind moved to other things. "Is your visit to Her Majesty yet arranged?" he asked.

"No. I was given to understand that Your Eminence wished to see me first."

"That is true. With a pregnancy so important as this, no risks can be taken. The child, if a boy, will be heir to the most powerful kingdom in the world. I could hardly allow the Queen to be disturbed by a hysterical nun with a faked relic."

I said, "There is something I should have said, my Lord Cardinal, before this. I and all my sisters at Loudun are most grateful for the support you gave us in the time of our most dire need. We could easily have starved."

"Oh," he said, "that pittance! Well, if it comforts you at all, it will continue so long as I live. And thanks to you—and to Saint Joseph—I feel more like living now than I did an hour ago."

He blessed us and dismissed us.

I LAY BACK IN the carriage, breathing the untainted air, content not to talk.

But Seraphima chattered. "Reverend Mother, I was so *glad* that you gave the answer you did."

"Which one?"

"About vanity, and shutting the world away. Sometimes I worry. I can see that you belong in this outer world. Grand people are your proper company. So I worry as to what might happen if . . . if the world claimed you back." She brought out the last words in a rush.

"I hope I should remember my vows."

"Whatever the persuasion?"

Suddenly I was out of temper with her. I said, "Seraphima, I chose you to come with me to be a comfort. Not to nag at me like a governess. Why should you think I regard my vows lightly? Because I ate meat on Friday? Such indulgence is allowed to travelers, as you should know. *You* stuck to the rule and ate that mud-flavored fresh-water fish. I admire you for it, and for washing in cold water. But I fail to see why you suspect me of reneging on my vows, whatever the persuasion, as you call it."

Her eyes filled with tears but she blinked them back. And I was angry with myself for speaking sharply. She was not to blame. What was to blame was my own untamed nature with its willful knowledge.

I did not want to go back to Loudun!

How FAST THOSE in power can move! We were hardly back in Monsieur de Laubardemont's house when he himself was with us, extremely subservient, saying that on the morrow we should go to visit Queen Anne at Saint-Germain-en-Laye, where she had gone for the benefit of purer air.

CHAPTER SIX

N O WOMAN SHOULD be judged by the way she looks when pregnant. But Anne of Austria was a Hapsburg, and I could remember my father saying, in his caustic way, that all Hapsburgs entered a room chin first, the outjutting lower jaw well in advance of any other part of the body. In her this peculiarity was not pronounced, but her face was bloated and heavily pigmented about the eyes.

Her Majesty greeted us most kindly from the sofa on which she lay, and offered us refreshments. Seraphima would neither eat nor drink, but I took a glass of wine and a small saffron cake.

The Queen then took my hand and held it, staring, for what seemed a full hour. She traced the letters with a fingertip, but otherwise subjected me to no test. Finally she said, "How can anyone disapprove of a thing so marvelous? A thing that inspires so much devotion? Those who decry this miracle are the enemies of the Church. Now, may I see the chemise of which Madame de Laubardemont speaks so highly?"

Seraphima took it from its bag and shook it out. I handed it to the Queen, who handled it most reverently and sniffed the balsam, saying, "Fragrant! Very fragrant! I have no pain now, but it will come." Terror flared in her eyes. She gathered the garment into small compass and pressed it to her breast. "You will allow me to keep it, Madame Prioress?"

I knew that the slightest wish expressed by a royal personage was a command to a mere subject. But I also knew that what she asked was impossible. I prayed, and the answer came.

"Your Majesty, were it mine to give, it would be yours already! But I am only its custodian. It works *through* me, so long as I obey orders. However, one thing I can promise. When your hour comes, I will bring it back."

"Then I must be content with that," she said, sounding far from content; but she returned it to me. Then she said to Seraphima, "Open that door. You will find one of my ladies. Tell her that I wish to see the King."

He came, inspected my hand, and made an ambivalent statement. "I never doubted," he said. "Now I am convinced." Then he made a rather feeble joke about his brother, Prince Gaston, having been cured of swearing and went away. He was glad to go, I thought.

We would have gone, too, but the Queen insisted that we stay. Dinner would be served shortly.

The meal was of the kind of which Seraphima much disapproved. Such shocking waste, she had complained. I had tried to explain to her that what was not eaten at the main table went to feed the staff, and that what was then left was given to the poor who daily waited at the gate of any great house. She listened but did not understand.

Unlike Seraphima, I obviously harbored a streak of gluttony in me; not for quantity, for quality: delicate food, so presented as to be pleasing to the eye as well as to the palate. Yet for all these years, ever since I had joined the Ursulines at Poitiers, I had been content with coarse fare, and during our early days at Loudun, a near-starvation diet.

The lady-in-waiting who had fetched His Majesty and then stayed in the Queen's apartment to share the meal—brought in on wheeled tables—was Madame la Marquise de Lacratelle; once pretty, middle-aged now, but well preserved and very elegant. Her hair was dressed high and the heels of her shoes must have measured at least four inches.

When the last table was wheeled away, the Queen said, "Marguerite, you know what I wish the lady prioress to see." The marquise rose, towering over me. I stood up and Seraphima would have risen, too, but Her Majesty waved an imperative hand. "No! Stay with me. Tell me about Loudun. I have never seen it."

And what indeed had Seraphima seen of it? She'd walked to that old, said-to-be-haunted house, walked from there to the Protestant College. I could imagine the Queen of France being entertained by a lively description of Seraphima's new kitchen.

The marquise and I went through a magnificent garden, passed a pool full of water lilies and a lake on which swans floated. I had no difficulty in keeping pace with her, for her heels made her totter. We followed a turnoff in the path and were confronted by a tall red-brick wall with an iron gateway in it. It stood open and we moved into what must have once been an exquisite garden, neglected now, but not so overgrown as that of our first house in Loudun. Men were working at its restoration, scything and then shearing the lawn, tidying and weeding the flower beds.

The house which this garden embraced was of a moderate kind, built for comfort and private living. And the furniture partook of the same moderate character. Nothing ornate, all for ease.

The marquise dropped down into the first chair available and kicked off those ridiculous shoes.

She said, "Look where you will. I know that Her Majesty will be most interested in your opinion."

"But in what regard?"

"Who can say?"

I walked about, noting that the house had been recently, and very hastily, cleaned; on some surfaces I saw the betraying semicircle of polished surface and the surround of dust. But the kitchen was wonderfully equipped and there were three latrines on each floor. Only one room puzzled me because it was completely empty. It was large and high ceilinged and had no hearth.

I was back in the Queen's room in time to hear Seraphima say, ". . . and with golden eyes. I miss her very much. But perhaps that is why we are not encouraged to keep pets."

"Yet you have your beloved cat."

"With the permission of Reverend Mother, Your Majesty."

They became aware of me. I curtsied, and the Queen sent Seraphima out into the anteroom. Then she said, with more humor than I should have expected, "A most entertaining half hour, though limited to two themes—your saintliness and the un-catlike qualities of Sister Seraphima's cat. And both themes are related in a way to what I have to propose to you. I assume that you do not hold that to be fond of an animal is to endanger one's soul."

I became a little wary. The Hapsburgs had not gained the greater part of Europe, and all that was worth having in the New World, by being stupid!

I said, "I think it is a matter of degree, madame. Saint Francis regarded his donkey as his brother and addressed him as such; in default of other audience, he preached to birds and to fishes. But the rule—though not always enforced or even approved—may be wise. A nun, of whatever order, should be devoted to God, and to Him alone."

"You allowed Seraphima her cat."

"She is of a peasant family. She is over seventy and has proved her devotion through very troubled times. She once told me that she longed for a cat. Yes, I gave her permission."

Abruptly she said, "And what do you think of the House Beyond the Lake?"

"I thought it most pleasant."

"Give me your hand again. And listen carefully. How would you like to have it for your own? To combine with me in the founding of a new order of nuns. The Sisters of Saint Joseph. Josephines. You would be abbess. You could write your own rules." Her hold on my hand tightened. She said, "I know of so many women—widows who have no wish to be married again, but who, alone in the world, could be forced to; young women who have no liking for the man chosen for them, and no refuge but a convent. A few who have—shall we say?—suffered disaster. But they fear the strict regime, the severance from the outside world, the lack of comfort, even the meager diet. Is it necessary to deny every human instinct in order to acquire grace in God's sight?"

"Madame, that is a difficult question. I can only say what I was taught: self-denial is part of the discipline needed to subdue the body. And a nun is bound by the rules of her order."

"I visualize a house ruled firmly—but humanely—by you."

"Madame, I took the vows and the veil of the Ursuline order sixteen years ago."

"They could be revoked. Even if it involved asking papal consent." Her mouth twisted. "Cardinal Richelieu approves of you, and if *he* made a request to Rome, there would be no quibble, no delay."

I thought of the warning of Saint Joseph. *There will be adulation and flattery, attacks upon your integrity. You must not allow your head to be turned.*

Nonetheless, the temptation was severe. Within my own order there was no hope of promotion. If every Ursuline abbess dropped dead at a given moment, my record would be held against me.

"You would have no financial worries," the Queen said coaxingly. "I would endow the house generously; and most of those who joined you would be women of good family and not without means. It could be a most happy establishment."

She was pregnant, and all France hoped for an heir. Pregnant women should not be upset.

I said, "Madame, may I have time to think about it? As you can imagine, this comes as a great surprise to me. I am—overwhelmed. It is a most generous and dazzling offer."

"Then pray think upon it favorably. And now . . ." Still holding my hand, she again asked me to allow her to keep the chemise. I repeated my arguments. This time she was more persistent.

"If, as you say, it works only through you, remain with me yourself. I am greatly in need of congenial companionship. People take their turns on duty, but they would far rather be in Paris. You and I could talk of so many things. Converting the ballroom of that house into a chapel. Stained-glass windows," she said enticingly.

I said, "Your Majesty, how delightful you make it sound! But first I have determined to go to Annecy. I wish to see the grave of Francis de Sales and I must take the chemise with me because so many people will benefit."

"Then at least allow me to house it properly."

She released my hand and indicated a table which stood on the far side of the room; on it were several small chests, all beautiful, all costly. None, of course, of wood, which was the substance I associated most closely with Saint Joseph. So I chose by size. Most relics are small, but a chemise, however well folded, has bulk; I chose the largest. Made of crystal, with ivory carved into a lacelike delicacy, the whole of it was set and held firm by borders and corner struts of gold. Saint Joseph, a craftsman himself, would have admired the workmanship.

Our leave-taking was rather touching. The Queen said, "Remember me in your prayers."

I said, "And please, madame, remember me in yours."

She kissed my hand, upon which the names stood out with exceptional brilliance that day, but when, taking leave, I would have kissed hers, she moved it, took my face in both her hands and kissed me on the forehead.

That evening Monsieur de Laubardemont came and gave me five hundred crowns, a gift from the cardinal to help with our traveling expenses.

IN MANY WAYS our journey to Savoy was a repetition of our one to Paris: the same crowds, the same enthusiasm. Evening after evening I sat at a window, or on a balcony, my hand extended; evening after evening Seraphima opened the reliquary and took out the chemise. Occasionally I fainted from sheer exhaustion. Seraphima worried, and began to speak wistfully of the time when we should be back in Loudun, the place I wished never to see again.

We came to Lyons where the archbishop was Cardinal Alphonse Richelieu, the great cardinal's brother, some years older but in good health. He was said to be very jealous of his brother, to whom he owed everything. That I could understand; a favor often breeds as much rancor as a grudge.

Because the great churchman had seemed to accept me, this man was hostile. I knew it the moment we entered the room. I knew it by the way he glanced at my hand. Yet I was unprepared for his next move. He whipped out a pair of scissors and, grabbing my hand, said, "Let us see if they can be cut off."

"My lord, you are hurting me!" I said, and I prayed: Help me! Help me! I meant: Give me courage. I did not expect any supernatural intervention.

My aid came from Seraphima, who stood a little distance away, opening the reliquary, preparing to shake out the chemise for inspection. Swift, silent as her beloved cat, she moved, went behind the cardinal's chair and laid hold of his right elbow in a grip known to women who have been obliged to defend themselves against superior physical power.

The cardinal's arm gave a convulsive jerk; the scissors fell to the floor. Seraphima gave them a kick which sent them sliding under a cabinet. Then she began to staunch my wound with the lower edge of the chemise, which hung over her left arm.

Rubbing his arm and grimacing, the cardinal said, "Perhaps scissors were not ideal. But I have, in the next room, a surgeon. Very skilled. Will you agree that he should attempt to shave the names off?"

Seraphima gave a horrified cry. I, however, replied with a steady voice. "*I* should have no objection," I said. "But I should, of course, need the consent of my superiors before lending myself to such an experiment."

"It shall be obtained," he said grandly. "Who are they?"

"At the moment my immediate superior is your brother, my lord."

His face turned such a dangerous purple that I felt he might shortly need the attention of that skilled surgeon himself. He managed to splutter, "Go away! And take your devils with you!"

We curtsied and withdrew.

In the anteroom I handed the chemise—now with blood on it—back to Seraphima and twisted my handkerchief tightly around my hand.

"Truly," she said, "you are a match for them all!"

"You were a match for *him*, Seraphima! Another snip and he could have severed an artery! Once again you have saved my life. Do you remember the first time? When you hauled my head out of that bucket?"

"Ah. Life was hard then, but so peaceful. Who would ever have dreamed . . . ? But when we get back, Reverend Mother, there will be peace again." I knew that she was thinking of her cozy kitchen and her cat purring in her lap.

NEXT DAY WE SET out in the direction of Grenoble and had not gone very far before we saw two Jesuits coming toward us, moving at a snail's pace. One was so old, so decrepit, that even with a staff in his left hand and his right resting on the arm of his companion, he seemed scarcely able to set one foot before the other. I remember thinking: Poor old man! He should not be walking! And then, with a terrible shock, I recognized him.

It was Father Surin.

I screamed to our driver, "Stop! Stop!" and he reined in.

Seraphima said, "What is the matter?" and Father Paul asked, "What now?" I was out of the carriage, down in the dusty roadway, on my knees before the man who had freed me at such cost to himself.

Perhaps I had changed, too, for he seemed not to recognize me. A blank stare, and then, below the surface of his face as it were, the ghost of a smile. A tremulous hand extended. But no word.

The younger man said, "He is dumb."

It was a plain statement of fact; yet there are varying ways of saying things and I detected something, a lack of sympathy, a kind of scorn, more the attitude of a keeper than of a companion; a hint of patience long tried.

Father Surin was already scrabbling about in the pouch which hung from his waistband. From it he produced a small square of slate like that used by children first practicing their letters. And the same kind of slate pencil.

He wrote the letters, shaky and broken-backed: "I am not mad. Help me."

"I most assuredly will," I said. "Trust me." And turning to the driver, I told him to halt at the first decent-looking place.

It was quite a small carriage, but we all squeezed in, and the horses, good and fresh, did valiantly. In no time at all we had reached an isolated wayside inn which seemed the kind of place that could produce some food at any hour, even if no more than a bowl of soup and a piece of cold meat. Father Surin had always been thin, almost emaciated; now he looked starved, with the starveling's gray pallor and sunken eyes. His companion, who had introduced himself as Father Thomas, was well fleshed. I wondered if they had been sent into the world with insufficient money and Father Thomas had been taking the lion's share of the food. It would have been difficult for a dumb man to complain. And I was not happy to think that the first words Father Surin wrote to me were: *I am not mad.* Somebody, somewhere, must have suggested that he was. There again, I suspected Father Thomas, and after entering the inn asked for the use of a private room for an hour. I also asked what food was available. As I had hoped, there was broth, and as I had not dared to hope, cold boiled fowl. I ordered wine also. Then Father Surin, Seraphima and I went into a small parlor.

I had wronged Father Thomas. The woman of the house brought in a laden tray, tastefully arranged. Father Surin took two sips of wine, two spoonfuls of broth, ignored the rest and wrote, the pencil squeaking: "I will starve out this devil."

"The one you took from me?"

He shook his head and wrote: "I soon rid myself of him."

"Has this one a name?"

"I do not know." He turned over the little slate and wrote on the other side: "I cannot remember. I cannot pray. Help me."

I said, "I wrote you a letter—about my hand. And Saint Joseph's finger marks on a chemise."

He looked at me with complete lack of understanding. Either he had never received that letter or had forgotten. I signaled to Seraphima, who opened the reliquary and unfolded the chemise. She had washed it overnight, but unless immediately put into salt water, or treated with bleach, blood leaves a pale, muddy mark, so that the chemise now looked soiled and rather squalid. Still, the fingerprints were as clear as ever. I put it into his hands. "It has shown healing properties," I said, "and now I will pray . . ."

I did so, mustering all the faith, all the devotion, I could attain to, pleading with Saint Joseph to intercede with the Holy Trinity and with Mary the Mother on behalf of this good man.

And it worked. With a suddenness and swiftness that left me momentarily at a loss for words.

"I can speak! Oh, thanks be to God! And to Saint Joseph. I am healed!" He began to chant, as though leading a large congregation, the *Te Deum*.

And the door opened; Father Thomas looked in, a little cautious, but conscientious. "Are you having trouble?"

Father Surin could now answer for himself. "No trouble, Thomas, unless a miracle can be so called. I am freed! What I need now is a pulpit from which to proclaim the truth. I must *preach*."

I thought he looked far too frail even to mount the steps of a pulpit, but I said nothing to discourage him. I merely pointed out that now he could take some food. "Ah, yes," he said with that noticeably sweet smile, "I have withstood a long and bitter siege. And been delivered." He set about the now tepid broth, ate the chicken and the coarse bread, drank the wine. Then he began to talk.

It was natural enough for a man whose voice had been restored to wish to make full use of it, but it seemed to me after a while that he was talking too much, his tongue outrunning his thoughts. He went from subject to subject with no obvious connection. Now and then he halted abruptly and looked bewildered. "I forget the rest," he would say and start off helter-skelter on something quite irrelevant.

He was determined to come all the way to Annecy with us and completely ignored Father Thomas' protests that they would be expected back at Bordeaux on a certain date or soon after.

Before we reached Grenoble, where he intended to preach his first sermon, I began to have misgivings. Would he ramble, become incoherent or forgetful when in the pulpit? Would he collapse? A few good meals had improved his appearance, but only very slightly.

I need not have worried. In Grenoble Father Surin preached not one sermon but three. And all, I was told, were masterly and held his audiences spellbound. I was obliged to rely upon hearsay, for he refused to allow me to attend. "I intend, for once," he said, "to speak the whole truth about certain matters. And that might be painful hearing for you."

"About my having been possessed? I assure you, no reference to that time would embarrass me."

"There is a graver matter. And I am not speaking of embarrassment." He suffered one of his little lapses and drifted off into another subject.

What Father Surin thought might make painful hearing for me was his justification of the fate of Urbain Grandier.

Strictly speaking, his sermons were not sermons at all; they were stories, but with a moral, like parables or fables; his theme being the indivisibility of belief. To disbelieve in the Devil, in witchcraft, in enchantment, in miracles, was to disbelieve in God.

I was told that in the pulpit he was most impressive as well as highly entertaining; even Father Thomas admitted that, though he disapproved of the whole procedure. "It is setting the clock back to the Dark Ages," he said. "Not so long ago the doctors of the Faculty of Paris published their doubts about witchcraft, demoniac possession, enchantment—and kindred subjects. Unless the Church goes in step with enlightened opinion it will lose all authority and become the province of silly old men and hysterical women."

I did not even bother to argue. I said, "Look from the window, Father Thomas."

And there they were, a multitude of people of every condition, every age. In other places the crowd had been thick; here, because of Father Surin's sermons—and he had not hesitated to name me or to speak of the miracle which had restored his speech—the crowd was multiplied tenfold.

We speeded up the endless procession by refusing to allow people to apply their own articles to the chemise. And Father Thomas helped to keep the crowd moving by issuing an order that there was to be no kneeling. Anyone who knelt was in danger of being trodden upon.

And so we came at last to Annecy.

EVEN IN HIGH SUMMER Annecy is a cold place. Cold air streams down from the mountains, cold air rises from the gray surface of the lake. Colder than either was my reception at the convent of the Nuns of the Visitation—the order founded by Francis de Sales and Madame de Chantal, now head of this house and called abbess.

To begin with, she kept us waiting. And the accommodation assigned to Seraphima and me was definitely poor. Even the most impoverished religious house—such as ours at Loudun—makes some effort to entertain visitors with a modicum of comfort. Here we were treated as though we were young nuns just entering upon our novitiate. And the contrast was more striking because ever since we had left Loudun we had been given, whether in private home, religious house or mere inn, the best that the place had to offer.

When at last the abbess, having finished her prayers, her accounts, her interviews, was free to receive us, it was like walking into an underground icehouse. She merely glanced at my hand and dismissed it as of no importance. Then she asked to see the chemise, calling it a shift.

She said, "It is much soiled. I will have it washed."

I thought: Yes, and retain it, handing us back a similar garment without fingerprints. And I wondered why she should be so inimical. I gave Seraphima a look which she understood. She would oversee any laundering.

. And then, when the abbess and I were alone, she exposed to me part of her grudge; her story was almost as strange as my own.

Bishop Francis, as she called him, had been recognized as a saint by, among others, his valet who, every time the ailing man had been bled by a surgeon, had collected the blood and preserved it. It had not gone sour and stinking; it had crystallized into a powder.

"And I myself," she said, "made a little ball of it and placed it under Father Surin's tongue to restore his speech. But it was quite ineffectual. Yet it seems the shift was successful. Which Father Surin immediately uses to exalt you. And to continue the masquerade."

"What masquerade?"

"Oh come," she said. "In your position a woman would have to be very stupid not to see the truth."

"About what? I was possessed. I was freed—by Father Surin. Then, by the grace of God, I found favor with Saint Joseph."

"But surely you remember Urbain Grandier."

"Of course . . . I still . . . I still pray for his soul."

"As you should, having been the instrument of his destruction! Are you prepared to tell me that you did not realize how you were being *used?*"

She had, as was her right, kept me standing, but I had reached the point where will failed me; I must sit down or fall down, the pain in my back was so excruciating. I said, "Madame, may I have permission to sit? It has been a tiring day. And my back is not strong."

"Could the shift not help you?" she asked nastily. But she did indicate a stool. As I took it, I thought how pleasant it would be if we could talk as friends, comparing notes of the successes and failures of the relics of which we were custodians. I had never met a woman in a position even remotely resembling my own, and perhaps never should again. I should so gladly have discussed why Saint Joseph seemed to fail with congenital afflictions, yet had succeeded in restoring Father Surin's speech. And doubtless the abbess could have reported cases where the dried blood *had* been effectual.

But the only conversation she wanted with me was to scold. She reverted to Urbain Grandier.

"That trumped-up witchcraft charge—to which you contributed so largely—was merely an excuse," she said. "Grandier's real offense lay in being anti-Cardinalist. And you must have known that."

"Madame, I was then, and still am, completely ignorant of politics."

"A dangerous admission from the head of any religious house, however small. Bishop Francis trained me. *He* saw where Richelieu was heading! Nothing would gratify the cardinal more than the reintroduction of the Inquisition. That is why, of all the orders, he favors the Capuchins and the Jesuits. They also would welcome back the rack and the thumbscrews. Bishop Francis was different. A most devout Catholic himself, he preached tolerance. He often said that if one began by persecuting a man for a difference of opinion, one ended by condemning him for the cut of his coat. And as a result of this tolerance, Bishop Francis had unprecedented success with the Huguenots. He converted thousands."

"So I understand. But—perhaps after all I *am* stupid—I fail utterly to see the connection with Urbain Grandier. Or why you appear to be so displeased with *me*."

She thought for a few seconds and then said, "You whip up superstition with your talk of possession and enchantments, of miraculous names on your hand and a shift which works wonders. You lash mobs into a frenzy—and frenzy can take ugly forms. Bishop Francis said, 'One day shout: *Burn the witch*, and tomorrow it will be: *Burn the heretic!*' And that would suit the cardinal. The treasury is empty and heretics' property is confiscated by the state. But perhaps nobody ever told you that."

Suddenly I had had enough of being scolded and derided. I said, "Where is the difference between my chemise, which you scorn, and the dried blood of Bishop Francis, which you revere?"

The answer came with crushing promptitude.

"In the *handling*," she said. "I know that the blood of so holy a man has miraculous healing virtues, but I don't go about hawking it, making display, gathering mobs. Forgive plain speaking, but I think the time has come for it. At every turn of this sorry affair your chief aim has been self-advertisement."

I said, "That is grossly unfair! I have always sought advice, acted only under instruction. I never wanted publicity—it was thrust upon me. Tell me"—I held my hand so that she must look at it—"how would you have handled such a sign of extraordinary grace?"

"With the utmost suspicion," she said; but at least she did now look at the names closely, before issuing a verdict which completely mystified me. "They are tattooed."

"What does that mean?"

"Some old pagan practice, now much in vogue among seafaring men, partly as a means of identification and as proof of fortitude. It is painful. The pigment is literally driven into the skin by needles. Nothing less than a surgical operation can remove such marks."

I thought of the cardinal's brother with his surgeon in the next room! I said, "But, madame, I should have known, if the process is painful."

"Before Father Surin became dumb he talked to many people—including Father Thomas, who passed on some information to me. When you were in that state of advanced hysteria which you chose to call demoniac possession, there were intervals when you were not—or at least one *hopes* you were not—in full possession of your senses. At such times anything could have happened."

She sounded so sure of herself, and her manner was so crushing, that I could not rouse enough spirit to argue anymore. I asked leave to withdraw, and retired.

There was a little comfort in the fact that under Seraphima's watchful eye some sisters of the Visitation had scrubbed the chemise and the marks were still there, as fragrant as ever.

Next day, dispirited and miserably cold, I went to the place where Francis de Sales was buried. The spot was marked by a stone, but of the simplest kind. Kneeling, I made the ritual prayer for the dead and then appealed to Saint Joseph, asking for strength and for guidance.

CHAPTER SEVEN

FATHER SURIN AND Father Thomas left Annecy with us and we traveled together as far as Briare, where they went west, toward Bordeaux, and we headed north for Paris. Father Surin still had the use of his voice and he preached with great vigor and fervor, but he continued to look very ill and walked feebly.

In a curious way our roles had been reversed: he was the one who had urged me to be humble, and sent me to work in the kitchen; now I was exhorting him to take care of himself. I had knelt and thanked him for delivering me from the demons; now he held my hand and thanked me for delivering him from the dumbness.

I had hoped to avoid crowds on this journey. The scornful words of the abbess about self-advertisement worked like yeast in my mind. But somehow word of my approach, or of my arrival, spread like wildfire and the people gathered and simply could not be ignored.

Because of the crowds and the fact that one day the coach in which we were traveling lost a wheel, I arrived in Paris later than I had intended. The Queen had felt the first labor pains during the night and it was almost ten o'clock in the morning when I literally forced my way into her chamber.

There are many ways in which queens lead enviable lives: they live in comfort, have beautiful clothes, glittering jewels, much adulation. But when the moment of parturition comes, they are worse off, I swear, than a poor peasant woman attended by a village midwife or a neighbor. The one thing that surely every woman needs at such a moment—privacy—is denied them.

Surrounding the Queen were courtiers, officials, doctors who could *do* nothing yet whose position demanded that they be there. Many were drunk; some were yawning, some complaining about the labor being so protracted. The King himself was far from sober, but he was sensible enough of what was going on behind the flimsy, totally inadequate screen to greet every moan of pain with a loud cry.

I went straight to the bed where the Queen lay moaning and said, "Your Majesty, I have brought the chemise to help you."

"Quick! Such pain . . . I cannot bear . . ." That pang passed. She said with reproach, "I thought you had forgotten."

"We were delayed."

She was wearing a loose open-fronted muslin wrapper, and as Seraphima handed me the chemise I caught a glimpse of something blue. I opened her robe a little and saw, tightly tied about the bulging abdomen, a faded blue cord.

"What on earth?" I exclaimed.

"It is the girdle of Our Lady, lent by Notre Dame," said the midwife in charge.

Our Lady must have worn it before she was pregnant, or after the Holy Child was born and she had regained her figure. It was so far too short for its present purpose that it could not be merely looped or tied in a bow. Somebody—with very strong hands—had managed to knot it, and the pressure of straining had tightened the knot until it could not be unfastened. It was now plainly a hindrance rather than a help, and the source of extra discomfort.

I said, "Give me a pair of scissors. Quick!"

The Queen moaned again, and from beyond the screen the King cried as though he had been stabbed.

"To cut the girdle of the Madonna would be sacrilege and an invitation to disaster."

I said, "I will take full responsibility."

Nobody moved, except Seraphima who found and handed me a pair of scissors which I used, not easily; the cord was tough. But it fell away at last, revealing the deep red furrow it had made. I then placed the chemise across the Queen's body and said, "May Saint Joseph help you to quick and successful delivery."

I would have stood back then, but the Queen, after another cry, said, "Your hand! Give me your hand!"

I gave her the one with the names inscribed upon it and she took it in both hers, which were slippery with sweat. I prayed. She suffered two more fierce pangs during which she cried, "It is not working for me!" and wrenched hard at my hand. Then she said, "Oh! Better! Better!" and with three more, almost painless thrusts, the baby was born. A boy; the heir for whom everyone longed.

(This is no part of *my* story, but the child at whose birth I had, to stake the mildest claim, assisted, became Louis XIV, the Sun King, the most glorious and absolute ruler France has ever known. On one occasion Father Surin wrote: "Thus it was that Saint Joseph demonstrated his mighty power, not only in sending the Queen a happy delivery, but in presenting France with a king incomparable in power and in greatness of mind. . . .")

On that auspicious morning, loud with bells and heralds' cries and courtiers galloping to carry the news, the Marquise de Lacratelle came to me. She told me that before the Queen had been brought to

bed she had directed that when I came I was to be taken to the House Beyond the Lake and there accommodated.

A good deal had been done to the house during my relatively brief absence. Everything had been thoroughly cleaned, some old things replaced by new. And it was fully staffed.

The greatest change had been made in the very large and formerly empty room. There was an altar, grandly furnished, and the big west window was now full of stained glass. It was very beautiful—the Flight into Egypt: Saint Joseph clad in brown, leading a white donkey upon which the Madonna, in her favorite blue, sat as on a throne, holding the golden-haired Child.

I stared at it for a long time, realizing that for me the moment of decision had come. Her Majesty had already gone some way toward putting her plan into operation, and since I had arrived in time and the chemise had both eased and shortened her labor, she would be all the more eager to honor Saint Joseph by founding an order in his name.

Why was I so hesitant?

THAT NIGHT SERAPHIMA and I dined in almost regal splendor and for once she refrained from criticizing; in fact, she praised, in a way, saying how pleasant it was to have an unhurried meal for a change. Then, quite inadvertently, she said a cogent thing.

Paris, though inland, is near enough to Le Havre, a big fishing center, to be provided with saltwater fish. Having enjoyed her portion, Seraphima looked at the remains on her plate and said, with feeling, "How my little cat would have enjoyed a lick round that plate."

I saw then the wisdom of the no-pet rule. A woman as devout as Seraphima, having renounced the world and abandoned all prospect of husband, of children, concentrated overfondly upon her golden-eyed cat. No real harm in that, but imagine a convent where every nun was allowed to keep a pet; where dog chased cat or cat scratched dog. There would be ill-feeling, perhaps open quarrels. And had I not, in my conversation with the Queen, almost promised to run a lenient house?

And what of these women who would call themselves Sisters of Saint Joseph? Not one in a dozen would have any real vocation; most would be seeking refuge from a worldly situation which they found unpleasant. They would all be women of good family and not without means. They would expect luxury and resent discipline.

Was I equipped to govern such a ménage? And without an established house to support me? Admittedly, at Loudun I had relaxed certain rules, granted a little indulgence here and there, and some favors. But the general Ursuline rule had always been there behind me, to be fallen back upon in case of need.

And I had a sudden soul-wrenching thought: Had Mother Bernard remained in command at Loudun, would any of this ever have happened? Would she not somehow have ignored the devils as resolutely as she had ignored that wailing child ghost? Were those who blamed me for everything so far short of the mark?

The mind, like a pendulum, swings in one direction and then reverts, taking the other side. Mine did, putting forward some shrewd arguments: but for the devils, I should never have met Father Surin, who had directed me to Saint Joseph; my hand would never have been inscribed, nor my chemise blessed with its healing quality. And what the abbess at Annecy had so derided as lashing up the superstitious frenzy of the mob had another side to it: it had stirred the apathetic people and made them aware of otherworldly things. Was that so bad?

Sometimes I thought in more material terms. Life in the new convent would be very comfortable—and I enjoyed comfort. It would also, with the Queen as patron, be secure. Loudun would enjoy a small pension as long as Cardinal Richelieu lived, but that time might be short. What would come after?

I thought. I prayed. I hoped for guidance. Every night for four nights I went to bed hoping that Saint Joseph would come to me and decide for me. He had warned me not to let my head be turned by adulation and I could truly say to him, in my mental prayers: See, I have not had my head turned or I should not now be in this dilemma. So help me! Please help me! He remained as remote as the stars. I was alone.

On the fifth day I received a message that Her Majesty wished to see me.

She was in bed, of course, but looking far better and happier and healthier than she had on my first visit. Ladies-in-waiting hovered about, gay as butterflies. In front of them all she reached out both hands and kissed me, once on my left hand, once on my cheek. Then she ordered them all away. Of the baby prince there was no sign.

I did not until that moment know what I would say to the Queen. And then I did.

People who mock at anything they have not themselves experienced—and whose experience is confined to what they call reality— may jeer at this. I saw between the far side of the Queen's bed and the window Sister Mathilde. And I heard her voice saying that she would have handled things differently. And certainly much better.

Sister Mathilde vanished as inexplicably as she had appeared, but she had tipped the balance of my mind and I knew suddenly exactly what to say.

The Queen asked, with a light, almost conspiratorial air, "Well, and what do you think now of the Josephine house?"

"It is even more beautiful than when I first saw it, madame. The west window in the chapel is truly magnificent."

She looked pleased. "I am delighted to hear it. I could not, of course, exercise personal supervision, but I chose reliable people. And I had several quite long talks with the man who designed the window. In his first sketch the donkey was gray, and in proximity to Saint Joseph's brown robe the effect was drab."

I was glad to think that the preparation of the house had provided her with interest during a difficult time.

"And now, have you thought over my proposal?"

"Very thoroughly, Your Majesty. And I have come—most reluctantly—to the conclusion that I am not suitable."

I think I had never before seen such an expression of mingled shock and affront on any countenance. Her brows came together in a fierce scowl, her eyes flashed, her heavy chin and lower lip became very prominent.

"Do you realize what you are saying? I do not make a habit of choosing *unsuitable* people to serve me!"

I said, "No. No, of course not. But Your Majesty cannot know me as I know myself. Perhaps I should have used the word *unworthy*." Then I rushed headlong into self-abasement, trying to explain, and appease. I told her things I had never told anyone, not even a confessor. I said, "I never had a vocation; I took the veil and the vows in a fit of pique. I have tried to be devout, but I am unstable. Too easily swayed. Of all our community I was the one worst possessed, being the most susceptible—"

She said, "Stop!" and made an imperious gesture with her hand. "I asked for your decision, not your life story." That was nastily said, but after a second or two her expression became amiable again and she spoke coaxingly. "Come, come! We must not quarrel. We will forget this foolish babble. Surely you can allow me to judge of your worthiness. I should imagine that my experience of the world is somewhat wider." She smiled. "So, I put it to you again. Yes or no?"

I said, "Your Majesty, with more regret than I can possibly express—no." She was again angered. And I, too hastily, and most incorrectly, began recommending Sister Mathilde.

The Queen cut me short, saying in the coldest possible voice, "You forget where you are!" She allowed that rebuke to sink in, and went on: "I do not foresee any great difficulty in finding a suitable person for the post you have refused. You may go."

I curtsied, moved backward to the door and there curtsied again. Her Majesty was looking at me with intense disfavor. Something perilously near hatred.

I was genuinely puzzled. Why did it matter so much to her?

I went through the garden—still scented, though summer was aging now—past the water lily pool and toward the lake where the swans were still admiring their reflections. To divert my mind, I thought how Seraphima's face would light up when I said, "We are going home tomorrow." And then I had another thought, a heart-stopping one: Was Her Majesty angry enough to make me the subject of a *lettre de cachet*? This was a document authorizing the arrest and imprisonment of the person named in a space that had been blank when the King signed and sealed the paper. Such sealed letters were for sale for quite moderate sums of money, and the whole system was open to the most shocking abuses. I thought: The Queen would not even have to buy her *lettre de cachet;* she had only to ask!

I quickened my steps and when I found Seraphima said, "We are going home today." She looked delighted, which I had expected, but also deeply relieved, which I did not then understand.

Now in addition to our change of linen we had the reliquary to carry. I asked Seraphima to borrow a kitchen cloth and tie it like an ordinary bundle. "It will be easier to carry that way," I said. "And on this journey I want as little commotion as possible."

A sharper contrast than that between our first entry into Paris and our final exit could hardly be imagined. I now had little money left, but I spent some on hiring a carriage to take us as quickly as possible to the end of the first post stage. There we alighted and proceeded on foot. "We will avoid the main road," I told Seraphima. Near Paris, minor roads were easy to find since so many villages had links with the capital. Later on, in less populated areas, there was a choice between the main road and mere tracks through fields or woods.

While the weather remained mild we slept in the open, reserving what money we had for nights when rain fell or the seasonal gales began to blow.

For a journey of this kind Seraphima was the perfect, God-sent companion. Snug in her own kitchen, she had been prone to mention her age and stiffening joints; now she literally renewed her youth, was invariably cheerful and infinitely resourceful. Even her countrified voice was of service; peasants in cottages, keepers of small drinking places, warmed to her and would sell very cheaply, or even give, recognizing her as one of them.

My back resented the treatment it was getting. Too much walking and no bed. I suffered as I had during our early days at Loudun, sleeping on bare boards. I never actually complained, but Seraphima knew, and always did her best to find some straw or hay, even heather, to put between me and the ground.

I suffered some misery of spirit as well. It seemed to me that by refusing a high office I had shown the humility of spirit of which Saint Joseph should have approved; yet he never came near me, either in a dream or in that closeness of spirit when I prayed. Except for his name—still plainly visible on my hand—there was no longer any sign that he was my own particular saint. Kept awake by discomfort, I would look at the stars and think that if I had not heeded his admonitions I might now be lying on a feather bed with a down-stuffed satin cover and velvet curtains. I would appeal, in my mind: Have you no sign of kindliness for me?

One came, but from an odd quarter and in curious form.

We were in the vine-growing district and the vintage was well under way when one afternoon the sky clouded over and rain threatened. I counted my remaining money and saw that we could afford lodging, a proper meal, a reasonably comfortable bed.

These we found at a little hostelry which had its own vineyard. The first pressing had just been completed and there was an air of jubilation about the place. Even the rain, now falling heavily, was regarded as a blessing. It would plump out the grapes awaiting the later harvest, and the experience of generations proved that clouds held off frost, that most deadly enemy of the second vintage.

Seraphima and I were assigned a tiny parlor, served with coq au vin of superb quality, and—unasked for—a huge jug of the new wine. Since leaving Paris we had drunk nothing but water, except on one occasion when a charitable woman had given us a cup of goat's milk. Tonight even Seraphima ate and drank heartily, and became rather flushed and expansive. True to character, she spoke about her cat and how she had missed it, how glad they would be to see each other again. Then she said, "And there was another reason why I was so glad when you said, Reverend Mother, that we were to return home. I know how much you dislike gossip, but . . ." She proceeded to tell me what she had learned from talking to the servants in the House Beyond the Lake.

It had, until about ten years earlier, been a kind of adjunct of the court, but all very secret; a place where lovers could meet with some degree of privacy, a place where bastard children could be born. And the large room, now the chapel, had been the scene of masked balls where nobody was supposed to recognize anybody else.

"There was so much scandal," Seraphima said, "that the cardinal closed the place and thus angered the Queen, who liked the company and rather enjoyed a romp herself."

"Oh," I said, "and who told you all this?"

"A woman who helped in the kitchen in those days, and is back now. She said she only hoped the new ladies would be as generous as the others. She also said that for once the Queen had outwitted the cardinal, because the place was to be a convent and you, madame, its abbess because you stood so high in the cardinal's favor. I told her straight out that at Loudun we had had our share of trouble—and mysteries—and miracles, but that you would never lend yourself . . ."

I saw then, through kitchen chatter, why the Queen had been so disproportionately infuriated. I also saw how right Saint Joseph had been in his cautionary talk to me. And now, I supposed, with the dreary inward feeling of being rejected once more, he felt that he had done his duty by me and must pay attention to some other suppliant.

THREE DAYS LATER Seraphima and I reached Loudun, not this time in the rain but in the golden glow of an autumn afternoon. The huddle of roofs, the massive tower—all that remained of the great castle—and the spire of Saint Peter's stood dark against the sky of rose and apricot and saffron. Seraphima said joyously, "We are home!" and quickened her step. I felt no such joy, no sense of homecoming. But the choice had been mine and I must abide by it. Still, as the heavy door thudded shut behind us, it sounded to me like the door of a prison.

The convent atmosphere engulfed me. I might never have been away. And I need never have returned! All was in perfect order; Sister Mathilde had justified my choice of her as my deputy. And the Queen, if she was sincere in her wish to found a new order and not really intent upon running a disreputable house under the screen of religion, had missed an able collaborator.

(Perhaps I may as well say here that there never was a Josephine order established. The cardinal defeated the Queen once again and refused his sanction. There were, he said, quite enough religious orders in France. Whether he would have done otherwise had I been concerned is a matter of mere speculation.)

I talked to Sister Mathilde, in private, just before supper on the day of our return. I congratulated her on her meticulous accounts, far better than mine, far more resembling Mother Bernard's! And then I asked, "Have you received any official visitors?"

That idea of the *lettre de cachet* had haunted my imagination. I knew about the system, but not how it worked. Sometimes in a nameless village, couched on straw, I had visualized officials, well mounted, thundering down the adjacent highway. And I had also been concerned about Father Paul. In my scuttle from Paris I had forgotten him completely; I had not even left him a message.

But Sister Mathilde said, "No. No official callers." In fact, things had been very quiet. A few—she stressed that word—a few people had come hoping to see my hand and chemise. "I did not encourage them," she said; and I had a mental flash of just how discouraging she had been.

I said, "I have had a most exhausting experience and need rest. I should be grateful if you would remain in charge, at least for a time."

Apart from showing the beautiful reliquary and saying that it was a gift of the Queen, I made small mention of my days of glory. I was sunk in apathy. Even my prayers lacked force. Some people still came to the convent wishing to see me and my hand, but, with Sister Mathilde's full approval, I refused to display myself anymore. Visitors could go into the chapel and see the chemise in its reliquary, which now stood in the center of the table below my picture of Saint Joseph. In the area of Loudun, at least, he now had an established reputation as a helper of pregnant women.

One such woman had been tardy in her pilgrimage and was in labor when she arrived. Then I, with experience gained in places as diverse as the infirmary at Poitiers and the palace at Saint-Germain-en-Laye, proved useful as midwife. I delivered her of a fine boy who would be, of course, baptized with the saint's name. It was also, I reminded myself, Father Surin's name. I must write to him.

That night I went to bed very tired, and that night Saint Joseph did not come to me; I went to him. I was in his workshop, which was exactly as I had painted it, even to the tools on the wall and the shavings and sawdust underfoot. I could hear the quiet sound of the plane on wood. And I could smell, not only the scent of cedar, but, if it is not an irreverence, healthy human sweat.

And it was hot. I could now see more than I had seen in my mind's eye while I painted. A door stood open to the left of his workbench, but the air it admitted was hotter and drier than that of France, even in the height of summer. And it was odorous with spices.

Saint Joseph gave me a glance of recognition and a kind smile, but he did not immediately cease work. He ran the plane along to the end of the plank, tested the smoothness with his thumb and seemed satisfied. Then he straightened up, but kept the plane in his hand. A busy man, interrupted at work, prepared to give brief, patient attention, but anxious to resume work as soon as possible. Not very encouraging. I plunged straight in.

I said, "You deserted me! Why? What did I do, or fail to do?"

"Nothing. You did very well."

"Then why have you been so unheedful of me? I have prayed . . ."

"I know. All prayers reach their destination. My seeming heedlessness was—necessary."

"Why?"

"To strengthen you. To prevent too great a dependence. But I think you are ready now."

"For what?"

"The writing of that book, the honest account about which we once spoke. Remember, spare nobody. Least of all yourself . . ."

Before I could answer, the bright scene vanished and I was in my own bed, breathing not the hot, spicy air of Palestine but the chill, fog-flavored air of Loudun in midwinter.

I lay for the rest of the night, remembering, reliving events, deciding what must be included to make an honest account and what could be omitted. This last was very important, for if I included irrelevant things—as people tend to do when reminiscing—I should end with a book thicker than a Bible!

That morning, for the first time since my return, I welcomed the dawn, for the day it ushered in had shape and purpose.

Immediately after breakfast I went to the cupboard where such things were stored and took a supply of the better-quality paper. In my own little parlor I cut myself a new quill, saw that ink was plentiful, and fresh.

Then I faced the question: Where to begin? Not with my unhappy but unremarkable childhood. Nor with my time at Saintes or Poitiers—for nothing really worth recording had happened in either place. No, this story concerned what had happened in Loudun. So where better to start than with our arrival there?

I dipped the quill, shook off the surplus drop and in my best script wrote the first sentence—

We came into Loudun in the rain.

EPILOGUE

THE PRIORESS LIVED until 1665. By that time she had acquired a reputation for saintliness and had also become a kind of local sibyl who could be consulted upon almost any subject and whose advice

was generally found to be good. One hopes that those who profited from her good counsel showed gratitude in a material way, for Cardinal Richelieu died in 1642 and the pension ceased.

After her death the Ursulines did a thing which, bizarre as it sounds, suited one who had always at heart been an exhibitionist. They had her head cut off and mummified and enclosed in a glass-and-silver reliquary. During the next few years the head is said to have performed more miracles than the chemise.

In 1772 the Ursuline house at Loudun was dissolved and what happened to its relics nobody knows.

The place of Sister Jeanne's burial is known. Her decapitated body lies under the floor of what is now a cinema. In life she was not without a certain wry humor, and perhaps she would be amused that people should walk over her in order to view melodramas—none the equal of her own story.

THE REMARKABLE
DANIEL DUNGLAS HOME

The Remarkable
Daniel Dunglas Home

by
Julian Symons

ILLUSTRATED BY GUY DEEL

Born in Scotland in 1833, Daniel Home traveled first to America, then to England, the Continent and Russia. Everywhere he went he caused a flurry of excitement and speculation. He had visions of the future, he caused furniture to move about and instruments to play by themselves. He floated through air unaided, and he communicated with spirits. And wherever he went there were those who believed in what he did, and those who disbelieved.

Julian Symons, known worldwide for his insightful books on crime and a contributor to a previous Reader's Digest anthology, *Great Cases of Scotland Yard,* has long been interested in mysteries and puzzles. "When I dipped into spiritualism," he says, "it seemed to me that most mediumistic feats were or could be fakes. Daniel Home was, and for me remains, an exception." In this fascinating recreation of Home's life Symons recounts the astonishing feats achieved by the medium and ponders the question: Was he genuine?

Chapter One: IN THE BEGINNING

FROM THE FIRST some of the villagers of Greeneville, just outside Norwich in Connecticut, felt there was something strange about Daniel Hume, or so they said in later years. Of course, they all went to church on Sundays, as was right and proper, but was it natural for a boy in his teens to take the interest in religion shown by Dan? He attended every prayer meeting, and was so much affected by the Methodist services that his aunt, Mrs. Cook, said he must no longer go to them. Thereupon he joined the Congregationalists, but they too had meetings that stirred him so deeply as to make him weep during and after them. The lad was always wandering about in the woods outside the village, was said to have seen a vision of a friend three days after the friend died, and was known to be delicate, with a persistent cough.

In the year 1849 visions were not uncommon, and it was agreed by eminent divines that the end of the world and the Second Coming of Christ could not be long delayed. There were folk in Greeneville who thought that young Daniel's visions, the little lectures he sometimes gave on sin, prayer and death, and rumors about curious powers he possessed, all indicated that he was one of the beings whose gifts were portents of the Second Coming.

His Aunt Mary thought nothing of the kind. She and her husband, John, had been worried recently by the furniture in their home moving about, so that in the morning chairs and small tables would not be in the places where they had been left the night before. Obviously Daniel must have shifted them in the night to tease his uncle and aunt, but he denied doing so, and they could not catch him at it.

The climax came one morning when he came down to breakfast looking paler than usual and said he wanted nothing to eat.

"Are you not well, Daniel?"

"I am not unwell, aunt, but I had an experience last night."

Aunt Mary sniffed. "Another vision?"

"Not a vision. I heard three blows struck on my bed. Loud blows, as though they had been made with a hammer."

"I'll tell you something, Daniel. Last night you went to one of those prayer meetings, is it not so? You sang hymns, and I don't doubt there was a sermon warning you against the Devil—"

"But, aunt, it cannot be wrong to pray."

"I do not say it is *wrong*. But to one of your delicate constitution it is—dear Lord, what is that?"

A sound of rapping appeared to be coming from all over the breakfast table.

"You are making that noise, Daniel."

"Aunt, I have nothing to do with it."

There was another fusillade of raps. "Then it is the work of the Devil," his aunt cried. "You have the Devil in you, Daniel Hume, and he must be driven out."

Aunt Mary had come from Scotland and was a member of the Kirk, but there was no minister of the Church of Scotland in Greeneville. There were Congregationalist, Methodist and Baptist divines, however, and she called on them all. The Congregationalist, whose services Daniel attended, said that he was perhaps the purest-minded boy in the whole village, and should not be persecuted for something he could not help. The Baptist, the Reverend Mr. Mussey, thought differently.

"You must understand, my boy, that it is Satan who has possessed you. What have you done to bring him to you?"

"Nothing." The boy dropped to his knees beside a chair. "Oh, sir, I have done nothing."

"Then this is your misfortune, not your fault. Let us join together in a prayer to cast him out."

They began to pray. As they did so, gentle taps sounded on Mr. Mussey's chair, and when God's love and mercy were mentioned, the taps became louder. They seemed to agree with all the clergyman was saying, and after a minute or two he gave up in confusion.

Later the Methodist minister arrived. Perhaps the fact that Daniel had left his congregation influenced him. In any case, he told Mrs. Cook curtly that the rappings and visions were Satan's work, and that he feared the sixteen-year-old boy was a lost sheep.

What was to be done? Perhaps the raps had a meaning and could be interpreted. This was suggested by another relative of Daniel's, a widow who lived nearby. In recent years several spiritualists had appeared in America, and Mrs. Williams had heard that if an alphabet was placed near the tappings, they would indicate the letter intended by each tap, and the letters would form a message. No sooner was the alphabet used and the taps interpreted than messages began to come through, with remarkable results.

Young Daniel sat in a chair, sometimes with eyes open, sometimes with them closed and apparently unconscious. Taps sounded, on the chair or a nearby table. The messages gave one villager the name of the town where a long-lost sister was living, then a missing brooch was found, then some title deeds to a house were discovered. The villagers began to besiege the Cooks' parlor so that they could ask Daniel questions. Aunt Mary was worried almost out of her mind. She consulted with her husband, then spoke to the boy.

"Daniel, I am sure that this gift, if it is such, is not godly. Nor do I believe it comes from Satan. I believe that you are deceiving us in some way."

"But, Aunt Mary—"

"Allow me to finish. Either you will stop this nonsense, or—"

At that moment taps sounded, as it seemed from below the chair in which he sat. They were too much for her.

"You will leave this house now, Daniel Hume," she cried. "I will not have you under this roof for another night."

She went up to his room and threw his things out of the window. Daniel did not resist her, and said nothing harsh in reply. He stood beneath the window, tried to catch the things as she threw them out, and put them in his bag. His Sunday suit dropped to the ground, and he dusted it carefully before putting it away.

When she told her husband what she had done he did not reproach her, but said only that she should have found a place where Daniel could stay.

She snorted. "That boy will never lack a place to lay his head."

In that Aunt Mary Cook was perfectly right.

AN EXTRACT FROM THE Springfield *Republican*, March 1852, reporter Jacob France:

Your reporter paid a visit yesterday to the home of Mr. and Mrs. Rufus Elmer, those greatly respected inhabitants of our town, to interview their houseguest, young Mr. Daniel Hume or Home, who is said to have worked all kinds of wonders in the séances, as they are called, which take place almost daily in the Elmer residence. The result of my visit astonished me, but first I must set the scene.

I found the young fellow at ease in a sitting room. So far from being in a trance, he was wide awake and smiling, and expressed himself pleased to see me.

The young man is tall and slim, with a fair complexion and hair neither red, brown nor auburn, but like a silk made of all three colors. His eyes are blue, his face pale, his hands long, white and well kept. His manner is easy and almost aristocratic, although there is nothing of the snob about him. On the contrary, he seems artless and affectionate.

I asked what was his background, and he told me that his parents came from Scotland. His father, indeed, was the natural son of the tenth Earl of Home, so that Daniel Dunglas, which is his full name, has some reason for his aristocratic air. Daniel was born in 1833, and adopted in his infancy by an aunt who had no children, Mrs. Mary Cook. He came to this country when he was nine years old. The rest of the family had emigrated to Waterford, Connecticut, a year or two earlier, but Daniel sees little of them. He felt himself, however, much attached to his mother.

"She was gifted with second sight, which I have inherited," he told me. "She often predicted the deaths of relatives, and was never known to be wrong. Two years ago she came to me in a vision and told me that in four months she would pass on. My aunt said that the vision was the effect of a fevered brain, but in four months, to the day and almost to the hour, my dearest mother moved to the other world."

Coming back to the affairs of this one, I remarked that his father spelled the name Hume, but he said that although this was the pronunciation, the spelling should be H-o-m-e, which is the way that the tenth earl spells it. I then asked what were his feelings about his aunt, who is said to have thought he was playing tricks and turned him out of the house. His smile in response was ready and sweet.

"I think my dear aunt's reaction was quite natural, and am sorry that I gave her so much trouble. I have said always that the gift is not under my control."

"After leaving her house, what did you do? How did you live?"

Again that sweet smile, and a wave of the elegant hands. "If we trust the Lord, He will always provide. I have been fortunate in my friends. I have moved from town to town here in New England, and have found myself embarked, somewhat against my will, on the tempestuous sea of a public life."

I now asked a question which has been the subject of vexed discussion. "It is said you refuse payment for your appearances. Is that so?"

He replied earnestly, "I have never taken a cent in payment, and never shall. And it is wrong to speak of appearances. I make no appearances in public halls. I give séances in the houses of my hosts, and they invite a few friends, that is all."

I pressed the point a little. "There are certain necessaries essential to life—an overcoat, say, or a suit of clothes." I had noticed that he was well, even fashionably, dressed.

"I owe these clothes I am wearing to the kindness of my hosts, and I am deeply grateful. I have found generous hospitality everywhere."

"You know that other mediums make public appearances, and charge for them? Some are said to be frauds."

Again that sweet smile. "I certainly would wish to say nothing unkind about other mediums. I can only assure you of my own good faith. Perhaps you have heard of the visit paid here recently by several gentlemen from Harvard, Mr. Bryant and others. You may like to see the report they wrote after their visit."

I said that I knew of the visit, and of course the town has been buzzing with it. Mr. William Cullen Bryant is one of our greatest living poets, and one of those who accompanied him, Professor Wells, is a most distinguished member of the university. The other two gentlemen are also respected figures at Harvard, and I was naturally interested to read their report, which was headed "The Modern Wonder— A Manifesto." It will shortly appear in full, but I am privileged to quote two or three brief paragraphs, about the movement of the table at which they sat:

"The table was moved in every possible direction, and with great force, when we could not perceive any cause of motion.

"Mr. Wells and Mr. Edwards took hold of the table in such a manner as to exert their strength to the best advantage, but found the invisible power, exercised in an opposite direction, to be quite equal to their utmost efforts.

"Three persons, Messrs. Wells, Bliss and Edwards, assumed positions on the table at the same time, and while thus seated, the table was moved in various directions."

In conclusion they say that the room was well lighted, a lamp often placed on and under the table, and finally: *"We know that we were not imposed upon nor deceived."*

It has perhaps been clear that I came to the Elmer residence in a spirit of skepticism, but I will confess my doubts to have been somewhat shaken by reading this report. I had come in the hope of seeing a demonstration, and said as much to the young man. He said with his sweet smile that such happenings could not be ordered, and that he felt no "influence" at that time. Mr. and Mrs. Elmer came in, sat down, asked me if I had seen what they called the "testament" of Mr. Bryant and his companions, and the conversation became general.

Now comes the part of my visit that will stay in my mind forever, and turned me from a skeptic to a convert.

We were chatting, quite easily and generally, as I have said, and I was thinking it was time for my departure. I noticed Mr. Home was taking no part in the conversation, and Mr. Elmer said suddenly, "He is in a trance."

The young man was sitting upright in his chair. His features were what I can only call tense, though that gives a faint impression of the intensity of his expression. It was as though all the skin on his face had been drawn tight, so that one almost feared it might crack under the strain. Then he spoke. He said, "Deborah France is here."

To say that I was astounded is to understate the case. *Nobody* in that room knew of my sister Deborah. Still, I was not now convinced of her presence. *Mentally* (I did not say a word, although Mr. and Mrs. Elmer looked at me expectantly) I asked myself, How may I be certain it is truly Deborah? Give me some assurance.

Mr. Home, who seemed entirely oblivious of our presence, rose from his chair and wandered about the room. He wrung his hands and groaned. His utterance was not fully coherent, but phrases came through. "Oh, how dark," he cried. "What dismal clouds, what a frightful chasm. Deep down I see the fiery flood. Save them—oh, save them from the pit."

He went on his knees, struck himself on the forehead again and again, got up and roamed around the room like one in torment. Mrs. Elmer rose in alarm, but her husband gestured for her to leave the medium alone. "I see no way out," Mr. Home cried. "Light, light, there is no light. The clouds roll in, the darkness deepens, oh, this darkness of the night is terrible."

The scene, of which I give only a fragmentary impression, lasted nearly half an hour. At the end of it Mr. Home returned to his chair, almost collapsed into it. He opened his eyes. The tautness of skin I have mentioned was no more, and gradually the deathlike look of his features changed and was replaced by his normal pallor. He knew nothing of what had happened, but Mr. and Mrs. Elmer turned to me for an explanation. I gave it to them, as I do to readers of this journal, without further comment.

Deborah was my sister. She was a highly gifted and sensitive woman. But—some ten years before the *birth* of Daniel Home—she became insane from believing in the doctrine of endless punishment for the wicked. All the horrors so vividly enacted by the medium had been spoken by her when I last visited her in the asylum. To listen to them again was to have the past rise before me in the present.

Here were no rappings, no shifting of tables. But after such an experience, how could I withhold belief?

IN THE THREE YEARS after that day at Springfield young Dan Home (his friends never called him anything but Dan) traveled the eastern United States. He stayed always in the houses of those friendly to the spirit movement, and there he gave as many as five or six séances a day. They were always in private houses, never in public halls, and the young man never accepted payment for them. He welcomed skeptics, and told those gathered together to chat about anything they liked. Occasionally he asked that the lights be dimmed but, unlike other mediums, was often content to work in broad daylight. During séances his hands and arms sometimes became rigid, and at times his whole body stiffened like a board. When the séance was over, he relaxed, sweating or shivering, often in a state of distress. He said always that he knew nothing of what had been said or done while he was in a trance.

What was said, what was done? There were knockings and rappings, and sometimes messages sent through them to a member of the group. Furniture quivered, and was sometimes said to move across the room or to be raised from the floor; at times the very walls and floor seemed to shake. Bells brought into the room rang with no agency there to ring them, and in dusk or darkness hands would appear out of what seemed silvery clouds, and might touch the head, shoulder or leg of somebody around the table, or even shake hands with them. Music might be heard, or a draft of air cold as ice water be felt. The music came from accordions, guitars or concertinas if they were left in the room, and it was said they played whether held in one hand by Dan, by somebody else, or not held at all. Or they might travel about the room playing, with no hand seen to touch them, but this was at twilight or in darkness, never in full light.

And there were occasions when nothing happened at all. As Dan said, he could not control the spirits.

But was Daniel Home genuine? There were doubters, and their number increased as some of the other mediums were proved to be frauds. Yet he still had many believers and benefactors. One sent him to complete his sketchy education by taking courses in German and French. He began also to study medicine, but this had to stop when a New York doctor found his left lung to be diseased, and said that he was likely to die soon unless he moved to a different climate. Where should he go? His choice fell, strangely enough, on England—strangely, because the dampness of the climate there was thought bad for tubercular patients. Again, there were those who said that it was nonsense about his affected lung, and that he was going to England because mediums were little known there.

Rufus Elmer and his wife were not among these doubters. When Dan came to pay them a farewell visit, they were shocked by his haggard face and persistent cough. They sent him straight to bed, canceled the séances that had been arranged (there was a crowd hoping for marvels everywhere Dan went) and came to a decision about a matter they had talked over many times. They told him of it the next day, in the very sitting room where Bryant and his friends had tested the medium, and where the Springfield reporter was contacted by his dead sister.

"Dan," said Rufus Elmer. He was a portly old gentleman with fine side whiskers, which he tugged now in embarrassment. "You know that my dear wife and I have not been blessed with children." The young man bowed his head. "And that we feel toward you as if you were our son."

"I have always thought of you as my papa and mama. You know that my dear mama moved to the spirit world nearly five years ago. Since I have known you—" He did not complete the sentence, but went across to Mrs. Elmer, dropped to his knees and kissed her hand.

"I will come to the point," her husband said. "Dan, we should like to make you our son in fact as well as in feeling. That is, we wish to adopt you by law. You would take our name, you would live comfortably here with us in Springfield, exercising your gifts only when your health is recovered, and you would be my heir. I know you do not care for money, but still, I am a wealthy man."

Tears sprang to the young man's eyes as he embraced first Mrs. Elmer and then her husband. "It is the most wonderful, the most generous offer that I have ever heard of, and it shows the beauty of your souls. You are truly my mother and father."

"And you accept? You will be our son?"

Daniel shook his head slowly from side to side. "I cannot do that," he said. "It is not to be. I was born Daniel Dunglas Home, and that will always be my name. And I cannot stay here. My spirit voices call me to England."

Rufus was a believer, but also a man who prided himself on his common sense. "But, Dan, you know what the doctors say. You will die if you don't take care of your lungs. The spirits surely cannot wish that."

Dan clasped the old man's hands in one of those boyish gestures that had won many hearts. "There is no death, my dear Papa. We move to the other place, that is all. You must never grieve for me, there is no cause. And I shall treasure always the memory of your noble offer. It makes me truly proud."

They talked about it further, but to no effect. Nor would Dan take any money to pay for his early days in England, as they wished. As for his fare across the Atlantic, friends in Boston were providing for that. When he left Springfield two days later it was to the accompaniment of the warmest embraces, and to floods of tears.

A week later he sailed from Boston harbor.

As they neared England after nine days at sea, Daniel looked around at the faces of his fellow passengers, all glowing with pleasure, all with friends and families awaiting them. "A sense of utter loneliness crept over me," he recorded in his memoirs. "I sought my cabin, and prayed to God to vouchsafe one ray of hope to cheer me. In a few moments I felt a sense of joy come over me and when I rose, I was as happy as the happiest of the throng."

Chapter Two: DOUBTERS IN ENGLAND

IN PRACTICAL TERMS Daniel Home had no immediate need to worry. He had been recommended to Cox's Hotel on Jermyn Street in London, whose owner, Mr. William Cox, believed in the spirits. He greeted young Dan warmly and said that he should make the hotel his home as long as he wished.

Mr. Home's fame had spread across the Atlantic, and where in America he had made his temporary home with rich businessmen and sober divines, here he was waited on soon after his arrival by titled London hostesses. He gave séances in the houses of Lady Waldegrave and the Marchioness of Hastings; was carried off for country weekends at grand estates; was invited by the famous novelist and student of magic Lord Lytton to his home at Knebworth. Daniel was the success of the season.

There were also, of course, séances in Mr. Cox's back sitting room, and it was Mr. Cox who one day mentioned the names of Lord Brougham and Sir David Brewster.

"I do not know them, William," Dan said in his artless way. "You will forgive an American's ignorance, I hope."

"Lord Brougham was once chancellor, a very important man in the country. Of course he is old now, but he is known to be interested in the spirits."

"And the other gentleman?"

"Ah ha." Mr. Cox wagged a warning finger. "Sir David Brewster is a scientist, and a famous one, a Fellow of the Royal Society. His writings are too much for a simple fellow like me to follow, but it seems they are to do with the properties of light, and what are called optics. I should warn you that, although he is ready to inquire into anything, he is a doubter about the spirits. And he is a Scotsman."

"Well, I am a Scotsman by birth, although I think of myself as an American. If we could win him over to the cause, would you think that to be important?"

"More important than all your society ladies," Mr. Cox said with a touch of sharpness, for he had noticed signs that young Dan's head might have been turned a little by the attentions of the Countess of this and Lady that.

On a fine day in June Lord Brougham and Sir David Brewster descended from their brougham (this one-horse closed carriage was the invention of Lord Brougham and had been named after him), His Lordship with the care that befitted his eighty-odd years. Sir David, who was in his early seventies but very sprightly, pulled his nose, which was a way he had, and said with a grim smile, "Now then, we must be prepared for anything. If I may say so, it's as well that I'm on hand to assist in finding out the trick."

Lord Brougham grunted. Brewster was a clever fellow, no doubt, with his treatise on optics, his theories about the polarization of light and his invention of the kaleidoscope, which was a pretty toy as well as a scientific marvel, but at times he was too full of himself.

Inside the hotel they were met by a distressed Mr. Cox, who told them that Mr. Home's health was delicate. He had had a bad night, and was not yet risen.

Brewster rubbed his hands. "The demonstration is off, then?"

Not at all, Mr. Cox said. If they would be kind enough to wait a few minutes, Mr. Home would be with them. And in five minutes he appeared, looking quite astonishingly pale, but composed. His cough was very evident.

"Our sitting will be conducted in this room. If you would like to inspect it for 'machinery,' as I believe it is called, or make sure nothing is concealed on my person, I shall be happy for you to do so."

His Lordship shook his head. Sir David said, "Not necessary, Mr. Home. Do you propose to draw the curtains, make the room dark?"

"Not unless you wish it. Anything that happens will do so in full light. Mr. Cox, however, is deeply interested. Do you consent to his presence?" They made no objection. "Then let us sit at this table. I should like you to examine it thoroughly."

The table was an ordinary card table, with a cloth on it which extended over the sides. The four of them sat down and placed their hands on it.

The table shuddered. Rappings came from it. Brewster gave an exclamation, perhaps of surprise, perhaps of disbelief.

Home did not speak, but lifted his own hands from the table and gestured that they should do the same.

The table began to rise. Not very far, perhaps no more than four inches, but its feet were definitely off the ground.

The medium was very pale. He groaned. "The spirits," he said. "They are torturing me."

Before they began the séance a small hand bell had been placed on the carpet, its mouth down. Now as they sat there, with nobody near it, the bell rang.

"Shall I put it on the other side?" Mr. Cox whispered eagerly.

"The spirits," Home said. He put his hands to his head and rocked, as though in pain, then pushed downward as if trying to force away something hostile. Cox got up and laid the bell on the carpet on the other side.

The bell did not ring again, but began to move. It came to the edge of the table, then rose in the air and moved into Sir David's hand. He looked at it with astonishment. The bell moved away from him, and seemed to try to nudge itself into Lord Brougham's hand.

"Good heavens," Brougham said, pushing his chair back and letting go of the bell, which fell with a jingle. The table, meanwhile, had descended to the floor again.

Home opened his eyes and began to cough. He searched desperately for a handkerchief, put his hand to his mouth, rose. "Gentlemen, I must ask you to excuse me for a moment."

He hurriedly left the room. Brougham said that he hoped Mr. Home had not been taken ill.

"It is his complaint. I fear he may have been coughing blood, which is unhappily common with him. I am sure he will be back very soon."

And indeed he was, holding a handkerchief to his mouth, and apologizing that he had lacked one. "The lung disease from which I suffer has disagreeable effects. I thought I felt a rush of blood in my mouth, and had no handkerchief. It proved no more than excessive salivation. I think, after such an interruption, there is no use in trying to continue. I hope you have seen something of interest."

"Most remarkable," Lord Brougham said. "Mr. Home, Mr. Cox, I am obliged to you."

"Sir David, I am eager to know your reaction."

Brewster pulled his nose. "It was a strange and interesting occasion. I am glad to have been present."

That night Sir David wrote to his family about the afternoon, and told the tale of what had happened. Perhaps it was not very startling, but still he acknowledged that although neither he nor Brougham believed it was the work of spirits, "we could give no explanation of the happenings, and could not conjecture how they could be produced by any kind of mechanism."

Yet the more he thought about it, the more certain the scientist became that trickery had been at work. When he heard that the "conversion" of Brougham and himself was the talk of London society, and that he was said to have remarked that what he had seen "upset the philosophy of fifty years," he wrote an indignant letter to the press. In it he made a guess at how he had been deceived. How were the raps caused, what made the table rise—or appear to rise?

"This result I do not pretend to explain, but rather than believe that spirits made the noise, *I will conjecture* that the raps were made by Mr. Home's toes . . . and rather than believe that spirits raised the table, *I will conjecture* that it was done by the agency of Mr. Home's feet. . . ."

Sir David attended another séance, about which he made equally skeptical observations. He positively refused the offer to come a third time and take any precaution he wished, even holding the medium's feet throughout if so desired. The result of this first attempt at a test by a scientist was that believers still believed and doubters remained doubtful.

In the meantime Dan received invitations by the dozen, and accepted many of them. The resources of Cox's Hotel became a little strained, and Dan went to stay with John S. Rymer, a lawyer living in Ealing, a borough of West London.

THE QUESTION OF SPIRITUALISM was one of the few matters about which Robert Browning and his beautiful but sickly wife, Elizabeth Barrett, were divided. Both were poets, with finer sensibilities than most of mankind. Should they not keep their minds open to all kinds of possibilities in the world, outside the humdrum routine of ordinary life? Elizabeth thought so, and Robert did not disagree. He simply said that spiritualism was all nonsense.

They spent winters in Florence, partly for her health and partly because they both loved Italy, and there Elizabeth surrounded herself with what she called "visionary friends," persons who believed in spirits as she did. One of them, a rich Bostonian named Jarves, was a medium himself, and even Robert admitted that he was not a fraud.

Now while they were in England, Elizabeth had obtained an introduction to the Rymers, and they were to meet Mr. Home. The brightness of Elizabeth's great eyes on such occasions, and the eagerness and delicacy of her expression, always touched her husband's heart. As they set out for Ealing she placed a hand on his arm.

"Robert, dearest, whatever happens, do not be angry."

"Not angry, Ba. But the excitement you feel at seeing this man is something I cannot share. You know that perfectly well."

"But you cannot *deny* the spirits. So many of your friends believe in them."

"So many of my friends are—" He did not complete the sentence, but stood frowning for a moment, then smiled.

"You believe yourself, just a little, isn't that so? Say it is so."

"I believe that some mediums are genuine, though many are cheats. That is not to say I trust the messages that come from them."

"You will find Mr. Home is genuine. He is the most interesting person to me in the whole of Europe. Except one, of course."

"Then I must try not to be jealous of him."

Within the hour they were at the Rymers' house, and were welcomed with a warmth suitable to the reception of England's premier poets. Home held Elizabeth's thin hands in his, and showed her the clematis wreath that had been picked by him and one of the Rymer girls and placed in the room.

He made on her an impression of youth and delicacy, and she found something ethereal in his face. Robert, on the contrary, thought the man disgustingly affected. He wrote to a friend later: "Mr. H. says he is twenty"—in fact, he was twenty-two—"but properly adds that he looks much older." Home behaved, he said, like a little child, calling Mr. and Mrs. Rymer papa and mama, and forever kissing the young children. All this Browning found detestable.

Then came the séance, which since it was nighttime took place in semidarkness. There was no doubt about what happened, but the reactions of Elizabeth and Robert were entirely different.

They sat around the table, the Rymer family, two friends of theirs, the Brownings, and Daniel Home. There were raps and noises. Then a hand, clothed in white loose muslinlike folds, appeared from the edge of the table. This hand picked up the clematis garland and placed it on Elizabeth's head. As she saw it, putting up her lorgnette to look more closely, the hand was of the largest human size, white as snow and very beautiful. She asked that the wreath be given to Robert, and this was done. Robert was touched several times on the knees and hands, and then an accordion, held first by Home and afterward by Robert, played some music rather indifferently.

Home now went into a trance, and began to address Mr. Rymer in the character of his son, who had died at the age of twelve. The medium whispered in a child's voice as he began, "Dear Papa—is not God *good*, isn't He *lovely*?" Slowly the voice changed to Home's natural tones. The message from the dead boy went on for some time, and the medium asked all but the Rymers to leave, because what would be said would be private to them. When the others returned, it was to find that (as nearly as could be seen in the semidarkness) the table was raised several inches from the floor. The hand reappeared, and then the séance came to an end.

"To me it was wonderful and conclusive," Elizabeth wrote later to her sister Henrietta. "I am confirmed in all my opinions, and I believe that the medium present was *no more responsible* for the things said and done, than I myself was."

Robert was equally convinced that the whole thing was a fraud. He suggested that the tricks had been carried out by what he called "the scoundrel's naked foot," or something attached to it. Daniel Home became a taboo subject in their home.

Robert made his feelings very clear a few days later when Mrs. Rymer called on the Brownings, with her husband and Dan. They were shown into the drawing room, where Robert shook hands with Mrs. Rymer and her husband, but ignored the medium. Elizabeth stood by, pale and agitated. She put her hands in Home's when he approached her.

"Oh, dear Mr. Home, do not, do not blame me. I am so sorry, but I am not to blame. Do pray sit down."

They sat down, but the trouble was not over, for Robert, ignoring the medium, now addressed Mrs. Rymer. "I have to inform you, Mrs.

Rymer, that I was exceedingly dissatisfied with everything I saw at your house the other night."

The lady looked in agony from the poet to the medium, and spread her hands wide in helplessness. Home intervened.

"Mr. Browning, that was the time and place for you to have made objections regarding the manifestations. I gave you every possible opportunity."

Browning turned to him for the first time, his look savage. "I am not addressing myself to you, sir."

Mrs. Rymer thought Dan might be about to faint, but he did not give way.

"It is of me you are speaking, and it would be only fair and gentlemanlike to allow me to reply."

The poet merely glared and said nothing. When the visitors rose to leave a few minutes later, Elizabeth apologized again, and when they were gone, she reproached her husband. "Robert, you should not have treated Mr. Home in that way. It was extremely rude."

"Did I ask the man to pay a visit here, or foolish Mrs. Rymer to bring him? The man is a fraud."

"Do you mean that the Rymers conspired with him to deceive us?"

"I don't say that, don't say it at all. The Rymers are honest enough, but they are the dupes of that man. He is a humbug, Ba, and I wish to hear no more of him."

They did not see Home again, but it was difficult not to hear of him. He had left England and gone to Florence, where all those friends who had formed Elizabeth's circle welcomed him, and many more besides. She heard a good deal about him, in eagerly awaited letters from friends, letters that she did not always show to Robert. They said that although many stood in awe of the medium's gifts, he was not greatly liked in Florence. He had come out with one of the Rymers' sons, all expenses paid by them, but had cut the young man as soon as he had no further use for him—so it was said. It was said also that some of the Italians thought he was a sorcerer. There were rumors that his life had been threatened. Elizabeth, who enjoyed all the gossip, summed things up in a letter to her sister: "Everybody would be delighted to disbelieve in Home—but they can't. They hate him, and believe the facts." And then, in February 1856, she had the most incredible news. It was said that Home's powers had left him, and that for twelve months at least he would have no more ability to summon up spirits than any ordinary man in the street. And there was a further story, that he was to be received into the Catholic faith. Could these tales be true?

Like so many of the strange things said about Daniel they were indeed true, or at least they had a basis in fact. He had had trouble in Florence, and much of it sprang from his most extraordinary success. There were tales of phantom hands which picked up a fan, of spirits, of messages from the dead. One of the most amazing stories concerned an Englishwoman called Georgina Baker. Mrs. Baker lived with her unmarried sister and their mother, Mrs. Crossman, in the Villa Colombaia, which in the distant past had been a monastery. Part of it was still an old chapel, and Mrs. Baker's rooms were above this chapel. She became convinced that at night she was not alone. There were rustling sounds around the bed, and a draft of cold air, although the windows were closed. When she moved into the next room the sounds followed her, and with Home's arrival in Florence they became louder.

She and her sister made the medium's acquaintance, and asked him to stay for a few days at the villa. He came, and charmed all three ladies with his easy manner and his deference. They would hold a séance in the room she now occupied, and see what happened.

"But, Mr. Home, will you not be afraid?" Georgina Baker asked. "I have been very frightened, and although I do not know the nature of the spirit, I feel it to be evil."

"Dear lady, there is no reason why I should feel fear. It is not I who will encounter any spirit that may be here, but the power who works through me. I know nothing of what happens."

At eleven o'clock that night he went down to the chapel, and returned to say that all was quiet there. Then Georgina and her sister Mary sat with Dan (which is what he had asked them to call him) at a small round table in the bedroom. They were near a blazing fire, yet all three felt intensely cold. There was no other light in the room.

They sat with hands upon the table. All three heard a bell, which seemed at first to be tolling in the chapel and then came nearer, ringing close to Georgina, loudly and, as it seemed to her, angrily.

"Is a spirit present?" Dan asked. From the table came loud raps saying, "Yes."

"And is the spirit a good one?" A volley of taps, and the bell rang more angrily. "The spirit is evil, or perhaps in torment." Dan sat with eyes closed, his face very pale in the firelight.

Suddenly Mary Crossman screamed. "He is here. Look at that chair."

An old-fashioned high-backed chair which stood away from the table was slowly drawing nearer to it. Mary whispered that the spirit was sitting in the chair, but none of them saw a figure. A rustling sound could be heard beneath the table, as though somebody were moving there in a heavy cloak. Then the cloth on the table was raised, as though by a hand.

"He is trying to reach us," Georgina said. "It is his hand pushing up the cloth. In the shape of a fist—he threatens us. Dan, what is the matter?"

The medium had given a hoarse cry. His back arched as though he were in great pain. Then he writhed from side to side, and his hands beat the air in an apparent attempt to keep away something terrible. He began to speak falteringly, the words coherent, but the sentences incomplete.

"I cannot—oh, there is darkness and torment—water, swirling water and I cannot—cannot reach out—relief of torment—oh oh." He sank back in the chair.

"Dan, can you ask why it persists in visiting me, what it wants of me?" Before he could respond, the rappings came, and again seemed angry.

The medium spoke in a feeble voice. "Leave us, please, leave us tonight and return tomorrow. I lack strength to continue." More rappings. He raised his voice. "I adjure you, in the name of the Holy Trinity, leave us. Leave us, but return."

There was a single, and as it proved departing, rap. Afterward Dan lay on a sofa for an hour, white as a linen sheet and too fatigued to move. Yet he agreed that they must continue and discover the secret of the chapel.

They did so in two more sessions at night. Mary had been too frightened to come a second time, but they were joined by two men who, according to Georgina, were of "dispassionate judgment." There were again signs of anger as a bell rang violently, a nearby table was pushed forcefully about the room and a dagger appeared—

although it was not truly a dagger, but a sharp-pointed paper knife belonging to Georgina. This was drawn from its sheath, thrown about under the table and rubbed against Dan's knees.

Then Georgina felt, and saw, the hand. It grasped her by the elbow with long yellow skinny fingers. Its touch was clammy, as though, she felt, it had recently left the grave. The spirit promised to return on the following night.

And on that third night, with the spirit gentler and communication easier, all was revealed. Perhaps this was because Georgina had the inspired idea of asking questions in Italian. The replies came back in the same language through Dan, and although they were erratic in their spelling, it was later discovered that some of the odd spellings were those used in the sixteenth century.

"Who are you?" Georgina asked.

And the answer came. "My name was Giannana. I was a monk who lived here many years ago. I died in the room which you now occupy."

"Why do you trouble me?"

"I am myself in torment. I have wandered about this house for many years, trying to find peace."

"How can we help you? Shall I ask that masses be said for you?"

"No, no." (Agitated.) "I have done much wrong."

"Is the wrong connected with a dagger—is that why you made so much use of my stiletto paper knife?" (This question was repeated several times before an intelligible answer came.)

"In life I used the dagger too often, and too well. Pray for me."

"Is that how I can best help you?"

"Yes. Pray that my soul finds repose."

"Will you then cease to trouble me?"

"I will."

That was the last séance with Giannana, and after it Georgina found that the evil influence had vanished. Through Dan the rooms above the chapel had, as she wrote, "undergone a complete *purification,* and I feel that whatever painful influence did once exist there, has disappeared wholly, and as I trust for ever."

This exorcising of an unquiet spirit—for that is what it amounted to—was the talk of the English community in Florence. The great majority were impressed, although there were a few who whispered that they had heard Mr. Home once took a course in Italian. The Florentines were impressed too, but not as Dan had hoped. They had no doubts about his powers—but felt no doubt, either, that they came from the Devil. Servants crossed themselves when he came into the room, and he received several anonymous letters saying that he should leave Florence if he valued his life. He ignored the letters, but had proof of their seriousness when he was returning home on a December night. He wrote down what happened himself. He had almost reached his rooms when . . .

> I observed a man stepping from the doorway of the adjoining house. I was on the steps leading to my own door, and was looking up at the window to see if the servant was still up, when I received a violent blow on my left side, the force of which threw me forward breathless in the corner of the doorway.
>
> The blow was again repeated on my stomach, and then another blow on the same place. The assassin cried out, *"Dio mio, dio mio,"* and turning with his arm outstretched, he ran. I distinctly saw the gleam of his poignard, and as he turned, the light of the lamp fell full on his face. I did not recognize his features. I could not cry out or make any alarm, and stood thus for at least two minutes, after which I groped my way along the wall to the door of a neighbor, where I was admitted.

He thought that he must be badly hurt, but on examination found that Providence had saved him. The first blow had struck the door key, which happened to be in his breast pocket. Another blow had gone through the folds of the fur coat he wore, then through his suit coat, vest and waistband, without inflicting a wound. The third blow had also gone through coat and trousers, inflicting a slight wound. Altogether, he was more shaken than hurt.

He reported the attack on the following morning to the Guardie di Pubblica Sicurezza, and was ushered in to see Captain Canaglia, who stroked his mustache and regarded Daniel with what seemed suppressed amusement as he listened to the story.

"You are Signor Daniel Home, who brings back the dead to life. Is that correct?"

"Only the name is correct. I do nothing of the kind. I have gifts as a medium, that is all."

"I have heard of you. It is said you are a rich man. No doubt somebody attempted to rob you."

"That also is untrue. I am a poor man, with no fortune of my own."

"I hear you have received a ruby ring from one person here, a gold watch from another. And other gifts. Is that correct?"

"Some friends have been most kind, most generous."

"You see. It was a robber. We will look for him."

"But he made no attempt to rob me. This was an attack on my person, an attempt to kill me."

The captain shrugged. "As you say, Signor Home. Fortunately, you were almost unhurt."

"Is that all you have to say? I saw the man clearly, I could identify him."

Captain Canaglia leaned across the table. "Signor Home, Mr. Home, Home the medium. I have heard your name often, and what I hear is not good. I do not believe all the tales, I am a man of the world, but many of our people are simple peasants. This attack, perhaps it was a robbery. Perhaps you were mistaken for somebody else. Or perhaps—" A finger wagged, his speech slowed. "—Perhaps one of our simple people believed you to be in league with Satan. You smile, but they do not smile when they hear the things you do."

"What things?"

"I shall not discuss details," the captain said. He sniffed. "Do you smell anything, Signor Home?"

"Nothing unusual. It is a little musty in here."

"I smell something else, an unhealthy smell for foreigners. Do you understand me?"

After this interview Daniel had little expectation that the Guardie would ever find his attacker, but he was not prepared for the request he received a month later to report to Signor Landucci, minister of the interior, or for his reception. Signor Landucci had a bushy gray beard, and peered at him through little gold-rimmed spectacles. His manner was polite but frosty.

"I have a report on my desk which says that you were attacked here in the street four weeks ago. I am happy that you suffered no serious injury, and hope that you are fully recovered."

"Thank you, yes."

"Your attacker has not been found. However, I have other reports." He picked up several sheets of paper, looked through them briefly. "They suggest, among other things, that you administer the sacraments of the Catholic Church to toads and other creatures. You do so, it is said, to raise the dead by spells and incantations. Is there truth in these accusations?"

"None whatever. They are ridiculous."

"Nevertheless, you claim to have raised the spirits of the dead."

Daniel spread out his hands. "I am a medium, and unknown powers act through me. I make no attempt to raise spirits."

"Let us not bandy words." The minister's manner became frostier. "I have several letters about your behavior, angry letters. I must request that you do not walk about the streets either by day or night, and that at night you always keep the curtains of your rooms drawn."

"But that means you are asking me to leave Florence. I have many friends here."

"Then by all means stay with them. I am advising you not to walk about alone in the city. If you do so, I cannot be responsible for your safety."

That was one source of trouble. Another came from the fact that while recuperating from the attack he had stayed in a villa belonging to one of his admirers, Lady Katherine Fleming. She was living apart from her husband, and Daniel's presence as a guest in her villa turned some of the English colony against him. Daniel was both distressed and financially embarrassed. Because of his steady refusal to accept payment for séances, he had very little money, and so readily accepted the invitation of two friends he had made in the city to travel with them on a tour of Europe. Count Branicka was a young Polish nobleman, and his mother a niece of the great Russian statesman Potëmkin.

And then, on the same day he had agreed to travel with the Branickas, Daniel was told by the spirits that his powers would leave him for a year. He at once repeated this to the count and his mother, feeling that their interest in him would now be at an end. But they valued him, as he said, "for myself, even more than for the strange gift I possessed," and so he joined them on the tour.

We know nothing of this curious loss of power except what Home himself said in his memoirs—that the powers had left him, so he was entirely dependent on his friends. As he went with the Branickas from Florence to Naples, and then to Rome, he was in a position many would have found embarrassing. At times he received gifts—in Naples the King's brother gave him a ruby ring shaped like a horseshoe—but he refused to sell such presents. For Daniel, however, the position of a member of the household was one into which he slipped naturally. He was always ready to perform any little service, to gossip good-naturedly, to pronounce elevating sentiments. The Branickas, mother and son, were devoted Catholics, and there was much talk of religion. Daniel had been brought up as a Christian, but not in a particular form of worship. Now, when he thought about the friends who had turned against him, and of the power that had vanished for a time, he read all he could find about the Catholic faith, and was converted.

But would he be accepted into the Church? While in Naples he had a letter from Mrs. Crossman of the Villa Colombaia warning him that if he went to Rome, he would be expelled as a sorcerer. Nevertheless, he visited the city with the Branickas and met with no trouble, perhaps because they were an influential family. He was instructed by an English prelate, Monsignor Talbot, and was confirmed on Easter Monday of the year 1856, in the chapel of the English College. Count Branicka was one of his sponsors, the Italian Countess Orsini the other.

Afterward Monsignor Talbot took the young man aside. "My son, I am instructed to say that the Holy Father has asked that a prayer should be offered in thanks for your conversion to the faith. And something more. He has expressed a readiness to grant you an audience."

"I am deeply honored."

And so Daniel Dunglas Home, the child who had been brought from his native Scotland to America, who had amazed many people in America, England and Italy and affronted many others, was received in audience by Pope Pius IX. The Pope questioned him about his past life and about the gift which had now left him, and Daniel answered with the utmost coolness, as Count Branicka noticed with astonished admiration.

"My child, this gift that has left you, if it was given by God, has been taken away by Him. All that happens is by God's will." The Pontiff pointed to a crucifix which stood on a nearby table. "Never forget that it is upon what lies over there that we place our faith, and not upon gifts granted to any individual. Do you stay in Rome?"

"I am traveling with my friend, Count Branicka. In a few days we leave for Paris."

"We wish you to take for your confessor there one of the most excellent priests known to us, Père de Ravignan. Will you promise to consult him when you reach Paris?"

"I will."

"My child, go with our blessing." He extended his hand, the neophyte kissed it and the audience was over.

WITHIN A FEW DAYS they were in Paris, and soon after their arrival Daniel suffered a recurrence of his consumption and was ordered to bed. Perhaps Count Branicka had tired of his company, perhaps he had expected that Daniel's gift would return. In any event, he paid the expense of installing Daniel Home in an apartment and continued on his travels.

The news that the medium was in Paris became known instantly in French society. The Brownings were in the French capital, and Elizabeth was frightened that there might be trouble if they met Daniel. Robert, however, promised that he would be "meek as a maid" for her sake. If they met in the street, why, he would pass by and pretend not to see the fellow. Fortunately they did not meet, but Elizabeth heard that the medium was very ill. "I hear that he is dying or dead of congestion of the lungs," she told her sister.

That was not true. Daniel was slowly getting better, but was he a figure of any interest now that his powers had gone? The answer was emphatically *yes*.

Paris under the rule of Napoleon III and his beautiful wife, Eugénie, was passionate for pleasure and novelty. Crowds thronged the Champs Elysée, where Daniel had his rooms, to see the endless line of carriages—victorias, landaus, phaetons, barouches and the rest—going on the fashionable drive around the Lac Inférieur, the largest of the lakes in the Bois de Boulogne. The Emperor was often to be seen there, with many of the country's aristocrats, and also with the more famous of what was called the *demimonde,* those ladies of pleasure who were undoubtedly courtesans yet would have been indignant to be called prostitutes. It was, indeed, these *demimondaines* who gave the scene much of its color. Their carriages were upholstered in satin and colored peacock blue or dazzling orange, and they paraded in daring clothes and with hair dyed to match the color of their carriages. The *demimondaines* and the nobility often greeted one another, and the Emperor himself had been known to tip his hat to the more famous of them. "I need my little amusements," he said, and he meant that his appetite for women was endless. Queen Victoria had been enchanted by Napoleon when he visited Windsor, but it is not surprising that she disapproved of the life he led in Paris.

Napoleon required novelty in other things than women. He was both quickly interested and easily bored. He was himself a good amateur conjurer, and was confident that he would be able to spot any cheating on the part of a spiritualist medium. The Empress Eugénie's interest was of a different kind. She had been fascinated to learn of Daniel Home's origins, for her own family was Scottish, her great-grandparents having come from Scotland to try their luck as traders in Spain. The luck had been good, for Eugénie's mother, Manuela, had married a Spanish grandee. Eugénie grew up a red-haired beauty, with skin like alabaster and lovely down-slanting eyes. Her spirits were high, her conduct often reckless. When Napoleon first saw her, at a Fontainebleau hunt, she wore high-heeled patent leather boots, a felt hat in which an ostrich feather was fixed by a diamond clasp, and a habit in which a wide skirt covered gray trousers. Her whip had a handle set with pearls, and she sat astride her horse like a man instead of riding sidesaddle. After that he pursued Eugénie, paying off his current mistress with a title, and within a few months they were married.

She was now twenty-seven, eighteen years younger than her husband, and had been married for three unhappy years. She had almost died in giving Napoleon an heir to the throne. She detested her husband's little amusements, and often made scenes which were all the more embarrassing because Napoleon never lost his temper. Yet if Eugénie was frustrated and disillusioned, she abounded in energy, and was eager for any revelation bearing upon the spiritual life. Napoleon's desire for novelty and Eugénie's wish to discover new spiritual fields made their court an ideally receptive place to demonstrate the gifts of Daniel Home.

In the meantime, Daniel had seen Father de Ravignan. They had long conversations, and in a personal sense they became very friendly, but the father confessor did not find the results of the meetings altogether satisfactory. The spirits, Daniel said, would return, for he had been told his power would be gone for a year, no more. Father de Ravignan felt this was worrying, and tried to reassure the young man.

"You must have no fear that these forces will regain their ascendancy while you observe the sacraments and attend confession."

"But, Father, I cannot believe that the gift is evil. Why should I fear its return?"

"I have told you before, Daniel, that an encyclical has been issued by the Holy Office refuting all forms of sorcery and forbidding their practice."

"With respect and great humility, Father, I have never practiced sorcery. My gift has sometimes brought blessings, and never done harm."

"Nevertheless, the Church does not permit its practice. It is not right that you should reason with me about such matters. You must accept the Church's doctrine. What you call the gift will not return unless you desire it."

They argued in this manner for hours, and although Father de Ravignan made all possible allowances, their talks left him deeply concerned.

How was it that all Parisian society seemed to know the precise date, February 10, 1857, on which Daniel's "gift" might return, if he had not made clear the date himself? When Father de Ravignan went to Home's apartment on the morning of the eleventh, the young man met him with a smiling face, took the priest's hand in both his own and said, "Father, wonderful news. The spirits have returned."

"Oh, my child, my child. When did this happen?"

"Last night at midnight. I was in bed when I heard loud rappings. I felt a hand on my brow, and a voice said, 'Be of good cheer, Daniel, you will soon be well.' You know that I have been troubled by my cough. After hearing the voice I slept quietly and peacefully, and today—tell me if I do not look well?"

It was true that Daniel seemed in better health, but the priest did not say so. He spoke earnestly.

"Daniel, these are not visions but hallucinations. You must resist them, close your ears to them. What is that?"

That was the distinct sound of rapping, which seemed to come from the ceiling, the floor, or both. Father de Ravignan left in despair without giving absolution. As he was leaving, he passed the

Marquis de Belmont, chamberlain to the Emperor, who had been sent to inquire whether Monsieur Home's powers had returned.

When told that they had, he asked Daniel to present himself at the Tuileries as soon as possible. At the same time he informed Monsieur Home that Count Alexandre de Komar would be delighted if the medium would be a guest at his residence, the Hôtel de Vouillemont. Two days later Daniel made his first appearance at the French court, and soon afterward Father de Ravignan was replaced as his confessor by the Abbé Deguerry, who, although disturbed by the nature of Daniel Home's gift, did not deny him absolution.

Chapter Three: THE CONQUEST OF EUROPE

THERE IS NO RECORD of what young Daniel felt when the Marquis de Belmont's carriage drew up outside the Tuileries and he saw the gardens festooned with colored lanterns and every window of the palace blazing with light. He was no more than twenty-three years old, and was about to be received by the ruler of what many thought was the most important country in Europe.

Whatever may have been his feelings, the young man showed the utmost poise. With the marquis at his side he walked up the grand staircase, through the Salon Louis XIV where the Emperor and Empress received guests on great occasions, through the equally magnificent Salle du Trône, to the Salon d'Apollon, where Napoleon and Eugénie waited to receive him. A large part of the court was gathered in the salon. There were handsome young army officers covered with braid and gold lace, and the ladies attending the Empress, some wearing dresses that showed the satin flesh of the shoulders and were cut to reveal a glimpse of breasts. The sound of their voices was loud, but it died away as Daniel Home, pale and slender, bowed low to the Emperor, and kissed the hand of Eugénie.

If Daniel looked at Napoleon, he saw a figure by no means so impressive near at hand as he looked when observed from a distance or on horseback. The third Napoleon was squat, with short legs and a head that seemed too large for his body. He had a waxed, pointed mustache and a neat little beard which had been named an imperial especially after his style of wearing it. His calm was monumental, and

his face normally so impassive that the British ambassador Lord Cowley had said it was impossible to divine his intentions or fathom his thoughts. Tonight, however, his features were unusually lively. The Emperor looked forward to enjoying himself.

"We await an exposition of your powers, Mr. Home. I hope everything here is as you wish."

"I fear that it is not, Your Majesty." Eugénie frowned, Napoleon looked amused. "I cannot conduct a séance with so many people. There must be no more than eight."

Eugénie made a gesture at the ladies behind her. "These members of my suite will all sit at the table with us."

"I regret that is not possible. Even with eight people I cannot be sure of results, and with so many more it would be hopeless."

The Empress stared at him incredulously, then turned on her heel without a further word and left the salon, followed by her ladies. Napoleon, who seemed more amused than ever, asked whether any other special conditions must be observed.

"None, Your Majesty. We will sit at any table you may indicate, and at some time the first party of sitters may be replaced by an equal number of others. I am deeply distressed that I could not comply with the Empress' wishes."

"Never mind. The results are the thing." He dismissed a number of the court, so that only eight of them sat at a large round table, their hands placed on top of it. The room was lighted by gas chandeliers, one of them almost directly above the table. Suddenly the table vibrated, then rocked. Then it rose some three or four inches from the ground.

"Murat," the Emperor said.

Prince Joachim Murat said apologetically to Daniel, "We have heard that these are tricks, performed in some way by your legs. Do you permit that I hold them?"

With the medium's assent the prince dropped down and took hold of Daniel's boots. The table had settled on the floor again, but now raps began to come from it. The alphabet was produced, and Napoleon began to ask questions, most of them quite simple. The answers were sensible and accurate but, more important, the raps answered questions Napoleon put mentally. It was his unspoken thoughts to which the raps made replies.

"Extraordinary," Napoleon said. "Mr. Home, the Empress must see this. I shall go myself to find her."

It was a little while before he returned with Eugénie. She said to Daniel, "I have returned alone, Mr. Home, but next time I shall insist that all my party be present."

She replaced the Marquis de Belmont at the table. The rappings began again. Napoleon, with a word of apology, looked under the table where Prince Murat still held Daniel's feet. In the meantime Eugénie was asking questions. She suddenly gave a cry.

"Something is pulling my robe."

"It is a spirit, Your Majesty, one who wishes to approach you. If you will consent to put your hand under the table, I am sure it will not harm you."

Eugénie put a hand below the tabletop. What happened after that she described in a letter to her sister, the Duchess of Alba:

> As we sat round the table a hand never ceased to press mine or to pull my dress. Surprised by such importunity, I said to it: So you love me? The response was a very distinct pressure of my hand. Had I known you? Yes. Tell me your name on earth. Spelling the letters came the reply: Today is the anniversary of my death. Those present asked me who it was, and I replied: My father. Then the hand pressed mine with great affection and allowed me to press his. Then it made with a finger three signs of the cross on my hand, and disappeared.

How could she be sure she had been touched by her much-loved father's hand? Because Don Cipriano Guzman de Palafox, Count de Teba, Eugénie's father, had emerged with one eye, one sound leg and one sound arm from his campaigns with the great Napoleon. He had been left with only three good fingers, and she had felt the same defect in the hand that pressed hers.

So the séance that had begun so doubtfully ended in triumph. Eugénie said that she would be happy for the number of people around the table to be just as many as Mr. Home wished, and longed only for him to come again. Napoleon thought that some of the phenomena might be caused by electricity. Would Mr. Home consent to a professor from the Sorbonne being present at their next meeting? Mr. Home had no objection at all. The professor, however, did not attend a séance because, when consulted, he merely said that the Emperor could not possibly have seen the things he described. They were outside nature, and so trickery must have been used. Napoleon was annoyed, and there the investigation ended. He asked whether there were any special conditions for further séances. Daniel said only that he would prefer them to be held in a smaller room.

So they took place in the much smaller Salon Louis XV. Napoleon took the precaution of having the room and the furniture examined in advance for wires or electrical devices, but nothing was found. Nor was collusion possible, for the company around the table was comprised wholly of Napoleon and Eugénie plus members of the French nobility. The happenings were surprising. A large table rose to a height of three feet and then gently settled again on the ground. Having been light, so that Napoleon could move it with his fingers, on command it became so heavy as to be immovable. The crystal pendants of the chandelier shook and tinkled with the unknown force that filled the salon. There were the usual rappings and messages, the usual movement of bells.

There was more. An accordion firmly held by the Emperor played melodiously without any apparent outside agency being present. At one séance a luminous haze gathered, and in it a man's hand wrote "Napoleon." The Emperor declared the writing to be that of his great ancestor. On another occasion a similar haze became a child's hand. It moved toward the Duchess de Montebello, who shrank away terrified. The Empress said that she was not afraid, and caught hold of the hand, which seemed slowly to melt in her grasp. Throughout all these happenings—and also the evenings when nothing happened at all—Daniel Home remained pale and unmoved. There was something strange in his expression, Eugénie told her sister. He talked very little, and when questioned about what might happen, answered always, "I cannot tell you. I am only an instrument."

If he was pleased by all the attention paid him, by the flattery of the ladies and the eagerness of the court chamberlain to be seen parading arm in arm with him, he did not show it. He politely refused many offers to appear for money, while taking it for granted that anything he asked for, whether it was a carriage or a new coat, would be given him.

In a society eager for scandal and novelty, he was the scandalous novelty of the year. Newspapers carried caricatures of him, as Faust or Manfred, or the notorious swindler Count Cagliostro. Gossip writers suggested that he was a sorcerer who had transformed a scarab ring into a living beetle, and had made a dead girl materialize so convincingly that her former lover had died of fright. The stories spread abroad. In England *Punch* carried an irreverent cartoon of a Tuileries séance; in America *Harper's Weekly* said that "the wicked tongues of Paris" were busy with the medium's constant presence in Eugénie's apartments.

Daniel dined at the Tuileries at least once a week, and was so much in favor that he was bound to make enemies. The most important of them was the foreign minister, Count Walewski, son of the great Napoleon and his Polish mistress Marie Walewska. The count had attended one séance, but his skepticism was known, and one of the first messages conveyed by the rappings was that he should withdraw. Walewski had the secret police watch Daniel, in the belief that he was a spy employed by an Italian state, perhaps by Tuscany. The police found nothing to confirm the suspicion, but Walewski still complained bitterly to Napoleon.

The Emperor listened patiently, which was one of his gifts. He asked whether the other Cabinet members agreed with Walewski, and was told that they did. A few days later Daniel Home left for America. It was said by some that he had been expelled, by others that he had feathered his nest thoroughly and thought it time to go. In fact, Daniel had been told by Napoleon and Eugénie that it would be discreet for him to leave France at present, but that they would be delighted if he returned in a month or two. He took with him many gifts, including valuable jewelry. He had taken to loading his fingers with more rings than was thought quite gentlemanly, although he removed them for séances.

WHILE IN AMERICA Daniel revisited old friends in Hartford and Springfield, including the Elmers. The Hartford *Courant* called him "the most remarkable man living," the Springfield *Republican* said that the medium's visit would be brief because he was so much in demand. The Elmers met their dear Dan with open arms, and repeated that loving hearts and a good home awaited the young man whom they would always regard as their son. Dan called them his dearest papa and mama, but made it clear that he must return to Europe.

BACK IN FRANCE AGAIN, he was as much in favor as ever. He was now a permanent guest at court, going with Napoleon and Eugénie to Saint-Cloud and Fontainebleau, paying a visit to the Grand Duchy of Baden-Baden, and then returning by royal command to Biarritz, where Eugénie and much of the court were spending the summer. In these months he met many members of Europe's royalty, and impressed them all. At Fontainebleau, Napoleon and Eugénie took him to a little island in a boat, in the company of old King Maximilian of Bavaria, and at a kiosk on the island raps sounded and a message was received for Eugénie. Later when a table on a railway train moved of its own volition, the King was alarmed and fled. At a court ball a few days later he made a point of talking to the medium for several minutes because, as he said, it would be a terrible thing if Mr. Home decided to send some of his spirits to Bavaria.

Russia's Grand Duke Constantine, the Russian ambassador Baron Bodiska, the prince regent of Prussia, Lord Howden, the British ambassador at Madrid, princesses and countesses by the dozen came, saw and were conquered. Daniel performed some extraordinary cures, like that which removed the deafness of Madame de Cardonné's son. The boy, who was fifteen, had been deaf since suffering typhoid four years earlier, and had been given surgical treatment without success. When Daniel put an arm around Emil and passed a hand gently over his head, the boy said, "Mama, I can hear." The grateful mother wrote afterward of "a devotion that I shall carry with me to the grave," and the story was repeated everywhere, losing nothing in the telling.

Nor, of course, did what happened at the séances. One of the most remarkable was recorded by Princess Pauline Metternich, wife of the Austrian ambassador. The princess was hideously ugly by some accounts, with yellow skin, pop eyes and thick lips, but she was clever, audacious and noted for wearing amazing dresses and doing astonishing things. She was a close friend of Eugénie's, and one night the two of them dressed up as men and rode around Paris in a horse-drawn bus. Pauline drank, smoked cigars, and was eager for anything that would avert boredom. She was not bored by Daniel Home.

This particular séance took place at a house in the Rue de la Paix belonging to Monsieur and Madame Jauvin d'Attainville. Madame d'Attainville was devout and had at first refused to receive Daniel because she felt he practiced black magic, but she relented when she learned he was a Catholic. Perhaps, anyway, she was curious.

When the door of the drawing room opened and Prince Murat appeared with Daniel Home at his side, Pauline Metternich examined the medium closely. She saw a tall slim young man who looked, in his dress suit and white tie, like a gentleman of the highest social standing. He was pale, with sleepy china-blue eyes, his hair was reddish and thick, his expression one of gentle melancholy. There was nothing remarkable about him except his unusual pallor.

The room was richly furnished, and although it was evening, all was bright as day, with chandeliers and lamps blazing. Fifteen people were present, more than Mr. Home usually cared for, but he made no objection. They sat at a round table with a cloth on it, in no particular order. Some sat close to the table, others a little farther away, Home himself three or four yards from it. He did not know, he said, whether the spirits were present. He rested his head on the back of his chair and his pallor became extreme. Prince Murat whispered that the trance was beginning.

The medium said, "Bryan, are you there?" Two sharp taps came from the direction of the table, far away from Home. "Bryan nearly always comes when I call him. He was my best friend."

The lusters of the chandeliers began to move. A chair came from the back of the room and stopped beside Home.

"They are here," the medium said. "They will reveal themselves, and every one of you will be convinced of their presence."

The princess felt as if an iron hand had gripped her knuckles. Others felt the same. Although the grip was hard, it caused no pain.

The tablecloth was gently raised. There seemed to be a hand beneath it. The men present tried to clasp the invisible hand, but it seemed to vanish. The cloth was lifted—nothing there. One or two looked under the table—nothing there either. They went back to their seats.

Taps sounded from the table. Prince Metternich, Pauline's husband, sat under the table, determined to discover the source of the taps. From where he sat he called out, "Don't rap from above—no jokes, please." But, of course, nobody had been rapping from above.

Home called out that the spirits were all around. "One is near you. You surely feel it, like a light breath." It semed to them that they felt such a breath. "One is approaching the piano. I'll ask him to bring you the bunch of violets that one of you has left there."

The violets glided over the piano, unsteadily traversed the empty space between piano and table, and fell into Pauline's lap. Her husband seized them, looking for a thread or some kind of fastening. Nothing.

Home asked if there was an accordion in the room. "The conditions are so favorable that it is possible they may play on it."

Two of the company went out to buy an accordion. While they were gone, Home rose from his chair with difficulty and crossed the room to speak to Pauline. The lusters continued to tinkle, taps sounded from the table and walls. Home asked her whether she did not find communication with the spirits agreeable.

"Frankly, I prefer the living," she answered.

"Yet there is something comforting here, for nothing more is needed to convince unbelievers that the soul is immortal."

"But I am convinced already. I see no need to live with the dead."

He placed a finger on her mouth. "You must not speak of the dead. There are no dead. They live as you and I do, but in other spheres. Of such we must say that they have departed, not that they are dead."

Now the two who had gone out returned with a new accordion. The princess was told to hold it high above her head, standing alone in the center of the room. She did so, felt a tug as if somebody were trying to work the bellows, and then heard music "so soft and melodious that one would have said it was celestial."

With the sounds from this apparently bewitched instrument, the séance ended. Afterward they all had tea together and chatted quite normally, Daniel Home among them.

Such were the manifestations seen by Princess Pauline Metternich, a sharp and by no means credulous observer. To the end of her life she could not make up her mind about them, or about Daniel. The room was brightly lighted, everything took place in the simplest fashion, there was no preparation.

Was the answer some remarkable conjuring? Were they all hypnotized without knowing it, and without any of the usual preliminaries of hypnotism? Or were there truly spirits from another world at work? She could never make up her mind.

BUT DANIEL'S DAYS OF favor at the French court were ending. Soon after his arrival at Biarritz that summer he became ill and was put in the care of Dr. Barthez, physician to the baby prince.

Dr. Barthez was a total disbeliever in the spirits, and although Daniel had convinced many skeptics, he was made uncomfortable by a man who did not believe that even his illness was genuine. First impressions of Daniel varied from enchantment to extreme dislike, and Barthez found something repellent about him, as Browning had. His eyes and mouth, the doctor thought, were extremely disagreeable, and his hesitant, deferential air was no doubt assumed.

In writing to his wife about the doings of the court, Barthez acknowledged that he was unfavorably disposed toward Home because of his influence on the Empress. Eugénie, never one to do things by halves, spoke of Home always as a wonderful man, a miracle worker, someone with gifts beyond those of humankind. The doctor had heard about the séances, both from Napoleon and from Eugénie, until he was sick of them, but he had never seen the marvelous happenings. One night after dinner, however, he was present when Home went into a trance. And what happened? The spirits said that too many were present, and asked specifically that Dr. Barthez leave. No wonder that he went away with what he called "an incredulous smile on my face."

At later séances very little happened. Napoleon and Eugénie were disappointed, even though Daniel explained that when he felt unwell his power was low. A séance was stopped when one of those attending said the medium was doing everything with his toes—pulling at a dress, ringing a bell, rapping the table. Home indignantly denied it, showing his feet in their slippers, but he felt too unwell to continue. That night he became so ill that a priest was sent for, and the patient made confession. Eugénie, when she heard the news, sent along Dr. Barthez.

The doctor found Home in bed, his face swollen and his eyes red. His pulse, however, was normal. When the medium began to go into a trance Barthez shook his arm. "Come, Mr. Home, no nonsense," he said. "Let the spirits be. You know I don't believe in them." He reported to Eugénie that there was no need to worry, it was nerves. Home's power remained low, and there were no more séances. A week or two later he left France.

Rumors flew around. He had been exposed as a fraud, his manners had become altogether too free, he had upset both Napoleon and Eugénie by predicting that their son would never come to the throne, he had tried through the spirits to influence foreign policy. All of them seem to have been baseless. Daniel Home had provided a period of amusement for a court that feared boredom more than anything, but now perhaps he himself was in danger of becoming ever so slightly a bore, particularly since he had temporarily lost the power to enthrall and mystify. But the parting was friendly, he returned more than once to France, and was always received at the Tuileries.

THE DANIEL HOME WHO now went from court to court in Europe was a very different figure from the obscure young man who had come to England from America less than three years before. He traveled as an international celebrity to Holland, where he gave séances for Queen Sophia at The Hague, to Brussels, to Rome. There were a dozen noblemen and women anxious to be his hosts for as long as he cared to stay; gifts of jewelry and clothing were offered and accepted. Although he was adamant in refusing money, he moved always among the cream of European society. It was in the course of these wanderings around the Continent that he met the girl who was to become his wife.

In every city there were people eager for an introduction to the famous medium, an eagerness increased by the fact that Daniel was often unwell and went out very little. In Rome one of the people anxious to know him was a young Russian nobleman named Count Koucheleff-Besborodka, who arranged an apparently accidental introduction when Daniel was walking with a friend on the Pincio. The friend mentioned that a Russian family of distinction would like to know him, a passing carriage stopped—and there was Countess Koucheleff of the very family mentioned. Whether Daniel was deceived into thinking this a spiritual manifestation is uncertain, but he accepted an invitation to a late supper that night with the family. It was a very late supper, for they went in to eat at midnight, and far from being a small family group, it was a large and cheerful party.

The Koucheleffs (to abbreviate their name for convenience) were young and lively. They also belonged to a highly distinguished family, for both the countess and her young sister Alexandrina, who was called Sacha, were goddaughters of the Tsar. Daniel, the guest of honor, was placed at his hostess' right, and Sacha was on his other side. She was a pretty, small dark-haired girl of seventeen who had been educated in Paris, as was proper for Russian girls of good family. We have only Daniel's word for what happened at that first meeting, but he says that he knew immediately she was to be his wife.

At the table Sacha turned to him, laughing. "Mr. Home, you will be married before the year is ended. In Russia we believe that this must always be so when a gentleman is seated at a table between two sisters."

For Daniel Dunglas Home, son of a Scottish nobody, to think of marriage with a leading Russian family was a piece of presumption that might be thought absurd, yet in twelve days Daniel and Sacha were engaged. Sacha's father, who had been a general, was dead, but her mother, the Countess de Kroll, readily gave consent to the marriage. This astonishing result was not due to Sacha's belief in the spirits, for on the very day of their engagement she had asked him to tell her all about spirit rapping, as she did not believe in it, and had been rebuked by Daniel for talking lightly about matters which she had not seen, and so could not understand.

Reaction to the news was at first disbelief. Tsar Alexander II had to give his permission, and it was expected that he would refuse it because of Daniel's common birth. But Alexander greatly admired Napoleon III, and Daniel's friendship with the Emperor and Empress influenced him. The Tsar, to general astonishment, said yes. After that, views varied from the wholehearted delight of Daniel's admirers, who thought no woman good enough for him, to the comments of his detractors, who said that the spirits had certainly led him to riches. Now that he was settled among diamonds, pearls and rubies, it was suggested, he would find no further need to look into the next world. Somewhere between the two was the comment made by Elizabeth Barrett Browning that the young lady must have strange tastes. "Think of the conjugal furniture floating about the room at night!" But these observations proved untrue. The conjugal furniture did not float, there were many more séances, and Daniel did not make his fortune.

In August 1858 the marriage of Daniel Dunglas Home and Alex-

andrina de Kroll took place. There were two ceremonies, the first performed by an Orthodox priest in the Koucheleffs' private chapel, and then a ceremony in a Roman Catholic church. The novelist Alexandre Dumas, author of *The Three Musketeers*, acted as Daniel's godfather, and the Tsar was represented by two of his aides, and gave the bridegroom a diamond ring. The couple went on a six-week honeymoon, making a tour of the Koucheleff family estates.

The marriage was not accomplished without some excitement on the way. Daniel sent to Scotland for his birth certificate, but it came with the surname written as Hume instead of Home. Hume had, of course, been the spelling used by his father, and he had to go to his birthplace to persuade the parish clerk to make the necessary alteration. And during the whole of this period Daniel found it hard to invoke the spirits. When he received a summons to an audience with the Tsar he had the temerity to decline it, saying that he did not feel empowered. Alexander replied that he wished to see the prospective bridegroom, empowered or not, and Daniel spent a week at the summer palace of Peterhof, in a grandeur that exceeded the splendors of Versailles. There were no séances, but shortly after the marriage Daniel saw the spirit of his mother enter the bedroom, in the company of another spirit whom he instinctively knew to be General de Kroll. Sacha had been asleep, but she woke and, although she said that she was not afraid, she shrank away from the spirits and turned to her husband, trembling violently.

The first months of married life went happily in some ways, less well in others. Power returned to Daniel—he said that the dry atmosphere of Russia was partly responsible—and he gave séances by the dozen, in the presence of many of the Russian nobility. Tables rose and tilted at an angle without things on them falling off, bells rang, messages were received by raps, musical instruments played unaided. The Tsar, his brother Grand Duke Constantine, many generals, barons and counts and their wives were tremendously impressed. Something mystical about Daniel appealed to the Slavic temperament, and the trusting openness of almost everybody he met made Daniel flourish so that he became less pensive, more genial.

Daniel and Sacha were happy together, and just nine months after the marriage their first, and as it proved only, child was born. Little Gregoire, who was called Grisha, was born on a snowy night in Saint

Petersburg. An invisible bird was heard by the parents warbling in the room, and they also saw a bright light gleaming over the baby's head, and moving toward the door.

That was the good side. The bad was that Daniel fell ill again, so much so that his life was in danger. He recovered, however, and there was no Dr. Barthez in Saint Petersburg to suggest that his illness might have been partly assumed. When he was well they decided to go to England. Sacha had never been there, and perhaps Daniel was pleased to return to a country where he had been successful but not triumphant, now that he had married a Russian noblewoman. He had been accepted at the Tuileries and the Peterhof palace, but had not yet been received at the Court of St. James's.

They took a suite at Cox's Hotel, to the delight of old Mr. Cox, and fashionable London flocked to see him and to meet Sacha, whose charm, elegance and uncertain English (when she first met Daniel they had talked in French, which he spoke fluently) delighted women like Lady Shelley, wife of the poet's son, and Mrs. Thomas Milner Gibson, wife of a Liberal member of Parliament. Mr. Gibson was not interested in the spirits, and when he found a séance in progress would exclaim, "At it again, my dear," and close the door. But still, his enthusiastic wife sent out invitation cards for "spiritual séances," and the smiling Daniel did not rebuke her. Mrs. Milner Gibson acted as a kind of unpaid agent for him, sending him lists of "the best people" who would be coming on a particular occasion, and writing that there were two vacant places and twenty applicants. Could Lady Trelawney come? Or the Marchioness of Londonderry? At more than one of these séances the medium floated up to the ceiling.

One of the occasions was described by a journalist of repute named Robert Bell in William Makepeace Thackeray's *Cornhill Magazine*. Thackeray and Dickens were the two literary giants of mid-century Victorian England, and while Dickens had often expressed himself contemptuously about mediums in general and Home in particular, calling him "ruffian" and "scoundrel" among other names, Thackeray had been interested from the first. Dickens had never been present at a séance, but Thackeray had seen Daniel in his early American days and had been fascinated. That he should print an article called "Stranger Than Fiction" in the *Cornhill* showed that he took spiritualism very seriously, and the magazine was so highly regarded that the appearance of the piece did more than any other publicity to make Daniel respected by intellectual Britain, even though a number of readers expressed their regret that the distinguished *Cornhill* should see fit to publish such stuff.

Bell began by saying frankly that he would have refused to believe the things he had seen if it had been on the evidence of other people's eyes, and was not entirely sure that he believed his own. Then after describing his meeting with Daniel Home, Bell went on to the séance, which took place in Mrs. Milner Gibson's drawing room at Hyde Park Place. It was a room filled in the Victorian way with sofas and ottomans; the windows were thickly curtained and had shades. In the center of the room was a round table, and there the ladies and gentlemen sat.

There were soon "unmistakable indications" that the table should be moved near the center window. On the table were some sheets of white paper, lead pencils, an accordion, a hand bell and a few flowers. Rappings, interpreted by the alphabet, said that lights should be extinguished, and this was done. There was silence. They were in darkness, except for a faint light through the window and the flickering fire. Hands were placed on the table. "The stillness of expectation that ensued during the first few minutes of that darkness was profound." What was going to happen?

The tassel of the cord on one of the shades began to tremble. Then the shade was pulled down, slowly and uncertainly, and the darkness was increased.

A whisper went around the room that hands had been seen or felt. Bell felt a twitch at his knee, often repeated: sometimes a scratch, sometimes a kind of playful pat. Then this ceased.

What looked like a large hand appeared under the table cover. Bell reached for it, felt it, and—"it went out like air in my grasp." It seemed to him quite palpable, like velvet, and even solid, yet "pressure reduced it to air."

The accordion moved. Bell could not distinguish it clearly in the darkness, but he saw a mass rise toward the edge of the table and go down. It struck a single note as it descended, and later began to play as it lay on the ground. The music was sweet and wild, the execution "no less remarkable for its delicacy than its power." But it was the conclusion of the music that, as Bell said, "touched the hearts and drew the tears of the listeners." He added that "by what art the accordion was made to yield that dying note, let practical musicians determine. Our ears, that heard it, had never before been visited by a sound so fine."

Now came the most extraordinary event of the evening.

Home was sitting next to the window. In the semidarkness his head could be seen against the curtains, his hands on his lap. He spoke quietly.

"My chair is moving. I am off the ground. Talk of something else, don't notice me."

They began to talk, not very coherently, for it was difficult not to pay attention to the medium. Bell, sitting opposite him, saw his hands disappear from the table, and his head vanish into shadow. Then he spoke again, from the air above their heads. He had risen in his chair some four or five feet above the ground.

"I am being turned round very gently, like a child in the arms of his nurse. I have been laid down in my chair. I shall pass across the window and you will be able to see me in its light."

And indeed, they saw his figure pass from one side of the window to the other, feet foremost, lying horizontally in the chair.

"Now I shall turn the reverse way, and you will see me again."

He did so. What impressed Bell almost more than anything else was the tranquil confidence with which he spoke. Afterward he wavered around the circle for several minutes, now in the perpendicular position, and Bell felt something lightly brush his chair. It was the medium's foot. When Bell touched it, the foot was withdrawn with a cry and a shudder. "It was not resting on the chair but floating, and sprang from the touch as a bird would."

Now Home passed across the room to the other corner, and they could tell from his voice that he had risen farther, so that he was able to make a mark on the ceiling, which they all saw afterward. During the latter part of the levitation the accordion began playing in "a strain of wild pathos," not from beneath the table where they supposed it to be, but from a corner of the room.

All this, as Bell said, he was putting down in the driest and most literal manner, adding defiantly that the people around the table were all highly respectable. If evidence was trustworthy, it was no good saying that it was incredible. Facts should be collected and verified. "But this can never be done if we insist upon refusing to receive any facts, except such as shall appear to us likely to be true."

There had been similar performances, but the publicity given to this one caused a furor, with people expressing themselves as passionately for or against Home. He was challenged by the weekly *Spectator*, the editor and staff saying that they were ready to watch the furniture revolve and to be lifted in the air. *Punch* printed a hostile poem:

> *With a lift from the spirits he'll rise in the air,*
> *(Though as lights are put out we can't see him there). . . .*
> *He can make tables dance, and bid chairs stand on end.*
> *(But of course it must be in the house of a friend.)*

The skeptics, however, could not shake the faith of believers, and Daniel rose to the peak of his success. He was an accepted—no, welcome—guest in more than half the courts of Europe, he had married a charming and aristocratic wife who had an income amply sufficient to keep them in comfort, his position in society was assured. But although the most remarkable of all manifestations lay ahead, his future life was to be clouded with trouble: trouble which began when a doctor told him that Sacha, too, had tuberculosis, and that she had not long to live.

Chapter Four: THE DARKEST DAYS

IN AN ATTEMPT to save Sacha, Daniel took her to English health resorts, including Bournemouth and Folkestone, but without any good effect. They returned to London, where a constant stream of visitors came every day, including almost everybody of distinction in the Russian colony. Sacha remained sweet, delicate and charming, deeply in love with her husband. She believed that the séances helped her, both physically and emotionally, and they were held almost every night at their home. While in a trance Daniel saw a veiled spirit near his wife. The spirit reappeared almost every day, and each day the veil became shorter. In her last weeks Sacha also began to see spirits, and for the most part they gave her comfort, although one night she told Daniel of a strange, unpleasant spirit presence, and they learned in the morning that the son of a much-loved friend had died.

Sacha herself went to the spirit land in France, in July 1862. The last sacraments were administered by the bishop of Périgueux, who said that he had been present at many deathbeds, but never one such as hers. The veiled spirit made an appearance when Sacha had received the final sacrament. She tried to rise, opened her eyes wide, smiled, said, "Ah, now I see her," and then she departed.

Daniel was deeply distressed by losing her, and her departure brought trouble with it. Count Koucheleff and his wife remained friendly, but another branch of the family claimed the whole of Sacha's estate. A lawsuit developed, and Daniel's income was cut off. At the time this seemed of little importance, for he assumed the case would be quickly settled in his favor. Yet he had become accustomed to a style of living much more luxurious and more agreeable than that of the old days when he had depended on the hospitality of his friends. Money was necessary to maintain this way of life, and in a short time he produced a volume of autobiography, *Incidents in My Life*, written with the help of a friend. For the most part the book was fairly and reasonably reviewed, but although it had some success, he obviously had to look elsewhere for a permanent income.

He began to study sculpture with the aim, as he said, of making himself financially independent. Little Grisha and his nurse stayed with friends, and Daniel took lessons from Joseph Durham, a member of the Royal Academy, who had made a bust of Sacha. Durham then gave him letters of introduction to some of the leading sculptors in Rome, including the American William Wetmore Story. It should be remarked that if Daniel had wanted to make money quickly, he could have done so very easily by giving public séances. He never considered such an idea.

He went to Rome where Story, who was himself interested in spiritualism, got him a studio, although he said that he could not take a pupil. According to Browning, Home immediately wrote to friends that Story *had* taken him as a pupil. But Browning was not to be relied on, for he was now able to give his detestation of Home free rein. Elizabeth was dead, and the restraint he had felt bound to observe during her life no longer existed. He had published a long poem called "Mr. Sludge, The Medium." It was regarded as referring to Daniel Home, although it made no direct allusion to him, but attacked all mediums as frauds who obtained their effects by cheap tricks.

Daniel had already sculpted and sold some busts of friends, and his fame among the English and American colonies in Rome and Florence was such that he was certain to get many commissions. But he was foolish to come to Rome. He should have remembered the distress of the friendly Father de Ravignan at his refusal to regard the spirit manifestations as evil, and the severance of their relations after the return of Daniel's powers. No doubt he thought that his earlier troubles in Florence were forgotten now that he was a Roman Catholic, but he was much mistaken. The Catholic Church has a long memory and a long arm. In January 1864 he received one evening a letter ordering him to appear immediately at the central police station. There, after waiting for half an hour in a freezing anteroom, he was ushered in to the chief of police, Signor Pasqualoni.

The principal feature of the room, he noted, was a very large desk. There was a bust of the Pope done in plaster of paris, and an engraving of the Holy Virgin with some visiting cards stuffed into the frame. Signor Pasqualoni, a small peppery man, began a sharp interrogation.

"You are the author of a book, Signor Home, called *Incidents in My Life?*"

"That is so."

"Do you know that it has been placed upon the Church's Index of Prohibited Books?"

"I do."

The chief of police raised his eyebrows. "You admit it? Good. Now another question. You are thirty-seven years old?"

"No, sir, only thirty. Here is my passport."

Pasqualoni glanced at it, then looked at some papers. "According to my notes you are thirty-seven."

"Then I fear your notes are wrong."

Why was he in Rome? For his health, and to study sculpture. Then came the vital questions. Did he claim to be a medium, to become entranced and to see the spirits? He did. And did he hold communication with them? When they thought proper. How did they manifest themselves?

Daniel had opened his mouth to reply, when raps sounded on the table between them. Pasqualoni exclaimed in astonishment and asked what they were. The French consul, Gauthier, who had accompanied Daniel, said, "The spirits."

"*Spirits*," the chief of police repeated. He looked a little shaken, but continued the examination. Then the blow fell. Daniel was ordered to leave the city within three days. The reason? It was quite plain that he was a sorcerer, and the practice of sorcery was strictly forbidden by the Holy See. He was asked if he consented to his expulsion, and replied indignantly that he certainly did not. He was in Rome to follow the profession of sculptor, and had been doing so. He would protest through the British consul.

The British consul was Joseph Severn, who had been a friend of the poet John Keats. He was accustomed to helping British citizens who had fallen ill or been robbed, but a problem like Daniel's was quite outside his experience. When asked whether international law permitted expulsion on the ground of sorcery, he had to admit that he knew nothing about international law. However, he went to see the governor of Rome, Cardinal Matteuci.

"We have had him watched," the governor said. "He practices sorcery."

Severn protested that Home had behaved in the most strictly legal and gentlemanly manner during his stay in Rome.

"Nonetheless he practices, or has practiced, the black art, and there is a dangerous fascination in it. Whatever may be permitted in your country, the black art will never be permitted here."

Severn mentioned the number and importance of Home's connections, and the fact that he was *persona grata* at the courts of the French Emperor and the Russian Tsar. The governor cut him short.

"Those are temporal courts, Mr. Severn. This is the Holy City, and our laws have regard always to the preservation of the faith. But make no mistake. We have no desire to persecute Mr. Home, nor do we wish to make this matter public in an unseemly way."

"If you would be good enough to see Mr. Home yourself—"

"That is not necessary, nor perhaps desirable. Let Mr. Home enter into an engagement, through you, that he will desist from all communication with what he calls the spiritual world during his stay here. We ask nothing more than that."

Severn returned, happy that he had obtained this concession, to find that Daniel rejected it at once. How could he make such a promise when he had said many times that he was a passive instrument, with no control over the spirits? The two worked out a letter that seemed a reasonable compromise: "I give my word as a gentleman that, during my stay in Rome, I will have no séance, and that I will avoid, as much as possible, all conversations upon spiritualism. Daniel Dunglas Home, Palazzi-Paoli."

The letter, however, did not satisfy the government, and Daniel was ordered to leave Rome by the following day.

Once more he had created a furor—although, as he insisted, this was not by his own actions, but through the wrong interpretation placed on them. He left for Naples, and a crowd of distinguished sympathizers escorted him to the railway station and cheered his departure as if he were royalty.

In Naples royalty, in fact, received him in the person of Prince Humbert, who later, upon the death of Victor Emmanuel II, became the second King of Italy. Yet in spite of this triumphant departure and reception, the affair proved damaging. All forms of spiritualistic practice were forbidden to those of the Catholic faith, and this turned many away from him. And the papal ban, as it rippled out, had wider effects. Napoleon III was anxious not to offend the Pope, and did not receive Daniel when he went from Naples to Nice, and then to Paris.

After returning to England Daniel continued to give séances and Mrs. Milner Gibson still sent out cards inviting friends to meet the spirits, but how was Daniel to live? There were still many delighted to receive him as a houseguest, and Mr. Cox never thought of charging him for his room at Cox's Hotel, but this was not the style of living he had become accustomed to with Sacha, and the friend of emperors and princes surely deserved more than life as a permanent houseguest. He flitted from one country to another—England, America, Russia.

In Russia he was received with much warmth. The troublesome question of the will was not settled, but Tsar Alexander was more friendly than ever. Letters were addressed to Daniel c/o His Imperial Highness the Emperor of Russia, and he was loaded with gifts, among them more of the rings that he so much loved. On important occasions now he wore on his left hand an enormous solitaire diamond and a great sapphire above it; on his right hand, a large yellow diamond and a ruby set in brilliants. When told by the Tsar to ask for any favor he wished, however, he requested pardon for a political prisoner rather than another ring, and his request was granted. The Tsar agreed to be godfather when Grisha was rechristened in the Greek Orthodox Church, and Daniel himself was also received into the Orthodox faith a little later. Grisha was still cared for by friends, and saw his father only occasionally.

Daniel found Russia the country most sympathetic to his temperament, but he did not settle there. He returned to England, where he again gave séances, though it was noticed that they now seemed to leave him more worn and exhausted. One of the most remarkable took place at the Campden Hill home of Samuel Carter Hall and his wife, both of whom were engaged in journalism. Here Daniel began by playing the piano and singing the accompaniment. When he played a favorite air of Sacha's a chair slid up and moved beside him. Later the table rose in the air, the accordion played and knocks were heard all around the room. When the lights were put out, Mr. Hall's face shone as if with silver light, and the medium rose to the ceiling. He had no pencil, but when given one, he rose again and made a cross there.

Daniel gave more lectures and public readings—and he went on the stage, where his career was brief and a little mysterious. He began by playing the second lead in *Plot and Passion,* a blood-and-thunder melodrama, and the performance was praised. His voice was said to be not powerful but melodious, his elocution good and his figure an excellent one for the stage. This successful debut had been made at Worcester, and it was announced that he would next appear in London as Hamlet. This idea came to nothing, and he was then billed to appear at the St. James's Theatre in a play called *The Jealous Wife.* "Mr. Daniel Dunglas Home will make his first appearance in the character of Mr. Oakley." This, too, came to nothing, for at the last moment a notice was put up outside the theater to say that "owing to his sudden indisposition" Mr. Home would not appear. Was he unable to learn his lines? In any case, this was the end of his career on stage. Dickens said the truth was that the public had found out the scoundrel.

THE PROBLEM OF DANIEL'S future remained. He felt the power of the spirits less often now, and the strain of each séance was evident. What could be done for a man so sensitive that he absolutely refused to accept money? Some of his admirers came up with an idea. What the spiritualist movement needed more than anything else was a center which would be a rallying point for the faithful. Séances would be held there with several different mediums, a library would be provided, *conversazioni* would be held, followed by refreshments. The founding council included two barristers, a clergyman, a stockbroker and a wine merchant. Premises were found on Sloane Street, and more than a hundred people happily paid the subscription fee of five guineas (at that time about twenty-five dollars). There must, of course, be a secretary, whose expenses would be covered, and who would live on the premises. Who could fill the post better than Daniel Dunglas Home?

The Spiritual Athenaeum was officially opened in January 1867, with the exhibition of a portfolio of spirit drawings, executed by one of the members under the guidance of the Archangel Gabriel. Catalogues, printed on satin and bound in white calf, were sent to Napoleon III and to Queen Victoria. The Queen's attendance was hoped for, but neither now nor at any time did Victoria show an interest in the spirits. Daniel, who had been installed as secretary some three months before the opening, lived in an apartment above the rooms used for exhibitions and séances. Callers were delighted with his gentle politeness and his charm. The painter and poet Dante Gabriel Rossetti came to see the drawings, attended a séance and was much impressed by the raps.

But before the Athenaeum officially opened, events occurred which would ultimately cause its dissolution.

Fate took the unlikely shape of a seventy-five-year-old widow named Jane Lyon. Her husband had told her, shortly before his death in 1859, that in seven years' time there would be a great change in her life, and that they would meet again. She interpreted this as meaning that she would die when the seven years were up, but learned that if she were a spiritualist, her husband might come to her instead. She wrote asking to become a member of the Athenaeum, and followed up the letter with a call in person.

Mrs. Lyon was an eccentric. She was from the northern part of

England, the illegitimate daughter of a manufacturer. She had had little formal education, and her manners and language were crude. She was both intelligent and credulous, shrewd and silly. She lived cheaply, in lodgings over a stationery store. But, despite all appearances, she was rich.

On this first visit to the Athenaeum she asked to see the chief medium. Daniel took her upstairs to his rooms, where she exclaimed at the sight of the pictures on the walls and asked about them.

"That is the Grand Duchess Constantine of Russia and her family. She kindly gave it to me when I was staying at the grand duke's palace."

"Fancy that. You are a celebrity. And what about London, do you know a lot of great folk here?"

Daniel smiled. "You might say that I have been fortunate in my friends."

They settled down to a séance. By raps on the table and use of the alphabet, Mrs. Lyon received a message from her husband: "My own beloved Jane I am Charles your own beloved husband I am with you always I love love love you as I always did."

She asked if Daniel would call to see her, and he agreed to do so. On leaving, she remarked, "Well, I had expected to find you proud and stuck up from knowing so many great folks, but I like you very much and hope you will like me." She would be going to Paris next year, and asked if he would like to go with her. Daniel laughed and said yes. With that they parted.

From her dress and manner, he said afterward, he thought she might be a housekeeper, and certainly had no idea she was rich.

Another séance was held, this time in her shabby lodgings, and another loving message was received from Mr. Charles Lyon. The widow told Daniel it was a pity he was so poor, and she offered him a check for thirty pounds (about one hundred and fifty dollars at that time). He replied that he could not accept money, and she said that it was for the Athenaeum. She laughed when he still hesitated.

"This is nothing to me. I am very rich. I might live in great style, but prefer living as I do. I like you, and will be your friend."

In the lawsuit with which their relationship ended, Mrs. Lyon contended that Daniel came again to her lodgings, talked about

Sacha, and said that he had been happy with her, but that if he remarried, it would be to an elderly lady, and that he would be a loving and affectionate husband. She immediately rejected the idea of marrying him. According to Daniel, quite the contrary was true. She asked about his past life, and wanted to know whether another wife would be received by the grand people he knew.

Then, according to Mrs. Lyon, there was another table-rapping session at which she received a message from Charles: "Daniel is to be our son; he is my son, therefore yours. Do you remember before I passed I said a change would take place in seven years? That change has taken place."

Daniel denied that there had been any such séance, although he agreed that she spoke of adopting him, something he did not take seriously. She talked so much about being introduced to his friends, how she would allow him a thousand a year, and how it would spite her husband's family to see her among great folks that he began to wonder if she was in her right mind. He said that he did not like the idea of spiting anybody. At this she threw her arms around him, kissed him and said, "It shall be just as you like, darling."

Whatever happened at these meetings, there is no doubt that Mrs. Lyon was impressed by Daniel and was determined to give him some money. A week after their first meeting, she wrote to Daniel:

> I have a desire to render you *independent* of the world, and having *ample* means for the purpose without abstracting from any needs or comfort of my own, I have the greatest satisfaction in now presenting you with and as an entirely FREE GIFT from me the sum of £24,000 [$120,000], and am, my dear Sir,
>
> Yours very truly and *respectfully,*
> Jane Lyon

Daniel, with very little hesitation, decided that he would accept the offer, which on her calculations would bring him an income of seven hundred pounds (thirty-five hundred dollars) a year. In many ways he was an unworldly man, and he seems not to have understood what would to others have been plain from the beginning. Mrs. Lyon wanted to be his benefactor, but she wanted also to take over his life, and to show her late husband's relatives that the slights she had endured from them on account of her humble origins no longer applied. She came to Daniel's rooms at the Athenaeum almost every day with new plans and ideas. She arranged to clear off his debts, and said that stipends would be made to various members of his family. A cottage was bought for Aunt Mary, who had turned him out of her home many years before.

The thing Mrs. Lyon most longed for was that Daniel should change his name to hers, and become Daniel Lyon. This he refused to do, saying that it would look as if he were ashamed of his own name. But after a month of being coaxed and pleaded with, he gave way. On December 3 he changed his name legally to Daniel Home Lyon, and became her adopted son. She had succeeded where the Elmers had failed.

She said that on the occasion of his taking the name of Lyon she wanted to give him a little surprise. This was not a ring, a tiepin or a watch, but a gift of stock worth six thousand pounds (thirty thousand dollars). And that was not the end. She made a will by which she left Daniel all her property, and also assigned to him a mortgage worth thirty thousand pounds (one hundred fifty thousand dollars), keeping only the income on it for herself.

These matters were handled by a lawyer named Wilkinson, a friend of Daniel's, and he did his best to advise her to the contrary. When Mrs. Lyon was making the will, the lawyer urged her to include some provision for her relatives, but was told that they were all well off, and anyway it was none of his business. In relation to the mortgage, Wilkinson said that she had already placed her adopted son in a position only equaled in novels and romances, and that if she wished to give away the mortgage capital, it should be to hospitals. She said that she appreciated the warnings, but wanted her son to have the money. Wilkinson asked whether any spirit communications had affected her, and was told they had not. When the arrangement was completed, Daniel Home Lyon had a capital sum of sixty thousand pounds (three hundred thousand dollars). He was, for the first time in his life, a man of substance.

But not for long. The strain of living with his adopted mother—for after the change of name he spent the whole of most days with her from breakfast onward, going back at night to sleep in his rooms— told greatly on him. At the end of January he became ill and went south to Hastings to recuperate. He suggested, perhaps only halfheartedly, that she should go with him, but she refused. By the time he returned, she had taken a dislike to Grisha, who was now in London being educated by a tutor.

The quarrels between Daniel and Jane Lyon became frequent. In one he said he would have no more to do with her, and was sorry he had sold his soul to such a woman. She replied, "I have warned you not to turn my love to hate, for I will hunt you to the death, and there is no insult I will not heap on you. I will say it was all by undue influence you got what you have from me. I can pay whoever I please to give evidence for me, and you and your brat may go to the Devil."

He was so horrified by this outburst that he fainted. When he recovered, she begged him to forgive her, but within a week or two she was saying that she had made a pretty bargain in tying herself to a living corpse. In March she signed herself "Your affectionate mother" for the last time.

In the meantime, unknown to Daniel, Mrs. Lyon had been consulting several other mediums. The last of them was Miss Emma Berry, who succeeded in calling up the spirit of her husband. The conversation went like this:

"Do you know of this business with Daniel Home?"

"Yes."

"Do you approve of it?"

"No, it is an imposition."

"What shall I do?"

"Go to law at once, be firm and decided."

"Was your spirit ever with Daniel?"

"No, never."

Early in June Mrs. Lyon asked Daniel to return the latchkey to her lodgings. Now the break was very near.

Few of Daniel's letters to her have been preserved, but the tone of one he wrote after returning the latchkey shows his anxiety to remain on good terms. It begins "My darling Mother," is signed "Your affectionate son D. H. Lyon," and says he would like her to go with him to take the baths in Germany. He adds: "I will pay all expenses."

By now, however, she had begun a lawsuit, saying she had been cheated out of her money through his influence. At a final interview she said she had made up her mind to expose the whole swindle. Daniel wrote one more letter, offering to return the mortgage money if she would retract all charges against his honesty, agree that he should give up the name of Lyon, and "leave me and mine in undisputed possession of the [money] you in your noble generosity and kindness of heart gave me."

It was not to be. When he tried to leave England to take the waters in Germany, Daniel Home Lyon was arrested. He was released the next day, when he deposited in court the deeds covering the whole of the money he had received. The case of *Lyon v. Home* had begun.

IT WAS THE SCANDAL of the decade. The change of name had been advertised in the papers, as was legally necessary. It was picked up at the time in several journals on both sides of the Atlantic, and called "the strangest adventure in his singular career," among less polite phrases about the gullibility of elderly females. The case itself was a gift to press humorists, who played variations on the phrase "Daniel and the Lyon" and "In the Lyon's Den." The trial lasted ten days, and crowds lined up all night for the following day's hearing. Plaintiff and defendant made an extraordinary contrast, she voluble, often ungrammatical in her answers, but entirely uninhibited and showing at times a native shrewdness; he white as chalk, thin, elegant and dignified, with a look of suffering on his face that suggested he bore all the burdens of the world.

Mrs. Lyon on the witness stand was as good as a music hall act. She gave the whole of her evidence wearing a veil, and when pressed by Mr. Matthews, the defense attorney, to raise it, positively refused. "I can't take it up, and I won't take it up," she said. She absolutely denied that she had wanted to marry Home, saying it had been the other way around.

When it was Daniel's turn on the witness stand, he got on well enough in his examination. He talked in detail about spiritualism, and the goodness of the spirits, repeating as usual that his role was purely passive, and he had nothing to do with anything that happened. He described the movement of chairs and tables, and his own bodily lifting into the air.

Sir George Markham Giffard, the judge, intervened. "Do you mean that you were carried into the air by supernatural agency?"

"Yes, my lord."

The judge stared incredulously, and went on to ask whether the

chairs, tables and spirit messages by means of raps were also supernatural. He was told that they were.

"And what is the purpose of such manifestations, as you call
them?"

"We take it for granted, as in the call of the telegraph wire, that
there is an intelligence at the end of it."

Sir George shook his head dazedly as he made notes.

When Daniel was challenged by William James, Mrs. Lyon's attorney, to produce some raps, tilt the judge's chair or make a table rise
off the ground, he repeated that he was only a passive agent and
could do nothing by his own will. Many of the spectators, however,
were disappointed, and inevitably disbelieved in his powers: They
had come expecting, even looking for, raps and spirit presences.

Could the spirits give any information about the stock market, Mr.
James asked, and when the reply came that they were not concerned
with such matters, he said with a fine show of exasperation, "Can you
tell me, then, what practical use they are?"

The reply was weak. "They help with traveling and health sometimes. Generally, they try to patch up feuds and quarrels." Daniel
enlarged on their role. "If a spirit came and told me to cut my right
hand off, it would be an absurdity and I should not do it. If I had
cancer, and a spirit told me to consult a certain doctor, I should first
make sure he was expert in the subject."

"I see. What about their dress?"

"It seems to be similar to what they wore on earth."

"I am glad they are put to no extra expense in the other world.
When did you last see a spirit, Mr. Home?"

"Not for some time."

"Oh, come now. Can you not be more precise?"

"I would sooner not say. I may say that motives of delicacy prompt
my refusal. It was a relative of somebody present."

Mr. James raised his eyebrows. "Very well, I will press you no
further on the matter."

He went on, however, to ask many questions about Daniel's income.
The medium agreed that traveling expenses were provided for him,
and that he received anonymous gifts occasionally, but said that he
had no settled income. It was plain enough he had got money from
Mrs. Lyon, counsel said, but had he given her anything in return?

"I say I gave her rank and position, rank to associate with my friends, some literary, others in high positions in society."

"You call that rank, Mr. Home? And what would you say was your own rank in society?"

"I have no rank or position, only that which my friends give me."

The reply was sufficiently dignified, but Daniel cut a poor figure on the witness stand, in part because through him spiritualism itself was on trial. The only way in which the skeptical judge and counsel could have been convinced *was* by one of those manifestations which did not occur. In his judgment Sir George was scathing about Mrs. Lyon, saying that he could not credit a word she uttered without independent confirmation, and that much of her testimony had been discredited by her contradictory statements. He ordered her to pay Home's costs as well as her own.

But when it came to the defendant he was harder still. He said that spiritualism was "mischievous nonsense, well calculated to assist the prospects of the needy adventurer." In his eyes Daniel Home was such an adventurer. The gifts he had obtained from Mrs. Lyon were fraudulent and void, and must be returned. When it was all over, Daniel Home's brief glimpse of wealth had vanished.

And yet many friends remained loyal, some expressing their indignation at the way he had been treated, and others suggesting that he should return to the Catholic faith. He himself wrote to a friend that after the verdict he was well and happy. "I am sure this was all arranged by a higher power." Referring to the hostile demonstrations that had taken place almost every day, he added: "As to the mob, it was a paid one. Of that I am certain."

He emerged bruised, discredited, almost ruined. Yet the most astonishing achievements of his life lay ahead.

Chapter Five: THE GREATEST TRIUMPHS

BUT FIRST THERE WAS the matter of his debts, which were now more numerous than ever. To help clear them Daniel gave a course of public readings, making a tour of fifty cities in both England and Scotland. Such readings were fashionable in mid-Victorian days, and these were extremely successful. Home had many of an actor's qualities, and the pathos of his dramatic readings from Tennyson, and from Poe's "The Raven" and "The Bells," brought tears to many eyes, while his humorous stories "convulsed the audience with merriment," as one newspaper said.

Daniel gave an account of a typical reading in Edinburgh. The agent had been unwilling to engage him, saying that readings were not popular, and that other readers had been hissed off the platform. "I went on with fear and trembling," Home wrote. "Oh, the silence was fearful! I began my piece, 'Scotch Words,' and before it was over I had round after round of applause, and such an encore. My every piece was encored, and at the termination of the last I had to go on three times."

After the show there would be an invitation to supper, and often a séance followed. The manifestations were those with which we are familiar. Large spirit hands appeared, flowers were moved from one place to another, chairs and tables rocked and moved, all in a drawing room brightly lit with gas.

Now the manifestations, or some of them, were for the first time to be scientifically checked and tested.

William Crookes was a brilliant experimental chemist, the discoverer of thallium and an early exponent of the possibilities of wireless telegraphy. Now in his late thirties, he was a Fellow of the Royal Society, and was later to be knighted. He believed that nothing should be ruled out, everything must be tested. It was vital, he said, to have proper test conditions, and to make exact observations of every happening. Conclusions should be drawn after the tests, not before them. With such ideas in mind he tested two of the most striking phenomena surrounding Home: the playing of music with no apparent human agency, and the alteration in the weight of bodies—that is, the process by which a table could be heavy at one moment, movable with the fingertips at the next.

First, Crookes laid down certain conditions.

The tests were to take place in his own house, and under gaslight or in daylight.

Home was to bring no friends. Those present were to be another scientist, a well-known lawyer, the scientist's brother and Crookes's own chemical assistant.

Crookes himself took Home to the test, and was present while the medium dressed. "I am therefore enabled to state positively that no contrivance of any sort was secreted about his person."

The accordion was brand new, and had been bought by Crookes. It was placed inside a specially constructed wooden cage, which had fifty yards of insulated copper wire wound around it in a fine mesh. The cage would just slip under a table, but was too close to the top to allow a hand to be put in above it, or a foot inserted beneath.

In another part of the room an elaborate apparatus was made to test alterations in weight. Its basic features were a mahogany board, and a spring balance which checked the weight of the board. This weight was, in fact, three pounds. The tests then took place.

Two of the observers put a foot firmly on each of Home's feet, so that he could not move them. The accordion was drawn out from the cage. Home took it between the thumb and middle finger of one hand, at the opposite end from the keys. It was then put back in the cage and placed under the table.

The accordion began to play, first a few notes, then a simple tune. Crookes's assistant went beneath the table, and reported that the accordion was expanding and contracting. Home's hand, still holding it through an opening in the cage, remained still. His other hand rested on the table. His feet were anchored by those placed on them.

Now the accordion was taken out of the cage and put in the hand of the man sitting next to Home, who held it in the same manner, away from the keys. It continued to play, giving a rendering of "The Last Rose of Summer." It was put in the cage again, and floated around with no visible support.

So much for the accordion. The test of weight was less dramatic, but to those present equally impressive. At the mere touch of Home's fingertips the balance moved from three to six and a half pounds, yet he exerted no pressure at all. At one time it reached nine and a half pounds. Yet when Crookes himself stood upon the end of the board, where Home's fingers had been, and then jumped up and down, his whole weight depressed the balance by only two pounds.

Crookes concluded that something which he called "psychic force" was present in Home, something which ignored the laws of weight and touch. His investigation, he said, had been "as cold and passionless as the instruments I used," and hence he was totally convinced that "psychic force" existed.

The idea of the tests had been welcomed, in the expectation they would lead to an exposure of Home, but the results disconcerted both journalists and other scientists. There was talk of trickery and of conjuring. Various suggestions were made as to how the tricks were worked, among them that Home had a music box about him that made the sounds (a possibility contradicted by the preliminary search), and that in some way he placed weight on the spring balance. Crookes's request for the setting up of a commission to investigate "psychic force" was rejected, and his invitations to colleagues to attend further tests were declined. Undeterred, he made other tests himself, but since he was now a believer in "psychic force," these were not always monitored so thoroughly as the early ones. He and Home became friends, and though the scientist admitted in old age that he had often been deceived by other mediums, he never had any doubt about the genuineness of his friend Dan.

WHAT HAPPENED IN THE presence of Crookes, however, fades almost to the commonplace in comparison to the manifestations seen when Daniel was in the company of young Lord Adare.

Windham Thomas Adare was in his mid-twenties. He was an enthusiastic Irish guardsman, eager for any activity that promised excitement, like big game shooting or horse racing. He became a war correspondent for newspapers, not because he needed the money but to follow exciting events. When he met Home he had just returned from reporting the British war in Abyssinia. A monocled young sportsman sounds a most unlikely convert to spiritualism, but there were two special features in Adare's case. One was that his father, the Earl of Dunraven, was deeply interested in the occult, the other that a strong streak of Irish superstition was allied to Adare's eagerness for physical action. He was interested in everything and everybody out of the usual, and that included Daniel Home.

The two men got on well from the start, and half a century later Adare (by this time himself Earl of Dunraven) summed up the medium's character perhaps as shrewdly as it was ever done. He found Daniel emotional and vain—but then, perhaps the vanity was necessary if he was to hold his own in a world where many people made a joke of spiritualism. He was often depressed, subject to nervous crises difficult to understand, and although proud of his gift, was not happy in it. Altogether, as Adare summed it up, "He was of a simple, kindly, humorous, lovable disposition that appealed to me."

In fact, the friendship was much closer than Adare conveyed when writing of it afterward. Often Daniel stayed in Adare's London rooms in Buckingham Gate, or at the apartment of Adare's friend the Master of Lindsay, nearby in Ashley Gardens. The diary Adare kept at his father's request records eighty séances held in various places, some at the Dunravens' home in Ireland, Adare Manor, many at Buckingham Gate. The manifestations are of special interest because Adare put most of them down in great detail at the time, and because they are richer, more varied and more astonishing than any others. As he says, they took place in all conditions: "In broad daylight, in artificial light, in semidarkness, at regular séances, unpremeditatedly without any séance at all, indoors, out-of-doors, in private houses, in hotels." Often any prior preparation would have been out of the question, although it should be noted that many of the most remarkable happenings took place in semidarkness.

Some fifty people in all attended these séances, but among those who had the strangest experiences were the Master of Lindsay, and Adare's cousin, Charles Wynne. Most were young, but they were far from treating spiritualism as an amusement, as did some of the society ladies. All were looking for some truths outside those of the visible world, and believed that in the séances they had found them. Adare himself may seem credulous at times, but there can be no doubt of his total honesty, his desire to put down just what he saw and heard. He did not hesitate to note that the spirits sometimes talked nonsense or, as he puts it, expressed entirely erroneous opinions. When asked what the sun's rays were composed of, the spirits said they contained light and an elastic wave of electricity. At another time they said that the sun was not hot but cold, and on another still told the listeners that one spirit was trying to invent a powerful battery which would help the brain. "There are some physicists with large brains, who strain and wear themselves out through overwork. The brain becomes weary, loses its elasticity, disease sets in, preponderosis." It is one of Adare's merits that he puts down such things as they were said, without comment.

Two features of the Adare séances were new. One was Home's ability to elongate his body, the other his capacity to handle fire.

There was no doubt in the minds of those who saw the elongation that he grew taller, but they confirmed by tests the evidence of their eyes. Daniel's height was five feet ten inches, and he stood beside a man two inches taller; then he slowly added between six and eight inches to his height, with Adare holding his feet firmly on the ground. "Daniel will show you how it is," Home said, referring to himself in the third person, as he often did in a trance, and unbuttoned his coat to show elongation from his waist upward, with a space of four inches between his vest and the band of his trousers.

At another time one of the men present held his hand on Daniel's hipbone, and felt the lower rib pass under his hand and move upward, with the whole flesh and muscle apparently moving and stretching. Once Daniel was elongated and raised into the air at the same time. A luminous halo was seen around his head, and little globes of blue fire appeared in his hands.

Daniel could also pick up pieces of hot coal without hurting himself, and he was sometimes able to transmit his immunity to others. Once he stirred the embers of a fire into flame, then knelt down and placed his face among the burning coals, moving it about as though bathing it in water.

He moved away from the fire, held a finger for some time in a candle flame, then blew upon a piece of coal he had already handled, and picked it up. He walked slowly around the table.

"I want to see which of you will be the best subject."

A barrister named Jencken held out his hand. "Put it in mine."

"No, no. Touch it and see."

Jencken touched the coal with his fingertip, and was burned.

The coal was put very near two others in the circle. They flinched from the heat.

"Adare will be the easiest," Daniel said in a trance, "because he has been most with Dan. If you are not afraid, hold out your hand."

The young man did so. After making two rapid passes, Daniel put the coal into his hand. It felt "scarcely warm." Daniel took it away, laughed, and then said, "Why, some of them think that only one side of the ember was hot." He told Adare to cup his hands, put the coal in them, then placed his own hands on top. They held the burning coal there for some time, and to Adare it still seemed hardly warm.

"Do you realize that you have seen what is called a miracle, yet in reality it is no such thing? These phenomena show our superior acquaintance with natural laws, and our power over material substances," Daniel said, still in a trance. Afterward they examined him closely. Not a hair of his head was singed, nor was there a sign or smell of fire about him.

On several occasions this immunity from being burned was transmitted to others besides Adare.

Spirits often materialized during this time, Sacha among them. A typical occasion was when Lindsay, having missed a train, slept on a sofa in Home's room. He woke to see at the foot of the bed a woman standing in profile. She was dressed in a long wrap, not gathered at the waist. Home said, "It is my wife. She often comes to me." The next morning Lindsay recognized the face in a photograph.

There were séances at which little or nothing happened, others at which the medium was obviously in great pain, two at which he spoke in a language unknown to any of those present, one when he coughed blood. The most astonishing happening was undoubtedly his levitation in the open air, high above the ground. Adare, Lindsay and Wynne were present, and the first two were so awed that they wrote accounts of it. Wynne later confirmed what they had seen.

The place was Ashley Gardens on Victoria Street, and the occurrence took place on a dark night, with little or no moon. Nor was there light in the room, but they could see well enough to distinguish each other, and to discern the different pieces of furniture. Daniel went into a trance, and messages were received, one for Wynne, which related to the whereabouts of some missing papers. Then Daniel became excited and went out of the room. Before going, he said, "Do not be afraid, and do not leave your places." They were all at a table, their chairs facing the window. Lindsay suddenly spoke.

"Oh, good heavens! I know what he is going to do, it is too fearful."

"What is it?"

"I cannot tell you, it is too horrible. He is going out of the window in the other room and coming in at this one."

They heard the window in the next room go up.

Then they saw Daniel. He was standing upright in the air *outside the window*. He opened the window and walked in. They stared at him, spellbound. He sat down and laughed, and Charlie Wynne asked what he was laughing at.

"We are thinking," Daniel said in a trance, "that if a policeman had been passing, and had looked up and seen a man turning round and round along the wall in the air, he would have been much astonished. Adare, shut the window in the next room."

Adare went in and shut it, noticing that the window was open no more than a foot. On returning, he said he could not imagine how Home had managed to squeeze through such a narrow space.

"Come and see."

The two of them went back into the other room. Adare opened the window as it had been before, and then stood back. Daniel went through the open space head first, his body apparently rigid and almost horizontal. He came in again feet foremost, and they returned to the others.

When Home awoke, he was alarmed. He said that he had gone through a "fearful peril," and had felt a "horrible desire to throw himself out of the window." And still the evening was not over. Jets of flame were seen coming from his head. Then a bird seemed to be flying about the room, whistling and chirping. Lastly they all felt a strong wind. Its "moaning, rushing sound," according to Adare, was the weirdest thing he had ever heard.

Afterward they examined the area outside the windows. Each had a small balcony nineteen inches deep, bounded by stone balustrades eighteen inches high. The balustrades of the two windows were seven feet four inches apart, and the only direct connection between them was a stringcourse no more than four inches wide. It would have been impossible for a man to have walked or jumped from one window to the other. The rooms were seventy feet above the ground.

When these happenings became known, they were the subject of many theories, but the three young men were not to be moved. They agreed that the night was dark, but every one of them was positive that he had seen Daniel Dunglas Home do what no man had ever done before: float on air seventy feet above the ground.

There are other instances of levitation in the Adare séances, and they occurred in very varied circumstances. At a ruined abbey outside Adare Manor, Daniel was seen by several people to be floating horizontally off the ground for about ten or twelve yards, at a height which carried him over a two-foot stone wall. On another occasion Lindsay saw Daniel floating around the room pushing pictures out of their places as he moved along the walls. Altogether there were nearly a hundred cases of levitation, but the one outside that high window remained unparalleled.

After a period of nearly two years in which he saw a great deal of Home, Adare lost most of his interest in spiritualism because, as he said later, he made little progress after a certain point, and the study of the occult was not really congenial to him. Nevertheless, he wrote near the end of his life that "my belief in the genuineness of the phenomena remained unshaken, and my friendship with Mr. Home did not diminish or change."

A FURTHER ATTEMPT at scientific testing was made later in Russia. Home had gone to Saint Petersburg after witnessing the fall of Napoleon III's empire in the Franco-Prussian War, which he covered as foreign correspondent for both the San Francisco *Chronicle* and an English newspaper.

The tests were conducted by a committee headed by Professor von Boutlerow, professor of chemistry at the University of Saint Petersburg, and Dr. Karponitch of the Academy of Science. A room was furnished with various equipment, including a glass-topped table, at that time a considerable novelty. They all sat around this table—and nothing happened. Had the glass top prevented any trickery, or was it that the medium's power was greatly diminished?

At other sessions in von Boutlerow's home a bell hung in the air without support and a ring was drawn from the professor's finger and replaced, while both Home's hands were in full view on the table. Others were skeptical, but von Boutlerow was convinced. He had perhaps been influenced by the fact that Daniel was in favor with the Tsar. Several séances were held at the Winter Palace, and although official silence was preserved about them, a witness recounted two incidents. A spirit hand had opened a locket worn by the Tsar himself, which contained a portrait of his dead son. A series of raps on the locket said that the boy had been responsible for opening the portrait. And the Tsarina had received a message from her grandfather, who addressed her by a pet name he had given her in childhood. The Tsar acknowledged his pleasure by another gift of jewelry.

The greatest gift Daniel received on this visit, as he afterward said, was the hand of his second wife. Like Sacha, her connections were irreproachably aristocratic, her father being one of the Tsar's councillors of state. Like Sacha also, she was young, petite, dark and lively. When she first met Daniel she was agreeably surprised to find him wholly lacking in pretension. His smiling good humor pleased her, and like many women, she was delighted by his gentleness. Such conscious thoughts came afterward. When Daniel was presented to her she thought nothing, but heard a voice saying, "Here is your husband." Later she learned that he had received a similar message.

They became engaged. But rumors of the Lyon-Home case had been heard in Russia, and Julie's family was worried. Was Home still an acceptable figure in English society? Would their daughter be treated as she should be, when she was no longer Julie de Gloumeline but plain Mrs. Home? Von Boutlerow was her brother-in-law, and he made inquiries to a fellow scientist, William Crookes.

The reply was extremely favorable. The scientist said that "the life's happiness of a young lady was a serious matter," and he reported that Daniel Home seemed to be "peculiarly domesticated and affectionate. From the fascination of his manner, as well as the wonders of his mediumship, his company is eagerly sought by all classes. . . . In the intimate conversation of young men associating together as bachelors a considerable latitude of speech is frequently indulged in, but . . . I have never heard him utter a word which could not be repeated to a lady." Moreover, Crookes added, there were many titled ladies who would wish to call on Mrs. Home at the first opportunity.

This was enough. In October 1871 Daniel and Julie were married in Paris. The Tsar sent him a sapphire and diamond ring, the lawsuit about his inheritance from Sacha was settled in his favor, and Julie brought with her a considerable fortune. He was thirty-eight years old, and the difficult days were over.

WITH HIS MARRIAGE to Julie, Daniel's life changed almost totally. The couple went rarely to England, in part because Julie did not at that time speak a word of English, but it was true also that the Lyon affair still cast a shadow. Daniel's lung condition became worse, and they wintered every year on the Riviera, and traveled a great deal. He had an adoring and wealthy wife, and in Europe was now accepted as he had always felt was proper.

Nothing seemed more natural to him, as one friend said, than that he should be cosseted and cared for, providing in return amusing or thoughtful or sympathetic company. He basked in admiration, and was prepared to admire in return. If there were still some who disbelieved in his gifts, they were far exceeded in number and distinction by those who had faith. Mark Twain was anxious to meet him, and when Home was in London, Adare brought the American writer along, and recounted some of the wonders he had seen. Twain saw nothing strange, but he liked the medium, and was happy when Home managed to have one of the chapters from *A Tramp Abroad* translated into Russian. The translation seemed excellent, Twain said, looking at the bewildering Cyrillic characters. "At any rate, it looks funnier than it does in English."

And séances? They were now very few, and became rarer as Daniel's health continued to deteriorate. After Napoleon's death in 1873 Eugénie asked that Home be brought to see her, in the hope that he might make the Emperor's spirit form materialize. But Daniel asked to be excused, telling Princess Murat, through whom the request had been made, "In my broken state of health I dare not venture on a trial which, if I succeed, must use my strength and weaken me."

The Homes had a daughter whose beauty was, as Daniel said, "beyond belief." But she lived only a few days, and there were no more children. At the moment of the baby's death, all those present heard a hail of tiny sounds from the pillow where her head rested, and also the sound of music and voices.

His health grew worse, and in 1876 there was an announcement in a French paper that "D. D. Home has been found dead in a railway carriage while traveling between Berlin and Saint Petersburg." Obituary notices appeared, but Daniel survived, and took a cure in Russia, where he and Julie spent two summers in the southern city of Samara. There he drank nothing but mares' milk prepared in a special way. The cure was unavailing. Both his lungs were now affected, and he was also suffering from arthritis. Yet they continued to travel. In Paris, Geneva, Berlin, Moscow, Saint Petersburg, he would make his appearance every year, using a cane or leaning on Julie's arm, his secretary in attendance and a crowd of admirers around him. Even when his legs were attacked by paralysis and he was confined to a wheelchair, they still traveled to Russia, and he gave recitations at a charity performance organized by Countess Tolstoy.

At last in June 1886, after months of suffering, his life ended. He was buried, as he had wished, in the same vault with his infant daughter, Marie. At his request the funeral was simple and his desire that "all tokens and signs known as mourning be entirely discarded" was obeyed. Over his grave Julie erected a cross with the words: "Daniel Dunglas Home. Born to earth-life near Edinburgh (Scotland), March 20, 1833. Born to spirit-life, June 21, 1886."

There were no manifestations when he departed from earth-life, and none at the funeral.

POSTSCRIPT

THIS IS A DRAMATIZED version of Daniel Home's astonishing life. All of the incidents occurred, but I have sometimes turned a scene described by Home or somebody else into conversation. The only positive invention is the extract from the Springfield *Republican* in the opening chapter. The incident occurred as I have said, but to a clergyman. I changed him to a newspaper reporter for dramatic effect. I have given only a small selection of manifestations from the hundreds of séances Home held, but at the end of the story I think everybody is bound to ask: Was he genuine?

Remarkably enough, Home repeated in his autobiographical writings some of the criticisms made against him. His tone of amused scorn in recounting them may, of course, be considered as audacious bluffing. People accounted for the rappings in many ways, he says, "some beginning low down with the snapping of the toe joints, others getting up to the ankle, whilst some maintain it to be in the knees or thighbones. It has even been attributed to a strong beating of my pulse." And other effects? "Some say that springs are concealed in the table and about the room. It has been said that I have an electrical quality which I can use at command. I am an accomplished juggler according to others." He went on to list the bribing of servants, the use of agents to check records and so on. He did not deny that such practices were used, and when his own career had ended, he wrote a book, *Lights and Shadows of Spiritualism*, in which he launched his own attack on fraudulent mediums and their "brazen impostures." The essential thing, he said, was that séances be conducted in the light, and that if spirit figures manifested themselves, the medium should also be visible at the same time. But although Home worked more often in the light than any other medium, he held many séances in semi- or almost complete darkness. Few of his levitations occurred in full light. Those mentioned by the scientist Crookes—tantalizingly, he does not give full details—are exceptional.

Here are some of the explanations of Home's feats, offered by those who regard him as a fraud, with comments of my own.

ARTICLES STAYING ON TILTED TABLES: Gum or thread was used to prevent objects from falling off tables when they tilted. *(But there were many occasions when such preparation would have been impossible.)* Magnets were used under the table, so that on their release, the objects slipped, then could be checked again in their fall. *(More likely, but how and by whom were the magnets worked?)*

TABLE LEVITATION: This may be explained by the "human clamp" method. The table is steadied from above by the medium's hand, whether or not it is held by another person. The medium uses special shoes or boots which can be slipped on and off easily, and which have a specially strengthened toe, so a foot can be slipped out without this being perceived by the person who has a foot placed over the medium's. The table is gently rocked by all around it until the medium can put a toe under one table leg. After that, the table can easily be raised by combined hand and foot pressure. *(But wouldn't those who looked under the table have seen this?)* Or the medium wears a leather belt around his waist, with a hook attached. When the hook is fixed under the table edge, great power can easily be exerted on the table with comparatively little effort. *(A possibility. Home was often examined, but such examinations were fairly cursory, partly for motives of delicacy but also because they were carried out by believers. Even so, how did tables rise completely off the floor, to a height of three feet or more?)*

RAPS: There are many ways of making them, apart from those mentioned by Home. They range from simple operations like the use of thumb nails to sophisticated ones like an electrically operated tapping mechanism concealed in a shoe heel. *(Perfectly true.)*

PLAYING OF MUSICAL INSTRUMENTS: The Davenport brothers had an act in which musical instruments appeared to be carried around the room in the air and played, even though the brothers were manacled and bound to chairs. In fact, they freed themselves, and the instruments never left their hands. Other magicians can do similar things. *(Such deceptions would explain some, not all, of Home's musical feats.)*

LEVITATION IN GENERAL: It has been suggested that the boots people felt above their heads, as they thought, were in fact on Home's hands, and that the crosses on the ceiling were made by a telescopic rod with a pencil at its end. The use of "pseudopods"— extensions fitted onto hands or feet—was held by skeptics to be responsible for many phenomena. *(Pseudopods could have been used, but if they were, Home was lucky always to escape detection. And where did he keep these things?)*

THE ADARE LEVITATION: The great magician Harry Houdini offered two explanations for this. One was that Home went next door, opened the window, and in the dark crawled back again, inducing the watchers to believe that he was outside the window. The second, that Home had fixed a wire in advance outside the window, and swung from one window to another. Houdini offered to repeat the feat in similar conditions, but never did. *(The second suggestion is obviously possible, although Home ran a risk of the wire being found. It is possible also that Lindsay was in collusion with him—at least, that remark in advance about Home coming in at the window seems very strange.)*

These suggestions only scratch the surface of the literature that has grown up around Home's exploits. "The principal reason why he was never *completely* exposed was that he gave no public sittings," says the hostile Houdini, but the truth is he was never exposed at all.

It is easy enough to find things to criticize in Home. The messages he brought back were mostly vague, and given to highly credulous hearers. The spirit forms he evoked could easily have been faked, and so could the playing of musical instruments, although it is difficult to see how this was done in the case of Crookes's accordion test. Perhaps the table levitations were frauds. But when this has been said, a great deal remains—in particular, the extraordinary movement of furniture with the medium nowhere near it—that can be "explained" only by mass hypnotism, and there is not the slightest sign that Home ever prepared for or exerted such hypnotism.

I remain a skeptic about Daniel Home, yet how can one be altogether skeptical if one cannot offer complete explanations? He was and remains the most famous medium who ever existed, his achievements unequaled and still unexplained—unless one accepts that Home *did* have supernormal powers.

THE CAPTAIN'S RETURN

THE CAPTAIN'S RETURN

by
David Beaty

ILLUSTRATED BY RICHARD HARVEY

The airship R101, completed in Great Britain in 1930, was the largest dirigible ever built. She was to be the first in a fleet of lighter-than-air craft that would provide speedy travel to all parts of the British Empire, with a dependability and comfort impossible for the small airplanes of the time.

But even before her test flights were finished, R101 attracted a surprising amount of criticism, and there were a number of warnings about her safety. Incredibly, one of her most outspoken critics was an aviator who had been dead for more than two years, but had contacted his wife through a medium and given her an urgent message: *R101 is doomed!*

David Beaty, a British airman turned author, has written a number of novels involving flying, including *Cone of Silence* and *Excellency*. R101, surrounded by so many unanswered questions, has long fascinated him. Sifting through a mass of evidence, he came upon clues that led to several new discoveries. Now, incorporating these findings, he has recreated the suspense-filled story of R101 and her captain.

"IRWIN . . . NO, NOT IRVING . . . I–R–W–I–N."

Struggling to whisper his own name, Herbert Carmichael Irwin, captain of the airship R101, woke himself from an uneasy dream. It was one of those nightmares where the sleeper knows he must cry out but finds himself bereft of voice.

He turned his head on the pillow. Though he couldn't see his wife's expression in the predawn darkness, he knew she was gazing at him, her beautiful eyes wide. He knew that, like him, she had hardly slept, that she had heard the fitful rain and the rise of the wind.

"I had a dream," he said softly.

"Was it a bad one, Bird?" He could hear the anxiety in her lilting Scots voice, hear the extra tenderness as she spoke that personal nickname only she and his closest friends used. It was a nickname that embodied his delight, his aspirations, his dedication to the air.

"No, not a bad dream, Olive. A stupid one."

He squeezed her hand, and swung his legs over the side of the bed. The dream had indeed been stupid, though understandable. Irwin had dreamed that an incompetent clerk at the British Aviation Insurance Group had spelled his name wrong, and that the life insurance policy he had just taken out for R101's inaugural flight to India had therefore been declared invalid. As he sat on the edge of the bed, some superstitious voice at the back of his mind asked, "Does that imply a claim for the insurance will be made?" He shivered.

"Are you cold?"

Irwin felt his wife's anxious eyes on him, and when he shook his head, she asked, "Not time to get up already, is it?"

She sat up, cradling her arms across her chest, and stared accusingly at the thin crack of sky visible between the pretty patterned curtains where the darkness was beginning to pale. First light. Saturday, October 4, departure day, the day they had dreaded, had come.

" 'Fraid so." Irwin yawned and stretched his arms with apparent carelessness. Then he got to his feet and stood for a moment looking down at her. He was such a fine man, she thought with almost unbearable pride. Dark-haired with steady eyes and a well-boned face, he was even more handsome than when she had first met him, in Scotland at the East Fortune airship station. They had gone for walks along the cliffs to Tantallon Castle, watched the gulls settling on Bass Rock in the Firth of Forth and ridden horses from the farm at Haddington. He was an outstanding athlete who had represented his native Ireland in the Olympics. He was also a loving, tender husband, now leaning over to stroke her cheek gently with his forefinger.

"You stay where you are for a while, Olive." He began to put on the new double-breasted blue uniform specially designed for R101. "I'll go along and make us a cup of tea. I won't wake the others."

The others were Olive's older sister and brother-in-law, who were staying with them in Long Acre, the Irwins' white pebbled stucco bungalow on Putnoe Road in Bedford. They had come to watch R101's departure and to keep Olive company. They planned to stay with her until her husband returned safely.

Irwin tiptoed carefully past the guest room door. Last night he and his brother-in-law had sat for a while chatting over a beer, ostensibly waiting for the girls to finish with the bungalow's single bathroom. In reality, Irwin was telling his brother-in-law of his financial arrangements for Olive "just in case"—the insurance policy he had taken out, his pension, his small savings. Their conversation had naturally shifted to R101, her state of unreadiness, the cutting in half of her vast frame for the insertion of an additional hydrogen bag into her gut, and the strong political pressure on Irwin to fly her to India before proper tests had been completed. Irwin had downplayed all this to Olive, and had not told her the latest development—a personal telephone call from Lord Thomson himself.

Even in the cool calm of morning Irwin still burned with anger about that call. Lord Thomson, R101's most distinguished passenger-to-be, was in Irwin's opinion trying to use the airship as his personal chariot. Secretary of state for air, closest personal friend of Prime Minister Ramsay MacDonald, Lord Thomson was a power in the land. He was not accustomed to being contradicted.

Word had obviously reached Thomson that Irwin considered last Thursday's test flight inadequate. Hence the call to Irwin's office in Number 1 shed. Irwin could still hear that cold, calculating, cultivated voice ringing in his ears, reminding him that Major Scott was perfectly satisfied, and charging in a tone of relentless contempt, "You are an obstructionist, Irwin."

"I am the captain."

"And I, Irwin, am the secretary of state for air."

Irwin's hand trembled with anger as he filled the kettle at the kitchen sink. Then he lifted his eyes to the window and saw her.

The huge lighter-than-air craft R101, now tethered to her mooring mast, was visible for almost twenty miles around. From the slight eminence of Putnoe Road Irwin could see right across the southwest corner of Bedford, across the curve of the Ouse River, to Cardington and the two-hundred-foot mast. That view had been one of the reasons Olive and he had rented Long Acre, but lately the view had pleased them less.

For all that, the airship was a fine and splendid sight, her seven hundred seventy-seven feet of silver skin gleaming softly in a watery dawn. He was proud of her. Proud to be her captain but immensely conscious of the burden of command. He pursed his lips as he measured out the tea.

Irwin, born in County Cork and educated in Dublin, was a hard-working Irishman. He was clever, quiet spoken and a strict disciplinarian. Knowing but modest. Olive often teased him that he was more a Scot than she. But he had the Irishman's respect for things he didn't know or understand. For Destiny. For Fate. And the airman's respect for the awesome dimensions of the sky that man was only just beginning to comprehend.

"I thought you were never coming with that tea," Olive said, walking into the kitchen, tying the cord of her dressing gown. Irwin poured a cup, held it in both hands as if to warm them, then passed it to her and stared out of the kitchen window across the valley to the airship.

"I hear they're taking on a special consignment of sardines and salmon for Lord Thomson's hors d'oeuvres," Olive said. She made a brave attempt at laughter, and Irwin smiled broadly.

"Who told you that?"

"Lily."

At the mention of Lily, Irwin's smile faded slightly. Lily was Olive's closest friend, the wife of Ralph Booth. Ralph had commanded the airship R100 on the successful double crossing of the Atlantic to Canada and back. The Booths and the Irwins shared a deep friendship, a friendship that was ironically instrumental in Irwin's finally agreeing to the flight to India today. For at one point he had been so concerned about the unreadiness of R101 and the indecent haste with which she was being dispatched to India that he had decided to throw in his hand. He would flatly refuse to take her, resign if necessary.

Having made that decision, Irwin had inquired whether or not the flight would thus be postponed. Certainly not, had come back the answer. Squadron Leader Booth would be ordered to take the flight.

"But surely he won't take it either!" Irwin had told Olive. "Find out from Lily if he would refuse, too."

The two wives had met for coffee. Lily had shaken her head. "The RAF is Ralph's career. If he was ordered to take R101, he would."

So the decision was out of Irwin's hands. You either went into danger or you sent your friend. There was no choice but to go.

He watched Olive take down the frying pan, light a burner and begin to fry a couple of slices of bacon. "I suppose," Olive said, smiling bravely again, "we should be glad it's sardines and salmon and not some girl friend Thomson's taking with him. There's some Rumanian princess he's supposed to be madly in love with . . ."

Irwin put a finger reprovingly over her lips and then kissed them. Suddenly she relinquished the pan and flung her arms around his neck, kissing him wildly.

"I know Thomson's upset you. Mrs. Johnston says he's pressing you. Everyone knows the ship isn't ready. The ground staff know. Colmore does really, though he doesn't like to say so. So does Scottie in his heart of hearts. So does Atherstone. So do you."

"I know nothing of the sort. I know my bacon's getting ruined. Listen . . . " He put his hands on her shoulders and turned her around. "I'm the captain. *I* have the final say."

Someone other than his beloved Olive might well have replied: But *do* you have the final say? Hadn't that been the subject of so many arguments? Arguments that were still not resolved. Who really was in charge? Was it Irwin or was it Major Scott? Good-humored, clever George Herbert Scott, who had already been with Booth on R100 to Canada and back. Scott who, like Thomson, had his ambitions. Scott who should already have been knighted for his contributions to British aviation.

But Olive loyally and lovingly said nothing. She pretended to be comforted. "Just so long as you remember to see *they* remember that."

She held his right hand in both of hers and squeezed it. After that minor outburst she seemed restored to her normal gentle self. She fried him an extra egg with his bacon, and some mushrooms her brother-in-law had picked in the meadows beyond Putnoc Road. She wondered if her sister and brother-in-law would be coming down soon for breakfast, then guessed they were staying in bed late to give her more time alone with Bird.

Time. She glanced at the clock on the mantelpiece of the small dining room as she carried in the tray. Irwin followed the direction of her eyes. The clock was flanked by the silver trophies he had won. But she wasn't staring at these. Her eyes focused on the face of the clock and the second hand sweeping inexorably around, spinning away their last minutes together.

"Remember to put the clock back tonight." He smiled, struggling to keep the conversation level. "Summer Time ends at 3:00 a.m."

"Yes, of course, I shall get up in the middle of the night and personally put it back." She tried to laugh. But a great weight of gloom seemed suddenly to descend on her. She wondered what they would each be doing at 3:00 a.m. and whether either of them would get any sleep that night.

"Try to get some rest this afternoon," she said, watching him push his empty plate away. "Departure is between six and seven?"

"Thereabouts. I'll rest if I can." He stood up and ruffled her wavy brown hair. "But we've got Air Vice-Marshal Dowding coming up."

"The man who has to give you your Certificate of Airworthiness?"

"Officially, yes."

"Maybe he won't."

"I think he will."

"But he flew on Thursday's air test, didn't he? He must have known of the trouble with the engine."

"He was asleep at the time. Colmore said it was best not to disturb him. He's undoubtedly been told about it by now—maybe . . ." Irwin suddenly stopped speaking and smiled reassuringly at his wife.

"Do you think the weather will be good enough to go?" she asked.

He shrugged and checked his watch. "That's what I'm going to find out. Giblett, if I know him, will have been in Met since the crack of dawn."

M. A. Giblett was the meteorological officer who would be preparing the forecasts before and during the flight. He was clever and conscientious, and Olive brightened at the mention of his name. "At least Lord Thomson can't control the weather."

"He might well be trying to." Irwin pointed at the sky where patches of blue were beginning to show through the thinning clouds. Then he picked up his uniform cap with its R101 badge embossed in gold, gave her a warm kiss and walked out to his car. Tooting the horn in farewell, he edged the car onto Putnoe Road.

Now that he was committed, now that departure day had begun, his spirits rose as they always did before a flight. The air with all its complexities and challenges beckoned him. No real achievement was without its dangers, and perhaps he had been unduly pessimistic. Perhaps Scottie was right, he was overcautious. Scottie seemed relaxed and confident about this India flight.

Rounding a corner, past a clump of hazel and hawthorn, suddenly Irwin had to step sharply on the brake. A large brown hare had run out from the hedgerow in front of the car. Irwin squeezed the horn impatiently, but the hare continued loping in front of him. With a chill of foreboding he remembered an old Irish superstition, and his mind inevitably went back almost a year to October 12, 1929.

OCTOBER 12, 1929—that was before the Air Ministry had decided to expand her to carry more hydrogen. R101 had been shorter, but still enormous and still beautiful. The day of her first public appearance had been a cold October morning like this, and even before six the lanes were crowded with cars and bicycles and sight-seeing buses. Punctually at first light the great double-tracked hangar doors had been opened, and Irwin had given the order to *Walk*.

It was a happy day for Bedford and Cardington. Hundreds of unemployed had been taken on to help. The airship project was booming. And the megaphones and whistles that controlled the numerous working parties had sounded like a fanfare.

It had also been a happy day for Irwin. During the Great War he had served in the Royal Navy, flying dirigibles over the Aegean. Recently he had been in a dead-end job as head of balloon training in Salisbury Plain. He had been delighted when he had been temporarily released from his responsibilities there to become the captain of R101.

Standing in the control car, he had felt so proud commanding her, a strangely beautiful Gulliver, with those tiny workmen holding on to her ropes. With only inches to spare, she cleared the hangar doors. Yet she was so finely balanced that she seemed to float out as light as a dandelion puff.

A wind, like the one beginning to blow now, might at that critical stage have dashed her against the metal of the hangar. A grand cheer had gone up as her tail cleared the door, and the walkers began effortlessly to lead her across the frosty grass to the mooring mast.

Irwin remembered the sun had come up just as they maneuvered to leeward of the mast. He had given the order to pay out the main haul cable, and once that had been connected with the masthead cable, ordered the side guy wires to be run out to the ground positions. As she lay tethered by the triangle of ropes, Major Scott had pleased the crowd by climbing directly into the control car from the ground.

What had pleased Irwin less was that Scott had insisted on taking over the controls for the tricky maneuver of locking on. That had been his first indication of trouble. Scott had commanded an earlier airship, R34, safely across the Atlantic in 1919, and it was now clear that he would regard himself as captain of any airship he flew in.

After that 1919 success for lighter-than-air craft, disaster had come in 1921. The Cardington-built R38, manned mostly by an American crew, had broken in two over the Humber River and caught fire, killing all but five on board. Several years later, R33 with Ralph Booth in command was torn away from her mooring mast by high winds. Her bows crushed, she spent thirty hours being buffeted over the North Sea before the skill of her crew was finally able to bring her home. The government, disenchanted with airships, had diverted the taxpayers' money to airplanes.

Then onto the scene had come the first Labour government with Ramsay MacDonald as Prime Minister and his friend Christopher Thomson as secretary of state for air. Airships were in again. The privately financed R100, designed by Barnes Wallis, and the government-funded R101, designed by Vincent Richmond, were begun.

So also began an unholy race between nationalized and private industry, between capitalism and socialism, while all along the Germans were winning worldwide with their triumphant contender, the *Graf Zeppelin*. And starting simultaneously was a race between airships and airplanes. Airshipmen were confident of winning because airplane engines were too small to provide long-range air links to all the countries of the British Empire. The birth of R101 in the opinion of many airshipmen meant another nail in the coffin of the airplane. Already the even bigger R102 was being designed.

All seemed to go well on that day in October when R101 made her first public appearance. At least at first. After a nod from Scott, Chief Coxswain "Sky" Hunt gave the order by megaphone for the working party to let go. Up the ship rose, but meeting a layer of warmer, lighter air above, she bumped against it like a toy balloon against a ceiling. The water ballast in the nose was released in a great shower that sent the watching ground crew scattering for shelter.

Then suddenly the crew were running after something else. Irwin peered down. Three hundred men were rushing in front of R101's nose, to chase away . . .

What?

He shaded his eyes against the red glitter of the dawn. With a sense of foreboding, Irwin saw dashing across the grass a hare, that age-old harbinger of death by fire.

THE WHOLE SCENE FLASHED vividly through his mind as now, a year later, he drove toward the bridge across the Ouse, with the hare still loping ahead of him. Not till he was on the Cardington side did the animal veer to the left and disappear into the hedge. In Irwin's mind as he turned toward the airship sheds were all the things that had happened in the train of that earlier hare.

Every sort of problem. In the design, Richmond had incorporated all sorts of innovations: new valves for the gasbags, diesel railway engines instead of gasoline engines, a luxury lounge, a smoking room (the first ever in an airship), more cabins, triplex glass for the windows. Many of these had had to be removed to cut down weight when it was found that R101's lifting capacity was half what had been expected.

There had been engine trouble on many of the test flights. About three months ago, at the Hendon Air Display, when her nose had been dipped in salute, a gasbag harness broke. It was after that that she had been cut in two and an extra forty-four feet of length built into her stomach to hold an additional gasbag.

About all these events Irwin wrote detailed reports, carefully keeping carbon copies in his office desk.

Then the privately owned R100, commanded by Booth with Scott on board, had flown across the Atlantic to Montreal and back. That was over two months ago. So it had become imperative in the eyes of the socialist secretary of state for air, newly created *Lord* Thomson, for the government airship to show she was even better with a flight to India. Thomson intended to return in triumph on his magic carpet for the Imperial Conference of all the Empire's prime ministers, due to start in a fortnight's time. Indeed he had made it clear to Wing Commander R. B. B. Colmore, director of airship development, that unless R101 went to India before the winter, there would be no more Treasury money for airships and the workers who built them.

After the newly elongated R101 had gone on her one and only test flight, Richmond and Colmore were delighted with the new porpoise shape, the apparent extra lift. Scott was also satisfied. For Irwin's part, the sixteen-hour trial in perfect weather was totally inadequate after such drastic surgery. He had drawn up a careful program of tests, culminating in a forty-eight-hour final flight which was to include six hours at full speed in bad weather. His views had been communicated to Lord Thomson.

Endowed with a passionate sense of duty, Irwin now tried to weigh all the factors in his command as he drove through the flat Bedford-shire countryside.

A flurry of brown leaves from the sycamores scurried in front of the car. Autumn already. Winter was closing in. If R101 was to get to India before the tottering Labour government fell and Thomson was replaced as air minister, today was the last chance.

Everything pivoted on him, one of the most junior officers on board, yet the captain of R101. Throughout his early naval days Irwin had had drilled into him the classic definition that a captain "is the officer in charge of the vessel, and all persons whether officers, crew or passengers are, by virtue of their being embarked, subject to his commands in all matters affecting the safety of the vessel and the well-being of the community on board." As he passed the graveyard in Cardington, he saw one of those who would be "subject to his commands"—Samuel Church, a rigger in the crew of R101.

October 4, 1930   *1015 British Summer Time*
                                                              0915 GMT

SEEING IRWIN NOD, Samuel Church gave a stiff little salute. He was wearing his new blue double-breasted tight-fitting uniform, with a red cloth R101 badge on his cap. In a knapsack he was carrying most of his worldly possessions, including the brown coveralls and light rubber-soled shoes he would gladly change into when he got on board.

Although togged up like naval petty officers bound for the tropics, the crew were nearly all civilians. The officers were a mixture of Army, Navy and Air Force, illustrating the continuous interservice battle over who controlled the sky. Church was the local blacksmith's son, a regular attender at the Methodist Chapel, and engaged to a Bedford girl, Irene Capon. He had walked from his home next to the graveyard, past Cardington Green, past Saint Mary the Virgin Church, and now he turned left up the hill toward the vast gray cathedrals of airship hangars the Admiralty had built thirteen years before.

As Samuel Church went, he smiled cheerfully. He greeted Mrs. Potter, wife of the assistant coxswain, and her daughter in their garden. He smiled at Mrs. Rudd, wife of a fellow rigger, scrubbing her front doorstep. He smiled at Sky Hunt, the chief coxswain, a burly figure striding along in his rubber boots, and received in return a wide toothy grin.

Now he was in a crowd of men rushing to catch a bus to the mooring mast nearly a mile away. All around him he could feel exhilaration. Everyone was joking and laughing.

"Weather looks all right, then?" Church called across to Arthur Bell, who with his mate Joe Binks manned the aft engine car.

"Not bad, Sam."

"What about your engines, though?" Walter Radcliffe, a Bedford rigger, asked Bill King, who came from Tonbridge. It was a laughing reminder of the number of times the heavy diesel engines had failed during the last year, culminating in an oil cooler failure on their sixteen-hour test flight.

"What about your gasbags?" King retorted with not quite so much jocularity. The seventeen enormous gasbags were made of "gold-beater skin"—membrane from the intestines of a million oxen secured to cotton, through which hydrogen leaked at a considerable rate. Worse, when they had cut R101 in two, they had found hundreds of holes in the bags where they had chafed against the nuts and bolts of the latticelike metal frame. The points of chafing had now been bandaged by four thousand pieces of cloth, as ordered—unwillingly, it was rumored—by the Air Ministry.

"What about a drink more like?" another rigger interrupted as they all scrambled into the bus. Such bandaging was fairly standard in airships and they all leaked, but with five and a half million cubic feet of hydrogen to keep them up, what was the worry? "Me for Betsy's!"

Betsy's was the Bell Inn at Cotton End, another half mile beyond the mast, kept by Miss Betsy Bunker, and a favorite of the engineers and riggers after they had returned from a trip.

Men in coveralls were streaming along the road. Buses bringing sightseers had already begun to arrive. Somewhere in the Royal Airship Works a warning signal blared. There came the distant whine of hydraulics. The huge doors of the empty R101 hangar stood open. In the next hangar the silver snout of R100 was visible. Everywhere noise—the accelerated whir of the engines being tested, the whine of the elevator going up and down the mast. Everywhere excitement—the air vibrant, pulsating. The whole busload of R101 crew members was caught up in the momentum of it all.

As the bus conductor collected fares, the hilarity continued. They went past the hangars toward the shed containing the engine that controlled the swiveling masthead from which, like an enormous silver pennant, flew R101—lean as a greyhound, her steel and aluminum skeleton showing through her thin silver skin. Even the five engine cars sticking out from her sides, with the pusher propellers behind them, and the control car under her belly, did not spoil her streamlining. Longer than most oceangoing ships, more graceful than any airplane, larger than a cathedral, she was a shimmering phantom merging with the intermittent clouds, now highlighted in a sudden brief shaft of sunlight.

The bus stopped abruptly at the base of the mast. N. G. Atherstone, the curly-haired first officer, stood beside his faithful Alsatian dog, supervising the beginnings of "gassing up"—filling the gasbags from the underground hydrogen pipes to make up for seepage during the night.

"What's all this stuff for His Lordship, then, sir?" Arthur Disley, the electrician, indicated men unloading rolls of carpet from a truck.

Atherstone laughed. "Lord Thomson wants to add a touch of ceremony to our arrival in India."

"What about the weight, sir?" engineer Bell asked. "What about the weight of his valet, come to that? The lads are being allowed only fifteen pounds of luggage each."

"Never mind, Bell. Think of the pearls you'll be able to bring back from India for your girl."

"Rubies, sir! She wants rubies."

Atherstone caught sight of the chief coxswain getting out of the bus. "Check the movement of all controls, Hunt."

"Right, sir."

"Engines been tested, Gent?"

"Everything in top shape, sir," the first engineer told him.

"No oil cooler trouble this time?"

"No sign of any, sir," said Assistant Coxswain Potter.

Potter had been one of the survivors of the R38. He had also helped bring home the breakaway R33, as had Bill King, now standing beside him.

"And the gas valves?" Atherstone asked a bunch of riggers.

Each of the hydrogen-filled bags had two valves halfway up to let hydrogen escape. As outside air pressure varied, they opened and closed, making a chattering noise.

"*Seem* all right, sir," one rigger told him. "We've checked all the seatings."

Some of the crew were already being weighed in, handing over their matches and changing into rubber-soled shoes before going up in the elevator.

MAJOR SCOTT, COMMANDER of R34 in 1919, now the assistant director of airship development (flying), walked leisurely over to the mast from the Manor House at Cotton End, which was his home. He was a plump, clever man with a high forehead and protruding eyes who looked and acted like a bulldog. An eternal optimist, he did not plan ahead for the worst, as Irwin did, and was not nearly so methodical and time conscious. Privately he regarded Irwin as a bit of a fusspot. He himself was ready to take risks. He had made it clear to his political masters that he would fly R101 all the way to South Africa, well beyond her range, provided a destroyer was on hand to tow her the last thousand miles.

As he came toward Atherstone at the mast, he was remembering old times. The day three hundred men had stood at Pulham for R34's return, grabbing at the steel line that trailed over the ground as they came safely back to earth. The months spent developing his invention, the masthead with its revolving top which kept airships pointing into the wind like a weathervane.

"How's things?" he asked Atherstone.

"Seem all right."

Scott stroked the head of Atherstone's dog. "Crew seem cheerful."

Atherstone said nothing for a while. Then hopefully—after all, this evening's departure might still be postponed—"How's the weather?"

"Just going to the Met Office to find out."

IRWIN HAD GONE STRAIGHT to the Meteorological Office upon his arrival at the Airship Works. He was standing beside the bespectacled Giblett, who would be coming with them on the trip, when Scott came in. Scott was a little put out to find Irwin in uniform being addressed as "Captain" by the meteorologist, now running his finger over the curving isobars on the weather map.

". . . a depression here over Tynemouth, but it's moving away."

"Good!" Scott said.

"What about this cloud over us now?" Irwin asked.

"Should be breaking up before evening."

"And this depression?" Irwin pointed to a cluster of concentric circles in the Atlantic off Ireland.

"It *is* moving east," Giblett admitted. "But—"

"—we'll be away before it reaches us," Scott finished for him.

"*The Times* weather forecast this morning wasn't so hopeful," Irwin said.

"*The Times* is always pessimistic."

"Nobody can accuse you of being the same, Scottie." Irwin's tone was jocular, but in fact he was remembering how Scott had taken R100 slap into a cloud buildup northeast of Montreal, where an updraft had rocketed her up twenty-five hundred feet, rent a twelve-foot tear in her outer cover and sent the supper plates careering down the corridor.

"Thank God I'm not," Scott retorted.

"And the wind this evening?" Irwin asked.

"Southwesterly, fifteen miles an hour."

"Cloud base over France?"

"A thousand to fifteen hundred feet."

"Bumpy?"

Irwin was doing too much of the talking. Scott lit his pipe and began puffing it thoughtfully. This captaincy business had never really been sorted out. In Canada people had taken him as second-in-command of R100, superseded by Ralph Booth. Since Scott was undoubtedly one of the world's most experienced airshipmen, this had hurt him, for underneath that jovial good humor he was very sensitive. He'd had a word with Colmore about the captaincy of R101. From Irwin's attitude now, clearly he'd have to have another.

"Looks to me as though the stuff's breaking up," he pronounced through a cloud of pipe smoke. "What do you say, Gib?"

"I think we shall see the sun this evening, Major Scott." Giblett smiled tentatively from one to the other. "After all our problems, it looks as though the gods are with us at last."

"Well, what are we worrying about then?" Scott led the way to the door. "Are you coming to this farewell do at the Bridge Hotel, Irwin?"

"Yes."

"Could you give me a lift?"

"Of course."

The two men walked to Irwin's car.

Just before Irwin got into the driver's seat, he felt on his cheek like the brushing of a moth's wing a drop of light rain.

October 4, 1930   *1150 British Summer Time*
1050 GMT

"HERE THEY COME!" Navigator Johnnie Johnston got to his feet and led the roar of greeting as the two airship pilots entered the bar. "Gangway for the skippers to the bar, gentlemen, please."

Good-humoredly, the crowd parted. A way was made for Irwin and Scott to join the navigator and Colmore and his wife at the counter. Johnston's tankard was already empty. The entire male population of Bedford and half the female seemed to have gathered in the Bridge Hotel. Situated by the stone bridge on the London Road, the hotel had a marvelous view across the wide river Ouse.

People patted Irwin and Scottie on the arm, grasped them by the shoulders, and wished them Godspeed. The owner, a keen amateur singer, interrupted his humming to greet them warmly, while through the windows a group of wide-eyed youngsters, most of them with autograph albums, peered at the great men and the historic gathering inside.

Johnston, a burly man with a small toothbrush mustache, stared at the children indulgently. A devoted father himself, he enjoyed the youngsters' adulation. Without any undue pride, he knew that he was the greatest navigator of his time—no other man could find his way as surely as he did. As surely in fact as the swallows and the swifts. A product of the Merchant Navy, he had won his Master Mariner's Certificate at the age of twenty-three, was made an examiner for other master mariner candidates, and had then joined the infant RAF. He had been lent to Imperial Airways to navigate their first ever London–India flight—so airplanes could be said to have

beaten airships. But he didn't owe his navigation to books or charts or even the blessed stars which he knew so well. He owed it to a strange sixth sense that never failed him. Even after a few drinks he could navigate blindfolded.

"Another for you, Johnnie?" Irwin's voice held a certain lack of enthusiasm. Johnnie had been accused of striking a crewman at the end of the successful R100 return flight to Canada. He reportedly had had more than a drop then, and he'd been tired and tense. Irwin ran a tight ship, and he had no intention of allowing the breath of any such scandal.

Johnnie smiled to himself. Irwin was the best skipper in the business, but a bit of a stickler. As a flight lieutenant, he was Johnston's junior in rank, yet Johnston respected him profoundly. But that didn't mean he wasn't going to have another drink.

"Your drinks are all on the house, sir!" The innkeeper put his hand on Irwin's arm, reached across and scooped up Johnston's tankard and poured another round. Then he held his own tankard aloft. "To the crew of 101! Drink up! And don't any of you go! We've got a surprise for you. A small presentation."

While a buzz of speculation went around the bar, Johnston half closed his eyes and let his mind drift forward. If this flight was the success it must be, their careers would be forever made. It would be roses, roses all the way.

Roses. This morning before he left, he had said to his wife, "I'll bring you back something nice from India. What'll it be? Silk for a dress? A gold necklace? A ruby ring?"

She had replied fancifully, like the princess in Grimm's fairy story, "The first rose that touches your hat." Then she had broken off a white autumn rose and had pushed it for luck into his buttonhole. Late roses never lasted. Its petals had already fallen.

"What was the Met forecast like?" he asked Irwin suddenly.

Irwin shrugged. "Not too bad. There's a depression we'll have to watch coming in from the Atlantic off Ireland."

"This sort of stuff?" Johnston jerked his head at the window where intermittent raindrops had prickled the glass. What would old Hinch say to that, he wondered.

He took a swig from his tankard. Why the hell had he thought that? Raymond Hinchliffe had been one of the best early civil pilots,

Johnston's friend and comrade. But Hinch had lost sight in one eye in the Great War, and had been refused a British Civil License. That's why he had gone to Holland, where he had met and married Emilie. After the birth of their daughter, he began to worry he would not be able to support his family, as Dutch medical examinations for civil pilots were becoming more stringent. So to win fame and fortune, he had tried two and a half years ago to be the first to fly eastbound across the Atlantic, against the westerly gales. Accompanied by his financial backer, the shipping heiress Elsie Mackay, he had set off in a little Stinson—on March 13, of all days, considering Hinch had always been madly superstitious. The weather forecast had been appalling. Why ever had they gone? One message over Ireland reported them battling terrible head winds. Then storms—and silence.

But not total silence—that is, if Hinchliffe's widow, Emilie, could be believed. Spiritualism—the belief that the dead communicate with the living through séances, Ouija boards or mediums—was gaining quite a following just then. Emilie Hinchliffe believed she was in touch, through a medium, with her husband, on the "Other Side."

One day Emilie turned up at Cardington, solemn and straight-faced, and told Johnston she had a message for him.

"For me, Emilie?" he asked. "Who from?"

"From Hinch," she said calmly. "From the Other Side. He says I'm to warn you of the great danger you are in."

Kindhearted though he was, Johnston almost laughed. Poor old Hinch! Poor Emilie! Only her earnest, trusting face prevented him.

"It really *was* him, Johnnie. I know his voice. And he begged me to warn you. R101 is doomed! Don't go on her!"

Johnston didn't believe a word of it. He was all for live and let live. Or rather die and let die, and rest in peace. Emilie Hinchliffe wasn't deterred by his attitude. She came again. This time she brought with her no less distinguished a person than Sir Arthur Conan Doyle himself. Johnston had been delighted to make his acquaintance. He was an admirer of Doyle's Sherlock Holmes stories. But the great man had not come to talk of detective fiction. He had become very interested in spiritualism, and had come to lend weight as a spiritualist to Emilie's message from Hinchliffe. Sir Arthur could vouch for the integrity of the medium Emilie had consulted, Eileen Garrett, a woman who had apparently seen visions since she was a child. "You must believe Eileen Garrett," Sir Arthur had said. "You must trust her."

"My philosophy is Cromwell's," Johnston had replied. "I trust in God and keep my powder dry."

In his case, his powder was R101's navigation instruments. He was not completely happy about them. Shortly after Emilie's visit he had been in touch with Eckener, the German zeppelin expert, and with the instrument makers Hartmann and Braun, to see if they could help. But they couldn't—not in the time available.

"Try to warn Johnnie in time," Hinch had said, according to Emilie. Now he remembered the words again, today at the Bridge Hotel, and suddenly he felt a cold blast. But its origin was not spiritual. It came as the door was thrust open by Atherstone, accompanied, as he always was, by his Alsatian dog.

"Are you all here now, lads?" the innkeeper asked.

"What's the hurry with him?" Atherstone queried in his version of an Australian accent which he put on occasionally in his favorite pubs. Atherstone had been beguiled back from Australia by the Air Ministry, which had searched the world for airship experts and found him farming peacefully in Australia. Though Australian by adoption and inclination, Atherstone had Russian blood. Born in Saint Petersburg, he had been educated in England. He was meticulous in his duties, a first-class officer and a charming companion. "What's up with the innkeeper? He's nearly as impatient as our beloved Lord Thomson!"

Irwin smiled, but Colmore, still sitting at the bar with his wife, looked embarrassed. "There are reporters here, you know," he whispered mildly.

"You don't say!" Atherstone grinned unrepentantly. "Then maybe I should repeat that."

Colmore flushed. Very slightly, Irwin shook his head and Atherstone shrugged apologetically. "Only kidding."

"He's not in the mood for kidding. Dowding's coming this afternoon. He'll be fagged out before we begin!"

Though why he should defend Colmore, Irwin sometimes wondered. Colmore should have taken a tougher line with Thomson, and a less rosy view of that last test flight.

Noticing Atherstone's frown, Major Scott winked with apparent good humor. Frowns were out. It was essential for the crew to put on a public appearance of enthusiasm.

Atherstone, in fact, was simply resigned to events taking their course, for, like Irwin, he couldn't see how he could duck out of them. Airships had had a rotten press. The Canadian air ace Billy Bishop, who had shot down more German planes than any other Royal Flying Corps pilot except the Irishman Mannock, had called them in the *Daily Express* six months ago a "squandering of public money." He had added that an airship commander's "great machine can be in two kinds of weather at once, the nose of it fighting a clockwise gust, and the tail of it attacked by something quite different."

Now Atherstone caught Scott's eye, got the message, winked back and put on a big smile. Then, after draining his tankard, he asked, "So what *has* our innkeeper got up his sleeve for us?"

What he had became immediately visible. The innkeeper rolled out a most elegant nine-gallon ale cask of what looked like polished oak. The rims of the cask were edged with silver, while on its widest part the letter and numbers *R101* were engraved in silver, the two crossed flags of Great Britain and India beneath them.

There was a friendly wavering as to who should take charge of the handsome gift. Scottie puffed smoke at the ceiling and opened his arms. Richmond, the designer, leaned forward. But it was to Irwin the innkeeper turned.

"Here you are, Skipper!"

He thrust the cask toward Irwin, and then climbed up on the bar and began a presentation speech. It was highly laudatory of the crew, whom he said he was proud to serve, proud that they'd made the Bridge Hotel their second HQ. He spoke of their contribution to Bedford, to aviation, to science, called them a Band of Brothers.

Then the innkeeper concluded with those lines of Faust on the dream of flight:

> *Yea, if a magic mantle once were mine,*
> *To waft me o'er the world at pleasure,*
> *I would not for the costliest stores of treasure—*
> *Not for a monarch's robe—the gift resign.*

Irwin replied in his usual modest but oddly impressive way.

But Johnston, the navigator, didn't hear him. He was listening to someone else. A man just behind him in the crowded bar was proudly telling his companion how he had helped fashion the cask. He had done it on his own time after he had finished his shift at the undertaker's.

October 4, 1930   *1320 British Summer Time*
                                                         1220 GMT

"I'LL TAKE CARE of that."

Wing Commander Colmore, director of airship development, put his arms around the nine-gallon cask and lifted it off the counter. Then, helped by Lieutenant-Colonel Richmond, designer of R101, he carried it out the door to the cheers of those remaining, and deposited it on the back seat of Richmond's car, leaving his own for his wife to use.

Colmore was the administrator of the whole project. His role was that of a general at the battlefront of scientific knowledge. Theoretically he should have been an expert on airships, but actually he knew less about them than Richmond, the assistant director of airship development (technical), who had started as an engineer.

Colmore's contribution to scientific knowledge was a brilliant scheme for combating U-boats with the combined use of aircraft and surface ships, which was to remain a cornerstone of British sea defense policy. His job here was to juggle the endless problems, keep everyone happy, and get the government airship flying, linking the British Empire by air and justifying the enormous expense.

"Scottie didn't look his usual amiable self," Richmond said as they set off at a brisk pace back to Cardington.

"He's all right," Colmore replied. "Just thinking about the trip."

"Didn't look too happy to me."

Richmond was as artistically touchy and autocratic about his baby as all designers are. The trouble was that he had avoided well-tried German zeppelin ideas and had gone in for a lot of new inventions like the valves, diesel engines and gasbag harnesses. He wouldn't hear a word against any of them. Colmore knew the test flights R101 had had were not enough to prove the worth of Richmond's ideas. Still, when he had seen Lord Thomson in his office last Thursday, Thomson was all for R101 leaving for India on Friday evening,

October 3, insisting that he must be back in time for the Imperial Conference. This put Colmore in a fix since Irwin had demanded rest for the crew. Thomson had then tried for Saturday morning. That was out because the captain wanted to dock at Ismailia, Egypt, in the cool of the evening. Finally Colmore and Lord Thomson agreed to a departure between six and eight Saturday evening, October 4.

"Is Thomson quite happy now?" Richmond asked.

"Perfectly."

"What about Brancker?"

Sir Sefton Brancker was the government's director of civil aviation, and would be one of the passengers.

"Didn't have time to see him."

"Brancker has never shown his nose much up here," Richmond went on. "Always struck me as more pro-airplane than airship."

"He's been very good at trying for more airship masts along the route," Colmore, the peacemaker, pointed out.

Richmond simply grunted.

As they drove through the Cardington gates Colmore looked at his watch. Only another four hours to go and they would be away. As far as he could see, the loading appeared to be going well. Twenty-five tons of diesel fuel and five hundred gallons of drinking water had gone on board as well as cases of sardines and twenty different sorts of cheeses, wines, spirits and cigars. A radio microphone had been set up, and a Movietone cameraman was filming R101 as she lazed at the masthead. The fields were already filled with cars and buses and waiting people.

Bearing the nine-gallon cask of ale and smiling broadly, Colmore made his way to his office. There more problems awaited him. Richmond had been right. Scottie, who had arrived back in Cardington just minutes before Colmore and Richmond, *was* unhappy.

"It's about the press note I wrote," Robertson, the press officer, told Colmore. "Scottie reckons he's made to look simply a passenger."

Scott had apparently got hold of a copy of the press release for R101's flight. There he had found himself well down in the passenger list as assistant director of airship development (flying) while Flight Lieutenant Irwin headed the crew as captain.

"We'll have to add something to the first communiqué," Colmore suggested to Robertson. "Meanwhile go along and calm Scott down. Tell him we'll do something."

The press officer found Scott in the briefing room standing by a large-scale map, explaining R101's route to a group of journalists.

"We'll be passing right over London on the way to the southeast coast. Then our probable direction"—he stretched out his arm and drew his finger rapidly across the map—"will be between Rouen and Paris, then southwest via Tours to Bordeaux, turning southeast to Narbonne. We'll fly via Malta across the Mediterranean to the mast at Ismailia."

"Isn't that a very long way around?" one of the reporters asked.

"Why don't you go direct over the Alps?" queried another reporter.

"Is it because you have to zigzag to avoid high ground?" a third reporter suggested.

"*Probable* direction, I said," Scott pointed out. "The actual route *I* choose will, of course, depend on the weather."

The *I* had been heavily emphasized.

In the lull while the journalists were scribbling it all down, Robertson approached Scott and in a low voice told him that his position was going to be made quite clear in an addition to the first press communiqué.

The frown left Scott's big bald forehead. "Good! If anything happens on the trip, *I* will be held responsible."

October 4, 1930   *1415 British Summer Time*
                                              1315 GMT

FEW PEOPLE SEEING Sir Sefton Brancker on October 4 would have thought that he was anything but his usual cheerful, charming self. The dapper little director of civil aviation was the most popular of R101's distinguished passengers—especially with women, to whom he showed a bubbling champagne side, dancing all night and insisting when a flapper asked about his adventures, "My dear young lady, my heavenly adventures are all on the ground!"

That was certainly a cover-up. Brancker's adventures both on the ground and in the heavens had been legion. Trained in the Army, he had become obsessed with flying while he was in India. On his third flight, in an engine-driven box kite piloted by the French Major Jullerot, he had had his first of many crashes. His face was scratched, but his eyeglass had remained intact.

He had tried to become a pilot in the Great War. The medical examiner had written: "He is so shortsighted that he will be a danger to himself and everyone else if he is allowed to fly." But he wangled his way into the Royal Flying Corps by pulling strings at the War Office—an exercise at which he remained adept all his life.

His eyes were so bad that even when he had advanced to air vice-marshal, his young pilots were given instructions not to let him take over the controls. But the doctor was wrong in the sense that mattered. Far from being shortsighted, Brancker had the most tremendous vision. He could see into the future. He became the John the Baptist of aviation, its champion and its prophet. To him, flying was both romantic and invaluable to man's communication with man.

He had had many near squeaks. In 1923 he had tried to fly from Paris in a British plane, but it was full. He found a seat available on a French aircraft, but then the pilot of the British plane offered to drop his engineer in order to take Brancker along. Brancker hesitated, but in the end agreed. The French aircraft crashed near Amiens with the loss of all on board.

Nothing daunted, Brancker continued to fly—with the one-eyed Hinchliffe inspecting continental air routes; with Johnston on the first Imperial Airways flight to India—often sick, for he was afflicted with airsickness, but always joking. He had been terrified out of his wits at times, but he had known that he would survive, that his luck would hold until his number came up.

Women were more lethal. He had often told his friends that when his end finally came, he hoped to God it would be in the air and not in bed.

In fact he had repeated that remark not so long ago to a somewhat enigmatic lady he had met at a party. A delectable friend called Auriol Lee, a theatrical producer, had introduced him to Mrs. Eileen Garrett. This handsome woman with large hazel-brown eyes that were both compelling and disturbing had told him without preamble that she had had a vision. A vision of an airship crashing in flames.

He had been so taken aback that he had asked, as if he believed her, "Which airship? There are several."

And she had answered, "R101."

Brancker had immediately recovered himself. "Well, my dear young lady, let me tell you I shall be flying aboard that ship to India in just over a week's time."

He had gone on to tell Auriol Lee that he would perform his favorite trick of eating his monocle if the flight was canceled. But Auriol Lee hadn't laughed.

"I hope it *is* canceled," she had said, and then added in a low voice, "I had my horoscope cast. It said I had a dear friend"—she put her hand on his arm—"a very dear friend . . . who would perish"—the last two words had been scarcely audible—"by *fire*."

"I've told you, my dear, many times, a French astrologer cast mine. She said I had nothing to worry about for six years."

"But how long ago?"

He had shrugged. "I forget." But he had not forgotten. It was in 1924. She had said she could see nothing after that. Amazing how time went by! He had then gone on to make the remark about his own end, and the woman with the strange eyes had said no more about R101.

Just now Brancker was at Henlow airfield watching the arrival of the car belonging to his friend Major Oliver Villiers, who was to take him to Cardington. Villiers had a distinguished war record, winning the Croix de Guerre, Legion of Honor and Distinguished Service Order. Now he was editor-in-chief of civil aviation publications at the Air Ministry. He knew Brancker well enough to see beneath the jokes, to detect an abstracted air about him today, as they greeted each other. They said little as they got into the car. But on their way toward the airship Brancker told Villiers what had been on his mind, speaking quietly of his latest interview with the secretary of state for air.

Brancker did not mince words. He was not afraid of Lord Thomson. The two men were alike. Both were determined. Both were brave men. Both enthusiastic. Both born publicists. But Sefton Brancker wanted to publicize aviation, while Lord Thomson wanted to publicize himself.

"I told Lord Thomson that Colmore wanted more mooring masts along the route," Brancker said to his friend. "I told him the airship wasn't ready. I told him this flight should be postponed. That with the Imperial Conference coming up, it was better to leave R101 at her mooring mast. Let the delegates see her, dine aboard her, get her measure. I told him he was hurrying the crew. That they hadn't done a proper test. That they'd asked for more time for rest and for repairs."

"What reply did you get to that?" Villiers asked.

"I got rapped over the knuckles, and I got no change. He repeated all his old arguments over again."

"That he'd announced he'd be there and back in time for the conference?"

"Yes. We have already done the first flight to Canada, he said. We must also do the first flight to India. So that when we approach the Dominions for further cooperation in the scheme, I can say we have done Canada, we have done India, and now you can see what airships can do!"

Brancker stopped speaking abruptly and bit his lip. He could not tell even the trusted Villiers of Thomson's most wounding remark, "Of course, if you're afraid, you need not come along!"

The memory of that remark held him in an angry silence as the flat Bedfordshire countryside slipped past. Was he afraid? he asked himself. Air vice-marshal, knight commander of the Most Honourable Order of Bath, holder of the Air Force Cross, officer of the Legion of Honor, commander of the Order of Leopold, commander of the Order of the Crown of Italy, commander of the Order of Saint Stanislaus, member of the Order of Saint Vladimir—had he now begun to be afraid?

Was he afraid of that distant silver shape just now coming into view? No, he decided in all honesty, he was not. He thought the whole flight a damned misbegotten adventure, but he was not afraid, certainly not for himself. He was apprehensive for the men who would be flying on her. He didn't honestly believe R101 had been sufficiently tested and he didn't want the project spoiled by haste.

But he wasn't afraid. He simply felt he was in the clutches of something he could not avoid.

As they approached the mooring mast, they were being hemmed in by cars and crowds. Oliver Villiers had to drive at a snail's pace. People peered in through the car, recognized Brancker, smiled, and banged on the hood of the car approvingly. The guard waved them through, direct to the airship. Publicist as always, Brancker paused for photographs, spoke to the crewmen, to the loaders at the bottom of the mast, while the newsreel cameramen wound their film.

"This is Air Vice-Marshal Sir Sefton Brancker," said a reporter into a microphone, "director of civil aviation. May we have a few words, sir? For British Movietone News?"

As he spoke, Brancker's own pride and enthusiasm for R101 were rekindled. He pointed out the observation platform and the dining room, whose lights were already glowing. He spoke of the dinner they would be eating after slipping the mast, of the special silver and Wedgwood china, of the glassware cut with wings.

Suddenly life seemed very good. Who would have thought when young Sefton Brancker was spending an undistinguished three years at the Bedford School that he would one day return to the town in such triumph and that he would serve the people of Bedford so well?

He paused for a moment while several crates of champagne were loaded. A young journalist suddenly asked, "When did they christen her?"

Brancker shook his head. "They didn't," he said. The omission had never struck him till then.

The youth opened his mouth to say "That's unlucky," and then thought better of it.

The tempo of the preparations was rising fast. Men were shouting through megaphones. At the masthead there was a hissing as the gas filling continued. From inside R101 could be heard the ringing of the ship's telegraph being tested. It was as though the airship had sucked in breath from the scurrying hundreds around it and was palpitating with a living excitement. Preparations had now slipped beyond the point of no return.

At 1503 GMT another meteorological report had been issued from the Air Ministry: "The occluded front over France this morning has now passed eastward while a trough of low pressure off western Ireland is spreading in quickly. Cloud is increasing and falling to 1000 feet. Rain will spread in from the west, probably reaching Cardington tonight. . . ."

Even Scott now began hurrying people up, saying, "We've got to get off as soon as possible. Where the hell are the rest of our passengers?"

October 4, 1930   *1745 British Summer Time*
                                                             1645 GMT

LORD CHRISTOPHER BIRDWOOD THOMSON was watching his valet Buck pour tea at the village inn in Shefford.

"Come and sit down, man!" Thomson told Buck. "And for God's sake stop looking so long-faced!"

Buck was being difficult as only a great man's valet could be. But neither Buck nor Brancker, nor for that matter R101, was on Thomson's mind, as, finding themselves approaching Cardington ahead of schedule, he had told Buck that he had no intention of arriving early. They would stop for afternoon tea.

On Thomson's mind was Princess Bibesco of Rumania. A bachelor still at fifty-five, tall and strikingly handsome, Lord Thomson had never lost his romantic idea of women. His love affair with the princess had been the gossip of Europe.

Thomson had been born the son of a professional soldier, in India, the country to which he intended to fly today in triumph. Ramsay MacDonald had almost promised to make him viceroy of India. After this successful flight, Thomson would point out to the Prime Minister, it would be opportune to announce the appointment.

Thomson's life was studded with opportune moments and seized opportunities. While still very young, serving with the Royal Engineers in the South African War, opportunity had come his way when an enormous jam of railway freight cars delayed General Kitchener on the approach to Kimberley. The furious general had ordered Thomson, then a very junior officer, to do something. With the inexorable thrusting determination that was to become his hallmark, Thomson had rounded up gangs of men to overturn the freight cars and allow the general through. Kitchener was impressed and Thomson's military future assured. During a subsequent assignment to the War Office he made other powerful friends. He widened his interests, wrote prose and poetry, a romantic novel, mixed with the literati. Then he was appointed military attaché to Rumania.

At a palace reception he met and fell in love with Princess Bibesco. She was the embodiment of his most romantic imaginings—not just a beautiful and vivacious princess, but a woman of outstanding gifts, a writer like himself of no mean talent. He knew he would love her till his dying day.

The whole Rumanian royal family took the dashing and cultured soldier-diplomat to their hearts, and it had been Thomson's military knowledge and sagacity that had helped persuade them to bring Rumania into the war on the Allies' side.

It was then that Thomson had realized he possessed that strange quality known as charisma. When he had decided to forsake the Army for politics, and had joined the Labour party, that charisma had stood him in good stead. Though the rank and file of the party viewed him with suspicion, Labour's leader, Ramsay MacDonald, took an instant liking to him. They had become close personal friends, and when MacDonald became Prime Minister he had made Thomson a baron and appointed him secretary of state for air.

Two days ago Ramsay MacDonald had sent for him. At first Thomson had thought it was to give him his last briefing before the flight to India. Instead, the Prime Minister had put his hand on Thomson's arm and asked that he cancel his trip.

Ramsay MacDonald was an emotional man who knew how to sway his hearers with his vibrant voice, but rarely had he spoken thus to his friend. In some surprise Thomson had inquired stiffly, "Is this an order, sir? Are you *ordering* me not to go?"

The Prime Minister had shaken his head. "No. No. I won't order you. But I would feel happier if you stayed here."

Gratification at MacDonald's obvious solicitude and need of him had jostled with contrary emotions. Thomson was mildly alarmed that MacDonald, the political seer of the Highlands, should feel so disquieted about the flight. He also felt slightly irritated at the possible thwarting of his plans. But most of all he felt triumph at his own power over his Prime Minister. For a second, he hesitated. The fate of many men and women for many years to come hung in the balance. Then that opportunist streak in Thomson decided . . . give in now, and he would lose face. MacDonald and everyone else would think less of him.

"You wouldn't really want me to cancel at this stage, sir." He smiled. "I feel sure of that, for I am quite committed. I have every confidence in airships. And I wish to go." Despite his concern, the Prime Minister had looked at him with admiration.

"Try to be back in time to dine at Chequers on the sixteenth," MacDonald had said. "And at latest by the twentieth."

"I will, sir. I give you my word." They had shaken hands.

Princess Bibesco would have been proud of him. India was a special stepping-stone for him, a magic carpet to a glamorous new career. They had toasted each other at a farewell-for-India party, drunk champagne out of her dainty silver slipper. Now that slipper reposed safely in his sturdiest trunk, a token of her love and pride in him. It was a good-luck symbol and his most treasured possession.

Sitting in the little pub parlor in Shefford, Thomson noticed that Buck's hand was shaking as he passed him his cup of tea. He knew his valet had never flown before. "What's wrong with you, man?"

"The weather's getting worse, m'lord," Buck said in a tone which Thomson would have tolerated in no one else. "Rain's coming."

Without replying to Buck directly, Thomson said with exaggerated patience, "I seem to be surrounded by people dragging their feet."

Buck, who would have followed his master into the jaws of hell itself, flushed a dark angry red but said nothing.

"No, we won't require any more, thank you." Lord Thomson turned his unfailing charm on the innkeeper, who, aware of the great man he entertained, was hovering with a plateful of his wife's caraway seed cake. "We shall be dining early on board. Our bill, if you please."

"I'll keep this for luck, my lord," the innkeeper said, holding the half crown Lord Thomson had pressed into his hand. "You'll be coming over this way, they tell us, my lord. We'll all be outside to cheer, be it wet or fine."

It will be wet, Buck thought, opening the door of Thomson's car. Even in the time they had been inside the inn, the wind had risen, and the clouds had lowered. What would rain do to those miles and miles of gut and cotton that went into R101? To the soft skin that would be all there was between them and Kingdom Come? He remained silent, and to his master's thinking, sullen and sulky, all the way to Cardington. But it wasn't the reproof which kept Buck silent, it was his master's acts over the last few days.

Buck went over them in his mind. First his master had suddenly decided in the middle of pressing Cabinet business and with all the hullabaloo about the coming Imperial Conference that he must drop everything and go to see his old mother in Teignmouth. It hadn't been all that long since he'd seen her. Mrs. Thomson, who was nobody's fool and who trusted Buck implicitly, had phoned him personally to ask if her son was overdoing things.

Then there was the insurance. His master had taken out this big policy. Worse still, he had taken out one for Buck himself. Finally, just yesterday, his master, who had always sworn he would never make a will, had gone into his office, sat down and made one out, leaving all he had—not that it was much—to his brother.

Not a nice way to begin a journey.

October 4, 1930   *1855 British Summer Time*
                                                     1755 GMT

"CAREFUL WITH THOSE BAGS, man! Especially that one!" Lord Thomson pointed to the heavy brassbound box that contained the silver slipper.

"Thinks he's the blooming Prince Charmin' himself," Buck said, but not aloud. He averted his eyes from the huge whalelike airship that was about to swallow them all up, and set the cases down reverently one after the other, all dozen of them, enjoying with uncharacteristic malice the aghast expressions of the loaders at the extra weight.

Unlike the rest of those going aboard, Lord Thomson did not have his baggage weighed. Buck was searched for matches, while Lord Thomson stalked on ahead and was immediately surrounded by reporters, newsreel cameramen and photographers. He paused for a moment, tall, handsome, urbane, impeccably dressed in dark gray homburg and velvet-collared overcoat.

"Shall you be making the entire round trip on R101, sir?" asked a reporter.

"Why not?" Lord Thomson smiled. "I am under orders to be back in London by the twentieth, and I don't expect I shall have to change my plans."

From the control cabin Major Scott and Flight Lieutenant Irwin watched His Lordship's arrival, Scott with unconcealed impatience to be off, Irwin with gritty determination.

"Why doesn't he hurry himself!" Scottie exclaimed. "Can't he see the sky? Does he think this is just a bus ride?" Though Scottie didn't share Irwin's view that they should postpone the flight, he was worried by the strengthening wind and the gathering clouds.

Irwin said nothing to Scott. Scottie knew Irwin had already told Brancker of the worsening weather and that Brancker had reluctantly agreed to have a word with Lord Thomson. So when Irwin told Atherstone to take over and climbed the ladder into the chart room, Scottie knew exactly what Irwin was going to do.

In the chart room Giblett and Johnston were bending over the navigator charts. Giblett looked up and without being asked volunteered, "Weather's deteriorating, Captain."

Irwin said nothing. He walked pale-faced and grim out into the corridor, past the smoking room and up the stairs to the passenger lounge. There, as he had expected, was Brancker, standing by the window with a half-empty glass of champagne in his hand. He looked somehow older and smaller.

"Lord Thomson has arrived, sir," Irwin said tersely.

"So I see." Sir Sefton squared his shoulders and screwed his monocle into his eye. "So this is it! Well, I'll have another go at him. Though I can't promise any luck."

LUCK! LIEUTENANT COMMANDER Atherstone was thinking of luck as he awaited Irwin's return to the control car. In front of him stood the height coxswain, his hands ready on the wooden spokes of the wheel. Immediately in front of the coxswain was the instrument panel.

Atherstone stared at it. Johnston had had some trenchant criticisms to make of that panel, of the inadequate rise-and-fall indicator, and the altimeter that perversely read counterclockwise. Hung on the panel was a lucky cat mascot which no one would admit to putting there but which no one would allow to be removed, and a small icon brought from Italy, called Our Lady of the Fair Winds. It was beautifully painted, the face expressive though sad, and Scottie sometimes joked that Our Lady had a calming and benign influence.

Atherstone was hoping she would have one that night. They would need to be lucky with the winds and weather. Like the rest of the crew, Atherstone had had his moments of acute doubt. But he still believed that with luck they could do it. Only last night he had written in his diary: *We all feel the future of airships very largely depends on what sort of show we put up. There are many unknown factors, and I feel that thing called "luck" will figure rather conspicuously in our flight. Let's hope for good luck and do our best.*

Fifteen minutes later Irwin came back into the control car. He had waited in the lounge for Brancker's return. "I have done my best," Brancker told him. "But Thomson is adamant."

"CREW TO LEAVING STATIONS!"

The megaphoned order broke through engineer Binks's account of the number and size of Lord Thomson's bags. "Fifteen pounds they allow us," he said in his Sheffield accent, "and his nibs must've 'ad as many as fifteen bags. Tell us we can't have parachutes, must watch our washing water, and His Lordship takes a blinking magic carpet."

Hearing the order repeated, Binks padded out of the crew's quarters to his station in the aft engine car. He couldn't help a proud feeling of excitement as he hurried past the riggers toward the stern of the ship. He cracked a joke or two with them. Told them not to put their big flat feet through the gasbags. Then he opened up the hatch and climbed down the long ladder to the engine car. He could smell the cut grass and feel the rising wind, and almost as if he were in a big circus tent, he heard the gasp of the crowd.

His mate Bell was already crouched beside the huge eight-cylinder Beardmore engine. These were the first diesels ever to power an airship, and weighed nearly twice as much as R100's gasoline engines. But much safer, the crew was told, the heavy oil being practically unburnable. They'd even been given a demonstration in the hangar of a gasoline fire being put out by diesel oil.

"Late as usual!" Bell grumbled. "Joe Binks, you'd be late for your own funeral!"

October 4, 1930   *1930 British Summer Time*
1830 GMT

THE GROUP OF WIVES standing near the foot of the mast heard the ringing of the ship's telegraph. The clouds were gathering and night was falling. On top of that mast up which their men had disappeared,

red warning lights were flashing, casting an intermittent glow over the throat of the airship. Like blood, Lieutenant Colonel Richmond's mother thought. A symbol of the attacks that had been made on her son's design. How he had been castigated for too much innovation! He would show them! There he was now, waving down at them as he stood beside Lord Thomson on the promenade deck!

"Keep the flag flying," he had said to her and his wife, Florence. They would. And so would he. As if in answer to her proud thoughts, the pale blue flag with its RAF emblem broke from the ship and a cheer went up from the thousands of spectators.

The air smelled of exhaust fumes, diesel oil, rubber—and newly baked bread. Up in the galley Megginson, the galley boy, arranged the food for tonight's dinner. His mother had begged him not to go, but he wouldn't be denied this chance of a lifetime. He loved the ship, the company of the crew and the excitement.

On the ground Arthur Savidge, the chief steward, was carrying the gift of the proud people of Bedford to their own ship—a horseshoe arrangement of white heather with spots of purple for the nails.

I don't like it, Mrs. Atherstone thought. It looks more like a funeral wreath than a table decoration. She tried to tell herself that horseshoes were lucky. They would all be wishing for good luck, praying for fair winds and no rain, she thought, glancing around at the faces of the wives and relatives, huddled together. She noticed, a little to her left, a man and an elderly woman, standing rather apart, as if they knew no one. Instinctively she smiled.

"We have come to see off Squadron Leader O'Neill," the woman said, as if grateful to talk to someone. "Bill is my son. This is his brother. Bill's wife, Elsie, is in the hospital, you see. And it's only by the most remote chance that he's on this trip. He had to get back to India. And Sir Sefton Brancker managed to wangle him a lift aboard. It's a very long story."

Mrs. Atherstone smiled and nodded. She knew the story. Mrs. William O'Neill had come to England from India some months ago to have an operation performed by the famous royal gynecologist Sir Henry Simson. Alas, at that time the Duchess of York, wife of the future King George VI, was about to give birth, so Mrs. O'Neill's operation was postponed. The duchess was safely delivered of her second daughter, Margaret Rose, and Mrs. O'Neill was booked to enter the hospital at Hammersmith. Her husband was torn between his desire to remain with his wife and the necessity of returning to his duties as deputy director of civil aviation in India. Then, by chance, he met Sir Sefton Brancker. Brancker promised to wave his magic wand. O'Neill could stay at his wife's side till the operation was over, for instead of making the long trip to India by sea, he would travel aboard R101 in some capacity or other.

"I'm sure we're all very grateful," Mrs. O'Neill said. "Bill was so keen to get on this airship. And Elsie has had the operation. She had all sorts of misgivings about this flight. But really, I think . . . "

She didn't say what she thought. And Mrs. Atherstone whispered to Mrs. Hunt, who was standing on her right, "I think I can hear Sky's voice from here."

Everyone liked Sky Hunt, with his booming voice and his comforting presence. Only his young son knew that just before he left, he had said quietly, "If anything happens to me, look after your mother." And there was Sky Hunt now as if he hadn't a care in the world, leaning over the side, blinking his flashlight to them.

Everywhere lights were flashing as at a fairground. Car lights, rotating lights, searchlights. Now that Lord Thomson was aboard, the crowd was getting impatient, feeling that departure was imminent. Then someone was pushing through, waving a paper.

At least three wives thought it was a last-minute reprieve, that the flight was to be postponed. But no, it was the belated Certificate of Airworthiness. More telegraph bells rang.

"Start engines." Crouched in their aft car, Binks put up his thumb to Bell. The gasoline starter motor was going. Then the first of the great diesels began to boom. But the forward starboard engine remained dead. Engineer King struggled with it, the sweat breaking out on his forehead. It coughed and backfired. He could see the shower of red sparks fly menacingly past the car. Finally it caught. The giant airship quivered as the engines gathered power. The five propellers spun, turning the lights into iridescent catherine wheels.

"Stand by to slip!"

The crowd cheered. Men took off their hats and waved them in the air. A child screamed. At the top of the mooring mast the order was received, "Slip!"

The pin securing the release lever was whipped out. There was a metallic clatter as R101 was freed from the mast, cut loose from the earth.

"All engines slow astern," Irwin spoke into the voice tube and moved the telegraph lever.

Another cheer went up, but somehow ended in a sigh. R101's nose should have risen. Instead, it dipped.

Olive Irwin clenched her hands until the nails bit into the palms. There was not a wife present who didn't know the danger. Irwin had perilously little room to maneuver such a huge overladen ship above the heads of all those thousands of people. Even a small dip could bring her bow down among the spectators.

In the cars the engineers had opened up the throttles. The huge diesels thundered, but still her nose did not rise. Irwin gave the order to release water from the ballast tanks in her bow. Seven times, as the watchers on the ground counted, a cascade descended, the water chopped by the propellers into fine rain.

Slowly, reluctantly, wearily, the big ship backed away from the mast.

"We're away, lads," Sky Hunt called loudly.

The crew began to signal farewell with their flashlights. The crowd cheered enthusiastically and stamped in unison as the giant airship cleared the top of the mast and, illuminated by the searchlights, gently turned.

Irwin guided Bedford's ship right over Bedford itself, dipping her nose in salute. Her white lights, her red lights, her green lights, wrote her passing on the wide river, on the wet roofs, on the streets of her native city.

Then Irwin climbed, leveled her out and set her on course for her passage to India.

October 4, 1930   *2005 British Summer Time*
                                                         1905 GMT

"To our passage to India!" Lord Thomson raised his glass of champagne as the lights of Bedford slipped beneath R101's belly. As a delicate compliment to R101's designer, His Lordship clinked glasses first with Lieutenant Colonel Richmond, then with the rest of the assembled passengers.

"To India!" they all replied.

Now that they were airborne and away, a pleasant euphoria filled the magnificent white and gold lounge, around which the stewards padded on rubber-soled shoes, proffering canapés and topping up crystal glasses, hand-cut with the RAF wings. With the five engines running, the heaters worked comfortably and the lounge was warm. It was decorated with exquisite flower arrangements, and a number of the pillars had been clad in blue-green velvet. But warmer and more attractive than any of the physical surroundings were Lord Thomson's smile and his manifest confidence and pleasure. Under the spell of his peculiar charisma, not one of the assembled company felt anything but confident. Past fears and doubts were pushed aside. Irwin, who might have remembered, was in the control car with Atherstone.

"Had we but the partners, we could dance our way to India," Lord Thomson said. His mind harked back to that previous champagne party, and to Princess Bibesco's tireless silver slippers. Those were certainly capable of dancing to India and back. One day, who knew, perhaps she might accompany him. Certainly when he had achieved his ambition he could in all propriety entertain her.

Aloud he said, "Come along, gentlemen! Drink up! I shall give you another toast!" Lord Thomson waited till the glasses were drained and then refilled. Then he raised his own. "To our absent partners! To the ladies, God bless them!"

Thomson's light gray eyes traveled around the assembled audience. He had been told by Colmore why O'Neill was aboard, and with his facility for what Brancker called "charming the birds off a tree," he asked him, as if he really cared, "Good news of your wife, I sincerely hope, O'Neill?"

"Splendid, sir, thank you."

For the moment Thomson was ignoring Brancker. He was not pleased with him. He could not abide people who dragged their feet.

He turned to compliment Richmond on the design of the lounge, the feeling of spaciousness. He asked Colmore if "Stuffy" Dowding had not been similarly impressed.

"Indeed, yes, sir. Being an airplane man, he was very impressed with the marvelous passenger accommodations." Colmore did not at that stage see fit to mention that Air Vice-Marshal H. C. T. Dowding had been somewhat perturbed about their failure to do a high-speed test on all engines, and had suggested a full test as soon as practicable after slipping the mast.

A test was out of the question just now. Perhaps when they were lighter, when they had lost some of the burdensome weight of fuel, when crew and airship had shaken down together, when it was less bumpy and when the weather forecast was better. But not yet.

"Come along, Scottie, gentlemen . . . your glasses are empty!"

There was a momentary pause in the conversation while more champagne corks popped and the wine fizzled into the glasses. In it, they heard a sound which had escaped them before but which had already been heard by Irwin and Atherstone in the control car—the steady drum of rain.

October 4, 1930   *2032 British Summer Time*
                                           1932 GMT

As THE BBC ANNOUNCER enthusiastically described R101's departure, Emilie Hinchliffe was at the home of the friend who had first communicated with Emilie's dead husband and had been instrumental, along with Sir Arthur Conan Doyle, in arranging her meetings with the medium Eileen Garrett.

The BBC man was describing how the crew had come on board the airship in good spirits, Squadron Leader Johnnie Johnston, the navigator, cracking a joke with reporters before going up in the elevator.

Emilie Hinchliffe turned her head and looked at the night outside. Darkness had fallen early. The sky was overcast and inhospitable. She was filled with a sense of failure at having been unable to convince Johnston of her husband's warning.

Now she heard the announcer describe the vast lounge, the blue-green carpet, the velvet-covered pillars, the Wedgwood china and silver of R101's dining room. He told the listening millions how R101 had slowly slipped the mast, how suddenly her nose had dipped and cascades of water had descended on the onlookers.

Emilie's sense of foreboding deepened.

Hoping to be reassured, she and her friend laid out the Ouija board and the planchette—a heart-shaped piece of wood on casters with a pencil attached underneath. They would try to contact Emilie's husband.

Together they waited.

But when the pencil moved, it wrote the words Emilie most dreaded: *Storms rising. Nothing . . . can save them now.*

October 4, 1930   *2055 British Summer Time*
                                       1955 GMT

AT HITCHIN, SEVENTEEN MILES southeast of Cardington, Mrs. Shane Leslie, wife of a well-known writer, heard the servants screaming and ran out of the house into the rain. R101 was coming up the mushroom field directly at her, lighting up the whole house with a ghastly glare. As the red and green tail lights moved away, an inexplicable horror descended on her household.

Overhead in R101's aft engine car, the oil pressure reading had dropped and Arthur Bell had shut the engine down. It was started up again as Bell went off duty and Joe Binks, on the eight o'clock watch, relieved him.

Watched by thousands, the airship droned on toward the vast smudge of lights that marked London. She passed over New Barnet while the clock was striking the hour—very low, white light on her nose, navigation lights on her shoulders.

The oil gauge in the aft car again showed falling pressure. Engineer Short, first engineer Gent, and Leech, the engineer officer, descended into the car and shut down the engine at exactly the same time as Atkins, the wireless operator, tapped out in Morse: *Over London. All well. Moderate rain. Base of low cloud 1500 feet. Wind 240 degrees 25 mph. Course now set for Paris. Intend to proceed via Tours, Toulouse and Narbonne.*

On only four engines, R101 continued south. In the forward port car William King was standing beside the gasoline tank of the starter engine, looking out of the small window. They should be about over Bodiam now, and he was trying to work out from the scattering of lights over the dark countryside where it lay.

Bodiam was green and cool and quiet. Bodiam was where he had spent his childhood. The eldest of seven children, he had been brought up by his grandparents there.

He saw a town over on his left now, its lights blurred by rain. They were flying low. He caught sight of a river.

His sister Winifred used to come and stay during her school holidays. They picked wild watercress and searched for plovers' eggs to cook and eat.

He had a feeling the town wasn't Bodiam. Below was a road, and he could see the twin beams of a car. Soon R101 would overtake those lights. But as he watched, he saw them draw well ahead, the rear lights becoming twin pricks of red . . . and then nothing. He now recognized the town. It was Sevenoaks, about twenty miles north of Bodiam—they *must* be flying slow.

Back in the aft engine car the engineers were still too busy to look out of the windows.

Rolling and pitching under the cloud base, still on four engines and with the head wind increasing, R101 flew even slower and lower.

October 4, 1930   *2230 British Summer Time*
2130 GMT

LAWRENCE KIRBY OF Berwick House, Fairlight, saw the airship begin to cross the English Channel about 10:30 p.m., making little headway against the strong wind and drifting sideways. As she passed out to sea, with her nose south, he reported having sight of her below the level of the Channel cliffs. A Hastings fisherman thought her so low that he nearly telephoned the Eastbourne lifeboat.

In R101's tiny wireless cabin Chief Operator S. T. Keeley was sending a message given him by Johnston. *Crow (four engines running). At 2135 GMT crossing coast in vicinity of Hastings. It is raining hard and there is a strong southwesterly wind.*

In the aft car Binks, Gent, Short and Leech were still all cramped together. Isolated in that metal cell of unaccustomed quiet, reeking of diesel oil, they were conscious of nothing except the stopped engine.

Rigger Rudd was halfway up the ladder into the bowels of the ship,

inspecting the gasbags for leaks and looking at the seating of the valves. The galley boy, Megginson, chosen out of five hundred applicants, was placing the cold meat on plates for dinner, and handing up surreptitious cups of cocoa to the crew.

In the port amidships car below, engineer A. J. Cook could see the big white tongues of spume blowing back toward land. We're low, he thought. Not more than seven hundred feet, less than our length.

The electrician Disley walked down the now swaying corridor to have a word with the operator on watch in the wireless cabin. All the lights had suddenly gone out after leaving London. It had only been the circuit breaker, but the incident had unsettled him.

Below in the control car he caught sight of the height coxswain at the elevator wheel, with Atherstone, the officer of the watch, standing beside him. Behind was the shadowy figure of navigator Johnston with his eye to the drift sight.

Perhaps it was the grouping of the three figures. Or perhaps it was the gloom down there punctuated by the phosphorescent spark of the needle on the big tilt indicator—reading three degrees nose up just then. But he sensed a tension, an echo of his own feelings in the sudden darkness. The altimeter read nine hundred feet.

Then he saw Atherstone grab the wheel from the height coxswain and wind it back, saying, "Don't let her go below a thousand feet!"

Behind Atherstone, Johnston adjusted the drift sight and peered down the eyepiece. Not a sign of a light float! Either they were in a cloud or there was so much rain and moisture around that it was misting up the lenses. No point staying here. He had to find some indication of their drift, and the only place to do that was the lonely observation post completely aft. He threw two flares down the chute. Then, climbing up the metal rungs from the control car, he made his way along the corridor, past the smoking room and the crew quarters, past the engine cars, on and on, clambering up into the tapering tail cone, past the elevator fins and the base of the giant rudder out into the tiny aft lookout—a tight metal cup connected to the vast ellipse of the airship.

This was where he would come with his sextant to shoot the stars. No good trying to get an astro-fix tonight! Hair blowing right back over his head, rain stinging his eyes, navigator Johnston took stock of his tiny world.

The storm was worse. Solid overcast above. Seven hundred feet below, a thousand whitecaps were being whipped by the wind. Ahead of him the propeller of the aft car was still stopped. In the glow from the red and green navigation lights he could see the silver envelope weeping with water. R101 was crabbing to port, sixteen degrees at least—he spotted the muzzy blobs of the flares in the dark water behind them. And they were crawling along—not more than twenty-five miles an hour.

Looking down at the raging sea, Johnston suddenly thought of Hinchliffe.

October 4, 1930   *0000 British Summer Time*
2300 GMT

THE WATCH CHANGED. The engineers and riggers gulped down cocoa and sandwiches and then slithered along the oily companionway to their positions. In the aft car, where Scott had now joined Gent, Short and Leech in trying to get the engine started, Bell relieved Binks.

While his fellow rigger went off, Samuel Church took up the forward station, inspecting the valves and gasbags, control wires and fuel lines. He peered down the open hatches at the furious sea not very far below, as the relieving engineers scrambled down to their engine cars.

The low which that morning had made its first appearance on the Cardington weather map over the eastern Atlantic had deepened. As R101 struggled through the rain with one engine still out, the storm had begun racing up the English Channel toward her. French fishing boats turned back to port at Le Havre and Dieppe. A wind twice the speed of the original forecast caught the tops of the waves and sent them crashing down in long white arrowheads of spume.

But guilefully as a poker player, the storm played its cards cleverly. The wind died down. The rain stopped. The cloud ceiling rose. There was even a glimpse of the moon ringed by a halo through thin gray cirrus.

R101 stopped rolling. The chattering of the gas valves ceased.

Back in the aft car the senior engineers at last got the engine working, wiped the sweat off their faces, said good night to Bell. As they climbed thankfully up the ladder back into the envelope, they could see the lights of France, diamond-bright ahead.

So could the distinguished passengers looking out the dining room windows.

"A historic sight, gentlemen." Lord Thomson thrust back his chair, tossed his napkin on the table and stood staring down through the windows of the dining room. These windows were cunningly designed to give a view across the intervening promenade deck to the terrain below. In this case it was the coast of France, the flashing beam of the lighthouse near Pointe de Saint-Quentin, and the indentation, silvery in the intermittent moonlight, that was the estuary of the Somme. "We have crossed the French coast," Thomson went on. "The first time a British passenger-carrying airship has flown to Europe. This will not go unrecognized"—he paused—"either by history or by this government."

"Shall you take coffee here or in the smoking room?" Colmore asked him. He found the hint that honors were in store for them so pleasant he could not respond to it adequately.

"In the smoking room, of course! We shall have a final cigar, I suggest, and then turn in. It has been an exciting and splendid day. But we shall have a tiring schedule in Egypt."

Trooping after Lord Thomson into the metal-lined smoking room on the deck below, Sir Sefton Brancker felt a return of the queasiness that had bedeviled him all through his flying career. The champagne had eased his airsickness a little, but the thought of sitting amid cigar smoke was not greatly to his liking. The Channel crossing had made him feel ill as well as apprehensive. He had half hoped that the loss of the engine would favor their return. The great dirigible had rolled more like an underkeeled hulk, and the whitecaps had looked dangerously close. There had been some nasty moments.

But as they grouped around the great man in the smoking room, R101 seemed to have found her element. The weather was steadier.

"You may compliment the chef on the dinner, Scottie." Lord Thomson cut a cigar. "The Inverness salmon was excellent." So had been the hors d'oeuvres, the cold saddle of lamb, the peach melba, the mushroom savory. He sniffed brandy out of a great balloon glass and ran his finger over its winged emblem.

"I'm particularly happy that you"—he turned to O'Neill—"should arrive in India by this splendid means. As deputy director of civil aviation, the experience is invaluable."

He expounded to O'Neill about his own plans for air links with India. They talked about the huge airship mast that had been built at Drigh Road airport near Karachi, and the shed which was even larger than Cardington's.

Though Brancker had served longer than O'Neill in India, he was somehow excluded from the conversation.

"They had rotten luck building that mast," Brancker cut in. "Several workmen fell to their death."

"The price of progress," Thomson said curtly. "Luck doesn't come into it. We make our own luck."

Then, having snubbed Brancker, Thomson turned to the others, once more benign and good-humored. He appeared to have taken a liking to O'Neill, and spoke again to him, smiling expansively. "I'd like you to send your wife a goodwill message from us all."

O'Neill colored with embarrassed pleasure. "She would be delighted, sir."

"Go and do it now, man!"

"I'll come with you," Brancker offered.

He was glad to get away from the fumes of the smoking room. The catwalk was cooler, and tiny stabs of light could be seen from the dark countryside below. Certainly they were in more stable air now. The crew and the airship seemed to have shaken down together. He began to envisage the excitement of their arrival in India.

In the wireless cabin Atkins was sitting at the console with his headphones on.

Brancker told Atkins, "We want a message sent. Squadron Leader O'Neill will write it." He handed O'Neill a message slip from the pad which Atkins gave him, and watched him carefully pencil it out.

Brancker was thinking of Mrs. O'Neill and her pleasure at receiving it when suddenly he was reminded of Auriol Lee. He felt an acute longing to talk to her, an awesome feeling that he wasn't going to see her again. On impulse he penciled out a message to her at the Hotel Elysée, New York: *Off at last . . . blessings . . . B.*

"Shall we go back to the smoking room?" O'Neill asked.

"No, thanks. You go back." Brancker adjusted the monocle in his eye. "Being a nonsmoker, I dislike the fumes. I'll look out for a while and then turn in."

He looked out for several minutes—how long he didn't know. He wondered what all the people down there in the French villages were thinking as R101 passed overhead. Did they hear the engines, did they look up from the fertile farmlands that had once been the battlefield of the Somme?

He sighed, feeling suddenly very alone. He was too wide awake to sleep, but reluctant to return to Lord Thomson and the smoking room. He walked the few paces to Johnston's cubbyhole and pushed open the door. There was something cheering about the lights and the maps and the charts, and Johnston himself. This wasn't the first trip to India they had made together. Johnston would navigate them there if anyone could. But even as Brancker stood in the doorway, he could feel the airship begin to roll and yaw and heave again.

"Hello, Brancks." Caught in the light of the desk lamp, Johnston's face looked somehow different.

"Thought I'd just drop in, Johnnie, and say good night."

"Looks as if it might be a rough one."

"Bad forecast?"

"Not good." He pointed to the new weather map Giblett had made out. "Took us two hours to cross the Channel."

"Where are we now?"

"Abeam of Amiens."

"Amiens." Where the French plane he had almost taken had crashed. "And what's this town ahead?"

"Beauvais."

"Beauvais! We're passing over *Beauvais*?"

"That's right." Johnston turned his head around. "Why, what's the matter?"

"Nothing. *Absolutely* nothing." The ghost of a jaunty little smile crossed his face. "Just that . . . two and half years ago . . . I had a little contretemps over Beauvais."

In a sudden vivid flash he saw it all happen again: the Imperial Airways Paris–London plane dropping like a stone in sudden turbulence, passengers flying upward, ceiling damaged, people injured. He had checked with the meteorological office on landing: a down current, he had been told, on the leeward side of Beauvais ridge caused by strong westerly winds associated with unstable polar air moving quickly east from the Channel.

"Coincidence, of course . . . but the weather then was nearly the same as our forecast tonight."

October 5, 1930   *0101 British Summer Time*
                                                                   0001 GMT

OUT TO THE WORLD went Scott's reassuring wireless message: *After an excellent supper, our distinguished passengers smoked a final cigar and having sighted the French coast have now gone to bed to rest after the excitement of their leave taking. . . . Essential services are functioning satisfactorily, and the crew have settled down to watch-keeping routine.*

The weather was certainly better. In comparative peace Harry Leech and Bill Gent, after their successful efforts to start the aft engine, were having a drink and a smoke in the now empty smoking room.

Then the storm was upon them again. In the midst of the south-westerly gale the ground speed was down to just nineteen miles an hour. Back came the rain, drumming on the drenched envelope like machine-gun fire.

Heavy and storm-tossed, R101 sank lower, in spite of the efforts of the height coxswain.

At the Poix airfield the manager, Monsieur L. A. Maillet, ran out into the rain when he heard her engines. There she was over to the west, a gray wraith wreathed in wisps of cloud at no more than three hundred and fifty feet.

In the chart room Irwin asked Johnston, "What's our ground speed now?"

"I'll get a bearing from Le Bourget."

Back it came from the Paris airfield . . . three hundred and forty-five degrees true.

Johnston drew the line on the map.

"Still around twenty miles an hour."

"Winds strengthening as we approach Beauvais?"

"Yes."

Scott had said of the forecast of worsening weather received over

London, "It'll get better." The lull as they had crossed the French coast had appeared to support him. Now Irwin went down to the control car and told him, "We're crawling along."

"Probably a bad bearing."

"Doubt it." Irwin saw the height coxswain struggling with the wheel. "Oughton's having trouble maintaining height."

"It'll improve," Scott repeated.

"Or get worse." Irwin paused. "Scottie, I think we should go back."

"Go *back?*"

"With this wind behind us, we'll be home in no time. My view—"

"Get a position," Scott said curtly. "An *accurate* position."

It struck Irwin as he climbed back to the chart room that to Scott, turning back was the ultimate disgrace. Experienced, courageous, skillful and now keyed up with the euphoria of going and doing, Scott would never admit the weather had beaten him. With so much to gain by going on and so much to lose by turning back, Scott shared with Thomson the inability to see that the superior courage was sometimes in retreat.

At 0150 GMT Johnston calculated their position as one kilometer north of the landing field at Beauvais.

"Wind's well over fifty," Irwin told Scott back in the control car. "So now . . . "

"Now what?"

"Back."

"No."

Irwin drew a deep breath. "I'm the captain. I'm responsible for the ship's safety."

"No."

"Scottie, we're going back! It's my responsibility and—"

"You're wrong." Scott reached for the clip of signals sent to the ship from the ground. "Here! Look at that!"

It was the communiqué of the voyage sent worldwide from Cardington. Thinking it was simply a copy of the previous press release, Irwin hadn't spared the time to read it.

"R101 left Cardington at 1836 hours GMT . . . on the first stage of her flight to India," he now read, "under the direction of Major Scott."

Way below the list of passengers and Royal Airship Works officials was Irwin's name designated captain.

"This isn't what I agreed to," he said sharply. "It's been altered."

"Altered by Colmore. I had a word with him before we left."

"Nobody told me. The ship's safety—"

"—is my responsibility," Scott snapped. "The flight is under my direction. And I direct that our course be maintained."

Then he turned and climbed up to the chart room.

Silence settled in the control car, broken only by the rumble of shuffling gasbags and the creak of girders as the airship rolled.

The minute hand of the clock clicked toward 0200 GMT. Just before the hour, the new watch, led by Atherstone, came clattering down the ladder.

"I'll stay on watch with you," Irwin told his first officer. "Weather's worsening . . ."

At precisely the same time as he said those words, the wind vane at the Beauvais weather station swung from south to south-southwest.

October 5, 1930   *0200 GMT*

DOWN IN THE TOWN of Beauvais, the clock on Saint-Etienne Church was just striking two.

Monsieur Woillez, hearing the engine of R101, woke his children. They went to the windows and saw the lights of the airship passing behind the cathedral spire. The wind was blowing in squalls and the airship seemed in difficulty, flying slowly and turning to the left.

Out for a night's poaching, Monsieur Rabouille, an employee at the local button factory, was just setting up his rabbit traps among the trees of the Bois des Coutumes when he heard engines rumbling above him.

Louis Tillier, a shepherd in the clover field at Bongenoult, heard them too. The door of his hut was halfway open, and looking out toward the woods, he saw the airship lights in a row, like the illuminated windows of a passing train.

As HIS MATE CAME in through the hatch of the forward port engine car, William King took out his watch, opened it up and said, "Bang on time. Thanks!"

The watch was a gold one that had been presented to him and

others of the R33 crew by a government grateful for the safe return of this breakaway airship after its thirty-hour battering by North Sea gales. In the back he kept his postage stamps—those left after sending a postcard of R101's dining room to his parents in Tonbridge on Friday with the message *Shall see you soon.*

As King climbed out, a blast of cold wet air greeted him. He hurried up the ladder into the ship and along the companionway to the washroom. After running cold water into a bowl, he took off his jacket and doused his hot face.

In the starboard midships car, Victor Savory had taken over for A. C. Hasting, while on the port side, A. J. Cook had relieved Robert Blake. Revolutions were eight hundred and twenty-five per minute, oil pressure fifty pounds in, seventy-one out—everything normal.

Except for Bell in the aft car, all the engineers had been relieved.

October 5, 1930   *0201 GMT*

"COME ON, JOE!" engineer Short was shouting. "You're late!"

Warm in his sleeping bag, Binks opened his eyes reluctantly.

All around him men were scrambling into trousers and canvas shoes. Through a haze of sleep Binks remembered their trouble. "How's our engine?"

"Okay now," Short told him. "But hurry!"

The floor was crowded with jostling bodies as the galley boy came in with a tray of sandwiches and cocoa.

"No room to swing a cat!" Binks grumbled. He untangled his feet from his sleeping bag and jumped down. His mouth was dry.

He shuddered. "Cheese sandwiches again!" Around him men of the previous watch were clambering into warm bunks their mates had just vacated.

Binks took a mouthful of cocoa, feeling it warm and sweet in his mouth, before going out into the corridor. R101 was rolling. He could hardly keep his balance as he made the long walk to the rear. Halfway along he passed Squadron Leader F. M. Rope keeping an eye on the snuffling gasbags and the chattering valves.

When he reached the aft hatch, Binks swung himself out onto the steel ladder and began descending.

Rain stung his face. Wind tore at his jacket. Close by his right shoulder the big propeller whirled.

Looking down, he thought: We're low. Street lamps, headlights, a spire, shadowy roofs—quite a big town just below him.

Two more rungs, then he felt the warmth of the engine car through the soles of his canvas shoes. Breathless and thankful, he crept in.

"Binks," Bell shouted at him above the noise of the engines, "you're late!"

"Only a few minutes," Binks yelled back at him.

The reek of hot engine oil was overpowering.

"Suffocated! Deafened! Thirsty! Hungry! Binks, you have a nerve!"

"You fuss about nothing, Arthur."

"Nothing! I tell you this, Binks—"

"Pressures okay?"

"Pressures are fine. It's you—"

"Temperatures okay?"

"Temperatures fine. It's you—"

There was a sudden lurch forward.

Binks tried to grab a stanchion and missed. Bell fell against the starting engine.

"What the hell . . . ?"

October 5, 1930   *0206 GMT*

LYING IN HIS BUNK beside the electrical panel, Disley felt himself slipping forward.

In the smoking room Harry Leech watched glasses and a soda siphon slide down the table onto the floor.

Resting at last in the crew room rigger Radcliffe was flung off his bunk.

Forward in the nose Samuel Church was just coming off watch when R101 suddenly nose-dived and the companionway seemed to give way under him.

Standing beside Atherstone at the back of the control car, Irwin grabbed the wheel from the height coxswain and spun it backward.

"Hunt!" he called to the chief coxswain. "Release forward ballast!"

"Aye, aye, sir!"

"And release ballast here!"

But the experienced Hunt was already pulling the release toggles on the panel.

Creeping relentlessly downward, the needle on the altimeter indicated seven hundred, six hundred fifty, six hundred . . .

Limp and lifeless, the ship sagged, not responding to the wheel. Searching for the cause, Irwin glanced forward, then aft to the dark underbelly.

"Hunt . . . Atherstone! *Look!*"

But both had already seen. Both *knew*.

Even as the steering coxswain at the nose reported reassuringly, "She's leveling, sir!" Hunt was racing up the ladder from the control car, two rungs at a time, calling out, "We're down, lads!"

"WE'RE DOWN, LADS!"

Sky Hunt's stentorian bellow echoed again and again down the lower deck.

In his cubbyhole Disley could hear the chief coxswain calling. Yet everything now seemed perfectly normal. The ship had resumed the horizontal, had even begun to climb.

In the smoking room Harry Leech got up, picked up the siphon and glasses from the floor and put them back on the table.

The next moment glasses and siphon were again swept off. Again the nose went down, this time more steeply. The ringing of engine telegraphs echoed through the ship, and Sky Hunt still roared out his warning, "We're down, lads!"

The captain's message to release the half ton of forward water ballast had found Samuel Church just going off watch. Immediately Church turned around and went back to the nose. Steeper and steeper R101 dived. Panting, sweating, gasping, Church had to cling to the stanchions at the side of the catwalk to keep himself from falling. But still he fought his way forward toward the nose ballast tank.

He had almost reached it when he felt under him the slightest impact. The ship shuddered, gave a little jump, then crunched quite softly to earth.

Church could hear the cracking of girders like fir trees falling. Then there was a *whoof.*

Suddenly a white sheet of flame enveloped him.

October 5, 1930   *0210 GMT*

IN THE WASHROOM engineer King could hear above the roar and crackle of the flames the sound of many feet running desperately up and down, as men struggled to find a place to get out of the airship. When he tried to join them, the washroom door jammed. He was trapped inside.

He banged his hands frantically against the burning walls, yelled for someone to try to free the door. But another explosion like a rumble of thunder drowned his voice. Sweat was pouring into his eyes. There seemed to be no air to breathe.

Using his shoulder like a battering ram, he shoved against the scorching hot walls. Then suddenly the walls were in flames. Liquid fire, like burning candle wax, dripped all around him. His only escape was through the furnace. Shielding his face with his right arm, he rushed out head down. He stumbled unseeingly over girders, ducked under a red-hot stanchion, jumped down through a blazing hole. Something ripped at his arm, red hot or cold he didn't know. He put out his other arm to steady himself, and clutched a bunch of sodden hazel leaves.

That same small hazel tree cushioned the desperate fall of Harry Leech. Realizing he had to fight his way out of the smoking room or be roasted alive, he had seized anything that came to hand to try to smash in the bulkhead. He cursed the metal lining of the room, scrabbling at it desperately with his nails. A thinner piece of the partition began to give way. Smoke poured in, then sheets of fire. But he had got out somehow and made it into the hull on the starboard side.

Everywhere were smoke and flames and the stink of burning. Everywhere he heard screams.

He was just thinking he was trapped in the hull when, not caring what was on the other side, he hurled himself through blazing windows onto the wet tree. His hair was singed and his face and arms were burned, but he staggered to his feet and rushed around to see if there was anyone else alive.

Engineer Cook was alive in the port midships engine car. He had stopped his engine as soon as he had seen the ground rushing up. He managed to get out immediately after the explosion. The white light of it almost blinded him. He had a momentary sight of Irwin heroically at his post giving orders, "making no attempt to save himself," Cook afterward said, before a sheet of flame enveloped the control car.

Flames were on the point of enveloping Binks and Bell in the aft car. Bell had just obeyed the urgent ringing of the telegraph and reduced speed to four hundred and fifty rpm when the crash came. Bumping along the ground as R101 telescoped, the car bottom caved in. The engine stopped. The light went out. But they needed no lights. The whole interior was illuminated by the blazing inferno. Flames were licking around the car, around the door, advancing toward the gasoline tank for the starter motor.

"If that goes up, we're done for, Joe!" Helplessly, they began stamping on the flames. Open the door and they knew they would explode in a puff of smoke.

"It's all up with us anyway, Bell."

Now they realized smoke was all they had to breathe. The burning hydrogen was consuming all the oxygen. Sweat ran down their faces. Their eyes stung. Their limbs felt heavy. Bell gasped to Binks, "We're suffocating."

"Better than being roasted, Bell."

"So R101 wouldn't catch fire, eh Binks?" As they stamped with increasing feebleness on the flames, and a pointed yellow flame licked at the already warm gasoline tank, Binks said, "This is our lot."

Bell nodded.

Solemnly and with great finality they shook hands. Binks thought of his parents in Sheffield, of his friends in Betsy's bar. Then, in what was to seem forever afterward to be the miracle of his life, water poured down over his head. A few drops at first, then a cascade deluging the top of the car as a ballast bag burst in the disintegrating carcass above them.

The flames hissed down. The smoke thinned. A way of escape was opened for them.

After pausing a moment to press rags soaked in the downpour over their faces, Bell and Binks leaped clear to help find their comrades in the howling inferno.

HELP WAS ALREADY on its way. From Beauvais, from surrounding villages, from lonely farmsteads. A British racehorse owner, George Darling, and his friend, the musician Marcel Debeaupuix, were setting out on an early shoot, and had been admiring the sight of the airship. Then had come the terrible explosion and the column of flames shooting up into the sky. They jumped immediately into the musician's car and Debeaupuix stepped on the accelerator. Guided by the soaring flames, he left the road for the last half mile and went bucketing over the fields. They passed villagers carrying lanterns hurrying toward the crash, and were the first to reach the scene.

To Leech and Binks and Bell, who were staggering among the red-hot girders, the flaps of burning fabric, the black smoke, the stench of burning flesh, their ears filled with the screams of their friends, the arrival of the auto was the continuation of a miracle. They had been joined by Disley, who had managed to trip one of the electric circuits as the airship crashed. Between them they had dragged Radcliffe clear, obviously badly injured.

Now here were Darling and Debeaupuix. Joans of Arc, Binks called them in his report. He christened Darling "Strong Man," and referred to him ever after as that. "Cannot speak too highly of him."

Shoving red-hot debris aside, they ran in and out of the fire searching and calling. The villagers had arrived, and the flames were ringed now by their bobbing lanterns. The wind flung the great column of flames from side to side like some huge tree. The rain still poured down, powerless against the heat of the burning hydrogen, gasoline and oil. With the rain, like leaves, fell white-hot debris flung up by the explosion.

Savory, from the starboard midships engine car, was found staggering helplessly. Villagers swept him off to the Catholic hospital. Church was found by Debeaupuix. The Frenchman realized he was seriously injured, made him comfortable in the back seat of his car and drove him straight to a private hospital.

King was about to be taken to the same hospital. A middle-aged Frenchwoman was helping him. His face was badly burned and there was a deep gash across his arm. Before getting into the woman's car, he turned to take a last look at the airship. He saw a human figure staggering in the heart of the flames. King ran from the car back into the fire. He did not return.

Nor did anyone else come out of the flames. Disley hurried off to find a telephone and tell the Air Ministry of the disaster. Reluctantly the others went to the Beauvais hospital. The villagers were joined by gendarmes and men of the 51st French Infantry stationed at Beauvais. The restive neighing of horses, disquieted by the smell of fire and the flicker of dying flames, replaced the human screams and the roar of the fire. Now they searched not for survivors but for bodies.

Most were burned beyond recognition. Nearly all had their fists clenched and some had their arms bent. A village priest chanted a Miserere over each. The searchers found a few personal possessions. Watches, all but one stopped at 2:09. W. H. King's watch, inscribed by a grateful government in honor of the R33 crew, was still going. And the postage stamps at the back were still perfect, even though his body had been found in the heart of the fire.

Perfect, too, was the silver slipper in the brassbound trunk.

And a monocle. Fire had come as predicted for Sir Sefton Brancker. And at Beauvais, in a storm.

October 5, 1930   *0215 GMT*

AT THE BUNGALOW ON Putnoe Road Olive Irwin sat in her dressing gown, watching the last flames in the sitting room fireplace die away. The confident all's-well midnight message from R101 had been telephoned through to her. She felt only slightly easier in her mind, though she tried to pretend to her guests that she was reassured.

"You get some sleep," she had told her sister and brother-in-law. "I'm going to bed presently."

But she had been reluctant even to try to sleep. It was as if she ought to keep watch. As if in some way she could help keep Bird safe by watching and waiting.

Suddenly she heard the chimes of Bedford Church, and remembered she had not put back the clock for the end of Summer Time. As she opened the clock face to turn the hour hand, she was pierced with a sense of loss so certain and grievous that she subsided into the chair again and sat for minutes with her face covered in her hands, all thoughts of sleep and rest completely gone.

Few of the wives slept that night. In her red-brick house half a mile from the Airship Works, Mrs. Short was unable to quiet her young son, who kept crying for his father.

Over at Kempston Mrs. Atherstone fell into an uneasy sleep only to be wakened by the howling of her husband's Alsatian. It was a terrible sound, underlining the sob of the rising wind. She tried to comfort herself with the thought that sometimes dogs howled at the full moon, but stroking his quivering neck, seeing his manifest distress, she knew that was not the cause.

Like Mrs. Irwin, she kept repeating to herself the soothing message from R101 that had been phoned to all the officers' wives. She lifted the receiver now with the idea of telephoning to see if there was any further message, and then decided against it.

In the guardroom the duty watchman had dozed off in front of his coke stove, happy that the airship was safely on her way. A middle-aged man, he had known years of unemployment, and like so many thousands of other Bedfordians, his security was bound up with R101. He woke in an unaccountable sweat. The stove had died down and the room was cold. He had the feeling he had heard some tremendous noise, an explosion like thunder. But he must have dreamed it, for the night was quiet, except for the gusting of the wind.

Yet some sound had wakened him. He sat for a moment listening. Then he identified it: the insistent click of the switchboard signaling that someone was trying to make an outgoing call. His first feeling was of relief. He swung his chair around to plug in the call. Then his relief turned to dismay, as he saw the signal came from Flight Lieutenant Irwin's office—the office he knew would be kept empty and locked till the captain returned.

October 5, 1930   *0300 GMT*

THE TELEPHONE SHRILLED at the Air Ministry.

"R101 has crashed in flames near Beauvais. Nearly everybody has been killed. This is Disley, the electrician."

Dean, the duty officer, could just make out the anguished words on the line from Beauvais. He reached for the Emergency Instructions, and called 10 Downing Street.

"This is the duty officer, Air Ministry. I'm sorry to disturb you at this time in the morning, but I regret to say R101 has crashed in France."

The Prime Minister was informed. His sorrow was manifest and heartfelt. At dinner a few hours previously, he had confessed his uneasiness for R101 and admitted that his apprehensions would "not be set at rest until I know for a fact that the great airship has safely arrived in India."

Dean then called Cabinet ministers, members of the Air Council, high officials at the Air Ministry.

The French wireless was sending out the news all over the world. The telephone lines from Beauvais to London were jammed with calls. A priority call from the gendarmerie reached Dean. Immediately he sent the information to Cardington: *Ship lost, seven survivors.* (This information was not entirely accurate, for at this point there were eight survivors.)

Fifteen minutes later Squadron Leader Booth, captain of R100 and Irwin's close personal friend, was apprised of the news and asked to report immediately to Cardington.

Ismailia, feverishly preparing for the day's splendid doings, had been informed by priority signal. So had Karachi. The lights blazing in the offices at Cardington had started rumor of the disaster speeding around the town. Shadowy figures began hurrying up the hill. Groups of wives in dressing gowns waited at the gates like women at a fishing village after a ship has been lost.

Deeply distressed, Booth waited in an office at the Royal Airship Works hoping against hope for news of more survivors. He thought of those brave comrades, many of whom had served with him. Of Johnston, Scottie, Atherstone. Of Potter, who had also survived the breakup of R38; of King, who was so inordinately proud of that presentation watch. And of Irwin, of course.

Booth stood up. It was getting toward dawn and nothing more had come through. When Olive heard the news, it must be from him.

After stopping to pick up his wife, he drove to Putnoe Road and brought the car to a halt some yards short of the entrance to the

Irwins' bungalow. Hoping to break the news gently, the Booths tiptoed up the drive and tapped on the window of the guest room.

Whispering that they brought bad news, they asked Olive's sister to meet them at the front door. Rounding the corner of the bungalow, however, they saw that the front door was already open, and that a dressing-gowned figure stood framed in the glass porch.

Characteristically, Olive seemed almost sorry for them. Gently, she put her hand on Lily Booth's arm. "Please . . . don't worry. And don't tell me. I know. I have known for certain since just after two."

October 5, 1930   *0602 GMT*

FIRST LIGHT AT BEAUVAIS illuminated what looked like a gigantic carcass of a dinosaur picked clean of flesh by vultures. R101 lay on the brow of the ridge, her nose in a little wood, still fitfully burning. Wisps of smoke rose steadily from the skeleton and the ground around was churned into a mass of mud. Bits of gilded promenade deck hung down from her girders. The staircase that had once led up to the grand lounge now led up to nothing. Half the electric oven lay in a shambles of broken metal. The only signs of the seventeen gasbags were the chain harnesses to hold them in place; the big round valves that "chattered" too often when the ship rolled—Irwin's nightmare—still hung on the latticework. Pieces of blue and gold crockery, cutlery, broken cups and glass littered the burned grass.

Only R101's flag was relatively unscathed. It still flew over the wreck, its blue cotton stiff in the breeze, the RAF emblem clearly visible. Captain Wilson, the *Daily Mail* pilot who flew a reporter and a photographer to Beauvais, said to one of the gendarmes, "I am a British officer. I claim the Royal Air Force flag." It was handed over to the British air attaché in Paris, and later put on the altar at Saint Paul's for the memorial service.

In the wood, covered in white sheets brought by the villagers, forty-six bodies lay in rows. French soldiers were trying to identify them. Little piles of blackened belongings—keys, money, watches—had been placed beside them, together with flowers the women of Beauvais had brought. Some of the women had lit candles. Sisters of Mercy kept an all-night vigil of prayer.

An all-night vigil was also kept by the bedsides of those who had escaped. Together in one ward of the Catholic hospital were seven of the survivors. Cook's eyes could be seen staring out from his bandaged head. Beside him, Radcliffe was asleep. In the private hospital, Church lay unconscious.

An Air Ministry investigation team led by Air Commodore F. V. Holt and including Ralph Booth and F. M. McWade, the Cardington inspector, flew to Beauvais that morning.

Cardington was a ghost town. The curtains of all the houses were tightly drawn. Dispatch riders on motorbikes roared around the silent roads bringing their dreaded news.

The families of the two critically injured survivors were preparing to go to their bedsides. Mrs. Radcliffe was arranging for someone to look after her two children. Church's father, and the rigger's fiancée, Irene Capon of Bedford, were planning to go to Henlow to board an airplane for France.

Arthur Bell's wife had gone to the house of Mrs. Short and was trying to comfort her.

Some families, made desperate by the lack of detailed information, joined the crowds besieging the offices of the Bedfordshire *Standard*. Through the Bedford streets marched the Salvation Army Band playing the "Dead March" from *Saul*.

Major and Mrs. Villiers had been informed of the tragedy. They were deeply grieved, but not surprised. They had left the Airship Works the previous night unhappy and puzzled, worried about the way R101 had dipped her nose as she slipped the mast, about the rising wind and the weather. For hours after he heard of the disaster, Villiers kept hoping that Brancker would be among the survivors. But a telephone call to the Air Ministry in London told him that his friend's body was among those recovered.

October 5, 1930   *1000 GMT*

THE WHOLE COUNTRY MOURNED. Everywhere in London flags were flying at half mast—down Whitehall and in the Strand and Kingsway and above government offices and foreign legations. Ironically, the squally wet and windy weather had disappeared. The calmer weather served only to emphasize the gloom and shock felt in the capital. Newsboys carried posters lettered in thick black, R101 DISASTER. They shouted out their wares: "Pictures! Read all about it! Mystery of R101."

The Sunday *Dispatch*, whose first edition had described the successful departure and the sight of the airship over London as being like a pale gray ghost merging with the sky, had by evening brought out another edition, thick with mourning black.

R101 was on everyone's tongue. From many a pulpit the sermon was about the sacrifice made by the brave men on board. The bishop of London said, "Those who have perished were among the bravest and best men in England." At the Temple Church, Canon Carpenter said, "The fact that they died like heroes does not take away the sorrow of their friends, but it touches that sorrow and that sacrifice with the glory of the supernatural world."

It was to that supernatural world that at least one friend of the crew turned for comfort that afternoon. Emilie Hinchliffe had not been able to get Johnston out of her mind since the news had come over the wireless. She kept going over what she ought to have said to warn him instead of what she actually had said. If only she could have persuaded him, convinced him as she herself was convinced, that she was in communication with her husband, then Johnnie would be alive today.

Sadly, the very fate of R101 was abundant proof to any doubters that messages could come from beyond the grave. So distressed was she by Johnnie's fate that she couldn't bear to buy a paper. She sat staring out unseeingly as the bus took her to her appointment with the medium Eileen Garrett.

Mrs. Garrett lived in a big Victorian brick house at 13B Roland Gardens, South Kensington, with her daughter and an Irish maid called Minnie. Stone steps led up from a checkerboard pavement to the front door. Mrs. Garrett's apartment on the first floor contained three small bedrooms and a large attractive living room, with the walls painted a gold sunset color. On each side of the fireplace were wall lights of half bowls of alabaster. Grapes flowed over the top, through which the light reflected soft patterns on the ceiling.

When Mrs. Garrett opened the door she greeted Emilie without a smile, and when Emilie opened her mouth to say something about

R101, Mrs. Garrett shook her head fiercely. Without preamble she sat down in a chair, her eyes staring through the window, her feet crossed, her hands lying loosely on the arms of the chair.

The seconds ticked by. Then Mrs. Garrett lifted her right hand, pinched her nostrils, and began breathing through her mouth. Each breath became louder and harsher, as she sank into a trance. Very slowly her right hand dropped to the arm of the chair, her eyes closed.

Almost at once the voice of her spirit guide, Uvani, began speaking, but before he had time to do more than identify himself, he was brushed aside by the well-known cadences of Hinch.

"Will you believe me?" asked Hinch's voice. Then in bitter, helpless anger, "They had their doubts themselves. That damned job could not stand up under air pressure and currents, and was caught and had to battle for two hours against the elements. If I, not heavily loaded . . . could not stand up against what I met, what the devil could they expect? . . . They had their meteorological chart. I do blame them. No right to take chances. From beginning to end they had trouble, before they put off, but on account of public opinion they did not turn back."

October 6, 1930 *1200 GMT*

SURVIVING BUT IN CRITICAL condition, the rigger Radcliffe was too badly burned to make a statement. On Monday his wife, just about to leave for Beauvais, was told that he had died.

The weather was too bad for Mr. Church and Irene Capon to fly from Henlow, so they went by train and boat to Beauvais. At the hospital a nun took their hands and told them sadly that Samuel Church had died.

October 7, 1930 *1000 GMT*

THE DESTROYERS *Tribune* and *Tempest* were sent to Boulogne through stormy seas to pick up the remaining six survivors and the bodies. On Tuesday morning in the square at Beauvais the French

Premier and air minister and thirty thousand people assembled to see the procession of twenty-four carts, each carrying two flower-decked coffins. Bell, Binks and Leech, still in their coveralls, walked behind the carts to the railway station. There was a salute of one hundred and one guns. Forty-eight French Air Force planes flew in formation overhead as the procession made its way to the train which would take the coffins to Boulogne.

The Channel crossing was again stormy. It was dark by the time the destroyers docked. The Air Force guard of honor presented arms.

The next morning the Prime Minister of England would wait, gray-faced, on the platform of Victoria Station with ten thousand others to receive his friend Lord Thomson and the other dead of R101.

October 7, 1930   *1500 GMT*

THE DEAD OF R101 WERE not on the mind of Ian Coster, assistant editor of *Nash's* magazine, as he kept an appointment for a séance with Eileen Garrett. Coster was curious to discover if Sir Arthur Conan Doyle, who had died in July, would be able to communicate from the Other Side, as he had promised to try to do.

Mrs. Garrett had been recommended to Coster as a woman of great integrity by the well-known debunker of mediums Harry Price. She had agreed to a séance with Coster, with Price himself and his secretary, Ethel Beenham, present.

Eileen Garrett was not told the purpose of Coster's visit, nor did she know his profession or his interests.

The session began.

Mrs. Garrett talked in a strangely accented voice: "It is Uvani, I give you greetings, friends. Peace be with you and in your life and in your household."

At first there was no sign of Sir Arthur Conan Doyle, and Price had warned Coster that he must not prompt. Then, abruptly, Mrs. Garrett became obviously distressed. Her face contorted, her eyes opened, filled with tears.

"I see . . . ," said the voice of Uvani, "I see someone called . . . Irvin . . . no, he says . . . not Irving . . . Irwin . . . he spells it: I–R–W–I–N."

Then the entity, or whatever it was taking over, said very faintly as if from a distance, "Irwin."

Coster leaned forward, as the secretary was doing, to catch every word that fell from Eileen Garrett's lips. There followed a jumble of sentences spoken by a rather faint voice in great distress. "Must do something about it . . . apologize for coming . . . the whole bulk of the dirigible was entirely too much for her engine capacity."

The voice got stronger, as if mastering an unfamiliar mode of speaking: "Engines too heavy. Useful lift too small. Gross lift computed badly. . . . And this idea of new elevators totally mad. Elevator jammed. Oil pipe plugged."

Astonished, Coster heard the technical jargon that meant little to him fall naturally from Eileen Garrett's lips. Yet it no longer seemed to be a woman who was talking. The voice was staccato, male and fervent, nothing like Mrs. Garrett's.

"Flying too low altitude and could never rise. Disposable lift could not be utilized. Load too great for long flight. Cruising speed bad and ship badly swinging. Severe tension on the fabric, which is chafing."

The voice paused. In the silence the listeners held their breaths, totally absorbed. Coster didn't know the language of aviation, but he was sure that whoever was speaking did.

"Cannot rise. Never reached cruising altitude. Same in trials. Too short trials. No one knew the ship properly. Airscrews too small. Cooling system bad. Bore capacity bad. Fuel injection bad. Did not allow mixture to get to engine. Backfired. Pressure and heat produced explosion. Three times before starting. Not satisfied with feed. Already a meeting, but feel desirous to push off and set our course.

"Fabric all waterlogged and ship's nose down. Impossible to rise. Cannot trim. Two hours tried to rise, but elevator jammed. Almost scraped the roofs at Achy. Kept to railway. At inquiry to be held later, it will be found that the superstructure of the envelope contained no resilience, had far too much weight. . . . I knew then that this was not a dream but a nightmare. The added middle section was entirely wrong . . . made strong but took resilience away and entirely impossible. Too heavy and too much overweighted for the capacity of the engines."

For several minutes Coster and Price were hardly aware that Mrs. Garrett was silent and that her breathing rhythm had changed, her face become less tormented. Both were absorbed in their own thoughts, while Price's secretary was hurriedly finishing her shorthand.

Suddenly Mrs. Garrett spoke again. This time Coster could easily recognize Uvani's voice. "There is an elderly person here saying there is no reason in the world he should attend you, but he has here an SOS sent out five days ago. He is tall, heavy, has difficulty walking, is amusing and at times very difficult." The voice changed again, this time to an elderly tone; the diction became that of a well-educated Englishman. "Here I am. Arthur Conan Doyle. Now, how am I going to prove it to you?"

But for Coster, the case was already proved.

October 10, 1930   *1200 GMT*

NOW THAT IT WAS too late, the government could not do too much. The coffins lay in state for two days in Westminster Hall, the traditional last resting place of kings. A memorial service was held in London at Saint Paul's Cathedral at noon on Friday. It was attended by the Prince of Wales and the Duke of York, himself an officer of the Royal Air Force. Behind them stood Ramsay MacDonald and his Cabinet.

Up in the gallery were the reserve crew of R101, the crew of R100 in their blue dress uniforms, and Bell and Binks and Leech. That gray cold noontime seemed a far cry to them from the inferno of five days ago.

From where they sat, they could look down on R101's flag spread over the high altar. The black-clad relatives seated on the main floor could see it too. Mrs. Richmond kept her eyes on it as the band of the Royal Air Force played softly, mutedly, selections from Handel, Mendelssohn and Gounod. "Keep the flag flying," her husband had said. And there lay his flag now.

Beside her, Olive Irwin struggled to maintain her composure as the gentle music of the RAF band melted away. Noon chimed with awful solemnity. There was a moment's silence. Then down the aisle came the procession. At the end walked the bishop of London, and following him, the archbishop of Canterbury.

The band played the national anthem. The first verse was sung by the congregation packing the cathedral and by a second congregation waiting patiently outside. Then "I Am the Resurrection and the Life" was sung, and the hymn "Rock of Ages" and the "Twenty-third Psalm."

Most of the wives were too numbed by grief to pray for more than that they would get through the service without breaking down.

Olive Irwin tried not to think of Bird's anxiety over the airship and fixed her eyes on the exquisite colors of the dome, now intermittently lit by faint autumn sunshine. Standing to sing one of her favorite hymns, "Jesus, Lover of My Soul," she still kept her eyes upward.

> Let me to Thy bosom fly,
> While the nearer waters roll,
> While the Tempest still is high!
> Hide me, O my Saviour, hide,
> Till the storm of life is past;
> Safe into the haven guide;
> O receive my soul at last!

At the end of that verse she saw a faint movement in the dome. A pale gray bird was fluttering high above her. As she and the others watched, the pigeon flew down the nave and up again. Then, drawn by a bright beam of sunlight coming through the south window, it disappeared.

Olive felt oddly and profoundly comforted. When the archbishop stood at the high altar and pronounced the Benediction, praying in it for the preservation of "those on the pathways of the air, in their going out and their coming in," she remained dry-eyed. Bird had found his immortality.

October 11, 1930   *0130 GMT*

THAT SATURDAY THE MEN of R101 returned to Bedford. A year ago almost to the day, R101 had been triumphantly brought out of her shed for the first time and manhandled to the mooring mast, while men chased a hare across the field.

Now the gates of the cemetery were open wide to receive forty-eight coffins, destined for one vast common grave.

When the burial service was over, three rifle volleys rang out, and the trumpeters sounded the "Last Post." One minute later, from the far side of the cemetery, another band of trumpeters sounded "Taps."

Bedford had paid her last respects to her dead. But she had not forgotten or forgiven. Throughout the city there was talk of manslaughter and murder. In an agony of sadness and fury the Bedford *Record* thundered: "Bedford's indictment, in a word, is this . . . that the disaster that filled the countryside with grief and horror need not have happened. . . . R101, as reconditioned, was a new ship. . . . Her trials should have been as exhaustive as the new conditions obviously demanded. Instead, she was rushed off in a hurry to her doom. . . . Who did it?"

October 28—November 13, 1930

"WHO DID IT? Who's to blame?" Major P. L. Teed, counsel for Olive Irwin, put down his briefcase and sat beside her. "That's what the inquiry is here to find out!"

It was cold in the great hall of the Institute of Civil Engineers. Shafts of pale October sunlight slanted through the grimy windows. Sitting in the section reserved for relatives of the dead, dressed in a cloche hat and a black coat with a fur-lined collar, Olive Irwin looked out sadly at the scene below. The section was sparsely occupied because most wives were too distressed to come to the inquiry. But she, Mrs. Colmore and Mrs. Richmond were fiercely protective of their husbands' reputations. Olive had heard that they might try to blame Bird as R101's captain. Her brother-in-law had repeated Bird's account of Lord Thomson's telephone call the day before departure. She wanted to be quite sure that incidents like that would be revealed.

"The standard rule," Major Teed was saying to Mrs. Irwin, "is that the captain of a ship, like your husband, or the minister in charge of a program, like Lord Thomson, must accept the blame for actions for which they are nominally responsible."

As the clock ticked toward ten on Tuesday, October 28, 1930, the bustle in the crowded hall increased. Air Ministry officials and witnesses were crammed into one block of benches, reporters struggled for space behind them. All the seats allocated to the public were filled.

At the front of the hall Major Villiers adjusted a silver model of R101 hanging from the ceiling. Numbed by the disaster, he had worked listlessly at the Air Ministry since the crash.

Three nights before the inquiry began, Villiers had had a strange experience. Though he was not psychic, he had the layman's natural interest in the paranormal. Alone by the living room fire late at night he had had a strange feeling that someone was beside him. In his mind it was as though a voice were calling out, "For God's sake, let me talk to you." He recognized the voice as Bird Irwin's.

Next morning he told a friend who had studied psychic research. The friend arranged for him to consult a medium with an excellent reputation at 7:00 p.m. on Friday, October 31—incognito. Because of his position at the Air Ministry, it was vital that his name and the nature of his business be revealed to no one. The medium was Eileen Garrett.

The noise in the great hall subsided. Villiers made a last adjustment to the model airship.

In came Sir John Simon, president of the court, a Liberal MP as well as a highly successful lawyer.

Seated behind the desk on the dais, Sir John spoke. "What happened to R101 just after 2:00 a.m. on October 5 over Beauvais? The Crown authorities are providing all the information and papers they can. But I am asking now for any other clue that might assist us to solve the mystery, from whatever quarter it might come."

Item by item, the extraordinary history of R101 began to unfold.

"Who gave the authority to shorten that final test flight to only sixteen hours?" Sir John asked. "Surely there is a report on it?"

The attorney general rose. "Sir, there is none in existence."

In the hush of incredulity that followed, Olive Irwin leaned over and whispered into her counsel's ear, "But *surely* there must be some report?"

The silence went on and on.

Finally Major Teed rose to his feet. "Sir . . . I am informed that the captain of R101, Flight Lieutenant Irwin, kept a manifold book in which he drafted his reports to his superiors. These reports should be in existence, and the carbon copies would be left in Captain Irwin's office."

But the reports were not found.

Air Ministry letters, reports and files on the only trial flight of the altered R101 had also mysteriously disappeared.

What did emerge was Irwin's report on R101's troubles at the Hendon Air Display in June. The heaviness of the ship, the loss of gas through holes in the bags, the bad "chattering" of the gas valves, the flapping of the outer cover, even the need to fix a dining room table—all were mentioned.

"What strikes one very much," said Sir John, "is that Captain Irwin evidently gave a most detailed report of the behavior of the ship during her flights in June, and I am still very anxious to know whether there is not some material somewhere which shows how the ship behaved on the final trial flight."

Professor Leonard Bairstow, R101's aerodynamic expert, gave evidence on the large differences between design and actual construction, saying that when the gasbag wires were altered, he had asked Richmond, the designer, what would happen if a gasbag burst in the nose at the same time the ship encountered a violent downward gust. Richmond had replied that calculations on that had never been asked for in any airship.

Was the structure faulty? That was the cause first given to the press by Air Commodore Holt's investigation team after they landed at Beauvais, though the statement was subsequently retracted.

The Court immediately ruled that cause out entirely. Yet fragments of metal frame were discovered far from the crash, and part of a girder was found about a hundred yards away. And the aerodynamic experts had not had the time to examine R101 properly after her stomach operation before a Certificate of Airworthiness was issued.

Was it the elevators? American experts told Major Teed that R101's vertical control was the worst of any British airship. Since a cable was found broken, that looked like the cause until tests showed the break had occurred after the fire. Yet if that was so, why were some pieces of fabric only inches away quite unburned?

Why was the wreckage on the ground pointing southwest when the airship's course had been southeast? Had they turned to starboard in an effort to go home? Was the altimeter misreading? Their messages reported heights of one thousand and one thousand five hundred feet, yet R101 was seen from the ground flying very low.

On Friday, October 31, the survivors gave their evidence.

"What happened to you after the midships engine car struck the ground?" the attorney general asked engineer Cook.

"I tried to get out of the doorway of the car towards the ship. I found it was just one mass of flame and the heat was terrific, so I turned back to the outboard side of the car. There were two sliding doors where we could climb alongside the engine to examine the cylinder heads. . . . But . . . a girder had fallen across the opening there. . . . I thought I was completely trapped in the car. I lay down on the top of an oil tank that was there and gave things up. In a second, I must have been driven absolutely desperate, and I got up and put my hand up and pushed the girder on one side with the back of my hand. I then jumped over the side of the car and found that I had landed in some trees."

THAT FRIDAY EVENING, as he adjusted the model airship hanging from the ceiling of the great hall while different degrees of dive were reported by the survivors, Major Villiers' mind was really on his seven o'clock appointment with Eileen Garrett.

He had been asked to submit a written statement to the court of his last drive with Brancker when the director of civil aviation had related his row with Thomson. But Sir John had not asked him to testify.

Villiers arrived at 13B Roland Gardens, South Kensington, rather apprehensive, ready to take notes of what he might hear. Eileen Garrett's appearance reassured him. After explaining to so obvious a novice what might happen in the trance state and about her spirit control, Uvani, she closed her eyes and began breathing deeply.

Within minutes she was in a deep trance. But only Uvani's accented voice came through, talking of nothing Villiers could understand, going on and on. Nothing, he thought, is going to emerge from this.

And then suddenly, "Irving . . . Irwin . . ."

The accent had changed to the jerky staccato voice of the captain of R101 that he remembered so well from his visits to Cardington.

". . . one of the struts collapsed and caused a tear in the cover . . . the rush of wind caused the first dive and then we straightened again and another gust surging through the hull finished us . . . the forces she can be subjected to in bad weather and wind currents are too strong for the present system of calculations. . . ."

Certainly that made sense and was true. Villiers was not sure what "strut" meant (he was no expert on airships), but he had heard at the inquiry that a girder had been replaced during R101's trials and part of one had been found about a hundred yards from the crash.

He was so impressed he made another appointment. That Sunday, November 2, the spirits of Brancker and Scott were present and spoke of a conference before departure, of the desire to postpone the flight, of the dangerously leaking gas valves and of a cracked girder that split the outer cover.

Villiers took longhand notes as best he could, filling them out to make a coherent record the next day. He recognized undoubted mistakes and errors of fact, but he did not correct these, preferring to leave everything he wrote at the séance.

As he left Roland Gardens that November night, the sky was dark and overcast and the wind was rising.

FRENCH WITNESSES WERE brought across the Channel to give evidence. "At the time of the crash," Rabouille, the rabbit poacher, said, "there was a tempest from the west!"

No other British airship had ever encountered such weather over land. The director of the Meteorological Office at the Air Ministry now produced the weather charts of that night, which showed the low moving in over France with rapidly deteriorating weather. Weather recorders at Beauvais had recorded at about 2:00 a.m. a sudden veering of the high wind from south to southwest. "As to the question of Beauvais being a particularly bad spot for aviators," he said, "it might be of interest if I handed to the court a memo from Sir Sefton Brancker on the subject of the weather he encountered when flying over Beauvais in February 1928."

The memo read:

At about 12:30 p.m. on Saturday, February 11, I was flying from Paris to London on an "Argosy" belonging to Imperial Airways when we encountered a most exceptional down current. I estimate that the airplane fell like a stone for about two hundred feet. The ceiling was damaged by the impact of passengers flying upward, one emergency exit was torn and blown off, chairs were broken, and two passengers were slightly injured.

During the rest of the voyage we had a very heavy head wind, and the bumps were from time to time unpleasant but, generally speaking, conditions were not very bad. The weather was thick, and I am not sure of our location when this incident occurred, but it must have been in the neighborhood of Beauvais. Could you give me any meteorological explanation of this particular disturbance? I have never experienced anything quite so bad on the London–Paris service, though in the East, when flying over mountains, similar incidents are not infrequent. The sky was overcast and we were close under the clouds at about two thousand feet.

Back had come the reply: a down current on the leeward side of the Beauvais ridge, caused by strong westerly winds associated with unstable polar air quickly moving east from the Channel.

Almost the identical weather R101 had experienced.

But Sir John would have none of such aerial whirlpools. The alarming loss of ground speed to around twenty knots as R101 approached the storm passed by without comment. Weather was virtually dismissed as a primary cause.

As one factor after another was ruled out by the inquiry, Harry Price, at his National Laboratory of Psychical Research, was wondering whether Irwin's utterances through the medium Eileen Garrett might help find the cause. He knew nothing of her continuing séances with Villiers. The last thing he had heard was that she was going to America.

Useful lift, gross lift—he could guess what those terms meant, but the words would never have slipped quickly off his tongue in the right context, let alone that of a woman who had even less technical knowledge. *Engines too heavy*—reports published more than three weeks after the séance said they were nearly twice as heavy as R101's gas engines. *Elevator jammed*—the elevator cable had been reported broken, which would mean it could not work. The trials *had* been too short; there were paragraphs in the paper to that effect.

Scraping the roofs of Achy—numerous reports indicated the airship was very low. Price searched the maps of France but could find no mention of the place. Then he found it at last, a tiny railway junction near the village of Poix. Poix was where the airport manager had seen the airship struggling dangerously low in the storm.

Price sent a copy of the séance transcript to the Air Ministry, and wrote to Sir John Simon: *I have thought the matter over carefully, and I consider it my duty to acquaint you with the following facts, however bizarre you may regard them, or in fact, they may be.* He then summarized Irwin's statements delivered through Mrs. Garrett.

BUT WHY EVER HAD R101 departed in the first place, and who had authorized her departure? A memo from Lord Thomson had been read out: "I must insist on R101 being ready by the end of September, as I have made my plans accordingly."

Further evidence emphasized his obsession. R101 had flown only one hundred and twenty hours since her launching. And on several of these trips engine trouble had been experienced. The attorney general said that Lord Thomson never knew the last test had been cut short. Colmore had seen him just after the trial flight, and Thomson had asked if they could leave on the following Friday. Colmore, knowing Irwin wanted more time for his crew to rest, urged a later departure date. They finally agreed that R101 would leave on Saturday evening.

"Not one of those very experienced officers—Irwin, Scott and Colmore—suggested to Lord Thomson that it was desirable that the flight to India should be delayed or that further tests should be made," the attorney general contended.

Olive Irwin's pale face flushed and her eyes sparked with anger. She turned to her counsel. "Bird said the flight should be delayed. He told Thomson!"

Major Teed wrote to Sir John, informing him that as far as Irwin was concerned, the attorney general was wrong.

Three documents on the leaking gasbags had at last turned up: Irwin's report that hundreds of holes had been caused by chafing, a letter from Richmond to Scott putting the loss of lift at one ton per square inch of opening each twelve hours, and a letter from the Cardington maintenance inspector, Mr. F. M. McWade, addressed to the secretary of the Air Ministry stating that the points of fouling throughout the ship amounted to thousands. McWade went on to say that until a proper remedy was undertaken, he could not recommend the extension of the present permit to fly or the issue of any further permit or certificate.

McWade was called to give evidence. "What would you have done," Sir John asked him, "if it had been left to you whether the ship should have a Certificate of Airworthiness?"

"Had it been left to me, sir," McWade replied, "I'm afraid they would never have got it."

"After her trial flight on October 2, the responsibility had really passed to Flight Lieutenant Irwin, the captain, since the ship was now delivered from the Royal Airship Works?"

"Yes, sir."

"We must give due weight to that," said Sir John.

As Olive Irwin listened to these words her heart sank. They were going to divert attention away from Lord Thomson and put all the blame on Bird after all.

On the last day of the evidence she watched Ralph Booth take the stand. White-faced and drawn, he still managed to look across at her and smile.

He related that Irwin had drawn up a three-and-a-half-page list of trials to be done *after the ship received its Certificate of Airworthiness.* These included tests in the shed and on the mast occupying five days and numerous flying tests, finishing up with a flight of "forty-eight hours under adverse weather conditions to windward of base. Ship to be flown for at least six hours continuous full speed through bumpy conditions, and the rest of the flight at cruising speed."

All R101 got after the agreement to issue that certificate had been a two-hour inspection which McWade had agreed was "just a friendly visit."

Nobody would listen to Irwin—except his friend Booth, the captain of R100, and he could not influence events.

"Have you any reason to think," Sir John asked, "that after her calm-weather flight of sixteen hours, Irwin changed his previous view that a more elaborate trial in bad weather was needed?"

"No, I have no reason to think that he changed his mind."

"In your view, if you had been responsible, do you think that the trial of R101 before she started for India was adequate?"

Booth hesitated. It was a very tricky question that might condemn his friend. He pointed out that the officers concerned had more experience of the ship than he, before resolutely continuing, "At the same time, I feel that the decision—or agreement—to leave at that time for India was biased by the fact that the Imperial Conference was being held. If the conference had not been coming off, they would have insisted on more trials."

November 14, 1930—April 28, 1931

THE INQUIRY BROKE UP for a three-week recess to give Sir John and his assessors time to consider the evidence.

During that time Villiers had four more remarkable sessions with Eileen Garrett. He was told of missing documents, and of a conference on board among the officers and Brancker on whether they should leave. So impressed was Villiers that he had come to the momentous decision, particularly brave in that he was an Air Ministry employee, that he must contact Sir John Simon immediately. Sir John invited him to lunch. He listened gravely to Villiers' account of the séances, and asked for copies of his notes. Sir John took the messages sufficiently seriously to send his secretary to search Cardington for the missing documents named in the séances—but none were found.

Throughout the inquiry it had been Irwin, *Irwin*, IRWIN. The captain of R101 had been shown repeatedly right. Yet it seemed to Olive Irwin that Sir John, though he brought such evidence out, was always putting it back again in the shade. The question of command, Scott's insistence on his position, had been ignored, as had Lord Thomson's "strafing" on the telephone, accusing Irwin of being an obstructionist. When was her counsel going to bring up all that?

Major Teed repeatedly reassured Olive Irwin that the court would never blame her husband. But she was not so sure.

On November 27 Major Teed wrote to Sir John, suggesting Olive's brother-in-law could give evidence regarding Lord Thomson's telephone call to Irwin. Sir John replied: *I may say that I am personally completely satisfied that there is no possible ground to cast any reflection on [Irwin]. . . . We ought to consider whether any official purpose would be served.*

Major Teed was thinking along the same lines. He agreed it would have been difficult for a junior officer to refuse to fly with the secretary of state, and even such a refusal would not "in all probability have stopped the vessel from going when it did, for there were at least two and possibly three alternative captains, one of whom would have been prepared to take a chance which might well be associated with an award."

The long-overdue knighthood for Scott was implied. Matters were left as they were. The last three days of the inquiry passed uneventfully. Ramsay MacDonald's government was collapsing, and to shore it up and to soothe public opinion, the report was produced in double-quick time.

The cause of the disaster, it stated, could have been many things, but the most likely was that a forward gasbag had suddenly burst, bringing the nose too far down for the coxswain to control it.

There was no mention of missing documents. There was no condemnation of the Air Ministry or the Royal Airship Works. The only real criticism of Lord Thomson was Ralph Booth's courageous statement, appropriately paraphrased: "It is impossible to avoid the conclusion that R101 would not have started for India on the evening of October 4 if it had not been that reasons of public policy were considered as making it highly desirable for her to do so if she could."

Irwin was not blamed, but neither were his lonely efforts to protect the ship and all who flew in her properly highlighted. To absolve him from the traditional responsibilities of captain, the report would have had to state bluntly that the government in the person of its secretary of state and with the help of its Air Ministry had assumed full responsibility for the safety of the airship.

If Irwin was to get his proper due, Lord Thomson's name would have had to be blackened. A junior officer would have had to be shown as a solitary prophet crying in the wilderness.

"We have reached the truth without offending anyone," Sir John Simon said of his report. He wrote to Teed: *I am pleased to receive a grateful letter from Lord Thomson's sister, saying how greatly our report has relieved the minds of herself and her mother. It is a trying business for these people to be landed into poverty when with a turn of the wheel, they might have been out with the new viceroy of India.*

Now suddenly had come out the *real* reason why R101 went that night—Thomson's ambition to rule India.

Irwin was still on Sir John's mind when he wrote on April 13, 1931, to Teed: *One of the things about which I am particularly pleased is that Irwin's record and reputation stand out beyond challenge. Poor Mrs. Irwin must get such consolation as this affords.*

1931 and after

THE TRUTH? THE FEELING gradually gained ground that the inquiry had been nothing but a gigantic Whitehall whitewash designed to save the memory of Lord Thomson, and the faces of the Air Ministry and the Establishment.

Once the official report was published, Harry Price felt free to publicize the account of the October 7 séance with Eileen Garrett, for it seemed clear that the séance got closer to the truth. R101 was too heavy, her lift was too small, the elevator might have jammed, her trials were too short, she was difficult to trim, the added middle section was entirely wrong. *The New York Times* of May 31, 1931, quoted Price as saying that experts within and without the Air Ministry had told him that only someone familiar with the details of the airship could have made that analysis. "No one will accuse me of being particularly credulous," Price asserted, "but on the evidence, I feel I must accept Irwin's explanation in preference to the official findings of the court of inquiry."

In August 1931 E. F. Spanner, an engineer, published *The Tragedy of R101*, a two-volume work. Spanner considered that the airship had "hogged"—that is, become deformed. She had suddenly encountered a head-on gust of about sixty-six miles an hour when her nose was slightly down, and this gust had caused a rapidly increasing downward-pitching motion. To correct the dip, the fins were gradually moved to a fully up position, and the airship began to rise. While this was taking place, the lower girders in the added center section of the airship gave way. In Spanner's view, R101 broke her back through structural weakness.

That conclusion seemed to support the evidence of Villiers' séances.

The British airship program ended. The mast was dismantled—

the wooden parts used for fencing, the lift made into cigarette boxes and ladies' jewel cases. R100, the private enterprise competitor of R101, was flattened with a steamroller. Britain turned her aviation expertise to heavier-than-air craft, particularly fighter planes. Leader of the campaign to build a strong military air force was Stuffy Dowding—by the time of the aerial Battle of Britain in 1940, Air Chief Marshal Lord Dowding, RAF chief of Fighter Command.

Major Villiers received little promotion, and was retired from the Air Ministry as an unestablished officer with no pension. His eyes began to trouble him, and he eventually became blind, but he still managed to live a disciplined, fruitful life well into his nineties. The Garrett séances had totally convinced him of life after death, and it was the spreading of this profound conviction that guided and informed and upheld his life until 1981, when he died.

Eileen Garrett, on whose integrity much of the story hinges, left England for America, where she established herself as a medium of great power. Her psychic gifts were studied at Duke University and elsewhere. She also formed a close friendship with Frances Bolton, congresswoman from Ohio, and with her help founded the Parapsychology Foundation in New York, which has attracted interest and encouraged experiments all over the world.

Today the airship sheds at Cardington—bigger than Westminster Abbey, taller than Nelson's Column—are in none too good repair. They are used for experimental balloons. Workers and visitors must wear steel helmets for protection from the pieces of metal that fall like bullets from the vast rusting roof. Nevertheless from all over the world people still come to see the sheds. Officials say they are so huge and so strange that they have their own weather—sometimes foggy when the weather is clear outside, or fine when outside it is wet and windy. Once it even snowed in Number 1 shed when there was no snow outside. They seem to exist in some time and weather warp all their own.

To these sheds, a few years ago, returned Air Marshal Sir Victor Goddard, an airship commander in World War I, a friend of Bird Irwin's, and one of the officers who had been considered for captain of R101. Sir Victor had become deeply involved in spiritual studies, and had decided he ought to try to contact the spirits of his dead friends, or perhaps discover that they had never revisited earth at all.

He therefore invited the distinguished medium Helen Greaves to attend a reunion of airshipmen at Cardington.

That day Sir Victor and Mrs. Greaves walked into the cold, eerie Number 1 shed and crossed the concrete floor. Above them towered the iron-raftered roof. Footsteps and voices echoed in the vast emptiness. It was the perfect atmosphere for a spiritual visitation.

Alas, Helen Greaves experienced nothing. No voices, no visions, no sensations—nothing.

Disappointed, they returned to the hotel where they had booked accommodations for the night. It was while the medium was alone in her room that the visitation came. Effortlessly and without preamble, as if he moved freely now and without struggle, the spirit or entity of Irwin materialized. Mrs. Greaves had no doubt it was he. "Irwin," he said, "I–R–W–I–N," as he had said all those years ago.

Gently and with great compassion, the voice of Irwin asked that no further attempt be made to contact him or any of those who had perished in the R101 disaster. He gave Mrs. Greaves to understand that Lord Thomson had realized what had been wrong, that he and all the others were doing useful work. But now—Irwin conveyed to the medium a profound feeling of sweetness and love—they needed to be left in peace.

STRANGE AFFAIR AT STRATFORD

STRANGE AFFAIR AT STRATFORD

by
Barbara Michaels

ILLUSTRATED BY NORMAN WALKER

On March 10, 1850, something invaded the home of the Reverend Dr. Eliakim Phelps on Elm Street in Stratford, Connecticut, and began to terrify the Phelps family. Furniture was rearranged when no one, or at least no person, was there to rearrange it. Clothing wasn't where it should have been. Even food mysteriously disappeared from the kitchen, only to turn up later on the bookshelf. At first it seemed a simple joke, and Dr. Phelps was determined to get to the bottom of it. He would not allow his new young wife and her children to be frightened by mischievous pranksters.

But this was no joke. And no one was able to get to the bottom of it. Not Dr. Phelps or any of the other clergymen he called in to help. Not the newspapermen, not the "spiritualist consultants." No one could stop the intruders.

Who or what were they?

Author of many gothic mysteries and suspense novels, including *The Master of Blacktower* and *Ammie Come Home*, Barbara Michaels is also an Egyptian historian who has written several nonfiction books about ancient Egypt.

PROLOGUE

IT SEEMS SO LONG ago. Over a century—one hundred and thirty-three years. Yet think of it in terms of generations and the distance is not so great; an adult living today might have heard the story from the lips of an eyewitness. Still, we do not have all the facts. We will never have them now. We have only fragmentary reports, distorted by the prejudices of the observers. The family of the Reverend Dr. Eliakim Phelps did not desire notoriety. He was a man of the cloth, his wife a lady of good family. Once the bizarre business had ended, they were eager to have it forgotten.

We will probably never know for certain what eerie force invaded the quiet manse in Stratford, Connecticut, in the year 1850. But this is how it might have happened . . .

CHAPTER ONE

WHEN I FIRST SET eyes on Stratford, I thought it was such a quiet, peaceful little town. Now I hate it. What have we done to bring this horror upon us? The ladies still speak to me when I meet them in the shops or on the street; they can hardly fail to do so, when my husband is their clergyman. But they cluster in little murmuring groups after I pass; the buzzing of their gossip follows me like a swarm of angry bees.

They say our invisible tormentors are devils, damned souls sent to punish us for some hidden sin. Andrew (he said I might call him Andrew) insists they are spirits of good. I wish I could be sure. When he spoke, when I was in his presence, I believed him. He has such a wonderful voice. His fiery dark eyes, his handsome features, his tall, youthful frame—his entire being vibrates with such sincerity that I am carried away by it. But he has gone now—never to return? I wish I had never left Philadelphia. I wish I had never married again. But what else could I have done? I was alone—grieving for my deceased husband, helpless as women always are without a strong man to lean on; my children suffering from the lack of a father's care. When the Reverend Dr. Phelps proposed marriage, my answer was, in some degree, influenced by the needs of my children. But not entirely— oh, no. I thought Dr. Phelps a fine man. Fine looking, too, for sixty. He is so serious and scholarly. I respect him very much.

We talked, I know not how long, in the parlor of my house in Philadelphia. When I told him I would be his wife he kissed me gently on the brow. Then he took his leave, promising to return that evening to greet the children as their new papa.

After he had gone, I stood in the hall, looking up the stairs. The weather was dreary, dark and chill; snow hissed against the windows like whispering voices. I was conscious of a strange and inexplicable reluctance to ascend those stairs. As I hesitated, my hand on the knob of the newel post, it seemed to me that there was something up there, just out of sight. A dark shapeless shadow loomed on the wall of the landing.

I know now that it was a portent, a foreshadowing of what was to come. It could have been nothing else. No danger awaited me at the top of the stairs, only the nursery and my darling children. The two little ones, Sara and Willy, would be tucked in their cribs now; but I had promised to come to Harry after Dr. Phelps left.

The nursery was bright and cheerful. A fire crackled on the hearth. I reminded myself not to call it "the nursery." Harry disliked the word. He was too old, he insisted, for a nurse or a nursery. Soon he would be all of twelve!

He sat on the rug before the fire, his legs crossed and his chin propped on his hands. He was playing with his little toy theater, his favorite plaything of all the ones I had given him. It was an elaborate affair, though it was made of pasteboard and the characters were cut out of paper. It had real red satin curtains and a small stage. Harry often put on performances for me, taking all the parts himself and moving his paper people around the stage as he spoke in voices that moved from gruff to falsetto. *Hamlet* and *Julius Caesar* were among his favorites—in greatly abridged versions, of course. Apparently some new play was being plotted, for there were only two cardboard personages on the stage—a slender, ringletted female who usually represented the heroine, and a villainous-looking person who had been Cassius and Hamlet's wicked uncle in his time.

Harry looked up. His face brightened when he saw me, and he brushed a lock of unruly brown hair from his eyes.

"Mama," he cried, running to embrace me, "you were so long!"

I put my arms around his sturdy little shoulders, noting, with half a smile and half a sigh, how tall and strong he was growing. He would not be "Mama's dear little boy" much longer.

"I am sorry, my darling. Dr. Phelps has just this moment left."

"Why does he come so often and stay so long?" Harry demanded. "I wish he would not come."

"Harry, you mustn't say such things," came a quiet voice from the corner of the room. It was Marian, my daughter, five years older than Harry. Marian always sits in corners and speaks in a quiet voice. It is easy to forget that Marian is in the room. But she has a good heart. Her devotion to her brother is the finest part of her character.

"Never mind, Marian," I said. "Harry only means that he misses his mama. I miss you too, Harry. But I hope you will be polite to Dr. Phelps. You will see more of him. . . . I mean to say . . . You don't really dislike him, do you, darling? He is a good man—"

"I hate him!" Harry stepped back. Fists clenched, face crimson, he looked challengingly at me.

Marian rose, putting down the book she had been reading.

"He doesn't mean it, Mama. Don't be upset. He only says it to vex you."

"Why, Marian, how spiteful you are!" I exclaimed. "Harry would never wish to vex me."

"Never, Mama." With one of his sudden changes of mood, my son flung his arms around me. "I love you, Mama."

"And I love you, my dearest."

"So you will tell that nasty old man to go away and leave us alone?"

"Darling, he is not old, or nasty."

Harry clung to me, his face hidden in my skirts. Marian said in a flat, expressionless voice, "Are you going to marry Dr. Phelps, Mama?"

I do not know why the question rang in my ears like an accusation, or a threat. I don't know why I took so long to answer.

When I said, "Yes, I am," I had my explanation all prepared. Their need of a father's love, my need of a husband's care. I had actually started my speech before I realized there was no need for it. In the same strange voice Marian murmured, "I wish you happiness, Mama."

Harry said nothing. He moved away from me, dropped to the floor before his little theater and began moving the figures around the stage. His face was quite calm.

"There," I said to myself. "You see how it is—there was no need to worry. He has taken it well."

CHAPTER TWO

So MUCH FOR THE rumor put about by malicious persons that my children refused to accept their new papa. Harry's single outburst was only natural. Marian does not feel deeply. Much as I hate to say it of a child of mine, she is rather shallow. The younger children were only six and three, too young to care for anything beyond their own little world. But Harry and I had always been close.

Certainly he did not fail in courtesy to Dr. Phelps after that, and I am frank to admit that some of the credit for their good relationship must go to Dr. Phelps himself. He treated my children as though they were his own. Well, not quite; after all, his children are fully grown, with families of their own.

Before we were married he informed me we would not be living in Philadelphia, as I had assumed. He had accepted a position as pastor of the Presbyterian church in a small town in Connecticut. Knowing what I know now, I marvel that a shudder did not pass through my body when I heard the name Stratford. But at the time—despite what some people have said—I was not reluctant to make the move. I had always loved Philadelphia, but the death of my first husband had cast a gloom over the city where we had lived together; I saw little of our former friends. Besides, it is a wife's duty to follow cheerfully and uncomplainingly wherever her husband leads.

Dr. Phelps kindly explained the reasons for his decision. His duties as pastor of the congregation in Huntington, New York, combined with his position as secretary of the Presbyterian Educational Society in Philadelphia, involved considerable travel to and fro. He found it increasingly wearisome; and now that he was about to contract new familial ties, he had decided to find a quiet country town in which to settle.

He assured me I would love my new home. His eyes shone with the enthusiasm that is his most youthful and attractive characteristic.

"It is a very old town, my dear—founded in the early seventeenth century. Washington was constantly there. He has become such a legend it is difficult to remember that he died—why, it is exactly fifty years ago, in 1799. I talked with residents of Stratford who well remember his final visit to that city. Mrs. Benjamin Fairchild was able to serve him potatoes from her garden, which he relished very much."

I wonder, I thought to myself, if they still grow potatoes in their gardens, the good people of Stratford. And why should they not? Potatoes are a suitable product for a village garden.

In fact, my first sight of Stratford was a pleasant surprise. The train was not very nice—they make such a terrible noise—but the Connecticut scenery was lovely. Rich meadows and grand old trees, picturesque vistas crowned by majestic hills, tinkling streamlets of pure water running down to the blue waters of Long Island Sound, which sparkled in the spring sunlight. Upon the southern horizon rose the outline of Long Island itself, called Sewanhacky—the Island of Shells—by the Indians who once inhabited this idyllic region. Dr. Phelps, as excited as a boy, told me this fact and others of historical interest. The history of Stratford is as peaceful as its appearance; the bloody skirmishes of war have passed it by, except for encounters with the aborigines. The community's chief claim to fame derives from the visits of General and Mrs. Washington.

Stratford was as charming as Dr. Phelps had claimed and not so bucolic as I had feared. I saw two churches, a number of shops and many elegant houses. Our house was on Elm Street, and when the carriage turned into this thoroughfare I found it broad and spacious, lined with fine old trees whose shade was welcome on the warm afternoon. Of course it was not a paved street, one could hardly expect that. But the dwellings of our new neighbors were large and handsome, with wide green lawns that, like our own, stretched down behind the houses to the Housatonic River near where it flowed into the Sound. We had—so Dr. Phelps told me—a property of some three and a half acres. Ideal for the children, I agreed, but I expressed some natural maternal concern about the nearness of the water. Dr. Phelps brushed this aside.

"Henry must learn to swim. It will be good for the boy. You have made him something of a namby-pamby, my dear. Quite natural; but it is time he learned more manly pursuits. As for the younger children, they can hardly get into trouble with you in close attendance, not to mention the servants."

It was a pleasant house, gleaming with fresh white paint, its façade adorned with a fine portico supported by tall Grecian pillars. Inside, the house was equally immaculate. We had sent servants ahead to prepare for our coming and Dr. Phelps said the good ladies of the congregation had been tireless in their assistance. He had told me little about the place, beyond assuring me it was elegant and spacious; when I stepped into the hall, I suppose my face must have displayed my surprise, for he smiled.

"Is it not handsome?"

"It is so *long*," I said. "And what a peculiar arrangement for a staircase."

He stood with his feet apart, viewing the hallway with the fond pride of a new proprietor.

"It was built for a sea captain," he explained. "His wife supervised the construction while he was on his final voyage to China. She did not want him to miss the sea, so she designed the hallway to be exactly the dimensions of a clipper ship's deck—seventy feet long by twelve wide. The twin staircases carry out the same idea of allowing the captain to fancy himself still aboard his beloved ship. After pacing the main deck, he could climb one stair to the hurricane deck, and then descend by the other stair."

"A pretty notion," I said.

And a peculiar notion, I added—but to myself. What is well in a ship does not always suit a house! However, when Harry began running up one staircase and down the other, expressing his loud approval, I was able to contemplate my extraordinary hallway more favorably. It was certainly a splendid place in which to play. Harry gleefully announced his intention of being up and down the stairs all day long. When Dr. Phelps heard this his expression was decidedly solemn. The room he intended to use as a library was on the "main deck," just to the right of the stairs. But he said nothing at that time, and I promised myself I would persuade Harry to be considerate of his new papa's need for quiet.

Harry was equally approving of the rest of the house. He declared that it was perfect for hide-and-seek, with its many corridors and chambers.

When winter came and the icy winds swept across the Sound, some of the deficiencies of the house became evident. The parlor chimney smoked abominably upon occasion, and since this was apparently caused by a certain velocity and direction of wind, nothing could be done about it. The house was a cold house. I was constantly shivering in icy drafts that no one else seemed to feel. Dr. Phelps did not object when I ordered heavier draperies for all the windows, and kept the carpenter busy caulking and refitting window frames; but one day in mid-January, when he saw how the woodpile had shrunk, he took me to task for extravagance.

"It is all your imagination, my dear. None of the rest of us is affected by these drafts. You are a little hothouse plant, I am afraid."

I *was* the only one to complain of the cold. But I do not believe now that it was solely my imagination.

Dr. Phelps's pastoral duties were not onerous. He was at home a great deal. Snow and freezing weather kept us constantly indoors, and I envied him his ability to amuse himself with one hobby or another. One of his interests, however, caused me some concern as the long months of winter dragged on. He had never made any particular secret of this interest, but it was not one he advertised abroad. He knew some of his parishioners would not approve of their pastor dabbling in what he called "spiritual philosophy." They would have had other names for it—and so did I. Once I peeped into a journal he had been reading, and found that it was full of references to apparitions and mysterious rappings, phantoms and eerie voices. I could hardly believe that my husband, so serious and so intelligent, was engrossed in such matters. But the journal also spoke of wonderful messages from the Apostles and the Old Testament prophets.

When I mentioned the subject to Dr. Phelps, his face took on a dreamy, far-off look. "Imagine hearing," he said, "from the lips of Saint Luke or Isaiah a description of the realm of the blessed! But it is all speculation; there is as yet no real proof that these communications are genuine."

The dull days dragged on. I kept myself busy, sewing and playing with the children, and practicing on the piano, which I had sadly neglected in Philadelphia. The ladies of Stratford were assiduous in Good Works. I served on a dozen committees—to educate the heathen and supply them with modest clothing; to call on the sick; and to improve the lot of servants, children and fallen women. We did not entertain or go out a great deal. Dr. Phelps seemed more than content closeted in his library for hours on end.

Then, one February evening, came the event that was to bear such dreadful fruit.

I had been up with the children, helping to tuck them into bed. After they were snug in their little cots I read them a story and kissed them good night.

Harry was no longer a resident of the nursery. He had firmly announced that he was too old for the company of babies and had demanded a room of his own, just like Marian's. There was no difficulty about that; the house had three floors and a sufficiency of bedchambers. Being older, Harry was allowed to sit up later than the younger children so long as he remained in his room, quietly reading or playing. Usually I went to talk with him for a while after the little ones were in bed. It was for me the best part of the day, and unfortunately it was all too short; I knew my husband awaited me in the parlor, and although he usually read to himself and spoke little, he liked me to be there.

That evening there was a change in the routine. As I left the nursery I saw Harry coming along the hall. He was fully dressed.

"Why, Harry!" I exclaimed. "What are you doing here? You know Papa would disapprove."

Harry gave me a bewitching smile. "It is by his orders that I am freed from prison this evening, Mama. I am to attend him in the library."

"Oh, Harry, have you been naughty again? I begged you—"

"Nothing of the sort." Harry's boyish smile broadened. "I am surprised you have so little faith in me, Mama. I assure you, I am not expecting a beating or a lecture."

"But, Harry—"

"Oh, Mama, don't fuss. You are always fussing."

He scampered away. Filled with the direst forebodings, I started after him. Dr. Phelps may laugh at my premonitions, but I solemnly swear I felt an icy chill run through me. I went after the boy, trying to catch up—all in vain, of course. Harry is very agile when he does not wish to be caught. He was in the best of spirits; he teased me by waiting on the landing till I had almost touched him, and then slipped down one of the twin stairs as I started down the other.

I was pleased to see him merry, but I had cause for concern. Harry had not been well. Physically he seemed in excellent health; his new papa pointed out, rather smugly, how tall and rosy-cheeked he had grown since we came to Stratford. But his behavior the past few weeks had worried me. He showed a kind of nervous excitability. Harry was always volatile—it is the sign of a highly intelligent and artistic character—but of late I fancied his moods were more intense and more rapidly changing. I had had the physician. He was no help at all. After listening to my description of Harry's behavior and examining the boy, he had laughed and proclaimed him a thoroughly healthy specimen.

"All he needs, ma'am, is a good touch of the stick. They are limbs of Satan, these young fellows, and they are worse at this time of year when the festivities of the holiday season are over and they see nothing ahead but dreary weather and long months of school. Whack him, ma'am, whack him often and soundly. That will cure his trouble."

Is it any wonder, then, that I was concerned about any unusual event involving Harry? His spending time with his papa in the library was certainly unusual.

Needless to say, I followed him into the room. My husband did not appear overly pleased to see me.

"You said you had work to do this evening," he reminded me.

"Some sewing task for the Women's Institute that must be finished before tomorrow."

"I have plenty of time," I replied. "You cannot blame me for being curious; what are my two favorite gentlemen planning to do in this mysterious interview?"

"There is nothing mysterious about it," he said. "I simply saw no reason to mention it to you. Henry has not been himself of late. I have been subjecting him to a course of Pathetic Medicine."

"Harry?" I exclaimed. "Medicine?"

Harry threw himself into a big leather chair and crossed his legs. "It is great fun, Mama."

"The term is misleading," Dr. Phelps went on. "There are no drugs or medicines involved. It is a correct Theory of Mind assisting the spirit to heal itself."

I sat down. "I will help you, Dr. Phelps."

"I hardly think it will interest you, Mrs. Phelps."

"If it is to do with Harry, it will interest me. Pray make allowance, Dr. Phelps, for a mother's natural feelings."

He could not deny me after that. He has a great deal to say in his sermons and elsewhere about parental love.

I am ashamed to admit what ill-defined fears crowded my mind. I was soon disabused of them; the proceedings appeared harmless enough. With the room in semidarkness, Dr. Phelps took out his watch and held it before the boy's eyes. In a low, soothing voice he bade him follow the gleaming surface as he moved it to and fro.

After a while he said softly, "Can you hear me, Henry?"

"Yes," was the reply, in a voice equally soft.

"How do you feel, my boy?"

"Very calm. Very well."

A few more sentences were exchanged, of the same order. Dr. Phelps kept repeating the words *calm* and *well*. Finally he said, "You are calm, you are at peace. You will continue in that state, Henry. Wake now."

Harry rubbed his eyes. "Is it done?"

"Yes, all done. Off to bed now. Sleep well."

"Yes, sir. Good night. Good night, Mama."

When he had gone, Dr. Phelps turned to me. "Well, my dear, I trust you are now convinced that I am not abusing the boy."

"I never thought—"

"Lying is a sin, Mrs. Phelps. You suspected me. I confess it hurts me deeply."

In some confusion I apologized, adding, "Indeed, Dr. Phelps, I have never known you to be unkind to anyone. But I don't understand what you were doing. Why did you tell him to wake? He was not asleep. He spoke to you, answered you; his eyes were wide open all the while."

"The process is too complex for you to understand," he replied. "It is a scientific process. I assure you, I have had considerable experience with it. I employed it on my own son, when he suffered from a heart condition, and was able to relieve him greatly."

I learned later that the method he employed is called Mesmerism; it is used, in Pathetic Medicine, to put the patient into a proper state of mind. Oh, but if that were all! There are doors unseen, opening into unimaginable realms. Once those doors have been opened, what creatures may enter in?

I remained uneasy. I could hardly forbid the treatments. I had seen nothing to complain of; but the uneasiness persisted, and next day I found myself mentioning the matter to Marian. Ordinarily I do not confide in her, but I knew that any problem concerning Harry would touch her.

Like the younger children, she seemed happy in Stratford—as nearly happy as Marian can be. She had entered into the various activities of the Ladies' Circle and was constantly busy. Having finished her education the year before, she had nothing else to do except look for a husband, and in that respect, I must confess, I found Stratford somewhat lacking. Marian is not pretty. In order to succeed in what must be any woman's chief endeavor she requires a broad circle of acquaintances. There were few young men of the right age and social position in Stratford. However, Marian did not complain.

She surprised me—it is one of the few times she has succeeded in doing that—when I mentioned Dr. Phelps's treatment of Harry.

"There is no harm in it, Mama. Indeed, I find it beneficial. It is like a pleasant sleep, and one feels so calm afterwards."

"What!" I exclaimed. "He has done it to you?"

"Papa does nothing except assist my own spiritual powers to

increase." Marian's thin cheeks were flushed. "I feel much better for it."

"You don't look better for it," I retorted somewhat sharply. "What have you been doing to yourself? You are thinner than ever, and there are shadows under your eyes."

Marian murmured something about sleeping badly.

"If that is all . . ."

"It is nothing serious. I . . . I dream sometimes."

"We all do," I said.

CHAPTER THREE

NEVER HAS THERE BEEN so long a winter. I awaited spring with such eagerness that tears came to my eyes when I saw the first snowdrops peeking bravely out of the bleak bare earth. But the weather was still chilly and blustery, the trees yet leafless, on that Sunday of March 10, when we prepared for church. The date is, I think, burned forever into the tissues of my brain.

There was the usual Sunday morning bustle. Dr. Phelps was ready first, as usual; as usual, he kept demanding irritably why we could not prepare for this ritual, now so familiar and long established, without such noise and confusion. Men never understand these things. My first husband was the same. Let them try to supervise the washing and attiring of four children—Marian was as bad as the rest, she has no taste in clothes and does not know what to wear—while trying to present a reasonably respectable appearance oneself.

I wore my new suit that morning. It was fine navy blue wool, a trifle light for the season, but I had waited so long for spring; I wished to do something to convince myself it was really coming. I had thought the pattern quite pretty when I chose the fabric and the delicate braiding that covered the front of the jacket in complex scrolls. However, the final result was somewhat disappointing. The village seamstress has not the accomplished touch one is accustomed to in a large city.

We got ourselves together and lined up in the hall for inspection, as was our custom. Dr. Phelps confronted us like a general on parade, running his eyes over us one by one. He had no comment for me. I had rather hoped he would say, "Very pretty, my dear," or something of that sort.

Marian, too, passed without criticism, though I thought her appearance quite dreadful; the dull maroon of her gown made her skin sallower than ever. Harry was subjected to a scathing critique. Everything was wrong, from his uncombed hair to his scuffed boots. The little ones, whom I held firmly by the hand, won a fatherly pat on the head.

We took the carriage, since the weather threatened, though the distance was short. Harry had to sit on the box with the coachman, which he did not mind at all.

I do not recall the text of the sermon. I do remember that Harry was restless—not unusually restless, no more than normal for a boy his age. Since the pastoral pew is just under the pulpit his actions did not go unnoticed, and I was constantly having to nudge and frown at him.

It is a wonder I remember anything of that frightful day except the event that turned it into a nightmare—the beginning, had I but known, of a long and continuing evil dream.

It always took us forever to get away after the service. Dr. Phelps must talk with everyone who wanted to chat. He insisted that we wait with him, which was difficult for the children. When we got into the carriage, the three younger ones behaved like little animals let out of their cages. Harry was not the only one in high spirits; Willy pinched his sister, who slapped him and burst into tears. Dr. Phelps exclaimed, as he frequently did, "One would think they had come from a zoological garden instead of a house of God!"

Everything was as usual. Nothing was different . . . until we reached home.

A cold drizzling rain had begun to fall. Anxious not to damage my new suit, I hastened toward the house. My entrance was facilitated for me, in no pleasant way. The front door was wide open. I stood staring at it rather stupidly until the others joined me on the portico. Marian had the smaller children by the hand. Harry was close behind her, followed by his papa.

"Why do you not go in?" Dr. Phelps inquired.

I gestured. "The door. Did you forget to close it?"

"Certainly not. I thought you—"

"No, it was like that when I came up."

He frowned. "I won't tolerate this sort of thing. Come along, Mrs. Phelps, we must have a word with the servants."

He strode into the house. One can almost measure his temper by the length of his strides. I followed, plucking at his sleeve. It was difficult enough to find decent servants in a small town; I did not want them upset unnecessarily.

"But, Dr. Phelps, the servants were at church. Nor would they have occasion to use this door."

"All the same, they must be questioned."

Naturally, the servants one and all denied being responsible. They had returned from church before us, on foot; but had used the back entrance and had not even gone into the front part of the house. The only exception was Cook, who had, of course, remained at home to complete the preparations for dinner. No one could suspect her; she was the most respectable of middle-aged females, and her indignation at being accused, even by implication, was obviously genuine. Even more convincing of her innocence was the terror that replaced her initial outrage.

"Burglars! That's what it was, criminals and burglars. We'll be murdered in our beds, we will. I won't stay in this house another minute!"

Having aroused this storm, Dr. Phelps left me to calm it, and it required some time to convince Cook that she was not in mortal danger—particularly when I was not too easy in my own mind. After leaving the kitchen I found my husband in the hall, about to mount the stairs.

"The doors to the library and morning room were also open," he said. "I am sure I closed the former, as I always do. Someone has been in the house. I am going to examine the upper chambers."

We went from room to room without finding anything amiss until we reached our own bedroom. Dr. Phelps preceded me. When he looked in, he uttered a loud exclamation.

"What is it, what is it?" I cried apprehensively.

Silently he stood aside. When I saw what had prompted his cry, my relief was so great I could have laughed aloud. Four chairs had been piled on top of our bed, their wooden legs forming a weird tangle.

He did not share my relief. In the low, stern voice that characterizes his angrier moods he said, "Mischief. Some trickster has done this."

And he turned to direct a cold, hostile gaze upon Harry, who, hearing our voices and sharing our concern, had come to see what was happening.

Observing the strange construction on the bed Harry burst out laughing. Indeed I could not blame him, but the effect was unfortunate. Dr. Phelps's face darkened. Before he could speak I said quickly, "It could not have been Harry. He was with us the entire time."

"He could have done this before we left the house," Dr. Phelps said.

"But he could not have opened the front door. You yourself closed it when we left, and you were the last to get into the carriage."

Harry's smile had faded. "I didn't do it," he cried. "Honestly—"

"This is a serious matter, Henry," Dr. Phelps said. "Give me your word that you know nothing of it."

"Honestly, Papa—"

"Very well, very well. I believe you."

It cannot be said that Sunday dinner was a pleasant meal. Cook's perturbation had resulted in a badly cooked joint of beef, and the housemaid was so nervous she dropped two plates. Marian looked like a ghost. Harry continued to speculate and wonder about the strange events until his papa cut him short.

"Let us hear no more about this, Henry. I will take steps to prevent its happening again."

When dinner was over we went upstairs to prepare to attend the afternoon service. Dr. Phelps did not come up with us; he had gone to the library. When I was ready I went to look for him and found, to my surprise, that he was stretched out on the sofa reading.

"You will be late," I said.

"I am not going."

"But—"

"As you know, I do not preach this afternoon. I mean to stay here and keep watch."

THE RAIN HAD STOPPED when we returned from church, but the clouds still hovered, and when we entered the house I saw with considerable irritation that the servants had not yet lit the lamps. Dr.

Phelps was still in the library. He sat up with a start when I entered. It was too dark for me to see his face, but I felt certain he had been napping.

"Has anything happened?" I demanded.

"It has been completely quiet," he said, trying to hide a yawn.

In some bitterness of spirit I summoned the housemaid and told her to light the lamps. After taking a candle, I started up the stairs. Dr. Phelps came out of the library and followed.

As I opened the door to our room, my candle died, extinguished by an icy draft. The fire burned low, cloaking the room with shadows. In the reddish glow I saw what lay on our bed—a motionless and dreadful form, shrouded for the grave. The candle dropped from my nerveless hand. A black mist threatened to envelop me. As I swayed, I felt my husband's hands support me. His sharp intake of breath told me the terrible vision was not the product of my imagination. He thrust me unceremoniously aside and ran to the bed. I let out a shriek when his hands touched the silent form. But worse was to come. With a muffled sound, more like an animal's growl than a human voice, Dr. Phelps began to dismember the corpse. Its head flew in one direction, its limbs in another.

I remember nothing more until I woke, my nostrils quivering with the sting of smelling salts, to find myself lying on that same bed. The shock to my system was so extreme that I feel it yet. Before I could spring shrieking from that infernal couch, my husband spoke.

"It was only a dummy, made of clothing wrapped in a sheet. For the love of heaven, calm yourself, Mrs. Phelps."

But it was the voice of my dear boy that saved my reason. Tears streaming down his face, he clutched my hand and implored me not to die—for, as he told me, so deathly was my pallor that he feared me on the brink of extinction.

"Dearest Harry, Mama will not die," I assured him. "I was only startled for a moment. I am well now."

"You would not do such a thing to frighten your mama, would you, Henry?" Dr. Phelps asked.

I clutched my boy to my bosom. "Harry was with me all afternoon. You know that. How dare you—"

"Very well! You are quite right and I own I am wrong. Are you recovered now? I must see what other mischief has occurred."

"My bed has been pulled out into the middle of the room," Harry volunteered in a voice still choked with sobs. "And Marian's small table is missing."

His face shone with tears. He gazed up at his papa with wide luminous eyes. I had never seen anyone so palpably innocent. Even Dr. Phelps was moved.

"It is very curious," he muttered. "I cannot account for it, unless . . . But no, that cannot be. Stay with your mama, Henry, and take care of her."

But Harry was understandably wild with curiosity to see what else had happened, and I forced myself to rise and accompany him. Close examination of the house produced some amazing discoveries. Marian's small inlaid table had been crammed into her wardrobe, crushing her frocks. Other pieces of furniture were disarranged or hidden; outcries from the kitchen proved to result from Cook's discovery that the loaf of bread she had set out for tea had disappeared. It was eventually found in the morning room, in a bookcase.

It was late evening before order was restored and the children sent to bed. I lingered long with them, afraid to leave them alone. Finally Dr. Phelps sent one of the maids to summon me to the library.

He had little to say, however. He spent most of the evening turning through various newspapers, as if in search of some particular article. When I tried to speak of the horrors that had occurred, he was brusque with me.

"I am taking steps, Mrs. Phelps. You need not concern yourself."

It was with extreme effort of will that I took my place beside my husband on our bed that night. In the darkness I felt the presence of the shrouded corpse between us.

My FIRST THOUGHT on waking next morning was to rush to my children. Harry looked at me in surprise when I asked if he was all right, and replied grumpily that he was not, for this was Monday and a long week of school stretched ahead of him.

This was reassuring. The sight of Marian at the breakfast table was less so. She crumbled her food instead of eating, and looked as though she had not slept a wink. Dr. Phelps noticed her distraction. After Harry had left for school he said, "Come to me in the library, Marian, and we will have another treatment."

"If Marian is ill, perhaps we ought to have the doctor," I said listlessly.

"You yourself informed me, Mrs. Phelps, that the man was an ignorant, sadistic quack."

"Did I? Well, Dr. Phelps, I am sure you know best."

So they went off together and I busied myself with the normal morning chores. I was in the parlor, dusting the china ornaments, which I prefer not to leave to the clumsy hands of the maids, when I heard screams from the floor above.

As I entered the hall Dr. Phelps came out of the library. The screams had stopped, but had been replaced by shuddering sobs that were almost as loud.

"Marian?" I asked.

"She has just left me."

The screams had indeed been uttered by my elder daughter. She was in a fit of hysteria when we found her, standing in the open door of her room. Its condition gave some excuse for her distress. The furniture was strewn about in utter confusion. The washstand, normally concealed behind a screen, stood blatantly in the center of the room with the towels draped over it. Next to the washstand was a trunk, one of the humpbacked type bound in brass, in which Marian stored extra clothing. Its lid had been tipped back, and atop the neatly folded garments was a heap of masculine clothing—trousers, vest, coat—which I at once recognized as belonging to Dr. Phelps.

He had to raise his voice to be heard over Marian's sobs. "Those are the garments that were used last night to create the form on our bed," he cried. "How did they come here?"

The uncouth gulping sounds coming from Marian scratched at my nerves, which, needless to say, were in a dreadful state. I turned and slapped her sharply on the cheek. This is of course the best cure for hysteria, and it had the desired effect. Marian's sobbing ended. Her hand at her burning cheek, she looked at me in shocked surprise. I had never struck her before. I do not believe in striking children.

"It was necessary," I said in answer to her wordless reproach. "Are you better now? Sit down—breathe deeply—and tell me what has happened."

Marian obeyed, jerkily, like a puppet. Still holding her cheek, she shook her head. "I found it . . . like this."

"These garments." Dr. Phelps held them out.

"They are yours, are they not, Papa?" Marian looked bewildered. "I don't know how they came here."

He tossed them back into the trunk. "This is beyond words."

"You cannot accuse Harry," I cried. "He—"

"He could have done this before he left for school. Marian is always early to breakfast and he is invariably late." Hands clasped behind his back, he walked around the room, peering closely at the disarranged furniture. I found myself doing the same, as if hoping some solution would suddenly leap out at me—a solution that would clear my boy, once and forever.

Suddenly there was another shriek from Marian. So overwrought was I that I echoed it. Whirling around, I saw her bolt upright in her chair, her arm outstretched, her finger pointing.

"The clothing," she gasped. "It is gone."

Sure enough, the suit of gentleman's clothes was no longer in the trunk. Marian began babbling. "I had covered my face with my hands—when I took them away, the things were gone—"

"Hush," I exclaimed. "Be still or I will slap you again. Dear heaven, I cannot endure any more of this."

Again Dr. Phelps searched the room. The missing garments were found under the bed.

At this discovery Marian began weeping. I jumped at her and shook her by the shoulders. It was not such a terrible thing to do, and I do not remember crying out; but Dr. Phelps said I was losing control of myself.

"I will put the clothes away," he said sternly. "Be assured this time they will stay there!"

He flung the garments into the trunk and carried it into the closet, which he locked. He ushered us from the room, then turned the key in the door lock.

"There," he said, putting the keys in his pocket. "Now we shall see."

Marian crept away, looking like a red-nosed frightened mouse. I felt I must lie down, so I retired to our bedroom. I ought to have been relieved. Harry could hardly be accused of hiding the garments under the bed. But I was shaking uncontrollably. How had the suit of clothing—which I devoutly hoped Dr. Phelps would never wear again—how had it moved from the trunk to the floor, and under the bed? Marian might have moved it while Dr. Phelps and I were looking elsewhere. But why should she do such a mad thing? And she had certainly appeared to be as alarmed as we. . . .

Had Dr. Phelps really been alarmed? Men must conceal their fears, if they feel them; but the more I thought about it, the more I suspected that his eyes had held a strange glint, a look almost of pleasurable excitement.

I decided I must have been mistaken. That was the last emotion one would expect to see in a man so tormented.

I heard his footsteps approach the door, which had been left ajar. To my surprise—for I had expected he would come to inquire how I felt—the steps did not pause, but went on past. They were very quiet, as if he were tiptoeing. The most incredible surmises troubled my mind. I rose and went to the door and peered out. Dr. Phelps stood by Marian's door. As I watched, unobserved, he took a key from his pocket and inserted it into the lock. I heard the sharp click as it turned. Gingerly he opened the door. The sound he made was not a gasp of surprise, but a long-drawn-out "ah!" I could bear the suspense no longer. I ran to his side.

On the floor of Marian's room, just inside the door, lay the suit of clothes which, scarcely fifteen minutes before, he had locked in the closet.

CHAPTER FOUR

I WAS PITIABLY SHAKEN. Indeed, I remember very little of what transpired thereafter until I found myself entering the library, leaning on Dr. Phelps's arm. After he had placed me in a chair he insisted I take a small glass of port, which was kept on hand for medicinal purposes. He was kind in his way, but when I asked that the maid be sent for a cup of tea, he refused.

"I don't want the servants brought into this until it is unavoidable. They are a superstitious, ignorant lot and will take fright."

I did not reply in words; but my glance, I believe, was eloquent. Dr. Phelps shook his head, almost playfully. I could not understand his mood.

"My dear Mrs. Phelps, I assure you there is nothing to fear. I may be excused in the beginning for failing to understand the truth; but the events of this morning put the matter beyond doubt. To think that I have seen with my own eyes phenomena I have often read about and often mistrusted!"

He went on in this dreadful vein of self-congratulation until I interrupted with a demand for an explanation. If my tone was somewhat shrill, I think that is excusable.

"I was reading just last night of a similar case," he said. "Have you not heard of the Rochester rappings? The newspapers have been full of them for months."

He then went on to explain, in his most tedious and pedantic manner. It seems that for some time two young women named Fox in Rochester, New York, had been producing raps and scratching sounds out of thin air. Some invisible intelligence was obviously responsible for the sounds, since it responded to questions, rapping for "yes," remaining silent for "no," and spelling out more complex answers by rapping when the correct letter of the alphabet was reached by a person reciting it. That the phenomenon was connected with the Fox sisters, and not with the house in which they lived, was proved by the fact that when the girls went elsewhere, the rappings broke out in those places also. Other persons had taken up the sport of calling on these invisible "spirits"—the word is that of Dr. Phelps—and had received answers to the most complex theological questions.

He would have gone on and on about the wretched girls and their raps if I had not interrupted.

"What has this to do with us? We have heard no—"

"Do you remember last Tuesday, when the door knocker sounded and the housemaid reported no one was there?"

"Some mischievous child. You said so yourself."

"I was mistaken. Phenomena such as we observed this morning, and also yesterday, are well known. Ignorant persons attribute them to ghosts, or 'haunts'; until recently, educated persons dismissed them as pure imagination. We now have reason to suspect they are demonstrations of some unknown force."

"A diabolical force," I cried.

"I cannot deny that possibility." Dr. Phelps looked grave. "But, I assure you, there is nothing to fear so long as we remain calm and secure in our faith. Who knows, we may have seen the last of these demonstrations already."

"Oh, I hope so!"

But I was not convinced by his explanation. Having denied, at first, the possibility of trickery, for fear Harry would be accused, I now clung to that theory as to a lifeline. It must be Marian who was responsible. I did not ask myself why she might have done such things, I only persuaded myself that she might have been able to do them, and promised myself a firm talk with her. However, when I expressed this intention to Dr. Phelps (without elaborating on my true reasons), he forbade me to see her—my own daughter!

"She is in an extremely nervous state, Mrs. Phelps. I took the opportunity of giving her another treatment of Pathetism, and she is now resting. Pray do not disturb her."

And, as it turned out, such a talk would have been unnecessary. That afternoon it was proved, beyond a shadow of a doubt, that neither Marian nor any other living creature was responsible for the terrors that afflicted us.

I did not see the first of the occurrences, but I heard the house-maid cry out. She was in the hall. Upon being questioned, she insisted that Dr. Phelps's umbrella had hurtled past her, half the length of the hall. No one else had been there.

Scarcely had Dr. Phelps succeeded in calming the girl when the door knocker sounded, and so stretched were our nerves that even Dr. Phelps started. But upon opening the door we beheld nothing more alarming than little Mrs. Platts, the music teacher, who had come to give Harry his piano lesson. Naturally I tried to behave as if nothing were amiss. Mrs. Platts is the worst gossip in Stratford, and I did not want her telling tales all over town. I called up to Harry—a reluctant musician at best, he was skulking in his room—and showed Mrs. Platts into the music room. Eventually I had to call Marian and ask her to fetch her brother, which she did. Dr. Phelps's treatment appeared to have helped her. She looked more alert than she had for some days.

It was necessary to chat awhile with Mrs. Platts, for Dr. Phelps insisted we treat her like the distressed gentlewoman she claimed to be. He made a point of coming in to greet her himself. We were talking idly when Mrs. Platts let out a cry and put her hand to her head. I had not been looking directly at her. My husband had. With the agility of a man half his age he sprang to her side and picked up a hairbrush from the floor beside her.

"Are you hurt?" he inquired.

Mrs. Platts rubbed her head. "No; it was not a hard blow. I am sorry; I must have knocked the brush from—er—its former place."

This was patently impossible, the only piece of furniture within arm's reach of Mrs. Platts being a low table. If the brush had been on it, it would simply have fallen to the floor instead of rising in the air and striking her on the head. I saw at once where her suspicions lay. She could not keep her eyes from Harry, who was standing on the other side of the room, as far from the piano as he could get.

Mrs. Platts rose and went toward the fire, rubbing her hands together and remarking on the chill of the day. Scarcely had she left her chair when there was a loud discordant crash from the piano. It sounded as if half a dozen of its strings had been violently snapped. Mrs. Platts squealed. Under other circumstances I might have been hard pressed not to laugh, she looked so comical with her large mouth ajar and her eyes bulging.

The first thing was to open the piano. Dr. Phelps did so, with Harry's assistance. He reached inside and lifted out a large block of wood and stood weighing it in his hand.

"Has it damaged the strings?" Harry inquired hopefully.

"That is hardly the vital question," Dr. Phelps replied.

Mrs. Platts was suddenly galvanized into action. "You will excuse me, I hope, I have just remembered . . . No, no, you needn't show me to the door, I will . . ." And she departed, uttering fragmentary sentences that sounded like sharp little shrieks of consternation.

I had been watching Harry. I had seen his hand move, just before Mrs. Platts cried out the first time.

But if *he* had thrown the brush, who had moved the block of wood through a closed lid and dropped it violently onto the piano wires?

It was too much for me. I managed to retain control of myself until Mrs. Platts had gone. Then I slid to the floor in a dead faint.

I KEPT TO MY bed next morning. I suppose it was childish—like hiding one's head under the covers—and if I had hoped thus to escape knowledge of new horrors, I was not allowed. Soon after breakfast Harry came running in to announce that further manifestations had occurred during prayers. He had been struck on the head by a key, and various objects, including a tin box, had been propelled across the room by invisible hands. When I demanded why he was not at school he snuffled unconvincingly and said Papa had agreed he was coming down with a cold.

Dr. Phelps did not visit me until later in the morning. I saw at once, by his face, that he had more news—bad news.

"I have just found a cloth spread on the floor, with a Bible and three candlesticks arranged—"

"I don't want to hear about it."

"You must get up, however, my dear. I have asked the Reverend Dr. Mitchell to spend the day, in the hope of getting his advice."

I protested. He was adamant.

"There is no chance of keeping these things secret any longer. I kept Henry at home to prevent him from gossiping to his friends, but he cannot remain secluded indefinitely. Besides, Mrs. Platts has undoubtedly told her tale to half the town. We owe it to ourselves to have the testimony of a man such as John Mitchell."

"His wife dislikes me. She will revel in—"

"In what, for heaven's sake? Our misfortune? I cannot believe anyone would be so uncharitable. Now, Mrs. Phelps, you must calm yourself. Your present state alarms me. I have been thinking you might profit from the treatments I have been giving Marian and Henry."

I was too weak and disheartened to protest.

It was the strangest experience. Apprehensive at first of I knew not what, I felt the most exquisite drowsiness gradually seize me as my eyes followed the slow swinging of his watch. After that it seemed but an instant before I was wide awake, with no recollection of any passage of time. I did feel better, and I told Dr. Phelps so.

"Good." He rose. "You will come down at noon for dinner, I trust. Dr. Mitchell will join us at the meal and remain for the rest of the day."

Without the treatment I am convinced I could never have endured the distress of Dr. Mitchell's presence. A tall, severe-looking man, he had always treated me with reserve; and as my husband narrated the strange events that had perplexed us, his cold gray eyes kept wandering in my direction, as if to say, "There is the culprit."

But I was vindicated. During dinner Dr. Mitchell was treated to a spectacle of knives and forks and other objects flying around the dining room. No sooner had his astonished eyes turned to follow one than another hurtled past him. One spoon struck him with a thump on top of his bald head; and I cannot say I was sorry to see it.

By four p.m. on the day of Dr. Mitchell's second visit—for you can be sure he was there early the following morning—we had counted over forty-five different objects that had been moved, some of them several times. On Thursday another Stratford clergyman, the Reverend Weed, was asked to be present. This was the first time we heard noises like the rappings Dr. Phelps had mentioned to me. Some of them were produced by a brass candlestick, which beat itself against the floor until it finally broke.

It was also on this day that the mysterious writings first appeared. They were scratched onto a turnip, of all things, which was thrown through the parlor window; Mr. Weed's bushy gray eyebrows rose clear up into his hair.

I could go on for many pages describing the other objects that moved, including the heavy mahogany dining room table. The writings continued to materialize, often on the most bizarre objects. Harry's cap, pantaloons and blue silk handkerchief were so adorned. I could only shake my head helplessly when they were shown to me. The characters were like none I had ever seen before and the clergymen, familiar with such ancient scripts as Greek and Hebrew, said the same.

By that time we suffered what I privately called a plague of pastors. Not only Dr. Mitchell and Mr. Weed, but several other gentlemen of the cloth from nearby towns had been summoned to assist us in our trouble. This was Dr. Mitchell's idea. He even went so far as to remark, in his pompous manner, that if there were evil spirits in the house, the presence of so many servants of God ought to intimidate them.

Quite the contrary! The reverend gentlemen inspired more outrageous outbursts than before. Objects continued to whiz around the house, and the large knocker on the outside door sounded constantly, without any human agency having touched it. One morning all the contents of the pantry were tossed into the middle of the kitchen, bags of salt and sugar emptied onto a heap of tinware and culinary instruments. Cook threatened again to leave and was persuaded to stay on only by promises of extravagant raises in salary.

Dr. Mitchell decided that the clergymen must keep a constant watch on all parts of the house. So they rushed from room to room, up and down the stairs and along the passageways, looking for all the world like a swarm of very large somber beetles in their dark suits and spectacles. It was unnerving in the extreme. I would be sitting with my embroidery in the morning room, trying to snatch a few moments of peace, when a clerical head would appear around the door frame and a pair of glittering eyeglasses would stare at me. I daresay it sounds very amusing. It was not.

The gentlemen had determined one day to subject the house to a rigorous search from cellar to attic. Heaven knows what they hoped to find—an infernal machine of some kind, perhaps, or confederates of ours, hiding in dark corners and waiting for an opportunity to play another trick. While they were busy with this I decided to retire to our bedroom, hoping that this sanctum at least would be free from their investigations.

Marian's room was down the hall. As I entered the corridor I saw her standing by her open door. She turned very slowly to look at me. I scarcely recognized her. Though her body was quite still, her arms hanging limply at her sides, her entire countenance quivered, as if every muscle in it had been subjected to a violent shock.

"Mama," she said quietly, "come and see this."

My involuntary cry of surprise brought my husband running. He summoned the others. Before long there was a sizable audience. The word is appropriate; the scene before us resembled a setting for a theatrical performance, complete with actors. Of all the strange events we witnessed in those terrible months, none remains so vivid in my mind as this awesome tableau.

Most of the furniture had been pushed aside—a task requiring no small strength in itself. In the space thus cleared a number of figures had been arranged in the most graceful and lifelike attitudes. They were formed from articles of clothing, padded out to resemble human forms. Most were female figures—the garments were both mine and Marian's—in attitudes of extreme devotion. Some knelt before open Bibles. Others were crouched, their "faces" bent to the floor in poses of utter humility.

In the center squatted a strange dwarfish figure whose basic constituent was my poor little Willy's best Sunday suit; but this had been so grotesquely adorned with artificial flowers and ribbons and other feminine articles that it resembled something out of a madman's nightmare. This was, however, the only repulsive figure; it almost seemed as though the lovely women's shapes guarded it, turning to devout prayer as a means of shielding the dwellers in the house from the malice such misshapen creatures are known to feel. This impression was strengthened by the last figure, which was suspended from the ceiling as if flying through the air, or hovering in benediction above the worshipers.

The ensemble was so strange and yet so picturesque that we were struck dumb. I cannot emphasize too strongly the lifelike appearance of the attitudes. The unknown arranger had been fiendishly clever in setting them up in such a way that the blank stuffed faces were turned away or hidden. One figure, fashioned from a gown of my own, knelt gracefully by the bed. I did not recognize the gown at first; it was an old one I had not worn for some time, and my first impression was only one of vague familiarity: "Where have I seen that woman before?" Then, behind me, I heard my little Willy whisper to his sister, "Mama is saying prayers." And I knew the figure was my own.

An icy chill pervaded my limbs. I remembered the old legend of the doppelgänger, or double. To recognize such a figure, the precise replica of oneself, is an omen of sudden death.

One of the clergymen was the first to break the awed silence.

"We ought to take a copy of this. A sketch."

It was a sensible suggestion, but no one moved to follow it. Mr. Weed murmured, "No need; I doubt that any of us will forget it."

He, I might add, was later to say the most insulting things about us, claiming he had seen nothing a three-year-old child could not have done, and implying that we ourselves had played tricks on him and the other clergymen. He referred, disparagingly, to the scene I have just described as "images or dolls dressed up the size of life." All I can say is that at the time he was as dumbfounded as the rest of us.

Everyone in the house, including the unfortunate servants, was subjected to a cross-examination. It was impossible to prove that each and every person had been under observation the entire day, but no one could understand how the ensemble had been created. Not a sound had been heard, not a person had been seen running to and fro with armfuls of clothing; and since the various garments, Bibles and other objects had been gathered from all over the house, the construction of the Chapel Scene, as my husband termed it, must have taken long hours of labor.

"And," Dr. Mitchell said, rubbing his bald head in perplexity, "we were all on the *qui vive* the entire day, looking for evidence of trickery. I can swear, gentlemen, that I saw nothing the whole time."

I HAD NOT VENTURED from the house since that awful Sunday. By the end of the week the weather cleared and Dr. Phelps insisted I do some shopping, as much for the exercise as the duty itself. Dr. Mitchell and the other clergymen were still prowling about, getting in everyone's way. All except Mr. Weed who had, quite suddenly, taken his departure, with unconvincing excuses of pressing business which he had not seen fit to mention earlier. It was obvious that the situation had gotten beyond him. Later, as I have said, he denied that there was anything extraordinary in the case. Perhaps by that time he had managed to convince himself that he spoke the truth.

Even after my morning treatment from Dr. Phelps, on which I had come to rely, I contemplated the trip into town with some apprehension. Men do not understand. They cannot realize the cruelties women inflict on their fellow women. The sidelong glance, the sly little smile, the seemingly harmless comments that raise smarting welts . . .

I knew what the good ladies of the church thought of me. From the moment of my arrival in Stratford I had from time to time overheard remarks: "Too young . . . too frivolous . . . he was mad to take on the responsibility of a new family at his age . . . and such a family . . . the older boy, they say, is quite wild."

The road was muddy from the recent rains. I had to keep to the grass edge. The walk itself was pleasant enough. The trees showed fat, promising buds and some of the lawns boasted brave displays of crocuses and an occasional courageous daffodil.

My rising spirits received a rude check when I reached the shops and saw that the ladies of the town were out in full force. It was the first fine day for almost a week; they were starved for gossip. Even

Mrs. Mitchell was there, the center of an avidly listening group. I tried to act as usual, nodding and smiling as I walked on. No one had the effrontery to question me directly—not then. There were murmurs of "How are you feeling?" and "I had heard you were unwell, Mrs. Phelps," to which I replied as casually as I could. By the time I reached the shop door my hands were shaking, and I was vastly relieved to find that the only customer at the counter was old Mrs. Babcock, who was avoided by the other ladies because her sole topic of conversation was the fifty-year-old visit of Mrs. General Washington. I had heard the story at least a dozen times, and had vowed I would never listen to it again. This morning I actually raised the subject myself, to prevent Mrs. Babcock from mentioning other matters.

Even she failed me. Properly nudged, she rambled on for a time about Mrs. Washington's chariot, drawn by four white horses ridden by black postilions in scarlet and white livery with white cockades on their hats. But the spreading gossip had penetrated even her senile brain. She broke off in the middle of a sentence to inquire, with the rudeness old ladies sometimes feel entitled to display, "What is going on at the manse, Mrs. Phelps? I have heard the most peculiar stories about all of you."

I don't remember what I said. When I finally reached home I found I had purchased red ribbons instead of blue, and had forgotten the buttons for Harry's trousers.

Even now I break out into a cold perspiration when I think of it. In some ways it was the hardest part of the whole affair. I did not see how I could go on.

Then, in early May, the miracle happened. Andrew came. Like an angel of mercy, he rescued me from my torment.

CHAPTER FIVE

I SMILE—THOUGH SADLY—when I remember how casually I responded to the first mention of his name. Of course I did not know who he was. When I heard of his projected visit he seemed like another of the vultures who came to feed their horrid curiosity on our suffering.

Nothing spreads so fast as gossip, and malicious gossip has a demoniac life all its own; it appears to die in one spot only to spring up, without apparent cause, in a dozen others. I am not certain how word of our troubles reached so rapidly beyond the confines of Stratford. I suspect Dr. Phelps wrote to some of the acquaintances who shared his interest in spiritualist matters. I could hardly believe he would do such a thing, but the promptness with which these vultures gathered was highly indicative.

I protested, as vigorously as my nervous condition allowed, when Dr. Phelps informed me we would be entertaining certain newspaper persons.

"It is our duty to science to report these happenings," he said solemnly. "Be realistic, Mrs. Phelps. The story will spread, no matter what we do. Is it not common sense to make sure that what is printed is the truth, instead of superstitious fancies?"

He had a way of putting things that made it impossible for me to disagree with him. My feelings told me he was wrong; but men do not have much regard for a woman's feelings.

So, once the plague of clergymen had passed, the second plague, newspaper reporters, descended upon us. At one time or another we had representatives of the New Haven *Journal-Courier,* the Derby *Journal* and the Bridgeport *Standard.* There was even a person from one of the New York papers, a Mr. Beach.

I actually developed a certain liking for one of the reporters—Mr. Newson of the Derby *Journal.* He was a nice-looking young fellow with thoughtful brown eyes and a modest manner. His newspaper—I was told—has a much more limited circulation than the others, so his professional position was inferior in consequence, I suppose. I don't think that fact accounts for his good manners, however; he seemed a naturally kindhearted and sympathetic man, and his unfailing courtesy to me—his instinctive comprehension of the difficulties of my position—could not fail to make a good impression on me. Nevertheless, I was distressed by the presence of so many strange men in the house.

One evening was particularly painful. The house reverberated to raps and thumps, coming now from one side of the room and now from another. The newspaper persons were impressed, but they were also incredulous. One of them insisted on sitting by Harry's side, and another—the person from the New Haven paper, I believe—never took his bold black eyes from me. Finally I could bear no more. I announced my intention of retiring for the night.

Even this expedient did not end my martyrdom. With Dr. Phelps's quick acquiescence the committee announced its intention of following us upstairs and taking up a position in the hallway. I verily believe Dr. Phelps would have consented to their entering our bedroom if they had insisted.

Under the circumstances I felt it would be more convenient, as well as more respectable, if I shared Marian's bed that night. Dr. Phelps did not object after I explained my reasons.

Marian and I spoke little as we prepared for bed. The door was closed; but I, at least, was uncomfortably aware of the presence of strangers only a few feet away. I had not even been allowed to lock the door. This was represented to me as a safety precaution, to enable help to reach us quickly if we were disturbed or frightened. But I knew it for what it was, a demonstration of suspicion. Marian did not complain, though I presume she shared my feelings. Both of us made haste to assume our nightgowns, removing the last of our garments beneath the concealment of their ample folds. It was an agonizing experience for a modest female. I had never felt so completely vulnerable.

I will say that for the most part the men kept their voices down, in deference to our need for rest. Now and then, however, we would hear a loud exclamation and thunderous footsteps along the passageway. Apparently the knocks and rappings had followed the investigators upstairs.

Having finished her ablutions, Marian knelt by the bed to say her prayers. In her long white gown and frilled nightcap, her thin face hidden in her hands, she looked very young and susceptible. When I knelt beside her for my own devotions, I was moved to touch her lightly on the head; and I would have said a few affectionate words if she had responded in the slightest way. She did not look up. Somewhat chilled, I mumbled through my petitions and got into bed. After emptying the wash water and blowing out the lamp, Marian joined me.

The window was tightly closed against the noxious night air and the room was uncomfortably warm. The muttering conversations and the footsteps outside kept jarring me out of the sleep I so desperately craved; but eventually I began to drift off. I do not believe I was sound asleep, only dozing, for when I heard the crash it jolted me awake in an instant. The sound was ear shattering, and seemingly at my very side. It was followed by the bursting open of the door. Four men crowded into the doorway. I believe there were only four of them; at that moment they looked like a multitude, and every eye was fixed on me with fierce intensity.

Mr. Newson ran to the bed.

"Ladies," he cried, "are you injured?"

Marian, uttering little whimpering sounds, held out her hands. Instantly he grasped them in his and went on, "We heard the most frightful crash against the door. We feared for your safety—please excuse this intrusion."

"Here is the cause of the crash," said one of the other men. He held up the heavy pitcher of white earthenware that made part of the set on the washstand. It was not valuable, but it had been in my family for many years; and it is so difficult to match a single piece without replacing the entire set. I was chagrined to observe that the handle had been broken off the pitcher.

"And here," the same person continued, "here is the result of the crash—an indentation in the boards of the door, where the pitcher struck it. It is a miracle the vessel was not shattered; it struck with such force as to leave a deep dent."

I looked at Marian, whose hands were still firmly held by Mr. Newson. Eyes downcast, she continued to moan faintly; but I had the impression she was not so disturbed as she pretended.

"Where was the pitcher when you retired?" asked the inquisitor.

He looked accusingly at me. I slid farther down in the bed and pulled the sheet up to my chin. Indignation was beginning to replace my initial feeling of shock. My annoyance was increased by the fact that Dr. Phelps made no attempt to remove the intruders, but stared as curiously as they.

"It was not in my bed," I said sarcastically. "You may think women lacking in intelligence, gentlemen, but I assure you I would have observed its presence, even in the dark, had Marian brought it to bed with her."

"Then Miss Phelps was the last to handle it?" the questioner went on, unmoved by my justifiable indignation.

"I put it in the corner, there," Marian said faintly. She turned her face aside.

Mr. Newson bent over her. "Your cheek is very red, Miss Phelps," he said respectfully. "Did the pitcher strike you in passing?"

"Something struck me," Marian whimpered. "I do not know what it was."

"It could not have been the pitcher." This time it was Dr. Phelps who spoke. He had gone to stand in the corner Marian had indicated, and as the others turned toward him he continued triumphantly, "Observe the path the pitcher must have taken. If thrown from here, it would have followed a straight line, striking either the corner of the room or the bureau there. In order to reach the door it must have followed a semicircular path."

"Impossible!" one of the men exclaimed.

"But true." Dr. Phelps rubbed his hands together in satisfaction. "The fact has been observed in other cases of this sort. It has also been noted that objects propelled through the air in this mysterious fashion often move with unnatural slowness. That would account for the fact that though the pitcher struck the door with extraordinary force, it did not shatter." He glanced at me. There was no compassion in his look, only the cold curiosity of a scientist. "What a pity, Mrs. Phelps, that the room was dark. I suppose you saw nothing of interest?"

"I was asleep."

One of the men made a small wordless sound and nodded significantly. I knew what he was thinking. So did Mr. Newson.

"Let me state at once, and for the record," he said firmly, "that neither of these ladies could have been responsible for the hurling of the pitcher. To hurl it with such force would be impossible for weak female muscles. Besides, we entered the room instantly, did we not—and found both ladies in bed with their hands under the bedclothes."

I remember Mr. Newson very kindly. He never retracted that statement, and he continued to insist that there was no physical explanation for the marvels he had seen. Some of the others were not so fair-minded.

ANOTHER RATHER GENTLEMANLY reporter was the person from the New York *Sun*, Mr. Beach. I gathered that he had some considerable reputation, for Dr. Phelps was childishly pleased to welcome him.

Mr. Beach had children and grandchildren of his own. He pointedly told us several stories about "the young rascals' tricks." I knew then where his suspicions lay, and I was sure of it when one night he asked if we might not talk with Harry for a while after the boy had gone to his room.

We all went upstairs—except the younger children, who were, of course, already asleep. Harry was in bed reading. He was delighted to see us.

We were talking quietly—I do not recall the subject—when Mr. Beach started and stared at a certain spot on the carpet. I could not see from where I sat, so I got up and moved to a better position.

The object at which Mr. Beach pointed was only a tin match box. But I am sure it was not there before or I would have noticed it, since it was four or five inches long and almost as wide.

As we continued to stare in wonderment at the box, it moved, sliding along the carpet toward the bed. Its lid flew open. A dozen or more matches jumped out onto the floor. Harry was as dumbfounded as the rest of us. Poor boy; he had been so often accused that his first exclamation was, "I didn't do it! It wasn't me!"

"That is quite all right, my lad," Mr. Beach said. He spoke soothingly—but at the same time his hand explored the empty air, as if expecting to find a string or thread running between Harry and the match box. He found no such thing, and I could not help but feel satisfaction when I saw his expression of chagrin.

Harry was extremely upset. Tossing and turning in his bed, he whimpered, "They want to burn me. That is what the matches are for—to burn me in my bed."

"Nonsense!" Dr. Phelps exclaimed. "Such womanly cowardice does not become you, Henry."

"He has been attacked before," I retorted indignantly.

"Minor things only—no more severe than the rest of us have endured."

"His clothes have been ripped off his body, his things marked and hidden—"

"Please, Mrs. Phelps. You forget we have a guest."

That was always his way, to suggest that I was losing my temper and forgetting my manners. His voice had been as loud and intemperate as mine.

We had turned our eyes and our attention away from Harry as our discussion became heated. A shriek from the boy interrupted us. He had pulled himself up to the very head of the bed and was crouched against the pillows. His trembling hand pointed to a bright yellow tongue of fire quivering on the bedclothes, not far from where his feet had been.

I felt my senses were about to leave me. Dr. Phelps stood frozen. It was Mr. Beach who sprang forward and extinguished the flame.

"A scrap of newspaper was set alight," he said, holding up the partially charred fragment. "Don't be alarmed, Mrs. Phelps. No damage was done; the sheet is barely scorched."

It was absurd to suggest I should not be alarmed. Any mother would be beside herself after such an experience. Harry, too, was crying and wailing. I was exceedingly wounded by Dr. Phelps's attitude. When I insisted I would spend the night at my boy's bedside he accused me of being hysterical. Was it hysterical to fear a repetition of this dreadful occurrence? If another fire started while the boy was sound asleep . . .

Mr. Beach came to my rescue by offering to take Harry into his bed that night. So it was arranged; and so far as I know the rest of the night passed peacefully. When Mr. Beach left us next morning he assured me he would be scrupulously fair in reporting what had occurred; and I must admit he kept his promise.

When I think of it now, the newspaper persons were not so bad as they might have been. The "spiritualist consultants," as they called themselves, were another matter. One of them was a certain Mr. Sunderland, the editor of Dr. Phelps's favorite publication, the *Spiritual Philosopher*. He had the impertinence to include us on a kind of psychic tour, whose main attraction was those same Fox sisters whom Dr. Phelps had told me about. As if we were in a category with those shameless girls who had made a public display of their tricks and had even taken money for performances!

Is it any wonder that when I first heard the name of Andrew Jackson Davis I took him for another of the vultures? That morning, when Dr. Phelps opened his mail and remarked, "We have attracted widespread interest. Mr. Davis himself proposes to call on us," I said only, "Not another of them!"

"Not another of anything," he said with a faint smile. "Mr. Davis may reasonably claim to be unique."

"You sound as if you do not approve of him, Papa," Marian said timidly.

"I don't know what to make of him. He calls himself the 'Poughkeepsie Seer,' which rather smacks of charlatanism; and he is only twenty-four years old, quite uneducated, from a respectable but lower-class family. Yet this untutored young man has produced an astonishing book in eight hundred closely printed pages—*The Principles of Nature, Her Divine Revelations, and A Voice to Mankind*. It consists of lectures delivered by Mr. Davis while in a state of trance. Some of the thoughts expressed are quite profound; they suggest an acquaintance with philosophical and scientific subjects far beyond the normal scope of such a man. It is certainly possible that he has been used as a vehicle by spiritual guides of great power and wisdom, as he claims."

At least, I thought to myself, he is not another of those elderly gray-bearded skeptics. Who knows, perhaps a man like that—young, flexible, spiritually gifted—can save us.

The morning of his arrival we were at the window watching for him. Other memories have vanished into the mists of time, but I remember perfectly the morning Andrew came. Every detail of his looks and his manner of speech remains fresh in my mind. I can even remember what he wore that day. His costume was smart yet gentlemanly—a black coat with a satin collar, brown-and-black-checked trousers, a scarf of green around his neck and a tan felt bowler. It suited his erect, youthful figure. His long springy steps required no assistance from the gold-headed stick he held in one hand. The other hand carried a portmanteau, which he swung to and fro with boyish exuberance, as if it weighed nothing. He glanced about him with obvious pleasure in the beauty of the day, and a sweet smile curved his lips. He was clean-shaven. His dark hair waved from under the brim of his hat, and when he removed the latter, as if to relish the freshness of the soft spring air, the sunlight woke golden highlights in the thick, glossy locks.

I wore my brownish-pink taffeta with bell-shaped sleeves embroidered at the cuffs and a collar of fine batiste. It was always one of my favorite gowns.

Soon he was among us, greeting my husband with graceful deference and bowing over my hand. Marian behaved like a moonstruck schoolgirl. She goggled and gaped and was incapable of sensible speech. Mr. Davis favored her with considerable attention, his eyes ever wandering back to her face, but it was obvious that his interest was strictly professional. He was not long in explaining it.

"The moment I entered this house I sensed the presence of spirits," he said solemnly. "And you, Miss Phelps—you feel them too, do you not? You are a clairvoyant of considerable power."

I made an involuntary sound of surprise and protest. At once our visitor turned his full attention upon me, sensing my need for reassurance.

"Don't be alarmed, Mrs. Phelps. There is nothing to fear. These forces are purely benevolent. They come to do you good. They are a mark of favor which few families have merited."

I cannot describe my sensations.

"Some claim they are evil spirits," Dr. Phelps said sharply. "Devils."

"Nonsense, nonsense. But we will discuss the matter at a later time. With your permission, I would like to wander about the house, absorbing its atmosphere and talking casually to all of you. I would also like to examine the notes I understand you have taken, Dr. Phelps. I am particularly interested in the mysterious writings; you have copies of them? Good. And of course I desire to meet young Master Henry."

It was all arranged as he had asked. He spent part of the afternoon sitting quietly in the parlor, his eyes closed, his face uplifted, the most angelic expression of smiling peace on his countenance. He roused at once when a clatter of boots on the porch announced the arrival of Harry, who was, for once, prompt in his return from school.

The meeting between them was fraught with significance. Harry's reaction to some of our other visitors had reflected my own feelings of resentment. He had been prepared to greet Mr. Davis with the same outer courtesy and inner contempt he had felt for others; but his reserve fell instantly before the warmth of Andrew's smile and his companionable clap on the shoulder.

Andrew asked Harry to show him around the grounds. They went off together and were gone for quite a while, returning with hearty appetites in time for tea.

When the shades of night were falling and we gathered in the library, Andrew was gracious enough to share his thoughts with us. He had requested that Harry make one of the party. Harry was delighted to oblige. He was already devoted to Andrew, and the air of innocent satisfaction with which he assumed his chair and crossed his legs, in imitation of his new idol, was delightful to behold.

"Let me assure you again there is nothing to fear," Andrew began. His smiling glance seemed to linger on me. "The spirits who visit you mean you only good. I know them. You know them too, Miss Phelps, if I am not mistaken."

"I—I cannot say," Marian muttered.

"I know them," Harry cried.

"Now, my boy." Andrew raised a finger in gentle admonition. "Like your sister, you are a natural medium, but you must not be led astray. Let me explain how the spirits operate. You have all testified that objects have been invisibly moved from one place to another.

The objects were carried by spirits. You, Henry, and your sister have attracted these spirits. You are both exceedingly surcharged with vital magnetism and vital electricity, alternating with one another. When magnetism preponderates in your systems, then nails, keys, books and so on fly toward you. When electricity preponderates, then the articles move away from you. Laughably simple, is it not?"

"Not at all," Dr. Phelps replied. "You said first that the objects were moved by spirits."

"Of course. But the direction taken by the objects is determined by the electrical or magnetical condition of Henry and Miss Phelps."

"I understand!" I exclaimed.

Dr. Phelps's expression said "I do not" as plainly as if he had spoken. With a benevolent smile Andrew continued, "Henry is naturally nervous. This encourages the accumulation of magnetic forces. Miss Phelps has been *made* nervous by fear—unnecessary though that fear may be—and is now, I believe, the more powerful clairvoyant of the two."

Harry stirred restlessly, as if he did not much care for this analysis. His papa looked keenly at him and then said, "Mr. Davis, your theory is most interesting. But it does not suggest what we are to do about the children's—er—magnetism. How can we rid ourselves of these unsettling effects?"

"Why, you cannot. They will pass of themselves when the desired end is attained."

"And that end is . . . ?"

Andrew drew from his pocket a sheet of paper that I recognized as one of those on which Dr. Phelps had taken copies of the strange writings.

"This script," he said calmly, "is like the inscription I read upon a scroll that was presented to my mind some seven years ago. The characters mean, 'You may expect a variety of things from our society.' And this other inscription—on a turnip, was it not?—I interpret as 'Our society desires, through various mediums, to impart thoughts.' "

"What society?" Dr. Phelps demanded.

Andrew smiled gently. "Can't you guess?"

"A society of lunatics, I suppose. Only a mind bereft of reason would conceive such bizarre antics."

Andrew was a trifle taken aback by the vehemence, verging on discourtesy, of my husband's tone. Mastering his surprise, he replied, with the same affable patience as before, "You are wide of the mark, Dr. Phelps. I hope to prove it to you before long. In fact, if you will permit me to attempt a demonstration now . . . ?"

"Why not?" was the ungracious reply.

Despite his vociferous objections Harry was dispatched to his bed; and, at Andrew's request, Dr. Phelps put Marian into a trance. As Andrew explained, Marian was more attuned to her papa's mental vibrations than to his, powerful though they were, and might be expected to respond more readily to Dr. Phelps's questions. This concession put my husband into a better humor. He took out his watch and went through the now-familiar performance, and looked childishly pleased with himself when Marian's face immediately took on the dreamy, peaceful expression I had seen before.

Andrew was proved right. When interrogated, Marian acknowledged the presence of five different spirits. The features of two of them were familiar to her; but when pressed to identify them, she fell into a state of confusion.

"Never mind," Andrew whispered. "Don't pursue the matter. Waken her."

"But—" Dr. Phelps began.

"Look at her."

Marian's face retained its look of unearthly calm; but her hands, which had been loosely clasped in her lap, clenched tightly and began to twist and writhe, as if imbued with a life of their own. The contrast between her peaceful look and her frantic hands was unnerving in the extreme.

"We will try again another time," Andrew insisted. "Waken her."

Dr. Phelps obeyed. Marian's hands at once relaxed.

She remembered nothing of what had transpired, but admitted to feeling a little tired. So she too was sent to bed, and I felt free to ask the question that was preeminent in my mind.

"You told me, Dr. Phelps, that this treatment was therapeutic for Marian's nerves. It seems to be something more. What have you been doing to her?"

A dark flush suffused Dr. Phelps's face. He seemed at a loss for words. Andrew kindly supplied them.

"It is therapeutic, Mrs. Phelps—very much so. In the trance condition the subject's mind is open to influences it would not be aware of in the waking state. Miss Phelps receives the pure and healthful thoughts of her father; they do her good." He glanced at Dr. Phelps and his lips curved in a roguish smile. "Thoughts may come from other minds as well, Dr. Phelps. You know that as well as I do. Don't fight them. Let them in!"

CHAPTER SIX

I LEARNED, TO MY disappointment, that the following day was the last Andrew would spend with us. He had other commitments and other duties. When Harry heard this he begged to be given a holiday from school. I was more than willing; Harry's attachment to Andrew could only be to his advantage. When Andrew added his pleas to ours, Dr. Phelps could not refuse. Andrew spent part of the morning with Harry. However, he seemed more interested in Marian, who followed him about the house like a puppy.

When we assembled for tea Harry was missing. He was usually prompt for meals, if for nothing else, and I began to be alarmed.

"We must find him," Andrew said seriously. "Without delay!"

Harry was not in the house. Andrew led the way into the yard. Some supernatural agency must have guided him, for he went at once to the orchard. And there—I still turn cold when I remember— there we beheld the form of my boy hanging limp and motionless from a limb.

Terror gave me strength. I was the first to reach him, but Andrew was close behind and was quick to reassure me.

"The rope is only under his arms. He is not harmed."

I flung my arms around Harry.

"Mama," he whimpered, "I screamed and screamed; why didn't you come?"

Thanks to Andrew, I was soon calm again. As he pointed out, no harm had been done. I wanted Harry to go straight to bed, but he insisted he felt quite well and proved it by eating a substantial meal. When he finished, I repeated my suggestion, and this time Andrew seconded me.

"I will come up to say good night," he promised.

When Harry had departed, Andrew drew his chair closer to the table. His face was grave. "I must leave you tomorrow; but I will try to come again soon, if my appointments permit. Remain receptive to the influences that surround you—"

"I mean to do more than that," Dr. Phelps interrupted. "I am sending Henry and Marian away for a few days to stay with friends of mine."

Andrew nodded, as if this plan came as no surprise to him. "And your reasons?"

"You yourself said the children were the cause—the innocent cause—of the disturbances."

"They are. But you wish to test my theory. Good; I have no objection. Do you, I wonder, have any other reasons?"

Dr. Phelps glanced at me.

"Speak," Andrew urged. "You underestimate your wife, Dr. Phelps. You do her excellent understanding an injustice when you attempt to spare her feelings."

"Very well," Dr. Phelps said, with another doubtful glance at me. "I will speak. I am uneasy about the circumstances surrounding Henry's desperate adventure this afternoon. He claims to have cried out. But if he had actually done so, the servants would have heard him; they were in the kitchen having their supper and the doors and windows were all wide open. Further, I examined the rope by which the boy was suspended, and I am forced to conclude that he could have tied himself to the tree. I am not saying he did; I am only saying he could have."

"You are quite right," Andrew said calmly. "He did."

I remained silent and motionless. Andrew gave me an approving smile. "Mrs. Phelps, permit me once again to commend your excellent understanding. And permit me to explain the mechanism of a process you instinctively comprehend without, perhaps, being fully cognizant of the details.

"You see, my friends, Henry did not know he was tying himself to the tree. A nearby spirit caused him to do so and deluded him into believing he had screamed aloud."

"And you presume to call them beneficent spirits?" Dr. Phelps inquired sarcastically.

"Exactly. From my superior condition I know that Henry was meditating some imprudent act—a swim in the river, perhaps, which might have caused him to take cold. The spirit intervened to prevent him. This 'adventure,' which appeared so 'desperate,' was just the reverse. You need have no fear for the boy. Send him away if you like; it will not put an end to these marvelous experiences, but it may help you by giving you a period of respite."

So, the following day, I bade farewell to two children and my friend—for such I hope I may call him. In some ways the next week was indeed a period of respite and relative calm. In other ways it was even more trying than the dreadful weeks that had preceded it.

It is hard to explain and harder, perhaps, to believe—but by sheer repetition we had become almost accustomed to uncanny events and eerie sounds. When a teacup flew through the air and smashed into bits against the wall, I would think: There it is again! I did not know what "it" was, but I was used to it. However, when my best scissors were missing from the sewing box, only to be discovered later on in the whatnot, I could not be sure whether "it" was playing tricks again or the incident was only one of those cases of absentmindedness that may occur in any household. That was the sort of thing that happened; and so I still do not know for certain whether the absence of the two children resulted in a cessation of the bizarre happenings.

I had gotten into the habit of remaining in bed late in the morning. For weeks my normal rest had been disturbed by terrifying events, my nerves had been wounded by shock after shock. Not only was I entitled to a period of convalescence; my system actually required it.

Therefore I was still in bed one morning when I heard a bustle within the house and a disturbance without. I rose, put on my wrapper and went to the window. The disturbance without resolved into the clopping of horses' hooves, the rattle of wheels and the bellow of a loud uncouth voice, shouting words that were as yet indistinct. From the far end of Elm Street an omnibus approached. Heads protruded from every window. A large glaring yellow sign had been nailed onto the side of the vehicle and as it drew nearer I was able to read the words painted upon it in prominent black letters: "Mysterious Stratford Knockings." It took me a moment or two to realize what it meant. Then a violent flush of shame and anger burned my cheeks.

The person on the box of the omnibus, flourishing a long whip, was the village hackman. His round red face and bulbous nose confirmed the rumor I had heard that he was habitually intoxicated. As I stared in horror the omnibus came to a halt immediately in front of our house, and the words the awful wretch was shouting became audible.

"Here it is, ladies and gentlemen, the house where it all happened! There you see the door that was thrown open by a skeleton hand; and there is the very identical spot from which the scissors grinder ascended mysteriously into the air, his wheels turning all the while, until he was lost to view, coming down next day in Waterbury. To your right—"

I clapped my hands over my ears. As I turned from the window the housemaid came running in.

"Oh, Mrs. Phelps, ma'am, have you heard—"

"Only a deaf person could fail to hear. Call the constable—call Judge Watson—call Dr. Phelps . . ."

"The pastor said as how he would go out to talk to them, ma'am."

I rushed back to the window in time to hear the front door open. The bellowing ruffian on the box of the omnibus stopped in midsentence and shrank back. Dr. Phelps walked slowly toward the gate, where he came to a halt. He did not speak; he only stood there, fists clenched. Slowly at first, then in a rush, most of the heads pulled back into the bus. A few of the bolder ones, including one woman with a coarse, painted face, stared back at Dr. Phelps with even more avid interest. Finally, however, his quiet dignity had the desired effect. The hackman's rubicund countenance turned redder, if such a thing were possible. He snatched up his whip and flicked the poor horses until they broke into a trot and the omnibus rumbled away. Not until it had disappeared among the trees did Dr. Phelps turn and walk slowly back to the house.

I suppose he could not have done anything else. A clergyman's dignity does not allow him to shout or call people rude names. I wished he had, though. I would have liked to do something—I don't know what—something violent. It would have relieved me to see him do it.

I had difficulty arranging my hair, my hands shook so—not with nervousness but with rage. I was determined to speak to my husband

at once. He must be persuaded to take strong measures to assure that such incidents never occurred again.

When I approached the library I realized that he had visitors. I heard not one but several voices raised loud enough to reach my ears, even through the thick panels of the door. Naturally I did not remain in the hall; and it was not until dinner time that Dr. Phelps

and I met. I saw at once that something had disturbed him. The presence of the servants prevented me from questioning him then; so after dinner I followed him into the library. He glanced up with an appearance of surprise from the book he held.

"Is something wrong, Mrs. Phelps?"

"You ask me that? After the degrading performance I was forced to witness this morning? What do you propose to do about it, Dr. Phelps?"

"There is nothing I can do. The road is a public thoroughfare. I cannot prevent people from using it."

"Indeed. Mr. Davis will be back in a few days; perhaps he can think of something."

Dr. Phelps's face darkened. "I had forgotten he was coming. Most unfortunate. But I suppose I can hardly retract the invitation now."

Such was my surprise at hearing these unkind words, spoken in the coldest possible voice, that I sank into a chair. "Why, Dr. Phelps! You welcomed Mr. Davis at first, and heaven knows he has already—"

"He has already done me considerable damage." It was so unlike him to condemn anyone so flatly that I gaped at him. He continued, "This morning I received a delegation of elders from the church who informed me that I must end these—their term was 'satanic operations.' "

"But what has Mr. Davis to do with it?" I cried. "As if he—and we—would not see the horrible business ended, if we could."

"The implication," said Dr. Phelps dryly, "is that I have encouraged these phenomena by my spiritualist researches. Mr. Davis is notorious in those circles, which means his very name is anathema to narrow-minded sectarians." He was silent for a time, his expression fading from severity to weariness. Finally he said slowly, "I am unjust to Mr. Davis. He is, I am sure, completely sincere. You must excuse me, Mrs. Phelps. The threat of a church trial—"

"Oh, no!"

"Alas, yes. It was nothing less than a threat. I am to be subjected to discipline if I do not succeed in putting an end to these phenomena."

I burst out weeping. It was not fear of the future that moved me. He had been for some time considering retirement from the ministry. He had the means to do so. But he had hoped to end his days in this peaceful village, enjoying the affection and respect of all who knew him. The stigma, the awful shame of dismissal—and under such circumstances. . . . We would never dare show our faces on the streets of Stratford.

He comforted me as a father might have, and I was grateful for his strength.

Every day that week odious curiosity seekers perambulated the street, stopping to stare openly at the house. Needless to say, I did not go out. Dr. Phelps refused to change his schedule, emerging every morning for his constitutional. He paid no attention to the gapers, but passed through them as if they did not exist.

On the following Monday morning he went to fetch the children. I was heartened by the fact that there were not so many people outside the house that morning. Overcast skies and threatening weather may have done something to discourage them, but I allowed myself to hope the worst was over. Even more cheering was the fact that Andrew was to arrive on the noon train. If only Dr. Phelps would be delayed in returning! It would do me good to have a private talk with Andrew.

That morning Sara, who is only six, had said she did not want to go to school. The other children had been teasing her. She would not or could not tell me what they had said. My heart ached for the child but I knew it would not be good for her character to let her retreat from unpleasantness.

Scarcely had she left the house when she came running back, waving a slip of paper. "Mama, see what I found on the ground near the gate."

It was a message written in the same strange characters I had seen before on numerous objects. With a thrill of horrified amazement I saw the ink was still wet. The child's hand had actually smeared it.

Sara was completely undone by this mysterious apparition and broke into such howls when I tried to send her off again that I gave in and let her return to the nursery.

I sat by the window in the parlor. I fear my embroidery did not progress noticeably. At long last I heard the whistle of the train. Dr. Phelps had not returned. I hoped he had decided to stay for dinner with his friends.

The station is only a short distance from the house—a few minutes' walk for a healthy young man. It seemed longer than that before I at last beheld the longed-for presence. I had had time to fear he would not come at all—that Dr. Phelps had written and told him not to come.

To touch his hand, to behold his smile, was like a soothing medicine. When we were seated, I handed him the paper.

"It was not yet dry when I took it from the child. You see, Andrew, that Harry could not have done this."

"I know. Harry is only the unwitting agent of angelic spirits, who may also act directly." He pondered the message for a time, his handsome face grave yet glowing. Then he closed his eyes. His lashes were very long and dark. "Yes," he whispered. "It comes to me now. A weak, a partial translation only . . .

> "Fear not, when he returns, fear not, all danger is o'er,
> We came, we disturbed thy house, but shall do so no more.
> Believe us not evil, nor good, till we prove
> Our speech to humanity—our language of love."

The words are exact. I copy them from the transcription he sent me later, after he had left us. But no copy can convey the tenderness and beauty of that deep, grave voice.

"Oh, is it true?" I whispered. "They mean you, of course; you are the one whose return means the end of danger."

"I believe so," Andrew replied humbly. "But you appear unwell— weary and distressed. What has happened in my absence?"

The sad tale poured forth in a cleansing flood. I may have wept a little. Before I finished, his hand was on my shoulder, gently pressing it.

"How well I know," he said, infinite sadness coloring his voice, "the bigotry of the ignorant—it is a cross all of us must bear who struggle to attain enlightenment."

"You, too?" I asked, wiping my eyes.

"Oh, yes. And," he added tranquilly, "no doubt I will see more of the same thing, for I do not intend to be moved from my chosen path. But it is more difficult for you—a lady's delicate, sensitive constitution . . ."

"It is. Oh, yes, it is. But few men, I daresay, have your strength of character."

He shrugged deprecatingly. "Few men have been blessed as I have been with spiritual aid."

I could have prolonged the conversation forever. Unfortunately we were soon interrupted by the arrival of Dr. Phelps with Marian and Harry.

My husband greeted our visitor with cold courtesy. Andrew tactfully ignored his changed manner.

"I understand you have had some unpleasant encounters with

certain of your fellow citizens on this plane of existence," he remarked.

"Nothing to speak of." Dr. Phelps's look at me was decidedly critical.

Andrew did not miss the look. The hidden emotions of the soul are an open book to him. "Do not blame Mrs. Phelps for confiding in me," he said. "The whole town is talking of your difficulties. I heard perfect strangers discussing the matter on the train, as we neared Stratford."

Dr. Phelps winced. Andrew continued sympathetically, "My dear sir, you know as well as I that the blind refuse to see and the deaf to hear. Pay no attention to narrow-mindedness. I bring comfort." From his pocket he took a sheaf of papers. "These," he said, tapping them with his finger, "are the translations of the messages I copied from your notes. Now I understand all, and I felicitate you on being chosen as a communicator of heavenly tidings. When you hear—"

Dr. Phelps started to his feet. "I beg your pardon, Mr. Davis. I cannot listen to your translations, as you call them."

"Dr. Phelps!" I exclaimed.

"They will calm you," Andrew urged, holding out the papers.

"No. I appreciate your good intentions. But I have reflected on this and have concluded that in some respects my critics are right. I have been misled. I must decline to continue in that error."

"Oh, Papa," Marian whispered.

Dr. Phelps started. I believe he had actually forgotten she was there. I know I had.

"Come, Marian." Dr. Phelps held out his hand. "This sort of discussion does not do you good. Come to your room."

"Wait!" Andrew exclaimed. "A moment, if you please . . ." Slowly he rose from his chair. His head turned; his eyes seemed to follow some invisible object as it crossed the room, from the door to the window. "They are here," he said quietly.

Dr. Phelps made an impatient gesture. "Mr. Davis—"

"One of them stands by your chair, Miss Phelps." In the most natural way possible Andrew's glance focused on a spot in empty air, behind and above Marian's head. She glanced up nervously.

"You feel his presence, do you not, Miss Phelps?" Andrew asked, still watching the unseen presence. Marian swallowed audibly but did not reply. Andrew went on, "Yes, I understand. He wishes me to describe him to you."

Dropping back into his chair, he pressed his hands to his eyes. His voice fell to a low, throbbing murmur. "He is a man of medium height and proportions, wearing a set of Dundreary whiskers. He has a rather long nose, slightly tilted; narrow lips; a broad, benevolent brow. There is a large brown mole on his chin."

I pressed my hands to my breast. A long shudder ran through Marian's body. But the one most affected by the identification was Dr. Phelps. Pale as a sheet, his lips quivering, he stared at Andrew.

"You know him, Dr. Phelps," said the latter. "He says he knew you, in life."

Dr. Phelps nodded painfully. "I knew him. Before. . . . He was Marian's father. The first husband of Mrs. Phelps."

EVEN AFTER THIS IMPRESSIVE demonstration of clairvoyance Dr. Phelps refused to listen to Andrew's reading of the messages. He did not forbid me to do so, however. They brought comfort, as Andrew had promised, as well as awe. To think that we had been chosen by a band of angelic spirits to testify to great truths!

Andrew explained. "The physical and electrical states of Henry and Miss Phelps made it easy for this class of spirits to furnish evidence of their presence. Thus they showed their desire to cultivate a closer acquaintance with humanity. It is a sort of magnetic telegraph, in short."

"But," I said timidly, "why do they do such peculiar things? Rapping and throwing crockery—"

"Oh, the means of communication may be imperfect at first," Andrew said.

My expression must have shown some of the reservations that still troubled me. He leaned forward and took my hands in his. "Dear lady, try to have faith. Some of these manifestations only seem peculiar because you do not understand their deeper meaning. Take, for example, the Chapel Scene you witnessed. I read in the newspaper a description of the figures kneeling in graceful attitudes of prayer. Believe me, these are not meaningless, or—as you may have suspected—mockeries of solemn gatherings. On the contrary! The figures pantomime an impressive lesson. 'Behold,' they are saying, 'there is no more substance in the mere ceremony of prayer than there is beneath these garments which compose us.' "

I do not understand how anyone can quarrel with the profound wisdom of this interpretation.

With Andrew's permission I went running off to explain it to Dr. Phelps. I could see he was struck by it; but for reasons I cannot understand he had conceived so strong a prejudice against Andrew that after a moment of reflection he shook his head and pronounced it, "Ingenious but without significance. Typical, I fear, of Mr. Davis' thinking."

"You cannot so easily discount his identification of Rob—of Marian's father."

"I can. He was all over the house on his earlier visit. I believe Marian keeps a portrait of her father in her room."

Against such a closed mind it was impossible to contend.

Andrew assured me that he did not curtail his visit because of any act or word of Dr. Phelps. Of course he is a busy man, much in demand. . . . All the same, I know he would have stayed longer if he had not been wounded by Dr. Phelps's coldness.

The morning of his departure was dark and drear. Even nature seemed to weep in slow persistent drops. His last words to me were a repetition of the blessed verse: "Fear not, all danger is o'er; we disturbed thy house, but shall do so no more."

And he was right—I know he was. If only we had believed him and followed the course he suggested! The grace of his presence, brief as it was, did bring about a cessation of the troubles. It was not his fault they broke out again later, more virulently than before. This time there was no doubt as to their satanic nature, for the tormenting spirits proclaimed their true identity in the very accents of hell.

CHAPTER SEVEN

AFTER ANDREW LEFT I was ill. A form of brain fever, the physician said; and for once perhaps the old humbug was right. I feel the effects of it yet.

My illness, a long period of pain and evil dreams, had one positive result. It aroused compassion in hearts that had been hardened against me, and my social status was somewhat restored. For the first time in months I entertained callers and returned to my work with the Ladies' Circle.

However, I did not receive anyone until I had made some attempt to improve my appearance. I looked terrible—hollow-eyed, pale, gaunt. I had lost so much weight all my gowns hung on me. I kept Marian busy for days taking them in. She was touchingly pleased to see me up and about again, and assured me that the manifestations had indeed subsided. A few panes of broken glass, an occasional rap—nothing more.

I was happy to accept this assurance. I wanted to believe it.

On the surface Harry was his dear self, and far less nervous than he had been. Yet I was conscious of a distance between us. He was always rushing off on some expedition when I wanted to talk to him. I mentioned this to Dr. Phelps. He brushed my fears aside. "The boy is growing up, Mrs. Phelps. You would not want him always clinging to his mama's skirts."

I fully expected that Dr. Phelps would suggest I leave the sickroom that had been specially set up for me during my illness and return to share our old room as soon as I was recovered. To be truthful, the idea was repugnant to me. Rest and privacy were absolutely essential to my nerves, and I was prepared to put forth this argument if he raised the subject. There was no need; he did not refer to it. I am convinced I could not have survived without those hours of privacy. It was wonderful to close the door at night and be quite alone, free to dream and read and think my own thoughts. Perhaps Dr. Phelps sensed this.

Or perhaps he had other reasons.

It was sometime in the middle of June, I believe, that Dr. Phelps called me into the library for the purpose of showing me a letter he had written. It was addressed to the editor of the New York *Observer*. When I read the opening lines my heart began to pound. "Public attention has been called of late to certain strange manifestations that have been denominated 'Mysterious Knockings.' "

Flinging the letter on the desk, I cried, "Are you mad? To call attention to this again?"

"Read the ending," Dr. Phelps insisted.

Sullenly I turned over the pages to the place he indicated, and read: "For some weeks past these annoyances at my house have been subsiding and now, as I hope, have ceased altogether."

"I felt that for your peace of mind you should be convinced of this," Dr. Phelps said. "You seem so much better—"

"I am perfectly well."

"I am glad to hear it."

I put the letter aside. Next to it, lying open on the desk, was a copy of that hateful periodical, the *Spiritual Philosopher*.

"You have not given up your interest in these matters, then," I said.

"There is nothing harmful in them. I refuse to accommodate myself to the demands of ignorant people."

I would have replied, but he gave me no opportunity. "There is one other matter I meant to mention to you. I have decided Henry should sleep in my room for a while. I have had a little cot put there for his use."

The change of subject was so abrupt I could only stare at him. He took my surprise for calm acceptance; with an approving smile he went on, "Henry is nervous, you know. Your friend Mr. Davis said it was his natural state. He sleeps better when there is someone with him."

Heaven forgive me—I did not question or inquire. I was not ready to receive the truth.

ONE DAY IN JULY Dr. Phelps saw fit to inform me that we were going to have visitors. I have complained of clergymen and newspaper persons, but this was the worst plague of all—Dr. Phelps's relations. They had spoken of coming before; but, like the rodents that desert a doomed vessel, they had been careful to keep their distance while we were enduring our agonizing experiences. Now that we had apparently been restored to favor, Dr. and Mrs. Joshua Phelps, and Mr. Austin Phelps, proposed to spend a few weeks in Stratford.

Joshua Phelps, my husband's brother, was a stolid, reserved gentleman who spoke very little, perhaps because his wife, Harriet, talked so much. She was the silliest of old ladies and had never approved of me or my children. But Austin was the one I dreaded. He was my husband's son by his first marriage and a man of absolutely terrifying respectability. His father was immensely proud of him, for he had followed his profession of theology and was already embarked on a distinguished career. I could have wished he was not so courteous to me; the icy correctness of his manner was almost worse than open resentment.

They arrived in the midst of a violent thunderstorm—another of those omens of nature to which I had become increasingly sensitive. Austin had not changed. When his hand touched mine in greeting it felt like an object carved of stone.

Harriet Phelps kept me constantly occupied for the next few days. She was unable to endure her own company—small wonder!—and followed me around the house, talking incessantly. I discovered that she was not the one responsible for keeping the family away while we were suffering; she was fascinated by the subject.

"Did the scissors grinder really ascend into the air?" she asked, round-eyed.

"Of course not. That was a complete fabrication."

"But windows were broken; Harry was carried through the air. Oh, I was most intrigued by it all," she went on, without giving me time to reply. "I would have liked to visit you then; but you know, Mrs. Phelps . . ."

"I know. Many of our friends abandoned us at that time."

It was perfectly safe to insult Harriet. She never noticed.

"Ah well," she said complacently. "People are very ignorant of spiritual matters. It is different with me. Oh, I do hope something will happen while I am here!"

They say that God is not the only one who grants wishes.

It was while I was attempting to escape Harriet for a brief time that I happened to overhear a conversation between Austin and his father. The gentlemen spent most of their time in the library, talking, as I supposed, of theological matters. How wrong I was in this assumption I was soon to learn.

Never before had I heard Austin raise his voice. The vehemence of his tones attracted my attention as I passed by the room; wonderment kept me motionless long enough to overhear his words.

"I am astonished at your attitude, Father. Surely you encourage matters that are better ignored."

"You have never doubted my word before, Austin," my husband said in tones of mournful reproach.

"I do not doubt it now. I am sure all the things you have described are literally true. I only wonder at your interpretation of them."

"You admitted last night that no one in the house could have been responsible for the sounds you heard."

I could bear it no longer. I flung the door wide.

"What sounds?" I cried. "What has happened? Dr. Phelps, you assured me the affair was over. You promised me!"

I think Dr. Phelps said something about eavesdroppers, but I was too overwrought to heed his words. The others were apologetic and kind. Austin made me take a chair, and Joshua Phelps stood by me, his hand on my wrist.

"You must tell her the truth, brother," he said to my husband. "It is far less alarming than the things she might imagine. Mrs. Phelps, your pulse is racing. Calm yourself."

Then they told me what had happened.

At midnight Austin had been awakened by a deep sigh breathed through the keyhole and repeated several times, quite loudly. This was followed by a tremendous hammering, outside in the hall. When he got up and struck a light he found dents on the banister. Then he went upstairs and found the children all asleep and the door communicating with the servants' quarters locked.

"Locked?" I interrupted.

"I have been taking that precaution for some time," my husband said. "It was necessary to eliminate the servants from suspicion."

"But my children and I are still suspects, I suppose!"

"No one suspects you, Mrs. Phelps," Joshua assured me.

"You heard nothing last night?" Austin asked.

"The medicine I take—for my nerves—contains laudanum. I sleep very soundly. . . ." But I could not go on. Was this why my husband had not objected to my having a room of my own? Was my door also locked after I retired?

Tears overflowed my eyes. Father and son exchanged glances. The latter said, "You have had a difficult time, Mrs. Phelps. But you could be of great help to my father if you would."

"What can I do? I swear I am innocent! I am a Christian woman, a member of the church—"

"I believe you." Austin sat down beside me. "I admit I came here with certain suspicions; but what I have seen convinces me that you are innocent of complicity. I hope this statement makes you feel better."

"It does, oh, it does. Thank you."

"Your active participation would be of great assistance to me," my husband said. "I have felt obliged to conceal certain things from you because of your highly nervous state—"

"You lied to me!"

"I have never lied to you. The statement I sent to the newspaper in June was correct. But when the rappings started again—"

"Why did they start?" I demanded. "You did something to bring them on!"

"Not until . . ." Dr. Phelps checked himself. "This exchange is unworthy of us, Mrs. Phelps. Can you not accept reality better now that we have the support of my family and the sympathy of many of our friends?"

I looked at Austin. He smiled—a warm, encouraging smile such as I had never before seen on his austere face.

"I will try, indeed I will. But my nerves will not stand much more."

"They need not endure indefinitely. I give you my solemn promise that if we have not put a stop to this business by the end of the summer, I will send you and the children away for a while—to Philadelphia, perhaps. Would you like that?"

"You need not talk to me as if I were a child, or bribe me with promises." I felt that I owed it to my self-respect to say this; but in fact the promise did hearten me. To foresee an end, however distant, makes any trouble easier to endure.

Dr. Phelps frowned slightly but did not reply to my criticism. He was too eager to explain the assistance he sought.

"Does the name de Sauvignon mean anything to you?"

The question was so contrary to anything I had expected I could only stare.

"No," I said finally. "Should it?"

"According to the information I have received, a man of that name was instrumental in cheating you in the settlement of an estate. Wait, I will spell it for you; it may be that my pronunciation has misled you."

When he had done so, enlightenment dawned on me. "You did pronounce it wrong; it is a French name. There was a clerk of that name—or one similar to it—in a law firm in Philadelphia. But how did you hear of him?"

My husband appeared a trifle embarrassed. After some hemming and hawing, he explained that one night, when the rappings had been particularly insistent, he had determined to ask questions, as had been done in other cases of the kind. To his surprise, he received intelligent answers, spelled out by means of letters of the alphabet—hence his mispronunciation of the name. The invisible respondent had informed Dr. Phelps that he was in hell, but had been permitted to report that an injustice had been done me. Dr. Phelps was all agog to check the accuracy of the information, but had been at a loss as to how to begin without my cooperation.

Needless to say, I was astonished at Dr. Phelps's folly. He had adamantly refused to encourage communication with the benevolent spirits Andrew had recognized. These spirits had now departed—I had Andrew's word for that. Then who—or *what*—had replied to Dr. Phelps's questions? But I knew the answer. It had identified itself as a damned soul. However, the astonishing accuracy of the information filled me with a sense of wonder that, for the moment, overcame my fears.

"Yes, indeed, there was such a man!" I exclaimed. "How amazing."

"Perhaps I should go to Philadelphia to see what can be done," Dr. Phelps said.

"Perhaps you should. It is not the money," I added seriously. "If a wrong has been committed, we ought to correct it and punish the wrongdoer. He may cheat others."

"Quite right." Dr. Phelps smiled approvingly at me. "You won't mind if I go away for a few days?"

"We will stay with you," Austin assured me.

"In that case," I said, "I shall be quite content."

WHILE WE AWAITED Dr. Phelps's return I found relief in talking with Austin, whose support comforted me a great deal. Of warmth he had very little, I think; but he did me justice and that was all I asked.

My sister-in-law, Harriet, was another matter. It was impossible to keep her from finding out that the rappings had begun again. She was disgustingly excited, and insisted on being allowed to speak personally to "the spirits." One afternoon I was entertaining a few ladies, who had called for the purpose of meeting her, when the wretched woman began telling my callers about the strange messages.

Mrs. Mitchell, who had become more friendly toward me since my illness, was among the visitors. My attempts to change the subject having proved vain, I glanced apprehensively at her—and saw that she was leaning forward in her chair listening as avidly as the others. Her lips were primmed disapprovingly, but her eyes gleamed with interest. I have often wondered whether strong desire can actually bring about a longed-for result. Though they would have denied it, every one of those respectable, proper ladies yearned for a demonstration of magical powers. Perhaps that is why their wish was granted.

There was a little distraction at the time, over teacups and hot water; no one actually saw the paper until it came drifting down onto the carpet. Harriet pounced on it with a squeak of excitement and read it aloud: "Sir Sambo's compliments, and begs the laddy's to accept as a token of his esteem."

Excited exclamations broke out. The grubby sheet of paper was passed from hand to hand.

The ladies stayed late that afternoon. But nothing else happened.

Dr. Phelps returned the following day. He had found enough evidence to confirm our suspicions, but not enough to justify taking the case to law. This annoyed me. Dr. Phelps, however, was inordinately pleased to have confirmation of his informant's accuracy.

When Harriet showed Dr. Phelps the epistle from Sir Sambo, he shook his head, smiling faintly. "Sir Sambo does not spell very well, does he? Seemingly there are tricksters in the spirit world as well as in this one."

"It must mean something," Harriet insisted.

"It means nothing."

"Then I wish he would write me a good letter," Harriet rambled on. "One that I could send to some of our relatives—the doubting Thomases, I call them—you know who I mean!"

She repeated this request, half jokingly, the following afternoon when the family was gathered in the parlor. Only a few minutes afterward a paper dropped onto the table. However, it was not addressed to Harriet. It began: "Dear Mary."

Harriet paused. Her eyes were not the only ones that turned

questioningly toward Marian, who, hearing a name so close to her own, dropped her embroidery and clasped her hands.

"Mama, truly, I did not ask—"

"No one has accused you of anything," I said. "Go on, Harriet. What does Sir Sambo say this time?"

"It is not from Sir Sambo," Harriet said seriously. "The letter goes on to say that the writer is well, and asks—"

"Never mind," my husband interrupted impatiently. "What is the signature?"

Harriet's eyes were round with awe. "H. P. Devil," she whispered. "Those are my initials—H. P. Do you think—"

"I think it is nonsense," Austin said, and Dr. Phelps agreed.

The imbecile communications continued, but erratically. We might receive two in one day; then a week would pass with no letter. They were so ridiculous I was unable to take them seriously, and though the raps and thumps continued, with an occasional broken pane of glass to enliven the proceedings, I no longer felt alarm. Familiarity had bred contempt, as Austin said. Harry had lost interest in the matter. He was out all day with his friends, swimming and playing ball, and Dr. Phelps assured me he was sleeping soundly at night.

Our visitors left in August. I would never have supposed I would be so sorry to see Austin go. I had come to rely on his sober composure, his quiet sympathy.

Things were somehow different after they left. I cannot describe the difference, though I felt it keenly. Perhaps the weather, which was unusually hot and muggy, had something to do with my restless mood. The nights were as stifling as the long hot days, without the slightest breeze; I would have found it impossible to sleep without my medicine. Marian began to show signs of sleeplessness; the rings under her eyes darkened daily.

The summer was drawing to an end. Harry complained of the imminence of school, and I began thinking about Philadelphia. Dr. Phelps had promised we would go if the rappings continued—and they had, though we had come to take them for granted.

I had another attack of illness at about that time—I cannot remember exactly when—the same thing as before, I think, though I believe the heat had a great deal to do with it. After the indisposition had passed, I felt better than I had for a long time. Waking one morning to find the air crisp and the leaves turning bronze, I had a burst of energy. When Marian came in, I was examining my clothes to see which needed refurbishing and which should be given to the poor.

"Mama, you should not tire yourself," she said in her low, breathless voice. "Sit down and tell me what I can do for you."

"Nonsense, I feel perfectly well," I said. "But you are quite faded, Marian. Are you ill?"

"No. . . . Not entirely healthy, perhaps."

"You will be better when we go to Philadelphia," I said. "We might consult Dr. Bishop—he always did you good. The doctor here is no use at all."

"Philadelphia! Are we going there?"

"Why, yes. Dr. Phelps said we would go in the autumn."

"He has said nothing to me."

I realized that my husband had not referred to the subject in recent days and decided I had better speak to him about it. To my chagrin, he equivocated.

"Do you feel it would be wise, Mrs. Phelps? Matters are fairly quiet now; people might start talking."

"Why should they? I have kin in Philadelphia and it has been a long time since I visited them."

"Well, perhaps."

"I want to get away from here."

I had not meant to say that. The sentence startled me almost as much as it did Dr. Phelps, who gazed at me with concern.

"Has anything happened that you have not told me about?"

"No. . . . But I feel—Dr. Phelps, it is not over. Something is going to happen—something terrible. You jeer at my premonitions—"

"No, Mrs. Phelps, I do not. What would you say to sending Henry away to school?"

A year earlier the suggestion would have roused me to anger and despair. Now I considered it coolly.

"Have you asked Harry what he thinks?"

"I have talked with him and he is not unwilling."

"Well, perhaps. In Philadelphia—"

"We will discuss Philadelphia at another time," Dr. Phelps interrupted. He picked up a book, indicating that our conversation was at an end.

I left the room. I had planted the seed in his mind and could only hope it would bear fruit. It would be good for Marian to spend the winter in Philadelphia—good medical attention, a wider circle of friends, perhaps even a suitor. Harry could go to school in the city and we could all be together.

I well remember my cheerful, optimistic mood that afternoon. I should have heeded the stab of premonitory terror that had pierced my heart, and not allowed it to be buried by hope.

I have tried to remember exactly when it happened. My memory is not good. Too many horrors have bruised it. And that horror, the worst of all, coming after a period of relative peace—just when my poor tired mind hoped a haven had been reached. . . .

Well, I cannot remember; but I know it was in the afternoon. I was sitting alone in the parlor, sewing on a new frock, when I heard a commotion in the hall. I went to the door, to see Dr. Phelps and Marian emerge from the library. He had put both arms around her in an attempt to guide her swaying, staggering steps, but she struggled and pushed at him. Her face was ashen pale, her eyes glazed; she babbled a string of nonsense syllables in a low hoarse voice. As I ran to assist my husband, Marian's limbs gave way entirely. She would have sunk to the floor if we had not supported her between us.

With the help of the servants she was taken to her room and placed on the bed. Smelling salts soon restored her; but when I questioned her she only murmured that she felt unwell and wanted to sleep.

I went to Dr. Phelps, who stood near the window.

"What happened?" I asked. "I have never seen her like this."

"I cannot imagine. We were attempting to . . . That is, I was giving Marian a mesmeric treatment—as I have done a hundred times— when she suddenly fell into a kind of fit."

"I have never approved of those treatments of yours. I knew they would do her harm!"

"You never said so," Dr. Phelps protested. His eyes fled from my accusing stare and turned anxiously toward the bed. He let out a cry of alarm. He pushed roughly by me. I turned. Marian's face was completely concealed by her pillow.

Dr. Phelps pulled it off. Marian's face, from being pale, had turned bright red.

"How did that happen?" I cried. "Did she do it herself?"

483

"I don't think so. . . . Good heavens! Now it is the sheet!"

I did not actually see it move; but suddenly it was over her face. Dr. Phelps removed it. Marian's eyes remained closed, her body unmoving, but now her breath came in long, harsh gasps.

"A pin," Dr. Phelps said. "Give me a pin."

I found two. Large safety pins. With hands that shook visibly Dr. Phelps fastened the sheet in place. Marian did not stir. My agitation was so great I started to shake her. Dr. Phelps took hold of my hands. I think I struggled with him. When I looked back at Marian, her face was once again concealed beneath her pillow. I snatched it off and clutched it to my breast, feeling as if I were grasping some animate, animal thing that might move again if I let go.

"Do something!" I cried. "She can scarcely breathe! Give her air! Open her collar!"

In fact she was wearing a gown with a low collar that did not in any way impede her breathing. Nevertheless, Dr. Phelps unfastened the top two buttons and laid the gown back from her throat. The harsh, painful breaths continued. In desperation Dr. Phelps untied the black ribbon she wore around her neck, though it appeared loose.

Under the ribbon was a narrow piece of tape. Dr. Phelps ripped it off, revealing a cord tied so tightly that it was imbedded in the flesh. Marian's breathing was like a series of death rattles, horrible to hear.

"Scissors, knife—something—quickly!" Dr. Phelps cried.

It seemed to take forever to find them. At last I located a pair of embroidery scissors. Dr. Phelps had great difficulty inserting the point under the cord; his fingers shook violently. But at last the cord was severed. Marian's breathing at once grew easier.

Finally she opened her eyes.

"Did I faint?" she asked weakly. "What has happened?"

THE TOWN IS WHISPERING again. Or did it ever stop, the buzzing grumble? I hear it constantly. It follows me even into my own room.

This time I cannot blame the gossips. He brought this on us with his tampering, his unholy curiosity. He has turned my daughter into some kind of monster; he has used my son as a subject for his dreadful experiments.

The first spirits were Angels, I am convinced of that. They departed, as they had promised—but the door was left ajar, and Dr.

Phelps opened it wide to other Visitors, damned souls from hell. The proof is in the result—a deliberate attempt on Marian's life. She would have strangled to death if we had not been with her. Nothing like that will ever happen again, if I can prevent it.

We leave tomorrow for Philadelphia. Harry is enrolled in school. Marian and I will stay with my aunt. Dr. Phelps will come later, perhaps. That is yet to be decided. I cannot see beyond the hour of our departure—our escape. I do not believe the demons will follow us; but will they linger here, haunting the empty chambers until we return, or will they go back to the hellish fires from which they came? Will I ever again dare to live in this house?

EPILOGUE

WHEN MRS. PHELPS and the children left Stratford, on October 1, 1850, the "demons" departed. They did not appear again when the family returned, in the spring of 1851. It is said, however, that the Reverend Dr. Phelps felt it prudent to separate the children. The following year Harry was sent away to school. Unlike the Fox sisters, who made a career of mediumship (and came to sad ends as a result), Harry is not mentioned again in spiritualist annals, nor is his sister. This strange and inexplicable interlude seems to have been their only adventure with the occult.

Naturally Mrs. Phelps's narrative reflects the opinions and knowledge of her time. It is tempting to poke fun at spiritual consultants like Andrew Jackson Davis; certainly his literary works, such as *The Great Harmonia*, are so stupefyingly dull and pompous as to be virtually unreadable. But the "Poughkeepsie Seer" was not as far off in his analysis of the Stratford case as one might think. He was shrewd enough to realize that Henry could, and possibly did, play some of the tricks himself. He also realized that this did not explain the mystery. His pretentious talk about spirits who caused the boy to act without his conscious knowledge becomes less absurd in terms of modern psychoanalytic studies of the subconscious. His references to "electrical and magnetic" forces are obviously nonsense; but laboratory studies continue today seeking to determine if there are other forces, as yet unknown, that can move objects just as Davis said.

A wiser man than Davis would have been confounded by the Phelps case. It remains to this day one of the most unusual and baffling of all poltergeist outbreaks. Skeptics cling stubbornly to the theory that the whole thing was a hoax; but if it was, it is hard to explain how all the tricks were perpetrated unless every member of the family was involved.

There have been those who suspected Dr. Phelps, but the favorite suspects were Henry and his sister. Almost thirty years later Austin Phelps, at that time professor of Theological Science at Andover College, admitted that initially he had felt the affair was contrived by his father's young wife and her older children. He went on to say that he soon became convinced they were innocent. Then, in a curt, shocking sentence, he added: "Mrs. Phelps was at that time in ill health from the first approaches of that malady by which she was subsequently bereft of reason."

"Bereft of reason." It was, in those days, literally a fate worse than death. The mentally ill were locked up for life in dreary institutions, or imprisoned in a room in some far corner of the house, where their screams would not disturb the family. A stronger woman than Mrs. Phelps might have succumbed to the strain and shock of those dreadful months. But was she a victim—or was she the unconscious perpetrator of a complex hoax, driven by her illness to commit acts that do indeed appear "bereft of reason"?

For over a hundred years the old Phelps mansion kept its strange secret. Dr. Phelps lived there until 1859; then he sold the place and moved to Plainfield, Connecticut. He finally died in New York State at the ripe old age of ninety. The house passed from owner to owner until, like so many large mansions, it fell victim to changing life-styles and to the turmoil of the Second World War, when it was turned into a nursing home. A few rumors of mysterious noises surfaced at that time. They can probably be dismissed as a combination of faulty wiring and active imaginations—for of course the eerie history of the rambling old house had never been forgotten.

There will be no more rappings in the Phelps mansion. After standing empty for several years it was attacked by vandals and by decay. In 1972 it was demolished.

A Novelization
of Events in the Life and Death
of Grigori Efimovich
RASPUTIN

A
Novelization
of Events
in the Life and Death of
Grigori Efimovich

Rasputin

by
Colin Wilson

ILLUSTRATED BY BEN WOHLBERG

The cold expanses of Siberia, the seething discontent of suffering Russian peasants and the terrible anxiety caused by the illness of a small boy provide the backdrop for the story of one of the strangest men of modern history, Grigori Efimovich Rasputin. Born a peasant, he was aware at an early age of extraordinary preternatural powers within himself. It was through these powers that he became a close personal friend and adviser of the royal family, thus gaining enormous political influence. Yet much of his life remains a mystery and the vast amount of material written about him contains discrepancies, inaccuracies and myths.

Who *was* Rasputin? To some, he was a saint, a miracle worker, a beloved friend. To others, he was an irreverent evildoer. In this compelling narrative Colin Wilson, author of *The Outsider* and *Rasputin and the Fall of the Romanovs*, draws an intimate portrait of Rasputin the man. We see his inner character, his remarkable personality, and we learn of his dreams, his desires, his fears, his disappointments.

CHAPTER ONE

ON JANUARY 1, 1917, THE TEMPERATURE in Petrograd was subzero and a light snow was falling. On the Petrovsky Bridge, over the river Neva, a few spectators watched a group of policemen who were standing around a hole in the ice. The head of a diver broke the black surface, and two policemen seized his arms and heaved him out. He was a big barrel-chested man whose body was caked with white grease to protect him from the cold; on his hairy chest it stuck up in little spikes like the icing on a cake.

The police now began heaving slowly on a thick rope that disappeared into the water. From the spectators on the bridge there was a gasp as a body broke the surface. When the corpse was pulled onto the ice, water drained out of the black beaverskin coat tied around it with ropes.

The police inspector bent and peered with disgust into the swollen face. The body was that of a bearded man in his late forties, the features strangely distorted by the ice that covered them. The man's arms and legs had been tied, but he had obviously succeeded in freeing one of his hands, which was raised above his chest, the fist clenched. It looked as if he were making the sign of the cross.

The inspector turned to the sergeant. "It's Rasputin, all right. You'd better telephone the minister's office." He noticed the look of satisfaction on the sergeant's face. "And stop grinning, you fool. Murder's no joke."

"No, Chief." But the sergeant made no attempt to hide his smile as he turned away.

When Protopopov, the minister of the interior, arrived about half an hour later, the body had been moved into a workman's hut on the riverbank. By now, the news had spread; cars and carriages lined the quays, and the bridge was crowded. The police had been given orders not to allow sightseers on the ice, in case it collapsed.

In the hut the doctor was dictating a report to his assistant. The inspector stood in the corner, warming his hands over a coke brazier. The body, which lay on a wooden bench, was now naked; melted ice had run to the floor. The doctor glanced at Protopopov, then went on dictating. "Bullet wound in the back, probably aimed at the heart. Another bullet wound in the head. Either should have been fatal. The left cheek is bruised and cut, probably from a kick. Handfuls of his hair are missing . . ."

Protopopov, a dapper little man with a neatly groomed mustache, peered down at the body, turned a sickly color and hastily looked away. He cleared his throat. "If the shots killed him, how did he succeed in freeing his hands?"

"Only one hand." The doctor was a burly gray-haired man with a gruff manner. "And the shots didn't kill him."

"How can you tell?"

"Because he died of drowning. Look." The doctor placed his hands on the naked chest and pressed down with his full weight; water gurgled out of the mouth, which was turned sideways. "The lungs are full of water, proving he was alive when he was thrown in."

Protopopov's face twisted, so that he resembled a child about to cry. He said tremulously, "What brutes. What filthy brutes." He hesitated, as if unsure what to do next. "They will be caught and punished. I'm going to report to Her Majesty."

The inspector said, "Pardon me, Minister. Can you definitely identify the body as that of Grigori Rasputin?"

"Yes, yes, it's him all right." Protopopov went out quickly, without looking back.

"He didn't stay long," the doctor grunted.

The inspector glanced out the door, to make sure the minister had gone. "He owed his appointment to Rasputin. Now, I daresay, he's worried he might lose it."

The doctor was pulling on his frock coat. "Any idea who did it?"

"Of course. Everybody knows. It was that young idiot Yussupov. With the help of Purishkevich. One of them rushed out and accosted a policeman, yelling, 'We have just killed Rasputin, the enemy of Russia and the Tsar.' "

The doctor whistled. "It sounds as if the Tsar may have been behind it."

"I doubt it. Why should he be?"

The doctor lowered his voice, nodding at the body. "They say he was the Tsarina's lover."

The inspector looked shocked. "Where did you hear that?"

"At my club."

"No, no, my dear chap. Not a dirty peasant like that." He glowered at the body. "I could believe he was a German spy. But not the Tsarina's lover."

The police sergeant looked in at the door. "The coffin's arrived. And the ambulance is trying to get through. The street's jammed with cars."

"Then make them move! That's what you're paid for." When the sergeant had gone, he asked the doctor, "Where's the body going?"

"The Chesma hospital. We'll do a postmortem there."

The coffin proved to be lidless; they had to cover the corpse with a blanket. Because of the crowds, the ambulance carriage had had to wait at the end of the quay; people struggled to glimpse the body as the men carried the coffin past. The doctor climbed into the back of the carriage and sat on the narrow wooden seat, his knees jammed against the coffin. The ambulance men, both middle-aged peasants (most young men were away at the front), looked at him respectfully, but said nothing. As the ambulance bounced and swayed over the cobbles, the doctor stared out the rear windows. In the Nevsky Prospect there seemed to be an unusual number of small groups. When the doctor had passed by two hours earlier, it had been half-deserted. Now people were talking eagerly, smiling, gesticulating; there was almost a carnival atmosphere. The news was spreading fast.

The blanket had slipped off the dead man's face, revealing the split cheek and the bullet wound in the head. As the doctor pulled it back again, one of the men said, "They must have hated him very much to treat him like that."

The doctor was struck by his thoughtful tone. He said, "Didn't you hate him?"

The peasant shook his round head ponderously; his guileless brown eyes made the doctor think of a large dog. "We had no reason to hate him, Doctor. He was a peasant, like us."

The other one added, "He was killed by the rich because he tried to help the poor."

The doctor stared at them in surprise; it was strange to hear a point of view so different from the one held among his acquaintances. The peasants looked down, as if they were embarrassed at speaking so frankly. The awkward moment passed as the carriage rocked violently, forcing them to clutch at the sides of the coffin; the carriage had turned onto the open road, and the driver had whipped up the horses. Under the blanket the dead man's raised hand gave the impression that he was about to push the covers away from his face and sit up.

SIBERIA IS A LAND of vast, empty steppes, of rivers so wide that the banks cannot be seen from the middle. Its forests are so immense that when a giant meteor exploded above them in June 1908, flattening eight hundred square miles of trees, it took many weeks for the news to filter back to civilization.

A great meteor also flashed through the skies of western Siberia on the night of January 23, 1871, when Grigori Efimovich Rasputin was born; his mother saw it through the bedroom window as she gave birth, and observed that it exploded into a shower like burning coals, then vanished. Through the pain of her labor, she wondered if the omen was for good or for evil.

Anna Egorovna was the wife of Efim Akovlevich Rasputin, a well-to-do peasant farmer. After ten years of marriage, life was pleasant and their affairs were prospering. It had not always been so. When they married, Efim Rasputin had been a coachman who drove the Imperial Mail, a man whose good looks and natural vitality attracted many women. He had married Anna out of a kind of bravado, because her demure gentleness seemed to contain a plea to be swept off her feet by a man who knew his own mind. Their first child, a daughter, was an epileptic; and the dashing coachman, finding married life something of an anticlimax, began to drink heavily. One night, as he slept drunkenly in the straw of an old barn, a thief stole one of his horses. Efim's superiors had already warned him about drinking; now the rumor that he had gambled away the horse in a card game led them to charge him with gross negligence. Such transgressions were treated harshly; Efim could have been flogged to death. But luck was with him; his punishment was six months in prison and the loss of his job. His wife and child moved back to her parents'.

The disaster made Efim Rasputin appreciate his wife; it also made him long for a stable home. On the advice of his father-in-law, he decided to emigrate to western Siberia. The government was anxious to encourage settlers in that immense, empty land; Efim was granted fifty square versts of land (a verst is about two thirds of a mile) and another ten square versts of forest. The land was good, and Efim enjoyed being a proprietor. With hard work, good management and a loan from his father-in-law, he soon became one of the most prosperous men in the village of Pokrovskoe. A son, Mikhail, born in 1869, was sturdy and intelligent, and spoke his first words before he was a year old. During the week when his second son, Grigori, was born, Efim Rasputin completed the purchase of a strip of meadowland from the government (at roughly two dollars a square verst) and was appointed headman of the village. Efim was a contented man, and never regretted the life of the open road, or the wayside taverns where he had played cards with other coachmen.

Grigori—abbreviated to Grisha—was as sturdy as his brother, but less placid. Misha accepted whatever life gave him; Grisha always demanded more. Misha enjoyed being caressed by his mother; Grisha struggled violently if anyone tried to kiss him. As a child, he always kicked off his bedclothes whenever he awoke in the night, so that during his first two winters his mother slept beside him in the kitchen, where the stove burned all night.

Although he was walking at the age of eight months, Grisha had still not uttered his first words by the time he was two. This was not lack of intelligence; his eyes sparkled with it. There was simply a lack of desire to communicate in language.

When he was just over a year old, Grisha disappeared one afternoon. His mother searched with increasing alarm until she found the stable door standing open. There was only one animal inside—a horse that had injured its leg in a fall. The animal was lying quietly in the straw; Grisha lay beside it, fast asleep. Anna picked the boy up and carried him back to the kitchen. At dusk her husband came back from the fields and sat drinking strong, sweet tea. The stableman, Ignaty, came in to smoke a pipe, and Efim Rasputin asked him about the horse, Kulat.

Ignaty shook his bald head. "Can't understand it. He seems all right."

"All right?" Efim hurried out to the stable. He came back shaking his head, but looking delighted. "That's amazing. The swelling's gone completely." Anna looked at Grisha, who was playing with a horseshoe, but said nothing. The idea that had crossed her mind seemed absurd.

From then on, the child spent a great deal of time in the stable and the milking shed. As soon as he was among animals, he experienced a deep sense of peace and contentment; moreover, he could convey the sense of peace to the animals when they were restive. When the pony pulled a hamstring, Grisha—who was then four—went and stood beside it, his eyes closed, his hand resting lightly on its rear leg. Then he smiled and said, "You're all right now," and went out. Ignaty, who had watched quietly from a corner without making a sound, led the animal into the yard; it walked without limping.

It was shortly after the incident of the pony that Grisha first began to suspect he was unlike other people. On a clear, sunny morning he and his brother were lying in their father's meadow, staring down into the glassy waters of the river Tura. The sun was behind them, so the water below was in deep shadow. Grisha peered down into the darkness and whispered, "There's a big fish."

"Where?" Misha craned forward cautiously, bringing his nose close to the surface; but he could see nothing. He said finally, "There's nothing there."

"Yes, there is."

"Can you see it?"

Grisha peered into the depths of the river; it was certainly dark, and the weeds formed a kind of curtain over the hollow in the bank below. He was not only aware of the fish; he was also aware of its alarm at the faces above.

Misha said in disgust, "There's no fish," and dipped his hand into the water. He shrieked as a large tench darted out from under the bank and into midstream. Grisha laughed, but it was not out of malice; it was out of the realization that he could sense the presence of the fish without seeing it, and that his brother did not share this ability.

One day in September his father came back early from the forest; Ignaty, the stableman, had been injured by a falling tree. The local midwife (Pokrovskoe had no doctor) had said his leg would take a few months to heal. As Grisha listened, he experienced a sudden foreboding—a certainty that Ignaty would never return to work.

In Siberia the autumn is brief; the hot summer turns quickly into icy winter. During this brief season the air is soft, heavy with memories of summer days and a sense of passing time. Two weeks after Ignaty's accident Anna Egorovna sat on the back porch, surrendering herself to the sounds of nature and to undefined regrets. Grisha sat by her feet, looking through a picture book of Russian saints. He asked suddenly, "Is Ignaty dead?"

She looked at him in surprise. "Why should he be?"

Grisha said, "I saw him come into the stable this afternoon when I was feeding Kulat."

"Was he limping?"

"No."

Anna said nothing more; but ten minutes later she walked down the street to make inquiries. Ignaty had died at four o'clock that afternoon—the leg injury had developed gangrene.

Anna Egorovna was disturbed and a little frightened. In country areas of Russia clairvoyance, or "second sight," is often taken for granted; but Anna had been brought up in a town. Her aunt Dunia, who was bedridden, also had the gift of "seeing things," and knew when there would be a death in the family. The ideas of clairvoyance and illness had become associated in Anna's mind, and she felt afraid for Grisha's health. This concern lasted until Grisha knocked over the milk jug while chasing his brother around the kitchen. With a child as mischievous—and occasionally destructive—as Grisha, there seemed no reason to worry about his vitality.

For in spite of his spells of dreaminess, Grisha was an altogether normal boy—that is to say, what the village priest, Father Pavel, called "a truant from holiness." He could be irritable, rough, petulant and self-centered. He was also affectionate, generous and completely honest. The Siberians are noted for their honesty; but Grisha told the truth for a reason of his own. He was so accustomed to knowing when other people were telling lies that he assumed they were able to see into his own mind. This habit of honesty persisted even after it finally dawned on him that other people lacked his insight.

In the 1870s there was no school in Pokrovskoe, so the boys grew up in complete freedom. Misha soon began borrowing books wherever he could find them. Grisha, however, preferred to wander in the *urman,* the immense forest of fir and pine, pick wild raspberries and red currants, or simply lie on his stomach and watch the wind ruffle the grass of the steppe. His father called him lazy; but he failed to understand that his son's wanderings were not due to boredom, or a desire to escape work. What drove Grisha outdoors in the summer dawn was an obscure hunger of the imagination. Lying in the grass, before the sun had evaporated the dew, he experienced a sense of deep peace, at the heart of which lay a curious excitement. It was as if the trees and the grass were trying to tell him something, but their whisper was just beyond the range of his hearing. On some days the earth itself seemed alive, and the peace inside him deepened. The feeling never lasted long; he became too excited and self-conscious.

One sunny morning in 1883, before the brief Siberian spring had turned into the stiflingly hot summer, Mikhail suggested that he and Grisha go on a picnic. They took chunks of black bread and onion, and bottles of homemade kvass, and made for a meadow not far above the waterfall where the river Tura joins the Tobol. It was a Sunday, and everyone seemed to have the same idea; the bathing place was crowded. They walked half a mile upstream to their father's meadow. The water was no longer calm and clear, but muddy and swollen with melting ice. Both of them knew that there was a broad shelf below the bank, where they could stand up to the waist in the icy water. Grisha was still taking off his clothes when he heard a cry from Misha. He rushed to the edge and saw Misha struggling in the water, several yards downstream, trying to grab a bush that grew out of the bank. Grisha jumped into the water, held on to the bush and reached for his brother. The freezing water numbed his legs. Misha gripped his hand and clung to it frantically, trying to turn in the fast current to grab with both hands. The jerk was too much, and Grisha lost his hold on the bush; he experienced terror as his mouth and nostrils filled with the muddy water. Misha was still clinging to his hand, and both boys were swept downstream.

Two hundred yards below, their neighbor, Arkhip Kaledin, the blacksmith, saw what had happened. Without hesitation, he jumped into the river, clinging with one hand to the grass of the bank. As Grisha went past, he gripped his forearm. Kaledin was a powerful man, but it took all his strength to hold on to both boys. He gripped Grisha between his legs while he pushed Misha up onto the bank; then he lifted Grisha after him. Kaledin then lost his balance and was swept fifty yards downstream before he managed to catch a projecting rock and pull himself ashore.

The boys were gasping, their teeth chattering, too miserable to be grateful. Shuddering with cold and shock, they allowed Kaledin to force them to walk home. Efim Rasputin made them drink a quantity of vodka, which made Mikhail sick. By evening both boys were delirious. Misha died two days later; the pneumonia that had set in was too much for him. Grisha was in a feverish sleep when it happened, his hair soaked with perspiration. His parents agreed to keep it from him, but it was impossible. As soon as he woke up, he asked, "Where's Misha?" Then he looked at his mother and said, "He's gone, isn't he?" and buried his face in the bedclothes.

For a few days Anna Egorovna believed she might lose Grisha too. But he was stronger than his brother. It was sorrow rather than illness that delayed his recovery. Summer came, and Grisha still looked pale and weak. At night he lay awake for hours, thinking about Misha.

His recovery came about through an event that amazed the whole village. On an evening in June, more than two months after the accident, a dozen peasants and their wives gathered in the headman's backyard, under a birch tree, to enjoy the coolness of the dusk and gossip about their neighbors; a steaming samovar stood on the bench that usually held milk churns. Grisha sat against the wall of the house, his knees drawn up under his chin. Since Mikhail's death, he had felt numb, and avoided these gatherings in his father's yard. This evening, for the first time, he felt a sense of awakening life.

The neighbors were discussing the loss of a horse that belonged to a local farmer. Two horses had vanished from his compound the previous night, and one had been found wandering near the river. The other had disappeared, leaving no marks on the hard earth. Some of the group were inclined to believe that the farmer, who drank too much, had forgotten to secure the gate and that the horses had wandered. When someone suggested that the missing horse had been stolen, he was contradicted by a peasant named Gvosdev: "In that case, why didn't the thief take them both?"

Suddenly Grisha spoke. "I can tell you." His heart was pounding with fear at the temerity of what he was about to say. Nevertheless he said it: "Because he didn't want people to think it was stolen."

The blacksmith, Kaledin, said, "Who's *he?*"

Grisha looked straight at Gvosdev, and saw him flinch; it confirmed what he already knew. He pointed. "*He* took the horse."

Gvosdev leaped angrily to his feet. "What's he talking about? Is he accusing me . . . ?"

Anna Egorovna said quickly, "Take no notice. The boy has been ill." She went over to Grisha, put her arm around his shoulders and said, "Come on, time for bed . . ."

Efim Rasputin apologized to Gvosdev, who accepted the apology with bad grace and left ten minutes later. Tactfully, the others refrained from mentioning what had happened. Yet all were thinking of what Grisha had said.

The next morning, as Grisha and his father crossed the farmyard, they saw three of the neighbors who had been at their house the night before walking through the gate; they looked tired but cheerful, and they were leading the farmer's horse.

"Where did you find that?"

The blacksmith clapped Grisha on the back. "Where do you think? At Gvosdev's place."

Interrupting one another, they told how, when they had left Rasputin's house the previous evening, they had begun discussing what Grisha had said and agreed that it was worth checking. Gvosdev had only been in the area for two years, and had already been accused of cheating a widow in a deal over land. The chief objection to the idea of theft was that it would be pointless to steal a horse from the same village; it was bound to be recognized. Then Kaledin remembered that there was a horse fair at Tyumen in a few days' time, and that gypsies there were not averse to buying stolen property. They walked to Gvosdev's small holding, three miles beyond the village, and lay in wait. Just before dawn they saw Gvosdev leave his house and go to a shed in an outlying field. When he came out leading the stolen horse, the three men fell upon him. In remote areas of Siberia horse stealing is regarded with more abhorrence than murder. They left Gvosdev unconscious on the ground, bleeding from the ears and nose; now they were leading the horse back to the farmer.

When the three men had left, Efim Rasputin turned to his son; his face was thoughtful, but he said nothing.

Grisha went back to the house for some bread and an onion. He stuffed them into his pocket and walked out of the village, along the bank of the river Tura. For the first time he was reconciled to Misha's death; he felt oddly changed, as if he were a different person. At a junction of the main stream and a tributary he sat watching the sunlight on the water until he felt hypnotized. Spaces seemed to be opening up inside him. In some indefinable way his heart seemed to be widening, and a stream of cool air was pouring in. Looking at the water, he was aware of the fish that swam in the green depths. Then, as the silence deepened, he could sense the movement of worms and insects in the earth. He could even feel the life of the trees, their leaves drinking the sunlight and sucking water up from the earth.

After half an hour this sense of kinship with the earth left him so tired that he lay down on the damp grass and fell asleep. He dreamed about Misha, but no longer felt any grief, for it seemed that his brother was not dead. When he woke up, the insight was still there. Death was some kind of illusion, a recombination of certain basic elements.

As these insights gave way to more normal feelings, he thought about his knowledge of the stolen horse, and glowed with satisfaction. He thought with pride of the words of Arkhip Kaledin, "That's a wonderful boy you've got—he'll make a name for himself." It was true. Now he knew it with a certainty that threatened to stifle his breathing. Suddenly, to his own astonishment, he felt an impulse to fall on his knees and press his hands together. The emotion choked his throat, and tears ran down his face. At the same moment he recalled something he had totally forgotten. When he was five years old, he had fallen ill with a fever. At the height of the delirium he had become aware of a woman sitting beside his bed. She was beautiful, had blond hair and was dressed in blue. When she laid her hand on his forehead, the fever left him and he fell into a peaceful sleep. There was a sense of complete security. Now, again, he experienced it: a sense of having an immensely powerful ally.

Walking home in the late afternoon, he felt that he had experienced a revelation. In some sense he had been "chosen." It seemed incredible: he, Grisha Rasputin, son of a peasant, confronted an important destiny. But what could it be? Would he become a saint? He could imagine himself living in a lonely hut in the forest, with pilgrims coming to visit him from all over Russia. It was deeply satisfying. Yet these daydreams were not wholly an expression of childish egoism. He felt a genuine longing to bring aid and peace to the suffering, to cure the sick, even to raise the dead.

Before he reached home, the character of his thoughts had changed. Suppose he was destined to become a great leader, or even, perhaps, an almighty tsar like Peter the Great? His imagination was on fire, and no dream seemed too absurd.

When he reached the village and people waved or said hello, he waved back gravely, with dignity, as befitted a man who had just been confronted by a dazzling future.

At midevening his mother went up to Grisha's bedroom to offer him a snack of salted fish and pickles, a habit she had slipped into since he had been ill. To her surprise, she found him reading—or at least he *seemed* to be reading. He had taken all the books from Misha's side of the room and placed them on the table beside his bed. They were an assorted lot: *The Life of the Archpriest Avvakum by Himself,* two odd volumes of Karamzin's *History of Russia,* a translation of a novel by Sir Walter Scott, a volume called *Family Miscellany* and a New Testament that Misha had been given by Father Pavel.

When Anna Egorovna told her husband that Grisha was trying to read *The Life of the Archpriest Avvakum* he was pleased; Efim Rasputin regarded himself as a religious man, and he often read the Bible aloud to his family on winter evenings. If he had known the thoughts aroused in his son by the life of the archpriest, he would have been less delighted. For Avvakum had traveled widely and had endured great perils. On the Tunguska River, in Siberia, his barge almost sank and his wife had to pull their children out of the water. After many tribulations Avvakum went to Moscow—"and the Tsar received me joyfully, as if I were an angel of God." Yet because he refused to forswear his faith in the old form of worship, he was thrown into prison and finally burned at the stake. Grisha was deeply stirred; he longed to visit these distant places, to see the churches of Moscow and the Altai Mountains and the vast expanse of Lake Baikal.

CHAPTER TWO

NOW THAT MIKHAIL was dead, it was the hope of Efim Rasputin that Grisha would one day take over the farm. Grisha was secretly determined to do nothing of the sort—at least not for a very long time to come. Relations between father and son deteriorated. As Grisha turned into a sturdy teenager, he was expected to work on the farm, digging potatoes, milking the cows, cleaning out the stable, reaping the wheat. He could, when he felt inclined, do a good day's work; but pulling up weeds and repairing fences bored him, and he usually left the job half done. At every opportunity he vanished to the forest, or out onto the steppe. There he would lie on his back, stare up at the sky and try to induce once more that mood of deep serenity. He experienced it in flashes; then his thoughts became commonplace again. His father was dissatisfied with him; he was dissatisfied with himself.

One Sunday he accompanied his parents to church. The church, with its onion dome, stood on a hill in the center of the village; on warm Sunday evenings—as this was—the doors were left wide open. Grisha sat where he could see out over the roofs of the village, to the forest. Father Pavel was not a good preacher, and his sermon this evening was unusually dull. Then something he read aloud captured Grisha's attention. "Neither shall they say, Lo here! or, lo there! for behold, the kingdom of God is within you."

He had heard the phrase many times before, but it had never meant anything. Now, recalling his experience on the bank of the stream, he suddenly understood. *That* was what he had glimpsed inside himself—the kingdom of God. The thought astonished him. When the service was over, he felt a compulsion to be alone. While his parents returned home, he walked out along the river until he came to the spot where he had experienced his earlier revelation. Once again, he tried to soothe himself into a state of peace and calm. His breathing became softer; his thoughts suddenly seemed to be within his control, no longer dragging him back toward the outer world. A sense of joy, of comfort, expanded inside him. Once again, he experienced the sensation of being able to look into nature. But this was still not the kingdom of God. He tried harder still, and his senses obeyed, allowing him to sink deeper and deeper inside himself. At that moment he felt a curiously pleasurable sensation at the base of the spine. It began to spread upward, until it entered his head, becoming a golden point of light. It became brighter, and he suddenly found himself thinking how strange it was that he should be sitting there, about to enter the kingdom of God. This thought was enough to destroy his absorption. The golden light vanished, and he found himself in the evening sunlight, sitting under a larch tree on the bank of the Tura. He went on his knees and prayed, trying to induce the vision again; but it had gone. He walked home slowly and sadly.

His mother was the only person to whom he tried to describe the experience. Her reaction was indignation. "Only the great saints see God. You'll be punished for the sin of pride." And she ordered him to speak of it to no one.

Rasputin now became absorbed in religious ideas, and it made him a better worker; he worked automatically, lost in his thoughts. Relations with his father improved. He also noticed that the girls of the village were becoming curious about him. At sixteen, he was tall, and the first growth of a mustache was appearing on his upper lip. Yet although he smiled amiably when people spoke to him, he seemed distant, engrossed in his own world.

ONE HOT JULY AFTERNOON Rasputin went down to the bathing meadow beside the river. Half the village was there already, lying around a natural pool. Those who had been in the water were naked, drying in the sun. Morality in Pokrovskoe was puritanical; yet generations of villagers had bathed naked and dried themselves in the open air, just

as in midwinter they shared the village steam bath and rushed out naked to roll themselves in the snow. In the water two girls began splashing him, and he made them scream by diving under the water and trying to seize their ankles. Later, when he came out, the girls came and lay nearby, their heads not far from his. He knew them well; they were sisters named Aksinia and Katia Gomozov, daughters of a peasant with some skill in veterinary surgery. During the winter Grisha had helped them deliver a calf.

The younger girl, Katia, now began to question him about his reputation for "second sight." The conversation was serious and proper, with no undertones of flirtation. They took care to look at each other's faces and not to allow their eyes to stray. It would have been regarded as an open breach of decency for people to stare at one another. Grisha explained that he sometimes had flashes of intuition about future events, but they would not work to order.

Three days later Grisha was returning from the turnip field, a hoe over his shoulder, when he encountered Katia again, leading a pony. The animal was limping; she told him she had been out riding when it had stumbled. Grisha placed his hand gently on its neck and raised its hind leg; soothing the flinching pony, he pulled out a fragment of flint from the hoof. "There you are, Katia. Now you can ride."

As he looked into her eyes, he felt a surge of desire that surprised him. Her own eyes became soft, almost frightened. He went on staring, savoring this new sensation, intoxicated by the surrender he saw in her eyes. Unable to resist, he bent down until his face was within an inch of hers; then, as she made no attempt to turn her head, he kissed her. His arms went around her, and he felt the warmth of her skin through the thin summer skirt. After a moment she pulled away, but made no attempt to break out of his arms. Suddenly, with embarrassment, he realized he had no idea of what to do next. He released her and said, "I'm sorry." It was untrue, but it relieved his awkwardness.

"I don't mind."

But he firmly rejected the temptation to kiss her again. They walked home together, trying to make casual conversation about horses.

Alone in his room, he thought about what had happened, and was overwhelmed with longing as he recalled the expression in Katia's eyes. But he had no desire to give up his solitude to share his evenings with this girl. It astonished him that his body could experience such a powerful need when his mind had no wish to get to know her better. Accordingly, he took care to avoid her for the rest of that summer.

THE FARMERS OF POKROVSKOE sold their wheat to the local miller, who in turn sold it back to them as flour. In August of 1887 Efim Rasputin's harvest was so good that he had an excess of wheat and barley. It would have to be taken to the market in Tyumen, a hundred and twenty versts away. Efim Rasputin had to supervise the farm; he decided to send Grisha to the market.

Grisha took the gray stallion, Ivan, the horse he liked best, and set out before sunrise on a morning in early September. The cart was well sprung, and he had padded his seat with furs. The sun was just rising as he left the village. For the first fifteen versts along the road the land on either side was cultivated, although the few farms he passed were in a poor state of repair and often the fences were broken.

It was a quiet morning, soundless except for the singing of birds. The grass was soaked with a heavy dew. At the wooden bridge over the river Grisha stopped the cart and stared down at the peaceful water, now low after the hot summer, and at the shadows of the fish. A deep sense of satisfaction descended on him. When Ivan snorted with impatience, he allowed the horse to amble on. The road was poor, full of holes, so it was necessary to proceed slowly.

After a few more miles Grisha reached a part of the road that he had never seen before; in all his years in Pokrovskoe he had never wandered more than a few miles beyond the village. Now, suddenly, western Siberia stretched all around him, the vast flat plains, the low rolling hills, the immense forests. The experience dazzled him; he had not expected the world beyond Pokrovskoe to be so breathtaking, so beautiful. More experienced travelers find western Siberia dull; to Rasputin, it seemed so rich and astonishing that it brought tears to his eyes. He wanted to pray, but was not sure what he should pray for, except to give thanks to God for making the world so enormous and varied. For hours he was in a kind of trance, too enchanted to get hungry. Occasionally he passed other peasants on the road, most of them with rags bound about their feet instead of boots—this was common in Russia at the time, and not necessarily a sign of extreme poverty.

By midafternoon he reached the village of Borki, midway between Pokrovskoe and Tyumen, and halted there to eat. In a neat white-painted building on the edge of the village he sat alone at a long table—big enough to hold twenty diners—and had a typical Russian meal of sardines with onion and tomatoes, hot mutton stew with highly seasoned dumplings, sour black bread, lemon tea and a huge chunk of melon. On a side table decorated with potted plants there were various bottles of wine with the prices written on each label. In the Rasputin household wine was seldom drunk; his father preferred to wash down his cheese and salt fish with vodka. Now he was surprised to see that the wine was so cheap, some of it as little as ten kopecks a bottle. Grisha counted his money—he had twenty rubles—and decided he could easily afford a bottle of wine. Timidly, half expecting a refusal, he asked the proprietress if he could buy a bottle; without hesitation, she set it in front of him, together with a wet glass. He tasted the wine, and found it sweet, with a delicious smell of some fruit that he could not place. After two glasses, an immense joy arose in him. He sat back in his chair like a Tartar overlord, surveyed the tavern as if he owned it, and thumped the table for a final snack of sour cream and cucumber.

That night he slept under the stars, wrapped in a blanket and a bearskin, while Ivan munched in a nearby field. As he stared up at the velvet arch with its blue and yellow stars, he told himself firmly that he would never settle in Pokrovskoe. He would travel the world until he had seen all its distant corners. His idea of geography was almost nonexistent; he only knew that an infinite variety of people and places stretched around him, and he wanted to see every single one of them.

He arrived in Tyumen shortly after midday, and found it large and rather intimidating, with its crowded streets, its wooden side-walks—Pokrovskoe had no such thing—its many churches and taverns. He asked about the market, and was told it had been held the day before. Rather downcast, he asked where the mill was, and was directed to a place that stood among gray, dusty fields on the edge of the town. Another peasant was ahead of him with a load of barley;

Grisha asked him the price of wheat, and was surprised to find it was much higher than in Pokrovskoe (where the miller held a monopoly). He sold his cartload without difficulty and, with a pocket full of rubles, found an inn for the night. After seeing Ivan settled in a stall, he walked around the town, marveling at its shops, its churches and, above all, its stylishly dressed women. He had never seen so many attractive women.

Outside a shop labeled *Modistka* he stopped to smell the delightful scent of perfume that wafted through the doorway. As he stood there, a woman came out—a pink-cheeked girl in her early twenties. She was wearing a purple silk gown, and blond curls were held against her cheeks by her bonnet. Instantly, in the space of a few seconds, Grisha Rasputin fell in love. The woman got into a droshky pulled by a smart brown thoroughbred that made Ivan look like a mule, and ordered her maid, sitting beside her, to drive on. Grisha stood and stared until they vanished around the corner. Then, with a heavy heart, he walked on. He could never hope to possess a girl like the one he had just seen. Life was unfair. Why should he, Grisha Rasputin, be doomed to remain a peasant? He looked at the young officers who walked smartly along the sidewalk and envied them.

The gloom was short-lived. He found a church that was dedicated to Saint Cyril and went in. The candlelit interior brought immediate peace to his disturbed spirit. Once again, he felt the presence of a secret ally, some guardian angel who meant well by him. He prayed devoutly for half an hour, then, uplifted, stepped once more into the dusty street.

When Grisha paid the bill the following morning and led Ivan back through the streets of Tyumen, he observed the prices of various goods displayed outside the shops and he noted that they, like the price of wheat, were a great deal higher than in Pokrovskoe. During the return journey he was oppressed by the thought that it would be another year before he would have the chance to travel this road again. Then he was struck by an idea. Many of the peasants of Pokrovskoe had excess produce—not just grain, but vegetables, herbs, smoked hams, dried beef, salt fish. Why not make regular trips to Tyumen to take advantage of the higher prices?

He was home before evening, the return journey being quicker with an empty cart, and was received like a general back from a successful campaign. His father was obviously delighted with the price received for the grain, although he grumbled when Grisha admitted he had made no attempt to bargain. His mother made him his favorite dumplings filled with herbs, and he ate an enormous meal. He knew his father well enough not to voice his idea about regular trips to Tyumen; but during the meal he spoke of the high prices, and mentioned that there must be other villagers with goods to sell. His father became thoughtful, then went out. An hour later he came back and asked Grisha if he would like to make another trip to Tyumen in about a month's time. Grisha pretended to consider the idea, then said he didn't mind, it was a pleasant drive. In bed that night he lay awake, hardly able to believe that life had suddenly become so interesting.

On the second trip, at the beginning of October, he drove the larger wagon, and needed a team of two horses. This trip was even more successful than the last. He forced himself to bargain, sold his goods at a price above the minimum specified by his father, and returned with a satisfactory profit.

A few weeks later, as Grisha was returning from his third trip, great drifting flakes began to fall gently from the gray sky. By the time he reached home it was snowing so heavily that he could not even see Ivan's head. It was going to be a long winter.

AND SO IT WAS. He was trapped in Pokrovskoe. At first he dreamed of distant places; then he grew too bored and depressed to dream. In previous winters he had been oddly contented, like a child listening to rain beating on the window; now he felt suffocated. His inner light dimmed, then went out. When he prayed, he felt nothing.

One cold, dull afternoon he delivered a load of sawn logs to the local tavern and accepted the proprietor's offer of a glass of slivovitz. The music of the accordion made him feel suddenly happy, and when someone began to do a Cossack dance, he joined in, performing with such vigor that everyone clapped. When he returned home for dinner that evening, he was mildly drunk, but he felt alive again.

Within a week the tavern had become a habit, and the seat near the stove was regarded as his. Because Grisha was the son of the village headman, people respected him; but they also seemed to like him for himself. As he played checkers or danced with the girls, his dreams of fame seemed absurd. Looking at the happy faces around him, he felt an immense love for the people of his own village.

In the second week of March the thaw set in. The snow melted and turned into mud. The ice on the Tura began to crack. The ditches were filled with roaring torrents of melting snow, and in all directions there was mud as far as the eye could see. The fields became sticky morasses that sucked at the boots, and the roads were almost as impassable as in the snowdrifts. But finally the monotonous brown was replaced by green. The earth smelled warm and fertile, and the birds returned.

Efim Rasputin was already calculating the amount of money he would make in the following year from his son's regular visits to Tyumen; he wanted an extension to his cowshed and a new pigsty; Anna Egorovna wanted a new porch at the back of the house and a seat around the birch tree. But when, in the last week of April, the big wagon was loaded and ready to go, the spring rain fell in torrents and again turned the roads into a shining expanse of water and mud. Then a tribe of gypsies arrived and announced that the road to Tobolsk was passable. Grisha, anxious to get out of Pokrovskoe, toyed with the idea of going to Tobolsk instead of Tyumen, but he was fascinated by the gypsies; they brought a smell of distant places, and he wanted to become better acquainted. Even his father agreed that a few more days would make no difference. Grisha would leave after the May Festival.

In Pokrovskoe, the morning of the May Festival is devoted to a church service followed by a procession through the village carrying icons and a crucifix. Tables with food and drink are set out in the street, and all the doors along the route of the procession are left open. There are few places in the world where this festival honoring spring is celebrated as joyfully as in Siberia, and by midday the streets of Pokrovskoe were crowded with dancers and the taverns with drinkers.

Grisha, enjoying the warm sunlight, the bright dresses of the women, the music of gypsy fiddles, sat down outside the tavern to drink a glass of beer. As he raised it to his lips, a tall blond girl came around the corner with an older woman and stood looking at the dancers and tapping her foot. Grisha took a thoughtful sip and put down the glass. In Russia blonds are unusual; this girl was also unusual in being tall and slim. Grisha was about to stand up and ask for a dance when another young man approached her and swept her off into the crowd. Grisha stood up to get a better view. She danced well—with grace as well as vigor—and with her flushed cheeks, she reminded him of the blond in the purple silk gown in Tyumen. The memory made his heart sink. When Aksinia Gomozov, the veterinarian's daughter, came and stood nearby, he asked her, "Who's the new girl?"

"Her name's Praskovia Dubrovina. She moved here last winter."

When the dance finished, Grisha found her standing a few yards away; he hastened over and asked her to dance.

"All right, when I get my breath back." With her white teeth and pink cheeks he found her dazzling. Another girl came up and talked to her. He stood there, watching her face. At close quarters she lacked the doll-like prettiness of the girl in Tyumen; but she had an air of good health that was even more captivating. Listening to her, it was impossible not to notice that she seemed better educated than most of the village girls, and her voice was well modulated and pleasant. With a kind of despair, he realized he was experiencing precisely what he had felt outside the *modistka* in Tyumen, and that he was about to fall in love.

The fiddles started to play. She turned toward him, holding out her hands. Suddenly he experienced a gleam of hope.

They danced well together. Grigori Rasputin was always a good dancer; it expressed his earthy vitality. She had more grace, and her movements made the bright checked dress swirl around her in a way that enchanted him. The girl seemed to like him, and he felt his confidence increase. When the dance was over, she made no objection when he led her to a drink stall and presented her with a glass of kvass.

"I'm Grigori Efimovich Rasputin."

"I am Praskovia Fedorovna Dubrovina."

"Where does your family come from?"

"Ekaterinburg."

His heart sank; he knew enough to know that Ekaterinburg was a large town, and that this probably accounted for her sophistication. But he rejected the sense of helplessness and stared into her eyes.

"You are very beautiful."

She blushed. "Don't be absurd." But he was thrilled to realize his eyes held hers, just as they had held Katia Gomozov's. With that curious inner certainty, he knew that this dazzling girl could be his. And this time he experienced no self-division. He wanted her as he had wanted the girl in the purple gown. But Praskovia Fedorovna was within his reach.

That night he walked her home to the other end of the village. It was one of the larger properties, bigger than the Rasputin farm. But now he was too confident to care. Firmly, as if to dismiss any objection, he pulled her into the dark shadows of the yard. She tried to turn her face aside until he took her head in his left hand and held it still. Then she allowed him to kiss her. He held her tightly, and felt a surge of pride as she submitted. When he released her, she made no attempt to move away. He whispered in her ear, "Tomorrow I have to go to Tyumen. But I'll be back in three days. Keep Thursday evening free for me."

As he walked home, he found himself unable to trust his luck. In his mind he ran through the whole day since he had met her, charting his progress toward that final kiss. And then, for the first time, he realized that he intended to marry her.

CHAPTER THREE

GRIGORI RASPUTIN MARRIED Praskovia Dubrovina not long after his nineteenth birthday; his bride was twenty-three. But the age gap made no difference; from the beginning he was master.

Praskovia moved into the Rasputins' house. Anna Egorovna liked her because she was an excellent housekeeper; she was sensible, competent, and knew her own mind; yet at the same time she was always gentle and pliable. Efim Rasputin was proud of her because she was so obviously a "lady"; when he looked at the blond head bent over sewing or carding wool, he often felt a flash of envy for his son's luck. It was dawning on Efim Rasputin that Grigori was somehow "different." If he tried to pin it down, he could only say that, with more education, his son might have become a schoolmaster or a priest. But it was now obviously too late.

The young couple found life with Grisha's parents in many ways frustrating. They were violently in love, but a custom of reticence forced them to conceal their feelings in front of others. They made up for it at night. Her body gave him the kind of pleasure he had imagined, but never believed he would experience.

THE FOLLOWING OCTOBER, Praskovia bore her first child, a son. They named him Mikhail after Rasputin's dead brother. The first time he took his son in his arms, Grisha was aware of the life in the tiny body just as he had been aware of the life of fish and birds as a child. He liked to hold the baby after Praskovia had finished giving him his bath, sitting with his shirt open to the waist, feeling the smooth, warm body against his naked chest. He would stroke the hairless head, holding the soft cheek against his own and laughing if the baby slobbered and made his face wet. His love was a strange mixture of pain and pleasure.

One night he was awakened from sleep by the sound of Praskovia's sobbing. He sat up, his heart pounding, and groped in the dark for some matches. "What is it?" he asked. But the fear in his heart told him the answer. As the light from the match lit the room, he saw his wife, sitting on the floor beside the cradle, holding the baby in her arms and rocking backward and forward in an agony of misery. "He's dead." Rasputin rushed across the room and seized the baby from her. But she was right; the body was already cold.

He raised her gently from the floor. "Come back to bed." He persuaded her to get into bed, where she sat, clinging to the body, rocking it against her breast. She was saying, "I can't understand it. It was only a cold—a slight chill." And he was thinking: I shouldn't have called him Mikhail. The pain was so great that he wanted to do something, to cry out or rush through the streets of Pokrovskoe. Instead he sat there, numb with misery, feeling once again all the helpless agony that he had experienced after his brother's death.

The next day was cold and gray. He went to the church to arrange for the burial; even the thought of burying his son twisted his heart so he wanted to groan. When he came back he went to their bedroom, lit the oil lamp in front of the icon of the Virgin of Kazan, and knelt and prayed. Slowly, the worst of the pain disappeared. God had not deserted him. Yet he still felt that the death of his son was some kind of punishment. He heaved himself to his feet, to go downstairs to comfort his wife. He was only twenty years of age; glimpsing himself in a mirror, he saw an old man.

The summer came. Praskovia was pregnant again. Grisha had recovered from his shock, but the sense of sin still pulled at his heart. He spent hours kneeling in prayer, and the prayers comforted him, although they brought no deeper illumination. About once a month he still made trips by cart to neighboring towns, to Tobolsk as well as to Tyumen, and sometimes even downriver to Kurgan by barge. Their affairs were prospering. With the help of his father and the village carpenter, Grisha began to build himself a house on the farm. The long, hard labor gradually eased the pain in his heart; so did the birth of another son, whom they called Dmitri. The child was unusually placid; he never cried. Because of his quiet disposition, it was a long time before they became aware that fate had visited them with a second tragedy: Dmitri was mentally subnormal.

ONE DAY, ON HIS way back from Tobolsk, Grisha was approached by a wealthy peasant who asked if he had any objection to going as far as the monastery in Verkhoture. Rasputin said he would go to Saint Petersburg, provided he was paid. The peasant—whose name was Arkadi Saborevski—explained that his son had decided to become a novice in the monastery. At age twenty-one, Mileti Saborevski had already attended a theological seminary, and was now convinced that he was destined for the life of a monk. Rasputin went back to Saborevski's house to meet the youth. Mileti was tall, sallow and clever. There was also a touch of the spoiled child about him. After eating a snack of salt fish and cucumber and drinking a tumbler of vodka, Rasputin and Saborevski agreed upon a price. Grigori would come for Mileti the following week.

On the first day of the journey neither spoke much. Rasputin thought about his home and his family, then simply stared at the wide, empty landscape, feeling as though it were flowing quietly through his heart, like a brook.

That night they stayed at a tavern—Saborevski's father was paying all expenses—and Rasputin suddenly asked his passenger why he wanted to become a monk. Saborevski said simply, "Because I want to live for God, not for myself."

Grisha smiled. "But God is inside you. You only have to listen to His voice. Why go to a monastery?"

Saborevski looked at him in surprise. "Inside me? What on earth do you mean?"

"The kingdom of God is within you," Rasputin said firmly.

He said it with such quiet conviction that Saborevski stared at him. Then he asked, "And how do you think you know?"

In the most matter-of-fact tone Rasputin related his experience on the bank of the Tura. As he spoke about the sensation that rose up his spine, Saborevski looked at him with a curious expression. It was a mixture of respect and envy. In Russia, as in India, there is a tradition of holy men who wander the roads, begging for their bread and praying at wayside shrines. Saborevski had talked with many of them, but few had impressed him as much as this tall peasant with the untidy hair. Saborevski asked curiously, "Don't you want to see God again?"

"Of course I do. I'd give anything for it to happen again."

"Then perhaps you ought to become a monk."

"No. I have a wife and child."

"How do you know God hasn't some important design for you?"

Rasputin laughed. "If He has, He hasn't told me what it is yet."

The next day, as soon as the wagon was rolling across the broad, empty landscape, with its distant forests, they again began to talk about religion. Rasputin realized that Saborevski thought all he had to do to get into heaven was to be good. For a while Rasputin kept this observation to himself. But as Saborevski asked him more and more searching questions, he spoke the thought that was in his mind.

"Why do you keep on talking about holiness? Holiness means being close to God. And you can't get close to God without really trying. You have to open your soul to repentance."

Mileti Saborevski frowned, his pale, youthful face looking like an unhappy child's. "But I've repented of my sins."

Rasputin could not prevent himself from laughing. "Then perhaps you haven't sinned hard enough."

The novice smiled ruefully. "You sound like one of the Khlysty."

"The what?"

"They are heretics. They think you need to sin in order to repent."

"Sounds sensible."

Saborevski snorted. "It's just self-indulgence."

Rasputin remained silent.

They arrived at the Verkhoture monastery at midafternoon on the third day. Rasputin was taken to the guest house where he was given food and a bowl of water to wash his feet. When he had finished the bread and soup, he went out into the courtyard and relaxed on a bench, enjoying the sunlight and staring up lazily at the spires and domes of the monastery. Through the gateway he could see monks working in the fields. He envied them their serene, unworldly existence.

Saborevski came out of the main building.

"Father Ignaty would like to see you."

"What does he want with me?"

"I don't know."

Father Ignaty was in his cell, high up in the monastery. It was a comfortable room with many books. The abbot was a huge gray-haired man who looked strong enough to lift an ox. He had striking blue eyes. Rasputin felt shy and awkward, not even sure how he should address an abbot; but Father Ignaty's genuine warmth soon put him at ease. The abbot offered him lemon tea from a samovar and asked after the health of Father Pavel, whom he had known at the seminary. Grisha found it easy to talk to the big, friendly man. He was also perceptive enough to know that Father Ignaty was summing him up. The abbot said suddenly, "Why don't you stay here for a while?"

Rasputin looked up eagerly. "May I?"

"Of course. We'd be glad of a bit of help—we're just getting the turnips in."

"I'd like to."

"Good. Stay as long as you like."

An hour later Rasputin accompanied Saborevski to vespers, then joined the monks at dinner in the refectory. After the opening prayers and a reading from the Bible, the atmosphere was as relaxed as at a party—perhaps because it was a Saturday and there was no work the next day. The food was good, and he was pleasantly surprised to find they drank cider and a sour white wine. After three days on the road Rasputin ate ravenously.

At the far end of the room he noticed a number of men who were obviously not monks; they were mostly bearded and dressed in peasant smocks. Rasputin asked the monk on his left, "Who are those men?"

"Ah, they're members of a sect called Khlysty."

"Khlysty? I thought . . . I thought they . . ." He was not sure how to put it without being offensive. The monk smiled.

"They are. Heretics. They've been exiled here. I suppose you could say they're prisoners."

Rasputin turned to Saborevski on his right and asked in a low voice, "Did you know those people over there are Khlysty?"

"Good heavens." Saborevski looked nervously at the bearded men in their blue smocks; a moment later Rasputin caught him surreptitiously crossing himself. He obviously thought he might catch heresy like a disease.

The next morning they were up at dawn for matins, then had breakfast, consisting of cold porridge, apples and tea. A novice named Peter had been assigned to show Saborevski the monastery and the nearby village of Verkhoture. Rasputin went with them. It was another mild, sunlit day, with a touch of autumn in the air. Verkhoture was slightly larger than Pokrovskoe, but less well kept. Nevertheless, everything seemed to Rasputin to have an indefinable charm, an aura of peace and holiness. Then, as they passed the church, people began to stream out, among them a number of attractive girls carrying their hymnbooks. Rasputin's thoughts about holiness vanished as he looked at them. For five days now he had been celibate, and his body longed for contact with female warmth. He sighed as he thought of the problems of achieving sainthood.

At that moment he heard the novice Peter saying, "Many people around here regard him as a saint."

"Who are you talking about?"

Saborevski said, "Father Makary. He's a hermit who lives in the woods. They say he used to be a learned man in Saint Petersburg before he experienced the call."

"Could we see him?"

Peter said, "Yes, I don't see why not."

It was a half hour's walk to woods beyond the monastery. On the way there Peter told the stories he had heard about Makary's youth—how he had been born into a wealthy family, had been an Army officer and become notorious for gambling, dueling and seducing shopkeepers' wives. One day, as a result of a bet, he had gone to live in a broken-down hut in a forest. After a month there he had won his bet, but had also decided that he had found his vocation. Now, after wandering all over Russia, he had settled near the monastery—where he was not much liked by most of the monks.

The hut stood in a clearing by a large clear pool. Rasputin thought he had never seen such a delightful spot. The building itself was a simple structure built of roughly hewn logs, with wooden shutters. Peter knocked on the door and called, "May we come in, Holy Father?"

"Yes, come in." The voice was deep and had a throaty resonance. Rasputin experienced a sudden cold feeling in his stomach.

The hut was divided in two by a curtain. On a low chair in the corner, beneath the open window, sat the hermit Makary, a striking-looking man with thin, ravaged features and a bald head. A few peasants, both men and women, were sitting opposite him on the floor. Makary said, "Ah, visitors from the monastery."

Peter knelt and kissed the hermit's hand. Saborevski also kissed Makary's hand, although his reluctance was plain. Rasputin went on both knees and kissed the hand with profound humility; Peter's stories had convinced him that he was looking at a saint.

Makary stared with interest at the good-looking peasant with his untidy hair and deep-set eyes. He reached out and took Rasputin's right hand in both of his, asking, "Where are you from?"

"Pokrovskoe, Father."

The old man's face was so white and strained that it looked like a skull covered with a rubber mask. But the dark eyes were full of life. These now stared into Rasputin's, as if trying to beat down their gaze. Rasputin stared back with fascination. He began to feel uncomfortable, but was unable to avert his gaze. The others, aware that something was happening, were silent. Then the hermit released Rasputin's hand and said quietly, "Come here, my boy." He gestured for Rasputin to come closer. Grisha moved forward. Makary spoke in a low voice, which was half drowned by the noise of the stream through the open window. He said, quietly and seriously, "You have a strange destiny. You are going to be a famous man . . ."

Rasputin, his lips dry, asked, "A holy man, Father?"

"Yes, a holy man. But you are going to be more than that." He

paused. Then he looked up and said in a strong, normal tone, "And if you're not careful, you are going to be a martyr."

Rasputin asked the question he had been longing to ask since entering the hut.

"Shall I find God?"

Makary said, "Only God could tell you that. But if you pray for guidance, He will help you. To strengthen your spiritual power, you should go to Greece and pray to the Virgin on Mount Athos."

A lamp was burning in front of an icon; Rasputin saw that it was the Virgin of Kazan, and felt that this was a good omen. He kissed Makary's hand again, then went to the corner and fell on his knees. Now, suddenly, he knew beyond all doubt that the aim of his life was to find God. Nothing else mattered.

On the way back to the monastery his companions talked normally; but he caught occasional glances that betrayed their intense curiosity. Finally Saborevski asked, "What did he mean about being a martyr?"

And Rasputin, ashamed of the depth of his experience, tried to make light of it. "He said if I'm not careful. But I intend to be careful."

After supper that evening Rasputin excused himself and went outside. In the courtyard it was cool; the sky was blue and clear. He sat on the bench outside the guest room and sank into peace. Someone came and sat on the other end of the bench; a gray-bearded man in the blue peasant smock of the Khlysty. Since the opportunity had offered itself, Rasputin decided to speak with him.

"Do you enjoy living here?" he asked.

The old man looked at him with mild blue eyes. "We accept whatever the Lord sends."

"Could you leave if you wanted to?"

"Only if we renounced our faith."

"And what is your faith?"

The old man looked at him searchingly, decided that the question was not impertinent or trivial, and said, "We believe that the spirit is good and that matter is evil. And we believe that Christ has returned to earth many times as a man. This is what He meant by His promise of resurrection."

Rasputin asked, "Where do you seek the kingdom of God?"

The old man answered promptly, "It lies within us."

Rasputin said with conviction, "You speak the truth."

"God cannot lie," the old man said gravely.

The abbot crossed the courtyard, talking with a monk. When he saw Rasputin and the old man on the bench, a shadow crossed his face. The old man noticed it.

"We cannot speak further. They don't like it." He said "they" as if speaking of some alien conqueror.

Rasputin said, "But where can I learn more about your teachings?"

The old man looked at him searchingly. Then he said, "Do you know the village of Neyvo Shaylansky?"

Rasputin had seen the name on a signpost the previous day. He nodded. The old man said, "Ask for Nikon Kostrovsky. Say Yemeljan sent you." He stood up and walked away. Rasputin noticed that the abbot was standing behind them, apparently staring into the distance, but obviously trying to listen.

The following day Rasputin left the monastery and by dusk he had found his way to Neyvo Shaylansky, a small farming community situated in a valley beside a stream. There he met a peasant woman carrying water and asked her where he could find Nikon Kostrovsky. She looked at him searchingly, then pointed down a dirt track to the water mill.

A middle-aged peasant with a straggly gray beard answered his knock.

"Nikon Kostrovsky?"

The man said cautiously, "Who are you?"

"Yemeljan sent me."

The man's face broke into a smile of welcome. He embraced Rasputin. "Come in, brother." They went across the room that housed the creaking waterwheel drive, into the living quarters; the place smelled of dust and corn flour. The man said, "To others, I am known as Dmitri Kuzmich. Only the pure ones know me as Nikon." It was clear that "pure ones" meant Khlysty.

Rasputin was invited to join them for supper. The family consisted of a youth of eighteen, a tall cross-eyed girl in her mid-twenties and a child of about nine. Kostrovsky explained that his wife had died.

They ate a simple meal of soup, black bread and vegetables, washed down with goat's milk. After the meal Rasputin bedded Ivan down for the night and then sat with the others and talked about religion. It was clear that these people found great pleasure in speaking about their beliefs. They told Rasputin of the group meetings that were held in the barn where the faithful danced wildly to the chanting of hymns, spinning around and around until finally they collapsed with exhaustion. They explained to him that sometimes, after the dancing, men and women would come together in sexual embrace, but they were no longer themselves. They belonged to God.

Rasputin listened intently and at a certain point, in answer to a question, he described again his experience by the river Tura. To his astonishment, the cross-eyed girl—whose name was Daria—came and knelt by his chair, kissing his hand.

At breakfast the next morning Kostrovsky said, "Do you wish to stay among us, Grigori Efimovich?"

"I must go."

"It is your choice."

As Kostrovsky spoke, Rasputin looked at Daria, who was drinking tea from a bowl. A strong force made him stand up and go behind her. Kostrovsky, aware that something was happening, became grave and watchful. Rasputin touched Daria's shoulder and pulled her back toward him, so her shoulders rested against his belly. Then he placed both hands over her eyes, pressing gently on the closed eyelids. The force flowed up through his fingertips. It was quite simple. He knew exactly what to do; he had done it before, as a child, when he had cured animals. He simply allowed the force to flow from inside him, changing her energies, straightening what was twisted, righting what was wrong. For perhaps five minutes he stood like this, while Kostrovsky sat with his head bent in prayer and the nine-year-old looked on with wide eyes. Then Rasputin knew it was done. He withdrew his hands, kissed her on top of the head as a mark of love, and sat down again. The girl was sitting still, her eyes full of tears. Then she jumped to her feet and ran out of the room and up the stairs. But Rasputin had had time to see that the eyes stared straight at him; the squint had gone.

Later that day, as the cart rattled along toward Pokrovskoe, he thought about what had happened and tried to understand it. It filled him with joy that this strange force had chosen him as its dwelling place. The certainty of it made him feel unshakable.

As if to emphasize that life still possessed its uncertainties, the wheel went over a rock and the cotter pin snapped; it took him two hours, and considerable ingenuity, to get the cart back on the road.

WHEN GRISHA RETURNED HOME, both his mother and his wife noticed that he was different. He looked older, more sure of himself. A certain boyish element had vanished, and would never return. His mother looked at him with pride; but his wife was less happy about the change. He seemed in some way harder. It was obvious that he still loved her; but it was in a more controlled way, without the abandonment.

Throughout that winter Rasputin spent hours of every day in prayer, hoping to perceive the kingdom of God he knew to be hidden somewhere in his own depths. On two occasions he entered moods of such profound peace that he felt the revelation to be close; but something inside him seemed to be resisting. And then, shortly after Christmas, he had an experience that again filled him with self-doubt and conflict.

Since the previous summer their neighbor, the blacksmith Arkhip Kaledin, who had once saved Grisha's life, had been running a small shop and general store, and his niece had moved from Yarkovo to help behind the counter. She was a young widow named Katerina, and she had one child, a boy. Katerina was an exceptionally pretty girl; and since the backyards of the two houses adjoined, she and Grisha often saw each other across the fence.

One freezing night in late December Kaledin knocked at Rasputin's door. The child was ill, the midwife was not at home, and the mother was desperate. Kaledin remembered that Grisha had a reputation as a healer and thought that his presence might at least comfort the mother. Rasputin dressed quickly and went next door. The child, a boy of about seven, was breathing harshly and his face was red; Rasputin thought it looked like pneumonia. He asked the mother and Kaledin to leave the room, then fell at the foot of the bed and prayed. Peace came upon him, then a feeling of strength. He laid one hand on the child's breast, the other on his forehead. He could feel the negative emanations flowing around the body. He allowed his own strength to flow from his fingertips. After a while the child's breathing became easier and the flush disappeared.

Rasputin went to the door and found the mother sitting there on the floor. He said, "You can come in now. He seems better."

The mother burst into tears when she saw the child's light, steady breathing; she dropped to her knees and kissed Grisha's hand. Embarrassed, he raised her to her feet and asked her to make him some tea. In the kitchen he talked to distract her, and half convinced her that the child had not really been ill at all; relief made her feel gay, almost light-headed. Then he realized it was nearly dawn and stood up to go. Again she took his hand and tried to kiss it; he pulled her to her feet, staring into her eyes to turn her thoughts elsewhere. He was too successful; he saw her helpless look of surrender, and had to place his hand behind her waist to stop her from swaying backward. As her body curved toward him, he experienced a rush of desire. There was a wooden settle behind her, covered with cushions. It seemed pointless to refuse what she was offering him in gratitude. He started to lead her toward the settle when they heard the voice of the child calling out, "Mummy." She rushed to the door. "Mummy, I'm thirsty. . ." Rasputin felt as if he had been awakened from a dream; he said good-by and hurried home.

The next day his own son, Dmitri, had a fever; it lasted only twenty-four hours, but it deepened his sense of guilt. He felt that he was failing to do what God wanted of him. Worse still, he was drifting into worldliness. He prayed for hours, but it brought no relief. Praskovia observed his torment and became pale and depressed. He felt helpless; he loved her, but his self-division made his life a misery. There were times when everything seemed unreal. He felt a powerful urge to do something but had no idea of what he should do.

SPRING CAME AGAIN. The sun dried away the floods; the birds sang and the sky looked newly washed. Yet nothing inside him responded to the coming of the new season. It was no longer guilt about Katerina; he now treated her in a friendly manner and made it clear that he regarded himself as a married man. She had only made him aware of the depths of his own dissatisfaction.

One day he decided to plow the meadow by the river. It was large, and he worked from dawn until late afternoon. His body was exhausted, but his mind remained disturbed. The horses were also tired, but in his misery he drove them on. Suddenly Ivan stumbled on a tree root and almost fell. Rasputin went to pat him and saw that he was sweating and trembling. The horse's distress made him clearly aware of his own. He said aloud, "What's wrong with me?" and allowed himself to sink to his knees beside the river. He was close to the spot where, fifteen years earlier, he had almost drowned. Now this thought only made him feel he might be better off dead. If God really had some purpose for him, why did He leave him in this state of confusion and bewilderment?

Then his heart seemed to expand and the sunlight grew brighter. He felt a presence above him, and as he looked up, the strong light solidified into the figure of a woman. She was hovering in the air, about twenty feet above his head, looking down at him with a serene smile. With astonishment, he realized he had seen her before— sitting by his bedside when he had been ill as a child. He half closed his eyes and allowed his gratitude to overflow as he stared up at the figure in purple and white robes. Then, as he knew it would, it slowly faded. He was left staring into the blue-washed sky.

Grisha rose slowly to his feet, and noticed that the knee of his trousers was soaked with blood. He had been kneeling on a sharp stone without noticing it. He unhitched the horses from the plow and limped slowly back to the farm. A sense of wild exultation was mixed with an element of anger, of self-contempt. Now that the Virgin had shown herself to him, his doubts vanished. What exasperated him was the thought that he had needed this revelation to remove his doubts. After what had happened at Makary's hermitage in Verkhoture, it should have been unnecessary. But at least he now knew what he had to do.

Praskovia took his decision to leave home with surprising calm. She had always felt that her husband was unlike other men, that he had to follow his own destiny. She was sad at the thought of losing him, worried at the prospect of managing the farm and bringing up a child alone, yet curiously serene in the knowledge that this was inevitable. If he had stayed at home and settled down to a lifetime of farming, she would have been disappointed.

In the hour before dawn they made love; then he pulled on his heaviest boots, packed a leather shoulder bag with food and left the house while it was still dark.

He walked all day, and by evening he was tired and homesick and felt strangely lost. The next day was worse; it rained all day, and he longed to be home with his wife and child. That night he slept in a broken-down barn. At dawn he knelt by the roadside and prayed. As he prayed, something inside him woke up. He became clearly aware that it was only his heart that longed for home. His mind told him he had to go on. It gave him a strange pleasure to crush his emotions, to turn his face again toward the south. He had an odd sensation, like looking down on himself from a height, as the Virgin had looked down on him in the field near the river. He was strong again.

CHAPTER FOUR

I N A SURPRISINGLY short time Grigori Rasputin became accustomed to the life of a wanderer. In Europe he would have been regarded as a tramp or beggar; in Russia he was a *strannik*, or pilgrim. The Russian peasants of his time were not a particularly religious people, yet they understood the urge that drives a man to leave his home and seek salvation. Thus few cottages or farms refused the wanderer food and rest. Besides, he brought a breath of the world beyond the village, and respite from boredom. Even if he merely sat by the fire and said nothing, his presence emphasized the brotherhood of man.

Occasionally Rasputin slept in a bed; more often it was in a hayloft or courtyard, or in the stable with the animals. He was always glad to enter the comfort of a home in the evening, and always glad to leave it for the open road in the morning. His greatest pleasure was to be alone in an empty landscape, with the rolling hills and forests stretching to the horizon. He loved to follow a river for miles along its course, to watch it narrow into a mountain stream or broaden into a lake or marsh. He became an expert at catching fish and roasting them over wood fires; from other *stranniki*, he learned what roots and berries could be eaten. When his leather boots wore out, and then burst, he made himself sandals of bark, or walked barefoot; when the weather became cold, he wrapped his feet in cloth.

Rasputin had always felt close to the land, yet now, as he watched the changes of the seasons, he noticed things he had never seen before. From day to day different trees and flowers bloomed. Sunsets varied from pastel shades of salmon pink and apple green to rivers of flame that ran down the sky like a torrent. There were summer nights when he deliberately turned aside from a village or farm to sleep in the forest or by a river, because he could no longer face human company. His heart felt the need to expand, to open itself to trees and stars.

IN POKROVSKOE RASPUTIN had become accustomed to making love to Praskovia every day, and the deprivation he now experienced often worried him more than physical hunger. When he was attracted by a woman, he fought it until the desire passed. But these struggles left him depressed and exhausted. He began to experience deep sympathy for the saints who had been tormented by female demons.

One night he fell in with a peasant on his way back from the fields, a big simple man who begged Rasputin to accept his hospitality. As soon as he saw the man's wife, Grisha felt desire. He controlled it and went to bed early. Not wanting to face the woman again, he left the house before dawn. As he walked along he prayed, "O God, why do you torment me with this lust? Why can I not be free of it? Show me the way . . ." He walked until the sun was high and he no longer felt chilled to the bone. At a wood not far from a village he found a stream at which he quenched his thirst. Then he closed his eyes and fell asleep in the long grass.

He was awakened by the sound of voices. He sat up cautiously. Fifty yards away, at the bottom of the slope, three girls were removing their clothes, laughing and chattering. Then one of them turned and saw him. She gave a scream of surprise and the others looked around. Then, to his relief, all three began to laugh.

They ran into the trees, and he heard splashes as they flung themselves into a pond. Since communal bathing was accepted as normal in all country districts, Rasputin joined them. They were obviously delighted that the stranger was young and attractive, and all three vied for his attention. As he wrestled and struggled with them, trying to avoid being ducked, his masculine desires flowed strongly again. But this time it seemed natural and acceptable.

A FEW DAYS LATER, at a cottage where Rasputin had asked for shelter, he learned the daughter was ill. She had fallen into the river, had been pulled out half-drowned, and had been feverish and delirious ever since. Rasputin remembered his brother, and felt his heart contract with pity. He asked to see the girl, who was scarcely breathing, then asked her parents to leave the room.

As soon as he touched her forehead, he knew he could cure her. The power welled up from deep inside him, stronger than ever before. He knelt by the bed, concentrated fully on the young girl, then allowed the energy to flow through him. Almost immediately the girl gave a deep sigh of relief and stretched her limbs. When he left her ten minutes later, she was breathing deeply and regularly.

He told the parents, "God has cured her. When she wakes up, she will be well."

The father embraced him and almost crushed the breath out of him; the mother kissed his hands. He was pleased they believed him and made no attempt to go and see the child. In the morning she was well enough to eat with them.

As he tramped on the next day, his bag again bulging with food, Rasputin experienced a curious, heady excitement that seemed to have no precise cause. If he concentrated and took a deep breath, the power welled up inside him. If he relaxed and simply looked at the scenery, he seemed to enter into it, to see it with a kind of urgency, as if it were speaking to him. He was changing; he was becoming different. He felt like a chrysalis about to turn into a butterfly.

Suddenly he again wanted to be back at home. Not, this time, out of misery and longing, but out of strength.

WHEN HE KNOCKED ON the front door, it was six-year-old Dmitri who answered, with Praskovia close behind him. Dmitri said, "Daddy!" and Praskovia hushed him to be silent and began to apologize; then she looked more closely and screamed, "Grigori!" She was hardly to blame for failing to recognize him at first. He was very thin, had skin like old leather, and his hair was shoulder-length.

"Oh, you've changed so much! You need fattening up."

Since Rasputin had left home almost two years earlier, Praskovia had acquired two female servants, Dunia and Katia. The farm had prospered, and there were now twice as many cows.

Within an hour the house was full of people. By then Rasputin had changed out of his long brown robe and Praskovia had trimmed his hair with the scissors. Dmitri was laughing and running about, delighted to see his father. The atmosphere was like Christmas. When Praskovia's father brought out a balalaika, Rasputin sang and danced. He seemed to be brimming with vitality.

Praskovia observed that the girls who came in found her husband attractive. The widow Katerina from next door blushed and stammered when he spoke to her. The maid Dunia Bekyeshova was also captivated. Before the evening was over, Praskovia had fallen in love with her husband all over again, and Dmitri thought he was the most wonderful man in the world.

The next day was Sunday; Rasputin went to church with his family. He learned that Father Pavel was dead; the new priest, Father Peter, was not greatly liked. In church it soon became clear why. He lacked charm and modesty; he had a harsh way of talking that verged on bullying. Rasputin could tell that he was a man with a touchy ego. After the service, when Rasputin introduced himself, the priest asked, "Well, did you find God?"

Rasputin answered, "No. But I heard His voice in the distance."

Father Peter looked puzzled and irritated at this reply; to him, it smacked of mysticism, which was another name for pretentious nonsense.

That evening the shoemaker's wife and her daughters came to Rasputin and asked him for spiritual advice. Praskovia listened as her husband spoke, and was astonished that he could talk with such authority about religion. So were the others who were present. Within a few days Rasputin had become the unofficial spiritual director of half the women in the village.

He attended church again the following Sunday, but found Father Peter unbearable, even stupid, without a grain of genuine devoutness. It was then that he decided to build his own chapel—to hollow it out from the earth underneath the barn. In the meantime, he constructed a small oratory in the yard, with an altar and an icon of the Virgin of Kazan. The following Sunday he retired there to pray. Then the shoemaker's wife arrived with her daughters and asked him to perform a simple service. Rasputin read to them from the Bible, talked for a while about the power of the Holy Spirit, then knelt and prayed aloud. When they left, the mother kissed his hand, and the daughters followed suit. Two years earlier he would have been embarrassed; now he felt it was natural. That afternoon the woman's husband came with his two brothers and offered to help dig out the underground chapel. Before evening they had dug a hole big enough for a horse and cart. Within weeks it was large enough to hold a dozen worshipers, and candles burned in niches in the walls. Yet as more people attended his Sunday morning worship, it became necessary to enlarge it.

In fact, Rasputin was benefiting from the intense dislike most people felt for Father Peter. After the gentle, self-effacing Father Pavel, this man seemed coarse, tactless and greedy. When he had moved into the priest's residence, he had brought his own house-keeper, and had promptly evicted the old woman who had devoted her life to Father Pavel; all the women of the village turned against him. They influenced their menfolk. So the arrival of the wandering *strannik* was a political rather than a religious event; it provided everyone with a method of showing dislike of the new priest. If Rasputin had been a self-seeking charlatan, the men would still have helped him build his chapel. As it was, he was obviously a true seeker of God, sincere, devout and compassionate. His healing powers were also remarkable; now whenever someone was ill, Rasputin was usually sent for before the midwife.

As his congregation diminished, Father Peter nursed increasing resentment. His anger grew until it became a canker that under-mined his judgment. After a Sunday morning service when his congregation totaled only nine old men and women, the priest sad-dled his horse and set out for Tyumen to lay complaints against Rasputin before the bishop. On the way he gave himself up to dreams of revenge and mentally prepared his case. Rumor told him that Rasputin took advantage of his women penitents, and that he had spoken of the Khlysty with tolerance and sympathy. Clearly, both these activities were unacceptable in a holy man.

The bishop, a genial old ex-missionary to Japan, was concerned rather than shocked by Father Peter's tales of a secret Khlysty con-gregation in Pokrovskoe. He pressed the priest for details, but could only elicit generalities. Yet the matter plainly deserved investigation. So the bishop ordered two monks from the local seminary to proceed to Pokrovskoe to find out what they could about Rasputin. As an afterthought, the bishop decided to also send two policemen, dis-guised as peasants.

The monks made their way to Rasputin's house and engaged him in theological discussion. As a layman, Rasputin had a natural and sincere respect for monks, and they were charmed by his hospitality and impressed by his fierce sincerity. They found his doctrines orthodox, and his knowledge of the Scriptures remarkable. When he preached his sermon on Luke 17:21, it was obvious that he spoke from personal experience.

Meanwhile, the two disguised policemen questioned Rasputin's congregation, both the women and their husbands, and heard stories about miraculous cures. Being policemen, they were skeptical; yet there were clearly no grounds for heresy. They also noted many complaints against Father Peter.

After six days the inquisitors left Pokrovskoe. A few days later Father Peter was summoned before the bishop. No one ever discovered the precise nature of the interview that took place; but Father Peter returned looking depressed and chastened. The authorities took no further interest in Rasputin's devotional activities.

The harvest that year was the best ever. After it had been gathered in, Rasputin made another journey to Tyumen, this time with three horses harnessed to the heavily loaded wagon. When he returned to Pokrovskoe, Praskovia told him she was pregnant again. The child, born the following spring, was a girl, who was christened Matriona— shortened to Maria.

TWO YEARS PASSED, and Rasputin's position in Pokrovskoe was an enviable one. He was virtually the village priest, but acknowledged no ecclesiastical authority. His devotees regarded him with an attitude bordering on adoration; yet Grisha insisted that they should look upon him as a brother rather than a father.

Rasputin did little work on the farm; it was unnecessary, since Praskovia ran it so efficiently. He spent his days like a priest, visiting his "parishioners," giving comfort and help, healing the sick, teaching the children to pray. Many young men regarded him as their spiritual mentor, and one of these, a clumsy brown-eyed giant named Peter Scherbatov—known as Petcherkine—was almost constantly in attendance, regarding it as a privilege to be allowed to help Praskovia with the housework. When a second daughter, Varvara, was born in 1900, Petcherkine became virtually her nurse.

Only Rasputin himself was less than happy. He remained constantly dissatisfied. His peaceful existence at Pokrovskoe was not what Makary had foretold. He remembered the old hermit's advice that he should go to Mount Athos to strengthen his spiritual power, and something inside him longed once more for the open road.

Praskovia recognized the symptoms; she had seen them before: the hours spent alone in prayer, the fits of abstraction, the occasional flashes of temper. One day as he sat at the table after the children had left, she asked him softly, "When will it be?"

"What?" He looked up irritably.

"When are you leaving?"

He stared at her, then his face broke into a smile of relief.

"Soon. Perhaps tomorrow." He pulled her to her feet and held her close. "Thank God I married you."

That evening Petcherkine found Rasputin praying in the chapel, dressed in his brown *strannik's* robe, his pilgrim staff beside him. His eyes widened in dismay. "Where are you going, Father?"

Rasputin showed no anger at being interrupted in his prayers. He placed his hand on Petcherkine's shoulder.

"To Mount Athos."

"I'm coming too."

"No, no, my boy. It will be a long journey."

Then, as he looked at Petcherkine's open, good-natured face, it struck him that it might not be a bad idea after all. Petcherkine had one great virtue: he knew when to be silent. Rasputin said, in his decisive manner, "All right. But tell no one. We leave before dawn."

They traveled in easy stages, first to Ekaterinburg, then to Kazan. Petcherkine, who had never been beyond Pokrovskoe, proved to be a born traveler. He acquired a cooking pot; and if night found them far from human habitation, he made a fire and cooked supper. In towns and villages it was Petcherkine—dressed in his brown monk's robe—who found them a night's lodging, and made himself so useful and agreeable to the mistress of the house that they were often asked to stay longer. And in the city of Kazan, ancient capital of the Tartars, it was Petcherkine who fell into conversation with a merchant named Katkoff, from whom he had begged the price of a loaf, and told him about the wonderful healing powers of his master, who was then praying to the Holy Virgin of Kazan in the cathedral.

Katkoff's wife suffered from arthritis; he asked Petcherkine, as a favor, to persuade the *starets* (holy man) to spend the night under his roof. Rasputin agreed. Neither he nor Petcherkine had ever been in such a place—a vast square house with four stories and fluted columns in front of the door. Katkoff's wife, a pretty, faded woman named Helene, came instantly under Rasputin's spell. He sat her in a straight-backed chair in the drawing room and placed both hands on her forehead from behind. Instantly she went into a hypnotic trance. He placed his hands on her joints, and told her that all pain would vanish. When she came out of the trance, she clenched and unclenched her fingers, flexed her arms, swung her legs back and forth, repeating, "It's gone, I'm cured."

Rasputin enjoyed Katkoff's generous hospitality, and was easily persuaded to stay on for a few days—particularly when Katkoff said he was driving to Odessa the following week and would take Rasputin and Petcherkine in his car. Rasputin had never been in a motorcar before.

Helene Katkoff invited many visitors to meet the *strannik*. All were impressed by his hypnotic gaze and his powers of healing. As word of his presence spread around Kazan, all kinds of people knocked on the Katkoffs' door—rich women and beggars, merchants and politicians, even the assistant to the chief of police, whose daughter had dislocated her back. After treatment by Rasputin, she was unable to move, her muscles apparently paralyzed; yet the next morning she was completely cured.

A week later, as Rasputin and Petcherkine left Kazan in the back of Katkoff's enormous open-topped roadster, Rasputin said to Helene, "I will return to Kazan. The Virgin has work for me to do."

CHAPTER FIVE

SEVEN MONTHS LATER, on a day of sleet and freezing gales, the two travelers arrived back in Kazan. Petcherkine was thinner; Rasputin, with his untrimmed beard halfway down his chest, looked like an Old Testament prophet. At Katkoff's house they were welcomed like royalty and placed in the finest guest bedrooms. Katkoff's wife was completely free of arthritis, and since they had last seen her, she had talked about Rasputin in Saint Petersburg. When she declared, with brimming eyes, that he was a saint, people smiled; but they were impressed all the same. Now it seemed half the gentry of Kazan were waiting to be introduced to him.

That day, at dinner, Rasputin seemed preoccupied. It was Petcherkine who described their journey from Odessa to Mount Athos in Greece, and then across Turkey to the Holy Land. He hinted that Rasputin had undergone some profound spiritual experience in Jerusalem. But when Helene Katkoff begged him to speak of it, Rasputin seemed to wake from a daydream and said to his host, "I hear that strange things are happening in the world."

"What things, master?"

"I am told there are murderers who want to destroy the Tsar and overthrow the Church."

Katkoff shrugged. "That is nothing new. I was in Saint Petersburg in March 1881 when Tsar Alexander was killed by a terrorist bomb. I heard the explosion and saw the gutter running with the blood of injured soldiers."

To Katkoff's astonishment, it was clear that Rasputin knew nothing of the assassination of Alexander the Second. Rasputin begged Katkoff to tell him the story in detail. Katkoff explained how the first bomb had only damaged the Tsar's carriage, wounding several Cossacks. The kindly Tsar made the mistake of getting out of his carriage to comfort the wounded men; a second bomb was thrown, shattering the Tsar's legs. The assassin himself was blown to pieces and twenty bystanders were killed. Katkoff, walking only two streets away, hurried to the scene and discovered that windows for hundreds of yards around were shattered. The Tsar was carried back to the palace, to die a few hours later surrounded by his weeping family. It had been Alexander who had signed the decree liberating the serfs.

Rasputin paled. He seemed unable to understand. "But why did they want to kill him?"

"They call themselves revolutionaries. They believe all authority is evil."

Rasputin lowered his head, as if about to pray, then said in a choked voice, "The world is becoming a madhouse."

The next day, before dawn, Rasputin left the house and went to the cathedral to pray. That afternoon Helene Katkoff, who had gone to his room to take him tea, met him in the hallway. She noticed that he seemed different. All the weariness had vanished. His eyes shone with joy, and he spontaneously took her in his arms and caressed her head against his chest. He said, "I must leave Kazan today."

"Today? But, master, we need you here."

He held her at arm's length, and his eyes were glowing with excitement. "Tell no one what I am about to tell you. The Virgin has spoken to me."

Helene dropped to her knees, and Rasputin knelt down, facing her.

"As I prayed in front of her image, she came to me from the center of a great light." His face was transfigured; he had difficulty preventing his voice from trembling.

Helene asked in a whisper, "She spoke to you?"

"Not with words, not with a voice. In here"—he pressed his heart with his fist—"she spoke and told me there was work for me to do."

"Here in Kazan?"

"No. Not in Kazan. Elsewhere."

"Where?"

"I don't know yet. When the time comes, I shall know."

Suddenly she seized his hands, "*I* know."

He looked at her in surprise. "Where?"

"In Saint Petersburg. Where the Tsar lives. The Grand Duchess Militsa wants to meet you. I talked to her about you."

A more sophisticated man would have wanted to know how the wife of a merchant had come to meet a cousin of the Tsar. The answer was that both Helene Katkoff and the Grand Duchess Militsa, the daughter of the King of Montenegro (now part of Yugoslavia), were spiritualists, and had met at a séance. Helene Katkoff had so far said nothing to Rasputin about her spiritualism, sensing that he would disapprove. In this she was correct. He would have regarded spirit communication and table rapping as a form of black magic.

Rasputin shook his head. "You may be right. But I must wait for a sign from the Virgin."

Helene Katkoff, convinced that what she was saying was divine inspiration, replied, "She may be telling you through me."

Rasputin stared at her for a long time; her eyes were adoring and candid. Then he stood up and went into his room. When Helene had mentioned Saint Petersburg, his heart had experienced a cold shadow, like the wing of a bird of prey.

IT WAS SNOWING on the November day when Rasputin arrived in Saint Petersburg for the first time, and the snow on the streets was so thick it muffled the sound of traffic like a huge white blanket. The air was crystal clear, and colder than Rasputin had ever known. Siberia was cold but dry. Saint Petersburg, built on the banks of the Neva by Peter the Great to provide himself with a seaport, was warm and moist in the summer and cold and damp in the winter.

Rasputin had made the journey from Omsk by train, packed in an uncomfortable third-class carriage. It was his first journey by rail, and he found it boring and depressing. The Trans-Siberian Express had electric lights, a restaurant, library and observation car; but there was an element of asceticism in Rasputin's nature that made him prefer the carriage, filled with peasants, to the train's "drawing room," with its piano and elegant waiters.

At the station in Saint Petersburg he asked about a cheap lodging house, and was directed to a place near the Fontanka Canal, a quarter of a mile away. As he plodded through the streets, at times up to his knees in snow, he was surprised by the number of drunken men he saw. The long straight avenues stretched ahead of him; the tall gray houses were like cliffs on either side, with their broad drainpipes emptying directly onto the pavement. Nothing he had seen in Kazan, or even Odessa, had prepared him for this vast, bleak, impersonal city. He stopped at a booth on a street corner to buy a glass of kvass; gloomy-looking men and women sat under the canvas awning, obviously making the drink last as long as possible before venturing again into the icy wind.

The lodging house overlooked a canal bridge and was next door to a hospital. The room, which was expensive, was on the top floor and smelled of fried fish and mothballs. He felt so lonely that he sat down and wrote his wife a letter, in his labored, childish scrawl: *This city is a bad dream of misery and dirt; there are more taverns on every street than in the whole of Tobolsk.*

That night Rasputin fell asleep to the sound of noisy shouts from the drunkards in the street.

When he woke early the next morning the bells told him—what he had forgotten—that it was a Sunday. He dressed hurriedly, ate the last of some oatcakes he had brought from Pokrovskoe and washed them down with water. He then went out into the deserted street. When he inquired from a beggar woman where he could find the cathedral, she asked, "Kazan or Saint Isaac's?" Kazan was the obvious choice, and she directed him to the Nevsky Prospect. But after plodding along an interminable avenue and trying to take a shortcut, he seemed to be lost. Soon he found himself on the waterfront, looking out over the vast expanse of the Gulf of Finland. On a quay facing Vassili Island a steamer gave a loud hoot as it prepared to leave. A notice tacked up on a nearby post said: *Steamers to Kronstadt Island—9 a.m. and 2 p.m.* The name was familiar. He had heard of Father John of Kronstadt, a man who was reputed to be gifted with the power of healing and prophecy. On impulse, Rasputin ran up the gangplank of the steamer just as the sailors were removing it.

The service at the church on Kronstadt Island had already begun when Rasputin arrived. He slipped in quietly at the back and knelt to pray. The congregation finished a hymn and sat down. Then a gentle, sonorous voice filled the basilica. The preacher had chosen his text from Saint Matthew. He spoke of an evil and adulterous generation, of modern faithlessness, of new doctrines that had come from Western Europe: the belief in spirits and communication with the dead, in Hindu and Tibetan masters, in decadent forms of mysticism. Although the voice was gentle, like the personality of the old man in the pulpit, there could be no doubting its fierce sincerity. This is what Rasputin had come to Saint Petersburg to hear. This is what had been running through his thoughts ever since that evening, two months before, when Katkoff had told him about the assassination of the Tsar. When the preacher spoke of the power of the Russian spirit, its ability to throw off these diseases of the decadent Europeans, Rasputin's soul shook with the force of its own awakened convictions.

The next part of the service surprised him. At a signal from the priest, members of the congregation leaped to their feet and began to cry out, "Forgive us our sins," and to name these sins explicitly. They turned around, addressing themselves to the worshipers who were praying, and spoke without inhibition about their wickedness.

Rasputin found it all strangely moving; these people at least were determined to live by the Holy Scriptures and the word of God. As he knelt and prayed, he suddenly knew that his destiny lay in Saint Petersburg. Great waves of peace and thanksgiving washed over him. Because he had experienced so much doubt and restlessness over the past week, this new conviction was like recovering from an illness. Tears ran down his cheeks; he felt himself immersed in a sea of bliss and forgiveness.

He sensed rather than saw that someone was standing beside him. He raised his head and realized that the church was now almost empty; the old man looking at him had mild, candid blue eyes, hair parted down the middle and a square beard that covered his chest. He asked without preliminary, "Who are you?"

"Grigori Rasputin."

"Ah!" The preacher obviously recognized the name. "So you are Rasputin . . ." He looked intently into Rasputin's face. "I am John of Kronstadt."

Rasputin scrambled to his feet. "I ask your blessing, Father."

"With all my heart." The priest obviously meant it. He gave Rasputin communion, and then asked, "Have you eaten?"

"Not yet."

"Come and eat with me."

As they walked back toward the monastery, John of Kronstadt said, "There is already talk about you in Saint Petersburg."

"How is that, Father? I know no one."

"Many seem to know you."

As they walked along a bare corridor toward Father John's room, the priest said abruptly, "Is it true you were once a great sinner?"

Rasputin gave a roar of laughter, and Father John looked at him with mischievous amusement. Rasputin said finally, "I'm afraid none of my sins could be called great. Who told you that tale?"

They entered the small bare room. Father John said, "Well . . . Madame Katkoff implied it."

"No!" Rasputin was astonished.

The priest laughed at Rasputin's puzzled face. "She says that you are a man of God, but she drops some fascinating hints about a life of sin followed by penitence."

And for the next hour John of Kronstadt questioned his guest about his life, his travels, his beliefs. He was amused by Rasputin's peasant honesty, his frank acknowledgment that he regarded most priests as parasites (an admission softened by Rasputin's obvious belief that his host was a true man of God). Then he became impressed by Rasputin's very considerable intelligence and ability to express himself. When Rasputin talked of his visions of the Virgin of Kazan, Father John had a sudden intuition that this man had been sent to him from God.

Father John Sergeieff was the son of a poor village deacon from Archangel, and he was neither a mystic nor an intellectual. His immense power and influence sprang from the fact that he was a good man, a man who loved the poor and the needy, and from his genius of prayer. And now, as Rasputin in turn began to ask questions, Father John answered from a heart that knew nothing of concealment or of pride. For the first time in his life, Rasputin knew he was speaking to a man like himself, one whose hunger for God made everything else seem unreal. For the first time in his life, he was meeting one who was truly his brother.

It was late that afternoon when they separated. As he tried to kiss Father John's hand, the older man said, "No, my son," and embraced Rasputin, the tears running down his cheeks. "Come see me again."

Rasputin returned to the lodging house, his soul filled with gratitude. Suddenly Saint Petersburg was no longer a nightmare; it was a city that was prepared to welcome him.

He awakened with a start the next morning as someone opened his door. The room was full of cold, snowy daylight, and snow was piled on the windowpane that sloped over his head. In the doorway stood his landlord, and beside him a figure he at first took to be a general. Then, as he sat up and rubbed his eyes, the magnificently dressed figure spoke and he realized it was a servant in gold-braided livery.

"Are you Father Rasputin?" (He pronounced it "Raspoutine" in the French manner.)

"Yes."

"A letter from the Grand Duchess Militsa."

Rasputin tore open the gold-embossed envelope. It took him several minutes to decipher the handwriting: *We are so excited to hear that you have come at last. Please treat my house as your home. Come this afternoon for tea.* The signature was a scrawl.

"Any reply?" The servant had a patronizing air.

"Tell her I'll be there."

When the servant had left, the landlord, who had remained near the open doorway, said, "I suppose you'll be leaving us now?"

"Not necessarily, my friend. By the way, what time is tea in Saint Petersburg?"

"About three o'clock—after they've finished lunch."

For the rest of that morning Rasputin walked around the streets. The sheer size of things astonished him: the gigantic squares, the boulevards like great broad rivers, the Neva itself, blue and immense, with the Peter and Paul Fortress dominating its farther bank. Now he no longer felt a stranger; he reveled in it all.

At about three that afternoon Rasputin mounted the marble steps of the house of the Grand Duke Peter Nicholaievich, cousin of the Tsar. As he rang the bell on the enormous front door, he wondered whether the servants would tell him to use the tradesman's entrance. He was not wearing his monk's robe, but a blue peasant smock and a coarse open-necked shirt. But his anxiety was unnecessary; the green-liveried footman, who looked as if he had stepped straight out of a German court of the nineteenth century, was obviously expecting him. He took his old sheepskin coat as if it were an ermine cape, then led him across to the great cream-and-gilt doors of the drawing room. He opened the doors and announced, "Father Rasputin."

There were only two people in the room, a man and a woman. The woman was dressed in a loose, flowing gown like an ancient Greek costume and had a chaplet of flowers in her hair. She hurried across the room, her hands outstretched. "Father Rasputin, I'm so honored to meet you."

Rasputin stared into the wide eyes and knew instantly that she was one of those he was born to dominate. He ignored her outstretched hands, grasped her by the shoulders and gave her a bear hug, kissing her on the cheek. Her face colored, but her eyes were bright.

The man had also started across the room; Rasputin saw he was dressed in a brown monk's habit. He was tall and thin, and had a narrow pointed face and intense eyes. The grand duchess said, "This is Father Iliodor—Father Rasputin."

Iliodor was the kind of man Rasputin instinctively disliked; the pale face, the tight lips, the intense eyes, revealed that he possessed a sensitive ego. Ten years before, Rasputin would have betrayed his mistrust. But his hours of meditation and prayer had given him the strength to control his reactions; he gave an open, kind smile and held out his hand. After a moment's hesitation the monk offered his own.

Rasputin sat in an armchair covered with silk and talked to Iliodor, who sat beside the Grand Duchess Militsa on a divan. The grand duchess described Iliodor as "the most brilliant man in Russia." This was an exaggeration; but, in fact, Iliodor, who was even younger than Rasputin, had established himself as one of the best theology students of his generation and as a preacher of remarkable power. He and Rasputin had much in common: both were sons of peasants, both were ambitious; but Iliodor's ambition was neurotic, intense and totally personal.

Iliodor was talking about his dream of building a monastery dedicated to the highest ideals of spirituality, a Russian equivalent of Mount Athos. Rasputin listened, and took in the room. Helene Katkoff's drawing room had been fine, but this was magnificent. The furniture was in pastel shades, the wallpaper was of olive silk brocade. It was the room of a woman who regarded herself as an arbiter of fashion. The faint perfume that hung in the air was distinctly of the Orient.

The grand duchess took him by surprise by asking suddenly, "What do you think, Father Grigori? Can Russia be spiritualized?"

It was the kind of question that made him irritable. He said, with a touch of sternness, "Russia *is* spiritualized. It is the priesthood and the aristocracy who need to be brought back to God."

She accepted the rebuke as if she deserved it, with lowered eyes. Iliodor, his face alight with enthusiasm, said, "That is true! The Russian peasant already knows God. The real traitors are the Russians who try to make us into Europeans." He turned to Rasputin, and his eyes glowed like those of a rat caught in the lamplight. "But these gentry are no longer having it all their own way. People like you and me will change all that."

"Mr. Alexander Scriabin." The footman had opened the door to admit a small pale man with neatly combed hair and a mustache that had been trained to curl at the ends. The grand duchess proudly introduced Rasputin to her new guest. Scriabin, apparently, was a composer; he looked up at Rasputin with a penetrating, mocking expression, and said in a surprisingly sweet voice, "Ah, the great sinner . . ."

Now other guests began to arrive. There were two writers, a lady opera singer, a traveler who had just returned from Africa, a conductor and a man who was trying to set up a film company. It was soon clear to Rasputin that everyone knew about him. But he had already divined that Militsa was an indefatigable propagandist who loved nothing so much as introducing new "celebrities" to Saint Petersburg society. And whether Rasputin liked it or not, the role in which he had been cast was that of a sinner who had received some kind of revelation and become a miracle worker. Scriabin, who had come from Moscow, seemed to be as curious about him as everybody else. He asked personal questions with an eagerness that would have been offensive if it had not been so frank. Rasputin was relieved when the grand duchess persuaded the composer to play the piano. Scriabin played his own compositions with a rapt, affected air that was an odd contrast to the schoolboyish curiosity of a few minutes earlier.

Rasputin turned his attention to Iliodor, who was leaning on the top of the grand piano, listening intently. Now that Iliodor's face was in repose, Rasputin became aware of an element of self-hatred in the man's character, a deep, nagging dissatisfaction like an open sore. Ambition, perhaps? Then, suddenly, with sad conviction, Rasputin knew this man would one day be his implacable enemy. He thought: Why do I know this about him? Why does my intuition reveal the future, while his fails to operate? And he at once saw the answer. Iliodor *did* know the future. Yet he was not prepared to listen to the inner voice that could reveal it. It was the same with all of them: with Militsa and with this self-centered little composer.

The music ended, and the guests clapped wildly. Then, when everyone had settled down, Militsa asked Rasputin about his healing powers. Somewhat embarrassed, Rasputin shrugged and said, "I do nothing. God cures."

"But through you," said Scriabin.

"God does most things through human beings. He seldom interferes in the course of nature. We are here to be used by God, as a housewife uses her broom or a farmer his plow." And since no one seemed disposed to interrupt, Rasputin allowed himself to be carried away on his favorite themes. He talked simply, with homely metaphors; it gave him pleasure to try to make these sophisticated city dwellers understand the truths of the inner life.

They in turn were fascinated by Rasputin, who seemed to bring the breath of the soil, the cowshed, the open steppe, into Militsa's scented drawing room. On that freezing November afternoon he reminded them of spring and summer.

At six o'clock guests began to leave. As Rasputin also prepared to go, Militsa whispered in his ear, "Stay behind. I have a surprise for you."

Rasputin and Iliodor were left alone in the room as Militsa saw off her guests. Rasputin said, "I wonder what the surprise could be?"

Iliodor said, "I think I can guess. You are to be examined by the high priests."

"High priests?"

Iliodor, who was looking out into the hall, said, "Ah yes. I was right."

Rasputin looked past him and saw the two men who had just entered; one was dressed in the purple robes of a bishop, the other in the black of a simple priest. Iliodor said, "The one in regalia is Hermogen, bishop of Saratov."

"And the other?"

"Father Theophan, inspector of the Theological Academy and confessor to the royal family."

There are times in a man's life when he encounters the situation for which he seems to have been prepared by fate. When this happens, he experiences an inner feeling of rightness, as if the wheels are turning in his favor. Since meeting John of Kronstadt, Rasputin had known this sense of rightness. Yet now, for the first time, he felt doubt, the ringing of some inner alarm bell.

Hermogen was a big man with a shrewd face and bluff manner. Theophan was simple, direct and rather shy. They were soon joined by the Grand Duke Peter, Militsa's husband, who seemed to be on the best of terms with the two church dignitaries, and who proceeded to show them all how to make a cocktail in the American manner—an art he had learned from a Hungarian barman in the Nevsky Prospect. When, half an hour later, they were summoned for dinner,

Rasputin had a sense of having become a member of a small club of the most influential churchmen in Russia.

After dinner, as they were drinking coffee in the drawing room, Peter inquired after the Tsarina, Alexandra Fedorovna, with whom Theophan had been that afternoon. Theophan talked simply and openly about her problems. The Tsar and Tsarina had been married for nine years, and by 1901 she had produced four daughters. After the birth of the fourth, Alexandra Fedorovna had begun to experience nervous depression; her failure to produce a male heir struck her as a disaster. At this point Militsa had introduced her to a "miracle worker" called Philippe Vachot, whom she had met in France. Dr. Philippe believed that the Tsarina's failure to conceive a son was due to nervous tension, and he started a course of hypnotic treatment. Soon the Tsarina's stomach began to swell. But when the court doctor examined her, he found no sign of pregnancy; her symptoms were a form of hysteria. The story quickly spread and increased the Tsarina's unpopularity. (She was a granddaughter of Queen Victoria, and was known as "the foreigner.") Dr. Philippe chose this opportune moment to return to France.

After Philippe Vachot there was a "prophet" named Mitia Koliaba, and numerous "miracle workers," including a French mystic, and even a herbalist who had studied Chinese and Mongolian and who hinted at secret masters in the remote mountains of Tibet. Some of them had brought comfort to the Tsarina, but there was still no sign of an heir. Only that afternoon Alexandra Fedorovna had burst into tears and asked Theophan to pray for Russia—by which he understood her to mean an heir to the throne.

Rasputin felt Militsa's eyes fixed on him, and deliberately avoided them. Suddenly he knew what she wanted to propose; and some instinct told him it was too soon. He was relieved when Hermogen asked, "Where are you staying?" When Rasputin told him, he said, "That's no good. Come and stay at the Kronstadt monastery. I'll make sure you get a comfortable room."

"You're very kind." Secretly he wondered how he could avoid the invitation; he had an instinct for independence.

At half past ten Hermogen yawned. "I must get back. It's been an interesting evening." He turned to Rasputin. "I can drop you off on the way."

As they moved toward the door, Militsa caught Rasputin's sleeve. "I must show you my own special icon. It won't take a moment." She drew him into a hallway, then into an attractive little room furnished in pink. She closed the door firmly and seized him by both hands. She stared earnestly into his eyes.

"Tell me, can you help her?"

Rasputin pulled back his hands. He was feeling sleepy and slightly drunk; he wanted to be allowed to go home to bed. He turned to sit on the pink chaise longue and pressed his hands to his head. Then, as he emptied his mind, the answer came. He looked up at Militsa, who was waiting patiently.

"She doesn't need my help."

"Why?"

"She is already pregnant."

"Are you sure?"

He heard himself speaking the words, yet had no idea whether they were true; they simply came into his conscious mind as if from some other source. His voice said quietly and firmly, "By next August she will have given birth to an heir to the throne."

Militsa gave a scream of excitement and started to fling her arms around him; then she thought better of it, dropped on her knees and kissed his hands.

There was a light knock at the door; the servant's discreet voice said, "The bishop's carriage is here, madame."

Rasputin said, "Tell no one." But he knew it was too much to ask of any woman.

CHAPTER SIX

DURING HIS NEXT FEW days in Saint Petersburg Rasputin was more interested in the strange processes that were taking place inside him than in the new acquaintances he made. That day at Militsa's had caused some decisive inner change. His vitality increased, and he had a new control over his moods. This feeling of health and power was at times so strong that he deliberately concealed it, as a rich man might want to conceal his gold watch chain when talking to a pauper.

At Hermogen's repeated invitation, he finally moved into the Kronstadt monastery. It proved to be more pleasant than he had expected; his reputation had gone before him, and everyone treated him with respectful curiosity. Within ten days his chief problem was finding enough time to get a good night's sleep. The Montenegrins, both Militsa and her sister Anastasia, who was married to another grand duke, Nicholas Nicholaievich, expected him at their soirees at least once a week, and exhibited him as their latest discovery. From these evenings other invitations followed, and they could not be easily refused.

Inevitably most of the people Rasputin met had relatives or friends who needed healing, so Rasputin held "surgeries" in the courtyard of the monastery for two hours every morning. Because of the freezing weather, only those in real need made the journey to Kronstadt Island. But it was easy to foresee the day when their numbers would multiply.

As Christmas approached, Rasputin found himself thinking increasingly about his family in Pokrovskoe. But it wasn't until early May that he was able to leave Saint Petersburg. He first went to Moscow, where he boarded the Trans-Siberian Express for Omsk and Tobolsk, and so back home.

ON HIS ARRIVAL in Pokrovskoe, Rasputin was surprised to discover that he had become a celebrity. Most of the "best people" of Tobolsk and Tyumen spent at least a few weeks of every winter in Saint Petersburg or Moscow; and it was impossible to spend much time in either capital without hearing something of the new miracle worker. Since most of the "best people" belonged—like the Katkoffs—to the merchant class rather than the aristocracy, they heard stories of Rasputin's triumphs secondhand, and inevitably exaggerated them. One story insisted that Rasputin was already intimate with the royal family.

For Rasputin, it was a relief to be home; he was glad to be able to spend hours at his prayers in front of the Virgin of Kazan. Yet he observed that it was a greater effort to sink into the depths at which prayer became naturally sincere; his mind often strayed to Saint Petersburg and to the Tsarina. His prophecy had been partially confirmed; she was to give birth in August. A part of him had no doubt she would produce a male heir; another part reflected on his loss of face if she did not.

The services in his underground chapel resumed, and people came from outlying villages to beg for his help. His healing powers were stronger than ever, and as the news spread, his life became increasingly crowded. During the summer he spent as much time as possible working in the fields or wandering in the forest; but there were always suppliants who would walk for miles to find him, or would wait for him no matter what hour he came home.

On the morning of August 13 there came a telegram from Militsa: *Heir born yesterday. Letter follows.* The letter described how, shortly after one o'clock on a warm August day, the cannon at Peterhof had boomed to announce the birth of the child; the cannon on Kronstadt Island had taken up the signal, and the guns of the Peter and Paul Fortress had told the citizens of Saint Petersburg of the arrival of the heir. Militsa had telephoned the palace and spoken to the court chancellor, who had confirmed that the baby was a handsome eight-pound boy with blue eyes.

The heir was born nine months to the day after Rasputin had foretold the event.

In the winter life at Pokrovskoe became quieter; heavy snow made the roads impassable, and Rasputin was again able to devote himself to prayer and to his own small congregation.

Spring came, and one day, as he was helping Praskovia plant potatoes, Rasputin received another letter from Militsa. In confidence, the Tsarina had told the grand duchess her distressing secret: the eight-month-old heir to the throne was suffering from hereditary hemophilia. Because his blood lacked an element essential to clotting, a bruise could lead to ugly blue swellings and fever, since the ruptured blood vessels would leak for hours. Small cuts or scrapes could be cured by bandaging tightly until the flesh healed over; but larger ones could lead to death. The Tsarina was now more reliant than ever upon various miracle workers and spiritual advisers.

Militsa urged Rasputin to return to Saint Petersburg by the next train. Yet he still felt an immense inner reluctance to meet the royal family. Instinct told him that such a step would alter the rest of his life. This may be why, in spite of letters from both Montenegrin sisters, Rasputin remained in Pokrovskoe. The farm prospered; he enjoyed his hours alone in prayer or wandering on the steppe. When gypsies arrived for the May Festival, he danced all night at their encampment, and then spent a day in bed with one of his rare hangovers, probably due to large quantities of a home-brewed wine laced with spirits. Through the summer and autumn of the year 1905 he felt serene and relaxed.

Friends in Saint Petersburg sent Rasputin newspapers containing political news. There was a rising tide of revolutionary violence, and many called upon the Tsar for stern action. In January 1905 a priest named Father Gapon had led a deputation of workers to the Winter Palace to present a petition to the Tsar for an eight-hour day and a minimum wage of a ruble a day. As the deputation marched through Saint Petersburg, it was joined by a growing crowd of supporters. But the Tsar had not bothered to wait in Saint Petersburg, and when the crowd arrived in front of the Winter Palace, the soldiers lost their nerve and opened fire at a distance of a few yards. The crowd panicked, scores of women and children were trampled to death. For days lines of peasants and workers marched through the improvised morgues to try to find missing relatives or children.

But it seemed the workers had not learned a lesson. There were strikes, demonstrations and more killings. The governor-general of Moscow was assassinated in front of the Kremlin; he was only one of hundreds of government officials murdered that year. The war with Japan, which had begun in February 1904, was going badly, and in late May the total defeat of the Russian Navy at Tsushima made the revolutionaries feel the end was very near. The sailors on the battleship *Potëmkin* mutinied in June. Even the corps de ballet in Saint Petersburg went on strike. Russian liberals insisted that the best way to avoid violent revolution was for the Tsar to grant the country a parliamentary government on the British model. The Tsar loathed the idea; but as things got worse, he was forced to start making concessions. In October 1905 he authorized the setting up of a parliament—it was called the Duma—but insisted that he was still the supreme ruler.

It was also in October that Rasputin received a telegram from Militsa: *Please come at once—very important.* She even telegraphed him the train fare. Rasputin was ready for the invitation. The women of his congregation had finally realized that the best place to find him alone was the chapel; as a result, he was likely to be interrupted in his prayers at almost any hour. The summons from Militsa offered an escape from the increasingly chaotic atmosphere.

FROM THE SAINT PETERSBURG station Rasputin took a cab to Militsa's house, arriving after dinner on an evening of wind and heavy snow. Militsa and the grand duke were dining alone. They treated him like an old friend, and insisted that he stay in their house for a few days. As Rasputin ate a belated meal, Peter Nicholaievich brought him up to date on the political situation. And what he had to say astonished Rasputin, who had not realized the trouble was so widespread. All over Russia peasants had murdered landowners and their families, and soldiers had taken violent reprisals. There had been mutinies at Sevastopol, Vladivostok, Kiev, Voronezh and Chita—even at Kronstadt. The Tsar had bought time by granting a parliament; but was it time that he needed? A parliament would only carry on the work of the revolutionaries. Some members of the court had advised Nicholas to grasp the nettle, to crush all rebellion, as his father, Alexander the Third, had crushed it. But the Tsar changed his mind from day to day.

Listening to all this, Rasputin felt slightly dazed. Here he was, actually being taken into the confidence of a man who was close to the Tsar himself. The worst of it was that he felt unable to offer any practical suggestions. Of course the Tsar ought not to hand over power to some gathering of woolly-minded liberals. On the other hand, Rasputin sympathized with the peasants and the workers. And the peasants and the workers were still loyal to the Tsar. Why couldn't the Tsar go straight to them, ignoring the treacherous intellectuals? If only he had stayed in the Winter Palace in January and talked to the crowd, instead of allowing his soldiers to slaughter them. The grand duke agreed; but now it was too late. The Tsar had promised to grant a parliament.

At this point they were interrupted by the butler; the Grand Duke Nicholas was on the telephone. Peter excused himself and went out. Militsa immediately invited Rasputin into her boudoir. She had listened patiently to all this political chatter; now she wanted to tell him important news.

The news was that Dr. Philippe was dead. He had died in Lyons, shortly after the arrival of a messenger from the Tsarina begging him to return to Russia. He had sent the Tsarina a deathbed message: *Tell her that she will not be alone for long. She will soon have another friend, who is greater than I.* This message had arrived ten days ago; Militsa had heard it from the Tsarina's own lips. Within an hour she had dispatched a telegram to Pokrovskoe.

Before she had finished speaking, Rasputin knew the moment had come. It could be delayed no longer. He asked, "Have you spoken of me to the Tsarina?"

"Many times. But only casually. I wanted to wait until she asked to meet you."

"Has she?"

"The other day. When she told me about the death of Dr. Philippe, she said, 'What was the name of that holy man from Siberia?' And when I told her, she said, 'Bring him to see me.' "

"When will you take me to see her?"

"I won't." She gave him her most mischievous smile. "She's coming here in the morning. That's why I want you to stay with us."

THAT NIGHT RASPUTIN slept badly; it was partly the exhaustion of the journey—he kept waking up and thinking he was on the train—and partly the expectation of meeting the Tsarina. At nine the next morning he woke out of a deep sleep as the maid brought him breakfast on a tray. He sat in the four-poster bed, the tray across his thighs, looking at the blue-brocaded wallpaper. Then, before eating, he closed his eyes and prayed. Immediately he felt stronger.

After eating, he bathed in the adjoining bathroom. Instead of the cake of violet-scented soap, he preferred to use a square chunk of scrubbing soap that some maid had left on the windowsill; scented soap offended his nostrils.

He was drying his beard when the butler knocked discreetly. "The grand duchess says her guest has arrived and she would like you to come down." It was sooner than he had expected. He combed his damp hair, donned his black monk's robe over his coarse peasant trousers, and hung around his neck the cross that had been given to him by John of Kronstadt. As he went downstairs he experienced a curious sense of exhilaration, as at the beginning of a journey.

He went into the drawing room without knocking. Militsa and her guest were seated on the settee near the fire that blazed in the hearth. Militsa said, "Ah, Father Grigori," and jumped to her feet. The other lady also stood up. Until this moment Rasputin had never asked himself how he ought to behave toward the Tsarina—whether to kneel, or kiss her hand. Now, as her eyes met his, he realized with astonishment that she was equally unsure of what to do. Her look was timid and uncertain. He walked up to her firmly, took her in his arms and crushed her against him, then gave her a kiss on the cheek.

What Rasputin saw was a tall and beautiful woman in her early thirties who looked about twenty-five. Her beauty had a quality of mournfulness; the mouth drooped downward at the corners; the eyes were gentle and contained a latent sadness. Oddly enough, his first reaction was a feeling that he had met her before. He had, of course, seen photographs; but these failed to capture her personality; and it was with her personality that Rasputin felt familiar.

They sat down. A servant brought tea. Rasputin felt completely at ease. With this woman, the intimacy was immediate and deep. For Rasputin, she was the kind of woman who seemed made for him, who responded to him with all her femininity. He was accustomed to women falling in love with him, but this woman was more desirable—because of a higher quality—than any woman he had ever known. Even the slight English accent made her lovelier.

Rasputin talked about prayer; but it made no difference what he talked about. She was not listening to what he said, but to his voice. She was drinking in his personality, his strength, his being. Everything he said fell on her soul like rain on a desert, bringing her peace.

When Militsa touched her arm and pointed to the clock, she seemed to come out of a trance. It was half past midday, and she was due to have lunch at the palace at one. She jumped to her feet, smiling shyly and apologetically. Rasputin stood up more slowly, and walked with her to the door. Militsa observed with a flash of jealousy that the Tsarina stood there, obviously waiting for Rasputin to embrace her again; and when he did, she momentarily buried her face in his shoulder. Militsa saw her out to her carriage, and as they embraced, the Tsarina said, "I don't know how to thank you, my dear." It was unusual for Alexandra, who was shy by nature, to call anyone "my dear." As she stepped into the troika, she said, "Bring him to Tsarskoe Selo tomorrow—no, the day after."

Militsa went back into the drawing room and found Rasputin stretched in the armchair before the fire, his legs akimbo. She asked him, "Well, what do you think of her?"

"She is beautiful." He added thoughtfully, "She needs my help."

THE HAMLET OF Tsarskoe Selo—meaning "the Tsar's village"—lies some twenty versts south of Saint Petersburg, in the Duderhof hills. Its two palaces had been used by the tsars as summer residences since the mid-eighteenth century. On Wednesday, November 1, 1905, Rasputin traveled there for the first time in the carriage of the Grand Duchess Militsa.

They were received by the Tsarina in the reception room at the Alexander Palace, which was crammed with photographs, ornaments and various bric-a-brac. Here, on her own territory, the Tsarina was more relaxed than at Militsa's. She made Militsa sit in an armchair, and sat herself firmly on the settee beside Rasputin; the symbolism was not lost on Militsa. As the two women talked about clothes and French hair stylists, Rasputin moved to the corner of the settee, where he could see the Tsarina better. Her skin was singularly clear and fresh. He was not offended that she ignored him; on the contrary, he recognized it as her way of showing him that she liked and trusted him.

A pretty child of about eight came in to ask her mother some question about a pony. This was the Tsarina's second daughter, Tatiana, a lovely girl who looked very much like her mother. When introduced to Rasputin—as "Father Grigori"—she took his hand and curtsied gravely; when he grinned at her and ruffled her hair, she looked startled, then gave him an open and charming smile. She went and stood by her mother, who put her arm around her.

As Rasputin watched them, he experienced a piercing feeling of sadness. Before he could explore it further, the Tsarina stood up. "It's nearly teatime," she said. "Would you like to see the nursery?" She took them up to the second floor. Here the nanny was already giving tea to the three youngest children—Maria, age six, Anastasia, age four, and the one-year-old boy, Alexis. The eldest girl, Olga, who was ten, was sitting by the window reading a book.

All four girls were pretty, but it was clear that the chubby Maria was going to develop into the most beautiful. The boy was seated in a baby chair, being given bread dipped in a boiled egg; he expressed his displeasure at the slowness of the procedure by grabbing a spoon and trying to demolish the egg with violent swipes. He was also startlingly attractive, with blue eyes, golden hair and his mother's transparent skin. Rasputin observed that the edge of the tabletop was padded so that he could not bruise himself. His sisters squealed and shouted with laughter as they watched; it was obvious they adored him.

At precisely five minutes to four the Tsarina said, "Time for tea. Come, Olga, Tatiana." She led the way downstairs, to a pretty room overlooking the terrace. A number of small tables were covered with white cloths, tea glasses and plates filled with hot bread and English biscuits. Almost as soon as they were seated, the door opened and the Tsar came in. The clock struck four. Rasputin and Militsa stood up, and Militsa curtsied. The Tsar beamed at them. "Do sit down." His wife said, "Nicky, this is Grigori Efimovich, the man I told you about."

Rasputin was not sure what to do; the Tsar saved him embarrassment by holding out his hand, which Rasputin shook in the European manner. The Tsar's hand was small and delicate.

Nicholas was very much a family man, and tea was a family ceremony. Tatiana sat on the floor and played with dolls; Olga began to do needlework. Rasputin found the whole scene delightful. The Tsar was a small bearded man with a friendly, democratic manner, and he immediately began asking Rasputin questions about peasant settlement in Siberia. Rasputin knew a great deal about it, and answered fully; he had to keep reminding himself that this simple, kindly man was the Tsar of all the Russias. When the conversation turned to religion and Rasputin described his vision of the Virgin of Kazan, the Tsar glanced at his wife, noted the absorption in her eyes and frowned meditatively.

At five minutes to five precisely the Tsar stood up. "I must return to work. I have two dozen visitors to see before dinner." Instead of shaking hands with Rasputin, he slapped him on the arm in a friendly manner. "They tell me you can see into the future," he said.

Rasputin smiled. "As we all can, sir."

The Tsar considered this for a moment, then said, "You are a man of the people. Do the people really want to get rid of us?"

Rasputin looked into his eyes and said with sincerity, "The common people love you. Besides, they are suspicious of change." The Tsar smiled involuntarily. Then Rasputin said, "It is the intellectuals who want to destroy Russia."

The Tsar shrugged; it betrayed nervousness. Then he went out without looking back.

The entry the Tsar made in his diary that night was noncommittal: *We have got to know a man of God, Grigori, from the Tobolsk province.*

CHAPTER SEVEN

MILITSA'S SISTER, THE Grand Duchess Anastasia, often visited the poorer parts of the city and organized the distribution of winter clothes. On the following afternoon Rasputin went with her, and ended the evening in the communal room of a cheap lodging house, listening to the conversation of down-and-outs and unemployed laborers. Unaware that he was connected with their "betters," they spoke frankly about their political views. Rasputin learned for the first time that "Bloody Sunday" had made the Saint Petersburg workers deeply and permanently suspicious of the Tsar. Before the massacre in front of the Winter Palace they had been willing to believe that he had their best interests at heart; now they regarded him as an enemy—or at least as a weakling in the hands of corrupt ministers. They were cynical about the new parliament, and about Prime Minister Witte, who had persuaded the Tsar to allow the formation of the Duma.

It struck Rasputin that Russian politics was a tragedy of misunderstanding. If the Tsar could only come here and listen quietly, he would understand how easy it would be to avert revolution. And if these workers were better informed, they would know that in Witte lay their chief hope. He resolved to say these things to the Tsar when he saw him again.

BUT THERE WERE NO more invitations to the palace, and Rasputin was too busy to wonder why. His disappearance from the Saint Petersburg scene in 1904 had aroused curiosity and speculation; now that he had returned, everyone wanted to meet him. During his absence

Militsa had quarreled with Iliodor, so now Rasputin was her chief protégé, and he soon became the center of her soirees. They were always crowded with people who wanted to meet him.

Then, in April 1907, Rasputin met Anna Taneyev, a plain, round-faced young lady who happened to be the Tsarina's closest friend. She was neither witty, aristocratic nor intelligent; but she was honest and unselfish, and the Tsarina trusted her completely. For a long time it had saddened Alexandra to see that her friend lacked a husband. Finally she found her a handsome young naval officer named Vyrubov whose nerves had been shattered at the Battle of Tsushima.

Anna found him attractive, but the thought of marriage frightened her. She confided in the Grand Duchess Militsa and said she wished she had a crystal ball to see into the future. "Quite unnecessary, my dear," Militsa had replied. "I know someone who can do it for you. His name is Father Grigori."

That first meeting was not entirely a success. Anna was shocked when Rasputin came into the room and gave the grand duchess three noisy kisses on her cheeks. When he turned his strange piercing eyes on her, she became tongue-tied; she left without asking him about her marriage. Later she phoned Militsa and asked her to seek Rasputin's advice.

Militsa relayed Rasputin's answer the next day. The marriage, he said, would take place; but it would not be a success. Their characters were completely incompatible.

When Anna told the Tsarina she had changed her mind, the Tsarina was hurt and upset. Everything had now been arranged. Anyway, Rasputin had never met Lieutenant Vyrubov, so how could he know? Anna allowed her misgivings to be overruled and married Vyrubov.

It was, as Rasputin had predicted, a disaster. On the wedding night Vyrubov got drunk, and his clumsy attempts at lovemaking made the bride nervous and uncooperative. Vyrubov ended by beating her and calling her names. Anna rushed to the Tsarina in the morning and made her promise that she need never see Vyrubov again. The two were divorced a year later. By way of an apology, the Tsarina gave Anna a small house next door to the palace and invited her with them on their yachting trip that year.

Anna soon came to adore Rasputin, who had so accurately foretold the failure of her marriage. She became one of his most devoted disciples and spoke of him often to the Tsarina.

AT THE KRONSTADT MONASTERY Rasputin became acquainted with a Dr. Mikhail Lebikov, who had been the surgeon of Tsar Alexander the Third. In January 1906 a group of revolutionaries opened fire on tents erected on the ice of the Neva, believing the Tsar to be inside one of them. No one was killed, and most of the revolutionaries were later rounded up by the police. Dr. Lebikov, who was in one of the tents, received a bullet in the leg, and the wound festered. Rasputin went to see him in the hospital, and placed his hands on the bloody bandages. The following day the wound began to heal. The grateful Dr. Lebikov tried to give Rasputin a large sum of money; Rasputin said he had no use for money, and that he always gave away presents to the poor. But the two men became friends.

It was now February 1908, the time of year when the Tsar and Tsarina prepared to leave Tsarskoe Selo for the beginning of their annual "migration," which would take them to Livadia in the Crimea, then to a villa on the Baltic, and then to the royal yacht in the Finnish fjords. They usually stayed away for the whole summer, returning to the Crimea in autumn, then to Tsarskoe Selo in November.

The afternoon of Thursday, February 27, was unexpectedly sunny; it brought happy crowds into the streets of Saint Petersburg. And at Tsarskoe Selo it was so warm by late morning that the children went out to play with their puppy. Only Alexei was not allowed to join in; he had to sit on a seat, under the eye of the nurse, an Englishwoman called Miss Eager. The children ran about on the damp grass, screaming with laughter as the puppy tried to dodge them. The tutor, Pierre Gilliard, came out and sat beside Miss Eager; he was carrying a French newspaper that had arrived from Paris that morning. As the two discussed the news from Europe, the dog ran up the slope of the lawn. Three-year-old Alexei, who had been watching all this with excitement, broke free from the nurse and tried to grab the dog. It was almost as big as he was, and knocked him over on his face. The child gave a shriek of pain, and the nurse and tutor ran to pick him up. The Tsarina, who was in a ground-floor room, rushed out.

The child was carried indoors to his bedroom, and the court physician, Dr. Botkin, was sent for.

Botkin, a big stout man, arrived half an hour later, and looked grave when he saw the extent of the damage. He immediately rang Saint Petersburg and sent for the children's specialist, Dr. Ostrogorsky. The train service was excellent, and Ostrogorsky was there within an hour. By late afternoon the child was crying with pain and his temperature was a hundred and six. A few hours later he was delirious, and both his eyes were swollen shut.

That night no one slept. The Tsarina sat by Alexei's bedside; the two doctors remained in the next room. At breakfast time the boy was bathed in sweat, twisting and moaning.

It was the Tsar who remembered that Lebikov had cured Maria of quinsy and who suggested sending for him. Botkin thought it was probably useless, but agreed. The Tsar's own motorcar was sent. From Saint Petersburg, the chauffeur telephoned to say that he could not find Lebikov at home, but thought he might be at the Kronstadt monastery; he was told to keep looking.

The Tsarina's state was pitiable; by the afternoon she was a nervous wreck. But she firmly refused to take the sedatives prescribed by Botkin, declaring that she needed to be wide awake in case her child needed her.

At five in the evening it was dark; the motorcar drew up outside. The Tsar himself, who had canceled all appointments, hurried out to meet Lebikov. To his surprise, Lebikov was accompanied by Rasputin. As Lebikov began to explain why he had been so long, Rasputin said quietly, "Where is the boy?"

The Tsar frowned. He objected to an outsider being present—he still fondly believed that the boy's illness was known only to the family and immediate circle. But he recalled that Anna Vyrubova had great faith in Rasputin. He said, "Do you think you can help?"

"I cannot help. But God may be able to."

Lebikov said, "Trust him, Your Majesty. He cured my wound."

In the boy's plain little bedchamber, with its brass bedstead, only the Tsarina was sitting by the bed. Nicholas came into the room, followed by Lebikov and Rasputin. The Tsarina's eyes brightened when she saw Rasputin. He crossed the room quickly, and stood by the bedside. Alexei was breathing painfully, with little moans. Rasputin laid the back of his fingers on his cheek, which was red and damp with sweat. Then, ignoring everyone, he went to the icon that was in the corner of the room and fell on his knees. Lebikov approached the bed, felt the boy's forehead and asked questions in a low voice. Then he went downstairs to consult Dr. Botkin.

Rasputin finished his prayers and went back to the bedside. He placed one hand on the child's forehead, and pulled back the bedclothes to lay the other on his shoulder. The child, who had been almost doubled up, sighed and stretched out his limbs. Rasputin stood there for about a minute, while the Tsar and Tsarina watched him without a word. Then, to their surprise, the boy opened his eyes, looked at Rasputin and smiled. Rasputin said gently, "There, you're going to be all right now, aren't you?" The boy nodded. At that moment Lebikov and Botkin appeared in the doorway; the Tsar motioned them to be quiet. Rasputin pulled up a chair by the bedside and began speaking to the boy in a low voice. He took hold of Alexei's hand and stroked it gently. The Tsar leaned closer to catch the words; Rasputin was asking the boy if he liked horses, and Alexei was nodding eagerly.

The Tsarina was crying, making no attempt to stop the tears as they flowed down her cheeks. Rasputin turned to her and said cheerfully, "No need to cry, Matushka [little mother]. He's going to be all right now." He was obviously trying to stop her from crying, in case it distressed the child.

The Tsar seized Rasputin's hand in both of his and stared into his eyes. He looked as if he were going to speak, but said nothing. To break the silence, Rasputin said, "They tell me all of you are to leave soon for the Crimea, Batiushka [little father]." The Tsar nodded, obviously unwilling to trust his voice. "Well, he'll be all right to travel in a couple of days."

Botkin, who had placed his hand on the boy's forehead, said, "I can't understand it. His temperature seems normal."

"Can I have some jam, Mama?" the boy asked. The Tsarina started to laugh, then burst into tears again and rushed out of the room. The Tsar dropped to his knees beside the bed and took the boy tenderly in his arms. Rasputin touched Lebikov on the shoulder. "Come," he said. The Tsar was so absorbed in the boy that he did not notice them leaving.

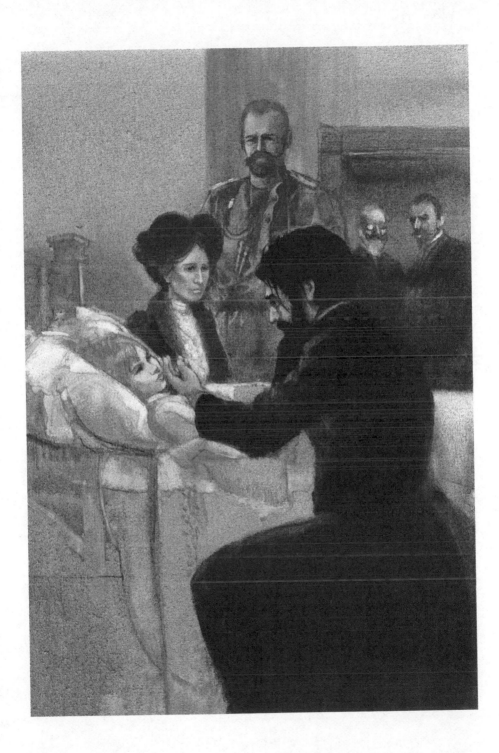

In the car on the way back to Saint Petersburg Rasputin said to Lebikov, "These people are in great trouble."

"They just have to take special care of the Tsarevich. He may improve as he gets older."

"That is only part of it. Their feelings are all wrong, their"—he struggled for the word—"their attitudes."

Lebikov looked at him curiously. "There are many who say this Tsar needs God's protection more than any of his predecessors."

"They live as if they were on the moon. But an emperor cannot afford to separate himself from his people. He should show himself. Otherwise he loses their trust."

Lebikov started to say something, then changed his mind. He could see the chauffeur was listening.

WHEN RASPUTIN HAD SAID the child would be ready to travel in two days' time, the Tsar had assumed it was an attempt to raise his spirits. But to Botkin's surprise, the boy's swellings had vanished by the next morning. At breakfast the child asked what had happened to "that funny man."

"Would you like to see him?" The boy nodded eagerly. So Count Fredericks, the chief minister of the Imperial Court, was told to contact Rasputin and ask him to come to Tsarskoe Selo.

When Rasputin arrived two hours later, he found Alexei sitting on the floor of his bedroom, surrounded by soft toys, while Anastasia showed him a picture book. The Tsar looked in shortly afterward, and saw both children sitting with their heads against Rasputin's knees while he told them a story about a little humpbacked horse. The Tsar withdrew quietly.

FROM THE TSARINA'S point of view, the acquaintance with Rasputin was an unalloyed blessing. Her first four pregnancies had all been difficult, and the boy's hemophilia was an immense drain on her emotional energies. She was shy by nature, and childhood illness had increased her tendency toward introversion. From the moment she had arrived in Saint Petersburg, she had felt unwanted. She was disliked by her mother-in-law, who virtually set up a rival court. Her distaste for social gatherings made her unpopular in Saint Petersburg, where she was regarded as a snob. The common people of Russia referred to her as "the foreigner." She felt safe and confident only when she was with her family; she and her husband adored each other. All these circumstances united to make her insecure and neurotic.

Rasputin's presence transformed her. On the evening before their departure for the Crimea Rasputin was invited to the Alexander Palace. The Tsar treated him as a friend, and addressed him as Grigori. He later noted in his diary: *Grigori arrived at 6:45. He saw the children and talked to us until 7:45.* As they were leaving the boy's bedroom, the Tsarina admitted to Rasputin, "I worry myself sick over him." Rasputin took her hand and replied, "While I am alive, you need have no fear for his life." And the Tsarina later confided to her husband, "I believe he has been sent to us from God."

IN THE YEAR 1908 the forty-year-old Nicholas the Second was a severely troubled man. Ironically, he would probably have made an ideal constitutional monarch. Intelligent, charming and extremely good-natured, he was liked by everyone he came into contact with. Allowed to show himself freely to his people, he would quickly have become the most popular man in Russia. But fear of assassins made this impossible, and marriage to the introverted Alexandra only made things worse.

The Tsar had one dangerous fault: he did not understand what was happening in his country. It never struck him to wonder why anarchists were making war on authority. He thought of the revolutionaries as wicked children who either had to be caught and punished or ignored until they decided to behave themselves.

These attitudes of the Tsar would not have mattered if he had been willing to leave the government in the hands of more competent men—like Prime Minister Witte. But he distrusted anyone who seemed to be willing to compromise with the revolutionaries. So Witte had been dismissed in May 1906 and replaced by a conservative nonentity called Goremykin, who assured the Tsar that he was still the absolute ruler. Within two months it was clear that Goremykin was a disaster; he resigned and was replaced by an ex-governor of Saratov, Peter Stolypin.

Stolypin was one of the bravest and most competent men in Russia. During the 1905 revolution he had traveled about the country restoring order and commanding respect everywhere by sheer courage.

Because he was a man of sense, Stolypin came to the same conclusion as Witte: Russia had to become more democratic. Inevitably, the Tsar regarded him with deep distrust. So did the revolutionaries.

Only three weeks after becoming prime minister, Stolypin was sitting in his study one Saturday afternoon when a tremendous explosion threw him out of his chair. There were screams and moans. When he rushed outside, he discovered that one wall of the house was missing. The exposed walls of the rooms were covered with blood and fragments of flesh; there seemed to be maimed and dying people everywhere. Thirty-two people were killed. Stolypin's young son, who had been playing on a balcony, was hurt, but not badly; his daughter was seriously injured. With incredible fortitude, Stolypin refused to be discouraged; the following Monday he was at work in his office.

In July 1906 the Tsar had dissolved his first parliament; the Duma had upset him by calling for land for the peasants and criticizing the corruption of his ministers. Half the Labor party had dashed over the border to Finland, and from there had called on their country-men to resist the government. Even the strongest reactionaries agreed that there had to be another parliament, so in March 1907 a second Duma had been formed. This time it contained far more radicals. The secret police, the Ochrana, did their best to destroy it by inventing terrorist plots. They succeeded so well that the second Duma lasted only until June. Troops were rushed into Saint Peters-burg to crush any protests. Meanwhile, the Tsar introduced new electoral laws that gave more votes to the gentry and less to the ordinary people.

The third Duma, as a consequence, consisted mainly of conserva-tives. But they didn't have it entirely their own way. Prime Minister Stolypin persisted doggedly with his plans to distribute the land among individual peasants—most of it belonged to village com-munes—and by 1910 he had taken most of the steam out of the revolutionary situation.

And at the end of August 1907 there had occurred an event to which no one paid much attention: the signing of an entente between England and Russia. Europe was worried about the buildup of Ger-man militarism. Still, it seemed highly unlikely that England and Russia would ever need to combine forces against the Kaiser.

CHAPTER EIGHT

NEWS OF RASPUTIN'S INTIMACY with the royal family spread quickly and made him the most-sought-after man in Saint Petersburg. Every morning he received a pile of letters and invitations, and while he had spent long wonderful periods wandering the roads alone, he also enjoyed good company. Now he found it very pleasant to feel he was conferring a favor by accepting someone's hospitality. When the politician Grigori Sasanov pressed him to move from the monastery of Kronstadt—which was inconveniently far from Saint Petersburg—into his own apartment, Rasputin accepted with pleasure, because Sasanov was obviously so eager to have him as a guest. When Aaron Simanovich—a jeweler whom Rasputin had met in Kiev— offered to become his unofficial secretary and take care of his correspondence, Rasputin again accepted with pleasure, because Simanovich was so obviously delighted to be at the right hand of a "famous" man.

Women, however, were continually a problem. Rasputin quite simply adored them. He once shocked Helene Katkoff by saying that the creation of the two sexes was God's most brilliant idea. Ever since he was a child, he had regarded women as objects of mystery and delight. Everything about them excited him. Their smell, their hair, the secrets concealed by their clothes.

Now in Saint Petersburg he suddenly had his choice of some of the most beautiful women in Europe. His male instincts were not prepared to withstand the abundance. In fact, there seemed no reason why he should try.

Stories spread about the Tsar's latest "friend and counselor," and these stories, together with rumors of his powers as a hypnotist, gained Rasputin many enemies. He began to acquire a reputation as a charlatan, an intriguer and a lecher. As a consequence, the royal family became still more unpopular and isolated. But wrapped in their private dreamworld, none of them even noticed.

IN THE SUMMER OF 1908, while the royal family were still at their villa on the Baltic, Rasputin returned to Pokrovskoe; it was his first visit home in over two years. This time he stayed for three months, and when he returned to Saint Petersburg that September, he took his daughter Maria with him.

Sasanov's apartment was clearly too small for two guests. Anna Vyrubova undertook to find Rasputin and his daughter somewhere to live, and located a large apartment on the third floor of 64 Gorokhovaya Street. From Rasputin's point of view, one of its more useful features was a back stairway, down which he could escape when the line of petitioners grew too long.

Maria, who was ten years old, found life in the capital bewildering. Even more bewildering was the endless activity that surrounded her father—the people who called at all hours wanting help or advice, the secret police who watched the house (on the orders of Prime Minister Stolypin, who greatly mistrusted Rasputin), the well-dressed ladies who came in crowds and sat listening for hours while her father talked about religion, the royal carriage that arrived several afternoons a week to take her father to the palace. Maria herself was received by the royal family, and became a regular visitor. Like her father, she was amazed by the simplicity of their way of life. The four young princesses were expected to work from morning until night at their studies, and they slept on plain camp beds. By comparison, Maria was spoiled.

IF ANNA VYRUBOVA was the high priestess of the Rasputin cult, its chief acolyte was a beautiful girl called Munia Golovina. When she met Rasputin, Munia had been suffering from a broken heart because her fiancé, Prince Nicholas Yussupov, one of the richest men in Russia, had been killed in a duel. Munia found comfort in religion. To her, Rasputin seemed a messenger from God; she believed him to be a saint, and asked nothing but to sit at his feet and listen to his voice. Rasputin, who felt genuinely sorry for her, treated her like a daughter.

It was Munia who talked about Rasputin to the younger brother of her dead fiancé, Prince Felix Yussupov, who, with the death of his brother, had become heir to one of the greatest fortunes in Europe. But this handsome young man was bored and unhappy. He had experimented with spiritualism, mysticism and yoga; all had left him dissatisfied. When Munia began to talk to him about Rasputin, it was not difficult to persuade Yussupov to meet the "saint." The meeting took place in the drawing room at the house of the Golovins. Felix was introduced to the *starets,* who embraced him amiably, made him sit down and began asking him questions. Rasputin was prepared to like anyone recommended by Munia. Besides, he felt protective toward this pale, attractive man, with his delicate features and nervous manner. On learning that Yussupov liked to play the guitar, he invited him to call on him at his apartment and bring the guitar. In fact, Yussupov found Rasputin intimidating; it would be years before the two met again.

By 1909, RASPUTIN HIMSELF was becoming increasingly dissatisfied. He had wandered all over Russia; he had become accustomed to the open air of the steppe. The atmosphere in Saint Petersburg stifled him. Half his disciples admired him for the wrong reason—because they thought he was a saint. Most of his enemies hated him for the wrong reason—because they thought he was a satyr. He was neither. He was simply a natural mystic, a man who feels strangely happy as he walks through a forest or climbs a hill. Unlike the great saints, he had no capacity for self-torment or self-analysis. Intrigue bored him. And the most successful people in Saint Petersburg were master players at the game of intrigue. Rasputin felt bewildered and out of place.

His secretary, the jeweler Simanovich, did his best to educate him. In this endeavor Simanovich called upon the help of one of the most skillful intriguers in the capital, a police spy named Manuilov. Manuilov loved money and power; he was also immensely likable. He had worked as a double agent in Paris and Rome, and, back in Saint Petersburg, had betrayed police secrets to the revolutionaries and revolutionary secrets to the police.

When Manuilov was introduced to Rasputin by Simanovich, he could hardly believe his luck. In Russia, as elsewhere, information was worth money. And Rasputin was ideally placed to gather secret information. Since the Tsar, except within his close family circle, kept his thoughts to himself, few people knew what he was thinking or what had passed between him and his ministers. Because Rasputin was a member of the Tsar's intimate family group, he was constantly overhearing state secrets that could make Manuilov a fortune.

And now, in his innocent way, Rasputin took an immense liking to

Manuilov. He told Manuilov anything he wanted to know, and he used his influence with the Tsar to do Manuilov favors. Rasputin was like a child playing at the game of intrigue; he could never convince himself that it really mattered. Manuilov sold the information provided by Rasputin, and made a great deal of money. Thus Rasputin's reputation grew; he became one of the most influential—and therefore most dangerous—men in Saint Petersburg.

The man who most wanted to see Rasputin's downfall was the prime minister, Peter Stolypin. And he was not entirely unjustified. For four years he had been struggling to reconcile the revolutionaries and conservatives, and to drag Russia into the twentieth century. The Tsar had learned to trust his judgment. But the Tsar was like a weathercock; he would agree to some controversial measure one day, and change his mind during the night. Stolypin believed Rasputin to be responsible for most of these vacillations. In fact, a police spy had overheard Rasputin boast that the Tsar was like putty in his hands. And whenever Stolypin would persuade the Tsar that Russia needed more parliamentary democracy, Rasputin would tell the ruler that he was the autocrat of all the Russias and ought to ignore the Duma. Then the Tsar would revoke his decision. Stolypin fumed, and vowed to get rid of the sinister intriguer.

Early in 1911 Stolypin took several police reports, all critical of Rasputin, to the Tsar, who listened carefully and was obviously shaken. Was Stolypin trying to tell him that Rasputin was just an ordinary hypocrite? No, said Stolypin triumphantly, he was not a hypocrite. He was secretly a member of the Khlysty, and the Khlysty believed in total sexual freedom.

When Stolypin left the Tsar that afternoon, he was convinced that Rasputin's career was at an end. He was reckoning without the Tsar's celebrated tendency to change his mind. When Stolypin brought up the subject at their next meeting, the Tsar remarked casually that he had given it some thought, but that it would only upset the Tsarina if Rasputin were forbidden to come to the palace; therefore it might be wiser to leave things as they were.

Stolypin left in a rage. Since it was impossible to show his annoyance with the Tsar, all his fury was directed at Rasputin.

The next morning Rasputin received a telephone call summoning him to Stolypin's office. The tone of the secretary made it clear that this was not a friendly invitation. Rasputin walked to the government building, and was shown into the prime minister's office. Stolypin looked up from his work, found Rasputin's strange eyes fixed on him and suddenly felt less confident. Making his voice curt and official, he said, "I shan't ask you to sit down. This won't take a moment. I have here"—he slapped a paper on his desk—"a report from Lukianov, procurator of the Holy Synod, which proves beyond all doubt that you are a member of the Khlysty."

Rasputin said quietly, "It is untrue."

"Do you deny that you have ever had any dealings with the Khlysty?"

"Of course not. I have come across most Russian sects in my travels. But I am not a member."

Stolypin found Rasputin's eyes unnerving; he remembered tales of his hypnotic powers. He said in a cold voice, "The evidence here would enable me to prosecute you as a member of a forbidden sect. But I prefer to avoid scandal. I shall expect you to leave Saint Petersburg tomorrow, and to stay away for at least six months. If you return before then, I shall have you arrested." He fiddled with a rubber stamp on his desk to avoid Rasputin's eyes. "Now get out. And don't bother to go whining to the Tsar. He already knows about this."

Rasputin was more shaken than he would admit. His wife had written to him from Pokrovskoe telling him about mysterious inquisitors who had been asking about his religious beliefs. And his father, who had paid Rasputin a visit in Saint Petersburg, had told him of some hostile comments made by his old enemy Father Peter during the course of a sermon, in which he had spoken about false prophets whose downfall would be as sudden and spectacular as their rise.

If the Tsar had now turned against him, there was no appeal. But this aspect of the affair hardly bothered Rasputin. Over the years his respect for his sovereign had steadily diminished, and he once told Simanovich that the Tsar was "an empty man." Besides, Rasputin was sick of Saint Petersburg. For a long time now he had felt a longing for the open road, for quiet evenings in monastery guest rooms or peasant kitchens.

So now that the blow had fallen, Rasputin felt oddly cheerful and relieved. He wrote a letter to the Tsarina, telling her what had happened, and he arranged for Maria to remain with Helene Kat-koff and her husband, who were staying in Kiev. Then, with just a few belongings in a small sack, he set out on a pilgrimage to the Holy Land.

The Tsarina was shattered. Her complete trust in Rasputin had never wavered. She saw this banishment as an attack on herself, an attempt to undermine her security. What if the Tsarevich fell down and injured himself while Rasputin was away? She wrote Rasputin a long and miserable letter, which caught up with him in Kiev. He wrote back immediately, telling her not to worry—he was certain the boy would remain well. He also promised to write to her from every monastery along the way. He kept his promise, and his words— scrawled in a barely literate hand on scraps of paper—brought the Tsarina a serene and total confidence.

Four months later, when Rasputin returned from the Holy Land to Pokrovskoe, the Tsarina herself recognized that it might not be wise for him to come back to Saint Petersburg. But she wrote to him almost daily, long, intimate letters. A police agent who managed to read one of the letters reported that it sounded as if Rasputin were the Tsarina's lover. That revealed a lack of perception. Rasputin's influence over Alexandra was far more powerful than that of a lover.

UNABLE TO GO TO Rasputin herself, the Tsarina asked Anna Vyru-bova to make the journey. Anna set out with a friend, Madame Orlov, in August 1911. They traveled to Tyumen on the Trans-Siberian Express, and were met by Rasputin. To their dismay, he was driving a large wagon—the one in which he had made his first journey to Tyumen so many years before. The women found the ride to Pokrovskoe bumpy and uncomfortably hot.

Anna was charmed by the Rasputin house—she wrote to the Tsar-ina that it was *almost biblical in its simplicity*. In fact, it was now the largest and most comfortable house in the village, an impressive two-storied dwelling. She described the simple evening meals, eaten around a bare wooden table, the servants who were treated as part of the family, and the four old friends who came in after supper and spent the remainder of the evening reading passages from the Bible and singing psalms. They fished and bathed in the Tura, took long walks in the forest and dozed in the meadows. For Anna, the month in Pokrovskoe only confirmed her view that Rasputin was a simple man who cared only for religion.

September came; Anna was due to join the royal family in Kiev, where they intended to make a ceremonial visit together with Stolypin and the minister of finance, Kokovtsev. Rasputin decided it would only be polite to accompany his guests; besides, he looked forward to seeing Maria and the Katkoffs again.

Their train arrived at eleven o'clock in the morning; Katkoff's chauffeur was waiting on the platform to help them with the baggage. "There's no hurry," he said. "We can't drive away until the crowd disperses."

"What crowd?" Rasputin asked.

"The Tsar and his ministers are due to drive past at any moment, on their way to the town hall."

Anna said, "What an amazing coincidence." Rasputin did not reply. His experience had taught him that coincidences usually had a deeper meaning.

They stood outside, at the edge of the station courtyard. Farther down the street, the crowd began to cheer. The imperial carriage came toward them, drawn by four magnificent chestnut horses. The Tsar was looking the other way. But the Tsarina looked straight at Rasputin, and her face lit up.

Ten yards behind the Tsar's carriage came another one, containing Stolypin and Kokovtsev. Stolypin was staring gloomily in front of him, his hands on the knob of his cane; most of the crowd had no idea who he was. Rasputin thought his face looked pale and death-like. Then, as the carriage drew near, the curious foreboding he had felt earlier seemed to explode into certainty. Stolypin's face became the face of a corpse, the eyes wide open and fixed.

Anna noticed Rasputin pale; she took his hand and asked, "What is it?"

Rasputin heard his voice saying, "Death is after him." At that moment Stolypin looked toward him. Rasputin pointed after the carriage and shouted, "Death is after him!"

In fact, Stolypin was feeling tired and discouraged. At the town hall, police surrounded the Tsar and Tsarina as they stepped from the carriage; Stolypin and Kokovtsev were left standing alone. Stolypin said irritably, "You see, we are superfluous."

That evening the royal party attended a performance at the Kiev Opera House. The Tsar and Tsarina sat in a box; Stolypin and Kokovtsev had been placed in the orchestra. During the second intermission of the opera—Rimsky-Korsakov's *Tsar Saltan*—Stolypin stood up, yawning, to stretch his legs. A young man walked toward him, looking as if he wanted to ask a question. When he was a few feet away from the prime minister, he reached into his pocket, pulled out a revolver and fired two shots. Both struck Stolypin in the chest.

The man who killed him, Mordka Bogrov, was a double agent, working for the police and the revolutionaries. He was later hanged.

WITH STOLYPIN DEAD, there was nothing to keep Rasputin away from Saint Petersburg; he returned with Maria to his apartment on Gorokhovaya Street. Simanovich and Manuilov were delighted to see him back again; so were the faithful disciples, who gathered to welcome him. When the royal family returned from the Crimea, the Tsarina immediately sent her carriage for him; the Tsar was amiability itself, and the Tsarina assured Rasputin that his banishment had been ordered without her husband's knowledge.

In early December, when the light was cold and gray and snow fell from the sky like eiderdown, there was a ring at Rasputin's door bell; Maria answered, and announced that it was a man called Iliodor. Rasputin was having tea with half a dozen female disciples; he hurried out of the room and embraced Iliodor, who was wearing a fur hat and had snow on his shoulders.

"What are you doing in Saint Petersburg?"

"I've come to try and raise money to complete the monastery. Can I put my coat in front of the fire?" Iliodor entered the sitting room, and stopped when he saw the women. He went suddenly pale, muttered something under his breath and walked out of the room. Rasputin hurried after him, and found him already opening the front door. Laughing, he seized him by the shoulders.

"Wait, you can't go yet! Come and have a glass of tea."

"I'm sorry. I have to leave." From the grim, set expression on Iliodor's face, he could see it was no use arguing. Iliodor tore himself away and went out. Rasputin stared at the closed door, then shrugged.

On returning to the sitting room, he encountered Olga Lokhtina, who had been introduced to the circle in the previous year; she looked pale and distraught, and was buttoning her coat. He asked in surprise, "What, are you leaving too?" She burst into tears. He asked helplessly, "But why?" She said something incomprehensible and rushed out.

The others were as puzzled by her departure as Rasputin. But the next day he learned the full story from Munia. Two years before, Olga Lokhtina—the wife of an Army officer—had been one of Iliodor's most devoted admirers. One day, after confessing to him, she was so upset that she flung her arms around his knees and tried to kiss his hands. Iliodor had reacted with incredible violence, grabbing her by the hair and slapping her face repeatedly. When some of his followers rushed into the room, Iliodor ordered them to take her out of his sight. They dragged her into the courtyard, stripped her and beat her. Then they tied her to the back of a cart and set the horse galloping off through the town of Tsaritsyn. As a result, Olga Lokhtina had suffered a nervous breakdown. Her husband had been transferred to Saint Petersburg; she had heard of Rasputin and had become a disciple. But she was too ashamed to tell him the story of her humiliation.

Rasputin was sympathetic, and not at all surprised. Since being appointed priest at Tsaritsyn, Iliodor had become increasingly fanatical. He was a preacher of great power, and had soon acquired an enormous following. His dream was to build a spiritual fortress called Mount Tabor, whose chief feature would be a tower from which he could preach. Hordes of devoted followers helped with the construction.

Two years before, Rasputin had visited Iliodor at Tsaritsyn and had been impressed by his achievement. But he found Iliodor's form of Christianity too intense and neurotic. When Iliodor had visited Pokrovskoe, Rasputin had taken a certain amount of pleasure in shocking him by drinking large quantities of his favorite sweet wine, and by kissing and embracing members of his congregation. Yet there had been no open quarrel. Now Rasputin decided that, when he met Iliodor again, he would refrain from mentioning Olga Lokhtina. There would be no point in widening their differences.

In late December Manuilov told Rasputin that Iliodor was spreading stories about him. Rasputin shrugged. "If he does, he's a fool."

Why should they quarrel with each other? The Lokhtina business was hardly important.

And then, one morning, Rasputin received a visit from Bishop Hermogen's secretary, a gloomy, officious man named Father Sergius. "Bishop Hermogen wishes to see you immediately."

The secretary's pompous tone irritated Rasputin. "What do you mean, immediately?"

"Today—this morning if possible."

"Well it's not possible. I have too many appointments. Tell His Eminence I'll be there this afternoon."

Father Sergius strode out, prim and offended.

Hermogen was staying at the Kronstadt monastery. When Rasputin arrived, he was made to wait about half an hour. Then Father Sergius announced importantly, "His Eminence will see you."

As soon as Rasputin walked into the room, he realized he was on trial. Hermogen sat behind a big mahogany table. Iliodor sat by the window. Also present were Mitia Koliaba, the "prophet" who had once been the Tsarina's adviser; a burly Cossack; and another man Rasputin did not recognize. The bishop—a big man, whose weight had increased notably since Rasputin first met him—stood up, facing Rasputin.

"Grigori Efimovich, I have asked you here to answer serious charges." And he proceeded to read from a paper that sounded very like the report Stolypin had acquired from Lukianov. It accused Rasputin of being a member of the Khlysty and of dishonoring various females. Rasputin listened quietly. The whole thing struck him as absurd. Hermogen concluded and then asked, "Is all this true?"

Rasputin said firmly but respectfully, "Some of it; most is exaggeration or lies."

Hermogen went red, and had some difficulty finding his voice. "If even some of it is true, you are . . . you are . . . a disgrace." He struggled for breath and added, "And a disappointment."

Now Rasputin was angry. "Pardon me, sir, but it may be a mistake to listen to the lies of people who are too cowardly to face me."

Iliodor spat out furiously, "I *am* facing you."

Rasputin said, "In that case, perhaps you will tell me why you've bothered to concoct this nonsense."

"You've just admitted it isn't all nonsense!"

Until this moment Rasputin had defended himself competently. Now he wanted to tell Hermogen that Iliodor was a fanatic, and that his accusations were based on envy; but he was too angry to articulate these charges. The interview turned into a shouting match. When Rasputin yelled, "I deserve a hearing!" Mitia Koliaba hurled himself upon him and started to hit him.

Hermogen came from behind the table and roared, "By the power invested in me by the Holy Church, I pronounce anathema on you!"

Rasputin shouted back, "Oh, shut up, you old fool! Keep your stupid curses to yourself."

Then, with a roar of rage, he struck out with both hands; Koliaba was hurled backward, and bowled over the bishop, who fell against the table. Iliodor, suspecting that he would be next, rushed behind a curtain. The Cossack tried to grab Rasputin, who, believing he was about to be attacked by everyone in the room, seized a chair from a corner and brandished it over his head. Everyone was breathing heavily. Then, seeing that no one intended to attack him, Rasputin said, "If you threaten me, I'll threaten you."

It was not an impressive exit line, but it served. He pulled open the door, and was grimly amused when Father Sergius fell into the room.

At teatime that afternoon Rasputin arrived at the palace. The Tsar said, "My God, Grigori, have you been in a brawl?" Rasputin's eye was swelling, and a tuft of his beard was missing.

Quietly and collectedly—he had had time to think out his words— Rasputin told them what had happened.

When he had finished, the Tsar placed his hand on Rasputin's shoulder. "Botkin's upstairs," he said. "Go and see him, and get him to put something on that eye. Meanwhile, leave this in my hands."

The following morning the Tsar's private secretary went to the Kronstadt monastery and inquired for Bishop Hermogen. He was told the bishop was ill in bed, but insisted on seeing him. In Hermogen's bedroom the secretary read aloud the Tsar's order of banishment. Hermogen was to go to the Zhirovetsky monastery, Iliodor to a monastery in Siberia. Hermogen, his face now very pale, said, "I have a right to be tried by a jury of bishops."

"The Tsar has overruled that right," the secretary replied.

Hermogen bowed his head.

Iliodor was already on his way back to Tsaritsyn. It was when he arrived there that he heard the order for his banishment. His reaction was hysterical. He wrote a long and violent letter to the Holy Synod, denouncing Rasputin as lewd and evil, and accusing him of being the Tsarina's lover. It was so intemperate that the Synod ordered his arrest. Iliodor was placed in a monastery near Saint Petersburg to await trial. There, rage and disappointment seemed to drive him to the brink of insanity. He now revealed that he had taken copies of various letters from the Tsarina to Rasputin—letters with phrases like "I love you always"—and sent them off to the Synod and to several newspapers. The Synod decided to avoid the scandal of a trial by unfrocking him. Iliodor then fled to Finland, started to write a book denouncing Rasputin and plotted a revolution to overthrow the Tsar.

Rasputin's triumph could not have been more complete.

Yet by the following spring fortune had turned against him. At first, it was merely a matter of rumor. It was said that a certain professor from Moscow had written a pamphlet denouncing Rasputin as a member of the Khlysty and saying he ought to be put on trial. An article saying much the same thing appeared in a newspaper owned by the president of the Duma, and soon the Saint Petersburg press was publishing daily insinuations about Rasputin and his misdemeanors.

In February Kokovtsev, who had surrendered his position as minister of finance to become prime minister after the murder of Stolypin, talked to the Tsar concerning Rasputin. The Tsar was affable and polite. He hinted that he himself knew all about Rasputin's questionable behavior, but that it did no harm. He ended by suggesting that Kokovtsev talk to Rasputin himself.

Rasputin was startled to receive a summons to Kokovtsev's house, and even more surprised to be escorted into his private study. Kokovtsev was a neat little man with a dry and rather stiff manner, and Rasputin was amused that the prime minister deliberately avoided his eyes—he had clearly been warned about Rasputin's hypnotic powers. Like an embarrassed schoolmaster, Kokovtsev explained that Rasputin's presence in Saint Petersburg was causing problems for everyone. While he was there, the liberal press used him as an excuse to attack the Tsar's policies, while stories about his debaucheries were embarrassing the Church.

Rasputin listened, and felt a wry sympathy for this awkward little man; an appeal to his good nature usually succeeded. He interrupted finally. "Please don't say any more. I'll leave Saint Petersburg."

Kokovtsev stared at him, then quickly looked away. "You will?"

"I promise—give me two more weeks. But before I go, I want to warn you about the railways. If Russia goes to war, our main weakness is the railway system. How can you move food and troops with inefficient railways?"

Kokovtsev said, "We all hope there will be no war."

"So do I. I'll tell you something in confidence. Two years ago, when the Duma was talking about going to war with Austria, the Tsar asked my advice. I told him that a war would be the end of Russia. I may be wrong, but I think my words made him think carefully. I don't know much about politics, but I know enough to realize that the Germans and the Austrians think we'd never dare to fight. So what do you think will happen next time the Duma gets an attack of patriotism and the Kaiser thinks they'll never dare to oppose him?"

Kokovtsev said, "Yes, yes, quite so. I'm . . . er . . . afraid I'm expecting another visitor now . . ."

After Rasputin had gone, Kokovtsev wrote in his diary: *When Rasputin came into my study and sat down in an armchair, I was struck by the repulsive expression of his eyes. Deep-seated and close-set, they glued on me, and for a long time, Rasputin would not turn them away, as though trying to exercise some hypnotic influence.*

THE WEATHER THAT YEAR was beautiful, and in September the royal family moved to Belovetchkaya, on the Polish border. Alexei, who had recently celebrated his eighth birthday, was growing up tall and strong. In recent years his health had improved steadily, and the Tsarina was convinced that this was due to Rasputin's healing powers. The boy was still not allowed to take part in any sport, and two large sailors from the Imperial Navy stood by to support him when he embarked on a boat or hurried down a flight of steps. But his health now seemed so good that they had gradually become accustomed to standing back and trying to be as unobtrusive as their immense bulk would allow.

One day, while the Tsar and his daughters were out riding in the forest, the sailors prepared to take Alexei for a row on the lake. As the boy was stepping into the boat, he tripped and his foot twisted under him. He landed against an oarlock, and cried out with pain. The alarmed sailors made him sit down and pulled up the leg of his short trousers. There was a small bruise on the thigh, just below the groin. Dr. Botkin, who examined him later that day at the hunting lodge, found a small swelling and ordered him to stay in bed. The boy cried and was feverish, but the swelling remained small. After a week it went away, and he was allowed to get up. The Tsar decided he was well enough for them all to move to his favorite hunting lodge at Spala. But Alexei was pale and unwell when he arrived. The tutor, Gilliard, tried to teach him French, but found him inattentive.

A few mornings later, when Alexei seemed better, the Tsarina decided to take him out for some fresh air; he drove off in the carriage, seated between his mother and Anna Vyrubova. The road was rough, and the carriage lurched and bounced. Suddenly Alexei cried out in pain; he became so pale that he looked as if about to faint. The Tsarina ordered the coachman to stop, then told him to go back to the house. Every bump on the way back made the boy scream with pain.

For four days Alexei suffered severe spasms of pain every quarter of an hour. Doctors arrived from Saint Petersburg, but they were ineffectual; it seemed that nothing could lessen the pain or remove the now enormous swelling. The Tsarina moved into the boy's bedroom. The Tsar continued with his household routine, but as the weeks dragged by, he became increasingly tired and lost weight.

In mid-October, more than a month after the original fall, the Tsar was sitting at lunch with the family when a servant handed him a note. He went pale, and hurried out. It was from the Tsarina and said: *I think he is dying.* Exhausted by weeks of pain, the boy was hardly breathing. The Tsarina, too overwrought to cry, looked at her husband from a gray face, and silently held out her hand. All afternoon they watched by the bed, expecting their son's breathing to stop. Toward nightfall the Tsarina tiptoed out of the room. When she came back, she said quietly, "I have asked Anna to send a telegram to Grigori."

The Tsar nodded. "But it will take days for him to come."

"No one else can help us."

Before midnight a servant knocked softly on the door, holding a telegram. The Tsar tore it open, read it and handed it to his wife. It said: *God has seen your tears and heard your prayers. Do not grieve. The Little One will not die. Do not let the doctors worry him.* It was signed *Grigori.*

The Tsarina buried her face in her hands and breathed deeply. Then she looked at her husband and said softly, "We can go to bed now."

The next morning Alexei was still alive, but the doctors declared that the hemorrhage continued. Then, toward midday, the boy began to breathe more deeply and easily. Botkin cautiously pulled back the thin sheet that covered him. Then he looked at the Tsarina. "I *think*—I'm not sure, but I think—that the hemorrhage has stopped."

She said, "I know." And for the first time in weeks she burst into tears.

By the next morning the swelling had gone down. Alexei looked thin and exhausted; but the color was returning to his cheeks. The Tsar took Anna Vyrubova aside. "Send a telegram to Grigori. Tell him we thank him from the bottom of our hearts."

CHAPTER NINE

THE YEAR 1913 MARKED the three hundredth anniversary of the Romanov dynasty, founded in 1613 by Tsar Mikhail. Nicholas ordered celebrations all over Russia, hoping that a wave of patriotism would put an end to revolutionary agitation. He was disappointed. Widespread strikes and civil disturbances disrupted the celebrations. And the shadow of war increased the sense of instability. In 1911 Italy had gone to war with Turkey; in 1912 Bulgaria, Serbia, Montenegro and Greece decided to join in the attack. The two Montenegrin sisters, Militsa and Anastasia, tried hard to persuade the Tsar to declare war on Turkey.

Rasputin was back in Saint Petersburg, more intimate than ever with the royal family. The Tsar was aware that his presence aroused hostility, but after the shock of the boy's illness, there was no more talk of banishing Rasputin to Pokrovskoe. When the royal family traveled to Kostroma, on the Volga, where the first Romanov Tsar, Mikhail, had been told of his election to the throne, Rasputin went with them. The cheering crowds they encountered everywhere convinced the Tsar and Tsarina that the mass of the Russian people was still loyal to the throne.

It struck Nicholas that a war against the Turks might not be a bad thing; there was nothing like war to stimulate patriotic feeling. But when he put the idea to Rasputin, the *starets* was blunt and emphatic. "No war is justifiable. But a war at this point would destroy Russia." The Tsar agreed to give it more thought.

That winter was one of the gayest ever seen in Saint Petersburg; there, at least, the celebrations had created an atmosphere of excitement and festivity. The Nevsky Prospect blazed with lights and decorations. The chief topic of discussion was the dancer Nijinsky, who had been expelled from the Diaghilev Ballet by Diaghilev himself. The two men had been intimate friends for years, and Diaghilev was outraged by Nijinsky's recent marriage, which he considered a betrayal. With scandals like this, no one was interested in politics. Revolution had never seemed more unlikely.

ON HIS RETURN FROM Pokrovskoe, Rasputin had brought his younger daughter, Varvara, as well as Maria and the maid Dunia. He enjoyed the quiet, domesticated routine they provided, for the events of the past two years had made him aware that he was surrounded by enemies. At forty-three years of age, he was beginning to think about the future.

Where his daughters were concerned, Rasputin was something of a prude. If they went out, they had to have a chaperone. Every night they had to be home by ten o'clock. The girls amused themselves with the telephone; they rang numbers at random, and carried on long and daring conversations with unknown males.

One day in May Maria received a telephone call from a man who told her he was in love with her. He explained that he had seen her in the street and had been following her for days. He described the walks she had taken and the people she had talked to, but he refused to tell her his name.

The unknown admirer called every few days. Sixteen-year-old Maria was not pretty—she resembled her father too much for that—

but she had a generous mouth, lively eyes and a good figure. The notion that someone thought her beautiful was enough to predispose her to return his feeling.

In the third week of June Rasputin suddenly announced that they would return to Pokrovskoe for the summer. The royal family were on their annual trip, and Alexei's health now appeared so improved that it seemed unlikely Rasputin would be needed. Besides, the *starets* had already displayed his ability to conduct his cures from a distance. On June 20, 1914, the Rasputins set out on the seven-day journey back to Pokrovskoe—five days on the train, two on the boat. At Tobolsk they took a river steamer for the final stage of the voyage.

As she stood on deck, enjoying the breeze from the steppe, Maria was approached by a dark-haired young man who told her he was a newspaper reporter. Something about his voice intrigued her. Suddenly it dawned on her—this was her unknown admirer. The young man, who said his name was Davidsohn, looked embarrassed and admitted it was true. Unable to spend the summer without seeing her, he had decided to follow her to Pokrovskoe. Maria was flattered. Davidsohn was not particularly attractive, being small and bespectacled; but it was pleasant to think she could inspire so much emotion. When they parted at the dock at Pokrovskoe, she was already feeling tender toward him. But she took care not to let her father see them as she allowed him to snatch a kiss.

Sunday, June 28, was a bright, calm day. Rasputin was in good spirits, delighted to be home. They attended church in the morning, and Rasputin showed no impatience with Father Peter's dull sermon. At lunch he kept everyone amused with lively stories about Saint Petersburg.

At two fifteen, while they were still sitting at the table, there was a knock at the door. It was the postman with a telegram. Rasputin read it, then left the house, saying he would walk to the post office to send a reply.

The sun had brought out most of the villagers; Rasputin walked through the crowded streets, acknowledging friends every few yards. Close to the post office, a lame woman dragged herself toward him, holding out her left hand. Rasputin felt in his pocket for a coin. As he did so, she drew the other hand from under her shawl and rushed at him. The knife in her hand drove into his stomach; then she dragged the blade upward. Blood gushed down Rasputin's clothes, and he turned to run. The woman lunged again, trying to stab him in the back. He seized a piece of wood that was lying in the gutter, turned again and struck her across the head. She collapsed in the road, then tried to crawl off. By this time passersby had noticed what was happening; several of them grabbed her and dragged her toward the police station. Rasputin, the blood gushing between his fingers, staggered back home.

Praskovia and the maid Dunia laid him on the kitchen table and removed his trousers. As they washed the wound, there was a knock at the door. Maria answered it and recognized the reporter, Davidsohn. He explained that he had heard about the attack and wanted to report it for his newspaper. As he tried to peer past her, Maria was struck by a horrifying recognition. This man was behind the attempt on her father's life. Angrily, she pushed him out and slammed the door.

Later that day the police called. The arrested woman was Kinia Guseva, and she had been lodging in the town for some days. Letters in her possession revealed that she was a disciple of Iliodor; the knife she had used actually belonged to the unfrocked priest.

Further investigation proved Maria's suspicion correct: Davidsohn had gone straight to Guseva's lodging when he had arrived in Pokrovskoe. Now he had disappeared.

JUNE 28, 1914, IS NOTABLE for another event besides the attempt on Rasputin's life. More than two thousand miles from Pokrovskoe, in the town of Sarajevo, in Bosnia, a young patriot of Serbian descent named Gavrilo Princip was following the movements of his intended victim, Archduke Ferdinand, heir to the throne of Austria-Hungary. The archduke had chosen a bad day for a state visit to Sarajevo, since it was the anniversary of a Serbian defeat. Of all the Slavic provinces within the Austro-Hungarian Empire, Serbia was the most nationalistic. Shortly after ten that Sunday morning a homemade bomb had been thrown at the archduke's car; it exploded and wounded several people. But the archduke and his wife were uninjured and went on to the town hall. As they left, half an hour later, the archduke remarked to his wife, "I've got a feeling there may be more bombs around." The car drove off. A few moments after eleven o'clock Gavrilo Princip watched its approach and clutched the Browning revolver in his pocket. Then, unexpectedly, the car turned off down another street. An official shouted, pointing out to the chauffeur that he had gone the wrong way. As the car began to turn back, Princip leaped forward, the revolver raised, and fired two shots. His aim was good; Ferdinand and his duchess died almost simultaneously.

Archduke Ferdinand was assassinated just past eleven o'clock in the morning; Rasputin was stabbed just after two fifteen in the afternoon. But Sarajevo and Pokrovskoe are separated by fifty degrees of longitude—a time difference of three hours. Kinia Guseva stabbed Rasputin very near the moment that Gavrilo Princip shot Ferdinand and his wife.

As RASPUTIN LAY IN the hospital, his life in the balance, consequences followed one another inevitably. Outraged at the assassination of the heir to the throne, Emperor Franz Joseph of Austria demanded reparations from Serbia, and permission for Austrian officials to interrogate Serbian officials to uncover the assassination plot. Serbia refused indignantly, and Austria declared war. The Tsar had a defense pact with Serbia. In this crisis he was clearly expected to declare war on Austria—which, in turn, had a defense pact with Germany. Was the honor of Serbia important enough to justify plunging Russia into war? In the past Rasputin had emphatically advised the Tsar against going to war for the sake of the Balkans. If he had been able to return to Saint Petersburg at the end of June 1914, he would undoubtedly have repeated that advice. But he was in the hospital, undergoing an operation to prevent peritonitis.

On July 29 the Austrians bombarded Belgrade, the capital of Serbia. The Tsar vacillated, but finally ordered a partial mobilization. The Kaiser, allied with Austria, sent him an insulting message, ordering him to cease military activity immediately or take the consequences. On August 1 Germany declared war on Russia.

It was a month before Rasputin had recovered sufficiently to pay attention to the news from the capital; he immediately wrote a letter to the Tsar beginning: *My friend: Once again I repeat, a terrible storm menaces Russia. Woe, suffering without end. . . .* But it was too late. Russia was already at war.

WHEN RASPUTIN RETURNED TO Saint Petersburg with his daughters in the autumn of 1914, the name of the city had been changed to Petrograd; Russians felt it was unpatriotic to call their capital by the German name chosen by Peter the Great. Rasputin hurried to see the Tsar, taking Maria with him. He was pale, and looked many years older; both his hair and beard were streaked with gray.

The Tsar and Tsarina received him kindly, and Maria sat at the Tsarina's feet, her head against the older woman's knees. But when Rasputin began to speak about the war, the Tsar became cold. "My friend, it is simply too late. There can be no going back."

"It is never too late to make peace."

The Tsar said irritably, "You are a man of God. You do not understand these things. Besides, it is a bad time to give up when we are winning."

This was not entirely true; the Austrians had won a great victory in August at Zamosc-Komarov, and the Germans at Tannenberg; but the Russians had won the Battle of Lemberg. The country thrilled with patriotism and victory; the Tsar was cheered whenever he appeared in public. There was no more talk of revolution. Rasputin struck Nicholas as a tiresome pessimist who was afraid to take risks. After explaining his point of view, the Tsar left the room.

When Rasputin departed from the palace that afternoon, he looked ill and exhausted. The war had done what his enemies had been unable to do: destroyed his influence with the Tsar.

THE NEXT FOUR MONTHS were the worst of Rasputin's life. Although the stab wound had healed, it had damaged his health; he felt permanently tired. Worse, he felt abandoned, not only by the Tsar, but also by God. Hours spent in prayer brought him no comfort. He began to drink heavily to dull the feeling of despair; every night Dunia watched him drink until he fell asleep in his chair, then helped him to bed.

It seemed to him an absurd irony that his enemies were more active than ever. There was a spy mania in Saint Petersburg that winter, and he soon discovered that someone had circulated a rumor that he was a German spy. For good measure, the rumor also insisted the Tsarina was his mistress, and that she was also a German spy. A current joke reported the Tsarevich as saying, "I don't know which side I'm on. When the Russians lose, Daddy looks gloomy, and when the Germans lose, Mama cries."

After September the war began to go badly for Russia. Her generals were incompetent, her ministers dishonest. There was open talk of profiteering, even of large-scale embezzlement of the money intended to buy arms; but no one did anything about it. Centuries of inefficiency and dishonesty had accustomed the Russians to thinking it was inevitable. The soldiers fought well, but they lacked weapons and died by the thousands. Moreover, as Rasputin had pointed out to Kokovtsev, Russia's railway system was poor; munitions and food piled up on the sidings. Even if Kokovtsev had wanted to heed Rasputin's advice, he would have had no time to do anything about it; the Tsar had dismissed him shortly afterward and appointed the old and muddled Goremykin in his place. The Tsar took advantage of the war to become the absolute autocrat he had always believed he ought to be. The Duma was not allowed to meet, and its six Bolshevik deputies were arrested. The sale of vodka was prohibited, to stop the troops from getting drunk; but this was unnecessary. Patriotic excitement had already caused a dramatic fall in the level of drunkenness. In those early months it was generally believed that the war would be over before the spring.

When the Tsar left Saint Petersburg for Russian military headquarters in Poland, Rasputin hoped to be summoned to the palace again. But no message came. In November 1914 Dunia returned to Pokrovskoe to tend her dying mother, and Rasputin began to spend his evenings at the Villa Rode, his favorite restaurant, where he could listen to gypsy music. The manager learned to send for a carriage to take him home when he began to snore.

As his health deteriorated, Rasputin felt that his powers were also deserting him. An old woman suffering from arthritis came to see him just before Christmas; her hands and arms were so twisted that they looked like burned wood. He held her hands in his and prayed; but nothing happened. The harder he tried to reach down to the hidden force in his depths, the less capable he seemed of concentration. He finally sent the old woman with a note to his friend Dr. Badmaev. Then he drank himself insensible.

When, a few days later, Dunia returned from Siberia, she was shocked by the change in him. He looked like a dying man. His skin was gray; his hands trembled when he tried to pour himself a drink. In spite of his protests she put him to bed and began feeding him a steady diet of thick vegetable soup.

On the afternoon of January 15, 1915, it was snowing heavily. Simanovich came to see him, and they began talking about the chaotic military situation. Suddenly the door burst open and Maria rushed in. Her face was pale. "Daddy, Anna Vyrubova's been killed in a train crash."

"Are you sure? Where did you hear it?"

"At Sasanov's."

Rasputin groaned and massaged his face with his hands. Then he said to Simanovich, "Get on the telephone. Find out if it's true."

Ten minutes later Simanovich came back. "It's not true. She's seriously injured, but not dead."

Rasputin struggled out of bed and began to dress. "Get me a car," he told Simanovich. "I'm going to her."

The snow was so heavy that it took the car two hours to reach Tsarskoe Selo. Rasputin went straight up the main steps of the palace, followed by Maria. Of the butler who came forward he asked, "Where is Anna?" He was directed to the sickroom.

The Tsar and Tsarina were standing by the bed. Rasputin ignored them. He took the hands of the unconscious woman, and was immediately aware that her life was ebbing. She was breathing shallowly, and her face was as pale as death. "Annyushka," Rasputin said in a strong voice, "Annyushka, wake up." There was no response. He leaned closer and repeated, "Annyushka, open your eyes." He felt her consciousness returning. Her eyelids fluttered and she looked up. It took her eyes a moment to focus; then she recognized him.

"Grigori," she said. "Thank God."

He said nothing more, but simply held her hands. Now, with his eyes closed, he entered her consciousness and was aware of the pain in her legs and hips. He deepened his concentration, and felt the power rising in his heart, flowing out again through his hands. He could sense her relief as the life flowed back into her. After about five minutes he placed her hands on the quilt. The color had come back into her cheeks. He looked across at the Tsar and Tsarina. "She will live," he said. "But she will be a cripple." Then he put a hand on Maria's shoulder. "Come."

They went out of the room. As soon as the door closed behind him, he felt his senses leaving him; he collapsed on the floor. Through the darkness he heard Maria say, "Get a doctor," and he managed to rouse himself enough to protest. "No," he said, "just get me home."

Later that day, as Rasputin slept, there was a ring at the door bell. It was a messenger with an enormous bouquet of flowers, and a basket of fruit so large that the police agent outside the door had to help him carry it up. The card on it said simply: *Love from Matushka.*

AS SOON AS THE Tsar went back to headquarters, the Tsarina sent a carriage to bring Rasputin to the palace. She wanted to ask his advice. She had heard a rumor that the commander in chief of the Army, Grand Duke Nicholas, was being referred to as "Tsar Nicholas the Third," and that he was the most popular man in Russia. Would it not be better if the Tsar himself took the supreme command? Should he give way to the pressure to allow the Duma to meet again? Which ministers could be trusted? Rasputin advised her against dismissing the commander in chief, but suggested that the Tsar should not mention his name in public proclamations.

On his way back to Petrograd it struck Rasputin that the Tsarina needed something to occupy her mind while the Tsar was at headquarters. In the Nevsky Prospect he passed a hospital convoy bringing the wounded back from the front, and saw the answer: she should become a nurse. It would give her a sense of helping the war effort, and it would keep her thoughts off politics. When he suggested the idea the next day, Alexandra was enthusiastic; not only would she become a nurse, but the two eldest girls would do so as well. They began training immediately, and for some months Rasputin heard no more about politics. When he told Maria about it, he chuckled and rubbed his hands like a pantomime villain. "Your father's getting cunning in his old age."

But nursing the wounded could not long prevent the Tsarina from worrying about the political situation. She bombarded her husband with letters (written in English) full of political advice. Her politics, however, consisted mainly of a series of violent personal dislikes. Her remarks about the Grand Duke Nicholas and her husband's kind heart implied that the Tsar was only leaving the grand duke in charge of the Army out of consideration for his feelings.

The Tsarina finally had her way; on September 5, 1915, the Grand Duke Nicholas was relieved of his post as commander in chief, and it was taken over by the Tsar himself. Suddenly Rasputin found himself in demand at the palace every day of the week, and the Tsarina's letters to the front contained an increasing number of phrases like: *Our Friend believes that the grace of God is in Hvostov, and that he would make an excellent minister of the interior.* Alexis Hvostov was a mediocrity with a gift for intrigue and flattery; but the Tsarina explained that *he stands up for our Friend, and would have himself chopped to pieces for you.* So Hvostov was made minister of the interior. The Tsar took his wife's advice about the Duma and closed it down in mid-September—a tactless move that led to a two-day protest strike among the workers of Petrograd. If he had been at home, the Tsar might have listened to less reactionary counselors and refrained from throwing oil on the flames of revolution. But while he was at headquarters, the Tsarina was in charge. And since Rasputin was her major adviser, he was virtually the Tsar.

ONE DAY, WHILE HAVING tea at the palace, Munia Golovina said to Rasputin, "Felix is back in Saint Petersburg." (Few people could get used to calling it Petrograd.)

Rasputin was at first puzzled. "Who's he?"

"Prince Felix Yussupov. You met him a few years ago. He wants to see you again."

Rasputin remembered the shy young man with the troubled stare. "Yes, I remember. He told me he played the guitar." The recollection produced a kind of sentimental affection for Yussupov, who had looked to Rasputin as if he needed help and advice. "I'd like to meet him again."

"He's coming to my house tomorrow afternoon. Could you come at teatime?"

"Good. I'd like to. Tell him to bring his guitar."

The following day Rasputin met with Felix Yussupov for the second time.

BY EARLY DECEMBER Rasputin found himself longing to return to Pokrovskoe for Christmas. He was sick of Petrograd and of endless intrigues. Politics bored him; yet he was obliged to think and talk about politics from the moment he woke up in the morning. Even his hours at Tsarskoe Selo were becoming a burden. He was clear-sighted enough to see that the Tsarina lacked the intelligence to judge the political situation, that she was guided again and again by her emotions. It was obvious, for example, that Prime Minister Goremykin was a disaster and ought to be dismissed as soon as possible; but the Tsarina liked and trusted him because he was so reactionary. Rasputin spent a whole afternoon arguing with him, trying to persuade him to recall the Duma and make various small concessions to the liberals; the old man would not listen. Rasputin returned home feeling exhausted and depressed.

To calm himself, he walked along the quays of the Neva until he was facing the Gulf of Finland. The great expanse of water gradually soothed his spirit. He found himself remembering that first day in Saint Petersburg, when he had stood in this same spot, looking out toward Kronstadt Island. It seemed a century ago. It suddenly struck him that he had at last achieved all he had dreamed of as a child: a position of power, and an intimacy with the Tsar even closer than that of the Archpriest Avvakum. The irony of the situation made him smile. He was trapped in a city he had come to hate, and in a way of life he found deadening to the soul.

When he returned to the apartment on Gorokhovaya Street, he told his daughters, "Tomorrow we take the train back to Tobolsk." Both girls began to dance around him in excitement. That night he telephoned Praskovia to tell her to expect them in about eight days, depending on the road from Tobolsk.

The next morning at eight o'clock Dunia woke him up. "It's the Tsarina on the telephone."

He snatched up the receiver and said irritably, "Hello, Matushka, what is it?"

"It's Alexei." Her voice was choked.

"I thought he was with his father?"

"He is. I've had a telegram. He's had a bad nosebleed and they're returning home."

"I'll come and see him as soon as he gets back."

He hung up the phone and said wearily to Dunia, "We stay after all."

Rasputin saw the Tsarina that afternoon. She looked weary and red-eyed. It seemed that the boy had caught a bad cold a week before and the constant blowing of his nose had caused a nosebleed that refused to stop. Now the eleven-year-old boy was again in a fever.

The following day there were more telegrams. Alexei was now in such constant agony that the train frequently had to be stopped. It would be at least another twenty-four hours before they would be home. Rasputin spent an hour soothing the Tsarina, and finally left her smiling and comforted. He felt exhausted.

He arrived home to find Felix Yussupov waiting for him. The prince jumped to his feet and, to Rasputin's astonishment, burst into tears. Rasputin put an arm around his shoulders. "Come, come, my friend. Sit down and tell me the trouble." As Yussupov wept on his shoulder, Rasputin experienced a flash of insight. He pressed him gently into an armchair.

"I've been trying to see you for the past week but you've been at the palace all the time . . ."

"Well, let's talk now. It's about your marriage, isn't it?" Yussupov looked at him in surprise. "I know the problem."

"You do?" Yussupov obviously wondered if they were speaking about the same thing.

"How long have you known . . . that you prefer men?"

Yussupov sighed with relief. "Ever since I was a child, I think. But I fought against it. Now . . . I don't want to fight anymore."

They talked together for over an hour. Rasputin's sympathy and warmth gave Yussupov the feeling that he was understood.

That night Rasputin went to the Villa Rode and danced to gypsy music. With his third bottle of wine, he fell asleep. When he woke up, he was in a car, being driven back to his own apartment. He had a leaden feeling in his stomach. When he climbed into bed half an hour later, the leaden feeling had turned into a burning sensation. He lay there for half an hour, feeling worse and wondering if he should send for a doctor, then he staggered to the washbasin and was violently sick. Finally he lay face down on the carpet, trying to make the nausea go away. The telephone began to ring in the next room. He ignored it. He had fallen into a doze when the bedroom light was switched on. It was Maria in her nightgown. She knelt beside her father and shook him.

"It's the Tsarina on the telephone. She wants you to go to the palace immediately. She says Alexei is dying."

Maria was not unduly perturbed to see her father lying on the carpet; she had seen him drunk before. But when he sat up, she looked alarmed. "You are ill." His face was ashen, his eyes bloodshot.

He heaved himself to his feet. "Never mind that. Help me to get dressed."

The dawn was breaking as the car arrived at Tsarskoe Selo. He had dozed on the way there; Dunia, who was with him, kept him covered with the car rugs and massaged his cold hands.

The Tsarina came running into the hall as he arrived; she had obviously been watching from the bedroom window. "Grigori, thank God you've come." She was so distraught that she did not notice how ill he looked. "Come quickly." She almost pulled him upstairs.

The Tsar was kneeling by the side of the bed, praying. The boy was awake, but looked hot and flushed. The pillow was covered with bloodstains. Botkin was standing by the window, looking out into the snow.

When Rasputin saw the boy's state, his own feeling of sickness vanished; the force inside him suddenly focused and concentrated. He went over to the bed and smiled; the boy tried to smile back at him. Rasputin put his hand out and touched his forehead; it was hot. "Well," he said, "you give me a lot of trouble, don't you?" He laid his hand on the boy's cheek. He looked down at the Tsar and said with mock roughness, "Why did you drag me out here? There's nothing wrong with him."

The Tsar said, "He's been bleeding . . ."

"But he's stopped now. He's all right." He ruffled the boy's hair. "Aren't you?" Alexei nodded, too exhausted to smile. Rasputin turned to the Tsarina. "I'm going back now. I'm tired." She accompanied him to the door. He gave her a kiss and whispered, "He'll be all right now." She flung her arms around his neck and hugged him so violently that he almost suffocated.

For the first time she noticed his face. "Are *you* all right?"

"Yes, I think so." He stopped himself from saying "I think someone tried to poison me"—it would only worry her. Instead, he said, "I need a holiday at home."

"Yes, of course. But not yet, please. Not until he's really better."

Rasputin slept all the way back to Petrograd.

The next morning Maria telephoned the palace. Alexei had had a peaceful night. There had been no further bleeding since Rasputin's visit.

CHAPTER TEN

ON THE NIGHT OF January 11, 1916, Rasputin woke up from a disturbing dream. He had been dreaming that he was a bear, hunted by huntsmen in red coats who wore top hats. He had been cornered in a cave, listening to the approaching shouts. Then a crowd of peasants, dressed in rags and animal skins, burst out of the trees. Rasputin rose on his hind legs, and the peasants fell down and worshiped him. Suddenly there was a roar of gunfire; he turned and saw that the hunters in red coats were behind him, inside the cave, and were pointing their guns at him. He woke up sweating.

He put on the light, struggling with a feeling of panic. Then he went to the table and picked up a pen. His fingers wrote hurriedly, as if of their own accord. When he had finished, half an hour later, he reread the opening sentences: *I write and leave behind me this letter at Saint Petersburg. I feel that I shall leave life before January 1.* He was too tired to read on. He climbed back into bed and quickly fell into a deep sleep.

The next morning he folded the letter without reading it and placed it in an envelope. On this he wrote: *To be given to the Tsarina in the event of my death.* He placed it in his drawer, hiding it under a piece of blotting paper. He no longer remembered what he had written. But he knew it was something he preferred not to know.

IN FEBRUARY 1916 THE TSAR decided to appoint a new prime minister. He chose a Rasputin candidate, Boris Stürmer. It was a generally unpopular decision: the people believed Stürmer to be a German; the Cabinet knew him to be incompetent and cowardly; the Duma rightly suspected that he owed his position to Rasputin.

In June a great Russian offensive was launched over a front of three hundred miles. The Austrians were taken by surprise, and retreated. The Tsar ordered his troops to keep up the offensive at all costs. They obeyed him, but the sacrifice was enormous—over a million men.

The Tsar's letters to the Tsarina detailed the military plans; he also sent her maps. Every letter contained injunctions to reveal these plans to no one; but she took it for granted that he meant no one but Rasputin. If Rasputin had been a German spy—as many people in Petrograd now believed—the Russian Army would have been decisively defeated in the summer of 1916. In fact, it continued to advance, but still with staggering casualties. Rasputin was shocked by the size of the losses, and repeatedly advised the Tsar to halt the advance and stop wasting men. The Tsar ignored him, feeling that victory was worth the price. It was a feeling that was not shared by his soldiers; by winter there was widespread disaffection in the Army.

IN PETROGRAD, MEANWHILE, Rasputin uncovered plans for his own assassination. The plans were originally betrayed to him by a crooked police agent called Beletsky, and their author was Rasputin's own appointee, Alexis Hvostov, minister of the interior. From the beginning, Hvostov had been looking for an opportunity to get rid of Rasputin, whom he regarded as a potential danger to his own ambitions. He discussed the matter with Beletsky, who suggested that the simplest method would be to lure Rasputin into a car or carriage, have him murdered in a side street and dump his body in the Neva. Beletsky, however, liked Rasputin, so he warned him not to get into any strange vehicles. The same evening a car stopped by Rasputin as he walked along the quay, and a police agent he recognized leaned out. "The minister begs you to come and see him. The matter is urgent."

"In that case, tell him to come and see me." Rasputin turned and walked off, leaving the police agent fingering the heavy bludgeon in his pocket.

Hvostov was enraged. He summoned Rasputin's special guard, Colonel Kommisarov, to ask his advice. Kommisarov said that the safest method to dispose of Rasputin was poison, and that he knew where to obtain it. But Kommisarov loathed Hvostov, and was rather fond of Rasputin. After a month of delays he brought Hvostov a large chest containing dozens of drawers, each labeled with a skull and crossbones. He spent two hours explaining the effects of the various poisons to Hvostov, who promised him a large sum of money when Rasputin was dead. In fact, the "poisons" were nothing more than ordinary household remedies, and Kommisarov had obtained his apparently exhaustive knowledge of poisons from an old book lent to him by Rasputin.

This particular joke rebounded on Rasputin. On that December evening when he went to the Villa Rode, one of Hvostov's agents sat at the next table; and when Rasputin nodded off to sleep for a moment, the agent slipped a teaspoonful of white powder into his drink. It was an old Latvian remedy for backache containing tartaric acid; it was this that had made Rasputin so sick the evening he had been summoned to the Tsarevich's bedside.

Hvostov was now beginning to suspect his two fellow conspirators. He decided that Iliodor would probably make a better assassin, and opened a secret correspondence with the unfrocked priest, who was still living in Finland. Hvostov offered Iliodor unlimited funds to organize the murder of Rasputin, and sent one of his agents, called Rzhetsky, to deliver the first installment. At the Finnish frontier officials inspected Rzhetsky's bag, and were curious to find such a large sum. They telegraphed to the police in Petrograd, who called Beletsky. Guessing where Rzhetsky was going and why he was carrying so much money, Beletsky ordered him arrested. Then he went to see Hvostov and told him with an innocent expression that he had just caught Rzhetsky, who was trying to abscond with the petty cash. Hvostov ground his teeth, but could do nothing about it. Beletsky and Rasputin spent the evening laughing and drinking.

At this point Beletsky brought about his own downfall by carelessness. He was tired of the police department and of working under Hvostov; Rasputin whispered a few words in the Tsar's ear, and Beletsky was appointed governor-general of Siberia. Before he left for his new job, he gave an interview to a Petrograd newspaper, in which he talked about the plot against Rasputin's life. However, the Tsar had issued an order that there should be no more stories about Rasputin in the Petrograd newspapers. When the story appeared, the newspaper was closed down and Beletsky lost his appointment. For good measure, the Tsar also dismissed Hvostov, and appointed Prime Minister Stürmer as a stopgap. Rasputin tried hard to get the decision reversed; he was grateful to Beletsky for giving him so much harmless amusement. But the Tsar was adamant, and Beletsky remained in disgrace.

Stürmer handed over the job of minister of the interior to Hvostov's uncle, an honest old man who was horrified to learn how much government money was vanishing into the pockets of corrupt officials. Hearing that Rasputin's friend Manuilov was one of the worst offenders, Hvostov arranged to trap him by offering him a bribe consisting of marked bank notes. Manuilov took the bribe and was arrested. He seemed completely unperturbed by his predicament; at his interrogation he merely hinted that if he appeared in court, some interesting disclosures about Rasputin would be made. The Tsarina was told about it; she sent a telegram to the Tsar. Hvostov suddenly found himself without a job. His place was taken by Rasputin's friend Protopopov.

In Petrograd discontent was spreading. Food prices had multiplied; even salt cost six times as much as before the war. Many people froze to death because of the fuel shortage. The problem, as Rasputin had always seen, was the railways; there was not enough transport to bring coal from the Donets region in the south. As the winter set in, Prime Minister Stürmer came in for an increasing amount of criticism. But the Tsar was unable to find anyone to replace him; the few competent men in Russia were hated by the Tsarina.

As the situation grew worse, even that objection lost its force, and in November 1916 Stürmer was dismissed. In his place the Tsar appointed Alexander Trepov, a loyal conservative. However, from the Tsarina's point of view, Trepov had one great drawback: he detested "our Friend." Moreover, Trepov thought that the recent appointment of Rasputin's friend Protopopov as minister of the interior was a disaster, and he made the Tsar promise to get rid of him. The Tsarina was frantic. She did her best to dissuade her husband. Finally the Tsar gave way to his wife's pleas and allowed Protopopov's appointment to stand.

ONE DAY IN EARLY DECEMBER Munia Golovina came to see Rasputin. It was shortly after Vladimir Purishkevich, a brilliant and well-liked member of the Duma, had made a violent speech against Rasputin and his evil influence. It was the most detailed and damaging indictment so far.

As Munia approached Rasputin's apartment, she found the door open. Rasputin was sitting in a chair by the window.

"Grigori, you shouldn't leave the door open. Anyone might walk right in."

"Who?"

"Somebody who wished you harm." At close quarters she could see he looked ill and tired. She pulled up a chair and took his hands.

"I've been talking on the telephone to Anna. She's had a letter from your wife."

Rasputin looked up in surprise. "What about?"

"Your wife says you've predicted you'll be dead soon."

"We may all be dead soon."

"But why say it now?"

He stared at her, and she saw there were black circles under his eyes. "If you really want to know . . . because I can smell death. I can smell disaster. Did you hear what Purishkevich said about me in the Duma?"

"Of course. Your friends know better than that."

"He says I hate democracy. But does he realize that the Duma is in session only because *I* begged the Tsar to allow it to meet again? And this same Purishkevich, who now calls me 'an ulcerated sore,' was trying to persuade me to get him the post of minister of the interior only six months ago."

She was relieved to see him becoming angry; his moods of depression worried and frightened her. "You've been attacked before and survived it."

He looked at her with an odd expression. "And do you believe what Purishkevich says about me?"

She said firmly, "Don't be silly. You know I don't." She stood up and placed her hand on his head. "But tell me the truth," she pleaded. "What made you tell your wife you thought you wouldn't see her again?"

"It happens all the time. I have a feeling. You know that when I am tired, I like to walk by the river. Yesterday it suddenly turned into blood."

"You mean in the sunset?"

"There was no sunset. It was real blood—the blood of grand dukes."

THE SPEECH, AND PURISHKEVICH'S sincerity, made a tremendous impression. And it made one member of the audience come to a decision. That man was Felix Yussupov, who had become increasingly convinced that Rasputin's influence over the Tsarina, and thus ultimately the Tsar, was responsible for Russia's military defeats. As he listened to Purishkevich's fiery speech, Yussupov decided that for the sake of Russia, Rasputin would have to be eliminated.

Since his visit six months before, Yussupov had been a constant visitor at Rasputin's apartment. His devotion to Rasputin seemed deep and genuine. On one occasion Maria saw him pick up a wine glass from which her father had been drinking and press his lips to it. A few days later, when Yussupov arrived with a severe headache, Rasputin sat him in a chair and stood behind him, pressing his hands against the younger man's forehead. The headache vanished, and Yussupov seized Rasputin's hand and held it against his lips.

On the afternoon of December 28, as Rasputin was leaving his apartment for Tsarskoe Selo, Yussupov telephoned. "Grigori," he said, "would you like to meet Irina?"

"Yes." Rasputin had not yet met Yussupov's wife.

"She's coming back from the Crimea tomorrow. Could you come for a late supper?"

"How late?"

"Midnight?"

"I suppose so. If you'll come and get me yourself."

"Of course."

"Come by the back stairway. I'll tell the watchman to open the door for you."

THE TSAR HAD ARRIVED back from headquarters that day. He was in a good mood, and joined the Tsarina and Rasputin for tea.

As Rasputin was about to take his leave, he asked the Tsar, "When do you return to headquarters?"

"The day after tomorrow."

"In that case I won't come tomorrow."

"Then give me your blessing."

Rasputin looked into his eyes; his own eyes were sad. "No," he said. "This time it is for you to bless me."

He knelt at the Tsar's feet, and Nicholas, looking slightly bewildered, made the sign of the cross over his head. When Rasputin stood up, he hugged the Tsar tightly, then kissed the Tsarina. He went out quickly.

RASPUTIN WOKE THE NEXT morning feeling strangely heavy and dull. He tried to pray, but his mind seemed wrapped in a cloud of darkness. The petitioners began to arrive shortly after ten; fortunately the weather was so cold that there were fewer than usual.

He was talking to the last petitioner, a banker who wanted a connection with the War Ministry, when Dunia came in. "Madame Vyrubova wants to see you. She says it's urgent."

Rasputin dismissed the banker, promising to do what he could. Anna hurried into the room; her cape and fur boots were covered with snow. She walked with a bad limp, an aftermath of her accident.

"Grigori, what's all this about going to Yussupov's house tonight?"

"He's invited me to meet his wife."

"Matushka says there must be some mistake. His wife is in the Crimea."

"I know. She's traveling back today."

Anna took both his hands. "Promise me you won't go."

"Does Matushka ask that?"

"No. I do. But she thinks it's very strange. And I talked to Protopopov this morning. He says there's a rumor going around that something is going to happen to you."

Rasputin pressed her hand to his cheek. "Annyushka, I can't let Felix down. I've promised."

She sighed and lowered her eyes. She was so accustomed to accepting what he said that she found it hard to oppose him. She said, "But why so late?"

"To keep the visit a secret from his parents. His father hates me."

"All right. You know best." She stood up and took his hand, staring into his eyes. "Or do you?"

He smiled at her; his face was weary.

An hour later Protopopov arrived. He had evidently been speaking to Anna. He repeated what she had said: that there were rumors something was about to happen to him, and he added that Purishkevich seemed to be behind them.

"But Felix doesn't know Purishkevich."

"Oh yes he does. My agents saw them together the morning after Purishkevich's speech at the Duma. They spent nearly an hour in his office."

"All right. I'll ask him about it when I see him. But Felix is too much of a coward to kill anyone."

Simanovich came in that afternoon to deal with the unopened letters. He also had heard the rumors. After tea in the kitchen with Dunia, Simanovich asked, "What's all this about going out at midnight?"

"Only to Yussupov's," Rasputin answered. "He's coming for me."

"Don't go."

"You're the third person to tell me that today. I've got to go. I've promised."

WHEN YUSSUPOV ARRIVED, shortly after midnight, Dunia was asleep in her armchair and the children were in bed. Rasputin slipped out quietly. Yussupov seemed subdued and looked pale. He was wearing a huge fur coat and a fur cap with earflaps.

Rasputin asked, "Why are you muffled up like that?"

"Didn't we agree to keep tonight a secret?"

"It's not much of a secret. Protopopov told me you might be planning to kill me."

"What!" Yussupov looked like a startled rabbit, and Rasputin roared with laughter. They climbed into the waiting car. Yussupov looked around out of the rear window before they drove off.

Rasputin, who had been feeling curiously uneasy, suddenly felt relaxed. He said, "Why don't we go to the Villa Rode and hear some gypsy music instead?"

"If you like. But my wife is expecting you."

"Oh, all right." He looked out of the window. "Why are we going this way?"

"In case we're followed."

"I've sent the secret policemen home. I told them I wasn't going out tonight."

Ten minutes later they pulled up to Yussupov's house on the Moika. He had moved in only recently, and there were scaffolding poles lying outside. The sound of an American jazz band floated out on the still, cold air.

"What's that? Are you having a party?"

"No. My wife has a few friends in. We'll go to the dining room and have some tea."

The house smelled of fresh paint. Yussupov led the way down newly carpeted stairs to the basement. Rasputin looked around him with curiosity. This room had also been recently painted and furnished.

"Tea? Or would you prefer wine?"

"Neither. I'll wait until your wife comes down."

"Then what would you like?"

"Play me something on your guitar."

As Yussupov played a plaintive Hungarian melody, Rasputin wandered around the room. He examined a large antique cupboard with close attention, opened its door, and looked inside at the many shelves and compartments. From above, the sound of music had now ceased.

Yussupov stopped playing suddenly. "I'll go and see if Irina's ready. Why don't you have some cake?"

"No thanks. I don't like cake."

"Sweet wine?"

"When your wife comes. I'll drink her health."

Yussupov went out of the room. Rasputin walked over to a large crystal crucifix that stood in the corner. As he examined the body of Christ, held on by silver nails, a curious sadness overcame him. He knelt in front of the cross, bent his head and prayed.

Yussupov returned, and stood still at the bottom of the stairs when he saw Rasputin praying. Then, with two quick steps, he crossed the room. Rasputin continued to pray quietly. From his pocket Yussupov drew a revolver. His face was very pale and his lips were trembling. He held the revolver at arm's length, closed his eyes and squeezed the trigger. The roar was deafening in the small room. Rasputin gave a strangled shout and fell forward. There was a sound of footsteps on the stairs, and four men rushed into the room. Foremost of these was Vladimir Purishkevich, a little man with a bald head and square beard. Purishkevich looked at Rasputin, who was lying face down, and shouted, "Good man! You've done it!" He thumped Yussupov on the back.

At that moment the light went out. Yussupov yelled with terror.

The light came on again; a young man in officer's uniform said, "Sorry, I caught the switch by accident."

Yussupov turned on him. "You idiot, do you want to give me a heart attack!"

A bearded man in a frock coat was kneeling beside Rasputin. He turned the body over on its back and felt the pulse. "He's dead all right."

Yussupov and Purishkevich flung their arms around each other. The other three men slapped Yussupov on the back. Purishkevich said, "Tonight you have saved Russia."

Yussupov was feeling generous. "*We* have saved Russia."

The fourth man—the Grand Duke Dmitri Pavlovich, Yussupov's close friend—said, "I need a stiff drink."

The five men went upstairs. In the hallway the young officer—a man named Sukhotin—donned Rasputin's heavy fur coat and cap and went out to the car. It was his task to drive back to Rasputin's house and enter by the back door, to give the impression to any secret policemen that Rasputin had returned home.

In the room above the basement Yussupov poured large measures of vodka. They all drank solemnly, "To Russia." Yussupov's hand was still shaking.

The man in the frock coat—a Dr. Lazovert—said, "When shall we move him?"

"Better wait until Sukhotin gets back with the car."

Yussupov wound up the gramophone and put on a record. Then, as the others began to talk excitedly, he slipped out of the room.

In the basement Rasputin was still lying on his back, as Lazovert had left him. Yussupov went cautiously across the room and knelt beside the body. As he did so, the body twitched. Yussupov looked up at the face and screamed. Rasputin's eyes were open, and they were staring at Yussupov in fury. With a jerk, he sat up, then lurched to his knees. As Yussupov tried to roll away from him, Rasputin grabbed him by the throat. Yussupov gave a wailing scream and fought like a cat. Suddenly he was free again.

He rushed up the stairs and met Purishkevich in the hall. "He's alive! He's still alive!" As Lazovert came out to see what was happening, Yussupov yelled, "You fool! You said he was dead!"

Purishkevich suddenly screamed and Yussupov looked around to see Rasputin scrambling up the stairs on all fours. When he saw the men above him, he began to shout and bellow—not words, but sounds that might have been made by a wounded bull. Purishkevich said, "Where's the revolver?" and ran back into the room.

Rasputin gained the top of the stairs, lurched to his feet and rushed for a side door. It opened, and a breath of night air blew in.

Purishkevich came back, brandishing the revolver. "Where is he?"

"Outside, in the courtyard."

Purishkevich ran out, followed by the others. Rasputin was crawling on all fours toward the gate. Purishkevich pointed the gun and fired at him. Rasputin collapsed face downward.

A moment later a policeman appeared in the gateway. "What's happening?" Yussupov hurried toward him, and the policeman recognized him. "Oh, it's you, Your Highness. I heard a shot." Yussupov seized him by the arm. "Yes, it's nothing. Just a stupid guest trying to show us how he shot a bear at close range." He laughed, but felt his voice cracking. He seized the policeman by the arm and led him back to the street. "It's really nothing to worry about. We don't want a scandal . . ." The policeman saluted smartly.

By now there were several more people in the courtyard, Yussupov's servants. Purishkevich was standing beside the fallen body. He said, "I think he's still alive. He just moved." He kicked the head with his pointed shoe; it made a dull sound. Yussupov said, "Let's get him back into the house."

They carried the body into the dining room and spread newspapers on the carpet to prevent bloodstains. While they were doing it, the door bell rang. The servant came in and whispered to Yussupov, "There's a policeman at the door—he wants to see you."

It was the same policeman who had been in the courtyard. He said, "Look, sir, I'm sorry, but I think I'll have to ask you for more details. I can't go back and—"

He stopped, startled, as Purishkevich ran out of the room and grabbed him by the arm. The little man's eyes were shining. He said in a strained high voice, "My man, have you heard of Rasputin?" The policeman nodded. "The man who has been betraying our country to the Germans, the Tsarina's lover?" Yussupov tried to interrupt, but Purishkevich raised his voice. "Well, he's dead. We've killed him. I am Vladimir Mitrofanovich Purishkevich, member of the Duma. We killed him to save Russia. And if you are a patriot, you won't breathe a word about it. You understand!"

The policeman nodded, too astonished to speak; Purishkevich's manner suggested he was drunk.

"Now leave us to our work!" The policeman allowed himself to be bundled out the front door.

Yussupov said, "Now you've done it! We'd better get him into the river as soon as we can. We'll have half the police force around in a minute." Purishkevich's obvious hysteria had made the prince feel calm and superior. He went into his study and took a truncheon from the desk. "This is in case he wakes up again!" As he spoke, Dmitri Pavlovich shouted, "Felix! Quick! He's alive!" Yussupov groaned, "Oh, no . . ."

Rasputin was struggling to sit up, his clawed hands tearing the newspaper underneath him. His face was covered with blood, and one cheek was torn where Purishkevich had kicked it. With a yell of rage, Yussupov rushed forward; he began to strike violently with the truncheon, screaming, "There, take that! That'll make you lie down." Rasputin collapsed without a sound. Yussupov stood above him, lashing out with the truncheon. Finally Dmitri Pavlovich grabbed his arm. "That's enough. He's dead. Do you want to get covered with blood?" Yussupov dropped the truncheon, turned away and suddenly began to cry hysterically. Then he looked around at the battered face, now totally inhuman, and fainted.

Purishkevich turned to the servants, who were standing in the doorway. "Get a blanket to wrap him in. Hurry up—the police may be here at any moment." They pulled him by the feet, the head bumping down the steps as they dragged him toward the car.

AFTERWORD

ON JANUARY 1, WHEN Rasputin's body was taken from the ice, Nicholas returned immediately to Petrograd to comfort his wife. Two days later Rasputin was buried in the Imperial Park at Tsarskoe Selo. By that time Maria had found her father's letter, prophesying his own death, and had handed it to the Tsarina.

It read: *I write and leave behind me this letter at Saint Petersburg. I feel that I shall leave life before January 1. I wish to make known to the Russian people, to Papa, to the Russian Mother and to the children, to the land of Russia, what they must understand. If I am killed by common assassins, and especially by my brothers the Russian peasants, you, Tsar of Russia, have nothing to fear, remain on your throne and govern, and you, Russian Tsar, will have nothing to fear for your children, they will reign for hundreds of years in Russia. But if I am murdered by Boyars, nobles, and if they shed my blood, their hands will remain soiled with my blood, for twenty-five years they will not wash their hands from my blood. They will leave Russia. Brothers will kill brothers, and they will kill each other and hate each other, and for twenty-five years there will be no nobles in the country. Tsar of the land of Russia, if you hear the sound of a bell that will tell you that Grigori has been killed, you must know this: if it was your relations who have wrought my death, then no one in the family, that is to say, none of your children or relations, will remain alive for more than two years. They will be killed by the Russian people. I go, and I feel in me the divine command to tell the Russian Tsar how he must live if I have disappeared. You must reflect and act prudently. Think of your safety, and tell your relations that I have paid for them with my blood. I shall be killed. I am no longer among the living. Pray, pray, be strong, think of your blessed family. Grigori.*

Dmitri Pavlovich and Yussupov were both members of the royal family, Dmitri by blood, Yussupov by marriage.

The Tsar did not return to the front. He seemed to be overtaken by a curious apathy.

In 1917 the Revolution began. In January there were strikes and protest marches. On March 8 there were riots about the shortage of bread. Three days later the police fired on crowds who were chanting, "Down with the German woman." The Volynsky Regiment revolted; other regiments followed; barricades went up in the streets. The Duma sanctioned the formation of a provisional government. When the Tsar tried to leave the palace, soldiers pushed him back with rifles, saying, "You can't go that way, Mr. Colonel." Nicholas had waited too long before heeding Rasputin's advice to be prudent and think of his safety.

On April 16 Lenin arrived in Petrograd by train. For a while he was merely another agitator. But in November the Bolsheviks seized the principal buildings of Petrograd. In due course the city was given another name—Leningrad.

In August 1917 the royal family was moved to Tobolsk; on the way there by riverboat they passed through Pokrovskoe and saw Rasputin's house, taller than all the others, facing the river.

Maria Rasputin was by now married, and her husband, a young mystic called Boris Soloviev, planned to rescue the royal family. Bishop Hermogen—who, ironically, had become bishop of Tobolsk—offered to help. But the Tsar refused to cooperate unless he received a promise that he would not have to leave Russia.

In April 1918, with the Bolsheviks now in command, the royal family was transferred to Ekaterinburg. On July 16, when there were rumors that the White Russian Army was advancing, the entire family was taken down to the cellar of the house and murdered. Nicholas was shot first; the Tsarina and the children fell to their knees, and were shot in that position. When the Princess Anastasia moved, she was battered with the butt end of a rifle. The woman who later gained international notoriety by claiming to be Anastasia insisted that she had only been knocked unconscious, and that she was the sole survivor.

The killers of Rasputin were never punished. Purishkevich died of typhoid in southern Russia after fighting with the Whites. Yussupov moved to Paris, where he wrote a book about Rasputin. His account of the murder contains obvious discrepancies. For example, he insists that he first gave Rasputin cakes poisoned with cyanide—apparently unaware that cyanide takes only a few seconds to kill. He claims that Rasputin was facing him when he shot him, failing to explain why the bullet entered Rasputin's back. Felix Yussupov died in Paris in 1967, at the age of eighty-one.

When I met Maria Rasputin in Los Angeles in 1969—after I had written a book about her father—she told me some of the true facts about him. These I have tried to present in this story.